READINGS
IN
MEDICAL SOCIOLOGY

Second Edition

READINGS
IN
MEDICAL SOCIOLOGY

Edited by

William C. Cockerham
University of Alabama at Birmingham

Michael Glasser
University of Illinois College of Medicine at Rockford

Prentice
Hall

Upper Saddle River, New Jersey 07458

Library of Congress Cataloging-in-Publication Data

Readings in medical sociology / edited by William C. Cockerham, Michael Glasser.—
2nd ed.
    p. cm.
  Includes bibliographical references.
  ISBN 0–13–027453–4
  1. Social medicine. 2. Social medicine—Cross-cultural studies. I. Cockerham, William
C. II. Glasser, Michael L., 1950–

RA418.R377 2000
306.4'61—dc21   00–033640

VP, Ed. director: Laura Pearson
AVP, Publisher: Nancy Roberts
Managing editor: Sharon Chambliss
Executive managing editor: Ann Marie McCarthy
Production liaison: Joan Eurell/Fran Russello
Editorial production/supervision
  and interior design: Joan Saidel/P. M. Gordon Associates, Inc.
Prepress and manufacturing buyer: Mary Ann Gloriande
Cover director: Jayne Conte
Cover designer: Bruce Kenselaar
Copy editor: Christina Palaia

This book was set in 10/12 ITC New Baskerville by DM Cradle Associates
and was printed and bound by Hamilton Printing Company.
The cover was printed by Phoenix Color Corporation.

 © 2001, 1998 by Prentice-Hall, Inc.
A Division of Pearson Education
Upper Saddle River, New Jersey 07458

Printed in the United States of America
10 9 8 7 6 5 4 3 2 1

ISBN 0-13-027453-4

Prentice-Hall International (UK) Limited, *London*
Prentice-Hall of Australia Pty. Limited, *Sydney*
Prentice-Hall of Canada Inc., *Toronto*
Prentice-Hall Hispanoamericana, S.A., *Mexico*
Prentice-Hall of India Private Limited, *New Delhi*
Prentice-Hall of Japan, Inc., *Tokyo*
Pearson Education Asia Pte. Ltd., *Singapore*
Editora Prentice-Hall do Brasil, Ltda., *Rio de Janeiro*

CONTENTS

INTRODUCTION

Medical sociology is the study of the social causes and consequences of health and illness. The field came of age in North America and Western Europe in the period following the end of World War II and now has practitioners and a vast literature spanning the globe. The intent of *Readings in Medical Sociology* is to bring together a collection of important articles addressing significant issues by medical sociologists and some of their colleagues in other fields. This reader is intended to serve as a companion volume to the eighth edition of William C. Cockerham's textbook *Medical Sociology* (Prentice Hall, 2001) or to be used independently.

The intended audience is people with an interest in reviewing studies in medical sociology to increase their understanding of how medical sociologists work and the nature of the research findings they disclose in explaining the relationship between health and society. Divided into 11 parts with 20 articles, the book is designed for a semester-long course in which one or perhaps two of the articles could be assigned weekly. The first part on social epidemiology (the study of epidemics from a social perspective) includes a paper on the social causes of disease and is followed by Part II on social demography with a paper on the link between education and health.

Part III deals with stress and contains a review paper on the sociological study of stress. Part IV is on health behavior (the behavior of people who wish to stay or be as healthy as possible) with a paper on sex stratification and health lifestyles. Part V on illness behavior (the behavior of sick people) focuses on first-person accounts of experiencing life-threatening or terminal illnesses and the cultural implications of anorexia nervosa. Part VI is on healing options, and the readings concern a study of religion, health, and a person's nonphysical sense of self and the meanings of health and health care to a group of African American women. That is followed by Part VII on the doctor–patient relationship. This section includes papers analyzing emotional expression during medical examinations and the increasingly important role of the Internet as a source of health information for the public. The next part is concerned with the physician in a changing society, including papers on professional dynamics and the changing nature of medical work and gender and the prestige hierarchy of medical specialties. Part IX contains a paper on the gendered experience of nursing and changes in the doctor–nurse relationship.

The reader concludes with two sections, one on health care delivery and social policy in the United States, and the other on health in selected countries. Part X has papers on health insurance and the working poor and the health insurance crisis in the United States. Part XI has articles on health care delivery in Canada, the Americanization of the British National Health Service, and the social determinants of the decline in life expectancy in Russia and Eastern Europe.

Taken together, these papers present research findings and critical discussions that define interests of medical sociologists, health practitioners, and policymakers throughout the world with respect to social links to health. They are intended to be timely, factual, and concise, thereby allowing the reader to have a good understanding of the broad range of research in medical sociology today.

William C. Cockerham

Michael Glasser

READINGS
IN
MEDICAL SOCIOLOGY

Part I
EPIDEMIOLOGY

Many medical sociologists work in the interdisciplinary field of epidemiology or use epidemiological methods in sociological research. Epidemiology—the science of epidemics—focuses on the health of communities and populations. The concern is not just with infectious diseases, but also with threats to the health of groups of people from any source, including chronic disease, environmental pollution, automobile accidents, alcohol and drug abuse, and violence.

Epidemiology draws on the skills and expertise of professionals from many fields, including medicine, public health, nursing, biology, statistics, anthropology, and psychology, as well as sociology. Epidemiologists are like detectives. They investigate what causes groups to become sick or injured and devise solutions. The principal role of medical sociologists in epidemiological work is to examine the impact of social factors on health. Typically, medical sociologists try to determine how age, gender, race, social class, and various forms of social behavior—such as sexual practices—place particular groups at risk for certain health problems. They go beyond biomedical explanations of illness and injury to the systematic scrutiny of social life in relation to health.

Despite its relative importance, Bruce G. Link and Jo Phelan ask us in their article entitled "Social Conditions as Fundamental Causes of Disease" to look beyond proximate or individually based causes of disease, such as hypertension, smoking, and diet, and to pay greater attention to social conditions if future health reform is to have a maximum effect. They argue that social factors such as socioeconomic status (SES) and social support are also fundamental causes of disease because they embody access or lack of access to important resources that affect health and disease outcomes, and maintain an enduring association with disease. Link and Phelan recommend contextualizing risk factors, which means going beyond proximate causes, such as unprotected sexual intercourse, sedentary lifestyles, or needle exchange, to understand how people's life circumstances contribute to unhealthy behavior and possible disease exposure. Ultimately, such an epidemiological conceptualization allows for broad-based social interventions and enhances the potential for substantial health benefits for the general population.

In closing, this article points to the primacy of social factors in epidemiology. Proximate or individually based risks provide only a partial etiological picture of the cause of important health problems, such as infant mortality, chronic illness, and AIDS. Inclusion of social conditions completes the portrait and deepens our understanding of health and illness among human populations.

SOCIAL CONDITIONS AS FUNDAMENTAL CAUSES OF DISEASE

Bruce G. Link
Columbia University and New York State Psychiatric Institute
Jo Phelan
University of California, Los Angeles

Over the last several decades, epidemiological studies have been enormously successful in identifying risk factors for major diseases. However, most of this research has focused attention on risk factors that are relatively proximal causes of disease such as diet, cholesterol level, exercise, and the like. We question the emphasis on such individually based risk factors and argue that greater attention must be paid to basic social conditions if health reform is to have its maximum effect in the time ahead. There are two reasons for this claim. First, we argue that individually based risk factors must be contextualized, by examining what puts people at risk of risks, if we are to craft effective interventions and improve the nation's health. Second, we argue that social factors such as socioeconomic status and social support are likely "fundamental causes" of disease that, because they embody access to important resources, affect multiple disease outcomes through multiple mechanisms, and consequently maintain an association with disease even when intervening mechanisms change. Without careful attention to these possibilities, we run the risk of imposing individually based intervention strategies that are ineffective and of missing opportunities to adopt broad-based societal interventions that could produce substantial health benefits for our citizens.

Epidemiology has been enormously successful in heightening public awareness of risk factors for disease. Research findings are frequently and prominently publicized in the mass media and in rapidly proliferating university-based health newsletters. Moreover, there is evidence that the message has been received and that many people have at least attempted to quit smoking, include more exercise in their daily routine, and implement a healthier diet.

Reprinted from the *Journal of Health and Social Behavior*, extra issue (1995), pp. 80–94, by permission of the American Sociological Association.

With few exceptions, however, the new findings generated within the field of epidemiology have focused on risk factors that are relatively proximate "causes" of disease, such as diet, cholesterol, hypertension, electromagnetic fields, lack of exercise, and so on. Social factors, which tend to be more distal causes of disease, have received far less attention.[1] This focus on more proximate links in the causal chain may be viewed by many, not as a limitation or bias, but as the rightful progression of science from identifying correlations to understanding causal relationships (e.g., Potter 1992). In fact, some in the so-called "modern"

3

school of epidemiology (e.g., Rothman 1986) have explicitly argued that social conditions such as socioeconomic status are mere proxies for true causes lying closer to disease in the causal chain.

This focus on proximate risk factors, potentially controllable at the individual level, resonates with the value and belief systems of Western culture that emphasize both the ability of the individual to control his or her personal fate and the importance of doing so (Becker 1993). This affinity between cultural values and the focus of contemporary epidemiology undoubtedly contributes to the level of public interest in epidemiological findings, and probably influences funding priorities as well. Thus modern epidemiology and cultural values conspire to focus attention on proximate, individually based risk factors and away from social conditions as causes of disease.

This is not to say that the role of social factors in disease causation has been neglected in all quarters. Medical sociologists and social epidemiologists have kept alive classical epidemiology's (e.g., Susser, Watson, and Hopper 1985) concern with social conditions and have made major strides toward documenting and understanding the connections between social factors and disease. However, we believe there are conceptual pitfalls that sometimes lead medical sociologists and social epidemiologists themselves to unwittingly reinforce the emphasis on proximate, individual-level risk factors. One of these pitfalls is that, in the process of elucidating the mechanisms connecting social conditions to health and illness—an important and desirable activity—we may, over time, lose interest in and come to neglect the importance of the social condition whose effect on health we originally sought to explain. Also, our tendency to focus on the connection of social conditions to single diseases via single mechanisms at single points in time neglects the multifaceted and dynamic processes through

which social factors may affect health and, consequently, may result in an incomplete understanding and an underestimation of the influence of social factors on health.

Our purposes here are to highlight the accomplishments of medical sociologists and social epidemiologists in advancing our understanding of social conditions as causes of disease, to underscore the critical importance of continued work in this direction, and to offer two conceptual frameworks that we hope will facilitate and enhance this research. First, we discuss the importance of "contextualizing" risk factors—that is, attempting to understand how people come to be exposed to individually based risk factors such as poor diet, cholesterol, lack of exercise, or high blood pressure—so that we can design more effective interventions. Second, we introduce the notion that some social conditions may be "fundamental causes" of disease. A fundamental cause involves access to resources, resources that help individuals avoid diseases and their negative consequences through a variety of mechanisms. Thus, even if one effectively modifies intervening mechanisms or eradicates some diseases, an association between a fundamental cause and disease will reemerge. As such, fundamental causes can defy efforts to eliminate their effects when attempts to do so focus solely on the mechanisms that happen to link them to disease in a particular situation. We conclude by discussing the implications of these ideas for research and social policy.

EVIDENCE LINKING SOCIAL CONDITIONS TO DISEASE

We begin with a brief review of the evidence concerning the connection between social conditions and illness. For the purposes of this paper, we define *social conditions* as factors that involve a person's relationships to other people. These include everything from relationships with intimates to positions occupied within the social and economic structures of society. Thus, in addition to factors like race, socioeconomic status, and gender, we include stressful life events of a social nature (e.g., the death of a loved one, loss of a job, or crime victimization), as well as stress-process variables such as social support.

Forty years of medical sociology have uncovered numerous examples of the social patterning of disease. Most obvious is the ubiquitous and often strong association between health and socioeconomic status. Lower SES is associated with lower life expectancy, higher overall mortality rates, and higher rates of infant and perinatal mortality (Buck 1981; Dutton 1986; Illsley and Mullen 1985; Adler et al. 1994; Pappas et al. 1993). Moreover, low SES is associated with each of the 14 major cause-of-death categories in the International Classification of Diseases (Illsley and Mullen 1985), as well as many other, health outcomes, including major mental disorders (Dohrenwend et al. 1980; Kessler et al. 1994). Other examples of the social patterning of disease are plentiful. Males have higher mortality rates at all ages (Walsh and Feldman 1981), as well as higher rates of coronary heart disease (Syme and Guralnik 1987), chronic respiratory diseases (Colley 1985), and ulcers (Gazzard and Lance 1982). There are pronounced gender differences in rates of various forms of cancer (Prout, Colton, and Smith 1987) and mental disorder (Dohrenwend et al. 1980; Kessler et al. 1994). African Americans have higher rates of overall mortality and infant mortality (Dutton 1986; Miller 1987), renal failure (Challah and Wing 1985), and stroke (Pedoe 1982) than do Whites . . . ; cancer rates also differ by race and ethnicity (Prout et al. 1987). Both physical and mental disorders vary with marital status and population density (Kelsey 1993; Benenson 1987; Robins et al. 1984), and certain religious groups such as Mormons and Seventh Day Adventists have lower risks of some types of cancer (Saracci 1985).

In addition, the tremendous growth and success of the stress paradigm have added considerably to the evidence for an association between social conditions and disease (Dohrenwend and Dohrenwend 1981; Pearlin et al. 1981; Turner and Marino 1994; Turner, Wheaton, and Lloyd 1995). Stressful life events have been linked to heart disease, diabetes, cancers, stroke, fetal death, major depression, and low birth weight in offspring (Miller 1987; Shrout et al. 1989). Research has also extended to the domains of social support (Berkman and Syme 1979; House, Landis, and Umberson 1988; Turner and Marino 1994) and coping (Pearlin and Schooler 1978), which have been shown to be associated with health and well-being in their own right.

The evidence reviewed to this point clearly establishes a strong and pervasive association between social conditions and disease. But medical sociologists and social epidemiologists have taken the field considerably beyond a description of the social patterning of disease. Important advances in establishing a causal role for social factors have focused on two major issues—the direction of causation between social conditions and health and the mechanisms that explain observed associations. In what follows we present prominent examples of work on these two issues.

Concerning the issue of causal direction, important controversies surround some of the relationships between social conditions and health. For example, does low SES cause poor health, or does poor health cause downward mobility? Does social support reduce morbidity and mortality, or does illness restrict social interaction and thereby lead to social-support deficits? Social epidemiologists have used three general strategies to address these questions.

One approach uses quasi-experimental strategies which involve locating conditions under which alternative explanations make different predictions about observable facts.

This approach is exemplified by Dohren-wend's (1966) quasi experiment designed to test social selection and social causation explanations for the association between SES and specific mental disorders. The two expla-nations make different predictions about rates of disorder in advantaged and disadvan-taged ethnic groups, when socioeconomic status is held constant. The recent culmina-tion of Dohrenwend's work on this problem, based on a large-scale epidemiological study in Israel (Dohrenwend et al. 1992), con-cluded that social causation was stronger than social selection in producing the inverse asso-ciation of SES to major depression in women and substance abuse and antisocial person-ality in men. For schizophrenia, however, the evidence was more supportive of the social-selection explanation.

In the second strategy, medical sociologists and social epidemiologists identify social risk factors that cannot reasonably be conceived as having been caused by an individual's illness condition. Exemplifying this strategy is a study by Hamilton and colleagues (1990) con-cerning the effects of plant closings on auto-workers' mental health. The investigators compared workers who were laid off because of a plant closing, workers who anticipated being laid off, and workers whose plant was not closing, and found that those laid off were more likely to experience negative mental-health consequences—particularly if they were minorities and of low SES. Since the illness condition of the workers cannot be thought of as having caused the plant closing, the differences between the groups studied are more clearly interpretable as the effects of social conditions on health. This strategy was also employed by Fenwick and Tausig (1994) in a study that used the Census-based unem-ployment rate for an individual's occupation in a longitudinal design to show that when unemployment is higher, workers' job satisfac-tion, decision-making latitude, and well-being are lower. Again, since workers' health cannot

cause the aggregate unemployment rate, the results are more readily interpretable as demonstrating the influence of social condi-tions on health-related outcomes. Finally, studies of stressful circumstance have used this strategy by identifying "fateful" life events that are unlikely to have been caused by an individual's behavior (e.g., death of spouse, plant closing). Thus when Shrout et al. (1989) found the odds of developing major depres-sion to be more than three times as high among people experiencing a recent fateful life event, the association was more clearly interpretable as an effect of social conditions.

The third strategy adopted by social epi-demiologists to clarify causal direction involves the use of longitudinal designs. When such designs can clearly place the emergence of an illness or an illness exacerbation before or after the social condition under study, a great deal can be learned about the direction of cause between the two. Unfortunately, some longitudinal studies do not allow clear inferences about time order and therefore do not provide the definitive evidence about causality that is sometimes attributed to them (see Link and Shrout 1992). Still, some notable studies have identified social condi-tions that clearly predate health outcomes and show that the social conditions predict morbidity and mortality even when com-peting risk factors are held constant. For example, Berkman and Syme (1979) used baseline data on social networks, collected in 1965, to predict mortality during the subse-quent nine years. They found a near doubling of risk for mortality among those low on a social-network index as compared to those high on the index. Although this study con-trolled for many competing risks (smoking, obesity, physical activity, etc.), it did not include measures derived from a physical exam. A subsequent study by House, Landis, and Umberson (1988) did include a baseline physical exam and controlled for blood pres-sure, cholesterol levels, and other biomedical variables. These investigators found associations between social relationships and mortality that were similar to those reported by Berkman and Syme. This line of work has continued to become more and more refined. For example, in a recent longitudinal study, Berkman and colleagues (1992) have shown that a measure of perceived support collected before the occurrence of a heart attack predicts survival following the heart attack net of an impressive array of biomedical and psychosocial control variables. Other social variables have also been effectively studied with longitudinal designs. For example, Catalano and colleagues (1993) related job layoffs to the emergence or reemergence of alcohol abuse, and Lin and Ensel (1989) and Ensel and Lin (1991) showed that stressful circumstances predicted subsequent health and mental-health outcomes.

Thus, while medical sociologists and social epidemiologists have not denied the possibility that illness affects social conditions (Johnson 1991), they have, at the same time, demonstrated a substantial causal role for social conditions as causes of illness.

Research identifying the mechanisms linking social conditions to disease has also done much to move social epidemiology beyond the description of social patterns of disease. Consider, for example, the job-stress model of Karasek and colleagues that provides evidence for one mechanism linking SES to coronary heart disease among men. These investigators have shown that "job strain," characterized by a combination of high job demands and low decision latitude, is more common in lower status jobs and is associated with coronary heart disease (Karasek et al. 1988; Schnall et al. 1990) and elevated levels of ambulatory blood pressure both on and off the job (Schnall et al. 1992). Another example is the work of Mirowsky and Ross (1989), who elucidate the mechanisms that might account for social patterns of distress. They present evidence showing that alien-ation and perceived control over life circumstances underlie many social conditions that put people at risk for elevated levels of psychological distress. Consider as a final example a study by Rosenfield (1989) that sought to understand mechanisms producing gender differences in symptoms of depression and anxiety. Rosenfield shows that women have higher symptoms of depression and anxiety. This work shows that women have higher symptom levels than men when they are overloaded by work and family demands or when they experience low power as a consequence of being out of the labor market. Moreover, the common mechanism underlying low power and role overload is a decreased sense of personal control, which is in turn related to symptoms of anxiety and depression.

Link and Dohrenwend (1989) explicitly advocate the approach of elucidating mechanisms because of its value in clarifying the relative merit of competing explanations for social patterns of disease. The rationale is that alternative explanations for these patterns, such as social causation and social selection, frequently imply different intervening mechanisms. Thus, evidence about which intervening mechanisms account for the association can help answer questions concerning causal direction and other competing explanations. Moreover, if causal links between distal factors (e.g., SES) and more proximal factors (e.g., occupational stress, diet) can be drawn, as Karasek et al. (1988), Mirowsky and Ross (1989), Rosenfield (1989), and others (Lennon 1987; Pearlin et al. 1981; Link, Lennon, and Dohrenwend 1993; Umberson, Wortman, and Kessler 1992) have done, it becomes increasingly clear that social conditions are causes exerting indirect effects on disease outcomes, rather than mere proxies, as Rothman (1986) and others might claim.

But are there unintended and undesirable consequences of an approach that focuses on intervening mechanisms? We believe there are. Despite the obvious benefits of such an approach, it is possible that in its enactment, one may inadvertently contribute to the focus on factors that are closer to disease in the causal chain. The intervening mechanism becomes the new and exciting "next step," while the social conditions become the old, passé "starting point."

The evolution of the stress paradigm is a good example of such an inadvertent downgrading of the issue which provided the initial impetus for research. The social causation/social selection controversy concerning the association between socioeconomic status and mental disorder spawned an interest in stressful life events as a direct operationalization of the adversity that might be experienced in lower SES contexts (Dohrenwend and Dohrenwend 1969, 1981). When a consistent but modest association between stressful events and illness was identified (see Rabkin and Struening 1976), investigators elaborated the model to consider social support and coping as potential modifiers. Now researchers are invested in understanding the mechanisms linking these factors with disease. Also, research on the biological consequences of stress (e.g., immune status and elevated catecholamines) is seen as an exciting new development (e.g., Cohen, Tyrrell, and Smith 1991). In general, interest has followed the most recent step in the progression toward disease outcomes, while concern with the earlier foci has dissipated to a point where some express disinterest in factors such as the causation/selection issue and the role of stressful life events in causing illness (but see Pearlin 1989; Dohrenwend 1990; Angermeyer and Klusman 1987 for dissenting views). Indeed Angermeyer and Klusman (1987) documented a sharp decline in the number of publications focused on social class and mental disorder in the period from 1966 to 1985, while the number of articles on stress and psychiatric disorders increased rapidly during the same period. To

the extent that interest in mechanisms increases at the expense of more fundamental social conditions, medical sociologists may unwittingly contribute to the emphasis on individual factors and play into the hands of those who argue that social factors have only a modest role in disease causation.

To this point, we have described two characterizations of social conditions as causes of disease that either advertently or inadvertently downplay their importance. One of these is the outright declaration that social factors are only proxies for true causes. This position is demonstrably unwarranted given the achievements of medical sociology and social epidemiology over the past few decades. The other characterization, which may be partially constructed by medical sociologists and social epidemiologists themselves, is the view that social factors serve as starting points whose main function is to point the direction to more proximal risk factors. We take sharp issue with both of these characterizations. In the next two sections, we develop two concepts that illustrate the critical importance of social factors in disease causation, provide conceptual frameworks for future research in this area, and point to the problems that may ensue if the role of social conditions is neglected by researchers and policymakers. These are the ideas of "contextualizing risk factors" and "fundamental causes."

CONTEXTUALIZING RISK FACTORS

We suggest that medical sociologists and social epidemiologists need to counter the trajectory of modern epidemiology toward identifying risk factors that are increasingly proximate to disease—ones for which "biological plausibility" can be argued. One way they can do this is by "contextualizing" individually based risk factors. By this we mean that investigators must (1) use an interpretive framework to understand why people come to be exposed to risk or protective factors and (2) determine the social conditions under which individual risk factors are related to disease. We present examples that illustrate both these principles.

First, an important strategy for reducing the threat of AIDS is to educate the public concerning the steps they must take as individuals to reduce their risk of contracting or infecting others with the HIV virus. Clearly, however, some people are better able to take advantage of this information than others. By contextualizing risk factors for AIDS, we may be able to understand why some people cannot avoid the risk. For example, homeless or other extremely poor women who turn to prostitution as a survival strategy may not have the options or resources that would enable them to refuse to engage in risky sexual behaviors, no matter how well informed they may be about the risks they face. This example suggests that medical sociologists and social epidemiologists need to contextualize risk factors by asking what it is about people's life circumstances that shapes their exposure to such risk factors as unprotected sexual intercourse, poor diet, a sedentary lifestyle, or a stressful home life.

Our second example concerns the increasing attention being paid to the public health problem posed by contamination of meat, poultry, and eggs with *E. coli* and salmonella bacteria. The public has been warned to rinse and cook meat and poultry thoroughly and to carefully wash hands, knives, cutting boards, and so on. Because some follow these safety guidelines more assiduously than others, one can imagine a risk profile of individual behaviors that might predict bacterial infection. These precautions are only necessary, however, when the food that reaches the marketplace is contaminated. Government actions in the 1980s that reduced the number of government inspectors and deregulated the meat-processing industry have created the need for vigilance on the part of individuals. While the current

approach to the problem focuses on the individual, it can readily be seen that economic and political forces shape individuals' exposure to this risk. This example suggests that medical sociologists and social epidemiologists need to contextualize by asking under what social conditions individual risk factors lead to disease and whether there are any social conditions under which the individual-level risk factors would have no effect at all on disease outcome.

While the importance of contextualizing risk factors may seem obvious, if we take a hard look at even some of the most influential areas of research in medical sociology, we will find that much more of this kind of contextualizing is needed. Consider again the stress paradigm. While there are hundreds if not thousands of studies relating stressful circumstances to health outcomes, until the recent efforts of Turner and colleagues (Turner and Marino 1994; Turner, Wheaton, and Lloyd 1995), there was very little even descriptive data about the social origins of stressful circumstances (but see Smith 1992; Goldberg and Comstock 1980).

Why is it so important that we strive to contextualize risk factors? One reason is that efforts to reduce risk by changing behavior may be hopelessly ineffective if there is no clear understanding of the process that leads to exposure. For example, there are powerful social, cultural, and economic factors shaping the diet of poor people in the United States. Consequently, providing information about healthy diet to poor people and exhorting them to follow nutritional guidelines is unlikely to have much impact. Without an understanding of the context that leads to risk, the responsibility for reducing the risk is left with the individual, and nothing is done to alter the more fundamental factors that put people at risk of risks.

This line of thinking suggests that medical sociologists and social epidemiologists should turn on its head the now-popular tendency to examine risk factors that are ever closer to disease in a causal chain. Rather, it suggests that it is just as important to face the other direction and search for the factors that put people at risk of risks. It exhorts researchers both to explore the social origins of risks and to ask whether individually based risk factors are context-dependent in the sense of influencing health outcomes only within the context of a specific set of social conditions.

FUNDAMENTAL CAUSES

In addition to the obvious need to contextualize risk factors, medical sociologists and social epidemiologists need to take as their task the identification and thorough consideration of social conditions that are what we term "fundamental causes" of disease. We call them "fundamental" causes because, as we shall see, the health effects of causes of this sort cannot be eliminated by addressing the mechanisms that appear to link them to disease. The possibility that some social conditions have this fundamental quality with regard to health was first presented by House and colleagues in a discussion of potential reasons for the persistent association between SES and disease (House et al. 1990, 1994). We elaborate upon these ideas to build our concept of fundamental social causes of disease.

The Case of SES and Disease

The idea that social conditions might influence health was forcefully asserted by nineteenth-century physicians who founded the field of social medicine. Virchow (1848), for example, declared that "medicine is a social science." And, of course, it was in part the strong association between indicators of poverty and health that supported this claim. The reasons for the powerful association were also thought to be apparent, residing in the dire housing, sanitation, and work condi-

tions of poor people at the time (Rosen 1979). With tremendous medical advances and extensive public health initiatives, the incidence of such diseases as diphtheria, measles, typhoid fever, tuberculosis, and syphilis declined dramatically. In addition, in modern welfare states, poor people's access to care increased substantially. By the 1960s, many of the factors that had been identified as linking SES to disease had been addressed, and one might have expected the association to wane and perhaps disappear altogether. Indeed, this is exactly the conclusion that Charles Kadushin reached in a 1964 article in *Sociological Inquiry* (Kadushin 1964). Startled that social scientists had not recognized the demise of the SES gradient in health, Kadushin reminded his readers that most of the mechanisms thought to produce SES differences in health in the United States had been addressed and that "as countries advance in their standard of living, as public sanitation improves, as mass immunization proceeds, and as Dr. Spock becomes even more widely read, the gross factors which intervene between social class and exposure to disease will become more and more equal for all social classes" (1964:75). As a result, Kadushin declared, Americans from the lower classes are no more likely to develop disease than those from the middle or upper classes.

Of course, Kadushin's prediction turned out to be dramatically incorrect as indicated by studies (cited above) documenting an enduring or even an increasing (Pappas et al. 1993) association between SES and many disease outcomes. But what was wrong with Kadushin's reasoning? Hadn't he engaged in logic that most of us not only accept but take for granted? Having implicitly drawn the path model with SES as the distal factor that is linked to disease by more proximal risk factors, and having observed that the proximal risk factors in the model had been largely eliminated as causal agents, he concluded that the SES-disease association should have disappeared. But it didn't.

On the face of it, the reason Kadushin's 1964 prediction turned out to be wrong is readily apparent when one compares the intervening risk factors he considered to the intervening risk factors identified by Adler and colleagues in their 1994 review of socio-economic status and health. The "gross" risk factors of sanitation and immunization that Kadushin mentioned are replaced in the Adler and colleagues' review by risk factors that include smoking, exercise, and diet, among others. Further, the evidence suggests that several of the risk factors mentioned by Adler and colleagues were not important intervening mechanisms when Kadushin wrote. Before the 1960s, for example, there was no evidence that rates of smoking were higher among lower SES individuals. Rather, the association emerged during the 1960s because people of higher socioeconomic status were likely to start smoking and more likely to quit if they had started (Ernster 1988; Novotny et al. 1988). Similar changes have occurred in other risk-related behaviors. For example, in considering the strong evidence that declines in coronary heart disease have been greatest among people of higher socioeconomic status, Beaglehole (1990) pointed to the fact that higher SES individuals have been better informed about and more able to implement changes in health behaviors like smoking, exercise, and diet. The result has been a widening of the gap in rates of heart disease between the rich and the poor (Beaglehole 1990). Thus studies of the association between SES and disease over the past several decades reveal an important fact—the risk factors mediating the association have changed. As some risk factors were eradicated, others emerged or were newly discovered. As new risk factors became apparent, people of higher SES were more favorably situated to know about the risks and to have the resources that allowed

them to engage in protective efforts to avoid them.

From one vantage point, this account of the association between SES and disease might be seen as a curious story in the history of social epidemiology—an instance in which unique historical events pulled the rug out from under an otherwise reasonable hypothesis put forward by Kadushin in 1964. Far more likely, however, is the possibility that the effect of SES on disease has endured—despite radical changes in intervening risk factors—because a deeper sociological process is at work. If so, what happened over the past several decades will continue to happen and if, at this partic-ular point in time, we presume that an under-standing of the SES-disease association lies in tracing the mechanisms that currently appear to link the two, time will prove to be as wrong as Kadushin was. This will occur, we argue, because SES is a fundamental cause of disease.

Fundamental Social Causes of Disease

Our discussion of SES to this point has focused on its persistent association with disease despite changes in intervening mecha-nisms. However, we have not yet explicitly indi-cated *why* SES, or any fundamental cause, might maintain this kind of enduring rela-tionship with disease.

The reason for such persistent associations, and the essential feature of fundamental social causes, is that they involve access to resources that can be used to avoid risks or to minimize the consequences of disease once it occurs. We define resources broadly to include money, knowledge, power, prestige, and the kinds of interpersonal resources embodied in the concepts of social support and social network. Variables like SES, social networks, and stigmatization are used by medical sociologists and social epidemiolo-gists to directly assess these resources[2] and are therefore especially obvious as potential fun-damental causes. However, other variables examined by medical sociologists and social epidemiologists, such as race/ethnicity and gender, are so closely tied to resources like money, power, prestige, and/or social connectedness that they should be considered as potential fundamental causes of disease as well.

An additional condition that must obtain for fundamental causes to emerge is change over time in the disease afflicting humans, the risks for those diseases, knowledge about risks, or the effectiveness of treatments for diseases. If no new diseases emerged (such as AIDS), no new risks developed (such as pollutants), no new knowledge about risks emerged (as about cigarette smoking in the 1950s and 1960s), and no new treatments were developed (such as heart transplants), the concept of fundamental social causes would not apply. In such a static system, as risk factors known to intervene between a social cause and disease are blocked, the association between the social cause and disease would decline in lockstep. But, of course, this is nothing like the situation humans have ever confronted with regard to health. In the context of a dynamic system with changes in diseases, risks, knowledge of risks, and treatments, fundamental causes are likely to emerge. The reason is that resources like knowledge, money, power, prestige, and social connectedness are transportable from one situation to another, and as health-related situations change, those who command the most resources are best able to avoid risks, diseases, and the consequences of disease. Thus, no matter what the current profile of diseases and known risks happens to be, those who are best positioned with regard to important social and economic resources will be less afflicted by disease.

The foregoing reasoning suggests two further attributes of fundamental causes. Because a fundamental cause involves access to broadly serviceable resources, it influences (1) multiple risk factors and (2) multiple disease outcomes. This is an important observation, because it alerts us to the possibility

that the association between a fundamental cause and disease can be preserved through changes either in the mechanisms or in the outcomes. The idea that multiple mechanisms may contribute to a persistent association between a cause and an effect comes from sociologist Stanley Lieberson. Lieberson (1985) proposed that some causes, which he called "basic causes," have enduring effects on a dependent variable because, when the effect of one mechanism declines, the effect of another emerges or becomes more prominent. We have already described the example of the changing role of mechanisms like smoking, exercise, and diet in relation to the association between socioeconomic status and disease. While these variables were no doubt always linked to disease, their connection to socioeconomic status changed when knowledge about their importance in health became available. We take the idea that a cause can affect multiple health outcomes from social epidemiologist John Cassel. Cassel (1976) points out that some social factors make individuals vulnerable, not to a specific disease, but to a wide array of diseases. As a result, investigations of the relationship of such social factors to specific manifestations of disease are of limited utility. Since only one manifestation of the social cause is measured in such studies, the full impact of the social cause goes unrecorded (also see Aneshensel 1992; Aneshensel, Rutter, and Lachenbruch 1991; Cullen 1984). However, in addition to underestimating the full impact of social causes at any given time, a narrow focus on one disease at a time misses the possibility that changes in particular disease outcomes can lead to enduring associations between fundamental causes and disease overall. When health surveillance or immunization systems fail and old diseases begin to reemerge (TB, measles) or when new diseases enter a population (AIDS), they do so in the context of existing social conditions that are ripe environments for producing mechanisms that link fundamental social causes to new or reemerging diseases. Thus, for example, before 1980, SES was linked to the intravenous use of drugs, which in turn had negative health consequences. But with the emergence of AIDS, this SES-linked risk factor came to have an even more potent effect on health. Indeed, AIDS will likely become a significant contributor to SES differentials in mortality in the time ahead due to the rapid spread of infection in low-income areas (Brunswick et al. 1993). Similarly, the reemergence of drug-resistant tuberculosis is striking poor inner-city populations to a far greater extent than it is in higher-status suburban areas.

In sum, a fundamental social cause of disease involves resources that determine the extent to which people are able to avoid risks for morbidity and mortality.[3] Because resources are important determinants of risk factors, fundamental causes are linked to multiple disease outcomes through multiple risk-factor mechanisms. Moreover, because social and economic resources can be used in different ways in different situations, fundamental social causes have effects on disease even when the profile of risk factors changes radically. It follows that the effect of fundamental cause cannot be explained by the risk factors that happen to link it to disease at any given time.

Research Implications

All too frequently, even those of us who believe that social conditions are important for health are lulled into thinking that the best way to understand and ultimately address the effects of social conditions is to identify the intervening links. Indeed, it is precisely this reasoning that Adler and colleagues use to assert that psychologists have an important role to play in addressing the SES-disease association—the risk factors they identified were individually based behaviors that psychologists are well-equipped to

address. But the concept of a fundamental cause sensitizes us to the possibility that fundamental social causes cannot be fully understood by tracing the mechanisms that appear to link them to disease. To be sure, a focus on mechanisms can help identify variables more proximal to health, and if such risks are addressed, the health of the public can be improved. However, in the context of a dynamic system in which risk factors, knowledge of risk factors, treatments, and patterns of disease are changing, the association between a fundamental social cause and disease will endure because the resources it entails are transportable to new situations. If one genuinely wants to alter the effects of a fundamental cause, one must address the fundamental cause itself.

There are two implications of this reasoning. First, medical sociologists and social epidemiologists need to be careful in interpreting and communicating the meaning of research involving social factors, intervening mechanisms, and disease. Specifically, if the social factor is a fundamental cause, one cannot claim to have accounted for its effects by having "explained" its association with the inclusion of intervening variables in a path or regression model. Second, to understand associations between fundamental causes and disease, medical sociologists need to examine the broader determinants of the resources that fundamental causes entail. This distinctly sociological enterprise will link medical sociologists to the broader discipline in a productive way as we seek to understand how general resources like knowledge, money, power, prestige, and social connections are transformed into the health-related resources that generate patterns of morbidity and mortality. . . .

CONCLUSION

The dominant focus in epidemiology and perhaps the American culture in general is on individually based risk factors that lie relatively close to disease in a causal chain. But this focus overlooks important sociological processes and, as a result, could lead us to actions that limit our ability to improve the nation's health. We have focused on two concepts—contextualizing risk factors and fundamental causes—that direct our attention to precisely those factors that are left unexamined in the currently dominant orientation to research on risk factors for disease. If future research by medical sociologists and social epidemiologists increases our understanding of the processes implied by these concepts, we will be better positioned as a society to further improve the nation's health.

consider a mastery orientation to be a resource that would be linked to many mechanisms and thus to many diseases. Similarly, at the biological level, the immune system might be conceptualized as a resource that would influence many specific mechanisms and thus many disease outcomes. In either of these cases, the association between the fundamental cause (mastery or immune system) and disease outcomes would likely endure even if the specific mechanisms were to change. Our main point regarding social factors as fundamental causes is not that fundamental causes should be taken seriously because they are often social, but rather that social conditions need to be taken seriously because they are often fundamental causes.

NOTES

1. Using the *American Journal of Epidemiology* as an indication of the current emphasis of epidemiological research, we reviewed the 240 articles published between November of 1992 and 1993. Excluding methodological reports ($N = 44$) and studies focused exclusively on descriptive epidemiology ($N = 15$), we found that only 13.3 percent (24/181) of the articles focused on risk factors that could be construed as social in nature. Moreover, because many of these articles examined race, ethnicity, or gender, without explicit reference to the social aspects of these characteristics, our figure of 13.3 percent should be considered an upper-bound estimate of the journal's focus on social factors.

2. We include stigmatization because it is so closely tied to the prestige system (Goode 1978). Prestige, or the general standing that an individual holds in the eyes of others, is an important resource that is likely to have many implications for health—either indirectly through resources like money, power, or social connections, or more directly through what a person and/or those around him/her believe he/she deserves from the social environment. Stigmatization is important because it involves the denial of the benefits of prestige.

3. We focus here on fundamental *social* causes of disease. It is possible to conceive of fundamental psychological or biological causes as well. For example, at the psychological level, one might

REFERENCES

ADLER, NANCY E., THOMAS BOYCE, MARGARET A. CHESNEY, SHELDON COHEN, SUSAN FOLKMAN, ROBERT L. KAHN, and S. LEONARD SYME. 1994. "Socioeconomic Status and Health: The Challenge of the Gradient," *American Psychologist* 49:15–24.

ANESHENSEL, CAROL S. 1992. "Social Stress: Theory and Research." *Annual Review of Sociology* 18:15–38.

ANESHENSEL, CAROL, CAROLYN RUTTER, and PETER LACHENBRUCH. 1991. "Social Structure, Stress and Mental Health." *American Sociological Review* 56:166–78.

ANGERMEYER, MATTHIAS and DIETRICH KLUSMAN. 1987. "From Social Class to Social Stress: New Developments in Psychiatric Epidemiology." Pp. 2–13 in *From Social Class to Social Stress: New Developments in Psychiatric Epidemiology* edited by M. Angermeyer. New York: Springer-Verlag.

BEAGLEHOLE, ROBERT. 1990. "International Trends in Coronary Heart Disease Mortality, Morbidity, and Risk Factors." *Epidemiologic Reviews* 12:1–16.

BECKER, MARSHALL H. 1993. "A Medical Sociologist Looks at Health Promotion," *Journal of Health and Social Behavior* 34:1–6.

BENENSON, ABRAM S. 1987. "Infectious Diseases." Pp. 207–26 in *Epidemiology and Health Policy*, edited by S. Levine and A. Lilienfeld. New York: Tavistock.

BERKMAN, LISA and LEONARD SYME. 1979. "Social Networks, Host Resistance, and Mortality: A Nine-Year Follow-Up Study of Alameda County Residents." *American Journal of Epidemiology* 109:186–204.

BERKMAN, LISA, LINDA LEO-SUMMERS, and RALPH HORWITZ. 1992. "Emotional Support and Survival after Myocardial Infarction: A Prospective, Population-Based Study of the Elderly." *Annals of Internal Medicine* 117:1003–9.

BRUNSWICK, ANN, ANGELA AIDALA, JAY DOBKIN, JOYCE HOWARD, STEPHEN TITUS, and JANE BANASZAK-HALL. 1993. "HIV-1 Seroprevalence and Risk Behaviors in an Urban African American Community Cohort." *American Journal of Public Health* 83:1390–94.

BUCK, CAROL W. 1981. "Prenatal and Perinatal Causes of Early Death and Defect." Pp. 149–66 in *Preventive and Community Medicine*, 2d ed., edited by D. W. Clark and B. MacMahon. Boston, MA: Little, Brown, and Company.

CASSEL, JOHN. 1976. "The Contribution of the Social Environment to Host Resistance." *American Journal of Epidemiology* 104:107–23.

CATALANO, RALPH, DAVID DOOLEY, GEORJEANA WILSON, and RICHARD HOUGH. 1993. "Job Loss and Alcohol Abuse: A Test Using Data from the Epidemiologic Catchment Area Project." *Journal of Health and Social Behavior* 34:215–25.

CHALLAH, SABRI and ANTHONY J. WING. 1985. "The Epidemiology of Genito-Urinary Disease." Pp. 181–202 in *Oxford Textbook of Public Health*, edited by W. W. Holland, R. Detels, and G. Knox. Oxford, England: Oxford University Press.

COHEN, SHELDON, DAVID TYRRELL, and ANDREW SMITH. 1991. "Psychological Stress and Susceptibility to the Common Cold." *The New England Journal of Medicine* 325:606–12.

COLLEY, J. R. T. 1985. "Respiratory System." Pp. 145–66 in *Oxford Textbook of Public Health*, edited by W. W. Holland, R. Detels, and G. Knox. Oxford, England: Oxford University Press.

CULLEN, FRANCIS T. 1984. *Rethinking Crime and Deviance Theory: The Emergence of a Structuring Tradition*. Totowa, NJ: Rowan and Allenheld.

DOHRENWEND, BRUCE P. 1966. "Social Status and Psychological Disorder: An Issue of Substance and an Issue of Method." *American Sociological Review* 31:14–34.

———. 1990. "Socioeconomic Status and Psychiatric Disorders: Are the Issues Still Compelling?" *Social Psychiatry and Psychiatric Epidemiology* 25:41–47.

DOHRENWEND BRUCE P. and BARBARA S. DOHRENWEND. 1969. *Social Status and Psychological Disorder*. New York: Wiley.

———. 1981. "Part 2. Hypotheses About Stress Processes Linking Social Class to Various Types of Psychopathology." *American Journal of Community Psychology* 9:146–59.

DOHRENWEND, BRUCE P., BARBARA S. DOHRENWEND, MADELYN GOULD, BRUCE LINK, RICHARD NEUGEBAUER, and ROBIN WUNSCH-HITZIG. 1980. *Mental Illness in the United States: Epidemiological Estimates*. New York: Praeger.

DOHRENWEND, BRUCE P., ITZHAK LEVAV, PATRICK SHROUT, SHARON SCHWARTZ, GUEDALIA NAVEH, BRUCE LINK, ANDREW SKODAL, and ANN STUEVE. 1992. "Socioeconomic Status and Psychiatric Disorders: The Causation Selection Issue." *Science* 255:946–51.

DUTTON, DIANA B. 1986. "Social Class, Health, and Illness." Pp. 31–62 in *Applications of Social Science to Clinical Medicine and Health Policy*, edited by L. Aiken and D. Mechanic. New Brunswick, NJ: Rutgers University Press.

ENSEL, WALTER and NAN LIN. 1991. "The Stress Paradigm and Psychological Distress." *The Journal of Health and Social Behavior* 32:321–41.

ERNSTER, VIRGINIA L. 1988. "Trends in Smoking, Cancer Risk, and Cigarette Promotion." *Cancer* 62:1702–12.

FENWICK, RUDY and MARK TAUSIG. 1994. "The Macroeconomic Context of Job Stress." *Journal of Health and Social Behavior* 35:266–82.

GAZZARD, B. G. and P. LANCE. 1982. "Peptic Ulceration." Pp. 211–19 in *Epidemiology of Diseases*, edited by D. L. Miller and R. D. T. Farmer. Oxford, England: Blackwell Scientific Publications.

GOLDBERG, EVELYN L. and GEORGE W. COMSTOCK. 1980. "Epidemiology of Life Events: Frequency in General Populations." *American Journal of Epidemiology* 111:736–52.

GOODE, WILLIAM. 1978. *The Celebration of Heroes: Prestige as a Control System*. Berkeley, CA: University of California Press.

HAMILTON, V. LEE, CLIFFORD BROMAN, WILLIAM HOFFMAN, and DEBORAH RENNER. 1990. "Hard Times and Vulnerable People: Initial Effects of

Plant Closings On Autoworkers' Mental Health." *Journal of Health and Social Behavior* 31:123–40.

HOUSE, JAMES S., KARL R. LANDIS, and DEBRA UMBERSON. 1988. "Social Relationships and Health." *Science* 241:540–45.

HOUSE, JAMES S., JAMES M. LEPKOWSKI, ANN M. KINNEY, RICHARD P. MERO, RONALD C. KESSLER, and A. REGULA HERZOG. 1994. "The Social Stratification of Aging and Health." *Journal of Health and Social Behavior* 35:213–34.

HOUSE, JAMES S., RONALD C. KESSLER, A. REGULA HERZOG, RICHARD P. MERO, ANN M. KINNEY, and MARTHA J. BRESLOW. 1990. "Age, Socioeconomic Status, and Health." *The Milbank Memorial Fund* 68:383–411.

ILLSLEY, RAYMOND and KEN MULLEN. 1985. "The Health Needs of Disadvantaged Client Groups." Pp. 389–402 in *Oxford Textbook of Public Health*, edited by W. W. Holland, R. Detels, and G. Knox. Oxford, England: Oxford University Press.

JOHNSON, TIMOTHY. 1991. "Mental Health, Social Relations, and Social Selection: A Longitudinal Analysis." *Journal of Health and Social Behavior* 32:408–23.

KADUSHIN, CHARLES. 1964. "Social Class and the Experience of Ill Health." *Sociological Inquiry* 35:67–80.

KARASEK, ROBERT, TORES THEORELL, JOSEPH SCHWARTZ, PETER SCHNALL, CARL PIEPER, and JOHN MICHELA. 1988. "Job Characteristics in Relation to the Prevalence of Myocardial Infarction in the U.S. Health Examination Survey (HES) and the Health and Nutrition Examination Survey (HANES)." *American Journal of Public Health* 78:910–18.

KELSEY, JENNIFER L. 1993. "Breast Cancer Epidemiology: Summary and Future Directions." *Epidemiological Reviews* 15:256–63.

KESSLER, RONALD, KATHERINE MCGONAGLE, SHANYANG ZHAO, CHRISTOPHER NELSON, MICHAEL HUGHES, SUSAN ESHLEMAN, HANS-ULRICH WITTCHEN, and KENNETH KENDLER. 1994. "Lifetime and 12-Month Prevalence of DSM-III-R Psychiatric Disorders in the United States: Results from the National Comorbidity Survey." *Archives of General Psychiatry* 51:8–19.

LENNON, MARY CLARE. 1987. "Sex Differences in Distress: The Impact of Gender and Work

Roles." *Journal of Health and Social Behavior* 28:290–305.

LIEBERSON, STANLEY. 1985. *Making it Count: The Improvement of Social Research and Theory.* Berkeley, CA: University of California Press.

LIN, NAN and WALTER ENSEL. 1989. "Life Stress and Health: Stressors and Resources." *American Sociological Review* 54:382–99.

LINK, BRUCE and BRUCE DOHRENWEND. 1989. "The Epidemiology of Mental Disorders." Pp. 102–27 in *The Handbook of Medical Sociology*, 4th ed., edited by H. Freeman and S. Levine. Englewood Cliffs, NJ: Prentice Hall.

LINK, BRUCE and PATRICK SHROUT. 1992. "Spurious Associations in Longitudinal Research." *Research in Community and Mental Health* 7:301–21.

LINK, BRUCE, MARY CLARE LENNON, and BRUCE DOHRENWEND. 1993. "Socioeconomic Status and Depression: The Role of Occupations Involving Direction, Control, and Planning." *American Journal of Sociology* 98:1351–87.

MILLER, C. ARDEN. 1987. "Child Health." Pp. 15–54 in *Epidemiology and Health Policy*, edited by S. Levine and A. Lilienfeld. New York: Tavistock.

MIROWSKY, JOHN and CATHERINE E. ROSS. 1989. *The Social Causes of Psychological Distress.* New York: Aldine de Gruyter.

NOVOTNY, THOMAS E., KENNETH E. WARNER, JULIETTE S. KENDRICK, and PATRICK REMINGTON. 1988. "Smoking by Blacks and Whites: Socioeconomic and Demographic Differences." *American Journal of Public Health* 78:1187–89.

PAPPAS, GREGORY, SUSAN QUEEN, WILBUR HADDEN, and GAIL FISHER. 1993. "The Increasing Disparity in Mortality Between Socioeconomic Groups in the United States." *The New England Journal of Medicine* 329:103–109.

PEARLIN, LEONARD. 1989. "The Sociological Study of Stress." *Journal of Health and Social Behavior* 30:241–56.

PEARLIN, LEONARD and CARMI SCHOOLER. 1978. "The Structure of Coping." *Journal of Health and Social Behavior* 19:2–21.

PEARLIN, LEONARD, MORTON LIEBERMAN, ELIZABETH MENAGHAN, and JOSEPH T. MULLEN. 1981. "The Stress Process." *Journal of Health and Social Behavior* 22:337–56.

PEDOE, H. TUNSTALL. 1982. "Stroke." Pp. 136–45 in *Epidemiology of Diseases*, edited by D. L. Miller and R. D. T. Farmer. Oxford, England: Blackwell Scientific Publications.

POTTER, JOHN D. 1992. "Reconciling the Epidemiology, Physiology, and Molecular Biology of Colon Cancer." *Journal of the American Medical Association* 268:1573–77.

PROUT, MARIANNE N., THEODORE COLTON, and ROBERT A. SMITH. 1987. "Cancer Epidemiology and Health Policy." Pp. 117–56 in *Epidemiology and Health Policy*, edited by S. Levine and A. Lilienfeld. New York: Tavistock.

RABKIN, JUDITH and ELMER STRUENING. 1976. "Life Events, Stress, and Illness." *Science* 194:1013–20.

ROBINS, LEE, JOHN E. HELZER, MYRNA M. WEISSMAN, HELEN ORVASCHEL, ERNEST GRUENBERG, JACK D. BURKE, and DARREL A. REGIER. 1984. "Lifetime Prevalence of Specific Psychiatric Disorders in Three Sites." *Archives of General Psychiatry* 41:949–58.

ROSEN, GEORGE. 1979. "The Evolution of Social Medicine." Pp. 23–50 in *The Handbook of Medical Sociology*, 3d ed., edited by H. Freeman, S. Levine, and L. Reeder. Englewood Cliffs, NJ: Prentice Hall.

ROSENFIELD, SARAH. 1989. "The Effects of Women's Employment: Personal Control and Sex Differences in Mental Health." *Journal of Health and Social Behavior* 30:77–91.

ROTHMAN, KENNETH. 1986. *Modern Epidemiology*. Boston, MA: Little, Brown, and Company.

SARACCI, RODOLFO. 1985. "Neoplasms." Pp. 112–29 in *Oxford Textbook of Public Health*, edited by W. W. Holland, R. Detels, and G. Knox. Oxford, England: Oxford University Press.

SCHNALL, PETER, CARL PIEPER, JOSEPH SCHWARTZ, ROBERT KARASEK, Y. SCHLUSSEL, R. DEVEREUX, M. ALDERMAN, KATHERINE WARREN, and THOMAS PIKERING. 1990. "The Relationship Between 'Job Strain,' Workplace Diastolic Blood Pressure, and Left Ventricular Mass Index." *Journal of the American Medical Association* 263:1929–35.

SCHNALL, PETER, JOSEPH SCHWARTZ, PAUL LANDSBERGIS, KATHERINE WARREN, and THOMAS PICKERING. 1992. "Relation Between Job Strain, Alcohol, and Ambulatory Blood Pressure." *Hypertension* 19:488–94.

SHROUT, PATRICK, BRUCE LINK, BRUCE DOHRENWEND, ANDREW SKODAL, ANN STUEVE, and JEROLD MIROTZNIK. 1989. "Characterizing Life Events as Risk Factors for Depression." *Journal of Abnormal Psychology* 98:460–67.

SMITH, TOM W. 1992. "A Life Events Approach to Developing an Index of Societal Well-Being." *Social Science Research* 21:353–79.

SUSSER, MERVYN, WILLIAM WATSON, and KIM HOPPER. 1985. *Sociology in Medicine*. New York: Oxford University Press.

SYME, S. LEONARD and JACK M. GURALNIK. 1987. "Epidemiology and Health Policy: Coronary Heart Disease." Pp. 85–116 in *Epidemiology and Health Policy*, edited by S. Levine and A. Lilienfeld. New York: Tavistock.

TURNER, R. JAY and FRANCO MARINO. 1994. "Social Support and Social Structure: A Descriptive Epidemiology." *Journal of Health and Social Behavior* 35:193–212.

TURNER, R. JAY, BLAIR WHEATON, and DONALD LLOYD. 1995. "The Epidemiology of Social Stress." *American Sociological Review* 60:104–25.

UMBERSON, DEBRA, CAMILLE WORTMAN, and RONALD KESSLER. 1992. "Widowhood and Depression: Explaining Long-Term Gender Differences in Vulnerability." *Journal of Health and Social Behavior* 33:10–24.

VIRCHOW, RUDOLF. 1848. "The Public Health Service" (in German). *Medizinische Reform* 5:21–22.

WALSH, JOYCE K. and JOSEPH G. FELDMAN. 1981. "Health of the U.S. Population." Pp. 583–602 in *Preventive and Community Medicine*, 2d ed., edited by D. W. Clark and B. MacMahon. Boston, MA: Little, Brown, and Company.

Part II
SOCIAL DEMOGRAPHY OF HEALTH

In this part, we present one article that deals with the social demography of health and illness. Demography, in its most basic form, involves the scientific study and analysis of human populations. Demographers systematically examine birth (fertility), death (mortality), and migration rates among different groups of people. Data come from a variety of sources, including vital statistics (birth certificates, death certificates), census taking (periodic gathering of information from designated populations), and empirical research. Demography is similar to epidemiology, in that it is interdisciplinary in nature and relies on sociologists, biologists, economists, geographers, and others to pursue relevant avenues of investigation. Medical sociologists who conduct demographic analyses are especially interested in profiling populations by social factors such as age, gender, race, and socioeconomic status (SES).

"The Links between Education and Health," by Catherine E. Ross and Chia-ling Wu, focuses on one aspect of socioeconomic status; namely, education. These researchers examine the association between education and health. Analysis of two separate data sets, both from national probability samples of U.S. households, uncovers a strong relationship between self-reported health and physical functioning. Someone who is highly educated and works full time in a subjectively fulfilling, high-income job with low economic hardship experiences good health. Furthermore, the well educated who report a greater sense of control over their lives, less smoking, more exercise, and moderate drinking are also more positive in their self-assessments of health, with higher levels of functioning. Overall, high levels of educational achievement seem to improve health directly and indirectly through work and economic conditions, social-psychological resources, and lifestyle.

THE LINKS BETWEEN EDUCATION AND HEALTH

Catherine E. Ross
The Ohio State University
Chia-ling Wu
National Taiwan University

The positive association between education and health is well established, but explanations for this association are not. Our explanations fall into three categories: (1) work and economic conditions, (2) social-psychological resources, and (3) health lifestyle. We replicate analyses with two samples, cross-sectionally and over time, using two health measures (self-reported health and physical functioning). The first data set comes from a national probability sample of U.S. households in which respondents were interviewed by telephone in 1990 (2,031 respondents, ages 18 to 90). The second data set comes from a national probability sample of U.S. households in which respondents ages 20 to 64 were interviewed by telephone first in 1979 (3,025 respondents), and then again in 1980 (2,436 respondents). Results demonstrate a positive association between education and health and help explain why the association exists. (1) Compared to the poorly educated, well-educated respondents are less likely to be unemployed, are more likely to work full-time, to have fulfilling, subjectively rewarding jobs, high incomes, and low economic hardship. Full-time work, fulfilling work, high income, and low economic hardship in turn significantly improve health in all analyses. (2) The well educated report a greater sense of control over their lives and their health, and they have higher levels of social support. The sense of control, and to a lesser extent support, are associated with good health. (3) The well educated are less likely to smoke, are more likely to exercise, to get health check-ups, and to drink moderately, all of which, except check-ups, are associated with good health. We conclude that high educational attainment improves health directly, and it improves health indirectly through work and economic conditions, social-psychological resources, and health lifestyle.

The positive association between education and health is well established, but explanations for this association are not. Well-educated people experience better health than the poorly educated, as indicated by high levels of self-reported health and physical functioning and low levels of morbidity, mor-

Reprinted from the *American Sociological Review*, vol. 60 (October 1995), pp. 719–45, by permission of the American Sociological Association.

tality, and disability. In contrast, low educational attainment is associated with high rates of infectious disease, many chronic noninfectious diseases, self-reported poor health, shorter survival when sick, and shorter life expectancy (Feldman, Makuc, Kleinman, and Cornoni-Huntley 1989; Guralnik, Land, Fillenbaum, and Branch 1993; Gutzwiller, LaVecchia, Levi, Negri, and Wietlisbach 1989; Kaplan, Haan, and Syme 1987; Kitagawa and Hauser 1973; Liu et al. 1982; Morris 1990;

Pappas, Queen, Hadden, and Fisher 1993; Syme and Berkman 1986; Williams 1990; Winkleby, Jatulis, Frank, and Fortmann 1992; Woodward, Shewry, Smith, and Tunstall-Pedoe 1992).[1] The positive association between health and socioeconomic status, whether measured by education, occupation, or income, is largely due to the effects of SES on health, not vice versa, and downward mobility among persons in poor health cannot explain the association (Doornbos and Kromhout 1990; Fox, Goldblatt, and Jones 1985; Power, Manor, and Fogelman 1990; Wilkinson 1986).

INEQUALITY AND HEALTH

Why is education associated with good health? Our theoretical explanations fall into three categories: (1) work and economic conditions, (2) social-psychological resources, and (3) health lifestyle. According to the first explanation, well-educated people are less likely to be unemployed, and more likely to have full-time jobs, fulfilling work, high incomes, and low economic hardship. According to the second, the well educated have social-psychological resources, including a high sense of personal control and social support, in addition to economic resources. According to the third, the well educated have healthier lifestyles; compared to the poorly educated, the well educated are more likely to exercise, to drink moderately, to receive preventive medical care, and less likely to smoke.

We focus on education as the aspect of socioeconomic status most important to health—not to the exclusion of work and income, but as the variable that structures the other two.[2] Education is the key to one's position in the stratification system; it shapes the likelihood of being unemployed, the kind of job a person can get, and income.

Sociologists study stratification out of interest in systematic differences in opportunities and quality of life. Although stratification research typically focuses on job-related outcomes such as occupation and earnings, ultimately the impact of social inequality extends beyond differences in jobs, earnings, prestige, and power, to the consequences of this inequality for individual well-being. If educational inequality leads to differences in health then it directly affects quality of life. Education-based inequality sorts people into different positions that are associated with different risks and rewards. Location in the stratification system shapes the ongoing stressors to which people are exposed, the resources available to help them cope with stressors, and lifestyle (Pearlin 1989). We argue that the advantages of the well educated in work and economic circumstances, social-psychological resources, and lifestyle improve health.

Although sociologists have called for research on the *explanations* for the association between socioeconomic status and health, little U.S. research has been done (Pearlin 1989; Williams 1990).[3] Those who study education's effect on the subjective quality of life often downplay its importance, claiming educational attainment is credentialism with little real value, and that education has a questionable payoff in terms of access to fulfilling and satisfying work (Berg 1971). A study by Leigh (1983), one of the few that examines the indirect effects of education on self-reported health in the United States, has limitations. First, it uses an economic, individual choice perspective which asserts that poorly educated people "chose" hazardous jobs due to lack of knowledge; second, it excludes the nonemployed, thus excluding people who are the most disadvantaged. Leigh finds that the relatively dangerous work done by the poorly educated explains some of the effect of education on health, but that income does not significantly affect health and therefore cannot explain any of the effect.

He concludes that income and medical care are inconsequential to health (he equates income with medical care and has no independent measure of the latter), as if the only drawback to poverty was the inability to purchase medical care. We question Leigh's conclusions. First, we view income and medical care as conceptually distinct, rather than as interchangeable explanations. Second, the *apparent* insignificance of income may reflect a truncated sample (of employed persons) that eliminates the most disadvantaged: those who are unemployed, engaged in unpaid domestic labor, and retired.

We include persons who are not in the paid economy, and thus, we do not measure work characteristics as occupational prestige, rank, or status. Because occupational prestige (or occupational status ranked from unskilled at the bottom to professionals, managers, and executives at the top) is relevant only to the employed, studies that use it exclude everyone who is not employed. Much of the *descriptive* research on social class and health is British, and almost all of it equates social class with occupation (e.g., Wilkinson 1986). By one estimate 42 percent of British women aged 16 to 64 were excluded from these studies because they had "no occupation" (Carstairs and Morris 1989). The exclusion of people not employed for pay eliminates the most disadvantaged, severely truncates variation in socioeconomic status, and attenuates the effects of educational and economic inequality on health.

"Social inequality" and "individual responsibility" are often considered rival explanations of health. The view that health is determined by individual behaviors, like smoking (Knowles 1977), is criticized by those who see health as a function of a social structure that allocates goods unequally (Crawford 1986). In contrast, in the theory we develop, social-psychological resources and health behaviors link structured inequality to health. Stressors, hardships, beliefs, and behaviors are not randomly distributed; they are socially structured. Smoking, exercising, drinking, or a sense of personal control are not *alternatives* to socially structured inequalities like unemployment, poverty, unfulfilling jobs, or economic hardships faced disproportionately by those with little schooling. On the contrary, they link education-based inequality to health.

Work and Economic Conditions

Education shapes work and economic conditions. Well-educated people are less likely to be unemployed than the poorly educated; they are more likely to work full-time, and their work may be more fulfilling. Their incomes are higher, and they experience less economic hardship. Thus, the work and economic conditions of the well educated may protect their health.

Employment. The well educated are more likely to be employed: Among persons aged 25 to 34 in 1991, 87 percent of college graduates were employed, compared to 77 percent of those with only a high school degree, and 56 percent of those with eight years of education or less (U.S. Department of Education 1992). The unemployment rate for college graduates was 3 percent, one-fifth of that for persons with some high school. Lack of education limits employment opportunities (Sewell and Hauser 1975), and it is the poorly educated who work at low-status, poorly paid jobs who have the greatest risk of losing their jobs in an economic downturn (Elder and Liker 1982). Among the employed, the well educated are more likely to work full-time. In comparison, part-time work offers less training, lower returns to experience, and fewer benefits (Holden and Hansen 1987).

Employment benefits men's and women's well-being, while unemployment is associated with ill health (Linn, Sandifer, and Stein 1985; Pearlin, Lieberman, Menaghan, and

Mullan 1981). Long confirmed for men, it has been established recently that among women the employed report the best physical health (Bird and Fremont 1991; Verbrugge 1983); housewives report lower health, and unemployed women report the worst health (Jennings, Mazaik, and McKinlay 1984). Part-time female workers have worse health than full-time female workers, although their health is better than the nonemployed (Herold and Waldron 1985). This positive association between employment and health is not simply due to selection of healthier people into the labor force (Kessler, House, and Turner 1987; Moser, Fox, and Jones 1986; Passannante and Nathanson 1985; Ross and Mirowsky forthcoming). We expect that the higher likelihood of and levels of employment among the well educated positively affect their health.

Income and Economic Hardship. Education shapes employment, income, and in turn economic hardship. Low educational attainment translates into low expected income (Sewell and Hauser 1975), which in turn is the major cause of economic hardship. Yet even at the same income levels, poorly educated people experience greater hardship than the well educated (Ross and Huber 1985). The effect of poverty and lack of education on economic strain is synergistic; each factor makes the effect of the other worse. Education provides skills and information to help people deal with the stresses of life, including a low income, while lack of education makes it more difficult to cope with an inadequate income.

Economic hardship negatively impacts health. The ongoing strain of paying the bills on an inadequate income takes its toll. When life is a constant struggle, when it is never taken for granted that there will be enough money for food, clothes, and shelter, people often feel worn down, depressed, and hopeless, which decreases resistance and makes

them susceptible to disease (Pearlin et al. 1981; Syme and Berkman 1986).

Work Fulfillment. We expect that education gives people access to subjectively rewarding work, but the evidence is indirect. Well-educated people are more likely than the poorly educated to experience autonomy on the job and nonroutine work, both of which increase psychological functioning and job satisfaction (Kohn, Naoi, Shoenbach, Schooler, and Slomczynski 1990; Ross and Reskin 1992). We expect that work done by people with a high school education or less is not as rewarding subjectively as work done by college graduates—that it is less enjoyable, provides fewer opportunities to learn new things and develop as a person, and results in less pride in accomplishments and less recognition from others. Work characterized by job insecurity, monotony, and exclusion from decision making may be less subjectively rewarding. However, the health effects of intrinsic work rewards among the employed are small, inconsistent, and not always positive (Hibbard and Pope 1987; House, Strecher, Metzner, and Robbins 1986). Past research on education, work fulfillment, and health is inconclusive.

Social-Psychological Resources

Education shapes two key social-psychological resources: a sense of personal control and social support—both of which may protect health.

Sense of Control. A sense of control over one's life may be an important link between education and health. Perceived powerlessness and lack of control is the belief that one's actions do not affect outcomes (Seeman 1983)—that outcomes of situations are determined by forces external to one's own actions such as powerful others, luck, fate, or chance. The opposite, belief in personal control, is a learned expectation that outcomes are contingent on one's own choices and actions—that one can master, control, or effectively alter one's environment. This sense of personal control appears in the literature in a number of related forms with various names, including locus of control (Rottel 1966), personal efficacy (Downey and Moen 1987), personal autonomy (Seeman and Seeman 1983), self-directedness (Kohn and Schooler 1982), mastery (Pearlin et al. 1981), and instrumentalism (Wheaton 1980).

Education, employment, and income increase the sense of personal control (Mirowsky and Ross 1989; Pearlin et al. 1981; Ross and Mirowsky 1992; Wheaton 1980). Through education, one develops capacities on many levels that increase one's sense of personal control, mastery, and self-direction: the habits and skills of communication (reading, writing, inquiring, discussing, looking things up, and figuring things out); and analytic skills (mathematics, logic, and, on a more basic level, observing, experimenting, summarizing, synthesizing, interpreting, and classifying). Because education develops one's ability to gather and interpret information and to solve problems on many levels, it increases one's potential to control events and outcomes in life. Moreover, through education one encounters and solves problems that are progressively more difficult, complex, and subtle, which builds problem-solving skills and confidence in the ability to solve problems. Education instills the habit of meeting problems with attention, thought, action, and persistence. In contrast, people with low levels of educational attainment and restricted employment opportunities and economic circumstances often learn that failure is built into their lives. Through experience, they come to perceive that powerful others and unpredictable forces control their lives and that they cannot get ahead no matter how hard they try.

The sense of personal control improves health, first, through enhancing health-related behaviors. People with high personal control are more knowledgeable about health, are more likely to initiate preventive behaviors such as quitting smoking or reducing alcohol consumption and, as a consequence, report better self-rated health and fewer illnesses than those with a low sense of control (Seeman and Seeman 1983; Seeman, Seeman, and Budros 1988). Second, lack of personal control affects health through physiological mechanisms, because experiences of uncontrollability and the resulting demoralization are associated with suppression of the immune system (Rodin and Timko 1992; Rowe and Kahn 1987).

Social Support. Social support is a sense of being cared for and loved, esteemed and valued as a person, and part of a network of communication and mutual obligation in which others can be counted on (Cobb 1976). The well educated have higher levels of social support than the poorly educated (Eckenrode 1983; Ross and Mirowsky 1989). Unemployment and economic hardship (associated with low educational attainment) decrease the sense of having a supportive spouse and increase domestic arguments (Gore 1978; Atkinson, Liem, and Liem 1986). Thus, the very people who most need social support to cope with their disadvantaged social positions are least likely to have it.

Social support improves health and decreases mortality (House, Landis, and Umberson 1988). The age-adjusted mortality for men with few social connections is 2.3 times higher than that for men with many connections; for women it is 2.8 times higher (Berkman and Breslow 1983). Social support improves health through psychological and behavioral mechanisms. It decreases depression, anxiety, and other psychological problems (Kessler and McLeod 1985; LaRocco, House, and French 1980). Over time, psychological distress worsens subsequent physical well-being (Aneshensel, Frerichs, and Huba

1984), and, in a 15-month follow-up, the severely depressed were four times more likely to die than others, adjusting for health conditions and physical functioning (Bruce and Leaf 1989). Also, social support may increase the likelihood of practicing protective health behaviors. For instance, married people experience more regulation of behavior than the unmarried (Umberson 1987), as one's spouse may discourage smoking, drug use, or heavy drinking.

Health Lifestyle

Compared to the poorly educated, well-educated people more frequently engage in positive health behaviors, like exercising, not smoking, and not drinking heavily— behaviors that may protect their health.

Smoking. The well educated are less likely to smoke than the poorly educated because they are more likely to have never smoked and because they are more likely to have quit (Helmert, Herman, Joeckel, Greiser, and Madans 1989; Jacobsen and Thelle 1988; Liu et al. 1982; Matthews, Kelsey, Meilahn, Kuller, and Wing 1989; Millar and Wigle 1986; Shea et al. 1991; Wagenknecht et al. 1990; Winkleby et al. 1992). Smoking negatively affects health. Of all the practices that affect health, smoking has the largest number of negative consequences (Rogers and Powell-Griner 1991). It increases the risk of coronary heart disease, stroke, atherosclerosis, and aneurysms; lung and other cancers, including esophagus, pancreas, bladder, larynx, and cervix; emphysema, bronchitis, pneumonia, and other respiratory infections; liver disease; and burns. Smoking is also associated with poor self-reported health (Abbott, Yin, Reed, and Yano 1986; NCHS 1989; Segovia, Bartlett, and Edwards 1989; Surgeon General 1982; U.S. Preventive Services Task Force 1989). Heart disease, cancer, stroke, and emphysema alone account for about 65 percent of all deaths (NCHS 1992).

Exercise. High levels of educational attainment are positively associated with physical activity (Ford et al. 1991; Helmert et al. 1989; Jacobsen and Thelle 1988; Leigh 1983; Shea et al. 1991), which positively affects many health outcomes. Compared to inactivity, any physical activity, aerobic or nonaerobic, reduces mortality (Berkman and Breslow 1983). Exercise reduces cardiovascular risk, back pain, osteoporosis, atherosclerosis, colon cancer, obesity, high blood pressure, constipation, varicose veins, and adult onset diabetes, and improves subjective health reports (Berlin and Colditz 1990; Caspersen, Bloemberg, Saris, Merritt, and Kromhout 1992; Duncan, Gordon, and Scott 1991; Leon, Connett, Jacobs, and Rauramaa 1987; Magnus, Matroos, and Strackee 1979; Paffenbarger et al. 1993; Sandvik et al. 1993; Segovia et al. 1989; U.S. Preventive Services Task Force 1989).

Drinking. The well educated are more likely to drink moderately than the poorly educated. In contrast, people with lower levels of education are more likely to abstain from or to abuse alcohol (Darrow, Russell, Copper, Mudar, and Frone 1992; Midanik, Klatsky, and Armstrong 1990; Romelsjo and Diderichsen 1989). Heavy drinking may temporarily relieve the stresses of poverty or low-level, high-risk jobs available to those with little schooling (Shore and Pieri 1992).

Compared to smoking and sedentary lifestyle, drinking as a risk factor is implicated in only 4 of the leading 15 causes of death— car accidents (one of the top 5 causes of death), cirrhosis of the liver, suicide, and homicide. Of these, only cirrhosis and injuries from car accidents affect self-reported health, making drinking far less ubiquitous in its health consequences than smoking or inadequate physical activity. Furthermore, research indicates a U-shaped relationship between drinking and illness. Both abstainers and very heavy drinkers have higher mortality and morbidity than do those who drink moderately (Berkman and Breslow 1983; Guralnik and Kaplan 1989; Midanrik et al. 1990). Moderate drinking, as compared to abstinence, is associated with lower risk of coronary heart disease, stroke, and hypertension, whereas very heavy drinking is associated with higher risk (Gaziano et al. 1993; Gill, Zezulka, Shipley, Gill, and Beevers 1986; Stampfer, Colditz, Willet, Speizer, and Hennekens 1988).

Health Checkups. The well educated are more likely to get preventive medical care—annual physical exams, immunizations, and screening—than are the poorly educated (Coburn and Pope 1974). They are more likely to have health insurance and to belong to social networks that encourage preventive behavior. Theoretically, annual physical exams help detect early signs of illness, thus forestalling more serious health problems. Little research has examined the efficacy of health checkups, but existing studies indicate little support for an association between annual physical exams and improved health (Canadian Task Force on the Periodic Health Examination 1979, 1988; U.S. Preventive Services Task Force 1989). Nonetheless, it is possible that one way education protects health is by increasing access to preventive medical care.

DATA AND MEASURES

Work, Family, and Well-Being

The Work, Family, and Well-Being (WFW) sample is based on a 1990 telephone survey of a national probability sample of U.S. households. Random digit dialing was used to ensure the inclusion of unlisted numbers (Waksberg 1978). Within each household, the person 18 years old or older with the most recent birthday was selected as respondent, which is an efficient method to randomly select a respondent within the household

(O'Rourke and Blair 1983). The response rate of 82.3 percent yielded a total of 2,031 respondents ranging in age from 18 to 90.

Measuring Education and Sociodemographic Characteristics. *Education* is coded as number of years of formal education completed. *Sex* is coded 1 for males; 0 for females. *Age* is coded as age in years. *Race* is coded 1 for whites; 0 for non-whites and Hispanics. *Marital status* is a dummy variable contrasting those currently married or living together as married (coded 1) with those who are single, separated, divorced, or widowed (coded 0).

Measuring Health. Health is measured as self-reported health and physical functioning. *Self-reported* health is the respondent's subjective assessment of his or her general health (coded 1 = very poor, 2 = poor, 3 = satisfactory, 4 = good, 5 = very good). Self-reported health is a valid and reliable measure of general physical well-being (Davies and Ware 1981; Mossey and Shapiro 1982). It combines the subjective experience of acute and chronic, fatal and nonfatal diseases, and general feelings of well-being, like feeling run-down and tired, having backaches and headaches. Thus, it measures health as defined by the World Health Organization—as a state of well-being, not simply as the absence of disease. Self-reported health is highly correlated with more "objective" measures, such as physician's assessments, and with measures of morbidity and mortality (Idler and Kasl 1991; Kaplan 1987; Mossey and Shapiro 1982), and it is a predictor of mortality over and above measures of chronic and acute disease, physician assessment made by clinical exam, physical disability, and health behaviors (Davies and Ware 1981; Idler and Kasl 1991; Liang 1986). In fact, self-assessed health is a *stronger* predictor of mortality than is physician-assessed health (Mossey and Shapiro 1982).

Physical functioning assesses physical mobility and functioning in daily activities.

All information in surveys consists of "self-reports," but physical functioning may not be as subjective as perceived health. Although self-reported health is highly correlated with morbidity, differences in the meaning, interpretation, or awareness of health and illness may shape socioeconomic differences in self-reported health. Therefore we also measure physical functioning, using an index of seven items. Respondents were asked "How much difficulty do you have (1) going up and down stairs; (2) kneeling or stooping; (3) lifting or carrying objects less than 10 pounds, like a bag of groceries; (4) using your hands or fingers; (5) seeing, even with glasses; (6) hearing; (7) walking?" (coded 0 = a great deal of difficulty, 1 = some difficulty, and 2 = no difficulty). The physical functioning index is the average of the 7 items, scored from 0 to 2. The low end of the scale reflects high physical impairment or disability; the high end reflects high physical functioning. This index is conceptually similar to Nagi's (1976) disability scale (alpha reliability = .804).

Measuring Work and Economic Conditions.
Employment status is measured using four categorical variables: employed full-time, employed part-time, not employed for pay (the comparison group in the regression analyses), and unable to work because of disability/illness. Inability to work because of disability or illness is included to control for the selection of some people out of the labor force because of illness, which will allow us to examine whether employment is associated with improved health, holding selection effects constant. *Household income* is coded in thousands of dollars per year. *Economic hardship* is measured as the response to three questions, "During the past twelve months, how often did it happen that you (1) did not have enough money to buy food, clothes, or other things your household needed; (2) did not have enough money to pay for medical care; and (3) had trouble paying the bills?"

Responses to each question were coded from 0 to 3 (0 = never, 1 = not very often, 2 = fairly often, and 3 = very often). The economic hardship index is the mean response to the three questions (alpha reliability = .82).

Work fulfillment is measured as fulfillment from work, either paid or unpaid. We asked employed and nonemployed persons to describe the work, tasks, or activities they most frequently do during the day. Respondents were then asked about the subjective rewards of their primary daily work. Paid work is considered the primary daily work of people working for pay 20 hours per week or more. Unpaid work includes reported activities such as housework, childcare, care for an ill or elderly family member, volunteer work, gardening and home repair, looking for work, and so on. Work fulfillment, or intrinsic gratification from work, includes pride in one's work, enjoyment of work, and the sense of learning and developing as a person through work. Work fulfillment is measured by responses to three questions: "How often do you finish your work/daily activities with a good feeling that you have done something especially well?" (coded −2 = never, −1 = once in a while, 0 = neutral, 1 = pretty often, 2 = very often); "How much do you agree with the statements: 'My work/tasks give me a chance to do things I enjoy'; and 'My work/tasks give me a chance to develop and to learn new things'?" (coded −2 = strongly disagree, −1 = disagree, 0 = neutral, 1 = agree, 2 = strongly agree). The work fulfillment index is the average response to these three questions; high scores indicate high work fulfillment.

Measuring Social-Psychological Resources.
Sense of control is the belief that you can and do master, control, and shape your own life. Perceived lack of control, the opposite, is the expectation that one's behavior does not affect outcomes. Sense of control is measured by a 2 × 2 index that balances statements

claiming or denying control over good or bad outcomes (Mirowsky and Ross 1991).

Social support is measured by responses to two questions about emotional support: "How much do you agree with the statements: 'I have someone I can turn to for support and understanding when things get rough,' and 'I have someone I can really talk to'?" (coded −2 = strongly disagree, −1 = disagree, 0 = neutral, 1 = agree, 2 = strongly agree). The social support index is the mean response; high scores indicate high support.

Measuring Health Lifestyle. *Exercise* is an index of walking and strenuous exercise. Walking is measured as the number of days walked per week. Respondents were asked, "How often do you take a walk? Would you say never (= 0), once a month or less (= .25), about twice a month (= .5), about once a week (= 1), twice a week (= 2), three times a week (= 3), more than three times a week (= 5), or every day (= 7)?" Strenuous exercise is measured by asking respondents, "How often do you do strenuous exercise such as running, basketball, aerobics, tennis, swimming, biking, and so on?" (coded the same way as walking, with the exception that more than three times a week is the highest response category). Our exercise index is the mean response to these two questions.

Smoking is coded 0 for nonsmokers, 1 for persons who have ever smoked seven or more cigarettes a week but who do not currently smoke, and 2 for persons who currently smoke seven or more cigarettes a week.

National Survey of Personal Health Practices and Consequences

The National Survey of Personal Health Practices and Consequences (Health Practices, or HP) sample is a national probability sample of U.S. households, collected by telephone in 1979; respondents were reinterviewed in 1980. Telephone exchanges were first randomly selected; next a random sample of telephone households were selected in proportion to the number of households served by each exchange; last, a sample respondent was chosen from each eligible household. There are 3,025 respondents, ages 20 to 64, interviewed in 1979; 2,436 were reinterviewed in 1980. Nonrespondents in 1980 do not differ significantly from respondents in terms of 1979 household income, education, employment status, or marital status. However, nonrespondents were younger and less likely to be white.

Measuring Education and Sociodemographic Characteristics. *Education* is coded ordinally in years of formal education completed (0 = none, 2.5 = 1 to 4 years, 5.5 = 5 to 6 years, 7.5 = 7 to 8 years, 10 = 9 to 11 years, 12 = 12 years, 14 = 13 to 15 years, 16 = college degree or more). *Sex* is coded 1 for males; 0 for females. *Age* is coded as age in years. *Race* is coded 1 for whites; 0 for non-whites. *Marital status* is a dummy variable contrasting those currently married (coded 1) with those who are single, separated, divorced, or widowed (coded 0).

Measuring Health. *Self-reported health* combines answers to two questions, "Would you say your health is . . . ," and "Compared to other people your age, would you say your health is . . . poor (= 1), fair (= 2), don't know (= 3), good (= 4), excellent (= 5)?" Self-reported health is the mean response to the two questions and is scored from poor to excellent health.

Physical functioning is a five-variable index. Respondents were asked "do you have any trouble or difficulties (1) walking; (2) using stairs or inclines; (3) standing or sitting for long periods; (4) using your fingers to grasp or handle; (5) lifting or carrying something as heavy as 10 pounds?" (coded 0 = yes, a great deal of difficulty; 1 = yes, some difficulty; 2 = no). The index is the mean response to the five items (alpha reliability = .846).

Measuring Work and Economic Conditions. *Employment status* is measured using four categorical variables: employed full-time, employed part-time, not employed for pay (the comparison group in the regression analyses), and unable to work because of poor health (coded 1 if retired because of health; 0 otherwise). *Household income* is measured according to the following categories: 4 = less than \$5,000, 7.5 = \$5,000 to \$9,000, 12.5 = \$10,000 to \$14,999, 20 = \$15,000 to \$24,999, 30 = \$25,000 or more. *Economic hardship* is measured by the responses to two questions: "Does it ever happen that you do not have enough money to afford the kind of medical care you or your family should have?" and "Please tell me if a serious financial difficulty or problem happened in your life during the past five years" (coded 0 = no and 1 = yes). The economic hardship index is the sum of responses.

Measuring Social-Psychological Resources. *Sense of control* is measured as the sense of control over one's future health. Respondents were asked, "How much control do you think you have over your future health?" (coded 1 = none at all, 2 = very little, 3 = some, 4 = a great deal). *Social support* is measured by responses to three questions: "How many close relatives do you have? These are people that you feel at ease with, can talk to about private matters and can call on for help"; "How many friends do you have that you feel really close to? These are friends that you feel at ease with, can talk to about private matters, and can call on to help" (coded 0 = none, 1 = one, 2 = two, 3 = three, 4 = four or more); and "Do you feel that you have enough close friends or relatives?" (coded 0 = no, .5 = neutral, 1 = yes). We standardize the three questions and take the average, so that the social support index is scored from 0 to 1. These items capture both the quantity and quality of social support, as respondents are asked about numbers of *close* relatives and friends—people one can really talk to and call on—and about perceived adequacy of this number.

Measuring Health Lifestyle. *Exercise* is measured by a seven-item index. Respondents were asked, "Please tell me how often you participate in these activities. How often do you (1) go swimming in the summer, (2) take long walks, (3) work on a physically active hobby such as dancing or gardening, (4) go jogging or running, (5) ride a bicycle, (6) do calisthenics or physical exercise, or (7) participate in any other active sports I haven't already mentioned?" (coded 1 = never, 2 = rarely, 3 = sometimes, 4 = often). The exercise index is scored as the mean response to the seven activities; high scores indicate high levels of exercise.

Smoking is coded in three categories (0 = never smoked, 1 = quit, 2 = current smoker).

Drinking is composed of a series of dummy variables: abstain from drinking, rare drinking, moderate drinking, and heavy drinking. Quantity/frequency drinking scores were computed by multiplying the number of days per week on which the person reports drinking by the number of drinks reported for the average day, and then categorized since the effect of drinking on health is probably nonlinear.

Health checkups are measured by the response to the question: "Some people get a general physical examination once in a while, even though they are feeling well and have not been sick. When was the last time you had a general physical examination when you were not sick?" (coded 0 = never, 1 = 5 or more years ago, 2 = 2 to 4 years ago, 3 = 1 to 2 years ago, 4 = less than 1 year ago). High scores indicate more recent checkups.

ANALYSIS

We propose that work and economic conditions, social-psychological resources, and health lifestyle are the links between education and health. To establish support for our model, education must be positively associated with health, and with work and economic conditions, social-psychological resources, and health lifestyle. We must also find that our three sets of explanatory variables are positively associated with health, and that they mediate or explain the observed association between education and health.

We first examine the mean levels of work and economic conditions, social-psychological resources, and health lifestyle among respondents with less than a high school degree, a high school degree to some college, and a college degree or more. (Education is categorized for these analyses only.)

Next, using multiple regression analysis, we examine the effect of education on health and the explanations for this association, cross-sectionally and over time. Equation 1 shows the total causal effect of education on health, adjusting for the sociodemographic precursors of sex, race, age, and marital status. Equation 2 adds the first set of explanatory variables—work and economic conditions—including employment status, household income, economic hardship, and work fulfillment. Equation 3 adds the variables measuring social-psychological resources—sense of control and social support. Equation 4 adds health lifestyle measures—exercise, smoking, drinking, and health checkups. The three sets of explanatory variables are added in an order that represents a proposed sequence in which work and economic conditions precede social-psychological resources, which precede health lifestyle. Although there may be reciprocal effects, longitudinal research shows that work and economic status affect sense of control and social support (Pearlin et al. 1981; Wheaton 1980), which in turn affect health behavior (Seeman and Seeman 1983). In each step of our analysis, we examine the effects of the explanatory variables on health, and whether the association between education and health is reduced with the addition of these variables, thus partially explaining[4] the association. We test our model using cross-sectional analyses with two data sets,[5] and using longitudinal analysis that examines changes in health over time. In the latter, change in health status is the dependent variable:

$$(Health_{1980} - Health_{1979}) = \\ b_0 + b_1\ Education + b_2\ Health_{1979} \\ + \sum_{i=3}^{k} b_i X_{i\ 1979} = u,$$

where change in health status over time is a function of education and the three sets of explanatory variables; sociodemographic characteristics and *health at time 1* are controlled. In this way, we address the causal order issue of whether education and the explanatory variables affect health, or whether health simply shapes educational attainment, employment, and so on.[6]

RESULTS

The Association between Education and Work and Economic Conditions, Social-Psychological Resources, and Health Lifestyle

Tables 1 and 2 show that in both samples work and economic conditions are significantly better among the college educated than among those with a high school degree or less. The college educated are significantly more likely to be employed full-time than are people with only a high school degree, followed by those who did not finish high school. In contrast, people who have not finished high school are the least likely to be employed. (People with a high school degree are more likely to work part-time than are people with a college degree or with no high school degree.) The college educated are least likely to be unable to work because of

TABLE 1 Means for Variables Measuring Health, Work and Economic Conditions, Social-Psychological Resources, and Health Lifestyle at Three Levels of Education: Work, Family, and Well-Being Sample, 1990

Variable	Less than High School Degree	High School Degree to Some College	College Degree or More
Health			
Self-reported health*	3.591	4.193	4.430
	(1.073)	(.851)	(.711)
Physical functioning*	1.599	1.847	1.905
	(.478)	(.261)	(.188)
Work and Economic Conditions			
Employed full-time*	.305	.511	.684
	(.461)	(.500)	(.465)
Employed part-time*	.063	.119	.101
	(.244)	(.323)	(.302)
Not employed*	.539	.350	.211
	(.499)	(.477)	(.408)
Unable to work*	.093	.021	.004
	(.291)	(.142)	(.064)
Household income^a*	25.439	36.507	50.290
	(17.761)	(23.362)	(31.821)
Economic hardship*	.616	.491	.250
	(.805)	(.704)	(.477)
Work fulfillment*	.784	.937	1.167
	(.780)	(.747)	(.700)
Social-Psychological Resources			
Sense of control*	.334	.664	.840
	(.437)	(.482)	(.475)
Social support*	.922	1.116	1.224
	(.812)	(.769)	(.768)
Health Lifestyle			
Exercise*	2.136	2.343	2.536
	(1.788)	(1.806)	(1.748)
Smoking*	.915	.788	.580
	(.880)	(.842)	(.743)

*Education categories significantly different at $p < .05$ (two-tailed tests).
^aCoded in thousands of dollars per year.

Note: $N = 2,031$; standard deviations in parentheses.

disability. Household incomes are highest among the college educated in both samples. In the WFW sample, the college educated had an average household income of $50,290, compared to $36,507 among those with a high school degree, and $25,439 among those who did not finish high school (see Table 1). Economic hardship is highest among respondents who did not finish high school, followed by those with a high school degree, and lowest among those with a college degree or more. In the WFW sample,

TABLE 2   Means for Variables Measuring Health, Work and Economic Conditions, Social-Psychological Resources, and Health Lifestyle at Three Levels of Education: Health Practices Sample, 1979

Variable	Less than High School Degree	High School Degree to Some College	College Degree or More
Health			
Self-reported health*	3.344	4.054	4.340
	(1.153)	(.904)	(.729)
Physical functioning*	1.731	1.898	1.955
	(.477)	(.272)	(.166)
Work and Economic Conditions			
Employed full-time*	.458	.599	.757
	(.499)	(.490)	(.431)
Employed part-time*	.073	.106	.063
	(.261)	(.308)	(.254)
Not employed*	.395	.275	.167
	(.489)	(.447)	(.373)
Unable to work*	.075	.019	.007
	(.263)	(.134)	(.084)
Household income*	12.672	17.200	21.345
	(7.860)	(8.138)	(8.703)
Economic hardship*	.361	.244	.179
	(.412)	(.356)	(.318)
Social-Psychological Resources			
Sense of control*	3.971	4.303	4.467
	(1.163)	(.962)	(.825)
Social support*	−.074	.020	.084
	(.723)	(.683)	(.659)
Health Lifestyle			
Exercise*	2.081	2.466	2.665
	(.643)	(.616)	(.565)
Smoking*	1.121	.906	.789
	(.893)	(.890)	(.841)
Abstain from drinking*	.432	.262	.139
	(.499)	(.440)	(.346)
Rare drinking*	.223	.280	.222
	(.416)	(.449)	(.416)
Moderate drinking*	.286	.418	.618
	(.452)	(.493)	(.486)
Heavy drinking*	.037	.024	.011
	(.188)	(.152)	(.103)
Checkups*	2.719	2.888	2.957
	(1.354)	(1.274)	(1.174)

*Education categories significantly different at $p < .05$ (two-tailed tests).

Note: $N = 3,025$; standard deviations in parentheses.

the college educated have significantly higher levels of work fulfillment than do people with a high school degree, followed by those who did not finish high school.

As education level increases, the sense of control over one's life and one's health increases (sense of control is measured as control over one's life in general in the WFW sample and over one's health in particular in HP sample), as does the level of social support. In both samples, the college educated are significantly more likely to exercise and significantly less likely to smoke. Table 2 also shows that the college educated are the least likely of the three educational groups to abstain from drinking or to drink heavily; they are the most likely to drink moderately. The likelihood of getting health checkups increases with educational attainment.

Explaining the Association between Education and Health: Cross-Sectional Analysis

Self-Reported Health. In both samples, the college educated report significantly better health than do those with a high school degree or less (see Tables 1 and 2 for unadjusted means). Equation 1 in Tables 3 and 4 shows that the well educated report significantly better health than the poorly educated, controlling for sex, minority status, age, and marital status. (In addition, people who are white, male, and married report better health than non-whites, women, and the unmarried, although the effect of sex is significant only in the WFW sample; and older people report worse health than younger.)

Work and economic conditions are added in equation 2. People who are employed report better health than the nonemployed. In both samples the positive effect of full-time employment is greater than that of part-time employment, and in the WFW sample, part-time employment is significant only at $p < .10$.

In both samples, we adjust for inability to work because of poor health or disability. Thus, the positive effect of employment on health is not due to the fact that some people in poor health do not work (a selection effect). Economic hardship has a significant negative effect on self-reported health in both samples. High household income is significantly associated with good health and low income with poor health in the HP sample, where household income affects health over and above economic hardship. In the WFW sample, economic hardship explains the effect of income, reducing its significance to .08. Part but not all of the reason income improves health is that it decreases economic strain: People with high incomes have little if any trouble paying for food, clothing, medical care, and monthly bills. Work fulfillment, a variable available only in the WFW sample, is significantly positively associated with health.

Social-psychological resources are added in equation 3 of Tables 3 and 4. A high sense of personal control over one's life in general (Table 3) and one's health in particular (Table 4) are significantly associated with good self-reported health. Social support is also positively associated with health, but is statistically significant only in the HP sample. Education is positively associated with a sense of personal control over one's life and one's health, and with high levels of social support, which in turn are positively associated with health. These associations help explain some of the association between education and health.

Health lifestyle is added in equation 4 of Tables 3 and 4. In both samples, exercise has a significant positive effect on health, and smoking a significant negative effect. The HP sample also has information on health checkups and drinking behavior. People who abstain from drinking report significantly worse health than those who drink moderately (the omitted category in the regression analysis). Compared to moderate

TABLE 3 Self-Reported Health Regressed on Education, Controlling for Sociodemographic Characteristics (Equation 1), Work and Economic Conditions (Equation 2), Social-Psychological Resources (Equation 3), and Health Lifestyle (Equation 4): Work, Family, and Well-Being Sample, 1990

Variable	Equation 1 b	Equation 1 Beta	Equation 2 b	Equation 2 Beta	Equation 3 b	Equation 3 Beta	Equation 4 b	Equation 4 Beta
Education	.076*** (.007)	.220	.041*** (.007)	.121	.036*** (.008)	.105	.031*** (.008)	.091
Sociodemographic Characteristics								
Sex (male = 1)	.114** (.038)	.062	.051 (.038)	.028	.054* (.038)	.029	.045 (.038)	.025
Race (white = 1)	.239*** (.056)	.089	.168** (.054)	.062	.156** (.054)	.058	.180*** (.054)	.069
Age (in years)	−.013*** (.001)	−.247	−.012*** (.001)	−.226	−.011*** (.001)	−.213	−.011*** (.001)	−.205
Marital status (married = 1)	.105** (.040)	.058	.043 (.037)	.024	.042 (.037)	.023	.055 (.037)	.030
Work and Economic Conditions								
Employed full-time[a]	—		.174*** (.044)	.098	.172*** (.044)	.097	.191*** (.044)	.107
Employed part-time[a]	—		.109 (.064)	.038	.108 (.064)	.038	.112 (.063)	.039
Unable to work[a]	—		−.835*** (.114)	−.150	−.827*** (.114)	−.149	−.779*** (.113)	−.140
Household income	—		.001 (.001)	.040	.001 (.001)	.033	.001 (.001)	.031
Economic hardship	—		−.172*** (.028)	−.133	−.169*** (.028)	−.130	−.158*** (.028)	−.121
Work fulfillment	—		.158*** (.024)	.134	.145*** (.025)	.122	.138*** (.024)	.116
Social-Psychological Resources								
Sense of control	—		—		.131*** (.038)	.074	.124** (.038)	.069
Social support	—		—		.015 (.024)	.013	.012 (.023)	.011
Health Lifestyle								
Exercise	—		—		—		.043*** (.010)	.088
Smoking	—		—		—		−.082*** (.021)	−.077
Constant	3.413		3.729		3.699		3.681	
R²	.152		.234		.239		.252	

*p < .05; **p < .01; ***p < .001 (two-tailed tests).
[a]Compared to not employed (for reasons other than health).

Note: N = 2,031; b = unstandardized regression coefficient with standard error in parentheses; Beta = standardized regression coefficient.

TABLE 4 Self-Reported Health Regressed on Education, Controlling for Sociodemographic Characteristics (Equation 1), Work and Economic Conditions (Equation 2), Social-Psychological Resources (Equation 3), and Health Lifestyle (Equation 4): Health Practices Sample, 1979

Variable	Equation 1 b	Equation 1 Beta	Equation 2 b	Equation 2 Beta	Equation 3 b	Equation 3 Beta	Equation 4 b	Equation 4 Beta
Education	.122*** (.007)	.312	.080*** (.007)	.204	.070*** (.007)	.179	.054*** (.007)	.139
Sociodemographic Characteristics								
Sex (male = 1)	.014 (.035)	.007	−.075* (.035)	−.037	−.062 (.034)	−.030	−.104** (.035)	−.051
Race (white = 1)	.281*** (.049)	.102	.141** (.045)	.051	.122** (.044)	.044	.102* (.044)	.037
Age (in years)	−.011*** (.001)	−.148	−.011*** (.001)	−.140	−.009*** (.001)	−.121	−.003* (.001)	−.040
Marital status (married = 1)	.145*** (.037)	.070	.021 (.037)	.010	.025 (.035)	.012	.050 (.035)	.024
Work and Economic Conditions								
Employed full-time[a]	—		.219*** (.040)	.108	.221*** (.039)	.109	.228*** (.038)	.113
Employed part-time[a]	—		.213*** (.059)	.062	.184** (.058)	.053	.156** (.057)	.045
Unable to work[a]	—		−1.254*** (.099)	−.210	−.1.131*** (.097)	−.190	−.981*** (.096)	−.164
Household income	—		.013*** (.002)	.114	.012*** (.002)	.102	.008*** (.002)	.073
Economic hardship	—		−.411*** (.046)	−.152	−.358*** (.046)	−.132	−.349*** (.045)	−.129
Social-Psychological Resources								
Sense of control	—		—		.176*** (.016)	.178	.151*** (.016)	.153
Social support	—		—		.094*** (.023)	.065	.067** (.022)	.047
Health Lifestyle								
Exercise	—		—		—		.295*** (.028)	.191
Smoking	—		—		—		−.046** (.018)	−.041
Abstain from drinking[b]	—		—		—		−.164*** (.041)	−.074
Rare drinking[b]	—		—		—		−.026 (.038)	−.011
Heavy drinking[b]	—		—		—		−.056 (.100)	−.009
Check-ups	—		—		—		−.014 (.012)	−.018
Constant	2.532		3.040		2.371		1.916	
R^2	.159		.271		.306		.339	

*$p < .05$; **$p < .01$; ***$p < .001$ (two-tailed tests).
[a]Compared to not employed (for reasons other than health).
[b]Compared to moderate drinking.

Note: $N = 3,025$; b = unstandardized regression coefficient with standard error in parentheses; Beta = standardized regression coefficient.

drinking, rare and heavy drinking are also associated with worse health, but not significantly so. Getting checkups does not significantly affect health. Thus, we find that smoking and exercise are more important determinants of self-reported health and explain more of education's effect on health than do drinking or getting checkups. Furthermore, abstaining from drinking does not improve self-reported health. Consistent with recent evidence on heart disease, stroke, and high blood pressure, we find that people who abstain from drinking report *worse* health than those who drink moderately. The well educated are more likely to exercise, less likely to smoke, and less likely to abstain from drinking, which explains some of the effect of education on self-reported health. Higher levels of preventive medical care—measured as health checkups—among the well educated do not explain any of the association.

All together, work and economic conditions, social-psychological resources, and health life-style explain 55 percent of the cross-sectional association between education and health in the HP sample ($[.122 - .054]/.122 = .55$) and 59 percent of the association in the WFW sample ($[.076 - .031]/.076 = .59$). Further, F-tests on the increments to R^2 for each additional block of explanatory variables are significant in both samples.

Physical Functioning. In both samples, the college educated report significantly better physical functioning than those with a high school degree or less (see Tables 1 and 2 for unadjusted means). Equation 1 in Tables 5 and 6 shows that the well educated report significantly better physical functioning than the poorly educated, controlling for sex, minority status, age, and marital status. (In addition, people who are married, young, male, and white report better physical functioning than unmarried people, older people, women, and non-whites, although

race is significant only in the HP sample.) The effect of education on physical functioning is as large or larger than its effect on self-reported health, and more of the association is explained in both samples (see Tables 4, 5, and 6).[7]

Work and economic conditions are added in equation 2 of Tables 5 and 6. In both samples, part-time and full-time employment are better for physical functioning than not being employed, even controlling for being out of the work force due to disability or poor health. Economic hardship is associated with poor physical functioning, although the effect of household income is not significant in either sample, adjusting for economic hardship. Work fulfillment (WFW sample, Table 5) is associated with good physical functioning.

Social-psychological resources are added in equation 3 of Tables 5 and 6. The sense of control over one's life and one's future health are both significantly associated with good physical functioning, whereas social support is not significant in either sample.

Health lifestyle, added in equation 4, has a much smaller effect on physical functioning than it does on self-reported health. Only exercise has significant effects in either sample, and the causal order here is problematic because a person with physical disabilities may not be able to exercise. Health lifestyle explains much less of the association between education and physical functioning than between education and self-reported health.

All together, work and economic conditions, social-psychological resources, and health lifestyle explain 71 percent of the association between education and physical functioning in the HP sample ($[.024 - .007]/.024 = .71$) and 46 percent in the WFW sample ($[.026 - .014]/.026 = .46$. Further, F-tests on the increments to R^2 for each additional block of explanatory variables are significant in both samples.[8]

TABLE 5 Physical Functioning Regressed on Education, Controlling for Sociodemographic Characteristics (Equation 1), Work and Economic Conditions (Equation 2), Social-Psychological Resources (Equation 3), and Health Lifestyle (Equation 4): Work, Family, and Well-Being Sample, 1990

Variable	Equation 1		Equation 2		Equation 3		Equation 4	
	b	Beta	b	Beta	b	Beta	b	Beta
Education	.026***	.222	.015***	.134	.014***	.125	.014***	.120
	(.002)		(.002)		(.002)		(.002)	
Sociodemographic Characteristics								
Sex (male = 1)	.032**	.052	.019	.031	.019	.030	.011	.018
	(.002)		(.011)		(.012)		(.012)	
Race (white = 1)	.018	.020	−.005	−.006	−.007	−.008	−.005	−.005
	(.018)		(.016)		(.017)		(.017)	
Age (in years)	−.006***	−.358	−.006***	−.325	−.006***	−.320	−.005***	−.311
	(.000)		(.000)		(.000)		(.000)	
Marital status	.061***	.100	.045***	.073	.045***	.075	.048***	.078
(married = 1)	(.012)		(.012)		(.012)		(.017)	
Work and Economic Conditions								
Employed full-time[a]	—		.058***	.097	.057***	.095	.062***	.103
			(.014)		(.014)		(.014)	
Employed part-time[a]	—		.060**	.062	.060**	.062	.063**	.065
			(.020)		(.020)		(.020)	
Unable to work[a]	—		−.488***	−.260	−.486***	−.259	−.477***	−.254
			(.036)		(.036)		(.036)	
Household income	—		.000	.002	.000	.002	.000	.003
			(.000)		(.000)		(.000)	
Economic hardship	—		−.044***	−.101	−.044***	−.100	−.043***	−.098
			(.009)		(.008)		(.009)	
Work fulfillment	—		.034***	.085	.033***	.082	.030***	.074
			(.008)		(.008)		(.008)	
Social-Psychological Resources								
Sense of control	—		—		.027***	.045	.021	.035
					(.012)		(.012)	
Social support	—		—		.004	.011	.004	.011
					(.007)		(.007)	
Health Lifestyle								
Exercise	—		—		—		.017***	.099
							(.003)	
Smoking	—		—		—		−.000**	−.000
							(.007)	
Constant	1.700		1.802		1.803		1.767	
R²		.226		.334		.336		.345

*p < .05; **p < .01; ***p < .001 (two-tailed tests).
[a]Compared to not employed (for reasons other than health).

Note: N = 2,031; b = unstandardized regression coefficient with standard error in parentheses; Beta = standardized regression coefficient.

TABLE 6 Physical Functioning Regressed on Education, Controlling for Sociodemographic Characteristics (Equation 1), Work and Economic Conditions (Equation 2), Social-Psychological Resources (Equation 3), and Health Lifestyle (Equation 4): Health Practices Sample, 1979

Variable	Equation 1 b	Equation 1 Beta	Equation 2 b	Equation 2 Beta	Equation 3 b	Equation 3 Beta	Equation 4 b	Equation 4 Beta
Education	.024*** (.002)	.189	.011*** (.002)	.086	.009*** (.002)	.073	.007** (.002)	.053
Sociodemographic Characteristics								
Sex (male = 1)	.050*** (.011)	.076	.032** (.011)	.049	.034** (.011)	.052	.025* (.011)	.037
Race (white = 1)	.059*** (.016)	.062	.005 (.014)	.005	.003 (.014)	.003	.004 (.014)	.004
Age (in years)	−.005*** (.000)	−.218	−.005*** (.000)	−.191	−.005*** (.000)	−.180	−.003*** (.000)	−.119
Marital status (married = 1)	.044*** (.012)	.065	.009 (.011)	.014	.011 (.011)	.015	.014 (.011)	.021
Work and Economic Conditions								
Employed full-time[a]	—		.057*** (.012)	.086	.057*** (.012)	.087	.059*** (.012)	.089
Employed part-time[a]	—		.070*** (.019)	.063	.066** (.019)	.059	.060** (.018)	.054
Unable to work[a]	—		−.750*** (.031)	−.387	−.729*** (.031)	−.377	−.693*** (.031)	−.358
Household income	—		.001 (.000)	.024	.000 (.000)	.017	.000 (.000)	.000
Economic hardship	—		−.155*** (.015)	−.176	−.147*** (.015)	−.168	−.148*** (.014)	−.168
Social-Psychological Resources								
Sense of control	—		—		.030*** (.005)	.094	.024*** (.005)	.075
Social support	—		—		.011 (.007)	.024	.004 (.007)	.008
Health Lifestyle								
Exercise	—		—		—		.079*** (.009)	.158
Smoking	—		—		—		.000 (.006)	.002
Abstain from drinking[b]	—		—		—		−.008 (.013)	−.011
Rare drinking[b]	—		—		—		.019 (.012)	.025
Heavy drinking[b]	—		—		—		.036 (.032)	.017
Checkups	—		—		—		−.005 (.004)	−.019
Constant	1.686		1.907		1.790		1.623	
R^2	.115		.324		.333		.351	

*$p < .05$; **$p < .01$; ***$p < .001$ (two-tailed tests).
[a]Compared to not employed (for reasons other than health).
[b]Compared to moderate drinking.

Note: $N = 3,025$; b = unstandardized regression coefficient with standard error in parentheses; Beta = standardized regression coefficient.

Explaining the Association between Education and Health: Longitudinal Analysis

Self-Reported Health.   Table 7 shows the effect of education on the change in self-reported health over one year, and the explanations for the association, controlling for health at time 1. The results are from the HP sample; time 1 is 1979 and time 2 is 1980. On average, the change in health over one year is negative. Thus, positive coefficients "slow" the decline in health between 1979 and 1980. Equation 1 reveals a large positive effect of education on change in health, controlling for health at time 1. In addition age accelerates the decline in health, and the better one's self-reported health is at time 1, the more negative it becomes, which probably indicates a ceiling effect.

Equations 2 through 4 add explanatory variables. Work and economic conditions are added in equation 2. Full-time employment and high household income significantly slow the decline in health over the one-year period, whereas part-time employment has no significant effect. Economic hardship significantly accelerates the decline. Equation 3 adds the sense of control over one's health and social support. A high sense of control over one's future health significantly slows the decline in self-reported health over time. Equation 4 adds health lifestyle. Exercise significantly slows the negative change in self-reported health over time. Smoking has little effect over a one-year period. Its effects are likely to be cumulative over a lifetime. Drinking behavior does, however, affect the change in health. Abstinence somewhat accelerates the decline in health over one year ($p = .07$), whereas rare drinking slows the decline. All together, work and economic conditions, social-psychological resources, and health lifestyle explain 43 percent of the total effect of education on the change in health ($[.037 - .021]/.037 = .43$). A signifi-

cant direct effect of education on the change in health over time remains, however, indicating that even after adjusting for explanatory variables, a higher level of education significantly slows the decline in self-reported health over one year.

One year is a short period of time; self-reported health does not decline much in one year ($-.036$ on a 5-point scale with a mean of 3.9 and standard deviation of .992 at time 1). It is somewhat surprising that we can predict this small change in health at all. The fact that education, work and economic conditions, sense of control, and health lifestyle significantly affect the change in health in over a year's time indicates the strength and pervasiveness of education's effect on health.

Physical Functioning.   Last, using the HP sample, we predict the change in physical functioning between 1979 and 1980 from education, sociodemographics, and physical functioning in 1979. Level of physical function changes even less in one year than does self-reported health ($-.004$ on a scale of 0 to 2). Given the small variance in this dependent variable, we do not report our results in a table. Nonetheless, education does have a significant positive effect on change in physical functioning over one year ($b = .006$, s.e. = .002, Beta = .049, $p = .004$). Education significantly slows the decline in physical functioning over time.

SUMMARY AND CONCLUSION

In two national samples, education is strongly and positively associated with two measures of health—self-reported health and physical functioning—both cross-sectionally and over time. For both health measures in both samples, a large part of the association is explained by our explanatory variables, but a significant direct effect of education remains: Adjusting for work and economic conditions, social-psychological resources, and health

TABLE 7 Change in Self-Reported Health between 1979 and 1980 Regressed on Education, Controlling for Health in 1979 and Sociodemographic Characteristics (Equation 1), Work and Economic Conditions (Equation 2), Social-Psychological Resources (Equation 3), and Health Lifestyle (Equation 4): Health Practices Sample, 1979–1980

Variable	Equation 1		Equation 2		Equation 3		Equation 4	
	b	*Beta*	*b*	*Beta*	*b*	*Beta*	*b*	*Beta*
Education	.037***	.125	.027***	.090	.025***	.082	.021***	.071
	(.006)		(.006)		(.006)		(.006)	
Sociodemographic Characteristics and Prior Health								
Health in 1979	−.348***	−.454	−.395***	−.515	−.413***	−.539	−.429***	−.559
	(.016)		(.016)		(.017)		(.017)	
Sex (male = 1)	.020	.013	−.036	−.023	−.032	−.020	−.040	−.026
	(.030)		(.031)		(.032)		(.033)	
Race (white = 1)	.034	.016	−.003	−.002	.0004	.0002	−.008	−.004
	(.041)		(.031)		(.040)		(.040)	
Age (in years)	−.004**	−.060	−.004***	−.069	−.004**	−.060	−.002	−.029
	(.001)		(.001)		(.001)		(.001)	
Marital status (married = 1)	.042	.026	.011	.007	.017	.011	.023	.015
	(.031)		(.032)		(.032)		(.032)	
Work and Economic Conditions								
Employed full-time[a]	—		.139***	.090	.144***	.093	.145***	.094
			(.035)		(.035)		(.035)	
Employed part-time[a]	—		.077	.029	.071	.027	.056	.021
			(.053)		(.053)		(.053)	
Unable to work[a]	—		−.245**	−.054	−.216*	−.047	−.179*	−.039
			(.091)		(.090)		(.090)	
Household income	—		.005*	.055	.004*	.051	.004	.042
			(.002)		(.002)		(.002)	
Economic hardship	—		−.191***	−.092	−.187***	−.090	−.192***	−.092
			(.042)		(.042)		(.042)	
Social-Psychological Resources								
Sense of control	—		—		.081***	.107	.076***	.100
					(.015)		(.015)	
Social support	—		—		−.005	−.005	−.011	−.010
					(.021)		(.021)	
Health Lifestyle								
Exercise	—		—		—		.088***	.075
							(.026)	
Smoking	—		—		—		−.007	−.008
							(.016)	
Abstain from drinking[b]	—		—		—		−.071	−.041
							(.038)	
Rare drinking[b]	—		—		—		.072*	.041
							(.036)	
Heavy drinking[b]	—		—		—		−.016	−.003
							(.093)	
Checkups	—		—		—		−.012	−.020
							(.011)	
Constant	.948		1.239		.969		.875	
R²	.175		.198		.208		.217	

*p < .05; **p < .01; ***p < .001 (two-tailed tests).

[a]Compared to not employed (for reasons other than health).

[b]Compared to moderate drinking.

Note: N = 2,436; *b* = unstandardized regression coefficient with standard error in parentheses; Beta = standardized regression coefficient.

lifestyle, education remains significantly associated with good health. This unexplained effect could be due to unreliability in our explanatory variables, to other factors not included in our model, or to direct physiological consequences of education. Education teaches a person to use his or her mind: Learning, thinking, reasoning, solving problems, and so on are mental exercises that may keep the central nervous system in shape the same way that physical exercise keeps the body in shape. On the other hand, some of the effect attributed to education's impact on knowledge, learning, and problem solving may have less to do with skills learned in school than the consequences of educational attainment for work. The jobs available to those with little schooling are more likely to be stressful, dangerous, and "dead-end" (Leigh 1983).[9]

Education improves health indirectly through work and economic conditions, social-psychological resources, and health lifestyle. The well educated are more likely than the poorly educated to be employed. Education gives people greater access to full-time rather than part-time work. It provides more of an opportunity for a fulfilling and enjoyable worklife and provides enough income so that economic hardship is low. Education boosts the sense of control, shaping the perception that one's life and one's health result from one's own actions and decisions. Well-educated people report more supportive relationships. And finally, the well educated have a more positive health lifestyle: They are more likely to exercise, less likely to smoke, more likely to drink moderately rather than abstain or drink heavily, and are more likely to get annual health checkups.

Compared to not working for pay, full-time employment, and, to a much lesser extent, part-time employment, are associated with good health. Fulfilling work and low levels of economic hardship are associated with good

health. The sense of personal control and, to a smaller degree, social support are associated with good health. Exercising, not smoking, and drinking some alcohol rather than abstaining are associated with good health. Of all the hypothesized mediating variables, only health checkups are not significantly associated with health in any of the analyses.

Although well-educated people are more likely to get checkups than people with less education, having regular checkups cannot explain any of the association between education and health because checkups do not significantly affect health. The goal of *primary* prevention is to *prevent the onset of disease* by reducing risks (through exercise, not smoking, or drinking in moderation). Annual checkups are secondary prevention. The goal of *secondary* prevention is to *catch disease early* to limit the consequences. Almost all prevention in our medical care system is secondary, not primary, despite better evidence for the health benefits of primary prevention. In fact, there is little evidence that checkups protect *adults'* health (U.S. Preventive Services Task Force 1989). The rationale behind annual physical exams makes four potentially false assumptions: (1) checkups catch disease early, (2) detecting disease early makes a difference in outcome, (3) checkups do no harm, and (4) the people who might benefit from checkups get them (Canadian Task Force on the Periodic Health Examination 1979, 1988). First, annual physical exams are not targeted to an individual's risk, so they are unlikely to find undetected disease. Second, early detection is not useful unless the treatment that follows is effective in slowing the course of illness, or ideally in curing it; this is rare for many chronic diseases. Third, screening that is not targeted at high-risk groups produces a certain percentage of false positives that can lead to dangerous and unnecessary treatments for nonexistent diseases, distress caused by the false diagnosis, and risks from the actual screening tests, which can expose people to risk of infection from invasive procedures, small amounts of radiation, and so on (Bailar and Smith 1986; Canadian Task Force 1979). Fourth, the people who need checkups the least are the most likely to get them, and vice versa. The well educated need preventive medical care least because they are at the lowest risk of illness: They are less likely to experience stress and economic hardship from unemployment or poverty, the resulting sense of fatalism and powerlessness, or the higher probability of smoking, heavy drinking, and of leading sedentary lives.

The hypothesized links between education and health are largely supported in our study, but are the relationships causal? We address causal-order issues in three ways: (1) outside evidence on established life course sequences, (2) controls for selection in cross-sectional data analyses, and (3) longitudinal data which we use to examine the change in health over time, controlling for health at time 1. First, the completion of formal schooling typically occurs by a respondent's late twenties. Although some people do return to school later in life, it is unlikely that most of the relationship between education and health is due to reverse causal order, in which people in poor health do not complete school (Davis 1985). It is more likely that education shapes a person's resources and opportunities, and thus shapes his or her health. However, some work and economic conditions, social-psychological resources, and health behaviors could be shaped by prior health.[10] Thus, second, in our cross-sectional data analysis we adjusted for the inability to work because of poor health. This controls for selection out of the workforce due to poor health. Significant associations between health and employment (and the consequences of employment for income and economic strain) are thus likely to result from the positive effects of employment on health. Nonetheless, some reciprocal relationships are possible. For example, the

sense of personal control likely shapes a person's health, which in turn affects the sense of control. We don't claim that reciprocal effects such as these do not exist, but we want to ensure that the proposed causal effects do exist. Therefore, third, we examine the change in health over time. If we find that a person's sense of control at time 1 significantly affects the change in his or her health between times 1 and 2 controlling for health at time 1, we know that sense of control affects health, and not simply that health affects the sense of control. This is the case for all variables examined.

The conclusions of our longitudinal analyses are substantively the same as those for our cross-sectional analyses, although there are a few differences. First, part-time employment, which is significant in three of the four cross-sectional analyses, is nonsignificant over time. Full-time employment appears to be best for health, while the benefits of part-time employment are smaller. Second, as in three of the four cross-sectional analyses, the effect of social support is not significant over time. The sense of control is a greater health-related social-psychological resource than is social support in these analyses. Third, in the cross-sectional analysis, rare drinking is not significantly different from moderate drinking in its effect on health. Over time, however, rare drinking is significantly better for health than moderate drinking. Nonetheless, in both analyses, abstaining from drinking is worse for health than rare to moderate drinking. Fourth, smoking does not significantly worsen health in one year's time, although cross-sectional analyses show very significant negative effects of smoking on self-reported health. The cross-sectional analyses capture the cumulative effect of a lifetime's smoking on health. Unfortunately the HP panel survey followed individuals for only one year; a three-year follow-up might have better revealed the impact of lifestyle on health.

Stressors, hardships, beliefs, and behaviors that affect health are not randomly distributed, they are socially structured. Smoking, exercising, and other individual health behaviors are not alternatives to socially structured inequalities, like the poverty, unfulfilling work, and economic hardships faced disproportionately by those with little schooling. The two are linked. Compared to people who are well educated, people with little education are more likely to be unemployed; if employed, they do not have equal access to fulfilling, high-paying jobs, and they experience greater economic hardship, all of which are associated with the belief that one is powerless to affect one's life and one's health, and with health lifestyle. If *efforts* seem useless, if health and sickness are seen as outside one's control, what is the point of exercising, quitting smoking, or avoiding heavy drinking (Wheaton 1980)? Compared to a sense of powerlessness, a sense of personal control has consistent positive effects on health in our analyses. Some of the effects are mediated by health lifestyle, and some are direct. Beliefs about personal control generally represent realistic perceptions of objective conditions (Mirowsky and Ross 1989). The failures structured into the life of a person who has not finished high school are likely to shape a sense of powerlessness, which ultimately affects health, in part through lifestyle and in part directly. Social-psychological resources and health lifestyle are not alternative explanations to structured inequality; they link inequalities in education, work, and economic circumstances to health.

NOTES

1. There are exceptions to this general pattern. For example, well-educated women have higher rates of breast cancer than the poorly educated, largely because they have fewer children, which increases risk. However, among women with breast cancer, well-educated women survive longer than the poorly educated (Lipworth, Abelin, and Connelly 1970).

2. Some researchers pit various aspects of socioeconomic status against one another, asking, for example, which is a better predictor of risk factors for cardiovascular disease—education, occupation, or income (Winkleby et al. 1992)? This ignores causal interrelationships among the three aspects of SES. Not only is education a strong predictor of health when occupation and income are adjusted, but a direct effect of education (net of occupation and income) underestimates the total effect of education that works indirectly by way of jobs and income.

3. In U.S. research, education is typically a control variable, statistically controlled in a study whose focus is on other variables (Pearlin 1989). Sociologists of health often ignore key sociological variables in studies of well-being, instead focusing on variables like life events, which are not grounded in the stratification system (Pearlin 1989:241). In contrast, social scientists studying the developing world see education as "the most influential investment" a country can make, improving skills, wages, economic well-being, birth control, hygiene, living conditions, health of children and adults, and life expectancy (Summers 1992:132).

4. We use the word "explain" in the statistical sense (Davis 1985).

5. The replications are almost, but not exactly, the same. The Health Practices sample (HP) includes measures of drinking behavior and checkups, whereas the Work, Family, and Well-Being sample (WFW) does not; WFW includes a measure of work fulfillment, whereas HP does not. Sense of control is specific to health in HP and general in WFW. Finally, WFW has no upper age limit, whereas HP includes only persons under age 65.

6. The model in which change in health (ΔY) is the dependent variable is equivalent to one in which health at time 2 (Y_2) is the dependent variable, and health at time 1 (Y_1) is controlled. (X_1 is an independent variable such as education at time $p1$.) Only the R^2s and the coefficients associated with health at time 1 ($b_1 Y_1$) differ in the two models, and the bs are linear transformations:

$$\Delta Y = Y_2 - Y_1$$
$$\Delta Y = b_0 + b_1 Y_1 + b_2 X_1 + U_{\Delta Y}$$
$$Y_2 - Y_1 = b_0 + b_1 Y_1 + b_2 X_1 + U_{\Delta Y}$$
$$Y_2 = b_0 + Y_1 + b_1 Y_1 + b_2 X_1 + U_{\Delta Y}$$
$$Y_2 = b_0 + (b_1 + 1) Y_1 + b_2 X_1 + U_{\Delta Y}.$$

In sum, b_1 when ΔY is dependent equals $b_1 + 1$ when Y_2 is dependent. The R^2s in the four equations in Table 7 are higher when health time 2 is dependent: .488, .498, .503, and .507.

7. The question of whether having a college degree has an effect on health over and above years of schooling per se can be examined in the WFW sample. Is the credential of a college degree as important or more important to health than years of schooling completed? We added a dummy variable for having a college degree to the first equations in Tables 3 and 5. Having a college degree did not have an independent significant effect on self-reported health ($p = .44$) or on physical functioning ($p = .27$), *over and above* years of schooling completed.

8. Before turning to longitudinal analyses, we ran three final cross-sectional analyses. We transformed the dependent variables to decrease nonnormality; we tested interaction terms to determine whether the effects of education on health are conditional on other variables; and we examined the effects of parental education on respondent's health.

First, the distributions of self-reported health and physical functioning are skewed. Skewness, or non-normality of the dependent variable, can produce heteroskedasticity. The consequence of nonnormal dependent variables is that heteroskedasticity produces the potential for inflated standard errors of the estimates, making the effects appear less significant than they really are. (Estimates are not biased in large samples.) We corrected for non-normality by raising the value of the dependent variables to a power. To determine what this power should be, we calculated the interquartile range (measure of dispersion) and the median (measure of central tendency) for both dependent variables at each level of education, and then regressed the log of the interquartile range on the log of the median. This yielded a coefficient (b) that we used to correct for heteroskedasticity (y to the N power, where $N = 1 - b$). In the WFW sample, N was 1.52 for self-reported

health and 2.25 for physical functioning. Using these powers we created two new dependent variables, self-reported health to the 1.52 power and physical functioning to the 2.25 power. These transformations decreased heteroskedasticity, so we reran the regressions for the WFW sample using the transformed dependent variables. In no case were the substantive conclusions different. Although some significance levels changed slightly, they did not change from the conventional levels reported for untransformed variables.

Second, education's positive effect on health may be conditional on other characteristics. We tested interactions of education with all sociodemographic and work/economic characteristics. Two interactions with education—age and household income—were consistent in sign and largely significant across all analyses. The positive effect of education on physical functioning increases with age, although the positive interaction of education with age only approaches significance ($p < .10$) in the self-reported health analyses. The positive effect of education on both health outcomes decreases significantly as household income increases.

Third, educational attainment is structured by parental socioeconomic status. The WFW sample measures parents' education. We reestimated a new equation 1 (Tables 3 and 5) that included parental education measured as the average of both parents' years of schooling completed. Next we added respondent's education, controlling for age, sex, race, and marital status. We found that parents' education positively affects respondents' self-reported health and physical functioning largely because it shapes a respondent's educational opportunities. The bivariate association between parental education and respondent's self-reported health is highly significant ($b = .060$, beta = .194, $t = 8.872$, $p = .000$). When respondent's education and sociodemographic characteristics are added to the equation, the association between parental education and health becomes nonsignificant at the $p < .05$ level, although it approaches significance ($p = .09$). When respondent's work and economic conditions are added, the effect of parental status is nonsignificant ($p = .19$). The bivariate association between parental education and respondent's physical functioning is also highly significant ($b =$

.021, beta = .202, t = 9.268, p = .000). When respondent's education and sociodemographic characteristics are added to the equation, the positive association between parents' education and physical functioning becomes nonsignificant (p = .611).

9. A narrow stratification approach to inequality looks at job status or rank; occupation-based social class; whether the job is in the core or periphery; has internal labor markets; exposes workers to dangerous conditions, and so on. We did not take this approach because the most disadvantaged are not included in these theories or research. People who have been fired or laid off, women engaged in unpaid domestic labor, the nonemployed elderly, and so on, are likely the most disadvantaged. Given our focus on the effect of social inequality on health, we did not want to exclude people from our analyses who were not in the paid economy. Furthermore, women are over-represented in the groups ignored by mainstream stratification theory and research. Almost all homemakers are women; because women live longer than men, the majority of nonemployed elderly are women; and as paid workers with relatively short tenure and low-level jobs, women are among the first laid off or fired in economic downturns.

10. Both economic hardship measures include difficulty paying for medical care, which could be a consequence, rather than a cause, of poor health in cross-sectional analyses. We deleted this item from the hardship measures in both samples and reran all analyses. We compared the effects in equation 4 in Tables 3 through 7. The exclusion of difficulty paying for medical care did not change substantive conclusions. Economic hardship remained significantly negatively associated with health (p < .001 in all cases), although the effects were smaller.

REFERENCES

ABBOTT, ROBERT D., YIN YIN, DWAYNE M. REED, and KATSUHILO YANO. 1986. "Risk of Stroke in Male Cigarette Smokers." *The New England Journal of Medicine* 315:717–20.

ANESHENSEL, CAROL S., RALPH FRERICHS, and GEORGE HUBA. 1984. "Depression and Physical Illness: A Multiwave, Nonrecursive Causal Model." *Journal of Health and Social Behavior* 25:350–71.

ATKINSON, THOMAS, RAMSAY LIEM, and JOAN H. LIEM. 1986. "The Social Costs of Unemployment. Implications for Social Support." *Journal of Health and Social Behavior* 27:317–31.

BAILAR, JOHN C. and ELAINE M. SMITH. 1986. "Progress against Cancer?" *New England Journal of Medicine* 314:1226–32.

BERG, IVAR. 1971. *Education and Jobs: The Great Training Robbery.* Boston, MA: Beacon.

BERKMAN, LISA F. and LESTER BRESLOW. 1983. *Health and Way of Living: The Alameda County Study.* New York. Oxford University Press.

BERLIN, JESSE A. and GRAHAM A. COLDITZ. 1990. "A Meta-Analysis of Physical Activity in the Prevention of Coronary Heart Disease." *American Journal of Epidemiology* 132:612–28.

BIRD, CHLOE E. and ALLEN M. FREMONT. 1991. "Gender, Time Use, and Health." *Journal of Health and Social Behavior* 32:114–29.

BRUCE, MARTHA LIVINGSTON and PHILIP J. LEAF. 1989. "Psychiatric Disorders and 15-Month Mortality in a Community Sample of Older Adults." *American Journal of Public Health* 79:727–30.

CANADIAN TASK FORCE ON THE PERIODIC HEALTH EXAMINATION. 1979. "The Periodic Health Examination." *Canadian Medical Association Journal* 121: 1194–1254.

———. 1988. "The Periodic Health Examination." *Canadian Medical Association Journal* 138:617–26.

CARSTAIRS, VERA and RUSSELL MORRIS. 1989. "Deprivation and Mortality: An Alternative to Social Class?" *Community Medicine* 11:210–19.

CASPERSEN, CARL J., BENNIE P. M. BLOEMBERG, WIM H. M. SARIS, ROBERT K. MERRITT, and DAAN KROMHOUT. 1992. "The Prevalence of Selected Physical Activities and their Relation with Coronary Heart Disease Risk Factors in Elderly Men: The Zutphen Study, 1985." *American Journal of Epidemiology* 133:1078–92.

COBB, SIDNEY. 1976. "Social Support as a Moderator of Life Stress." *Psychosomatic Medicine* 38:301–14.

COBURN, DAVID and CLYDE R. POPE. 1974. "Socioeconomic Status and Preventive Health Behavior." *Journal of Health and Social Behavior* 15:67–78.

CRAWFORD, ROBERT. 1986. "Individual Responsibility and Health Politics." Pp. 369–77 in *The Sociology of Health and Illness*, 2d ed., edited by P. Conrad and R. Kern. New York: St. Martin's.

DARROW, SHERRI L., MARCIA RUSSELL, M. LYNNE COPPER, PAMELA MUDAR, and MICHAEL R. FRONE. 1992. "Sociodemographic Correlates of Alcohol Consumption Among African-American and White Women." *Women and Health* 18:35–51.

DAVIES, ALLYSON ROSS and JOHN E. WARE. 1981. *Measuring Health Perceptions in the Health Insurance Experiment*. Santa Monica, CA: Rand Corporation.

DAVIS, JAMES A. 1985. *The Logic of Causal Order*. Beverly Hills, CA: Sage.

DOORNBOS, G. and D. KROMHOUT. 1990. "Educational Level and Mortality in a 32-year Follow-Up Study of 18-Year-Old Men in the Netherlands." *International Journal of Epidemiology* 19:374–79.

DOWNEY, GERALDINE and PHYLLIS MOEN. 1987. "Personal Efficacy, Income and Family Transitions: A Longitudinal Study of Women Heading Households." *Journal of Health and Social Behavior* 28:320–33.

DUNCAN, JOHN J., NEIL F. GORDON, and CHRIS B. SCOTT. 1991. "Women Walking for Health and Fitness." *Journal of the American Medical Association* 266:3295–99.

ECKENRODE, JOHN. 1983. "The Mobilization of Social Supports: Some Individual Constraints." *American Journal of Community Psychology* 11:509–28.

ELDER, GLEN H. and JEFFREY K. LIKER. 1982. "Hard Times in Women's Lives: Historical Influences Across Forty Years." *American Journal of Sociology* 88:241–69.

FELDMAN, JACOB J., DIANE M. MAKUC, JOEL C. KLEINMAN, and JOAN CORNONI-HUNTLEY. 1989. "National Trends in Educational Differentials in Mortality." *American Journal of Epidemiology* 129:919–33.

FORD, EARL S., ROBERT K. MERRITT, GREGORY W. HEATH, KENNETH E. POWELL, RICHARD A. WASHBURN, ANDREA KRISKA, and GWENDOLYN HAILE. 1991. "Physical Activity Behaviors in Lower and Higher Socioeconomic Status Populations." *American Journal of Epidemiology* 133:1246–55.

FOX, A. J., P. O. GOLDBLATT, and D. R. JONES. 1985. "Social Class Mortality Differentials: Artifact, Selection or Life Circumstances?" *Journal of Epidemiology and Community Health* 36:1–8.

GAZIANO, J. MICHAEL, JULIE E. BURING, JAN L. BRESLOW, SAMUEL Z. GOLDHABER, BERNARD ROSNER, MARTIN VanDENBURGH, WALTER WILLETT, and CHARLES H. HENNEKENS. 1993. "Moderate Alcohol Intake, Increased Levels of High-Density Lipoprotein and its Subfractions, and Decreased Risk of Myocardial Infarction." *The New England Journal of Medicine* 329:1829–34.

GILL, JASWINDER S., ALEXANDER V. ZEZULKA, MARTIN J. SHIPLEY, SURINDER K. GILL, and D. GARETH BEEVERS. 1986. "Stroke and Alcohol Consumption." *The New England Journal of Medicine* 315:1041–46.

GORE, SUSAN. 1978. "The Effect of Social Support in Moderating the Health Consequences of Unemployment." *Journal of Health and Social Behavior* 19:157–65.

GURALNIK, JACK M. and GEORGE A. KAPLAN. 1989. "Predictors of Healthy Aging: Prospective Evidence from the Alameda County Study." *American Journal of Public Health* 79:703–708.

GURALNIK, JACK M., KENNETH C. Land, GERDA G. FILLENBAUM, and LAUREN G. BRANCH. 1993. "Educational Status and Active Life Expectancy among Older Blacks and Whites." *New England Journal of Medicine* 329:110–16.

GUTZWILLER, FELIZ, CARLO LaVECCHIA, FABIO LEVI, EVA NEGRI, and VINCENT WIETLISBACH. 1989. "Education, Disease Prevalence and Health Service Utilization in the Swiss National Health Survey." *Preventive Medicine* 18:452–59.

HELMERT U., B. HERMAN, K.-H. JOECKEL, E. GREISER, and J. MADANS. 1989. "Social Class and Risk Factors for Coronary Heart Disease in the Federal Republic of Germany. Results of the Baseline Survey of the German Cardiovascular Prevention Study." *Journal of Epidemiology and Community Health* 43:37–42.

HEROLD, JOAN and INGRID WALDRON. 1985. "Part-Time Employment and Women's Health." *Journal of Occupational Medicine* 27:405–12.

HIBBARD, JUDITH H. and CLYDE R. POPE. 1987. "Employment Characteristics and Health Status among Men and Women." *Women and Health* 12:85–102.

HOLDEN, KAREN C. and W. LEE HANSEN. 1987. "Part-Time Work, Full-Time Work, and Occupational Segregation." Pp. 217–38 in *Gender in the Workplace*, edited by C. Brown and J. A. Pechman. Washington, DC: Brookings Institute.

HOUSE, JAMES S, KARL R. LANDIS, and DEBRA UMBERSON. 1988. "Social Relationships and Health." *Science* 241:S40–45.

HOUSE, JAMES S., VICTOR STRECHER, HELEN L. METZNER, and CYNTHIA A. ROBBINS. 1986. "Occupational Stress and Health among Men and Women in the Tecumseh Community Health Study." *Journal of Health and Social Behavior* 27:62–77.

IDLER, ELLEN L. and STANISLAV V. KASL. 1991. "Health Perceptions and Survival: Do Global Evaluations of Health Status Really Predict Mortality?" *Journal of Gerontology* 46(supp.):55–65.

JACOBSEN, BJARNE K. and DAG S. THELLE. 1988. "Risk Factors for Coronary Heart Disease and Level of Education." *American Journal of Epidemiology* 127:923–32.

JENNINGS, SUSAN, CHERYL MAZAIK, and SONJA MCKINLAY, 1984. "Women and Work: An Investigation of the Association between Health and Employment Status in Middle-Aged Women." *Social Science and Medicine* 19:423–31.

KAPLAN, GEORGE A., MARY N. HAAN, and S. LEONARD SYME. 1987. "Socioeconomic Status and Health." *American Journal of Preventive Medicine* 3(supp.):125–29.

KAPLAN, SHERRIE. 1987. "Patient Reports of Health Status as Predictors of Physiologic Health Measures in Chronic Disease." *Journal of Chronic Disease* 40(supp.):27–35.

KESSLER, RONALD C., JAMES S. HOUSE, and J. BLAKE TURNER. 1987. "Unemployment and Health in a Community Sample." *Journal of Health and Social Behavior* 28:51–59.

KESSLER, RONALD C. and JANE D. MCLEOD. 1985. "Social Support and Mental Health in Community Samples." Pp. 219–40 in *Social Support and Health*, edited by S. Cohen and S. L. Syme. New York: Academic.

KITAGAWA, EVELYN M. and PHILIP M. HAUSER. 1973. *Differential Mortality in the United States: A Study in Socioeconomic Epidemiology*. Cambridge, MA: Harvard University Press.

KOHN, MELVIN and CARMI SCHOOLER. 1982. "Job Conditions and Personality: A Longitudinal Assessment of Their Reciprocal Effects." *American Journal of Sociology* 87:1257–86.

KOHN, MELVIN, ATSUHI NAOI, CARRIE SCHOENBACH, CARMI SCHOOLER, and KAZIMEIERZ M. SLOMCZYNSKI. 1990. "Position in the Class Structure and Psychological Functioning in the United States, Japan, and Poland." *American Journal of Sociology* 95:964–1008.

KNOWLES, JOHN H. 1977. "The Responsibility of the Individual." Pp. 57–80 in *Doing Better and Feeling Worse. Health in the U.S.*, edited by J. H. Knowles. New York: W. W. Norton.

LAROCCO, JAMES M., JAMES S. HOUSE, and JOHN R. P. FRENCH. 1980. "Social Support, Occupational Stress, and Health." *Journal of Health and Social Behavior* 3:202–18.

LEIGH, J. PAUL. 1983. "Direct and Indirect Effects of Education on Health." *Social Science and Medicine* 17:227–34.

LEON, ARTHUR S., JOHN CONNETT, DAVID R. JACOBS, and RAINER RAURAMAA. 1987. "Leisure-Time Physical Activity Levels and Risk of Coronary Heart Disease and Death: The Multiple Risk Factor Intervention Trial." *Journal of the American Medical Association* 258:2388–95.

LIANG, JERSEY. 1986. "Self-Reported Physical Health among Aged Adults." *Journal of Gerontology* 41:248–60.

LINN, MARGARET W., RICHARD SANDIFER, and SHAYNA STEIN. 1985. "Effects of Unemployment on Mental and Physical Health." *American Journal of Public Health* 75:502–506.

LIPWORTH, L., T. ABELIN, and R. R. CONNELLY. 1970. "Socioeconomic Factors in the Prognosis of Cancer Patients." *Journal of Chronic Diseases* 23:105–16.

LIU, KIANG, LUCILIA B. CEDRES, JEREMIAH STAMLER, ALAN DYER, ROSE STAMLER, SERAFIN NANAS, DAVID M. BERKSON, OGLESBY PAUL, MARK LEPPER, HOWARD A. LINDBERG, JOHN MARQUAR, ELIZABETH STEVENS, JAMES A. SCHOENBERGER, RICHARD B. SHEKELLE, PATRICIA COLLETTE, SUE SHEKELLE, and DAN GARDSIDE. 1982. "Relationship of Education to Major Risk Factors and Death from Coronary Heart Disease. Cardiovascular Diseases, and All Causes." *Circulation* 66:1308–14.

MAGNUS, K., A. MATROOS, and J. STRACKEE. 1979. "Walking, Cycling, or Gardening, with or without Seasonal Interruptions, in Relation to

Acute Coronary Events." *American Journal of Epidemiology* 110:724–33.

MATTHEWS, KAREN A., SHERYL F. KELSEY, ELAINE N. MEILAHN, LEWIS H. KULLER, and RENA R. WING. 1989. "Educational Attainment and Behavioral and Biological Risk Factors for Coronary Heart Disease in Middle-Aged Women." *American Journal of Epidemiology* 129:1132–44.

MIDANIK, LORRAINE T., ARTHUR L. KLATSKY, and MARY ANNE ARMSTRONG. 1990. "Changes in Drinking Behavior: Demographic, Psychosocial, and Biomedical Factors." *International Journal of the Addictions* 25:599–619.

MILLAR, WAYNE J. and DONALD T. WIGLE. 1986. "Socioeconomic Disparities in Risk Factors for Cardiovascular Disease." *Canadian Medical Association Journal* 134:127–32.

MIROWSKY, JOHN and CATHERINE E. ROSS. 1989. *Social Causes of Psychological Distress.* New York: Aldine de Gruyter.

———. 1991. "Eliminating Defense and Agreement Bias from Measures of Sense of Control: A 2 × 2 Index." *Social Psychology Quarterly* 54:127–45.

MORRIS, J. N. 1990. "Inequalities in Health: Ten Years and Little Further On." *The Lancet* 336:49–93.

MOSER, K. A., A. J. FOX, and D. R. JONES. 1986. "Unemployment and Mortality in the OPXS Longitudinal Study." Pp. 75–87 in *Class and Health. Research and Longitudinal Data*, edited by R. G. Wilkinson. London, England: Tavistock.

MOSSEY, JOAN M. and EVELYN SHAPIRO. 1982. "Self-Rated Health: A Predictor of Mortality among the Elderly." *American Journal of Public Health* 72:800–808.

NAGI, SAAD Z. 1976. "An Epidemiology of Disability among Adults in the United States." *Milbank Memorial Fund Quarterly* 54:439–68.

NATIONAL CENTER FOR HEALTH STATISTICS (NCHS). 1989. *Deaths Attributable to Smoking, U.S., 1988.* Hyattsville, MD: Public Health Service.

———. 1992. *Advance Report of Final Mortality Statistics, 1989.* Hyattsville, MD: Public Health Service.

O'ROURKE, DIANE and JOHNNY BLAIR. 1983. "Improving Random Selection in Telephone Surveys." *Journal of Marketing Research* 20:428–32.

PAFFENBARGER, RALPH S., ROBERT T. HYDE, ALVIN L. WING, I-MIN LEE, DEXTER L. JUNG, and JAMES B.

KAMPERT. 1993. "The Association of Changes in Physical Activity Level and Other Lifestyle Characteristics with Mortality among Men." *New England Journal of Medicine* 328:538–45.

PAPPO, G., S. QUEEN, W. HADDEN, and G. FISHER. 1993. "The Increasing Disparity in Mortality between Socioeconomic Groups in the United States, 1960 and 1986." *New England Journal of Medicine* 329:103–109.

PASSANNANTE, MARIAN R. and CONSTANCE A. NATHANSON. 1985. "Female Labor Force Participation and Female Mortality in Wisconsin, 1974–1978." *Social Science and Medicine* 21:655–65.

PEARLIN, LEONARD I. 1989. "The Sociological Study of Stress." *Journal of Health and Social Behavior* 30:241–56.

PEARLIN, LEONARD I., MORTON A. LIEBERMAN, ELIZABETH G. MENAGHAN, and JOSEPH T. MULLAN. 1981. "The Stress Process." *Journal of Health and Social Behavior* 22:337–56.

POWER, C. O. MANOR, A. J. FOX, and K. FOGELMAN. 1990. "Health in Childhood and Social Inequalities in Health in Young Adults." *Journal of the Royal Statistical Society* 153:17–28.

RODIN, J. AND C. TIMKO. 1992. "Sense of Control, Aging and Health." Pp. 174–206 in *Aging Health & Behavior*, edited by M. Ory, R. Abeles, and P.D. Lipman. Newbury Park, CA: Sage Publications.

ROGERS, RICHARD G. and EVE POWELL-GRINER. 1991. "Life Expectancies of Cigarette Smokers and Nonsmokers in the United States." *Social Science and Medicine* 32:1151–59.

ROMELSJO, ANDERS and FINN DIDERICHSEN. 1989. "Changes in Alcohol-Related Inpatient Care in Stockholm County in Relation to Socioeconomic Status During a Period of Decline in Alcohol Consumption." *American Journal of Public Health* 79:52–56.

ROSS, CATHERINE E. and JOAN HUBER. 1985. "Hardship and Depression." *Journal of Health and Social Behavior* 26:312–27.

ROSS, CATHERINE E. and JOHN MIROWSKY, 1989. "Explaining the Social Patterns of Depression: Control and Problem-Solving—or Support and Talking." *Journal of Health and Social Behavior* 30:206–19.

———. 1992. "Households, Employment, and the Sense of Control." *Social Psychology Quarterly* 55:217–35.

————. Forthcoming. "Does Employment Affect Health?" *Journal of Health and Social Behavior.*

ROSS, CATHERINE E. and BARBARA F. RESKIN. 1992. "Education, Control at Work, and Job Satisfaction." *Social Science Research* 21:134–48.

ROTTER, JULIAN B. 1966. "Generalized Expectancies for Internal vs. External Control of Reinforcements." *Psychological Monographs* 80:1–28.

ROWE, JOHN W. and ROBERT L. KAHN. 1987. "Human Aging: Usual and Successful." *Science* 143:143–49.

SANDVIK, LEIV, JAN ERIKSSEN, ERIK THAULOW, GUNNAR ERIKSSEN, REIDAR MUNDAL, and KAARE RODAHL. 1993. "Phsycial Fitness as a Predictor of Mortality among Healthy, Middle-Aged Norwegian Men." *New England Journal of Medicine* 328:533–37.

SEEMAN, MELVIN. 1983. "Alienation Motifs in Contemporary Theorizing: The Hidden Continuity of Classic Themes." *Social Psychology Quarterly* 46:171–84.

SEEMAN, MELVIN and TERESA E. SEEMAN. 1983. "Health Behavior and Personal Autonomy: A Longitudinal Study of the Sense of Control in Illness." *Journal of Health and Social Behavior* 24:144–60.

SEEMAN, MELVIN, ALICE Z. SEEMAN, and ART BUDROS. 1988. "Powerlessness, Work, and Community: A Longitudinal Study of Alienation and Alcohol Use." *Journal of Health and Social Behavior* 29:185–98.

SEGOVIA, JORGE, ROY F. BARTLETT, and ALISON C. EDWARDS. 1989. "The Association between Self-Assessed Health Status and Individual Health Practices." *Canadian Journal of Public Health* 80:32–37.

SEWELL, WILLIAM H., and ROBERT M. HAUSER. 1975. *Education, Occupation, and Earnings.* New York: Academic Press.

SHEA, STEVEN, ARYEH D. STEIN, CHARLES E. BASCH, RAFAEL LANTINGUE, CHRISTOPHER MAYLAHN, DAVID S. STROGATZ, and LLOYED NOVICK. 1991. "Independent Associations of Educational Attainment and Ethnicity with Behavioral Risk Factors for Cardiovascular Disease." *American Journal of Epidemiology* 134:567–82.

SHORE, ELSIE R. and SHARON A. PIERI. 1992. "Drinking Behaviors of Women in Four Occupational Groups." *Women and Health* 19:55–64.

STAMPFER, MEIR J., GRAHAM A. COLDITZ, WALTER C. WILLETT, FRANK E. SPEIZER, and CHARLES H. HENNEKENS. 1988. "A Prospective Study of Moderate Alcohol Consumption and the Risk of Coronary Heart Disease and Stroke in Women." *New England Journal of Medicine* 319:267–73.

SUMMERS, LAWRENCE. 1992. "The Most Influential Investment." *Scientific American* 270:132.

SURGEON GENERAL. 1982. *The Health Consequences of Smoking.* Rockville, MD: Public Health Service.

SYME, LEONARD S. and LISA F. BERKMAN. 1986. "Social Class, Susceptibility, and Sickness." Pp. 28–34 in *The Sociology of Health and Illness,* 2d ed., edited by P. Conrad and R. Kern. New York: St. Martin's Press.

UMBERSON, DEBRA. 1987. "Family Status and Health Behaviors: Social Control as a Dimension of Social Integration." *Journal of Health and Social Behavior* 28:306–19.

U.S. DEPARTMENT OF EDUCATION. 1992. *Digest of Education Statistics (92-097).* Washington, DC: National Center for Education Statistics.

U.S. PREVENTIVE SERVICES TASK FORCE. 1989. *Guide to Clinical Preventive Services.* Baltimore, MD: Williams and Wilkins.

VERBRUGGE, LOIS. 1983. "Multiple Roles and Physical Health of Men and Women." *Journal of Health and Social Behavior* 24:16–30.

WAGENKNECHT, LYNNE E., LAURA L. PERKINS, GARY R. CUTLER, STEPHEN SIDNEY, and GREGORY L. BURKE, TERI A. MANOLIA, DAVID R. JACOBS, KIANG LIU, GARY D. FRIEDMAN, GLENN H. HUGHES, and STEPHEN B. HULLEY. 1990. "Cigarette Smoking is Strongly Related to Educational Status: The CARDIA Study." *Preventive Medicine* 19:158–69.

WAKSBERG, JOSEPH. 1978. "Sampling Methods for Random Digit Dialing." *Journal of the American Statistical Association* 73:40–46.

WHEATON, BLAIR. 1980. "The Sociogenesis of Psychological Disorder: An Attributional Theory." *Journal of Health and Social Behavior* 21:100–24.

WILKINSON, RICHARD G. 1986. *Class and Health: Research and Longitudinal Data.* London, England: Tavistock.

WILLIAMS, DAVID R. 1990. "Socioeconomic Differentials in Health: A Review and Redirection." *Social Psychology Quarterly* 53:81–99.

Winkleby, Marilyn A., Darius E. Jatulis, Erica Frank, and Stephen P. Fortmann. 1992. "Socioeconomic Status and Health: How Education, Income, and Occupation Contribute to Risk Factors for Cardiovascular Disease." *American Journal of Public Health* 82:816–20.

Woodward, Mark, Michael C. Shewry, W. Cairns, S. Smith, and Hugh Tunstall-Pedoe. 1992. "Social Status and Coronary Heart Disease: Results from the Scottish Heart Health Study." *Preventive Medicine* 21:136–48.

Part III
SOCIAL STRESS

Stress is a heightened mind-body reaction to stimuli that induce fear or anxiety (Cockerham 2001). The paper in this part helps us to understand the social aspects of stress—a major area of research for medical sociologists. This paper, "Stress, Coping, and Social Support Processes: Where Are We? What Next?" reviews and summarizes existing knowledge, unanswered questions, and new research directions in the areas of stress, coping resources, coping strategies, and social support. Peggy A. Thoits, the author, views stress as environmental, social, or internal demands that require the individual to readjust his or her usual behavior pattern. Coping resources ("social and personal characteristics upon which people draw when dealing with stressors") and coping strategies ("behavioral and/or cognitive attempts to manage specific situational demands which are appraised as taxing or exceeding one's ability to adapt") constitute intervening processes between stressors and reactions to stressful demands. Thoits suggests that the mechanisms by which resources such as personal control and perceived social support operate to promote well-being are poorly understood and require further elaboration. Additional research is recommended to assess the interplay between personal agency, structural constraints, and flexibility as an effective coping style.

Thoits observes that social support (feelings of being loved and cared for by significant others) has been closely scrutinized by medical sociologists. However, the determinants of seeking or receiving perceived emotional support, and the efficacy of solicited and unsolicited support remain unresolved. Advances in knowledge, as Thoits argues, rest on studying the relationship between the structural and functional dimensions of support, the perceived distribution of support, and the reciprocal influence of support and personality resources. In the end, Thoits suggests, the study of stress requires a fresh approach, employing such methodological techniques as qualitative comparative analysis, optimal matching analysis, and narrative analysis. Moreover, continued work, most notably in the area of social support, is imperative for the effective development of primary prevention and health promotion projects.

We all live with and will continue to live with stress. By pursuing the new directions in research outlined by Thoits and by exploring social support in greater depth, medical sociologists may in fact arrive at ways to help people successfully manage the stresses of both everyday life and extraordinary circumstances.

REFERENCE

COCKERHAM, WILLIAM C. 2001. *Medical Sociology*, 8th ed. Upper Saddle River, NJ: Prentice Hall.

STRESS, COPING, AND SOCIAL SUPPORT PROCESSES: WHERE ARE WE? WHAT NEXT?

Peggy A. Thoits
Vanderbilt University

I review existing knowledge, unanswered questions, and new directions in research on stress, coping resources, coping strategies, and social support processes. New directions in research on stressors include examining the differing impacts of stress across a range of physical and mental health outcomes, the "carry-overs" of stress from one role domain or stage of life into another, the benefits derived from negative experiences, and the determinants of the meaning of stressors. Although a sense of personal control and perceived social support influence health and mental health both directly and as stress buffers, the theoretical mechanisms through which they do so still require elaboration and testing. New work suggests that coping flexibility and structural constraints on individuals' coping efforts may be important to pursue. Promising new directions in social support research include studies of the negative effects of social relationships and of support giving, mutual coping and support-giving dynamics, optimal "matches" between individuals' needs and support received, and properties of groups which can provide a sense of social support. Qualitative comparative analysis, optimal matching analysis, and event-structure analysis are new techniques which may help advance research in these broad topic areas. To enhance the effectiveness of coping and social support interventions, intervening mechanisms need to be better understood. Nevertheless, the policy implications of stress research are clear and are important given current interest in health care reform in the United States.

Several decades ago, Selye (1956) focused research attention on noxious stressors and laboratory animals' patterned physiological changes in reaction to them. The systematic study of stress in humans began to flourish some years later with the publication of Holmes and Rahe's (1967) checklist of major life changes and their associated readjustment weights. Literally thousands of articles on the negative physical and mental health consequences of major life events were published subsequently. Since the late 1970s, a variety of new methods of measuring stress have been developed and refined (e.g., Bolger et al. 1989a; Brown and Harris 1978, 1989; Dohrenwend et al. 1993; Pearlin and Schooler 1978; Wheaton 1991; Zautra, Guarnaccia, and Dohrenwend 1986), and stress theory has been elaborated to incorporate factors which moderate or buffer the effects of stress on physical and mental health. Each of these moderating factors—coping resources, coping strategies,

Reprinted from the *Journal of Health and Social Behavior*, extra issue (1995), pp. 53–79, by permission of the American Sociological Association.

and social support—now has its own thriving literature.

A thorough review of each of these topic areas, including measurement and methodological problems, is beyond the scope of this paper. Since 1985, over 3,000 papers on "stress and health" have been published in psychological and sociological journals alone. I will instead summarize briefly what we know with some certainty (drawing heavily on reviews and key articles), point to unanswered questions, and discuss promising new directions in research on stressors, coping resources, coping strategies, and social support, taking each broad topic in turn.

The reader should be aware that much of the psychosocial literature on "stress and health" actually focuses on *mental* health conditions as outcomes. I will note wherever mental health findings also apply to physical health outcomes in the psychosocial literature. Because I have not delved into the medical or epidemiological journals where additional physical health findings are amassed and because my own expertise is in mental health, this overview and commentary will be heavily biased toward that subject area.

STRESSORS: EVENTS AND STRAINS

Definitions

"Stress" or "stressor" refers to any environmental, social, or internal demand which requires the individual to readjust his/her usual behavior patterns (Holmes and Rahe 1967). The term "stress reaction" refers to the state of physiological or emotional arousal that usually, but not inevitably, results from the perception of stress or demand. Theory generally holds that stressors motivate efforts to cope with behavioral demands *and* with the emotional reactions that are usually evoked by them (Lazarus and Folkman 1984). As stressors accumulate, individuals' abilities to cope or readjust can be overtaxed,

depleting their physical or psychological resources, in turn increasing the probability that illness, injury, or disease or that psychological distress or disorder will follow (Brown and Harris 1978; Dohrenwend and Dohrenwend 1974; Lazarus and Folkman 1984; Pearlin 1989).

Three major forms of stressors have been investigated in the literature: life events, chronic strains, and daily hassles. Life events are acute changes which require major behavioral readjustments within a relatively short period of time (e.g., birth of first child, divorce). Chronic strains are persistent or recurrent demands, which require readjustments over prolonged periods of time (e.g., disabling injury, poverty, marital problems). Hassles (and uplifts) are minievents which require small behavioral readjustments during the course of a day (e.g., traffic jams, unexpected visitors, having a good meal). Because most research attention has been paid to the effects of life events and chronic strains on physical and mental health, I will concentrate on these stressors in this overview.[1]

Major Findings and Gaps

It is now well established that one or more major negative life events experienced during a six- to 12-month period predict subsequent physical morbidity, mortality, symptoms of psychological distress, and psychiatric disorder (Cohen and Williamson 1991; Coyne and Downey 1991; Creed 1985; Kessler, Price, and Wortman 1985; Tausig 1986; Thoits 1983). It is relevant to note that Homes and Rahe (1967) originally proposed that the total amount of life change in a given period of time would overtax the physical resources of individuals and leave them vulnerable to illness or injury. With respect to mental health, Brown and Harris (1978) later argued that only negative changes (rather than all changes, positive and negative) would overtax the person's psychological resources and increase the risk of emotional disorder. Subsequent research consistently demonstrated that events that were negative or threatening *and* major or highly disruptive precipitated psychological distress and more serious forms of psychiatric disorder (especially anxiety and depressive disorders); positive or benign events and minor events were only weakly related to psychological disturbance (Thoits 1983). The physical health literature generally has followed the lead of the mental health literature, and focused on the effects of negative events rather than total events on health, without numerous comparisons of the relative predictive utility of negative versus total events (e.g., Cohen and Williamson 1991; Creed 1985). Although it appears that negative events are somewhat more strongly related than total events to disease and physical symptoms (e.g., Lin and Ensel 1989), further comparisons are warranted in the physical health domain.

Chronic strains or difficulties have been less frequently studied than life events, but the literature consistently shows that strains are also damaging to both physical and mental health (e.g., Avison and Turner 1988; Brown and Harris 1978, 1989; House et al. 1979, 1986; Liem and Liem 1978; Newmann 1986; Pearlin and Johnson 1977; Pearlin et al. 1981; Verbrugge 1989; Wheaton 1991). Physical health outcomes are most often examined as consequences of chronic unemployment or persistent job strains, while mental health outcomes are studied as consequences of a much wider array of chronic difficulties (e.g., marital, parental, occupational, financial). Thus, we know much less about the impacts of marital and parental strains on subsequent illness, injury, and disease than we do about the impacts of strains that derive from employment (and its lack or loss).

Findings differ regarding whether negative life events or chronic strains are more predictive of physical and mental health problems (e.g., Avison and Turner 1988; Billings and Moos 1984; Brown and Harris 1978; Eckenrode 1984; Wheaton 1991). Contrasting findings may be due to the ways in which events and strains have been measured across studies (Eckenrode 1984; Kessler et al. 1985). However, resolving the question of relative importance is probably less useful than better understanding the ways in which negative events and ongoing strains together influence physical and mental well-being. A number of studies show that negative life events produce significant increases in emotional problems only when the events themselves generate persistent or recurrent strains (e.g., Aneshensel 1992; Avison 1993; Gerstel, Riessman, and Rosenfield 1985; Pearlin et al. 1981; Umberson, Wortman, and Kessler 1992). Others indicate that negative events which occur in a domain that has been continuously stressful or conflicted can produce an onset of psychological symptoms (e.g., Brown, Bifulco, and Harris 1987). Still others show that losing a role which has been a source of ongoing difficulty (e.g., divorce, job loss) relieves, rather than exacerbates, psychological symptoms (e.g., Wheaton 1990a). These studies point to a need for further examination not only of the joint consequences of events and strains but of the consequences of specific event and strain *sequences*, a topic to which I will return below. I should note that these new studies of event/strain combinations have primarily examined mental health outcomes; whether similar findings might emerge for physical health outcomes remains an unanswered question. Physical health researchers seem much less interested in the *configurations* of specific events or chronic strains which might predict disease onset or susceptibility to infection (e.g., Rodin and Salovey 1989; Cohen and Williamson 1991).

Although most investigators have supposed that lower-status, disadvantaged groups experience more negative events and ongoing strains in their lives, the evidence indicates that only ongoing strains are consistently and inversely distributed by social status (e.g., Brown and Harris 1978; McLeod and Kessler 1990; Pearlin and Johnson 1977; Pearlin and Lieberman 1978; Turner, Wheaton, and Lloyd 1995). Lower-status persons are not always found to experience more undesirable events (e.g., Brown and Harris 1978; Eckenrode and Gore 1981; Lin, Dean, and Ensel 1986; Thoits 1982, 1984; Turner et al. 1995). The relationship between social status and life changes often depends on the types of events examined in a particular study (for example, whether events that can happen to members of one's social network are included). In general, people with many social roles are at risk of more personal losses and more network events than people with fewer social roles (Thoits 1987).[2]

Despite inconsistencies with respect to the relationship between social status and exposure to negative events, the stress literature indicates that members of disadvantaged social groups are especially vulnerable or emotionally reactive to stressors. When compared at similar levels or intensities of stress experience, women, the elderly, the unmarried, and those of lower socioeconomic status exhibit higher psychological distress or depression scores than their higher-status counterparts (Cronkite and Moos 1984; Kessler and Cleary 1980; Kessler and Essex 1982; McLeod and Kessler 1990; Pearlin and Johnson 1977; Thoits 1982, 1984, 1987; Turner and Noh 1983; Ulbrich, Warheit, and Zimmerman 1989; Wheaton 1982). However, disadvantaged groups are not *generally* vulnerable to all types of stress. When cumulative indices of events or strains are disaggregated into particular types of stressors (e.g., love loss events, income loss events, uncontrollable events, and so on), different groups appear to be vulnerable to specific subsets of stressors instead. Specifically, women seem to be more vulnerable to "network events" (events that happens to loved ones in their

social networks), while men may be more vulnerable to financial and job-related stressors (Conger et al. 1993; Eckenrode and Gore 1981; Gore and Colten 1991; Kessler and McLeod 1984; Turner and Avison 1989; but see Aneshensel, Rutter, and Lachenbruch [1991] and Thoits [1987] for exceptions). It should be noted that most examinations of differential vulnerability have focused on mental health outcomes: Whether social status and stressors interact similarly in their effects on physical health outcomes remains unexplored. That results may differ for physical health is suggested by Aneshensel and her colleagues (1991), who show that sociodemographic differences in reactivity to stressors depend not only on the types of stress examined but on the specific disorders serving as outcome measures.

Examining the social distributions of stress experiences and the social variations in emotional reactivity to stressors begs an important prior question, one that has not been thoroughly addressed by sociologists theoretically or empirically: What are the social origins of stress? In a seminal piece, Pearlin (1989) located individuals' experiences of ongoing strains and negative events within their social roles which are, in turn, products of sociocultural stratification by gender, race, and social class (see also Riessman 1990). Mirowsky and Ross (1989) point to structural powerlessness, alienation, and lack of control, again consequences of the stratification system. Aneshensel (1992) argues that the occurrence of social stress is a predictable, perhaps inevitable, outcome of social organization, in particular, systematic discrimination and inequity.

Despite attributions of the origins of stress to large-scale social structures or processes, few investigators have attempted to examine the links between macrolevel factors and microlevel experiences, preferring to assess, for example, status variations in role strains, powerlessness, or lack of control at the individual level only. An exception to the rule is a research program conducted by Dooley and Catalano (1980, 1984a, 1984b; Catalano and Dooley 1983; Catalano, Dooley, and Jackson 1981). These researchers have linked contractions in the macrolevel economic system directly to individual experiences of unemployment, financial difficulties, psychological symptoms, and psychiatric help-seeking. It may be because we have lacked similar studies examining the relationship between *other* macrostructures and microexperiences that stress research has been categorized as mere social psychology and less a part of mainstream sociology. Like the concept of "role," the stress construct provides a potentially valuable bridge linking large-scale organization and individual experience and action. It is also relevant that structurally induced chronic strains and collective coping efforts in response to them have played an important role in explaining the impetus for social movements and social change in more general sociological theory and research (e.g., Griffin and Korstad, forthcoming; Killian 1984; Smelser 1963; Useem 1985). In my view, we need to show to sociologists in general the relevance of our stress process research (which has been conducted primarily at the individual level) to broader sociological questions of structural persistence *and* social change.

Promising New Directions: Multiple Outcomes

There are a number of promising new directions in research on stressors and their health effects. One trend has been prompted by Aneshensel's (Aneshensel et al. 1991) argument that we drastically underestimate the impacts of stress and limit our understanding of specificities in stress-disorder relationships by following the usual practice of examining only one health outcome at a time in stress studies (e.g., depression, myocardial infarction). Aneshensel and colleagues' demonstra-

tion that one disorder is not a proxy for all disorders has prompted investigators to examine a variety of outcomes in the same study (e.g., Dohrenwend et al. 1992; Conger et al. 1993; Kessler et al. 1989; Thoits 1994b). Interestingly, this practice has been more routine in the physical health literature, which often includes measures of anxiety and depression along with physical health indicators (e.g., Cohen and Williamson 1991; Creed 1985; Lin and Ensel 1989). Emerging from the physical health literature is a fairly consistent finding that stressors are linked to physical illness or medical treatment-seeking *through* depression, anxiety, or generalized distress.

Although findings are inevitably more complex, I believe that inconsistencies among outcomes and uncovered specificities in relationships will eventually lead us to more refined theory, or at least to different questions. For example, stress researchers have attempted unsuccessfully for years to explain women's consistently higher depression scores compared to men. In contrast, we have given minimal attention to men's consistently higher substance use scores compared to women. If depression and substance use are *alternative* ways of reacting to stressors, then perhaps we should not be asking what it is about women's experiences that make them more depressed than men. We might ask instead what kinds of stressors lead to one psychological response as opposed to another. If we can identify the key conditions, *then* we might ask whether those conditions are distributed differentially by social status or explore whether alternative reactions to stressors are a product of differential socialization by social status.[3]

There is an additional reason for following Aneshensel's recommendation. I noted earlier that psychologists and sociologists have focused heavily on psychological outcomes (usually depression or psychological distress) in the stress, coping, and social support literatures. I believe that mental health researchers often presume that their findings can be safely generalized to physical health. But on a number of important issues, we simply have no information to warrant this. For example, we do not know whether members of lower-status groups are *physically* more vulnerable to the effects of stressors than members of higher-status groups, and we do not know whether specific coping efforts which ward off emotional distress also will ward off onsets of illness (or vice versa). There are good theoretical reasons to believe that the etiologies of chronic and infectious diseases differ from those of psychiatric ones (Cohen and Williamson 1991). Given such important gaps in the literature, it seems crucial to overcome our neglect of physical health consequences by analyzing physical *and* psychological dependent variables (as well as their interrelationships and comorbidity) within the same studies.

New Directions: Stress "Carry-over"

Another promising new direction in research involves investigations of what might be called "carry-over" effects of stressors—specifically, carry-overs across persons, role domains, and stages of life. For example, using daily diary data collected from husbands and wives, Bolger and colleagues (1989a, 1989b) found that stresses at work (e.g., overloads, arguments) spill over to increase stresses at home and vice versa, and that one spouse's spillovers affected the other spouse. Related to this, a number of researchers have examined cross-role interactions between work stressors and marital stressors. Stressors in one role sometimes exacerbate the negative psychological effects of stressors in other roles (Bromet, Dew, and Parkinson 1990; Liem and Liem 1990; Menaghan 1991; Wheaton 1990b). Other researchers are examining the cross-generational effects of stress and strain, in particular the impacts of parents' stressors and/or depressive states on their children

(Avison 1993; Coyne and Downey 1991; Menaghan 1991). New work in progress is exploring how events and strains in one stage of life can influence psychological well-being both in contiguous and much later life stages (Lin and Ensel 1993; Aneshensel and Gore 1991), including the negative consequences of childhood traumas (loss of parent, abuse, or neglect) for adult mental health (Coyne and Downey 1991; Kessler and Magee 1993; McLeod 1991; Turner et al. 1995; Wheaton 1991).

These "carry-over" studies are important for three reasons. First, they begin to capture some of the complexities of stress impacts that are familiar to us from personal experience but have long been neglected theoretically and empirically. Second, these studies begin to focus research attention on the consequences of particular *sequences* of experiences, both on a daily basis and over the much longer term (e.g., the life course). As a consequence, investigators may come to better understand the episodic, recurrent nature of some disorders, such as depression (Coyne and Downey 1991; Cronkite et al. 1993). Third, studies of longer-term consequences reintroduce the interesting possibility that although negative events and strains may be damaging in the short term, they may in the longer term prove beneficial (e.g., Elder 1974). I will briefly discuss recent developments in stress research related to these latter two implications.

New Directions: Stress Sequences

Earlier I mentioned that psychological distress is exacerbated when threatening events occur in a role domain which is already strained or conflicted (Brown et al. 1987). Psychological distress is ameliorated, however, when role loss occurs in an already stressful domain (Wheaton 1990a). I believe that these examinations of event and strain *combinations* are actually capturing the effects of particular event and strain *sequences*: ongoing strains followed by an acute threat in a role domain increase emotional upset while ongoing strains followed by role exit or role loss decrease upset. That the sequencing of experiences can matter importantly for mental health is also demonstrated by Jackson (1993), who examined the depression scores of men and women who acquired (and lost) marital, parental, and occupational roles in differing orders (controlling for the number and types of adult roles individuals held). White men and women who followed the statistically more frequent sequence of work, then marriage, then parenting were significantly less depressed than those who acquired these three roles in other sequences. Even the currently divorced and unemployed were less depressed if they had previously acquired these roles in normative order. (Jackson reasoned that previous transitions influenced individuals' coping resources and experiences of role strain at the time of each subsequent transition.) In short, examining experiential sequences, including more extended sequences of stressors over the life course, may help specify further the conditions under which stressors damage mental (and possibly physical) health (Albrecht and Levy 1991).

New Directions: Positive Effects of Stress

As is frequently noted in the literature, negative life events do not necessarily have negative health or mental health consequences, at least over the long run. In part this is because individuals often actively solve the problems which confront them. Less frequently recognized by stress researchers, individuals also learn and grow from negative experiences, even from those that cannot be reversed or escaped. Riessman (1990) offers a compelling demonstration, drawing from in-depth interviews with divorced women and men. Although her interviewees were more depressed or more likely to drink to excess during and immediately after divorce, both men and women also

described significant positive consequences which followed from their post-divorce adjustments. Women gained confidence in themselves and a stronger sense of control over their lives. Men acquired greater interpersonal skills and more willingness to self-disclose emotionally. Both sexes searched for and often found meaning and value in the divorce experience (see also Silver, Boon, and Stones 1983).

Along similar lines, Turner and Avison (1992) recently have drawn from crisis theory to argue that only unresolved negative events should have damaging psychological consequences. They define resolved events as experiences from which individuals are able to derive positive meaning for themselves and/or their futures. They showed that only events which were viewed by individuals as unresolved were associated with depression; resolved events were not. Similarly, work and love-relationship problems increased psychological symptoms only when individuals failed to solve them; successfully solved problems were unrelated to changes in symptoms (Thoits 1994b). These results add further support to Turner and Avison's (1992) argument that resolved or successfully solved life events should not be counted when estimating an individual's burden of stress.

Implicit in these studies is an important message which tends to be overlooked or, when acknowledged, often treated as a threat to validity in stress research: Individuals are activists on behalf of their own well-being (Thoits 1994b). That is, people purposefully engage in problem solving and/or actively reconstructing the meaning of their life experiences in order to sustain their sense of self-worth and alleviate anxiety or tension. This observation has several implications. First, as noted earlier, not all negative events will have negative consequences. Individuals may consciously and deliberately bring about negative events (e.g., divorce, getting fired) to solve otherwise intractable problems. Thus, some supposedly "undesirable" events are not stressors but instead problem-solving acts.

A second implication is that individuals are changing and changeable and thus less predictable than we typically assume. If people in fact observe and learn from their experiences, then they can decide to bring about change in themselves or their lives (Kiecolt 1994). Childhood traumas and subsequent stressful life experiences in adolescence or early adulthood may actually result in improvements in physical or emotional well-being in later life stages, not because people have become inoculated by or inured to or even more adept at managing stressors, but because they have simply decided and then acted to change things for the better.

Third, because individuals are presumably motivated to protect and enhance their well-being, they may deliberately engineer positive events in their lives to counteract or counterbalance those aspects which are negative. Brown, Lemyre, and Bifulco (1992) have documented that "fresh start" and "relief" events can promote recovery from depression and anxiety; Kessler, Turner, and House (1989) show that finding a new job eliminates the negative physical and psychological effects of unemployment. Thus, positive events may be just as important as negative ones for health and well-being (contrary to findings summarized earlier), but their effects might not be seen unless they are directly linked to preceding negative ones (suggesting once again the importance of examining experiential sequences).[4]

All of these implications seem to threaten the social causation perspective which explicitly or implicitly guides most, if not all, sociological stress research. Stress researchers cling to the idea that causation flows primarily from stressors to physical or psychological well-being; reverse causality (the social selection or drift hypothesis) is almost always viewed as an alternative explanation which must be ruled out (for exceptions see Dohrenwend et al. 1992; Turner and Gartrell 1978). Even researchers whose results clearly imply the effects of individual motivation or agency (e.g., Brown et al. 1992; Kessler et al. 1989) go to extensive lengths to show that individuals' prior levels of physical or psychological functioning do not fully account for the beneficial consequences of self-initiated change. Although considerable evidence supports the social causation perspective (e.g., Link, Lennon, and Dohrenwend 1993), social selection processes are both plausible and theoretically important. I will argue below that appreciating the individual as a psychological activist should not be seen as a threat to the social causation perspective, but instead as a challenging opportunity to explore more fully the interplay between personal agency and structural constraints.

New Directions: In Pursuit of Meaning

A final direction worthy of mention is a renewed interest in the meaning of stressors or, more generally, in the problem of meaning. Attempting to further specify which kinds of stressors should have harmful psychological consequences has stimulated this interest. Currently, there are four different approaches to meaning identifiable in the literature. The first two are well established, the latter two are more recent and exploratory.[5]

Lazarus and Folkman (1984) describe meaning in terms of appraisal: They ask, for example, whether a demand is perceived as a harm/loss, threat, or challenge, and whether a demand is perceived as controllable or not. Such appraisals should influence the number and types of coping responses that individuals will use. Brown and Harris (1978, 1989) assess the meaning of an event or chronic difficulty (its severity and emotional significance) by taking into account a person's biography, his/her plans and purposes, and the surrounding contextual circumstances (see Shrout et al. [1989] and Dohrenwend et al. [1993] for similar approaches). A contextual definition of meaning has been partially adopted by Wheaton, who examines preexisting chronic strains as the context in which events occur and which alter events' impacts (e.g., Wheaton 1990a, 1990b).

More recently, I have proposed that the meaning or significance of stressors depends on the salience to the individual of the role-identity domain in which they occur (Thoits 1992, 1994a; see also Brown et al. 1987). And Simon (1995) suggests and shows that the beliefs that individuals hold about the relationships among their roles influence the meanings they derive from experienced role demands. Individuals who believe that their work and family roles are interdependent report fewer role conflicts and feelings of failure as parents, spouses, and workers compared to those who believe that work and family roles are independent or unrelated.

These four approaches (using appraisals, context, identity salience, and belief systems), of course, do not exhaust the potential meanings of "meaning." Others likely will develop,[6] since there is little disagreement among researchers—in the field of mental health at least—that assessing meaning is crucial for further specifying which events and strains will have negative psychological impacts. My own work on the effects of identity-relevant stressors (Thoits 1994a) has convinced me that detailed qualitative information about surrounding circumstances, beliefs, and personal values is crucial for understanding the meaning and emotional impacts of negative events in identity domains that are important to the individual. Minimally, such qualitative details help distinguish major from minor events; maximally, they lead to new theoretical insights regarding the configuration of circumstances surrounding stressors which make them most damaging (e.g., Brown et al. 1987; Brown and Harris 1989).

As is often pointed out in reviews, even when refined specifications of stressors are obtained using qualitative information, the

relationships of events and ongoing difficulties with health outcomes are far from perfect. This observation has led researchers to consider other processes which intervene between stressful demands and reactions to those demands. I turn next to two related processes, the utilization of coping resources and coping strategies.

COPING RESOURCES AND COPING STRATEGIES

Definitions

Coping *resources* are social and personal characteristics upon which people may draw when dealing with stressors (Pearlin and Schooler 1978). "Resources . . . reflect a latent dimension of coping because they define a potential for action, but not action itself" (Gore 1985:266). In addition to social support (which is examined separately below), the two personal coping resources most frequently studied by sociologists are a sense of control or mastery over life (i.e., an internal or external locus of control orientation) and, somewhat less commonly, self-esteem.[7] These coping resources are presumed to influence the choice and/or the efficacy of the coping strategies that people use in response to stressors (e.g., Folkman 1984). It is for this reason that I review coping resources and coping strategies together in this section.

Coping *strategies* consist of behavioral and/or cognitive attempts to manage specific situational demands which are appraised as taxing or exceeding one's ability to adapt (Lazarus and Folkman 1984). Coping efforts may be directed at the demands themselves (problem-focused strategies) or at the emotional reactions which often accompany those demands (emotion-focused strategies).[8] Most investigators assume that people high in self-esteem or perceived control are more likely to use active, problem-focused coping responses; low esteem or perceived control should predict more passive or avoidant emotion-focused coping. A related concept is that of coping *styles*, which are habitual preferences for approaching problems; these are more general coping behaviors that the individual employs when facing stressors across a variety of situations (e.g., withdraw or approach, deny or confront, become active or remain passive) (Menaghan 1983).

Major Findings and Gaps: Personal Resources

A sense of personal control or mastery over life is the most frequently examined coping resource in the literature (with the exception of social support, discussed below). An impressive number of studies show that a sense of control or mastery both directly reduces psychological disturbance and physical illness and buffers the deleterious effects of stress exposure on physical and mental health (see reviews in Rodin 1986; Turner and Roszell 1994; also Kessler, Turner, and House 1988; Mirowsky and Ross 1990; Rosenfield 1989; Turner and Noh 1988).[9] Although self-esteem significantly reduces psychological symptoms (especially depression) and buffers the emotional consequences of stressors as well (Kaplan, Robbins, and Martin 1983; Shamir 1986; Turner and Roszell 1994), its role with respect to physical health outcomes has less often been studied.

Perceived control over life circumstances is inversely distributed by social status. Females, minority group members, unmarried persons, and especially those of lower education and income exhibit higher fatalism or a lower sense of mastery, personal control, or internal locus of control (see reviews in Mirowsky and Ross 1989; Turner and Roszell 1994).[10] Although less frequently studied by stress researchers, self-esteem is similarly distributed by social status (Turner and Roszell 1994). However, gender differences in self-esteem have less often been found in studies conducted since 1980 compared to earlier decades (Miller and Kirsch 1989); this shift may be due to women's changing labor force participation or to the influence of the Women's Movement more generally.

Because perceived control over life and high self-esteem are consistently observed to buffer the negative health effects of stress, researchers have reasoned that these characteristics probably increase the use of effective coping strategies, and that unequal distributions of these coping resources by social status probably account for observed demographic differences in emotional vulnerability to stressors (described earlier). Interestingly, support for each of these implications has been inconsistent. For example, although several studies show that individuals high in self-esteem and sense of control are more likely to use problem-focused coping strategies or to have an active coping style (Menaghan 1982, 1983; Menaghan and Merves 1984; Pearlin and Schooler 1978; Pearlin et al. 1981; Ross and Mirowsky 1989), most of these studies also show that problem-focused coping either has no effects on or in some cases can exacerbate psychological symptoms (see summary in Menaghan 1983:191). A close reading of these studies indicates that there is considerable complexity and inconsistency in the relationships among personality characteristics, choice of coping strategies, and the efficacy of coping outcomes. Far more work is required to clarify these relationships.

As mentioned earlier, differential vulnerability to stressors has usually been attributed to a lack of coping resources in lower-status groups—in particular, to lower self-esteem, lower perceived control, and lack of readily available social support. Although some studies confirm this reasoning (Kessler and Essex 1982; Turner and Noh 1983), several others do not (Brown and Harris 1978; Turner and Noh 1983; Thoits 1982, 1984, 1987). At present, we lack persuasive evidence that deficiencies in psychosocial resources reliably explain social status differences in emotional reactivity to stressors (Aneshensel 1992).

Major Findings and Gaps: Coping Strategies

Turning to research on coping strategies, a number of studies indicate that individuals typically use multiple tactics when coping with major life events or ongoing strains (e.g., Billings, Cronkite, and Moos 1983; Folkman and Lazarus 1980; Stone and Neale 1984). Folkman and Lazarus (1980) reported that in 98 percent of 1,300 stressful episodes, subjects used *both* problem-focused and emotion-focused coping strategies. These findings supported their contention that there are usually two sources of stress which must be handled, both situational demands and one's emotional response to those demands.

Not surprisingly, stressors which are appraised as more severe (e.g., as harms/ losses or as threats) evoke greater numbers of coping responses (Cronkite and Moos 1984; Folkman and Lazarus 1980; McCrae 1984; Menaghan 1982, 1983; Menaghan and Merves 1984). In general, problem-focused coping is more likely when situational demands are appraised as controllable; emotion-focused coping is more likely when demands seem uncontrollable (Billings et al. 1983; Coyne, Aldwin, and Lazarus 1981; Folkman 1984; Folkman and Lazarus 1980, 1985; Folkman et al. 1986; Forsythe and Compas 1987; Stone and Neale 1984; Thoits 1991). Although the perceived uncontrollability of a stressor consistently predicts the use of *emotion*-focused strategies, it should be noted that some studies find no association between perceived situational control and efforts to problem-solve (Stone and Neale 1984; Thoits 1991).

Coping researchers generally expect problem-focused coping to be more beneficial for well-being than emotion-focused coping. Despite this belief, there is no clear consensus in the literature regarding which coping strategies are most efficacious in reducing psychological distress or ill health (e.g., Aldwin and Revenson 1987; Mattlin, Wethington, and Kessler 1990; Rodin and Salovey 1989). Some studies find that problem-focused coping decreases psychological distress or promotes rapid recovery from illness while emotion-focused strategies do not; others report the opposite pattern. Indeed, Coyne and Downey (1991) have commented that across studies, coping strategies more often seem to have damaging rather than beneficial effects on well-being. One might be tempted to conclude that most forms of coping are usually ineffective, but this would be premature. Respondents may have already been distressed when they began coping with a specific problem, the specific stressor described may have been memorable because respondents were unable to handle it well, or the stressor may have been unusually severe. Adding further complexities to an already complex literature, some emotion-focused strategies (such as denial and alcohol use) have been found to be beneficial in the short run but to have deleterious consequences over the long run (Aneshensel and Huba 1983; Clark 1994; Rodin and Salovey 1989).

Probably no one coping strategy or coping mode is efficacious across all situations. In fact, research indicates that coping effectiveness depends importantly on the type of stressful situation that the individual confronts. Mattlin and associates (1990) found that efforts to cope with chronic difficulties were much less likely to reduce anxiety and depression than efforts to cope with acute life events. Like Pearlin and Schooler (1978) and Menaghan (1983), they also showed that specific coping strategies which reduced psychological symptoms in one stressful domain were ineffective or even detrimental when used to combat other problems. Generally speaking, the effectiveness of any one strategy or coping style may depend on abstract properties of a stressor (e.g., chronic versus acute, controllable versus uncontrollable), on specific subtypes of stressors (e.g., death of a loved one, illness, interpersonal problem), or perhaps on some combination of both aspects. Far more work will be needed to identify the types of coping which reliably reduce distress or ill health in response to particular types of situations.

A key question for sociologists is whether coping techniques and/or coping styles are distributed unequally by social status. With respect to gender, the answer seems to be a qualified "yes" (comparisons across studies are difficult because researchers use very different coping classifications and means of assessment—e.g., coping in response to a particular stressor versus measures of cross-situational coping style). Studies consistently suggest that men have an inexpressive, stoic style of responding to stressors and women have an emotional, expressive style (Milkie and Thoits 1993). Men more often report controlling their emotions, accepting the problem, not thinking about the situation, and engaging in problem-solving efforts. Women more often report seeking social support, distracting themselves, letting out their feelings, and turning to prayer. Women's greater propensity to seek social support is especially consistent across studies. But there are a number of exceptions in the literature with respect to gender differences in problem-focused coping (e.g., Billings and Moos 1984; Folkman and Lazarus 1980; Ross and Mirowsky 1989; Milkie and Thoits 1993). This may be because men's and women's use of problem-focused coping may depend upon perceiving control or power in a role domain—for example, men in the occupational arena and women in the family arena (Folkman and Lazarus 1980; Menaghan 1982; Pearlin and Schooler 1978).

To date, there are no reliable findings with respect to age differences in coping responses (Billings and Moos 1981; Folkman et al. 1987;

Folkman and Lazarus 1980; McCrae 1982; Rook, Dooley, and Catalano 1991). Racial and socioeconomic differences have rarely been examined. Some studies indicate that highly educated individuals are more likely to use or prefer problem-focused strategies, if thinking through the situation is treated as a problem-solving tactic (Billings and Moos 1984; Ross and Mirowsky 1989; Veroff, Kulka, and Douvan 1981). In general, social status differences in coping styles and in situational coping responses require further exploration.

My suspicion is that reliable differences will emerge (as they have for gender) despite considerable variability in ways of assessing stress and coping efforts across studies. Whether gender and other social status differences in coping can be attributed to exposure to different stressors, to differing appraisals of stressors, or perhaps to differential socialization become important questions to pursue (Milkie and Thoits 1993). Pearlin and Schooler found that women and people with low education and income were more likely to employ coping strategies which are relatively inefficacious in reducing role-related emotional distress. Thus, they suggest that "the groups most exposed to hardship are also least equipped to deal with it" (Pearlin and Schooler 1978:18). Whether social status differences in the use of coping strategies help explain status variations in health and mental health outcomes is a crucial issue which deserves far more research attention by sociologists.

Additional Gaps: Relationships between Coping Resources and Coping Strategies

Presumably, resources such as high self-esteem and an internal locus of control give individuals the confidence or motivation to attempt problem-focused coping in the face of stress. Presumably, too, the perception that a specific stressor is controllable increases the probability that the individual will attempt problem-solving responses (Folkman 1984). But the link between personality orientations and the perceived controllability of specific stressors has not been explored, to my knowledge. One could argue that people high in internal control or self-esteem should be more likely to appraise specific situations as controllable and thus to engage in problem-focused coping; those low in these personality resources should more often perceive problems as uncontrollable and thus engage in emotion-focused coping (Folkman 1984). Whether this reasoning is valid remains an open empirical question at this point. I emphasize here the unexplored links among personality characteristics, situational appraisals, and coping strategies to underscore a key point: To date, we have not developed adequate or detailed theoretical explanations of how or why self-esteem and a sense of control over life come to buffer the negative health consequences of exposure to stress.

Also unaddressed is the reverse question: What are the consequences of coping efforts for self-esteem and a sense of mastery (Cohen and Edwards 1989; Thoits 1994b; Turner and Roszell 1994)? Sociologists typically assume that life experiences both determine and modify personality characteristics. Personality characteristics should not only influence perceptions and coping behaviors, but the success or failure of coping efforts should also enhance or undermine self-esteem and a sense of mastery, respectively. We have rarely treated personality resources as *dependent* variables in the stress and coping process; doing so might help further illuminate the dynamics of the relationship between personality resources and coping.[11]

Moreover, the degree to which personality characteristics and coping behaviors influence the number and types of stressors that individuals experience is also unexplored (Cohen and Edwards 1989; Turner and Roszell 1994). People with high self-esteem and a sense of personal control may have the skills to avoid or prevent negative events or chronic difficulties. Alternatively, these characteristics may influence people's appraisals of events and strains, perhaps rendering them perceptually less threatening. Again, we have not yet spelled out theoretically or examined empirically just how personality resources and coping responses operate in the dynamics of the stress process.

Promising New Directions

I find it difficult to discern *new* directions in coping resources and coping strategies research. With respect to coping resources, this is probably because we have not yet developed theoretically detailed explications of how these personality characteristics actually work to reduce physical and emotional vulnerability to stress. New directions are also hard to identify in research on coping strategies because differing research designs and measurement schemes make comparisons across studies problematic and thus findings less cumulative.

I will highlight two potentially *promising* directions in current research. Since the mid-1980s, a number of investigators have begun to employ daily diary methods or panel survey methods with closely spaced assessments to study changes in stress, coping, mood, and physical symptoms (e.g., Bolger 1990; Bolger et al. 1989a, 1989b; Folkman and Lazarus 1985; Folkman et al. 1986; Stone, Lennox, and Neale 1985; Verbrugge 1985). Despite data complexities and inherent statistical problems, these studies are more faithful to the dynamic, unfolding nature of the phenomena under investigation, compared to experimental and cross-sectional survey designs. Such multiple-assessment, longitudinal designs might enable detailed examinations of coping sequences (which are rarely a focus) as well as the conditions under which individuals use the same or shift to different coping strategies in response to experiential feedback or changing situational demands (Menaghan 1983).[12]

A second development which has promise is the documentation of flexibility or versatility as an efficacious coping style. Pearlin and Schooler (1978) and Mattlin and associates (1990) found that people who routinely use a large number and variety of coping strategies in response to stressors experienced lower emotional distress. Mattlin and his colleagues also found that "passive coping," that is, routinely using few or no coping strategies, enhanced psychological adjustment to chronic difficulties (but not acute events). These general delineations of coping style seem important to replicate in future research. If replicated, interesting additional questions might be raised. What are the social and personality characteristics of people who display flexible and passive coping? If flexible/passive coping styles exist, do these styles influence peoples' subsequent experiences of stress?

I will close this section by briefly raising two additional issues which may be useful to pursue in future work. The first issue is our puzzling lack of attention to an obvious coping resource: money. We treat financial resources either as an indicator of socioeconomic status or, when resources are scarce, as an indicator of experienced chronic difficulty. We do not consider the possibility that financial resources themselves may serve as stress buffers, although everyday observation would suggest that people often draw upon their finances when coping with a variety of problems. Despite difficulties in operationally distinguishing the social status, chronic strain, and coping resource aspects of people's financial situations, this potential problem-solving resource deserves empirical attention, especially as it pertains to physical health outcomes through increased access to medical care.

A second issue concerns the influence of structural constraints. Earlier I argued that stress researchers tend, on the whole, to disregard or deemphasize the degree to which individuals are activists on their own behalf. But individuals' activism and motivation become obvious when we examine the effects of coping resources such as mastery and especially when we study the various coping strategies that people deliberately and consciously use. Ironically, in these areas of research, we may lose sight not of people's agency but of structural constraints on that agency (Menaghan and Merves 1984). As Pearlin puts it, "*Certain kinds of life exigencies seem to be particularly resistant to individual coping efforts* . . . [T]here are situations in which 'problem solving' is not a realistic option" (1991:267, emphasis in the original).

If we pursue questions about the relationships between personality resources and efficacious coping. I believe we will have to attend more closely to the objective features of individuals' situations that constrain action. Folkman (1984) has argued that for problem-focused coping to be effective, subjective appraisals of controllability must match the objective controllability of a stressor (conversely, for emotion-focused coping to be effective, situations should be objectively uncontrollable and accurately perceived as such). We have yet to take into account whether the specific problems with which people grapple are truly amenable to change. If we presume that individuals are activists, as I have advocated earlier, we must also, as good sociologists, simultaneously ask what are the limits on that activism? Research on coping resources and coping strategies seem ideal arenas in which to explore the interplay between personal agency and structural constraint.

SOCIAL SUPPORT AND SOCIAL INTEGRATION

Definitions

As mentioned in the previous section, social support is considered a coping resource—in this case, a social "fund" from which people may draw when handling stressors. Social support has been the most frequently studied psychosocial resource. Social support usually refers to the functions performed for the individual by significant others, such as family members, friends, and coworkers. Significant others can provide instrumental, informational, and/or emotional assistance (House and Kahn 1985). These various supportive functions usually are highly correlated and often form a single underlying factor (House 1981; House and Kahn 1985), summarized as perceived or received social support. The effects of *perceived social support* have most frequently been examined in the literature, especially the effects of perceived *emotional* support (i.e., beliefs that love and caring, sympathy and understanding, and/or esteem and value are available from significant others). The perception or belief that emotional support is available appears to be a much stronger influence on mental health than the actual *receipt* of social support (Dunkel-Schetter and Bennett 1990; Wethington and Kessler 1986).

Most investigators agree that structural and functional aspects of social support are different phenomena and should be assessed and examined as such (Barrera 1986; House and Kahn 1985). *Structural support* refers to the organization of people's ties to one another—in particular, to the number of relationships or social roles a person has, to the frequency of his/her contact with various network members, to the density and multiplexity of relationships among network members, and so forth. Network measures often capture the individual's level or degree of social isolation/integration or social embeddedness.

Major Findings and Gaps

Existing reviews of the social support literature (Berkman 1984; Cohen and Wills 1985; House et al. 1988; Kessler and McLeod 1985) lead to three major conclusions. First, measures of social integration are directly and positively related to mental and physical health, including lower mortality, but social integration does *not* buffer the physical or emotional impacts of major stressful life events or chronic difficulties in people's lives. Second, perceived emotional support is associated directly with better physical and mental health *and* usually buffers the damaging mental and physical health impacts of major life events and chronic strains. Third, the simplest and most powerful measure of social support appears to be whether a person has an intimate, confiding relationship or not (typically with a spouse or lover; friends or relatives function equivalently but less powerfully). Having a confidant significantly reduces the effects of stress experiences on physical and psychological outcomes (Cohen and Wills 1985). These conclusions generally hold for more recent studies of the effects of structural and functional support (e.g., Cohen 1988; but see Ensel and Lin [1991] for an exception with respect to stress-buffering).

How structural and functional aspects of social support are related to one another has not often been studied. It is possible that the number and structure of individuals' social ties matter less for *perceptions* of support than the possession of at least one tie that is close and confiding. However, Lin and Westcott (1991) argue cogently that network structure is crucial for *access* to various kinds of functional assistance. Indeed, the size of a person's social network, the cohesiveness of the network, and the types of relationships in a network (e.g., strong ties versus weak ties) have been shown to influence the *receipt* of various kinds of social support (Barrera 1986; Wellman and Wortley 1990). Received support, in turn, appears to promote perceptions of support availability (Wethington and Kessler 1986), particularly when help has been given with few strings attached (Uehara 1990). The propositions that network structure mediates access to received functional support which in turn enhances perceived support deserve further serious study.

Surprisingly little is known about the social distributions of perceived support. Studies generally show that women either report more perceived support than men or that men and women do not differ in this resource (Pearlin et al. 1981; Ross and Mirowsky 1989; Turner and Marino 1994; Turner and Noh 1988; Vaux 1988). This is a departure from the usual inverse relationship between social status and coping resources. Consistent with previous status patterns, however, are that married individuals report higher perceived support than the unmarried, and perceived support decreases with age and increases with indicators of socioeconomic status (Ross and Mirowsky 1989; Thoits 1984; Turner and Marino 1994; but see Lin et al. [1986] for exceptions by age and SES). Involvement in social networks also varies by social status. Men tend to have larger networks than women but women exhibit greater investment and intimacy in their relationships (Belle 1987). In other words, male participation in social networks across the life course is more "extensive" but less "intensive" than that of females (Belle 1987:260). Network size and participation decline with age and increase with employment status and socioeconomic status (e.g., Fischer 1982; Thoits 1982; Turner and Marino 1994). As discussed in an earlier section on coping resources, despite these social patterns, neither indicators of integration/isolation nor the degree of perceived support consistently explain differential reactivities to stressors by social status.

Despite considerable theorizing about how social support works to reduce ill health and psychological disturbance (e.g., Belle 1987; Berkman 1985; Pearlin 1985), we still lack studies which directly examine presumed intervening mechanisms. It has been argued with respect to mental health, for example, that supporters provide coping assistance (for example, by helping to reinterpret situational demands), that supporters' reassurances bolster self-esteem or a sense of identity, and that supporters' feedback and encouragement sustain a sense of mastery or competence. Yet very few studies to date have examined the actual influences of perceived or received support on individuals' choice of coping strategies or on individuals' self-esteem, identity, or mastery; the results of studies that have done so have been inconsistent at best (Brown 1978; Dunkel-Schetter, Folkman, and Lazarus 1987; Holahan and Moos 1987; Ross and Mirowsky 1989). Attention to intervening mechanisms seems a crucial next step if we wish to truly understand how social support influences psychological well-being.

The mechanisms through which social support can influence a target individual's physical health may be even more complex (Berkman 1985; Kaplan and Toshima 1990; Rodin and Salovey 1989). Supporters may encourage (or sometimes sabotage) individuals' attempts to control their eating, drinking, smoking, or exercising behaviors; actively monitor and regulate a target's health-related behaviors; model or be coparticipants in health-related activities; and urge medical treatment-seeking, among other possibilities. We still know very little about what support-givers actually do to encourage or sustain health-related changes. To add to the complexity, a significant other's sheer presence may regulate an individual's emotional state, which in turn may have implications for his/her immunological responses to stress (Cohen and Williamson 1991; House 1981). Until supportive processes and intervening mechanisms are better understood, the goal of designing effective interventions for people coping with specific stressors or attempting health-behavior changes will elude us (e.g., Gottlieb 1992; Heller et al. 1991a, 1991b).

Moreover, relationships among various psychosocial coping resources remain understudied (Gore 1985). Above, I argued that we know little about how social support affects individuals' personality resources. Conversely, we have rarely explored how personality resources affect perceived or received support and social isolation/integration (cf. Eckenrode 1983). It seems reasonable to suppose that individuals high in self-esteem and mastery also have greater social skills, which in turn should enhance their likelihood of having a support system in place and/or perceiving that support is available.[13] Ross and Mirowsky (1989) offer evidence, however, that perceived control and support are only moderately correlated and that they are alternative and functionally equivalent resources which directly reduce depression: one resource fills the gap if the other is absent. These interesting findings raise a more general question: Do personality resources and social support resources supplement (additively), augment (interactively), or simply substitute for one another as Ross and Mirowsky suggest? Clearly, we know very little about how these resources interrelate in their effects on physical and mental health.

Additional underexplored questions concern the effects of stress experiences on perceived or received social support over time. Obviously, some stressors simultaneously represent a loss of perceived and/or received support (e.g., death of a family member, conflict with relatives or friends, marital problems), so at least some stress experiences are likely to alter significantly the person's support system and/or perceptions of support availability. Despite this, we generally presume that troubles will result in support mobilization rather than curtailment (Eckenrode and Wethington 1990). Although acute stressors may cause support mobilization in the short run at least, chronic stressors may entail serious costs to the social network and thus erode perceived or received support over time (Lin and Ensel 1989). Some evidence corroborates this latter argument (Barrera 1986; Liem and Liem 1990; Quittner, Glueckauf, and Jackson 1990). However, when chronic

stressors are *mutually* experienced, collective mobilization (e.g., strikes and union formation and self-help groups) can develop instead (Griffin and Korstad, 1995). Speaking generally, we need further scrutiny and specification of the conditions under which stressors are likely to mobilize or erode social support. Moreover, we generally leave unexamined who marshals support—the stressed person or his/her significant others. When the stressor is an acute life event, are significant others more likely to intervene without the individual having to ask? Does the utility of support depend on whether the individual has had to solicit assistance or had it offered spontaneously? Does the individual's level of distress or illness influence the amount of support he/she receives? These remain unanswered questions.

Related to this, how do social ties and perceived support influence support-*seeking* (a coping strategy)? Some studies indicate that people who perceive their social networks to be dependable and intimate are the least likely to seek help for personal problems (Brown 1978). In contrast, Cutrona (1986) reported that persons initially high in perceived support actually received informational and emotional assistance following a stressful life experience more frequently (although she did not assess whether this assistance was actively solicited). Other studies indicate that perceived support leads to support-seeking, which in turn is associated with *higher* depression or distress (Coyne and Downey 1991; Pearlin and Schooler 1978; Ross and Mirowsky 1989). Clearly, the determinants of seeking or receiving support and the relative efficacy of solicited and unsolicited support for well-being need further investigation (Kessler et al. 1985).

Promising New Directions

Despite major gaps in our knowledge about social support and how it operates to enhance physical and mental health, there are several interesting new directions in recent research.

One new direction examines the costs as well as benefits of social relationships and support-giving. Despite the positive connotations of the concepts "social integration" and "social support," our social ties are not always or even necessarily positive influences in our lives and thus on our well-being (Rook 1992). Most obviously, the absence of social ties, or social isolation, may be a stressor in itself, producing chronic loneliness, lack of identity, or lack of behavioral regulation (Hughes and Gove 1989; Rook 1984, 1990). Some evidence indicates that obligatory social ties (e.g., spouse, parent, relative, worker) can produce stressful demands which may cancel or outweigh these roles' positive consequences for self-esteem, competence, or identity (Berbrier and Schulte 1993; Gove, Style, and Hughes 1990; Moen, Dempster-McClain, and Williams 1989; Rook 1992; Thoits 1992; Umberson and Gove 1989). In contrast, voluntary ties (e.g., friend, church member, group member) have more manageable or escapable demands, allowing those roles' benefits to exceed their costs.[14] Related to this, the results of several studies suggest that support-giving or caring for or about others can be costly; as discussed earlier, women seem emotionally more vulnerable to events that happen to members of their social networks. A recent focus on caregiver stress in the literature indicates that giving extended and extensive support indeed is physically and emotionally draining (e.g., Aneshensel, Pearlin, and Schuler 1993). In short, studies are beginning to show that there are important limitations on the degree to which the possession of social ties benefits physical or mental health.

Qualitative studies of support attempts that fail also reveal conditions under which received support can be nonbeneficial and at worst harmful (Harris 1992). Wortman and her colleagues (e.g., Lehman, Ellard, and Wortman 1986; Wortman and Conway 1985; Wortman and Lehman 1985) have documented the kinds of statements made by helpers which can offend or upset victims of life crises—for example, claiming understanding where there is no experiential basis for the claim. Wortman's research suggests that frequently the worst support-givers are family members who are themselves affected or threatened by the victim's life crisis. Family members may push too hard or too soon for evidence of recovery or, alternatively, may become so protective and overly helpful that the victim comes to resent his/her implied dependency. One ramification is that the most effective support-givers may be *similar other*—that is, individuals who themselves have successfully faced the same stressful circumstances that the victim is currently facing. In Cohen and McKay's (1984) terms, similar others are more likely to offer support that best "matches" the emotional and practical needs of the distressed person.

The hypothesis that the most efficacious type of support is that which matches the target individual's needs has not been definitely confirmed to date (Cutrona and Russell 1990). The idea of "matching" also has spawned several efforts to specify which support *sources* (e.g., spouse, friends, coworkers, professionals) are most efficacious in buffering the impacts of certain kinds of stressors (e.g., House 1981; Jackson 1992; LaRocco, House, and French 1980; Messeri, Silverstein, and Litwak 1993). These efforts have met with limited success, with one exception. Messeri and colleagues showed that people's preferred sources of support for instrumental tasks were members of primary or secondary groups which have properties (e.g., proximity, commitment, size, division of labor, etc.) which optimally match the structural characteristics of the task to be performed (e.g., cooking, bathing, job information, financial loans, 24-hour care). Clearly, the next step is to examine whether people whose sources of support optimally match their instrumental needs are in better physical or mental health than people whose matches are less optimal. Optimal matches between individuals' socioemotional needs and abstract sources of support (e.g., socially similar others, experientially similar others) might also be explored, following Cohen and McKay's (1984) original suggestion.

That there should be a match between what is needed/wanted and what is given is also suggested by recent qualitative studies examining the dynamics of mutual coping and support-giving between married couples—some sharing the common stressor of a chronically ill child (Gottlieb and Wagner 1991), others dealing with one spouse's work problems (Pearlin and McCall 1990; Weiss 1990). These studies strongly suggest that there are gender differences in preferred coping and support-giving strategies and in the types of support that men and women wish to receive; husbands are more likely to hide problems and give (unwanted) advice, less likely to ventilate, and more uncomfortable with their wives' emotional expressivity. Often what one spouse hopes to receive is incompatible with what the other spouse thinks it best to offer, which generates conflict and mutual dissatisfaction between them. These studies underscore again that there are limits to the helpfulness of support-giving and suggest that a match between an individual's needs and proffered support may indeed be important. Similarly detailed qualitative studies of age, race, and socioeconomic differences in preferred coping and support-giving strategies would be valuable for both theoretical and applied reasons. As Gottlieb (1992:300) notes, "[T]he strongest basis for planning support interventions lies in an examination of the interactional dynamics that shape judgments of perceived support."

It is important to note that most studies view social support primarily as an individual-level, or at best, interpersonal phenomenon. Recently, community psychologists have urged renewed attention to system-level or community-level structures and processes which promote social integration and perceptions of support (Felton and Shinn 1992; Heller 1989; Maton 1989a, 1989b). As Felton and Shinn (1992) point out, we have overlooked the possibility that instead of specific people, whole groups might function as sources of perceived support (e.g., churches, neighborhood associations, seniors' centers). A sense that one belongs and matters to others may depend on the homogeneity or cohesiveness of such groups. A focus on systems-level factors is certainly in keeping with a distinctively sociological approach to a social or interpersonal phenomenon and is worth further pursuit.

OTHER ISSUES AND POLICY IMPLICATIONS

In previous sections I identified many unanswered questions and research gaps in the stress, coping resource, coping strategies, and social support literatures. To briefly summarize with respect to stressors, we know relatively little about the complexities of stressors' effects on physical health outcomes compared to mental health outcomes, including differential *physical* vulnerability to stress by social status. The physical and mental health consequences of various event and strain *sequences* require empirical attention, including "carry-overs" of stress from one role domain or stage of life to another. Better specification of stressors' meanings to individuals might help to explain the physical and psychological damage *or* benefits that can follow from stressful experiences. In the psychosocial resources domain, the mechanisms through which a sense of personal control and perceived social support promote well-being remain poorly specified and require substantial elaboration and testing. How a sense of control influences coping behavior (and vice versa), the social determinants of various psychosocial resources, and the interrelationships among psychological and social resources need to be explored further. With respect to coping processes, studies of individuals' active efforts to cope with specific stressors may best reveal the complex interplay between personal agency and structural constraints on that agency. Additional studies of flexibility as an effective coping style and the social distributions of that coping style may be empirically and theoretically fruitful. Finally, in the area of social support, we need further work on the relationships holding among structural and functional dimensions of social support, the social distributions of perceived and received support, the ways in which support influences personality resources (and vice versa), the conditions under which supportive assistance is mobilized versus eroded, and the kinds of support which optimally match individuals' needs for help.

In addition to the above issues, there are a set of more general considerations which strike me as important to tackle in the near future. The first concerns our assumptions about the stress process. Most sociologists have implicitly adopted a fairly straightforward underlying model of the stress process, which can be summarized as follows: (1) Individuals' locations in the social structure differentially expose them to stressors which in turn can damage their physical and/or mental health; (2) this damage is generally moderated or lessened by individuals' social and personality resources and the coping strategies that they employ; and (3) the possession of psychosocial resources and the use of particular coping strategies are socially patterned in ways which at least potentially may leave members of disadvantaged groups more vulnerable to the harmful physical or psychological effects of stress. Although this model accords with common sense and portions

have been empirically verified (with some important gaps and exceptions, noted earlier), explained variance in physical and psychological outcomes has remained relatively modest. This leads me to speculate that the stress process is far more complex than we have envisioned and that we may need to consider additional data collection and analytic methods to explore these intricacies further.

One neglected theoretical possibility is that there are multiple pathways to the same health outcomes. Just as there may be different combinations of conditions across countries which lead to political revolution, there may be different configurations of factors across individuals which lead to heart attack or to the onset of major depression. But we have generally presumed that the factors leading both directly and interactively to particular illnesses are the same for all individuals (as in the three general statements listed above). The assumption of one process for becoming depressed or ill and the concomitant use of the general linear model to test it requires us to reject or ignore other possible processes which are less frequently observed and do not manage to achieve statistical significance.

How might one explore the possibility of multiple pathways to the same illness? One useful method is "qualitative comparative analysis" (QCA), developed by Ragin (1987) for the comparative analysis of historical cases. The QCA method and its accompanying software (Drass and Ragin 1988) are general and can be applied to data on large samples of individuals. Boolean algebra is used to isolate unique configurations of variables which are associated with specific outcomes (in this case, high depression scores or the presence of a specific disease). Although the technique has certain limitations (e.g., all independent variables and dependent outcomes must be dichotomous), its advantage is that it allows the researcher to ascertain the existence of distinct combinations of causal variables. Distinct causal configurations, in turn, suggest different theoretical pathways to illness or disturbance.[15]

Extending the logic of the QCA method one step further, different causal pathways may apply to individuals with differing configurations of social statuses (Aneshensel 1992; Weber et al. 1993). We tend to assume that our general stress process model applies equivalently to males and females, to blacks and whites, to the poor and the rich, and so on. We typically treat these social statuses as analytically separable and additive in their influences on each other and on other variables in the stress process. But people are not the simple sum of their statuses and those statuses are not independent of one another. Rather, people hold combinations of statuses which are "fused" in their life experiences (Griffin and Korstad, forthcoming) and which *taken together, interactively* determine their current locations in the social structure and influence their experiences, actions, and reactions. If we take this insight seriously, then, minimally, it seems imperative to examine the applicability of our general stress process model (as well as alternative pathways to distress and poor health) to groupings of individuals who hold similar status configurations.

Although the qualitative comparative method allows one to examine combinations of variables (including statuses) associated with a particular outcome, it is an essentially static analysis of what is normally conceived as a dynamic, unfolding process. Earlier, I argued that examining various sequences of events and strains might help further specify the conditions under which stressors damage health, and that detailed chronologies of coping and support-giving efforts might reveal some orderings which buffer the impacts of specific types of stressors. One simple but limited way to assess sequences is to employ a set of dummy variables to catego-

rize various orderings of interest. Or one can use stochastic models, such as discrete-state, first-order Markov processes and event history methods. But Markov and other stochastic models do not enable the identification of a typical sequence or sequences that might exist in one's data (Abbott and Hrycak 1990). Abbott and Hrycak suggest and illustrate the utility of "Optimal Matching Analysis," which is a statistical technique borrowed from the natural sciences used, for example, to identify DNA sequences. This technique isolates similar progressions in sequential lists of qualitative events or actions. Similar progressions then may be associated with particular outcomes of interest.

An intriguing and powerful approach to sequential *causal* analysis has been developed by Griffin (1993; Griffin and Korstad, 1995). To understand historical events such as lynchings and the rise and fall of a Southern union local, Griffin capitalizes on formal techniques of narrative analysis—in particular, the method of "event-structure analysis" with its associated software, ETHNO (Heise 1988, 1989). Event-structure analysis is a general technique which allows the researcher to examine and explain in a Weberian *verstehen* sense how a chronological sequence of individual actions and structural contingencies produced a particular outcome. Event-structure analysis easily could be applied to individuals' narrative accounts of their stress experiences, the sequences of actions they undertook to cope with them, and the outcomes of those actions (e.g., onset of depression, cessation of depression). The method also enables the investigator to abstract and generalize, to assess the applicability of a generalized explanation of one case to other cases, and to modify the general explanation to fit the concrete particulars of multiple cases.

The advantage of these various comparative and historical techniques of analysis is that they handle, in formal and replicable ways, data that are detailed, chronological, and qualitative. Chronological data are obviously essential to understanding unfolding processes and, as George Brown has maintained for many years, detailed qualitative data are crucial for understanding the meaning of stressful experiences to the individuals we study (Brown and Harris 1989). In my view, in order to advance and further elaborate stress theory, we need more qualitative research that focuses on the contexts and unfolding processes of coping and support-giving. In addition to the semistructured interviews and coding procedures developed by Brown and Harris and by Dohrenwend and colleagues, a variety of new formal qualitative methods is now available for use. These methods combine textual richness with sophisticated analytic techniques, merging important aspects of both qualitative and quantitative practices. This is not to say, however, that the traditional stress model, survey methods, or linear analyses should be abandoned. These are crucial for the replication of major studies, exploring unexamined relationships, and teasing out longitudinally a variety of causal sequences and time-lagged effects among the multiple factors in our refined stress models.

Policy Implications

There are four robust findings in the stress literature that, in principle, should have public policy implications: (1) The experience of negative major life events and chronic difficulties increases the probability of psychological problems and physical illness; (2) a sense of personal control over life circumstances both reduces psychological symptoms directly and buffers the psychological effects of negative events and strains; (3) social integration lowers the probability of morbidity and mortality; and (4) perceived emotional support both decreases psychological symptoms directly and buffers the physical and psychological impacts of negative events and chronic strains.

For political and economic reasons it is unlikely that massive social programs will be developed in the United States to control the occurrence in the population of major disruptive events or chronic difficulties (e.g., unemployment, poverty, divorce). Consequently, the applied implications of findings regarding the health-promoting effects of social integration, social support, and (to a lesser extent) personal control (as empowerment) have been emphasized. Researchers have been especially optimistic about designing interventions to boost or manipulate social ties and/or perceived social support for individuals who are confronting particular stressors. Indeed, the most frequent intervention strategy involves introducing new social ties. There is now a burgeoning literature on the physical and psychological effects of such social support interventions aimed at special populations—for example, the divorced, the bereaved, cancer patients, pregnant adolescents, abusive parents, caregivers for the elderly, and so forth (e.g., Gottlieb 1985, 1992).

Despite researcher optimism, support interventions have often floundered or produced weak, equivocal results (Gottlieb 1992; Grych and Fincham 1992; Heller et al. 1991a, 1991b; Ludwick-Rosenthal and Neufeld 1988; Okun, Olding, and Cohn 1990). This is because basic social support research presently provides only very general guidance for the planning and execution of interventions. Guidance cannot easily be extracted from the existing research literature in part because we still do not understand the mechanisms through which social relationships lessen poor health or buffer the impacts of stress, and in part because "the culture of intervention programs differs so strongly from the natural ecology in which supportive transactions take place" (Gottlieb 1992:307).

Despite these problems, a number of successful intervention programs have been designed to prevent a wide range of emotional, behavioral, and cognitive problems in children and adults and to promote health. The most carefully documented of these programs are described in *14 Ounces of Prevention* (Price et al. 1988), including the well-known Stanford Heart Disease Prevention Program. Successful primary prevention projects have several features in common. They target at-risk populations, they provide education as well as training in specific coping skills, they build in nonspecific social support from program staff (e.g., encouragement, validation, warmth) as a key component, and some attempt to strengthen existing natural family or community supports. Thus, the manipulation of social support is among several characteristics of an effective prevention/health promotion program and it may be the *combination* of support with training and information which enhances program success. Importantly, several of these projects have provided empirical evidence of their cost-effectiveness.

Kiesler (1985:362) has observed, "If a study is to be relevant to public policy, it must measure something of interest to public policymakers . . . such as reduced system costs, lowered incidence of disease, reduced morbidity, less use of (and charges to) the physical health system, reduced insurance costs, and the like." Social support and coping intervention studies rarely demonstrate their cost-effectiveness and/or practical utility in one or more of these terms. Doing so seems crucial in future research. We already know from amassed epidemiological and survey-based evidence that social support, a sense of control and self-esteem, and certain coping skills make a significant difference in preventing or reducing physical and mental health problems. Translating these findings into effective primary prevention and health promotion projects will be especially important given the proposed shift to universally available physical and mental health care in the United States. Effective primary prevention can ease pres-

sures on already overburdened and costly medical and psychiatric services, which may be in even greater demand with universal health coverage. Although some commentators (e.g., Kiesler 1985) have been cautious to pessimistic about our abilities to translate basic stress, coping, and social support findings into policies and programs, I am less so. Basic and applied researchers have mutually compatible goals: (1) understanding the mechanisms through which coping resources, coping strategies, and social support influence physical and mental health and (2) putting research results to use in real-world applications. A concerted focus on identifying intervening mechanisms in both basic *and* applied projects will be the passkey to more numerous, effective stress interventions.

NOTES

1. Many items intended to assess daily hassles and uplifts (Kanner et al. 1981) are indicators of life events, chronic strains, and physical or psychological symptoms. Such operational confounding makes the effects of hassles and uplifts questionable.

2. Coyne and Downey (1991) suggest that the nature of the dependent variable also influences findings. People with a diagnosed disorder may differ from those who score high on psychological symptom scales both in social characteristics and in life event experiences. Lower social status may be more reliably associated with serious, disruptive events and with clinical disorder.

3. Assessing multiple outcomes should also direct attention to the phenomenon of comorbidity—two or more health conditions present in the same person. The National Comorbidity Study indicates high prevalence rates of psychiatric comorbidity (Kessler 1993). This observation raises additional interesting questions: What are the properties of stressors which provoke multiple outcomes, and what are the social and personality characteristics of people with comorbid conditions?

4. It is also possible that positive experiences directly increase or enhance physical or psycho-

logical well-being. But most studies rely on symptom scales or clinical diagnoses as outcome measures. These assess the relative presence or absence of persistent problems rather than positive aspects of health or psychological well-being. Thus, they are truncated measures of well-being.

5. Turner and Avison's (1992) approach to meaning is somewhat different from the approaches to be described next. They ask whether the person has been able to find meaning in an event or not. The following approaches attempt to assess meaning itself—that is, meaning's content.

6. Pearlin (1991), for example, argues that the meaning of a stressor can depend on a person's value system (what he or she views as important in life), on the surrounding context (in Wheaton's sense), or on the secondary effects of the stressor (added life strains). Riessman (1990) assesses the meaning of divorce in terms of much broader sociocultural beliefs about the importance, permanence, and functions of marriage.

7. Psychologists additionally examine hardiness, a sense of coherence, and Type A characteristics such as impatience and hostility (see Cohen and Edwards [1989]; Rodin and Salovey [1989] for reviews).

8. Pearlin and Schooler (1978) distinguish what might be called perception-focused coping from other emotion-management strategies. Perception-focused coping consists of cognitive efforts to alter the meaning of stressful demands so that they seem less threatening or overwhelming (e.g., reinterpreting the situation, looking on the bright side of things). Lazarus and Folkman (1984) view perception-focused strategies as emotion-focused in nature because these efforts can reduce emotional reactions to demands but do not alter the demands themselves.

9. Self-efficacy, the belief that one is able to perform a specific behavior successfully, is also related to the notion of control or mastery. Behavioral self-efficacy has been related to health-promoting behavior and to positive physical health outcomes (e.g., Grembowski et al. 1993).

10. There are some inconsistencies in findings with respect to gender, however. Some investigators find no gender differences in personal control (Turner and Noh 1988; Ross and Mirowsky 1989);

numerous other studies report a significant gender difference. In their review, Miller and Kirsch (1987) conclude that there are few gender differences in causal attributions about stressful experiences. However, attributions about specific events are not equivalent to generalized beliefs about one's control or mastery over life circumstances.

11. That stress experience erodes a sense of mastery and self-esteem has been shown in a number of studies (see Turner and Roszell 1994). My question here is how coping successes and failures influence these personality resources. Some guidance in this topic area might be gained from the extensive learned helplessness literature.

12. These designs also may enable investigations of *combinations* of strategies that are more or less efficacious in reducing somatic or emotional reactions to stress, as well as strategies which may be equivalent in their effects and thus *substitutable* for one another (Ross and Mirowsky 1989).

13. How individuals cope with stressors might also influence whether or not support is offered and perhaps the types of support which are extended (instrumental, informational, emotional).

14. People's reports of low perceived support therefore may reflect either the absence of supportive ties *or* the presence of one or more conflictual, demanding relationships in their lives (Coyne and Downey 1991), which seems an important distinction to make.

15. The QCA method also seems ideally suited for investigating combinations of coping strategies that together most effectively reduce illness or distress in response to particular kinds of stressors.

REFERENCES

ABBOTT, ANDREW and ALEXANDRA HRYCAK. 1990. "Measuring Resemblance in Sequence Data: An Optimal Matching Analysis of Musicians' Careers." *American Journal of Sociology* 96(1):144–85.

ALBRECHT, GARY L. and JUDITH A. LEVY. 1991. "Chronic Illness and Disability as Life Course Events." *Advances in Medical Sociology* 2:3–13.

ALDWIN, CAROLYN M. and TRACEY A. REVENSON. 1987. "Does Coping Help? A Reexamination of the Relation Between Coping and Mental

Health." *Journal of Personality and Social Psychology* 53(2):337–48.

ANESHENSEL, CAROL S. 1992. "Social Stress: Theory and Research." *Annual Review of Sociology* 18:15–38.

ANESHENSEL, CAROL S. and SUSAN GORE. 1991. "Development, Stress, and Role Restructuring: Social Transitions of Adolescence." Pp. 55–77 in *The Social Context of Coping*, edited by J. Eckenrode. New York: Plenum.

ANESHENSEL, CAROL S. and GEORGE J. HUBA. 1983. "Depression, Alcohol Use, and Smoking over One Year: A Four-Wave Longitudinal Causal Model." *Journal of Abnormal Psychology* 92(2):134–50.

ANESHENSEL, CAROL S., LEONARD I. PEARLIN, and ROBERLEIGH H. SCHULER. 1993. "Stress, Role Captivity, and the Cessation of Caregiving." *Journal of Health and Social Behavior* 34:54–70.

ANESHENSEL, CAROL S., CAROLYN M. RUTTER, and PETER A. LACHENBRUCH. 1991. "Social Structure, Stress, and Mental Health: Competing Conceptual and Analytic Models." *American Sociological Review* 56:166–78.

AVISON, WILLIAM R. 1993. "Families in Poverty: A Stress Process Analysis of the Psychosocial Consequences." Paper presented to the American Sociological Association, Miami Beach, FL.

AVISON, WILLIAM R. and R. JAY TURNER. 1988. "Stressful Life Events and Depressive Symptoms: Disaggregating the Effects of Acute Stressors and Chronic Strains." *Journal of Health and Social Behavior* 29:253–64.

BARRERA, MANUEL, JR. 1986. "Distinctions Between Social Support Concepts, Measures, and Models." *American Journal of Community Psychology* 14(4):413–45.

BELLE, DEBORAH. 1987. "Gender Differences in the Social Moderators of Stress." Pp. 257–77 in *Gender and Stress*, edited by R. C. Barnett, L. Biener, and G. K. Baruch. New York: Free Press.

BERBRIER, MITCHELL and AILEEN SCHULTE. 1993. "Binding and Non-Binding Integration: The Relational Costs and Rewards of Social Ties on Mental Health." Paper presented to the American Sociological Association, Miami Beach, FL.

BERKMAN, LISA F. 1984. "Assessing the Physical Health Effects of Social Networks and Social Support." *Annual Review of Public Health* 5:413–32.

———. 1985. "The Relationship of Social Networks and Social Support to Morbidity and Mortality." Pp. 241–62 in *Social Support and Health*, edited by S. Cohen and S. L. Syme. Orlando, FL: Academic.

BILLINGS, ANDREW G. and RUDOLF H. MOOS. 1984. "Coping, Stress, and Social Resources Among Adults with Unipolar Depression." *Journal of Personality and Social Psychology* 46(4):877–91.

BILLINGS, ANDREW G., RUTH C. CRONKITE, and RUDOLF H. MOOS. 1983. "Social-Environmental Factors in Unipolar Depression: Comparisons of Depressed Patients and Nondepressed Controls." *Journal of Abnormal Psychology* 92:119–33.

BOLGER, NIALL. 1990. "Coping as a Personality Process: A Prospective Study." *Journal of Personality and Social Psychology* 59(3):525–37.

BOLGER, NIALL, ANITA DELONGIS, RONALD C. KESSLER, and ELAINE WETHINGTON. 1989a. "The Contagion of Stress Across Multiple Roles." *Journal of Marriage and the Family* 51:175–83.

———. 1989b. "The Microstructure of Daily Role-Related Stress in Married Couples." Pp. 95–115 in *Stress Between Work and Family*, edited by J. Eckenrode and S. Gore. New York: Plenum.

BROMET, EVELYN J., MARY AMANDA DEW, and DAVID K. PARKINSON. 1990. "Spillover Between Work and Family: A Study of Blue-Collar Working Wives." Pp. 133–51 in *Stress Between Work and Family*, edited by J. Eckenrode and S. Gore. New York: Plenum.

BROWN, B. BRADFORD. 1978. "Social and Psychological Correlates of Help-Seeking Behavior Among Urban Adults." *American Journal of Community Psychology* 6:425–39.

BROWN, GEORGE W. and TIRRIL O. HARRIS. 1978. *Social Origins of Depression: A Study of Psychiatric Disorder in Women*. New York: Free Press.

———. 1989. *Life Events and Illness*. New York: Guilford Press.

BROWN, GEORGE W., ANTONIA BIFULCO, and TIRRIL O. HARRIS. 1987. "Life Events, Vulnerability, and Onset of Depression: Some Refinements." *British Journal of Psychiatry* 150:30–42.

BROWN, GEORGE W., L. LEMYRE, and ANTONIA BIFULCO. 1992. "Social Factors and Recovery from Anxiety and Depressive Disorders: A Test of Specificity." *British Journal of Psychiatry* 161:44–54.

CATALANO, RALPH and DAVID DOOLEY. 1983. "Health Effects of Economic Instability: A Test of the Economic Stress Hypothesis." *Journal of Health and Social Behavior* 24:46–60.

CATALANO, RALPH, DAVID DOOLEY, and ROBERT JACKSON. 1981. "Economic Predictors of Admissions to Mental Health Facilities in a Nonmetropolitan Community." *Journal of Health and Social Behavior* 22:284–97.

CLARK, LESLIE F. 1994. "Social Cognition and Health Psychology." Pp. 239–88 in *Handbook of Social Cognition*, 2d ed., edited by R. S. Wyer and T. K. Srull. Hillsdale, NJ: Lawrence Erlbaum.

COHEN, SHELDON. 1988. "Psychosocial Models of the Role of Social Support in the Etiology of Physical Disease." *Health Psychology* 7:269–97.

COHEN, SHELDON and JEFFREY R. EDWARDS. 1989. "Personality Characteristics as Moderators of the Relationship Between Stress and Disorder." Pp. 235–83 in *Advances in the Investigation of Psychological Stress*, edited by R. W. J. Neufeld. New York: Wiley.

COHEN, SHELDON and GARTH MCKAY. 1984. "Social Support, Stress, and the Buffering Hypothesis: An Empirical and Theoretical Analysis." Pp. 253–67 in *Handbook of Psychology and Health*, vol. 4, edited by A. Baum, J. E. Singer, and S. E. Taylor. Hillsdale. NJ: Lawrence Erlbaum.

COHEN, SHELDON and GAIL M. WILLIAMSON. 1991. "Stress and Infectious Disease in Humans." *Psychological Bulletin* 109(1):5–24.

COHEN, SHELDON and THOMAS A. WILLS. 1985. "Stress, Social Support, and the Buffering Hypothesis." *Psychological Bulletin* 98(2):310–57.

CONGER, RAND D., GLEN H. ELDER. JR., RONALD L. SIMONS, and XIAOJIA GE. 1993. "Husband and Wife Differences in Response to Undesirable Life Events." *Journal of Health and Social Behavior* 34:71–88.

COYNE, JAMES C. and GERALDINE DOWNEY. 1991. "Social Factors and Psychopathology: Stress, Social Support, and Coping Processes." *Annual Review of Psychology* 42:401–25.

COYNE, JAMES, CAROLYN ALDWIN, and RICHARD S. LAZARUS. 1981. "Depression and Coping in Stressful Episodes." *Journal of Abnormal Psychology* 90:439–47.

CREED, FRANCIS. 1985. "Life Events and Physical Illness." *Journal of Psychosomatic Research* 29(2):113–23.

CRONKITE, RUTH C. and RUDOLF H. MOOS. 1984. "The Role of Predisposing and Moderating Factors in the Stress-Illness Relationship." *Journal of Health and Social Behavior* 25:372–93.

CRONKITE, RUTH C., RALPH W. SWINDLE, JR., JOAN TWOHEY, and RUDOLF H. MOOS. 1993. "The Role of Psychosocial Factors in the Long-Term Course of Unipolar Depression." Paper presented to the American Sociological Association, Miami Beach, FL.

CUTRONA, CAROLYN E. 1986. "Behavioral Manifestations of Social Support: A Microanalytic Investigation." *Journal of Personality and Social Psychology* 51(1):201–8.

CUTRONA, CAROLYN E. and DANIEL RUSSELL. 1990. "Type of Social Support and Specific Stress: Toward a Theory of Optimal Matching." Pp. 319–66 in *Social Support: An Interactional View*, edited by B. R. Sarason, I. G. Sarason, and G. R. Pierce. New York: Wiley.

DOHRENWEND, BARBARA SNELL and BRUCE P. DOHRENWEND, eds. 1974. *Stressful Life Events: Their Nature and Effects*. New York: Wiley.

DOHRENWEND, BRUCE P., ITZHAK LEVAV, PATRICK E. SHROUT, SHARON SCHWARTZ, GUEDALIA NEVEH, BRUCE G. LINK, ANDREW E. SKODOL, and ANN STUEVE. 1992. "Socioeconomic Status and Psychiatric Disorders: The Causation-Selection Issue." *Science* 255:946–52.

DOHRENWEND, BRUCE P., KAREN G. RAPHAEL, SHARON SCHWARTZ, ANN STUEVE, and ANDREW SKODOL. 1993. "The Structured Event Probe and Narrative Rating Method for Measuring Stressful Life Events." Pp. 174–99 in *Handbook of Stress*, edited by L. Goldberger and S. Breznitz. New York: Free Press.

DOOLEY, DAVID and RALPH CATALANO. 1980. "Economic Change as a Cause of Behavioral Disorder." *Psychological Bulletin* 87(3):450–68.

DOOLEY, DAVID and RALPH CATALANO. 1984a. "The Epidemiology of Economic Stress." *American Journal of Community Psychology* 12(4):387–409.

DOOLEY, DAVID and RALPH CATALANO. 1984b. "Why the Economy Predicts Help-Seeking: A Test of Competing Explanations." *Journal of Health and Social Behavior* 25(2):160–76.

DRASS, KRIS and CHARLES C. RAGIN. 1988. *QCA: Qualitative Comparative Analysis*. Evanston, IL: Center for Urban Affairs and Policy Research. Northwestern University.

DUNKEL-SCHETTER, CHRISTINE, SUSAN FOLKMAN, and RICHARD S. LAZARUS. 1987. "Correlates of Social Support Receipt." *Journal of Personality and Social Psychology* 53(1):71–80.

ECKENRODE, JOHN. 1983. "The Mobilization of Social Supports: Some Individual Constraints." *American Journal of Community Psychology* 11(5):509–28.

———. 1984. "Impact of Chronic and Acute Stressors on Daily Reports of Mood." *Journal of Personality and Social Psychology* 46(4):907–18.

ECKENRODE, JOHN and SUSAN GORE. 1981. "Stressful Events and Social Support: The Significance of Context." Pp. 43–68 in *Social Networks and Social Support*, edited by B. Gottlieb. Beverly Hills, CA: Sage.

ECKENRODE, JOHN and ELAINE WETHINGTON. 1990. "The Process and Outcome of Mobilizing Social Support." Pp. 83–103 in *Personal Relationships and Social Support*, edited by S. Duck and R. C. Silver, Newbury Park, CA: Sage.

ELDER, GLENN H., JR. 1974. *Children of the Great Depression*. Chicago, IL: University of Chicago Press.

ENSEL, WALTER M. and NAN LIN. 1991. "The Life Stress Paradigm and Psychological Distress." *Journal of Health and Social Behavior* 32:321–41.

FELTON, BARBARA J. and MARYBETH SHINN. 1992. "Social Integration and Social Support: Moving 'Social Support' Beyond the Individual Level." *Journal of Community Psychology* 20(2):103–15.

FISCHER, CLAUDE. 1982. *To Dwell Among Friends: Personal Networks in Town and City*. Chicago, IL: University of Chicago Press.

FOLKMAN, SUSAN. 1984. "Personal Control and Stress and Coping Processes: A Theoretical Analysis." *Journal of Personality and Social Psychology* 46:839–52.

FOLKMAN, SUSAN, and RICHARD S. LAZARUS. 1980. "An Analysis of Coping in a Middle-Aged Community Sample." *Journal of Health and Social Behavior* 21:219–39.

———. 1985. "If It Changes It Must Be a Process: Study of Emotion and Coping During Three Stages of a College Examination." *Journal of Personality and Social Psychology* 48:150–70.

FOLKMAN, SUSAN, RICHARD S. LAZARUS, CHRISTINE DUNKEL-SCHETTER, ANITA DELONGIS, and RAND J. GRUEN. 1986. "The Dynamics of a Stressful

Encounter: Cognitive Appraisal, Coping, and Encounter Outcomes." *Journal of Personality and Social Psychology* 50:992–1003.

FOLKMAN, SUSAN, RICHARD S. LAZARUS, SCOTT PIMLEY, and JILL NOVACEK. 1987. "Age Differences in Stress and Coping Processes." *Psychology and Aging* 2 (2):171–84.

FORSYTHE, CAROLYN J. and BRUCE E. COMPAS. 1987. "Interaction of Cognitive Appraisals of Stressful Events and Coping: Testing the Goodness-of-Fit Hypothesis." *Cognitive Therapy and Research* 11(4):473–85.

GERSTEL, NAOMI, CATHERINE KOHLER RIESSMAN, and SARAH ROSENFIELD. 1985. "Explaining the Symptomatology of Separated and Divorced Women and Men: The Role of Material Conditions and Social Networks." *Social Forces* 64(1):84–101.

GORE, SUSAN. 1985. "Social Support and Styles of Coping with Stress." Pp. 263–78 in *Stress and Health*, edited by S. Cohen and S. L. Syme. Orlando, FL: Academic.

GORE, SUSAN and MARY ELLEN COLTEN. 1991. "Gender, Stress, and Distress: Social-Relational Influences." Pp. 139–63 in *The Social Context of Coping*, edited by J. Eckenrode. New York: Plenum.

GOTTLIEB, BENJAMIN H. 1985. "Social Support and Community Mental Health." Pp. 303–26 in *Social Support and Health*, edited by S. Cohen and S. L. Syme. Orlando, FL: Academic.

———. 1992. "Quandaries in Translating Support Concepts to Intervention." Pp. 293–309 in *The Meaning and Measurement of Social Support*, edited by H. O. F. Veiel and U. Baumann. New York: Hemisphere.

GOTTLIEB, BENJAMIN H. and FRED WAGNER. 1991. "Stress and Support Processes in Close Relationships." Pp. 165–88 in *The Social Context of Coping*, edited by J. Eckenrode. New York: Plenum.

GOVE, WALTER R., CORLYNN BRIGGS STYLE, and MICHAEL HUGHES. 1990. "The Effect of Marriage on the Well-Being of Adults." *Journal of Family Issues* 11:4–35.

GREMBOWSKI, DAVID, DONALD PATRICK, PAULA DIEHR, MARY DURHAM, SHIRLEY BERESFORD, ERICA KAY, and JULIA HECHT. 1993. "Self-Efficacy and Health Behavior Among Older Adults." *Journal of Health and Social Behavior* 34:89–104.

GRIFFIN, LARRY J. 1993. "Narrative, Event-Structure Analysis and Causal Interpretation in Historical Sociology." *American Journal of Sociology* 98:1094–133.

GRIFFIN, LARRY J. and ROBERT R. KORSTAD. 1995. "Class as Race and Gender: Making and Breaking a Labor Union in the Jim Crow South." *Social Science History.* 19:425-459.

GRYCH, JOHN H. and FRANK D. FINCHAM. 1992. "Interventions for Children of Divorce: Toward Greater Integration of Research and Action." *Psychological Bulletin* 111(3):434–54.

HARRIS, TIRRIL O. 1992. "Some Reflections on the Process of Social Support and Nature of Unsupportive Behaviors." Pp. 171–90 in *The Meaning and Measurement of Social Support,* edited by H. O. F. Veiel and U. Baumann. New York: Hemisphere.

HEISE, DAVID. 1988. "Computer Analysis of Cultural Structures." *Social Science Computer Review* 6:183–96.

———. 1989. "Modeling Event Structures." *Journal of Mathematical Sociology* 14:139–69.

HELLER, KENNETH. 1989. "The Return to Community." *American Journal of Community Psychology* 17:1–15.

HELLER, KENNETH, MARK G. THOMPSON, IRENE VLACHOS-WEBER, ANN M. STEFFEN, and PETRI E. TRUEBA. 1991a. "Peer Support Telephone Dyads for Elderly Women: Was This the Wrong Intervention?" *American Journal of Community Psychology* 19(1):53–74.

———. 1991b. "Support Interventions for Older Adults: Confidante Relationships, Perceived Family Support, and Meaningful Role Activity." *American Journal of Community Psychology* 19(1):139–46.

HOLAHAN, CHARLES J. and RUDOLF H. MOOS. 1987. "Personal and Contextual Determinants of Coping Strategies." *Journal of Personality and Social Psychology* 52(5):946–55.

HOLMES, THOMAS H. and RICHARD H. RAHE. 1967. "The Social Readjustment Rating Scale." *Journal of Psychosomatic Research* 11:213–18.

HOUSE, JAMES S. 1981. *Work Stress and Social Support.* Reading, MA: Addison-Wesley.

HOUSE, JAMES S. and ROBERT L. KAHN. 1985. "Measures and Concepts of Social Support." Pp. 83–108 in *Social Support and Health,* edited by S. Cohen and S. L. Syme. Orlando, FL: Academic Press.

HOUSE, JAMES S., KARL R. LANDIS, and DEBRA UMBERSON. 1988. "Social Relationships and Health." *Science* 241:540–45.

HOUSE, JAMES S., ANTHONY J. MCMICHAEL, JAMES A. WELLS, BERTON H. KAPLAN, and LAWRENCE R. LANDERMAN. 1979. "Occupational Stress and Health Among Factory Workers." *Journal of Health and Social Behavior* 20(2):139–60.

HOUSE, JAMES S., VICTOR STRETCHER, HELEN L. METZNER, and CYNTHIA A. ROBBINS. 1986. "Occupational Stress and Health Among Men and Women in the Tecumseh Community Health Study." *Journal of Health and Social Behavior* 27(1):62–77.

HUGHES, MICHAEL and WALTER R. GOVE. 1989. "Explaining the Negative Relationship Between Social Integration and Mental Health: The Case of Living Alone." Paper presented to the American Sociological Association, San Francisco, CA.

JACKSON, PAMELA BRABOY. 1992. "Specifying the Buffering Hypothesis: Support, Strain, and Depression." *Social Psychology Quarterly* 55(4):363–78.

———. 1993. "The Context of Transition Events Across the Life Course: The Effects of Prior Event Sequencing on Adult Mental Health." Department of Sociology, Indiana University, Bloomington, IN. Unpublished doctoral dissertation.

KANNER, ALLEN D., JAMES C. COYNE, CATHERINE SCHAEFER, and RICHARD S. LAZARUS. 1981. "Comparison of Two Modes of Stress Measurement: Daily Hassles and Uplifts versus Major Life Events." *Journal of Behavioral Medicine* 4:1–39.

KAPLAN, HOWARD B., CYNTHIA ROBBINS, and STEVEN S. MARTIN. 1983. "Antecedents of Psychological Distress in Young Adults: Self-Rejection, Deprivation of Social Support, and Life Events." *Journal of Health and Social Behavior* 24(3):230–44.

KAPLAN, ROBERT M. and MICHELLE T. TOSHIMA. 1990. "The Functional Effects of Social Relationships on Chronic Illnesses and Disability." Pp. 427–53 in *Social Support: An Interactional View,* edited by B. R. Sarason, I. G. Sarason, and G. R. Pierce. New York: Wiley.

KESSLER, RONALD C. 1993. "The National Comorbidity Study." Paper presented to the American Sociological Association, Miami Beach, FL.

KESSLER, RONALD C. and PAUL D. CLEARY. 1980. "Social Class and Psychological Distress." *American Sociological Review* 45:463–78.

KESSLER, RONALD C. and MARILYN ESSEX. 1982. "Marital Status and Depression: The Importance of Coping Resources." *Social Forces* 61:484–507.

KESSLER, RONALD C. and WILLIAM J. MAGEE. 1993. "Childhood Adversities and Adult Depression: Basic Patterns of Association in a U.S. National Survey." *Psychological Medicine* 23(3):679–90.

KESSLER, RONALD C. and JANE D. MCLEOD. 1984. "Sex Differences in Vulnerability to Undesirable Life Events." *American Sociological Review* 49:620–31.

———. 1985. "Social Support and Mental Health in Community Samples." Pp. 219–40 in *Social Support and Health,* edited by S. Cohen and S. L. Syme. New York: Academic.

KESSLER, RONALD C., RICHARD H. PRICE, and CAMILLE B. WORTMAN. 1985. "Social Factors in Psychopathology: Stress, Social Support, and Coping Processes." *Annual Review of Psychology* 36:531–72.

KESSLER, RONALD C., J. BLAKE TURNER, and JAMES S. HOUSE. 1988. "Effects of Unemployment on Health in a Community Survey: Main, Modifying, and Mediating Effects." *Journal of Social Issues* 44(4):69–85.

———. 1989. "Unemployment, Reemployment, and Emotional Functioning in a Community Sample." *American Sociological Review* 54:648–57.

KIECOLT, K. JILL. 1994. "Stress and the Decision to Change Oneself: A Theoretical Model." *Social Psychology Quarterly* 57(1):49–63.

KIESLER, CHARLES A. 1985. "Policy Implications of Research on Social Support and Health." Pp. 347–64 in *Social Support and Health,* edited by S. Cohen and S. L. Syme. Orlando, FL: Academic.

KILLIAN, LEWIS M. 1984. "Organization, Rationality, and Spontaneity in the Civil Rights Movement." *American Sociological Review* 49:770–83.

LaROCCO, JAMES M., JAMES S. HOUSE, and JACK R. P. FRENCH, JR. 1980. "Social Support, Occupational Stress, and Health." *Journal of Health and Social Behavior* 21:202–17.

LAZARUS, RICHARD S. and SUSAN FOLKMAN. 1984. *Stress, Appraisal, and Coping.* New York: Springer.

LEHMAN, DARRIN R., JOHN H. ELLARD, and CAMILLE B. WORTMAN. 1986. "Social Support for the Bereaved: Recipients' and Providers' Perspectives on What is Helpful." *Journal of Consulting and Clinical Psychology* 54:438–45.

LIEM, G. RAMSAY and JOAN HUSER LIEM. 1978. "Social Class and Mental Illness Reconsidered: The Role of Economic Stress and Social Support." *Journal of Health and Social Behavior* 19:139–56.

LIEM, JOAN HUSER and G. RAMSAY LIEM. 1990. "Understanding the Individual and Family Effects of Unemployment." Pp. 175–204 in *Stress Between Work and Family,* edited by J. Eckenrode and S. Gore. New York: Plenum.

LIN, NAN and WALTER M. ENSEL. 1989. "Life Stress and Health: Stressors and Resources." *American Sociological Review* 54:382–99.

LIN, NAN and WALTER ENSEL. 1993. "Life History Analysis of Stress and Distress." Department of Sociology, Duke University, Durham, NC. Unpublished manuscript.

LIN, NAN and JEANNE WESTCOTT. 1991. "Marital Engagement/Disengagement, Social Networks, and Mental Health." Pp. 213–37 in *The Social Context of Coping,* edited by J. Eckenrode. New York: Plenum.

LIN, NAN, ALFRED DEAN, and WALTER M. ENSEL. 1986. *Social Support, Life Events, and Depression.* Orlando, FL: Academic Press.

LINK, BRUCE G., MARY CLARE LENNON, and BRUCE P. DOHRENWEND. 1993. "Socioeconomic Status and Depression: The Role of Occupations Involving Direction, Control, and Planning." *American Journal of Sociology* 98(6):1351–87.

LUDWICK-ROSENTHAL, ROBIN and RICHARD W. NEUFELD. 1988. "Stress Management During Noxious Medical Procedures: An Evaluative Review of Outcome Studies." *Psychological Bulletin* 104(3):326–42.

MATON, KENNETH I. 1989a. "Community Settings as Buffers of Life Stress? Highly Supportive Churches, Mutual Help Groups, and Senior Centers." *American Journal of Community Psychology* 17:203–32.

———. 1989b. "Towards an Ecological Understanding of Mutual-Help Groups: The Social

Ecology of 'Fit'." *American Journal of Community Psychology* 17:729–53.

MATTLIN, JAY A., ELAINE WETHINGTON, and RONALD C. KESSLER. 1990. "Situational Determinants of Coping and Coping Effectiveness." *Journal of Health and Social Behavior* 31:103–22.

MCCRAE, ROBERT R. 1982. "Age Differences in the Use of Coping Mechanisms." *Journal of Gerontology* 37:454–60.

———. 1984. "Situational Determinants of Coping Responses: Loss, Threat, and Challenge." *Journal of Personality and Social Psychology* 46:919–28.

MCLEOD, JANE D. 1991. "Childhood Parental Loss and Adult Depression." *Journal of Health and Social Behavior* 32:205–20.

MCLEOD, JANE D. and RONALD C. KESSLER. 1990. "Socioeconomic Status Differences in Vulnerability to Undesirable Life Events." *Journal of Health and Social Behavior* 31:162–72.

MENAGHAN, ELIZABETH G. 1982. "Measuring Coping Effectiveness: A Panel Analysis of Marital Problems and Coping Efforts." *Journal of Health and Social Behavior* 23:220–34.

———. 1983. "Individual Coping Efforts: Moderators of the Relationship between Life Stress and Mental Health Outcomes." Pp. 157–91 in *Psychosocial Stress: Trends in Theory and Research*, edited by H. B. Kaplan. New York: Academic.

———. 1991. "Work Experiences and Family Interaction Processes: The Long Reach of the Job?" *Annual Review of Sociology* 17:419–44.

MENAGHAN, ELIZABETH G. and ESTHER S. MERVES. 1984. "Coping with Occupational Problems: The Limits of Individual Efforts." *Journal of Health and Social Behavior* 25:406–23.

MESSERI, PETER, MERRIL SILVERSTEIN, and EUGENE LITWAK. 1993. "Choosing Optimal Support Groups: A Review and Reformulation." *Journal of Health and Social Behavior* 34:122–37.

MILKIE, MELISSA A. and PEGGY A. THOITS. 1993. "Gender Differences in Coping with Positive and Negative Experiences." Department of Sociology, Indiana University, Bloomington, IN. Unpublished manuscript.

MILLER, SUZANNE M. and NICHOLAS KIRSCH. 1989. "Sex Differences in Cognitive Coping with Stress." Pp. 278–307 in *Gender and Stress*, edited by R. C. Barnett, L. Biener, and G. K. Baruch. New York: Free Press.

MIROWSKY, JOHN and CATHERINE E. ROSS. 1989. *Social Causes of Psychological Distress.* New York: Aldine de Gruyter.

———. 1990. "Control or Defense? Depression and the Sense of Control over Good and Bad Outcomes." *Journal of Health and Social Behavior* 31:71–86.

MOEN, PHYLLIS, DONNA DEMPSTER-MCCLAIN, and ROBIN M. WILLIAMS, JR. 1989. "Social Integration and Longevity: An Event History Analysis of Women's Roles and Resilience." *American Sociological Review* 54:635–47.

NEWMANN, JOY P. 1986. "Gender, Life Strains, and Depression." *Journal of Health and Social Behavior* 27:161–78.

OKUN, MORRIS A., ROBERT W. OLDING, and CATHERINE M. COHN. 1990. "A Meta-Analysis of Subject Well-Being Interventions Among Elders." *Psychological Bulletin* 108(2):257–66.

PEARLIN, LEONARD I. 1985. "Social Structure and Processes of Social Support." Pp. 43–60 in *Social Support and Health*, edited by S. Cohen and S. L. Syme. Orlando, FL: Academic.

———. 1989. "The Sociological Study of Stress." *Journal of Health and Social Behavior* 30:241–56.

———. 1991. "The Study of Coping: An Overview of Problems and Directions." Pp. 261–76 in *The Social Context of Coping*, edited by J. Eckenrode. New York: Plenum.

PEARLIN, LEONARD I. and JOYCE S. JOHNSON. 1977. "Marital Status, Life Strains, and Depression." *American Sociological Review* 42:704–15.

PEARLIN, LEONARD I. and MORTON A. LIEBERMAN. 1978. "Social Sources of Emotional Distress." Pp. 217–48 in *Research in Community and Mental Health*, vol. 1, edited by R. Simmons. Greenwich, CT: JAI Press.

PEARLIN, LEONARD I. and MARY E. MCCALL. 1990. "Occupational Stress and Marital Support: A Description of Microprocesses." Pp. 39–60 in *Stress Between Work and Family*, edited by J. Eckenrode and S. Gore. New York: Plenum.

PEARLIN, LEONARD I. and CARMI SCHOOLER. 1978. "The Structure of Coping." *Journal of Health and Social Behavior* 19:2–21.

PEARLIN, LEONARD I., MORTON A. LIEBERMAN, ELIZABETH G. MENAGHAN, and JOSEPH T. MULLAN. 1981. "The Stress Process." *Journal of Health and Social Behavior* 22:337–56.

PRICE, RICHARD H., EMORY L. COWEN, RAYMOND P. LORION, and JULIA RAMOS-McKAY, eds. 1988. *14 Ounces of Prevention*. Washington, DC: American Psychological Association.

QUITTNER, ALEXANDRA L., ROBERT L. GLUECKAUF, and DOUGLAS N. JACKSON. 1990. "Chronic Parenting Stress: Moderating Versus Mediating Effects of Social Support." *Journal of Personality and Social Psychology* 59(6):1266–78.

RAGIN, CHARLES C. 1987. *The Comparative Method: Moving Beyond Qualitative and Quantitative Strategies*. Berkeley, CA: University of California Press.

RIESSMAN, CATHERINE KOHLER. 1990. *Divorce Talk: Women and Men Make Sense of Personal Relationships*. New Brunswick, NJ: Rutgers University Press.

RODIN, JUDITH. 1986. "Aging and Health: Effects of the Sense of Control." *Science* 233:1271–76.

RODIN, JUDITH and PETER SALOVEY. 1989. "Health Psychology." *Annual Review of Psychology* 40:533–79.

ROOK, KAREN. 1984. "The Negative Side of Social Interaction: Impact on Psychological Well-Being." *Journal of Personality and Social Psychology* 46(5):1097–108.

———. 1990. "Parallels in the Study of Social Support and Social Strain." *Journal of Social and Clinical Psychology* 9(1):118–32.

———. 1992. "Detrimental Aspects of Social Relationships: Taking Stock of an Emerging Literature." Pp. 157–69 in *The Meaning and Measurement of Social Support*, edited by H. O. F. Veiel and U. Baumann. New York: Hemisphere.

ROOK, KAREN, DAVID DOOLEY, and RALPH CATALANO. 1991. "Age Differences in Workers' Efforts to Cope with Economic Distress." Pp. 79–105 in *The Social Context of Coping*, edited by J. Eckenrode. New York: Plenum.

ROSENFIELD, SARAH. 1989. "The Effects of Women's Employment: Personal Control and Sex Differences in Mental Health." *Journal of Health and Social Behavior* 30:77–91.

ROSS, CATHERINE E. and JOHN MIROWSKY. 1989. "Explaining the Social Patterns of Depression: Control and Problem Solving—or Support and Talking?" *Journal of Health and Social Behavior* 30:206–19.

SELYE, HANS. 1956. *The Stress of Life*. New York: McGraw-Hill.

SHAMIR, BOAS. 1986. "Self-Esteem and the Psychological Impact of Unemployment." *Social Psychology Quarterly* 49(1):61–72.

SHROUT, PATRICK E., BRUCE G. LINK, BRUCE P. DOHRENWEND, ANDREW E. SKODOL, ANN STUEVE, and JERROLD MIROTZNIK. 1989. "Characterizing Life Events as Risk Factors for Depression: The Role of Fateful Loss Events." *Journal of Abnormal Psychology* 98(4):460–67.

SILVER, ROXANE L., CHERYL BOON, and MARY H. STONES. 1983. "Searching for Meaning in Misfortune: Making Sense of Incest." *Journal of Social Issues* 39(2):81–102.

SIMON, ROBIN W. 1995. "Gender, Multiple Roles, Role Meaning, and Mental Health." *Journal of Health and Social Behavior* 36:182–94.

SMELSER, NEIL. 1963. *Theory of Collective Behavior*. New York: Free Press.

STONE, ARTHUR A. and JOHN M. NEALE. 1984. "New Measure of Daily Coping: Development and Preliminary Results." *Journal of Personality and Social Psychology* 46:892–906.

STONE, ARTHUR A., SHELLEY LENNOX, and JOHN M. NEALE. 1985. "Daily Coping and Alcohol Use in a Sample of Community Adults." Pp. 199–220 in *Coping and Substance Use*, edited by S. Shiffman and T. A. Wills. Orlando, FL: Academic.

TAUSIG, MARK. 1986. "Measuring Life Events." Pp. 71–93 in *Social Support, Life Events, and Depression*, edited by N. Lin, A. Dean, and W. M. Ensel. Orlando, FL: Academic.

THOITS, PEGGY A. 1982. "Life Stress, Social Support, and Psychological Vulnerability: Epidemiological Considerations." *Journal of Community Psychology* 10:341–62.

———. 1983. "Dimensions of Life Events that Influence Psychological Distress: An Evaluation and Synthesis of the Literature." Pp. 33–103 in *Psychosocial Stress: Trends in Theory and Research*, edited by H. B. Kaplan. New York: Academic.

———. 1984. "Explaining Distributions of Psychological Vulnerability: Lack of Social Support in the Face of Life Stress." *Social Forces* 63:453–81.

———. 1987. "Gender and Marital Status Differences in Control and Distress: Common Stress Versus Unique Stress Explanations." *Journal of Health and Social Behavior* 28:7–22.

———. 1991. "Patterns in Coping with Controllable and Uncontrollable Events." Pp. 235–58 in *Life-Span Developmental Psychology: Perspectives on Stress and Coping*, edited by E. M. Cummings, A. L. Greene, and K. H. Karraker. Hillsdale, NJ: Lawrence Erlbaum.

———. 1992. "Identity Structures and Psychological Well-Being: Gender and Marital Status Comparisons." *Social Psychology Quarterly* 55(3):236–56.

———. 1994a. "Identity-relevant Events and Psychological Symptoms: A Cautionary Tale." *Journal of Health and Social Behavior* 36:72–82.

———. 1994b. "Stressors and Problem-Solving: The Individual as Psychological Activist." *Journal of Health and Social Behavior* 35:143–59.

TURNER, R. JAY and WILLIAM R. AVISON. 1989. "Gender and Depression: Assessing Exposure and Vulnerability to Life Events in a Chronically Strained Population." *Journal of Nervous and Mental Disease* 177(8):443–55.

TURNER, R. JAY and WILLIAM R. AVISON. 1992. "Innovations in the Measurement of Life Stress: Crisis Theory and the Significance of Event Resolution." *Journal of Health and Social Behavior* 33:36–50.

TURNER, R. JAY and JOHN W. GARTRELL. 1978. "Social Factors in Psychiatric Outcome: Toward the Resolution of Interpretive Controversies." *American Sociology Review* 43:368–82.

TURNER, R. JAY and FRANCO MARINO. 1994. "Social Support and Social Structure: A Descriptive Epidemiology." *Journal of Health and Social Behavior* 35:193–212.

Turner, R. JAY and SAMUEL NOH. 1983. "Class and Psychological Vulnerability: The Significance of Social Support and Personal Control." *Journal of Health and Social Behavior* 24:2–15.

———. 1988. "Physical Disability and Depression: A Longitudinal Analysis." *Journal of Health and Social Behavior* 29:23–37.

TURNER, R. JAY and PATRICIA ROSZELL. 1994. "Psychosocial Resources and the Stress Process." Pp. 179–210 in *Stress and Mental Health: Contemporary Issues and Prospects for the Future*, edited by W. R. Avison and I. H. Gotlib. New York: Plenum.

TURNER, R. JAY, BLAIR WHEATON, and DONALD A. LLOYD. 1995. "The Epidemiology of Social Stress." *American Sociological Review* 60:104–24.

UEHARA, EDWINA. 1990. "Dual Exchange Theory, Social Networks, and Informal Social Support." *American Journal of Sociology* 96(3):521–57.

ULBRICH, PATRICIA M., GEORGE J. WARHEIT, and RICK S. ZIMMERMAN. 1989. "Race, Socioeconomic Status, and Psychological Distress: An Examination of Differential Vulnerability." *Journal of Health and Social Behavior* 30:131–46.

UMBERSON, DEBRA and WALTER R. GOVE. 1989. "Parenthood and Psychological Well-Being: Theory, Measurement, and Stage in Family Life Course." *Journal of Family Issues* 10(4):440–62.

UMBERSON, DEBRA, CAMILLE B. WORTMAN, and RONALD C. KESSLER. 1992. "Widowhood and Depression: Explaining Long-Term Gender Differences in Vulnerability." *Journal of Health and Social Behavior* 33:10–24.

USEEM, BERT. 1985. "Disorganization and the New Mexico Prison Riot of 1980." *American Sociological Review* 50:677–88.

VAUX, ALAN. 1988. *Social Support: Theory, Research, and Intervention.* New York: Praeger.

VERBRUGGE, LOIS. 1985. "Triggers of Symptoms and Health Care." *Social Science and Medicine* 20(9):855–76.

———. 1989. "The Twain Meet: Empirical Explanations of Sex Differences in Health and Mortality." *Journal of Health and Social Behavior* 30:282–304.

VEROFF, JOSEPH, RICHARD A. KULKA, and ELIZABETH DOUVAN. 1981. *Mental Health in America: Patterns of Help-Seeking from 1957 to 1976.* New York: Basic.

WEBER, LYNN, ELIZABETH HIGGINBOTHAM, REBECCA F. GUY, and ANDREW BUSH. 1993. "Depression Among Professional Managerial Women: The Dynamics of Race, Class, and Gender." Center for Research on Women, Memphis State University, Memphis, TN. Unpublished manuscript.

WEISS, ROBERT S. 1990. "Bringing Work Stress Home." Pp. 17–37 *in Stress Between Work and Family*, edited by J. Eckenrode and S. Gore. New York: Plenum.

WELLMAN, BARRY and SCOT WORTLEY. 1990. "Different Strokes from Different Folks: Community Ties and Social Support." *American Journal of Sociology* 96(3):558–88.

WETHINGTON, ELAINE and RONALD C. KESSLER. 1986. "Perceived Support, Received Support, and Adjustment to Stressful Life Events." *Journal of Health and Social Behavior* 27:78–89.

WHEATON, BLAIR. 1982. "A Comparison of the Moderating Effects of Personal Coping Resources on the Impact of Exposure to Stress in Two Groups." *Journal of Community Psychology* 10:293–311.

———. 1990a. "Life Transitions, Role Histories, and Mental Health." *American Sociological Review* 55:209–23.

———. 1990b. "Where Work and Family Meet: Stress across Social Roles." Pp. 153–74 in *Stress Between Work and Family*, edited by J. Eckenrode and S. Gore. New York: Plenum.

———. 1991. "The Specification of Chronic Stressor: Models and Measurement." Paper presented at the Society for the Study of Social Problems, Cincinnati, OH.

WORTMAN, CAMILLE B. and TERRY L. CONWAY. 1985. "The Role of Social Support in Adapta-tion and Recovery from Physical Illness." Pp. 281–302 in *Social Support and Health*, edited by S. Cohen and S. L. Syme. Orlando, FL: Academic.

WORTMAN, CAMILLE B. and DARRIN R. LEHMAN. 1985. "Reactions to Victims of Life Crises: Support Attempts that Fail." Pp. 463–89 in *Social Support: Theory, Research, and Applications*, edited by I. G. Sarason and B. R. Sarason. Dordrecht, The Netherlands: Martinus Nijhoff.

ZAUTRA, ALEC J., CHARLES A. GUARNACCIA, and BRUCE P. DOHRENWEND. 1986. "Measuring Small Life Events." *American Journal of Community Psychology* 4(6):629–55.

Part IV
HEALTH BEHAVIOR

Health behavior is the activity undertaken by a person for the purpose of preventing health problems. Activities such as exercise, eating a healthy diet, wearing a seatbelt, and avoiding stress are forms of health behavior. This is an important area of study in medical sociology because health-oriented behavior does not pertain only to the sick and injured, but also to everyone who seeks to maintain a healthy physical and mental state.

The usual strategy that people pursue to maintain their health is to live a healthy lifestyle. A healthy lifestyle can be defined as collective patterns of health-related behavior based on choices from options available to people according to their life chances. These life chances include socioeconomic status, age, gender, race, and other variables that have an impact on choices. In other words, people have choices in their selection of lifestyle options, but these choices are constrained by the chances they have to realize them.

The paper by Catherine E. Ross and Chloe E. Bird entitled "Sex Stratification and Health Lifestyle: Consequences for Men's and Women's Perceived Health" points out that men are more likely than women to exercise strenuously and walk but also more likely to smoke and be overweight. Therefore, men are particularly at risk for poor health if their advantaged position in the marketplace (higher salaries and leadership roles) is accompanied by smoking, consumption of high-fat foods, and sedentary leisure activities.

SEX STRATIFICATION AND HEALTH LIFESTYLE: CONSEQUENCES FOR MEN'S AND WOMEN'S PERCEIVED HEALTH

Catherine E. Ross
Ohio State University

Chloe E. Bird
Rand Corporation

A representative national sample of 2,031 adults aged 18 to 90 was interviewed by telephone in 1990. Results showed that men report better health than women, but that the gap closes with age. We argue that a gender difference in labor and lifestyles explains sex differences in perceived health across the life course: Gender inequality in paid and unpaid work and the subjective experience of inequality disadvantage women, whereas lifestyle disadvantages men. Women are less likely to be employed and are more likely to work part-time, have lower incomes and more economic hardship, and to do more unpaid domestic labor than men, all of which except domestic labor *are associated with poor health. Domestic labor improves health, up to doing 60 percent of the housework. Women also have more distress and fewer subjective work rewards, both of which are associated with poor health. If women had the same levels of paid work, household income, economic hardship, work rewards, and distress as men, their health would equal that of men's and surpass it by age 59. Although we expected to find an overwhelming male disadvantage in lifestyle, we did not. Men are more likely than women to walk and to exercise strenuously, both of which are associated with good health. If women's labor and leisure-time physical activity equalled men's, women over the age of 54 would experience better health than men. Men's lifestyle disadvantage comes from their greater tendency to smoke and to be overweight, both of which are associated with poor health.*

Men report better health than women, but the gap closes with age. What explains the pattern of sex differences in perceived health across the life course? We expect that sex stratification in paid and unpaid work and the subjective experience of this inequality disadvantages women, while lifestyle disadvantages men. If women held the same positions as men in paid and unpaid work and experienced the same levels of subjective work rewards, personal control, and distress, would women's physical well-being equal or

Reprinted from the *Journal of Health and Social Behavior*, vol. 35 (June 1994), pp. 161–78, by permission of the American Sociological Association.

exceed men's over a larger part of the life course? Alternatively, if men had the same lifestyle as women, would men feel healthier at older ages?

Sociologists study stratification out of an interest in systematic differences in opportunities and quality of life. Although research on sex stratification typically focuses on work-related outcomes such as occupation and earnings, ultimately the impact of inequality extends beyond differences in jobs, earnings, prestige, and power, to the consequences of this inequality for individual well-being. If gender inequality leads to differences in health, then it directly affects quality of life. The sex-based division of labor in paid and unpaid work divides men and women into positions with different risks and rewards. In particular, employment may offer economic benefits and the rewards of achieved status, including low levels of distress, subjectively rewarding work, and high personal control, all of which may affect physical well-being. Unpaid domestic labor, on the other hand, may provide the disadvantages of economically and psychologically unrewarded work. We argue that, compared to women, men's relation to the means of production—their paid and unpaid labor—improves their physical well-being.

In contrast, men's and women's relation to the means of consumption, or lifestyle, disadvantages men. Although labor provides a crucial basis for stratification, status groups may differ according to the means of consumption available to them; that is, according to lifestyle—what people eat, where they live, and what they wear. Their leisure time activities, appearance, and possessions are also important. Ironically, men's access to the goods and benefits that come with advantaged position may worsen health, if advantage is accompanied by cigarettes, cars, high-fat foods, and values and norms associated with smoking, weight, or passive leisure-time activities. We argue that the differences in men's and women's relation to two com-

ponents of class—labor and lifestyle—explain sex differences in health over the life course.

SEX DIFFERENCES IN HEALTH

Gender and Health over the Life Course

Sex differences in health are paradoxical: Women report worse health than men, despite the fact that they live longer (Verbrugge 1985). Women experience more nonfatal illnesses of all kinds throughout life; men experience more life-threatening illnesses that develop with age. Even excluding reproductive conditions, women have more health problems than men (Waldron 1983). Women have more nonfatal chronic conditions (those lasting more than three months) such as varicose veins, hemorrhoids, constipation, gallbladder conditions, colitis, eczema, dermatitis, thyroid conditions, anemias, migraines, and arthritis. Women also have more acute conditions (those lasting less than three months), such as upper respiratory infections, gastroenteritis, and other short-term infectious diseases (Verbrugge 1985). Men's health advantage is smallest in later life when men begin to suffer from fatal conditions. Men have more life-threatening chronic diseases, including coronary heart disease, cancer, cerebrovascular disease, emphysema, cirrhosis of the liver, kidney disease, and atherosclerosis, all of which are leading causes of death (Verbrugge 1985). Of the 15 leading causes of death, diabetes is the only one for which women's rates even approach men's. Men die about seven years earlier than women: In 1989, life expectancy for women was 78.6, compared to 71.8 for men (National Center for Health Statistics 1992).[1]

National health statistics capture male health problems such as heart disease, cancer, and emphysema. Problems which women experience may be minor from a medical viewpoint, but they are not so in women's daily lives. Verbrugge calls this the "iceberg of morbidity": The visible tip of the iceberg is male, but the bulk of it is female (1985).

Implications for Measuring Health

As an indicator of the quality of people's lives, health may be best assessed by the subjective judgment of the individual. Self-assessed health combines the subjective experience of acute and chronic, fatal and nonfatal, disease; and general lack of well-being such as feeling run-down and tired, having backaches and headaches. Thus, it is not biased toward inclusion of only "male" or "female" problems. It measures health as defined by the World Health Organization: a state of well-being, not simply the absence of disease. Perceived health is highly correlated with more objective measures such as physicians' assessments, and with measures of morbidity and mortality, and it predicts mortality over and above measures of chronic and acute disease, physician assessment made by clinical exam, physical disability, and health behaviors like smoking (Idler and Kasl 1991; Kaplan 1987; Romelsjo et al. 1992). Self-assessed health is a stronger predictor of mortality than is physician-assessed health (Mossey and Shapiro 1982; Maddox and Douglas 1973) and, unlike measures of health based on physician diagnosis, it is not biased by differential diagnosis of a problem based on the person's gender. We use the term health to mean self-reported, subjective, or perceived health.

EXPLAINING SEX DIFFERENCES IN HEALTH

We first examine the basic pattern of gender and perceived health across age groups. We expect that women report worse health than men, but that the gap closes with age. At what age, if any, does women's physical well-being approach or surpass men's? Next we ask, what explains age-related sex differences in health? Our explanations fall into two cate-gories: (1) gender inequality in paid work and households, and the subjective experience of inequality, and (2) health lifestyle. Broadly speaking, we expect that the first disadvantages women, and the second disadvantages men.

Our explanations, if supported, potentially resolve the paradox of sex differences in health. The negative consequences for health of sex stratification manifest themselves over the adult life span. However, the negative consequences of health behaviors like smoking occur in later life, since most of the chronic diseases that ultimately kill take decades to develop. The disadvantaged statuses of women and the social stressors that stem from inequality worsen physical well-being—they produce acute illness and non-fatal chronic problems throughout life—but do *not* generate fatal disease, while the poorer health lifestyle of men produces life-threatening disease in later life.

Gender Inequality in Paid Work and Households

Men are more likely to engage in paid work than women, and employed men are more likely than women to work full-time. Men's incomes are higher and they experience less economic hardship than do women. In addition, men do less unpaid work at home. We expect that women's disadvantage in the division of paid labor and unpaid domestic labor negatively affects health.

Research indicates that employed women are physically healthier than nonemployed women, and participation in the labor force improves health over time (Bird and Fremont 1991; Marcus, Seeman, and Telesky 1983; Nathanson 1980; Verbrugge 1983, 1989; Waldron and Jacobs 1988). Follow-up studies of mortality that show substantially lower death rates among employed women than housewives support a causal interpretation (Passannante and Nathanson 1985). When women began entering the labor force at a growing rate, many speculated that women's employment would have a negative impact on their health and that women were better off staying home and avoiding the risks of employment. According to the argument, employment would expose women to work accidents, hazards, and the stress generated by competition and responsibility (Waldron 1983). Researchers discounted positive associations between employment and health as selection of healthier women into the labor force. Accumulating evidence indicates that, compared to not working for pay, employment improves health. Thus, we expect that women's lower likelihood of employment negatively affects their health.

Among the employed, men and women are segregated into different kinds of work (Reskin and Hartmann 1986). Women's jobs command lower pay, offer fewer opportunities for advancement, and have lower returns to experience and authority (England et al. 1988). Women who are employed full-time earn two-thirds as much as men (U.S. Bureau of Labor Statistics 1988), an economic disadvantage that may affect health (Bird and Fremont 1991). In addition, women are more than twice as likely to work in part-time jobs (26% of women compared to 10% of men in the employed civilian labor force) (U.S. Bureau of Labor Statistics 1988), which are even more segregated than full-time work, and offer less training, lower returns to experience, and fewer benefits (Holden and Hansen 1987). Part-time workers have worse health than full-time workers, but better than housewives (Herold and Waldron 1985).

Households and paid work are linked through household income and economic hardship. It is in the household that the larger social and economic order impinges on individuals, exposing them to varying degrees of hardship, frustration, and struggle. Women experience more economic hardship than men do, in part because they are less likely to be employed, are more likely to work part-time,

and they earn less than men. Because unmarried women's earnings typically constitute the total family income, they are the group most likely to be poor (Bianchi and Spain 1986). Even in intact families, women experience more economic hardship than men (Ross and Huber 1985). Wives usually have responsibility for maintaining the budget, doing the shopping, making sure there is food on the table, taking the children to the doctor, and paying the bills (Huber and Spitze 1983). The stress of trying to pay the bills and to feed and clothe the family on an inadequate income may take its toll in depression, anxiety, and susceptibility to disease (Pearlin et al. 1981; Ross and Huber 1985). Although we know of no research that examines the effect of economic hardship on health, we expect that women feel more economic hardship than men, which, in turn, worsens health.

Sex differences in earnings also affects the household division of labor. The lower an employed woman's earnings compared to her husband's, the more housework she does; women with no earnings do the most housework (Ross 1987). People who do housework describe it as monotonous, routine, isolating work, for which one receives little recognition and few rewards (Gove and Tudor 1973). According to this argument, it is exhausting work, done without pay, vacation, opportunity for advancement, or retirement (Bergmann 1986). Furthermore, lack of shared responsibility for housework produces a sense of inequity (Ross, Mirowsky, and Huber 1983). Few researchers have looked at the effect of housework on physical well-being, although Bird and Fremont find that the greater the number of hours spent in housework, the worse one's self-reported health (1991).

Distress, Sense of Control, and Work Rewards

Women's disadvantaged positions in paid work and households are one likely reason for their high levels of distress—especially depression and anxiety—compared to men (Mirowsky and Ross 1989). Women who are employed have lower levels of psychological distress than housewives, and the greater the responsibility for housework, the greater the distress (Gore and Mangione 1983; Gove 1984; Kessler and McRae 1982; Ross et al. 1983). Psychological distress, in turn, is associated with poor health (Gove and Hughes 1979). People who are depressed lack motivation and energy; they are less likely to quit smoking, to exercise, or to eat right, and they are more likely to drink heavily (Aneshensel and Huba 1983). Thus, distress has indirect effects on health, mediated by health behaviors. Distress also has direct physiological effects. For example, the fight or flight reaction triggered by anxiety can lead to ulcers and high blood pressure (Selye 1985). The helplessness of depression weakens the body's immune system, making it less able to fight off disease (Jemmott and Locke 1984). Consequently, psychological distress increases mortality (Somervell et al. 1989). We expect that elevated levels of psychological distress among women in part mediate the hypothesized link between sex and health (Gove and Hughes 1979).

We expect that men have a greater sense of control over their lives, due to their higher objective levels of control, opportunities, and rewards, and lower levels of dependency. Women are less likely than men to be paid for their work. Working for pay produces a cognitive connection between efforts and outcomes. Employment is associated with status, power, economic independence, and noneconomic rewards—for both men and women. In comparison, domestic work is done without economic rewards, and often without symbolic rewards, like recognition for a job well done (Bird and Ross 1993; Gove and Tudor 1973). Theoretically, the rewards associated with paid work and the cognitive connection between efforts and rewards increase the

sense of control. Furthermore, among the employed, men's jobs confer more autonomy, flexibility, economic rewards, advancement opportunities, and nonrepetitive work than do women's jobs (Wolf and Fligstein 1979)—qualities that increase the sense of control (Kohn and Schooler 1982; Wheaton 1980). Early research based on samples containing large numbers of Hispanics and nonemployed women found a significantly lower sense of control among women (Mirowsky and Ross 1984), although more recent research does not (Ross and Mirowsky 1989). We expect that women have a lower sense of control than men, which, in turn, affects health. People with a high sense of control know about their health, initiate preventive behaviors like quitting smoking, avoid dependence on doctors, and feel healthier than those with a low sense of control (Seeman and Seeman 1983).

We expect that men find their work more subjectively rewarding than do women, and that subjectively rewarding work is associated with good health. We know of no research that looks at subjective work rewards of the everyday labor done by men and women—both paid and unpaid. Among the employed, men report more intrinsic gratification from work and more work rewards than do women, although the health effects are small and inconsistent (Bokemeier and Lacy 1986; Hibbard and Pope 1987).

Health Lifestyle

Certain lifestyles reduce the risk of disease, even though lifestyles are not necessarily motivated by health concerns. We expect that women's lifestyles protect health; men's put their health at risk.

Of all the practices that affect health, smoking has the most consequences. Men are more likely to smoke than women, although the gap is closing (Waldron 1983; Wingard 1982; Verbrugge 1989). Smoking increases the risk of coronary heart disease, stroke, lung cancer, cancers at other sites (including esophagus, pancreas, bladder, larynx, and cervix), emphysema, pneumonia and other respiratory infections, aneurysms, bronchitis, atherosclerosis, liver disease, and burns; and it is associated with poor self-reported health (NCHS 1989; Rogers and Powell-Griner 1991; Segovia, Bartlett, and Edwards 1989; Surgeon General 1982). Heart disease, cancer, stroke, and emphysema alone account for approximately 65 percent of all deaths (NCHS 1992).

Other than smoking, fitness has the most health consequences. We examine three aspects of fitness: walking, strenuous exercise, and weight. (Walking, a moderate, nonaerobic exercise, is the most common physical activity, reported by about 20% of Americans [U.S. Bureau of the Census 1985].) Exercise and relative weight are linked because one of the ways in which exercise affects health is by decreasing or maintaining weight. Like smoking, lack of physical activity and its consequences for weight affect many health outcomes.[2]

Few studies have examined sex differences in walking, but some evidence indicates that women walk more than men (Ross and Hayes 1988). Compared to the inactivity of a sedentary lifestyle, any physical activity, aerobic or not, reduces mortality (Berkman and Breslow 1983). Walking reduces cardiovascular risk, back pain, osteoporosis, obesity, high blood pressure, constipation, varicose veins, and adult onset diabetes, and improves subjective health (Duncan, Gordon, and Scott 1991; Magnus, Matroos, and Strackee 1979; U.S. Preventive Task Force 1989).

Recent evidence indicates that men are more likely to be overweight than women (Verbrugge 1989). This is especially true in the middle and higher social classes and among non-Hispanic whites, where women are much less overweight than men (Ross and Mirowsky 1983). Women's concern with their weight may be part of the reason they stay thinner than men. Women are more con-

cerned with their appearance, are more likely to eat foods low in calories and fat, are more likely to eat fruits and vegetables, and are more likely to go on a diet than men (Hayes and Ross 1987). Being overweight is associated with poor perceived health, overall mortality, coronary heart disease, adult onset diabetes, hypertension, and lower back pain (Feinleib 1985; Manson et al. 1987; Segovia et al. 1989; Van Itallie 1985).

Strenuous exercise is an exception to the general prediction that men have a worse health lifestyle than women. Men engage in more strenuous physical activities—running, tennis, softball, basketball, and so on (Verbrugge 1989; Ross and Hayes 1988). Strenuous physical activity improves perceived health, and it reduces the risk of coronary heart disease, stroke, hypertension, atherosclerosis, colon cancer, osteoporosis, lower back pain, and adult onset diabetes (Berkman and Breslow 1983; Blair et al. 1984; Paffenbarger et al. 1993; Verbrugge 1989; Wingard 1982).

Acquired Risks versus Other Explanations

Our theoretical explanations fall under the general heading of "acquired risks" (Verbrugge 1985, 1989). In contrast to our view that sex stratification and lifestyle affect health, some researchers have argued that sex differences in health are an artifact of reporting, evaluating, and seeking help for symptoms. If health is measured as utilization of physician services, or as the probability of receiving a diagnosis from a physician, help-seeking tendencies could bias results. Doctor visits are a problematic measure of health because they are confounded with factors such as inclination to seek help, time, income, and insurance. Thus, we measure health as self-reports of physical well-being. Although sex differences in evaluating and reporting symptoms affect self-reports, there is little evidence for the ideas that women evaluate symptoms more negatively, are more aware of symptoms, complain more, or are more likely to report them than men. Gove and Hughes (1979) find that reported sex differences in health reflect real differences, rather than greater willingness among women to report illness, or to adopt the sick role.

METHODS

Analysis

Our goal is to explain the effect of sex on perceived health across age groups. First, we expect to find a significant, negative interaction between being male and age, indicating that men's health advantage diminishes with age. Second, we expect to find a crossover point: an age at which men's health advantage diminishes to zero and women's health equals men's. We then attempt to explain age-based sex differences in health by adjusting for sets of variables indicating sex stratification and its subjective experience, and health lifestyle. We develop a modification of the basic method of attempting to explain a total effect of sex on health. In the basic method, the goal is to decrease the regression coefficient associated with sex to insignificance, thus "explaining" the effect of sex on health. Here we are attempting to move the crossover point—the point at which women's health equals men's.

We examine the age at which women's health equals men's in the unadjusted equation, and then in the equation adjusting only for sociodemographic controls. Then we add sets of explanatory variables. First we add variables indicating sex stratification in paid work and households (employment, income, economic hardship, and housework). Next we add the social psychological experience of sex stratification (subjective work rewards, distress, and a sense of control). Next we add health practices (walking, strenuous exercise, overweight, and smoking). At each step we

solve for the age at which women's health equals men's. This will allow us to answer questions such as, "If women had the same levels of paid employment, income, economic hardship, and household work as men, at what age would women's health equal men's?" By adjusting for objective conditions and their subjective perceptions that disadvantage women, we expect to shift the crossover point to the left—to younger ages at which women's health would equal men's if women had the same advantages as men. By adjusting for lifestyles that disadvantage men, we expect to shift the crossover point back up.

The equation modeling the age-related effect of sex on health is:

$$y = b_0 + b_1(\text{male}) + b_2(\text{age}) + b_3(\text{age} \times \text{male}) \qquad (1)$$

Solving for males:

$$y_M = (b_0 + b_1) + (b_2 + b_3)\,\text{age} \qquad (2)$$

Solving for females:

$$y_F = b_0 + b_2(\text{age}) \qquad (3)$$

To solve for the age at which women's health equals men's, we set equations for men and women equal:

$$b_0 + b_2(\text{age}) = (b_0 + b_1) + (b_2 + b_3)\,\text{age},$$
$$b_0 - b_0 - b_1 = (b_2 + b_3)\,\text{age} - b_2\,\text{age},$$
$$- b_1 = b_3(\text{age})$$
$$- b_1/b_3 = \text{age} \qquad (4)$$

This is the age at which women's health equals men's and after which women's health exceeds men's, assuming the results show that b_1 is positive, b_2 is negative, and b_3 is negative (Aiken and West 1991). (In the regression equations age is measured as [age − 18] so that the intercept is the prediction at age 18, rather than zero. Thus $-b_1/b_3 = $ age $- 18$, and $[-b_1/b_3] + 18 - $ age$)$.

Ultimately, we are interested in the ways in which health changes with age for men and women. However, we are limited at this time to studying the cross-sectional variation in health across age groups. Longitudinal data are necessary to confirm whether sex differences in health across age groups reflect patterns of aging for men and women. Further, because the data are cross-sectional, they cannot be used to demonstrate the validity of causal order assumptions, nor are the processes we postulate meant to deny that there may be reciprocal effects. For example, distress and poor health may have reciprocal effects. The data, in combination with the assumptions, test the theory; that is, the data could fail to support the theory if, given our assumptions, we fail to find the hypothesized effects.

Sample

This research is based on a 1990 telephone survey of a national probability sample of U.S. households. Random-digit dialing was used to ensure the inclusion of unlisted numbers (Waksberg 1978). Within each household, the person 18 years or older with the most recent birthday was selected as respondent. (This is an efficient method to randomly select a respondent within the household [O'Rourke and Blair 1983].) A response rate of 82.3 percent yielded a total of 2,031 respondents, ranging in age from 18 to 90.

Measurement

Health is measured as the person's subjective assessment of general health. This self-report of health is coded very poor (0), poor (1), satisfactory (2), good (3), or very good (4). Self-reported health measures general physical well-being rather than simply the absence of morbidity, and is a valid and reliable measure (Davies and Ware 1981).

Sex is coded one for males. *Age* is coded in number of years. Control variables include *minority status* (coded one for non-whites and Hispanics); *education* (coded in number of years of formal education completed), *marital status* (coded one for persons who are married or living together as married), and number of *children* (coded as the number of children under age 18 living in the household).

Employment status is measured with three categorical variables: employed full-time, employed part-time, and not employed for pay (the comparison group in the regression analyses). *Household income* is coded in thousands of dollars per year. *Economic hardship* is measured as the response to three questions, "During the past twelve months, how often did it happen that you" (1) . . . did not have enough money to buy food, clothes, or other things your household needed?, (2) . . . did not have enough money to pay for medical care?, and (3) . . . had trouble paying the bills?" Would you say never (0), not very often (1), fairly often (2), or very often (3)? The economic hardship index is the mean response to the three questions and had a reliability of .82.

Housework is measured as the percentage of household work a person does, coded from 0 to 100. Respondents were told, "Think of all the things that have to be done for your household: cooking, shopping, housework, laundry, repairs, dish washing, budgeting and paying the bills, making arrangements such as doctor's appointments, and child care. What percentage do you do?"

Subjective work rewards include work fulfillment and recognition from others. We asked parallel questions of employed and nonemployed persons. Everyone was asked to describe the work, tasks, or activities they usually do during the day, and to report the subjective rewards of their primary daily work. Paid work is the primary daily work of people working for pay 20 hours or more a week. Unpaid work includes reported activities such as housework, child care, care for an ill or elderly family member, volunteer work, gardening and home repair, looking for work, and so on. Work fulfillment, or intrinsic gratification from work, includes pride in one's work, enjoyment of work, and the sense of learning and developing as a person through work. In addition to these intrinsic qualities of work, extrinsic symbolic rewards, measured as recognition from others, are assessed. Subjective work rewards are measured by the response to four questions: (1) "How often do you finish your work/daily activities with a good feeling that you have done something especially well?" (Coded never [−2], once in a while [−1], no opinion [0], pretty often [1], or very often [2].) "How much do you agree with the following statements: (2) My work (these tasks) gives me a chance to do things I enjoy; (3) My work (these tasks) gives me a chance to develop and to learn new things; and (4) My work (these tasks) gives me an opportunity to get recognition from others." (These were coded strongly disagree [−2], disagree [−1], don't know [0], agree [1], or strongly agree [2].) The index is the average response to the four questions and has an alpha reliability of .67.

Perceived control is the belief that one can and does master, control, and shape one's own life. Perceived lack of control, the opposite, is the expectation that one's behavior does not affect outcomes. Perceived control is measured by a 2 × 2 index that balances statements claiming or denying control over good or bad outcomes (Mirowsky and Ross 1991). Amount of agreement with each of the following statements was assessed. Statements (1) and (2) claim control over good outcomes: (1) "I am responsible for my own successes"; (2) "I can do just about anything I really set my mind to." Statements (3) and (4) claim control over bad outcomes: (3) "My misfortunes are the result of mistakes I have made"; (4) "I am responsible for my fail-

ures." Statements (5) and (6) deny control over good outcomes: (5) "The really good things that happen to me are mostly luck"; (6) "There's no sense planning a lot—if something good is going to happen, it will." Statements (7) and (8) deny control over bad outcomes: (7) "Most of my problems are due to bad breaks"; (8) "I have little control over the bad things that happen to me." Responses to the perceived control questions (1 through 4) are coded strongly disagree (−2), disagree (−1), neutral (0), agree (1), or strongly agree (2), and responses to lack of control questions (5 through 8) are coded strongly disagree (2), disagree (1), neutral (0), agree (−1), or strongly agree (−2). From these responses, a mean score perceived control index was created, coded from low perceived control (−2) to high perceived control (2). Alpha reliability is .68.

Psychological distress refers to depressed and anxious mood and the absence of positive emotions. We include only the mood components of depression and anxiety so as not to confound psychological distress with physical health. Thus, we exclude symptoms of malaise such as trouble sleeping, feeling tired, run-down, and listless. Depression and anxiety are highly correlated, and, as the two most common types of psychological problems which are experienced by everyone to some degree at some time, they are sensitive psychological barometers of life strains (Mirowsky and Ross 1989; Pearlin and Johnson 1977). The inclusion of positive psychological states (coded in reverse) results in an index ranging from psychological well-being at one end of the continuum to distress at the other. At the well-being end of the continuum, people usually feel happy and hopeful about the future; at the distress end, they feel sad and anxious. Respondents were asked, "On how many days in the past week have you: (1) worried a lot about little things; (2) felt tense or anxious; (3) felt restless; (4) felt sad; (5) felt lonely; (6) felt you couldn't shake the blues; (7) enjoyed life; (8) felt hopeful about the future; and (9) felt happy?" Items one through six are coded from 0 (never) to 7 (every day), and items seven through nine are coded in reverse. The index is the mean response to the nine items and has an alpha reliability of .85.

Walking is measured by asking respondents, "How often do you take a walk? Would you say . . . never (0), once a month or less (1), about twice a month (2), about once a week (3), twice a week (4), three times a week (5), more than three times a week (6), or every day (7)?" *Strenuous exercise* is measured by asking respondents, "How often do you do strenuous exercise such as running, basketball, aerobics, tennis, swimming, biking, and so on?" Responses are coded in the same way as walking, with the exception that more than three times a week is the highest code.

Smoking is coded zero for nonsmokers, one for persons who have ever smoked seven or more cigarettes a week but do not currently smoke, and two for persons who currently smoke seven or more cigarettes a week. Degree of *overweight* is measured by the Quetelet index (kg/m^2). Of the various weight-relative-to-height measures, weight/height^2 is the most adequate because it is the least correlated with height and is highly correlated with skinfold measures indicating body fat (Roche et al. 1981).

RESULTS AND DISCUSSION

Overall, men report significantly better health than women, as shown in Table 1. Men are significantly more likely to be employed than women, and, if employed, to work fulltime; men have significantly higher household incomes and experience less economic hardship; and men do a significantly lower proportion of household labor than do women. Men's objective advantages in paid work and households are reflected in their subjective experience. Men find their work significantly more rewarding than do women,

and men have significantly lower distress levels than women. Although men's sense of control over their lives is higher than women's, the difference is not significant. Women are disadvantaged in objective positions in paid work and households, and only in the sense of control do women's subjective experiences approach men's. Thus, our hypothesis is largely supported.

Men are significantly more likely to smoke than women and are significantly more likely to be overweight. On the other hand, women are significantly less likely to walk or to engage in strenuous exercise than are men (see Table 1). Thus, our hypothesis that men face a disadvantage in health lifestyle is only partially supported. We expected that women would be more likely to engage in the moderate exercise of walking, but this is not the case.

The regression analysis in Table 2 shows the effect of sex on perceived health at different ages and how this effect changes when explanatory variables are added. Equation 1 of Table 2 (graphed in the top panel of Figure 1) shows that men report significantly better health than women, but that men's advantage decreases with age, as indicated by the significant positive coefficient associated with being male [b_1], and the significant negative coefficients associated with age [b_2] and the age-by-sex interaction [b_3]. Solving for the age at which women's health equals men's produces a crossover point of 67.918 ($-b_1/b_3 + 18$).[3]

Gender inequality in paid work and households is added in Equation 2 of Table 2. High household income is significantly associated with good health, and economic hardship with poor health. The direct effect of income on health, controlling for economic hardship, indicates that household income affects health both by way of economic hardship and in other ways. Possibly, high income symbolizes success and achievement and increases self-esteem, over and above its economic importance to paying the bills and buying food, clothes, and medical care for one's family.

TABLE 1 Means and Standard Deviations (in parentheses) for Total
Sample, Women, and Men

	Female	Male	Total
Health	3.112	3.272***	3.171
	(.904)	(.853)	(.888)
Age	44.450	42.004***	43.548
	(17.174)	(16.961)	(17.133)
Minority	.169	.184	.175
	(.375)	(.338)	(.380)
Education	13.134	13.373*	13.222
	(2.505)	(2.732)	(2.593)
Married	.611	.597	.606
	(.488)	(.491)	(.489)
Children	.817	.628***	.747
	(1.115)	(1.006)	(1.080)
Family Income	36.713	41.917***	38.632
	(23.977)	(29.968)	(26.458)
Economic Hardship	.509	.346***	.449
	(.729)	(.585)	(.684)
Employed Full-time	.436	.681***	.526
	(.496)	(.466)	(.499)
Employed Part-time	.135	.058***	.107
	(.342)	(.235)	(.309)
Not Employed	.429	.260***	.367
	(.495)	(.439)	(.482)
Housework	76.869	58.110***	69.944
	(21.591)	(27.362)	(25.537)
Work Rewards	.873	.938*	.897
	(.707)	(.725)	(.714)
Sense of Control	.651	.682	.662
	(.486)	(.516)	(.497)
Distress	1.812	1.500***	1.696
	(1.614)	(1.509)	(1.583)
Walking	4.213	4.417*	4.288
	(2.576)	(2.679)	(2.616)
Strenuous Exercise	1.671	2.587***	2.009
	(2.211)	(2.360)	(2.310)
Smoking	.705	.847***	.757
	(.833)	(.820)	(.831)
Overweight	24.249	25.318***	24.651
	(4.943)	(3.841)	(4.589)
N	1282	749	2031

Significance of sex difference, 1-tailed test.

*$p < .05$; **$p < .01$; ***$p < .001$.

TABLE 2 Regression of Perceived Health on Sex, Age, and Their Interaction (Controlling for Sociodemographics) (Equation 1), Gender Inequality in Paid Work and Households (Equation 2), Subjective Experience of Gender Inequality (Equation 3), and Health Lifestyles (Equations 4 and 5).

	Eq. 1	Eq. 2	Eq. 3	Eq. 4	Eq. 5	
Sex (male = 1)	.230***	.215***	.215***	.181**	.217**	.049
	(.069)	(.068)	(.068)	(.068)	(.068)	
Age[a]	−.011***	−.010***	−.010***	−.009***	−.009***	−.208
	(.001)	(.002)	(.001)	(.001)	(.002)	
Sex × Age	−.005*	−.004*	−.005**	−.005**	−.005**	
	(.002)	(.002)	(.002)	(.002)	(.002)	
Minority	−.142**	−.114**	−.119*	−.124**	−.134**	−.057
	(.050)	(.048)	(.047)	(.047)	(.047)	
Education	.076***	.051***	.039***	.037***	.033***	.095
	(.007)	(.008)	(.008)	(.008)	(.008)	
Married	.123**	.062	.027	.037	.051	.028
	(.040)	(.043)	(.042)	(.042)	(.042)	
Children	.001	.023	.025	.029	.033*	.040
	(0.19)	(.019)	(.018)	(.018)	(.018)	
Family Income		.002**	.002**	.002*	.002*	.045
		(.000)	(.001)	(.001)	(.001)	
Economic Hardship		−.220***	−.138***	−.134***	−.119***	−.091
		(.029)	(.029)	(.028)	(.028)	
Employed Full–time[b]		.262***	.218***	.231***	.238***	.134
		(.045)	(.043)	(.043)	(.043)	
Employed Part–time[b]		.193**	.174**	.178**	.160**	.055
		(.065)	(.063)	(.063)	(.062)	
Housework		.012***	.011**	.011**	.010**	.107
		(.004)	(.004)	(.004)	(.004)	
Housework squared		−6.6E−5**	−6.2E−5*	−5.8E−5*	−5.1E−5*	
		(2.9E−5)	(2.8E−5)	(2.9E−5)	(2.9E−5)	
Work Rewards			.110***	.101***	.101***	.081
			(.026)	(.026)	(.025)	
Sense of Control			.104**	.085*	.094**	.053
			(.038)	(.038)	(.038)	
Distress			−.115***	−.113***	−.109***	−.195
			(.012)	(.012)	(.012)	
Walking				.018**	.017**	.051
				(.007)	(.007)	
Strenuous Exercise				.030***	.024***	.063
				(.008)	(.008)	
Smoking					−.080***	−.075
					(.021)	
Overweight					−.016***	−.082
					(.004)	
Constant	2.356	2.069	2.303	2.213	2.690	
Cross-over age[c]	67.918	66.903	58.945	54.134	62.731	
R^2	.149	.204	.261	.270	.280	

[a]Age = (age − 18).

[b]Comparison group is nonemployed.

[c]$(−b_1/b_3 + 18.)$ Crossover age calculations are based on coefficients of 6 decimal points (not the rounded coefficients shown above):

Eq. 1: $(−.229625/−.004600) + 18 = 67.918$

Eq. 2: $(−.214929/−.004395) + 18 = 66.903$

Eq. 3: $(−.215045/−.005252) + 18 = 58.945$

Eq. 4: $(−.180889/−.005006) + 18 = 54.134$

Eq. 5: $(−.217391/−.004860) + 18 = 62.731$

*$p < .05$, 1-tailed test ($p < .10$, 2-tailed test); **$p < .01$, 1-tailed test ($p < .02$, 2-tailed test); ***$p < .001$, 1-tailed test ($p < .002$, 2-tailed test).

Unstandardized regression coefficients with standard errors in parentheses are shown. The last column shows the standardized coefficients in the final equation.

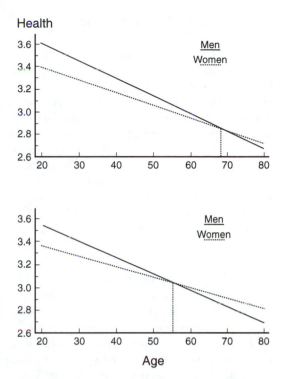

FIGURE 1 Men's and women's perceived health across age groups.

The top panel adjusts for sociodemographic controls only (Equation 1 of Table 2). The bottom panel adjusts for men's advantages in labor and in leisure-time physical activity (Equation 4 of Table 2). Equations 1 and 4 of Table 2 are graphed at the mean level of all control variables.

Compared to people who do not work for pay, full-time employment and part-time employment are both significantly associated with feeling healthy. People who are employed full-time report the best health, followed by those who are employed part-time; people who are not employed report the worst health.

The effect of housework was unexpected. In a linear specification we found that high levels of household labor were associated with good health. Because this was unanticipated, we then asked whether housework's positive effects were unlimited, or whether the positive effect diminished at high levels. Specifying a declining improvement in health with increas-

ing amounts of housework (modeled as housework + housework^2) proved significantly better than a linear specification. Housework is associated with good health up to a point (about 60% of the household labor), at which the positive effect levels off and then decreases somewhat. Whereas housework has negative effects on psychological well-being (Ross et al. 1983; Kessler and McRae 1982), we find that it has diminishing positive effects on physical well-being. Doing a large proportion of the housework could indicate involvement in unrewarding, onerous, and menial work, and inequity in the division of unpaid work at home, both of which probably worsen health. However, housework is also physical activity. Since, compared to being sedentary, any physical activity is good for health, this aspect of housework might improve health. Cleaning windows, mopping floors, vacuuming, and pushing a light power mower expend the same amount of energy as walking three miles per hour (Fox, Naughton, and Gorman 1972), and doing some unpaid work at home may be better for health than doing no work. Thus, housework could have trade-offs for physical health, improving it up to the point at which the psychologically negative aspects outweigh the physically positive ones. Since our results indicate that the positive effects of housework do not extend past doing about 60 percent of the housework, this is plausible. It is only after a person is doing the majority of the housework that the sense of inequity surfaces.

Women's lower average household incomes and level of paid work, as well as their higher levels of economic hardship explain some of the negative effects of being female on health. Women's higher levels of household labor do not explain any of this effect. Although women perform significantly more household labor than men do, housework is not associated with poor health. Because of this, we do not move the crossover point at which women's health equals men's—at least not much.

Work rewards, distress, and the sense of control are conceptualized as the subjective correlates of objective positions in paid work and households, and significant correlations generally support this view. Personal control correlates positively with full-time employment and high income, and negatively with economic hardship and housework ($r = .159$, .192, −.083, −.074, respectively). Distress correlates negatively with income and positively with economic hardship and household labor ($r = −.100$, .309, and .071). Subjective work rewards correlate positively with full-time employment and high income ($r = .166$ and .129), but are not associated with household labor.

Subjective experiences of inequality affect health, as shown in Equation 3 of Table 2. Compared to people who report that their everyday work is unrewarding, people whose work gives them a chance to develop and learn new things, who feel good about their work, who enjoy their work, and who get recognition from others report significantly better health. Women report fewer subjective rewards from their everyday work than do men. Unrewarding work, in turn, is associated with reporting poor health; rewarding work, with good health.

Compared to people who have low levels of psychological distress, those with high distress report significantly worse health. Women have significantly higher levels of psychological distress than men, and distress, in turn, is associated with poor health.

People who feel in control of their lives report significantly better health than those who feel their lives are not in their control. However, men do not have a much higher sense of personal control than do women. Because the sense of control is not highly correlated with sex, it cannot explain much of the effect of sex on health.

Together gender inequality in paid work and households and its social psychological correlates explain a significant part of men's

advantage in health over the life course. If women had the same levels of paid work, household income, economic hardship, subjective work rewards, and psychological well-being as men, their perceived health would equal men's at a much younger age. Adjusting for gender inequality and its subjective experience moves the crossover point at which women's health equals (and then surpasses) men's from 67.918 in Equation 1 to 58.945 in Equation 3. If women's positions in the stratification system and the subjective correlates of those positions equaled men's, women would experience better health than men for much of the late middle and later years.

Health lifestyle variables are added in two steps: those that advantage men (walking and strenuous exercise), and those that disadvantage men (smoking and overweight). Equation 4 of Table 2 adds walking and strenuous exercise. Although some had speculated that only strenuous exercise improves health, we find significant beneficial effects of walking, over and above the positive effect of strenuous exercise. Adding the exercise variables to the equation shifts the age at which women's health equals men's to 54.13 (as shown in Equation 4 of Table 2 and graphed in the bottom panel of Figure 1). If women had the same positions as men in paid work, households, and their subjective correlates, and if they exercised as much as men, their health would equal and then surpass men's for most of middle and older age. Since these are the years when most health problems and health concerns emerge, women's equality in labor and in leisure time physical activity would produce better health over most of the years in which health is a concern. By age 54, women's health would surpass men's.

In contrast to men's other advantages, they face a disadvantage in two lifestyle characteristics: smoking and overweight. Men are more likely to smoke and to be overweight than women, and these tendencies significantly worsen health (See Equation 5 of Table 2.) This lifestyle disadvantage is so great that it shifts the crossover point back up to 62.731. Men would maintain their advantage in health even longer in the life course if their levels of smoking and overweight equalled women's. Stated the other way, if women smoked as much and were as overweight as men they would lose most of what they could gain with equality in labor and leisure-time physical activity. The fact that this loss would offset much of the other gains is especially troubling since the hypothetical scenario is occurring: Women's smoking levels are approaching men's. Women may well offset any gains they make in employment levels, earnings, and economic well-being if with these gains they increase their smoking.

Other findings deserve mention. *Marriage* is positively associated with health in Equation 1. When household income and economic hardship are added in Equation 2, the effect becomes insignificant. This indicates that much of the positive effect of marriage on health is due to the higher household incomes and lower levels of economic hardship among the married. The fact that the number of *children* in the household has no effect on health until all explanatory variables are added in Equation 5, at which point children are positively associated with health, also deserves mention. Although we cannot specify this effect here, it indicates that children have both positive and negative effects on health, improving it in some ways and worsening it in others. For example, children increase economic hardship and they decrease the ability to take walks, thereby worsening health, but if parents maintain their economic well-being and opportunities to exercise, children have positive effects on parents' physical well-being. *Education* positively affects health. The advantage that the well-educated have in paid work and households and in the subjective experience of this advantage for work rewards, personal control,

and distress, and in their health lifestyle, explains most, but not all, of the health advantage of the well-educated. Almost 57 percent of the positive effect of education is explained, but a significant effect remains. Like the well-educated, majority group members report better health than *minorities*, even adjusting for all explanatory variables. Possibly because of discrimination, any given level of achievement requires greater effort and provides fewer opportunities for members of minority groups.

Because sex differences in self-reported health could be due to *response tendencies*, we next adjust for them. Response tendencies are measured in two ways: as the tendency to keep emotions to oneself rather than to express them; and as responsiveness, measured as the tendency to report both positive and negative mood. The first is measured as the amount of agreement with the statement "I keep my emotions to myself," coded strongly disagree (−2), disagree (−1), don't know (0), agree (1), or strongly agree (2). The second is measured as reporting both positive mood and depressed mood. People who score high on responsiveness report feeling sad, lonely, blue, *and* happy, hopeful, and enjoying life. Responsiveness is scored as the mean response to the six items, 0 to 7. Women are significantly more responsive than men ($\bar{x} = 3.376$ compared to 3.232), and significantly less likely to report that they keep their emotions to themselves ($\bar{x} = .008$ compared to .446). However, response tendencies do not account for age-based sex differences in self-reported health. Results are substantively the same with adjustment for response tendencies.[4]

Finally, we tested *interactions* of all theoretically relevant variables with sex. All interaction terms significant at $p < .15$ were added to Equation 5. None were significant at $p < .10$. However, the interaction of sex with part-time employment ($b = .232$) was significant—at $p = .12$, indicating that part-time work may have a larger positive effect on men's health than on women's. The interaction of sex with being overweight ($b = .014$) was significant at $p = .11$, indicating that overweight's effect on health (as measured by the Quetelet index) may be less negative for men. Nonetheless, the general conclusion of this analysis is that women and men are exposed to different work and household situations and lifestyles, and it is this differential "exposure," not sex differences in response, that affects health.

CONCLUSION

Throughout most of life men feel healthier than women, but men's health advantage decreases with age. In order to explain age-based sex differences in health, we examined gender inequality in paid and unpaid work, the subjective experience of inequality, and health lifestyle. Compared to men, women are less likely to work for pay, are more likely to work part-time rather than full-time, have lower household incomes, more economic hardship, lower subjective work rewards, and higher levels of distress. (Women's lower sense of control over their lives is not significantly different from men's.) These indicators of gender inequality and its social psychological correlates negatively affect health. Sex differences in lifestyles also affect health. Men exercise more than women, which is associated with good health. Together, sex differences in labor and in leisure-time physical activity explain a large part of women's worse health over the life course. Adjusting for these factors shifts the point at which women's health equals men's from 68 to 54. (Compare the top and bottom panels of Figure 1.) If women had the same levels of paid work, household income, economic hardship, work rewards, distress, and leisure-time physical activity as men, their perceived health would equal and then surpass men's by late middle-age. After age 54, women would experience better health than men. Thus, we conclude that women's equality in

labor and in leisure-time physical activity would produce better health over most of late middle and older age, the years in which health is of the greatest concern (Verbrugge 1986).

Women's potential health advantage in older age groups may be underestimated due to selection. Men have higher mortality rates than women. If the sickest men in the older age groups have died, this leaves a "residue" of healthier men in our sample. Since these are the ages in which women's health advantage appears (see bottom panel of Figure 1), women's health advantage would be even greater if these sickest men were still in the sample.

Nonetheless, men's health advantage persists in our model throughout the younger years. This could be due to biological differences; however, we know of no biological theory that implies that women's inherent advantage would appear in later life, while men would have the advantage in younger groups. If anything, the inherent advantage of women should be most apparent among women of childbearing years, since the argument for women's resilience is that women need to be strong and healthy because they are the ones who give birth.

Unexplained sex differences could also be due to unreliability in our explanatory variables, or to other social factors not included in the model. These factors could include attitudes and values that modify the effect of employment or housework on health, characteristics of men's and women's jobs not captured by work rewards, or other lifestyle characteristics such as drinking and drug use.

Our conclusions are based on cross-sectional data using self-reports of health. Although self-reports are highly correlated with morbidity and mortality for both men and women, there may be sex differences in the meaning, interpretation, and awareness of health and illness that affect self-reports. We have adjusted for two types of potential response bias in self-reports of health, but we have not been exhaustive in our controls for response tendencies. We are also limited to studying cross-sectional variations in men's and women's health across age groups. Longitudinal data are necessary to confirm whether sex differences in health across age groups (and the predicted crossover points in men's and women's health) reflect patterns of aging for men and women.

We find that women are much more likely than men to do unpaid domestic work. However, domestic work does not have a negative effect on health, and therefore cannot explain women's poorer health. Increases in household work, up to about 60 percent of the total work done in a household, improve health. Perhaps the physical activity involved improves health up to the point at which the psychologically negative aspects of housework outweigh the physically positive ones. Housework increases women's depression levels (whether they are employed or not), but it does not affect men's. Because women's housework varies between half and all of the housework, but men's varies between none and half, it may be that housework is not intrinsically ungratifying, but that a lack of shared responsibility increases the sense of inequity (Ross et al. 1983). Shared housework, which here means less than 60 percent, is not psychologically damaging and may have the health benefits of all types of physical activity. Since few studies have looked at the effect of housework on physical health, this finding should be considered tentative until replicated, especially since Bird and Fremont (1991) found that hours spent in housework worsened health. Research is needed to examine the independent health effects of the proportion of housework performed and the time spent doing it.

Research to date on sex differences in health has focused on utilization of physician services, reporting differences, methodological artifacts, symptom awareness, and acquired risks associated with social roles—in particular nurturant role obligations—concluding that

social roles, more than anything else examined, affect sex differences in health (Gove and Hughes 1979; Verbrugge 1985). However, nurturant role obligations, usually operationalized as being married and having children, cannot explain much of the sex difference in health, since marriage, and to a lesser extent children, are associated with good health for both men and women. Nurturant role obligations also cannot explain the consistent positive effect of employment on health, for both men and women, even when combining the work role with other roles such as parenthood, which might indicate role overload (Verbrugge 1983, 1989; Waldron and Jacobs 1988).

We find that sex differences in two components of class—labor and lifestyle—explain much, but not all, of the effect of sex on health over the life course. If women's paid labor (and its economic and psychological correlates) and women's leisure-time physical activity equalled men's, women over the age of 54 would feel healthier than men.

NOTES

1. As Verbrugge (1985, 1989) points out, the paradox is not simply that women have excess morbidity and men excess mortality. The excess mortality results from excess morbidity for life-threatening diseases.

2. By comparison, drinking is a risk factor for only one of the five leading causes of death—car accidents. It increases the risk of four of the 15 leading causes of death: car accidents, cirrhosis, suicide, and homicide. The latter two, although they are the eighth and tenth leading causes of death, respectively, will not show up in a health survey. Only cirrhosis and injuries from car accidents will affect self-reported health, making drinking far less ubiquitous in its health consequences than smoking or fitness. Furthermore, moderate drinking, as compared to abstinence, is associated with *lower* risk of coronary heart disease, stroke, and hypertension, whereas very heavy drinking is associated with higher risk (Gill et al. 1986; Stampfer et al. 1988). Since most of the variation in drinking among adults is at the low to

moderate end of the scale, drinking may not significantly worsen health (Verbrugge 1989).

3. With no adjustments, men report better health until age 80. We also tested a nonlinear specification (age − 18)^2 that models a steeper decline in health at older ages than younger. In Equation 1, this specification produces an R^2 of .1480 and a t-test associated with the age coefficient of −7.78 which, although very significant, fit no better than the linear model (R^2 = .1492; t = −7.70).

4. The unstandardized regression coefficients associated with sex, age, and their interaction with adjustment for response tendencies follow (all are significant). Eq. 1: .249, −.011, −.005; Eq. 2: .236, −.010, −.004; Eq. 3: .219, −.010, −.005; Eq. 4: .183, −.009, −.005; Eq. 5: .220, −.009, −.005. Comparison with Table 2 shows the similarity. All other results are substantively the same. (Analysis available on request.)

REFERENCES

AIKEN, LEONA S. and STEPHEN G. WEST. 1991. *Multiple Regression: Testing and Interpreting Interactions.* Newbury Park: Sage.

ANESHENSEL, CAROL S. and GEORGE J. HUBA. 1983. "Depression, Alcohol Use and Smoking Over One Year: A Four-Wave Longitudinal Causal Model." *Journal of Abnormal Psychology* 92: 134–50.

BERGMANN, BARBARA. 1986. *The Economic Emergence of Women.* New York: Basic.

BERKMAN, LISA F. and LESTER BRESLOW. 1983. *Health and Ways of Living: The Alameda County Study.* New York: Oxford University Press.

BIANCHI, SUZANNE M. and DAPHNE SPAIN. 1986. *American Women in Transition.* New York: Russell Sage Foundation.

BIRD, CHLOE E. and ALLEN M. FREMONT. 1991. "Gender, Time Use, and Health." *Journal of Health and Social Behavior* 32(2):114–29.

——— and CATHERINE E. ROSS. 1993. "Houseworkers and Paid Workers: Qualities of the Work and Effects on Personal Control." *Journal of Marriage and the Family* 55:913–25.

BLAIR, STEVEN N., NANCY N. GOODYEAR, LARRY W. GIBBONS, and KENNETH H. COOPER. 1984. "Physical, Fitness and Incidence of Hypertension in Healthy Normotensive Men and Women." *Journal of the American Medical Association* 252(4):487–90.

BOKEMEIER, JANET L. and WILLIAM B. LACY. 1986. "Job Values, Rewards, and Work Conditions as Factors in Job Satisfaction among Men and Women." *The Sociological Quarterly* 2(2): 189–204.

DAVIES, ALLYSON ROSS and JOHN E. WARE. 1981. Measuring Health Perceptions in the Health Insurance Experiment. Santa Monica: Rand Corporation. R-2711-HHS.

DUNCAN, JOHN J., NEIL F. GORDON, and CHRIS B. SCOTT. 1991. "Women Walking for Health and Fitness." *Journal of the American Medical Association* 266:3295–99.

ENGLAND, PAULA, GEORGE FARKAS, BARBARA STANEK KILBOURN, and THOMAS DOU. 1988. "Explaining Occupational Sex Segregation and Wages: Findings From a Model with Fixed Effects." *American Sociological Review* 53:544–58.

FEINLEIB, MANNING. 1985. "Epidemiology of Obesity in Relation to Health Hazards." *Annals of Internal Medicine* 103:1019–24.

FOX, SAMUEL M., III, JOHN P. NAUGHTON, and PATRICK GORMAN. 1972. "Physical Activity and Cardiovascular Health." *Modern Concepts of Cardiovascular Disease* 41(6):25–30.

GILL, JASWINDER S., ALEXANDER V. ZEZULKA, MARTIN J. SHIPLEY, SURINDER K. GILL, and D. GARETH BEEVERS. 1986. "Stroke and Alcohol Consumption." *The New England Journal of Medicine* 315(17):1041–46.

GORE, SUSAN S. and THOMAS W. MANGIONE. 1983. "Social Roles, Sex Roles, and Psychological Distress." *Journal of Health and Social Behavior* 24:300–12.

GOVE, WALTER. 1984. "Gender Differences in Mental and Physical Illness: The Effects of Fixed Roles and Nurturant Roles." *Social Science and Medicine* 19:77–84.

——— and MICHAEL HUGHES. 1979. "Possible Causes of the Apparent Sex Differences in Physical Health: An Empirical Investigation." *American Sociological Review* 44:126–46.

——— and JEANETTE F. TUDOR. 1973. "Adult Sex Roles and Mental Illness." *American Journal of Sociology* 78:812–35.

HAYES, DIANE and CATHERINE E. ROSS. 1987. "Concern with Appearance, Health Beliefs, and Eating Habits." *Journal of Health and Social Behavior* 28(2):120–30.

HEROLD, JOAN and INGRID WALDRON. 1985. "Part-Time Employment and Women's Health." *Journal of Occupational Medicine* 27(6):405–12.

HIBBARD, JUDITH H. and CLYDE R. POPE. 1987. "Employment Characteristics and Health Status among Men and Women." *Women and Health* 12(2):85–102.

HOLDEN, KAREN C. and W. LEE HANSEN. 1987. "Part-Time Work, Full-Time Work, and Occupational Segregation." Pp. 217–38 in *Gender in the Workplace*, edited by C. Brown and J. A. Pechman. Washington, D.C.: Brookings Institute.

HUBER, JOAN and GLENNA SPITZE. 1983. *Sex Stratification: Children, Housework, and Jobs*. New York: Academic Press.

IDLER, ELLEN L. and STANISLAV V. KASL. 1991. "Health Perceptions and Survival: Do Global Evaluations of Health Status Really Predict Mortality?" *Journal Gerontology* 46:S55–65.

JEMMOTT, JOHN B. and STEVEN E. LOCKE. 1984. "Psychosocial Factors, Immunologic Mediation, and Susceptibility to Disease: How Much Do We Know?" *Psychological Bulletin* 95:75–108.

KAPLAN, SHERRIE. 1987. "Patient Reports of Health Status as Predictors of Physiologic Health Measures in Chronic Disease." *Journal of Chronic Disease* 40:27S–35S.

KESSLER, RONALD C. and JAMES A. MCRAE. 1982. "The Effect of Wives' Employment on the Mental Health Married Men and Women." *American Sociological Review* 47:216–27.

KOHN, MELVIN L. and CARMI SCHOOLER. 1982. "Job Conditions and Personality: A Longitudinal Assessment of their Reciprocal Effects. *American Journal of Sociology* 87:1257–86.

MADDOX, GEORGE L. and ELIZABETH B. DOUGLAS. 1973. "Self-Assessment of Health: A Longitudinal Study of Elderly Subjects." *Journal of Health and Social Behavior* 14:87–93.

MAGNUS, K., A. MATROOS, and J. STRACKEE. 1979. "Walking, Cycling, or Gardening, with or without Seasonal Interruptions, in Relation to Acute Coronary Events." *American Journal of Epidemiology* 110:724–33.

MANSON, JOANN E., MEIR J. STAMPFER, CHARLES H. HENNEKENS, and WALTER C. WILLETT. 1987. "Body Weight and Longevity." *Journal of the American Medical Association* 257:353–58.

MARCUS, ALFRED C., TERESA E. SEEMAN, and CAROL W. TELESKY. 1983. "Sex Differences in Reports of Illness and Disability: A Further Test of the Fixed Role Hypothesis." *Social Science and Medicine* 17:993–1002.

MIROWSKY, JOHN and CATHERINE E. ROSS. 1984. "Mexican Culture and its Emotional Contradictions." *Journal of Health and Social Behavior* 25:2–13.

——— and CATHERINE E. ROSS. 1989. *Social Causes of Psychological Distress*. New York: Aldine de Gruyter.

——— and CATHERINE E. ROSS. 1991. "Eliminating Defense and Agreement Bias from Measures of Sense of Control: A 2×2 Index." *Social Psychology Quarterly* 54:127–45.

MOSSEY, J. M. and E. SHAPIRO. 1982. "Self-Rated Health: A Predictor of Mortality among the Elderly." *American Journal of Public Health* 72:800–808.

NATHANSON, CONSTANCE A. 1980. "Social Roles and Health Status among Women: The Significance of Employment." *Social Science and Medicine* 14A:463–71.

NATIONAL CENTER FOR HEALTH STATISTICS. 1989. *Deaths Attributable to Smoking, U.S., 1988*. Hyattsville, MD: Public Health Service.

———. 1992. *Advance Report of Final Mortality Statistics, 1989*. Hyattsville, MD: Public Health Service.

O'ROURKE, DIANE and JOHNNY BLAIR. 1983. "Improving Random Selection in Telephone Surveys." *Journal of Marketing Research* 20:428–32.

PAFFENBARGER, RALPH S., ROBERT T. HYDE, ALVIN L. WING, I-MIN LEE, DEXTER L. JUNG, and JAMES B. KAMPERT. 1993. "The Association of Changes in Physical Activity Level and Other Lifestyle Characteristics with Mortality among Men." *New England Journal of Medicine* 328:538–45.

PASSANNANTE, MARIAN R. and CONSTANCE A. NATHANSON. 1985. "Female Labor Force Participation and Female Mortality in Wisconsin, 1974–1978." *Social Science and Medicine* 21:655–65.

PEARLIN, LEONARD I. and JOYCE S. JOHNSON. 1977. "Marital Status, Life Strains and Depression." *American Sociological Review* 42:704–15.

PEARLIN, LEONARD I., MORTON A. LIEBERMAN, ELIZABETH G. MENAGHAN, and JOSEPH T. MULLAN. 1981. "The Stress Process." *Journal of Health and Social Behavior* 22(4):337–56.

RESKIN, BARBARA and HEIDI HARTMANN (Eds.). 1986. *Women's Work, Men's Work: Sex Segregation on the Job.* Washington, D.C.: National Academy Press.

ROCHE, ALEX F., ROGER M. SIERVOGEL, WILLIAM C. CHUMLEA, and ROGER WEBB. 1981. "Grading Body Fatness from Limited Anthropometric Data." *American Journal of Clinical Nutrition* 34:2831–38.

ROGERS, RICHARD G. and EVE POWELL-GRINER. 1991. "Life Expectancies of Cigarette Smokers and Nonsmokers in the United States." *Social Science and Medicine* 32(10):1151–59.

ROMELSJO, ANDERS, GEORGE A. KAPLAN, RICHARD D. COHEN, PETER ALLEBECK, and SVEN ANDREASSON. 1992. "Protective Factors and Social Risk Factors for Hospitalization and Mortality among Young Men." *American Journal of Epidemiology* 135(6):649–58.

ROSS, CATHERINE. 1987. "The Division of Labor at Home." *Social Forces* 65:816–33.

———— and DIANE HAYES. 1988. "Exercise and Psychologic Well-Being in the Community." *American Journal of Epidemiology* 127:762–71.

———— and JOAN HUBER. 1985. "Hardship and Depression." *Journal of Health and Social Behavior* 26:312–27.

———— and JOHN MIROWSKY. 1983. "The Social Epidemiology of Overweight: A Substantive and Methodological Investigation." *Journal of Health and Social Behavior* 24:288–98.

———— and JOHN MIROWSKY. 1989. "Explaining the Social Patterns of Depression: Control and Problem-Solving—or Support and Talking." *Journal of Health and Social Behavior* 30:206–19.

————, JOHN MIROWSKY, and JOAN HUBER. 1983. "Dividing Work, Sharing Work, and In-Between: Marriage Patterns and Depression." *American Sociological Review* 48:809–23.

SEEMAN, MELVIN and TERESA E. SEEMAN. 1983. "Health Behavior and Personal Autonomy: A Longitudinal Study of the Sense of Control in Illness." *Journal of Health and Social Behavior* 24:144–59.

SEGOVIA, JORGE, ROY F. BARTLETT, and ALISON C. EDWARDS. 1989. "The Association Between Self-Assessed Health Status and Individual Health Practices." *Canadian Journal of Public Health* 80:32–37.

SELYE, HANS. 1985. "History and Present Status of the Stress Concept" Pp. 17–29 in *Stress and Coping: An Anthology,* edited by R. S. Lazarus and A. Monat. New York: Columbia University Press.

SOMERVELL, PHILIP D., BERTON H. KAPLAN, GERARDO HEISS, HERMAN A. TYROLER, DAVID G. KLEINBAUM, and PAUL A. OBERIST. 1989. "Psychological Distress as a Predictor of Mortality." *American Journal of Epidemiology* 130(5): 1013–23.

STAMPFER, M. J., G. A. COLDITZ, W. C. WILLETT, F. E. SPEIZER, C. H. HENNEKENS. 1988. "A Prospective Study of Moderate Alcohol Consumption and the Risk of Coronary Heart Disease and Stroke in Women." *New England Journal of Medicine* 319:267–73.

SURGEON GENERAL. 1982. *The Health Consequences of Smoking.* Rockville, MD: Public Health Service.

U.S. BUREAU OF THE CENSUS. 1985. *Statistical Abstract of the U.S.* Washington, D.C.: U.S. Government Printing Office (p. 288).

U.S. BUREAU OF LABOR STATISTICS. 1988. *Labor Force Statistics Derived From the Current Population Survey, 1948–1987. Bulletin 2307.* Washington, D.C.: Government Printing Office.

U.S. PREVENTIVE TASK FORCE. 1989. *Guide to Clinical Preventive Services.* Baltimore: Williams & Wilkins.

VAN ITALLIE, THEODORE B. 1985. "Health Implications of Overweight and Obesity in the United States." *Annals of Internal Medicine* 103:983–88.

VERBRUGGE, LOIS. 1983. "Multiple Roles and Physical Health of Men and Women." *Journal of Health and Social Behavior* 24:16–30.

————. 1985. "Gender and Health: An Update on Hypotheses and Evidence." *Journal of Health and Social Behavior* 26(3):156–82.

————. 1986. "From Sneezes to Adieu: Stages of Health for American Men and Women." *Social Science and Medicine* 22(11):1195–212.

————. 1989. "The Twain Meet: Empirical Explanations of Sex Differences in Health and Mortality." *Journal of Health and Social Behavior* 30(3):282–304.

WAKSBERG, JOSEPH. 1978. "Sampling Methods for Random Digit Dialing." *Journal of the American Statistical Association* 73:40–46.

WALDRON, INGRID. 1983. "Sex Differences in Illness Incidence, Prognosis, and Mortality: Issues and Evidence." *Social Science and Medicine* 17:1107–23.

WALDRON, INGRID and JERRY A. JACOBS. 1988. "Effects of Labor Force Participation on

Women's Health: New Evidence from a Longitudinal Study." *Journal of Occupational Medicine* 30:977–83.

WHEATON, BLAIR. 1980. "The Sociogenesis of Psychological Disorder: An Attributional Theory." *Journal of Health and Social Behavior* 21:100–24.

WINGARD, DEBORAH. 1982. "The Sex Differential in Mortality Rates: Demographic and Behavioral Factors." *American Journal of Epidemiology* 115(2):205–16.

WOLF, WENDY C. and NEIL D. FLIGSTEIN. 1979. "Sex and Authority in the Workplace: The Causes of Sexual Inequality." *American Sociological Review* 44(2):235–52.

Part V
ILLNESS BEHAVIOR AND THE SICK ROLE

This part focuses on illness behavior, and on the social factors that influence people's definitions of illness and their decision to use professional medical services. As Cockerham (2001) points out, illness behavior can include self-care, or self-initiated and self-managed attempts at responding to perceived symptoms of illness. Sociodemographic variables such as age, gender, ethnicity, and socioeconomic status have been shown to influence people's use of health care services. Further, social–psychological models have been developed to explain how and why people engage in illness behavior, which includes the activities of defining illness and seeking relief. In this section, the concept of illness behavior is discussed through three papers that address such issues as structural versus social construction approaches to understanding illness behavior; the roles of social networks in defining and responding to illness; stages in the social construction of disease; self-definitions of chronically ill patients, specifically adults with traumatic spinal cord injury; and uncertainty as a variable in the illness experience and lives of persons with AIDS.

The first paper in this section, by Alan Radley, investigates the first-person accounts of people with life-threatening or terminal illnesses as they construct their own particular social world around their health problems. But given the seriousness of their afflictions, their stories are not just mundane reports of what it is like to be sick; rather, these are chronicles of the illness experience that go beyond the ordinary. They reflect the feelings of suffering, horror, and apprehension that accompany their predicament. Radley argues that medical sociology needs to give proper due to the expressive form of such accounts and the powerful symbols they project into the the world of the sufferer.

Sing Lee's paper notes the manner in which anorexia nervosa is no longer a Western culture–bound syndrome, but has been configured as an Asian problem as well. This ailment, marked by serious and life-threatening weight loss primarily among young women, has generally been regarded as a pattern of behavior connected to Western values ("the cultural pursuit of thinness"). Dr. Lee argues that the cultural construction of this disorder has clearly expanded to encompass Asia and psychiatric practices have contributed to this development.

David Rier, a medical sociologist in Israel, provides a unique account of the critically ill patient in which he analyzes his own experience. He suggests that Parsons's concept of the sick role, especially the dependent status of sick persons in doctor–patient interaction, in not necessarily out of date. Rather, he finds that there are times when seriously ill patients are too sick to nego-tiate their care and simply have to trust in the decisions of their doctors. Although the general trend is toward greater equality for patients in the doctor–patient relationship, there are times when this is not the case.

REFERENCE

COCKERHAM, WILLIAM C. 2001. *Medical Sociology*, 8th Ed. Upper Saddle River, NJ: Pren-tice Hall.

THE AESTHETICS OF ILLNESS: NARRATIVE, HORROR, AND THE SUBLIME

Alan Radley
Loughborough University, United Kingdom

First-person accounts of life-threatening or terminal illness appear frequently in the academic literature and in the media. This paper takes up the question of how these accounts might provide, for their authors, a sense of coherence and freedom, and for their readers a grasp of suffering and its potential. By focusing upon the horrors integral to such accounts, the argument is made that such horrors are basic to the sufferer's symbolization of an illness-world. This world, rather like the adventure, is torn from life, grounded in the sensuous fragments through which its elusory powers are expressed. Seen as the problematization of life as a work of freedom, the illness account can then be analyzed as an aesthetic project. The reading discusses this proposal, distinguishing between aesthetics and aestheticization as social phenomena. It uses this distinction to make a critical observation upon attempts to understand suffering in the modern world in terms of power or of myth.

INTRODUCTION

In recent years there have been a number of accounts of illness—almost always serious illnesses such as cancer—written by sufferers. These have appeared in the popular press and in books inviting a more intellectual reflection. At one level, these stories concern encounters with medicine and disease. At another level, each is a personal narrative of the way that the person has coped with the life changes consequent upon the diagnosis, and the likelihood of leading life in the shadow of what has happened to them (Couser 1997; Frank 1995). The accounts that have appeared in the popular media and books have been considered to the journalistic

pieces, albeit ones that seem to be creating a new genre, or answering what might be a previously unmet need among the public to know about illness experience (Greenslade 1997). As far as the medical sociology literature is concerned, such accounts can be viewed from several distinct but overlapping perspectives. In one way, they are narratives similar to those collected by researchers, which have an undisputed place in the work of medical sociologists and anthropologists (Hyden 1997; Kleinman 1988). Analyses of such accounts have centered mainly upon the type of narrative (Mishler 1995; Robinson 1990) or upon what the narrative accomplishes. This latter function concerns either the articulation of the person's illness experience or its contribution to the individual's social context. From this point of view, narratives are evidence of what Frank (1997a) has called a "potential consciousness of illness"

Reprinted from *Sociology of Health & Illness*, vol. 21, no. 6 (1999), pp. 778–96, by permission of Blackwell Publishers Ltd./Editorial Board.

that bears witness to suffering in ways that have implications for those who are well, in addition to those who are ill. This is because such stories are about matters of love and death (not just life and death), which stand "on that creative threshold between the sublime and the mundane, light and dark, what we can know and what we never will" (Gerrard 1996).

The relevance of these writings for social science studies of health/illness extends beyond the (important) claim that they reveal how people cope with serious and terminal disease. These accounts have been described as being more than simply revelations because, in an important way, the act of telling is a means by which the person engages with difficult experiences so as to reformulate them (Kleinman 1988). Telling about one's illness provides both a model for analytic writing about the body (a "communicative body") and an opportunity for writer and reader together to be brought into a new relationship to each other (a "lived ethics of bodies") (Frank 1997b).

This reading takes up this theme, extending the argument that such accounts are significant by proposing that they are essentially exemplifications of a way of living. This means that they do more than report events which the person has suffered, or even provide an account of the author as principal player in the story. The key difference is that, by bearing witness to their illness and its treatment, these authors are fabricating a "world of illness" (Radley 1993). As part of this world, they, too, are refigured in relation to both disease and health. The question arises as to how this is achieved, and what form of symbolization might be involved. I shall argue that this is achieved through a portrayal of how to live with illness, rather than by a specification of events or actions alone. It is in the course of this portrayal that there is a transformation of the mundane world of disease and its treatment essential to an under-

standing of suffering. This presentational act of "showing forth," summarized here as *exemplification,* has been proposed as key to all aesthetic acts (Goodman 1968).

Taking this view involves finding the aesthetic in features of illness that are not usually considered to be relevant to the fields of beauty and pleasure. However, this is not to argue that the aesthetic is some ethereal flight from the fears and difficulties of serious illness. In stark contrast, the claim is that we find the aesthetic where we least expect to find it—grounded in matters reported as horrific by the sick and feared by the healthy. As a particular form of symbolism, the aesthetic project involves a vital engagement with features of suffering, and it is through this engagement that the sublime aspects of illness experience penetrate the sensuous and material world of disease and its treatment. However, just as the aesthetic is not confined to the ethereal, so the treatment of disease is not merely a matter of mundane practice. How this is possible, and its significance for the articulation of the position of the patient in the modern world, are the main issues for discussion in the present reading.

At one level, accounts of serious illness describe or denote (literal) happening in the life of the particular author. At another, by exemplifying symbolic acts in the person's life, they show how anyone might live in the shadow of serious illness. Symbolizing the patient's world is achieved through a figurative display of qualities that are not only denoted as present (or, by the same token, denied, like heroism), but are in some way demonstrated in the telling. This demonstration involves a showing forth of qualities that the person exemplifies. Through communicating encounters with medicine and the world of health, they allude to qualities that figuratively capture the writer's spirit or outlook. This mode of symbolization is characteristic of all, but not at all restricted to, artistic endeavor (Goodman 1968). [It has, for example, been regarded as a key orientation of method in phenomenology (Toombs 1992)]. In that sense, to join with another in the witnessing of his or her own suffering from disease is also to engage in an aesthetic act, in which the countenancing of the sublime is achieved in the light of horror and of pleasure.

The expressive potential of the illness narrative lies not just in the fact of what it deals with, but in what it says about the exigencies of chance, necessity, and the ways of rising to the unknown. In this it shares something with Simmel's (1959a) idea of the "adventure" as an experience where there is a dropping out of the ordinariness of life, a brush with something alien that is yet connected to its center (Frank 1995).[1] Now, what Simmel had in mind when he spoke of "the adventure" was clearly not a bout of serious illness, and there are important differences between the romantic notions that this idea conjures and the sufferings of, say, the cancer patient. Indeed, authors of cancer stories often remove themselves explicitly from the role of hero and combatant in the course of setting out experiences—first as patients, then as survivors, and finally as witnesses of what befell them. The point is that illness narratives, by virtue of their exemplifying a world of illness, reach further into everyday life than the sphere of mundane illness management that appears to contain them. They say something about how life itself—in this time and place—might be conducted in an ethical way (R. Williams 1993). What emerges is more than an account per se, more than just a personal story. There is a refiguring of the person as a new patient in the modern world, one who takes responsibility for his/her life-with-illness, even when that illness has a terminal prognosis.

The transformational potential of illness stories goes beyond the distinction that has, for some time, been drawn in medical soci-ology between the reified concepts of medicine and the consciousness of the patient (Taussig 1980); between the voice of the lifeworld and the voice of medicine (Mishler 1995); or even the difference between the acute and the chronic patient who repairs the breaches in everyday life through narrative reconstruction (Williams 1984). A consideration of illness accounts as aesthetic projects raises questions not only about the mode of symbolization involved in these communications (effectively, to open up what is meant by the term *illness experience*), but also about their role in the fabrication of ideas about health. To address these issues, it is necessary first to acknowledge features of illness experience that are often overlooked. Then one can examine how their transmutation is key to understanding the construction of accounts that deal in matters beyond the issue of illness management.

ACKOWLEDGING HORROR

It is a feature of most accounts of serious or life-threatening illness that they begin at or near diagnosis. As a result, aspects of everyday life that went before this fateful moment are often only briefly described, so that they are effectively unavailable to the reader. The immediate mobilization of medical treatment, with its technical vocabulary and its promise of clinical intervention, displaces the everyday world right from the beginning. It is necessary here to give some thought to what is displaced, not in the sense of these matters having been lost (for then they are already transformed) but as powers that are now either out of reach, or which cannot be disposed of at will. This displacement might involve not only disrupted work capacities and social contacts (the stuff of much empirical research), but also includes such matters as the person's dreams, wishes, and fancies. These are not mere fancies but the taken-for-granted capacity to conjure the world as a fabulous, tragic, or a poignant place. For sufferers, it is perhaps not surprising that this way of apprehending the world—essentially that of everyday aesthetics—is marginalized to the point of extinction just after hearing of such a diagnosis. The disintegration of life under these circumstances arises not so much from a splitting of plans and routines, but from the altered significance of everything in life, where each fragment is drained of the totality of meaning that is the taken-for-grantedness which is summarized as a person's biography (Bury 1982). It is in that sense that each object attains a separate weight of obligation as part of a past prior to diagnosis, deriving from its place in the order of things that led up to it, or is its history. In that sense, one of the losses sustained in serious illness, sometimes termed a "loss of self" (Charmaz 1983), comes from the double movement of the draining of meaning from things and their additive weight as objects that have achieved an alien independence from the sick person.

What is referred to here is the loss of those powers that are normally considered aesthetic—the ability to engage in fancies, to contemplate beauty, and to create space and time for frivolous activity. This fall into the mundane presages a "colonization of the person" by medicine (Frank 1995). But it is not medical treatment as such that undermines these aesthetic powers. Rather, medicine attaches its separate initiatives to the objectified concerns (about one's body, about life) that are symptomatic of loss of self and the alienation of the mundane. It is for this reason that existential concerns are inextricably linked to uncertainties within clinical and scientific practice (Adamson 1997). Following the diagnosis, there then appear, simultaneously, the uncertainties and fears surrounding the future, so that out of this global anxiety are distilled particular concerns for loved ones, for friends, and for treasured pastimes.

It is against this background that speaking of aesthetics seems both inappropriate and perhaps morally offensive. However, I want to argue that it is precisely this context that provides the necessary conditions for fashioning accounts essential to the reestablishment of a sense of direction and coherence. Clearly, this means more than saying that people have to experience extremes of anxiety or suffering to write about them. Instead, my claim is that it is in the chasm between the mundane and the terrifying that the horrors of illness experience are forged. And it is the communication of these horrors, or rather the aesthetic form of this communication, that is essential to the symbolization of the world of suffering that we term the "illness account."

Horrors include specific events that are imbued with meaning deriving from the transmutation of the ordinary by the terrifying, often in the service of treatment. For example, Arthur Frank (1991) describes how, on returning to his hospital room during his treatment for cancer, he found a new sign on his door which read "lymphoma," a diagnosis of which he had not yet been told. Jackie Stacey tells of the moment when, after surgery for the removal of an ovarian cyst, a doctor gave her the diagnosis that it was malignant. This message was communicated to her among a group of nurses whom she believed were not prepared for this event. She goes on:

> I just make it down to the toilets, trailing the drip, hand on wound, surgical stockings on both legs. Away from those 20 or so strangers in front of whom I have just been given the worst news I could imagine, I look at myself in the mirror. Is this what a person with cancer looks like (1997: 105)?

And John Diamond describes how, before the operation for cancer of the tongue, the hospital dentist explains the use of a gel that he must rub on his gums once his salivary glands have been removed:

With half my saliva gone that neutralizing effect would be reduced and I'd need to rub the fluoride gel into my gums every night.

For how long?

Oh, you know. For the rest of your life (1998: 84).

These are examples of horrors, in the sense that I want to use the term. Their effect is achieved by the appearance of the unthinkable in the guise of the innocuous—the notice that simply informs, the nurses who would provide support, the information so casually given. There are two points to be made here. One concerns the effect of these movements upon the sufferers concerned. In each case these instances are carefully recorded in the accounts, and (in Frank's case certainly) are able later on to elicit an involuntary "tightening" of the body as a memory of their original effect. For that reason they stand as moments that symbolize the sufferers' sense of alienation or colonization by medicine, something that these accounts are partly aimed at overcoming. Such horrors are integral to the fashioning of the aesthetic in illness. This is not mere platitude, even though it is clear that an account of illness experience must be grounded in reports of suffering of some kind. However, the claim concerning the central role of horror turns upon the point that the aesthetic is grounded in the sensuous: It is not the creation of some ethereal sphere into which the author escapes from the pains of illness. From the point of view of ethics, in her account of living with terminal cancer, Gillian Rose (1995) adopts the recommendation to "Keep your mind in hell and despair not" as a way of remaining in the sphere of the sensuous, close to what she terms the "edges of life."

Second, the idea of horrors as being in part defined through their presentation in the context of the ordinary, or the unimpeachable, is not restricted to the sphere of illness alone. In her analysis of horror ("death infecting life"), Kristeva describes seeing in the museum at Auschwitz a heap of children's shoes, something she had seen elsewhere, "under a Christmas tree, for instance, dolls I believe" (1982: 4). And this matters, because the mode of presentation is key to understanding the kind of experience that is being set out for the reader of the illness account. In the examples given above, the telling of these moments is a concrete instantiation, a portrayal of that which is somehow made worse by the good intentions of medical staff, the casualness of a remark, or even the innocence of children. It is interesting that the nurse's use of medical terminology, far from eliminating metaphor as Sontag (1978a) supposed, becomes a metonym for a sense of depersonalization in Frank's experience.

The issue is one of how horror is elicited through the form of the presentation, either enacted or fashioned in the sufferer's account. The key lies, in some way, in a portrayal in which dreaded but unspecified events are figured in the benign, and especially in the innocent. Wittgenstein (1979) discussed a similar point in his commentary on Frazer's *Golden Bough*. The particular issue pertains to the Beltane festival, in which a cake baked with knobs on is divided among those present, the person drawing the slice with a particular knob being designated the symbolic sacrificial victim. Wittgenstein says that what is sinister about this account is not the history of it (i.e., that it truly represents something that once happened), nor that human suffering per se is implicated, but that, "the fact that for the lots they use a cake has something especially terrible (almost like betrayal through a kiss) and that this does seem especially terrible to us is of central importance in our investigation of practices like these" (1979: 16e). Questioning the experience of horror as being one of interpretation, Wittgenstein alights precisely upon the idea that horror is significant through its mode of appearance, that it is *made more ter-*

rible by virtue of the way it is portrayed, not in the way that it is explained.

It is in the allusive portrayal of the unwanted and unknown that horror is to be grasped (e.g., in the presentation of extreme pain, ultimate despair, or death). This form is presentational in the sense that the unknowable is symbolized through display rather than through denotation. Spelling it out (if one could) would belie the experience of horror as a "terror that dissembles" (Kristeva 1982). It fashions, not just a meaning, but a *world of being* into which the account admits us, as readers. That world is extensive across the sufferer's life, a totality that is at the center of everything he or she does; [John Diamond (1998) says he wrote about his cancer because at the time he could think of nothing else]. So, it is not the liberal statement (or the denoted act) that he will have to rub gel into his gums for the rest of his life that is horrific. It is the apprehension of his experience of which this stands as but a sample, though a fragment, which symbolizes the totality of his illness-world. Horrors are the stuff of elusive powers in human experience, made tangible in these accounts through the grasping of sensuous fragments that metaphorically express them.

In his interpretation of Edmund Burke's philosophy, Lyotard provides a commentary relevant to the ideas put forward here, in saying that, "there is another kind of pleasure that is bound to a passion far stronger than satisfaction, and that is suffering and impending death" (1984: 40). For Burke, this spiritual passion was synonymous with terror, and what is terrifying is that the ongoingness (the "happenings") of life will no longer continue to happen. Aesthetic conduct, by distancing this terror, produces a kind of "delight," so that thanks to it, "the soul is returned to the agitated zone between life and death, and this agitation is its health and its life." It is in this sense that we can speak of the sublime in the context of narratives concerning the horrors of extreme suffering.

ILLNESS: IMPRESSIONS OF THE SUBLIME

If the sphere of art per se is the domain where the sublime is witnessed, then autobiographical accounts of illness can be treated as evidence of the aesthetic in present-day society. There is no question here of equating illness (or its reporting) with art by fiat. Rather, there is an obligation on the sociologist to be attentive to "the different kinds of shape and significance that humans give to their creativity" (Osborne 1997). This is made possible by focusing upon exemplification as a particular form of symbolization, in which individuals are able to transform the world through displays that create their own sense of the present, and articulate significant features of social life. Catching up the threads of the moment to create the possibility of another way of living alludes to a totality, a way of being in the world, while at the same time lending significance to the specific things said or done. In terms of illness experience, this means that the illness account witnesses the sublime through the evocation of a world that is figuratively, as well as literally real. If the account were not of this kind—if it were only a story that recounted that this happened, or that the patient was told these things—the reader would neither be repelled nor moved by the evocation of how illness is borne.

The idea of accounts fashioning a "world of illness" implies a realm of experience that is distinguishable (if not wholly distinct) from what one might call the "mundane." Effectively, however, the mundane appears or is produced at the same time as the aesthetic sphere, in being that from which it can then be distinguished, rather like the "ordinary life" from which the adventure is torn. In this context, the evocation of the world of suffering and survival is achieved through a narrative form in which certain moments or events exemplify matters of life and death.

These are matters which cannot be adequately explicated. Such events might be drawn from times of treatment, or when with family, or from ideas that derive from other realms of everyday life. As in the configuration of any aesthetic sphere, signs or objects exemplify ideas that do not normally belong to them (Goodman 1968). In Geertz's words, expressive forms works because "properties conventionally ascribed to certain things are unconventionally ascribed to others, which are then seen to possess them" (1972: 26). This is most clearly seen in the case of descriptions of times or situations which symbolize for the person the state of their illness. For Arthur Frank, in chronic pain due to a failure to diagnose cancer, it occurred one night as he looked from a window in his home:

> Making my way upstairs, I was stopped on the landing by the sight—the vision really—of a window. Outside the window I saw a tree, and the streetlight just beyond was casting the tree's reflection on the frosted glass. Here suddenly was beauty, found in the middle of a night that seemed to be only darkness and pain (1991: 33).

Frank explicitly denies that the window was a (mere) metaphor, in that he says it did not figure the pain he felt. The view was just what it was. However, later in the book he goes on to say:

> In that frosted window I saw myself. Not the self I see in a mirror, but a world I am so completely a part of that is too is myself. The sight allowed me to exist outside my body's pain and at the same time to see why that pain was part of the same world as the window, as necessary to that world as the window's beauty was (1991: 141).

Frank offers a small poem to this experience and then makes two points that bear upon the argument being made here. First, the beauty of the window is experienced as a restoration of *coherence*, so that it is a fragment in which a totality of meaning is apprehended. And second, he argues that the coherence does not go without saying; it requires *expression*. Of course, not only the poem written at the time but the subsequent account of it is expressive. These two points—concerning coherence and expression—are central to the analysis of the aesthetic in social life (Frisby 1985; Simmel 1968). The first indicates the time-space boundedness of the experience, and the second the role of distance from the object in the fashioning of expressive forms. The fragment is what it is because in transcending the mundane its various aspects are sensuously related by properties that are metaphorically possessed. This notion of metaphorical possession becomes here a post hoc reflection: Phenomenally, what is figuratively real about this for Frank has the quality of a transparent vision (a sensuous realty), so that it is apprehended not merely as possessing truth, but as truth itself (for a similar argument from Simmel, see Frisby, 1985: 47).

The view that the aesthetic sphere is essentially distinct comes traditionally from the belief that art is separate from the everyday world, a view that was held by Simmel (1959b) and is still held today (Lyotard 1984). Illness accounts, in bearing witness to horrors and revelations, partake of both the mundane and the sublime, which are apprehended as such only in relation to each other, and which are irreducible one to the other. But the sublime is always apprehended by virtue of the mundane, in the sensuous grounding of the body in the world (Merleau-Ponty 1968). Arthur Frank's window partakes of both mundane and aesthetic worlds, which location defines it as a fragment in relation to the totalities of meaning it expresses. This situation can be elucidated by recourse to Simmel's (1959b) illustration of the vase, which he uses as an example of how certain artifacts stand in two worlds at one and the same time. More precisely, Simmel pointed to the handle (on the vase) as that point where these two worlds are both located. The handle is both the means by which the vase is grasped and is aesthetically pleasing, in part because its shape harmonizes the two worlds.[2] This underlines the experience of the sublime as being at once transcendent and immanent in the object, so that which is expressed in the account of illness is evoked by virtue of what happens to the person as an embodied being.

If illness accounts are a recovery of the sick person's sense of identity, having an ethical as well as an aesthetic dimension to them, then the handles that provide for the articulation of the sublime will sometimes be fortuitous fragments, not always major events. In the mundane world, these are likely to concern the effects of clinical diagnosis of serious disease, of medical treatment and of the impact of events upon the family and friends. That is, the fragment that exemplifies the sublime is not necessarily the beautiful or something that has been prejudged as significant. Indeed, reading these accounts, one is struck by how often they are presented as narratives in the sense of storied tellings with a linear plotline that yields to formal analysis (Hyden 1997; Mishler 1995; Robinson 1990). The everyday—and not so everyday—events that are strung together appear as mundane because, as previously argued, the horrors of illness are consequent upon the draining of positive significance from things in the person's world.

Seeing these accounts as narratives rather than aesthetic projects, the telling about horrors is a prelude to the story of living with suffering and surviving it. But from a perspective sensitive to aesthetic practice, events that evoke horrors offer the potential for a transmutation of feeling. What has been called a recovery of oneself from the colonizing attentions of medicine owes its ethical significance to this transmutation. And while *how* it is told is clearly important, under-

standing *what* is being said owes everything to our being embodied readers, for whom issues such as horrors and the sublime extend well beyond what can be said in words. For example, Arthur Frank describes his three months of chemotherapy as a time when "a foot of tubing was hanging out of my chest" in order that the drugs could be delivered and blood samples taken. This line he saw as "another flag planted by the medical system" on his body, something which he resented as much as he needed it:

> I needed the line not only for relief from pain, but also as a way of displacing my larger fears about cancer. I was able to refocus these fears— whether chemotherapy was working, how long it would go on—onto the daily problems of managing the line (1991: 77).

Here Frank identifies the line as something that connected him (literally) to the system that allowed fears to flourish, and yet as something that (both metaphorically and literally) provided scope for self-care. But there was more to this, in that, because the line and its exit site needed daily attention:

> The line also refocused the relationship Cathie [his wife] and I had fallen into. By the time it was installed, the hospital had pretty well taken me over. Although Cathie was usually with me during the physician's visit, the doctors and nurses never acknowledged her presence (1991: 77–78). . . . However, Cathie took over the disinfecting, flushing and bandaging, and these tasks became a daily ritual between us. We laughed that it was our special time together, but these moments of quiet in a hectic life were a gift. . . . When I went back to being an inpatient, Cathie and I joked about how much better her antiseptic procedures were than those of the nurses who dressed the line (1991: 78).

This incident shows how a part of the world of medicine (i.e., the line) that signified the terrors that illness can hold was apparently transformed into a fragment that exemplified another world, one which Frank shared with his wife. The other world is also a world of illness, but one that creates its own time-space that both of them could occupy. In the terms of the argument put forward here, this is an aesthetic achievement, a conjoint witnessing of the sublime. But it is not an achievement of other-worldliness, of an acorporeal, asensual existence. The line is more than a connection between Frank and his medical carers, more than a link between him and his wife: It stands in both the world of medicine and the world of illness which the Franks were able to conjure. The sensual, in this case, is grounded in the cleaning and disinfecting of the body, by virtue of which it is possible to instantiate, to conjure this different world. The line exists simultaneously in the mundane and in the aesthetic worlds, so that on reflection it could be said to stand for something, or to signify in a different way.

What this means is that the production of the aesthetic sphere—creating a world of illness that is not just a world of medical care—occurs by virtue of some specific aspect of the mundane that exemplifies properties which it does not usually possess. This indicates that the transmutation of horror does not have to be achieved separately for each incident alone. The occasion of the line reported by Frank produces a total world—albeit brief—that has the potential to color all of his experiences within and outside that other world, the one of medical care. This idea of the transmutation of suffering by virtue of our being embodied is reminiscent of the view put forward by Walter Benjamin:

If the theory is correct that feeling is not located in the head, that we sentiently experience a window, a cloud, a tree, not in our brains but, rather, in the place where we see it, then we are, in looking at our beloved, too, outside ourselves. But in a torment of tension and ravishment. Our feeling, dazzled, flutters like a flock of birds in the woman's radiance. And as birds seek refuge in the leafy recesses of a tree, feelings escape into the shaded wrinkles, the awkward movements and inconspicuous blemishes of the body we love, where they can lie low in safety. And no passer-by would guess that it is just here, in what is defective and censurable, that the fleeting darts of adoration nestle (1986: 68).

This excerpt can be read either as a view of perception or as a further example of the way that the sublime is grasped in the sensual, and that bearing witness to it is effectively made in the context of the transmutation of what is deemed abhorrent.

AESTHETICS AND NARRATIVE

Speaking of accounts of illness as being aesthetic projects moves beyond seeing them either as representations of past events or as narratives per se, as this latter term has come to be used in medical sociology (Hyden 1997). The idea of an aesthetic project has been introduced in this paper to point up the kinds of special features that these accounts display. Among these is the idea that writing the account is part of coming to terms with disease, illness and an altered health consciousness. This not only underlines the break with naive realism, but also with naive constructionism, in the sense that the account is taken as a text that is to be interpreted only through a formal analysis of its structure, type, or process. If treated in this way, those physical and ethical features that are essential to narrative's aesthetic significance are made to reappear within the analysis of the text. As a result, aesthetic issues are admitted as the vital but *theoretically* unacknowledged background that makes selected excerpts open to glossing. This retention of the aesthetic as a tacit component is necessary for any analysis of suffering wanting to show why anything said, or how it is said, should matter at all. This, however, is effectively a reification of discourse (and a marginalization of the sublime), and becomes possible once the ethical and elusory issues involved in the telling of such stories are excluded (Radley 1995, 1997).

One of the key issues, then, is the relationship between the account and the events that it describes. Seen as an aesthetic project, the account is just one communication (albeit a special one) in an ongoing reflection upon the illness condition. That is, it exemplifies a world of illness—an imaginary sphere—that finds reinstantiation time and time again in various contexts and moments of the person's life. So, in describing a significant moment (one that captures something important about being ill), the ascetic discipline of narrative shows forth this essence in literary form. It is not that some aesthetic essence is carried over, or better described, but that the meaning is achieved by virtue of being symbolized in the way set out above. This is indeed a kind of construction, but the idea is not reducible to the narrative forms or rhetorical devices that are essential for the achievement or ascetic distance, on which an aesthetic projection depends. Such a view separates the material and sensuous from the linguistic, so that the constructionist answer is given before, rather than following the analysis.

Once the illness account is conceived as an aesthetic project, it is no longer possible to see it primarily as a commentary, or even more important, as something that medical sociologists or others can reduce to hypothesis or to developmental explanation. This might appear to be a contentious claim given that, within their own accounts, several authors—among them medical sociologists—provide commentaries upon the experiences they recount. Certainly it is possible to offer explanations, but the key question here is whether what is significant in the story—the horror and the apprehension of the sublime—is given through explanation or primarily through the exemplification of the author's world? I propose that it is only

through exemplification that the recognition of suffering is given to the reader. Going one step beyond this, one can say that to understand the sufferer's situation requires no *further* explanation. This is true of all such experiences, as Wittgenstein argued from a different perspective:

> I think one reason why the attempt to find an explanation is wrong is that we have only to put together in the right way what we *know*, without adding anything, and the satisfaction we are trying to get from the explanation comes of itself. . . . An historical explanation, an explanation as an hypothesis of the development, is only *one* kind of summary of the data . . . (1979: 8e, emphases in the original).

Therefore, accounts of serious illness attain significance because they exemplify a life (a world), not just because they explain the experience of treatment. The response, which they evoke in the reader who comes to share in that world, follows because, in Wittgenstein's words, "*we* impute it from an experience in ourselves" (1979: 16e, emphasis in the original). In the terms of the argument presented here, that imputation is a form of symbolic communication that employs exemplification as well as denotation. This is showing forth or "seeing as," not just denoting what happened, when, where, and in what order. Sociological analysis—whether of a modernist or postmodernist variety—certainly illuminates the development of the circumstances under which certain kinds of illness experience become possible, but their explanations cannot substitute (nor remove the need for) the *portrayal* of the suffering that they seek to explain.[3]

This emphasis upon aesthetics provides a critical perspective upon approaches to illness that depend exclusively upon the study of history and governance, upon various kinds of formalist analyses of narrative, and upon the (medical) realism that remains if one sees only aestheticization, and hence romanticism in talk about illness (Sontag 1978a). As has already been acknowledged, illness talk—in its various forms and legitimation—is illuminated by historical analyses that uncover the various discourses that enable and hinder it. Indeed, because the potential space of (i.e., the call for) the aesthetic response is socially and historically contingent, it can only be explained by tracing out the changing means by which consciousness of our world is attained (Hunter 1996; Lasch 1996). This is similarly the case with respect to Sontag's exposure of romantic myths that contribute to a reduction in the dignity of the suffering. But both explanations—one based upon power, the other upon metaphor—*presume* the significance that aesthetic judgment *has already accorded the object* of their respective analyses. Because of this presumption, neither of them is able to show the significance of the aesthetic dimension in illness, and how this capacity to fabricate and to conjure is fundamental to the shared experience of human suffering.

AESTHETICS AND AESTHETICIZATION IN THE SPHERE OF HEALTH/ILLNESS

The argument has been made that accounts of illness are more than narratives—in the sense of storied tellings—inasmuch as they are exemplars of a way of being in the world. This should not be mistaken for a plea to see the illness narrative as a metaphor for life, which option is only there by virtue of a post hoc reflection upon narrative and life as if they were two aspects of a figure of speech. Instead, it is important to recognize that the performative unfolding of the account, its reading, initiates the reader into an aesthetic/ethical relationship with its object. While the illness experience is, in a sense, "torn from life," its form is not coterminous with the account, which both extends beyond events in the mundane world of disease, and continues beyond the end of treatment. The "account as a whole" (the account as read) fashions a distinct world lived as a totality, and this is achieved by virtue of the transmutations of the ordinary that have been discussed

above. What is "adventure-like" in the account of illness is that unfolding of events and actions that, dealing with chance and necessity, exemplifies significant meaning about life and how one lives it (G. Williams 1993). This analysis is useful as showing the way that illness accounts are always more than "stories about": they are also ways of "seeing as."

Nevertheless, this paper must address the question as to whether it is sensible to propose an aesthetic of illness, or whether such a treatment merely extends to this field the idea that aesthetics permeate modern society—the aestheticization thesis (Featherstone 1991; Maffesoli 1991, 1996). This issue has been crystallized by Osborne (1997), who asks whether the aestheticization of the problematic of social science is achieved only by the failure of critics to analyze art as an institution. The idea that, during the 19th century, imagination was emancipated from art makes possible the claim that in the course of the modern and postmodern eras the "unaesthetic is made, or understood to be aesthetic" (Welsch 1997: 7). In the sphere of health this would embrace those various lifestyles choices that equate good health with the consumption of what is thought to be beautiful, and which is believed to enhance the individual. This occurs at both surface and deep levels. For example, cosmetic surgery enhances personal appearance, while genetic engineering prizes open the fundamentals of life, making possible choices where there was previously only authority and fate. And as has been shown above, there has emerged a concern with the ethics of illness that provides a prima facie case for the analysis of the experience of illness in these terms.

One response to the consideration of the aesthetic is that illness is an inappropriate subject for treatment in these terms, because to undertake this analysis is surely to lead back to the romanticization of suffering criticized by Sontag (1978a) in her essay on illness as metaphor. Furthermore, the treatment of social life as the territory of homo aestheticus [the aesthicization thesis, Maffesoli (1991)] is arguably limited, in that it leads away from the analysis of the particulars of aesthetic practice that makes for an understanding of what is special about the modality. Contemporary societies may have undergone changes in their organizational forms that can be summarized under the term *aesthetic*. However, this takes us no nearer to understanding how, in the experience of illness, ideas are fabricated and directed toward issues that, in their significance, are believed to have some bearing upon the concerns of art.

Drawing upon commentators on the postmodern conditions, Osborne (1997) argues that what is required to understand the aesthetic is an analysis relating to the values which are attached to it: namely, the concrete shaping of freedom—or rather the aesthetic problematization of life as a work of freedom (Foucault 1984, cited in Osborne 1997); and bearing witness to the sublime, or to the inexpressible (Lyotard 1984). However, he is at pains to show the "comparative irrelevance" of these writers to the aesthetic sphere (thereby removing the analysis from the general postmodernist debate) in order to highlight the distinction between core aesthetic practices and the effects of aestheticization. Also, because the emergence of the aesthetic is a modernist as well as a postmodernist concern, this argument distances the asetheticization of social life from the attempt to take the aesthetic dimension seriously within sociological analysis (Simmel 1991; see also Frisby 1985). In part, this is because the analysis of the objectification of forms in the sensual life of the present acknowledges those ascetic values that are key to artistic endeavor (Benjamin 1970).

Where does this brief analysis bring us on the question of aesthetics and illness? First, it shows that one should not confuse asetheticization with aesthetic practice, even while acknowledging that the emergence of the aesthetic dimension in theorizing is contemporaneous with modernity and the postmodern. Illness experience has been shaped by the dis-solution of boundaries and the fragmentation of interests in which the diffraction of morality now appears as an "*ethos* that comes from below" (Mafffesoli 1991). This goes some way toward explaining the emergence of the self-caring patient in recent years, who then questions the authority of doctors and the expectations of the healthy. However, it falls far short of providing an account of the "problematisation of illness as a work of freedom," or of how individuals who have written of their experiences "bear witness to the sublime." To achieve this requires an attempt to engage with those aspects of the illness experience that share with the sphere of art those values held to be central to it. Paradoxically, this becomes possible only because of the social changes during the 19th century that released the aesthetic from art itself (Eagleton 1990; Buck-Morse 1989).

To sum up the orientation of this paper, while aestheticization must be recognized as a feature of modern life, this is quite different from assuming that it is synonymous with the aesthetic dimension in health and illness. Taking the latter dimension seriously means addressing those practices by which sufferers attempt to bear witness to what they have experienced and how these symbolize issues of life, death, and of living with illness in the modern world. The recognition of exemplification as key to understanding expressive forms is in line with the idea that the significance of social life is grasped through the example, through the "fortuitous fragment" (Simmel 1968). Generalizing this capacity, Frank (1997a: 134) draws upon the work of Goldmann (1976) to say that "the value of literature is to exemplify the limits that the thought of its age could extend to." In a similar vein, Sontag (1978b: 42) wrote (in her attack upon interpretation in art criticism), "for the modern consciousness, the artist (replacing the saint) is the exemplary sufferer. And among artists, the writer, the man of words, is the person to whom we look to be able best to express his [sic] suffering." This is consistent with the view espoused by Nietzsche that art is now the sole antidote to the dread and horror inspired by existential reality, replacing religion in this role (O'Toole 1996). However, the issues discussed here do resonate with the echoes of religion and the sacred, of which it has been reported that there are fragments in many biographies exhibiting a creative response to illness (R. Williams 1993).

Given the preceding, there is a need for medical sociology to give proper due to the expressive form of such accounts, going beyond interpreting them in terms of their content or even treating them in terms of their different formal characteristics. While accounts of illness are not to be assimilated to the general category "art," they do partake of symbolic powers that derive from that special sphere. An important outcome of this is the transparency of what is presented—experiencing the sensuousness, the horrors or the vitality of life itself. Thus, an account of illness experience should show not just what it means, nor just how it is what it is, but "that it is what it is" (Sontag 1978b). And insofar as these symbolic powers are there as a potential, they are not limited to the sick academic or journalist but are there for everyone threatened by serious illness.

NOTES

1. Robinson (1990) treats the adventure as one kind of account within a typology of narrative forms. Frank shows how an illness narrative can be analyzed as a journey or quest, breaking it down into three temporal stages of *departure, initiation,* and *return* (1995: 116–119). However, he is careful to distinguish the "quest narrative," with its risk of romanticization, from narrative as testimony (1995: 134–136).

2. Simmel (1959b) makes this point in relation to the handle of a vase, which exists both in the mundane world (it holds water) and in the aesthetic sphere, as a work of art. The handle is important for Simmel because it seems to harmonize these two worlds. While this might be true in relation to art per se, there are no grounds for arguing anything similar for the aesthetic dimension to illness.

3. In a recent chapter examining the role of governance in health, Petersen (1997: 190) says that authors such as Beck and Giddens, "can be criticised for their lack of attention to the aesthetic-expressive dimension of the modern self." And yet no mention of aesthetics in relation to health appears elsewhere in this volume.

REFERENCES

ADAMSON, C. (1997) Existential and clinical uncertainty in the medical encounter: an idiographic account of an illness trajectory defined by Inflammatory Bowel Disease and Avascular Necrosis, *Sociology of Health and Illness,* 19, 133–59.

BENJAMIN, W. (1970) *Illuminations.* Arendt, H. (ed) London: Jonathan Cape.

BENJAMIN, W. (1986) One-way street. In Demetz, P. (ed) *Reflections: Essays, Aphorisms and Biographical Writings.* New York: Schocken Books.

BUCK-MORSE, S. (1989) *The Dialectics of Seeing: Walter Benjamin and the Arcades Project.* Cambridge, Mass.: MIT Press.

BURY, M. (1982) Chronic illness as biographical disruption, *Sociology of Health and Illness,* 4, 167–82.

CHARMAZ, K. (1983) Loss of self: a fundamental form of suffering in the chronically ill, *Sociology of Health and Illness,* 5, 168–95.

COUSER, G.T. (1997) *Recovering Bodies: Illness, Disability and Life Writing.* Madison, Wisc.: University of Wisconsin Press.

DIAMOND, J. (1998) *C: Because Cowards Get Cancer Too . . .* London: Vermillion.

EAGLETON, T. (1990) *The Ideology of the Aesthetic.* Oxford: Blackwell.

FEATHERSTONE, M. (1991) *Consumer Culture and Postmodernism.* London: Sage.

FOUCAULT, M. (1984) *Dits et Ecrits.* Trans. IV, 1954–1988. Paris: Gallimard.

FRANK, A.W. (1991) *At the Will of the Body: Reflections on Illness.* Boston: Houghton Mifflin.

FRANK, A.W. (1995) *The Wounded Storyteller: Body, Illness and Ethics.* Chicago: University of Chicago Press.

FRANK, A.W. (1997a) Illness as moral occasion, *Health,* 1, 131–48.

FRANK, A.W. (1997b) Narrative witness to bodies: a response to Alan Radley, *Body and Society,* 3, 103–9.

FRISBY, D. (1985) *Fragments of Modernity: Theories of Modernity in the Work of Simmel, Kracauer and Benjamin.* Cambridge: Polity Press.

GEERTZ, C. (1972) Deep play: notes on the Balinese cockfight, *Daedalus,* 101, 1–37.

GERRARD, N. (1996) Hello darkness, my old friend. *Observer, Review,* 7, 9 June.

GOLDMANN, L. (1976) *Cultural Creation.* Bart Grahl, Trans. St. Louis: Telos Press.

GOODMAN, N. (1968) *Languages of Art: an Approach to a Theory of Symbols.* Indianapolis: Bobbs-Merrill.

GREENSLADE, R. (1997) Heading towards the exit, *Guardian, Media,* 6–7, 11 August.

HUNTER, I. (1996) Aesthetics and the arts of life. In Grace, H. (ed) *Aesthesia and the Economy of the Senses.* Sydney: University of Western Sydney.

HYDEN, L.-C. (1997) Illness and narrative, *Sociology of Health and Illness,* 19, 48–69.

KLEINMAN, A. (1988) *The Illness Narratives.* New York: Basic Books.

KRISTEVA, J. (1982) *Powers of Horror: an Essay on Subjection.* New York: Columbia University Press.

LASCH, S. (1966) The consequences of reflexivity: notes toward a theory of the object. Paper to conference on 'Signatures of Knowledge', Bielefeld University.

LYOTARD, J.-F. (1984) The sublime and the avant-garde, *Art Forum,* 22, 36–43.

MAFFESOLI, M. (1991) The ethics of aesthetics, *Theory, Culture and Society,* 8, 7–20.

MAFFESOLI, M. (1996) *The Time of the Tribes: The Decline of Individualism in Mass Society.* London: Sage.

MERLEAU-PONTY, M. (1968) *The Visible and the Invisible.* Evanston: Northwestern University Press.

MISHLER, E. G. (1995) Models of narrative analysis: a typology, *Journal of Narrative and Life History,* 5, 87–123.

OSBORNE, T. (1997) Review article: the aesthetic problematic, *Economy and Society,* 26, 126-46.

O'TOOLE, R. (1996) Salvation, redemption and community: reflections on the aesthetic cosmos, *Sociology of Religion,* 57, 127–48.

PETERSEN, A. (1997) Risk, governance and the New Public Health. In Petersen, A. and Bunton R. (eds) *Foucault, Health and Medicine.* London: Routledge.

RADLEY, A. (1993) Introduction. In Radley, A. (ed) *Worlds of Illness: Biographical and Cultural Perspectives on Health and Disease.* London: Routledge.

RADLEY, A. (1995) The elusory body and social constructionist theory, *Body and Society,* 1, 3–23.

RADLEY, A. (1997) The triumph of narrative? A reply to Arthur Frank, *Body and Society,* 3, 93–101.

ROBINSON, I. (1990) Personal narratives, social careers and medical courses: analysing life trajectories in autobiographies of people with multiple sclerosis, *Social Science and Medicine,* 30, 1173–86.

ROSE, G. (1995) *Love's Work.* London: Chatto and Windus.

SIMMEL, G. (1959a) The adventure. In Wolff, H.K. (ed) *Georg Simmel, 1858–1918: A Collection of Essays.* Columbus: Ohio State University Press.

SIMMEL, G. (1959b) The handle. In Wolff, H.K. (ed) *Georg Simmel, 1858–1918: A Collection of Essays.* Columbus: Ohio State University Press.

SIMMEL, G. (1991) The problem of style, *Theory, Culture and Society,* 8, 63–71.

SIMMEL, G. (1968) Sociological aesthetics. In Etzkorn, P. Trans. *Georg Simmel: The Conflict in Modern Culture and Other Essays.* New York: Teachers College Press.

SONTAG, S. (1978a) *Illness as Metaphor.* New York: Farrar, Straus and Giroux.

SONTAG, S. (1978b) *Against Interpretation: and Other Essays.* New York: Octagon.

STACEY, J. (1997) *Teratologies: A Cultural Study of Cancer.* London: Routledge.

TAUSSIG, M.T. (1980) Reification and the consciousness of the patient, *Social Science and Medicine,* 14B, 3–13.

TOOMBS, S. K. (1992) *The Meaning of Illness: a Phenomenological Account of the Different Perspectives of Physician and Patient.* Dordrecht: Kluwer.

WELSCH, W. (1997) *Undoing Aesthetics.* London: Sage.

WILLIAMS, G. H. (1984) The genesis of chronic illness: narrative reconstruction, *Sociology of Health and Illness,* 6, 174–200.

WILLIAMS, G. H. (1993) Chronic illness and the pursuit of virtue in everyday life. In Radley, A. (ed) *Worlds of Illness: Biographical and Cultural Perspectives on Health and Disease.* London: Routledge.

WILLIAMS, R. (1993) Religion and illness. In Radley, A. (ed) *Worlds of Illness: Biographical and Cultural Perspectives on Health and Disease.* London: Routledge.

WITTGENSTEIN, L. (1979) *Remarks on Frazer's Golden Bough.* Rhees, R. (ed) Retford: Brynmill.

RECONSIDERING THE STATUS OF ANOREXIA NERVOSA AS A WESTERN CULTURE-BOUND SYNDROME

Sing Lee
The Chinese University of Hong Kong

Based on Ritenbaugh's 1982 definition, this essay reconsiders the status of anorexia nervosa as a Western culture-bound syndrome (CBS). It argues that anorexia nervosa, in its culturally reconstructed fat phobic form, is no longer bound to specific Western localities. Instead, it may be conceived as being grounded in the transnational culture of 'modernity,' characterized by an internationalized socioeconomic stratum now found in many rapidly urbanizing parts of the world, and composed of increased affluence, as well as the globalization of fat phobia and diffusion of biomedical technology. Although the treatment implication of Ritenbaugh's CBS concept may appear to be misplaced from the clinician's pragmatic perspective, its salience for clarifying the interaction of individual and cultural concerns in self-starvation, as well as for fostering a needed self-scrutiny in psychiatry, is affirmed. A critique of the dialectical relationship between culture and psychopathology is then put forward. This addresses the apparently conflicting role of anorexia nervosa in enacting as well as combating the cultural pursuit of thinness, and ends by highlighting the inadvertent influence of the biomedical establishment in propagating the condition with measures intended, ironically, for preventing it.

We are as highly developed in psychopathology as in technology.

Jules Henry[1]

INTRODUCTION

Anorexia nervosa (AN), an intriguing condition that is characterized by food refusal, marked weight loss, and amenorrhea in young women, has customarily been regarded as a pattern of behavioral deviance that is generated and sustained by certain Western cultural values, expectations, and social organizations. Often called a Western[2] "culture-bound syndrome" (CBS), it is believed to be absent or extremely rare outside of Western Europe, North America, Australasia, and South Africa.[3-9]

Recent attention, however, has been drawn by researchers to the emergence of the cultural fear of fatness and AN not only in different socioeconomic levels and minority groups in Western societies, but also from diverse countries in Europe, Africa, India, the Middle East, and the Far East.[10, 11] In one

Reprinted from *Social Science & Medicine*, vol. 42, no. 1 (1996), pp. 21–34, by permission of Elsevier Science.

recent survey conducted among high school and college students in Nigeria, for example, Oyewumi and Kazarian[12] found that the prevalence of disordered eating attitudes was comparable to that of Western countries. They concluded that "nowadays abnormal eating attitudes associated with anorexic behaviour may be a universal phenomenon that transcends cultural boundaries, contrary to the earlier notion that they were restricted to western countries." Among Asian societies such as Hong Kong,[13] China,[14] Taiwan,[15] Malaysia,[16] India,[17, 18] and Singapore,[19] a growing number of reports of AN have indeed appeared in the past decade. In Japan which is a highly industrialized Asian society, eating disorders do not only appear in large numbers,[20] but also conform to typical Western styles, such as the multi-impulsive forms of bulimic disorder.[21]

As recently as 1990, Condit[22] remarked that AN is "virtually unheard of in China." However, to take the lack of reports in the English literature as evidence for the nonexistence of the condition in China is to oversimplify the matter. In the Chinese literature, Song and Fang[14] described nine female AN patients admitted to the Institute of Mental Health of Beijing Medical University between 1982 and 1988, while Chen[23] reported seven child AN patients in Beijing between 1979 and 1986. At the Shanghai Institute of Mental Health, seven out of 2,275 inpatients were discharged with a diagnosis of AN in 1990.[24] Recently, a follow-up study of 19 AN patients seen over a period of 30 years was reported from Nanjing.[25, 26] The comment, made by Prince[4] only a scant decade ago, that AN "just does not appear in many other cultures" has therefore become untenable.[27] Nasser even advanced that the power of the media to shape and homogenize public perceptions has made no society immune to eating disorders nowadays.[28] If this is so, a prudent reevaluation of the Western culture-bound status of AN is clearly in order.

THE CONCEPT OF CULTURE-BOUND SYNDROME

The notion that the distribution and manifestation of psychiatric disorders may be influenced by cultural factors is hardly new. More formally, the term CBS was coined by Yap to refer to exotic psychopathology that is produced by certain systems of implicit values, social structure, and obviously shared beliefs indigenous to certain geographical areas.[29, 30]

Despite its popularity, not all researchers have agreed on the definition and validity of this term.[4, 31, 32] It has been contended that there can be no true non-CBSs because the construction of every psychiatric category must be culturally fashioned, and that every disorder should mean something unique from its sufferer's point of view.[5, 33] The notion is therefore criticized for encouraging a pedantic contextualism which may severely limit cross-cultural comparison. Often defined as having "no major biological etiology,"[34] it is also said to neglect the neurobiological correlates of psychopathology, and hence create a spurious distinction between culture and physiology.[35, 36] For these reasons, the term is rarely applied to "authentic" biomedical categories, and does not find a niche among the diagnostic categories that are recognized in the DSM-III-R, DSM-IV, or the ICD-10.[9, 39–41] There is even the suggestion that it should be abandoned.[42]

But other researchers maintain that the concept usefully links an individual case of ill health to wider sociopsychological concerns and is a symbolic bridge for communicating a range of meanings for both the affected person and those around him/her. By problematizing the relationship between self and society[31] and by confronting the Neo-Kraepelinian assumption that currently describes psychiatric disorders as self-evident entities in the world, it does not only diminish the divide between psychiatry and anthropology,[3, 30] but also allows doctors to practice medicine with awareness rather than mechanically.[43] This awareness of the culture-bound nature of problematic ideation and/or behavior is particularly germane to contemporary psychiatry, which is said to remove human suffering from its cultural context, and to pursue a reductionist biological discourse uncritically.[44] As Cassidy[33] put it, "the clinical practitioner who knows the cognitive characteristics and limitations of his/her model, and realizes that the model may not be shared by clients, is in a more powerful position to do good." A comprehensive theory of human reactions and pathology, Hahn[35] submits, must take CBSs into account (p. 170).

Traditionally, CBSs were equated with exotic and flamboyant behavioral deviations found in localities far away from Western societies where psychiatric theory and practice were bred.[31, 42, 45] In the "new" cross-cultural psychiatry, however, anthropological researchers have unravelled that the cultural construction of psychiatric disease categories is pervasive, and have called into question culture-bound categories within Western biomedicine itself.[3, 30, 34] It is hoped that by presenting a stern challenge to the universalist view of mental illness, this broadened study of CBSs will reduce medicocentrism and contribute to the refinement of international classification of psychiatric disorders.[46]

Landy advised that "perhaps the place for the anthropologist to begin to understand culture-bound reactive syndromes is at home."[30] Swartz[5] thus concluded that AN was "so clear an example of a Cassidy/Ritenbaugh culture-bound syndrome" (p. 729). Prince[4] similarly referred to AN as "*the culture-bound syndrome which is most understandable to a Western audience,*" but emphasized a lack of information as to whether the illness was truly restricted to Western societies. By highlighting the medicalization of anorectic women's quest for spiritual disembodiedness in contemporary North America, Banks also made a plea for

investigating the presence of AN in non-Western cultures.[47] Conceivably, such a scenario and the attendant need for examples of culture-bound disorders within Western societies have motivated researchers to identify AN as an informative case of Western CBS. Not surprisingly, the past two decades have witnessed a massive outpouring of publications on AN, prompted ostensibly by the premise that Western cultural ideals associating slimness and beauty lead to AN.[27] As Bordo says, "anorexia calls our attention to the central ills of our culture."[11]

A quadplex definition of CBS, which will make biomedically defined conditions accessible to a meaning-oriented analysis, was provided by Ritenbaugh.[48] This has been employed to unravel the symbolic meanings of mild-to-moderate obesity, protein-energy malnutrition,[33] type A behavior,[43] and even adolescence.[49] Thus, an examination of type A behavioral pattern in relation to coronary heart disease indicated that it played an important role in resolving the conflictual moral values over achievement orientation, stressful lifestyles, and the obligation to keep good health in the United States.[43]

Using Ritenbaugh's criteria and data from both Western and Chinese sources,[50] this paper reevaluates the CBS status of AN.[51, 52]

Criterion One: It Cannot Be Understood Apart from Its Specific Cultural or Subcultural Context

The sine qua non of contemporary AN, as conceptualized in the DSM-IV or the ICD-10 biomedical discourse, is an intense fear of fatness which persists despite obvious emaciation in affected subjects.[9, 39, 40, 53] As a corollary of this epistemological assumption, the legitimate reason given for deliberate non-eating by an anorectic patient is expected to be "I don't want to be fat; I am already too fat." Some authorities have insisted that the resolution of such a "fat phobia" is a precondition to recovery.[54, 55]

Anorexia nervosa was previously regarded as a specific attribute of achievement-oriented, upper, and middle class individuals in Western countries.[10] Crisp,[56] for example, referred to "this skewed distribution of morbidity, in which the working class background seems to have a sparing effect" (p. 22), while Rothblum[7] asserted even in 1990 that "a desire for slimness is absent in developing nations." Recent anthropological writings perpetuate the view that most anorectic patients come from within the ranks of the upper classes.[53, 57]

But a sufficient accumulation of evidence has shown fat phobia and eating disorders to be "democratically" present in virtually all socioeconomic strata and ethnic groups in Western societies.[10, 11, 58] Similar attitudes and weight control behavior have also been found to be very common in second-generation Asian females living in the United Kingdom.[59] Notably, clinical and epidemiological information now exists that fatness is no longer valued by young women in many non-Western societies.[12] A recent two-stage survey in the Chinese society of Hong Kong, for example, showed that a cognitive fear of fatness was common among female undergraduates and, irrespective of social class, was universally present in those who had a biomedically normal body mass index of 20.5 kg/m² or more.[60] Contrary to traditional Chinese notions, no subject considered that corpulence was a sign of prestige, let alone physical attractiveness.[58]

Fat phobic concern is hardly confined to Chinese people in Hong Kong. In Chongqing and Shanghai, China, the majority of female college students were found in self-report surveys to exhibit fat phobia.[61] In both Taiwan and China,[14, 25] the clinical characteristics of Chinese patients with eating disorders were also reported to be broadly similar to those of their Western counterparts.[15] Gandhi and coworkers[62] in India noted that "anything beyond a well-fed look in an adolescent is very likely to subject her to ridicule from peers and family members, and may adversely affect her prospects even in the arranged marriage system." They found the view that slimness was not a requisite for beauty in the Indian culture was an oversimplification, and stressed that some of their anorectic patients demonstrated fat phobia.

Nasser has submitted that nowadays the transcultural comparison of any psychopathology may become less striking than before because the world has culturally shrunken by virtue of mass communication technology.[28] Television, for example, has made possible a mass deployment of images, so that few people can escape its shaping of their fantasy lives.[11] It is hardly to be denied that this rampant process of cultural assimilation has contributed to the globalization of fat phobia which, along with the elimination of food shortage and the increasing problem of obesity in non-Western societies undergoing modernization,[58] have obvious implications on the CBS status of AN. Kleinman[63] observed that CBSs should strike the observer as odd, inexplicit, or incomprehensible, while Hughes[42] referred to them as "'crazy' (to us) ways of being crazy" (p. 141). *Latah*, for example, is often regarded by Western people as an amusing idiosyncrasy.[31] By contrast, fat phobic AN is nowadays far from a strange aberration to many non-Western people. A recent survey showed that 72 percent of a large sample ($N = 895$) of Chinese undergraduates in Hong Kong accepted the cultural fear of fatness as one common cause of AN.[64]

Traversing both geographic and socioeconomic boundaries, AN thus appears to be no longer a Western CBS according to Ritenbaugh's first criterion.[65] However, this view has to be tempered by at least two provisos.

First, instead of arguing for a case of culture-boundedness categorically, we may consider whether AN is "more culture-bound" than other psychiatric conditions, or can be usefully understood using the CBS framework.[3] Stated differently, culture-boundedness is best considered a processual rather than static concept, and the words *bound to* should be interpreted as encompassing directionality, relativism, and an allowance for reworking, rather than as "bandaged" or "kept fast in bonds or in prison."[66] It is like a "West-bound train" moving toward and eventually reaching some point in the West. As anticipated by Ritenbaugh herself,[48] all diseases in all cultures can, to varying degrees, be culture-bound.

Second, inasmuch as AN develops in response to a complex orchestration of sociocultural elements including industrial capitalism, urbanization, immigration, abundance of food, rising population weight norms, advanced information technology, proliferation of body-oriented advertisements, decreased birth rate, and changing social roles of women,[6, 11, 22, 47, 53, 67] the condition may be considered to be bound to the culture of "modernity" rather than to specific geographical sites.[68] In this deeper sense, AN is still a CBS, albeit not necessarily a Western one by locality.

Since culture is never stationary, the CBS concept also raises the question of historical variability, which suggests that the same symptoms viewed at different times or in different contexts may be interpreted differently.[8, 31, 55, 69] DiNicola[70] has thus construed AN as a culture-reactive or culture-change syndrome. This transformative nature of AN is supported by the fact that fat phobic AN was more culture-bound to people of upper social class in Western societies 15 years ago,[56] and may be more so nowadays than 10 years from now, when fat phobic sensibilities and epistemologies will more deeply permeate non-Western societies and become truly globalized.[58] The CBS model is then an acculturation model, but it does not imply, ipso facto, that the immediate cause of clinical instances of AN must be blamed on culture.[5, 13]

Criterion Two: The Etiology Summarizes and Symbolizes Core Meanings and Behavioral Norms of That Culture

Apart from the motion of Prince[4] that notions of cause are inherently culture-bound, capricious, and should therefore be excluded from the definition of CBS, this criterion faces two other problems when it is applied to AN. First, it seems to assume simplistically a unitary etiology which is at odds with the multicausal conceptualization of AN.[22, 71] Second, it has been very difficult to establish etiology with regard to any psychiatric condition, let alone AN.

For all the extensive publicity given to fat phobia, which connotes a certain inevitability to dieting behavior, evidence is by no means conclusive that this aesthetic attitude is a sufficient, let alone necessary, cause of AN in the treatment context.[58, 72] Since most clinicians conceive psychopathology to reside within individuals and/or families, they focus their attention pragmatically on immediate psychological problems, and rarely find that fat phobia is the most significant cause of AN.

In Hong Kong, most young Chinese women are cognitively inclined to feel fat, but relatively few of them are propelled to determined weight control behavior. This is apparently because they are already slim when compared to their Western counterparts.[58] In addition to data from a number of non-Western societies which suggested that fat phobia was not a necessary cause of AN,[55] the view that AN may occur in the absence of a cultural drive for slimness has recently been endorsed by Western researchers themselves.[47] Thus, Yager[73] and Steiger[74] testified to the presence of non–fat-phobic AN in the United States and Canada, respectively. They conceded that in their clinical experience anorectic patients were often able to acknowledge their thinness, and that the disorder was not uniformly about a desire to be thin. Instead, the apparent pursuit of thinness was often explicable in terms unique to each subject. Schmolling[75] even asserted that the desire for slimness could symbolize an ego-syntonic drive for the realization of higher psychological needs in some Western women. Inasmuch as the link between fat phobia and AN is a variable one, the debate about whether fat phobia in a precise sense causes AN, based on a unitary model of causality, may be specious.

It may of course be argued that the validity of Ritenbaugh's second criterion depends on how one interprets causation in a multidetermined condition such as AN. By contrast to the mechanistic variety of causality that modern science has come to rely on, the Aristotelian version of causality, for example, distinguished between "efficient" cause and "final" cause. The former answers the question of how a particular act is emitted, whereas the latter provides an explanation for why a particular act is given off.[76, 77]

On a macrosocial level of analysis, if one accepts that a culturally based fat phobia is a *final* cause of AN among distressed young women,[58, 78] then Ritenbaugh's criterion is fulfilled because fat phobic AN embodies, as much as it caricatures, the normative fear of fatness in Western societies.[5, 48] Among Western people, slimness has come to symbolize not only attractiveness but also self-control, youth, and efficiency in both social and work-related domains. By contrast, fatness connotes ugliness, shame, and even sin. The pursuit of slimness has become a moral discourse and the body, a site for moral action.[48] Slimness also embodies an economic reality in that fat females may be more likely to be denied acceptance to colleges and to marry poorer husbands than their slim counterparts.[34, 67, 79] Inasmuch as fat phobic AN expresses a compelling cultural voice predicated on core Western values, it is considerably more culture-bound to Western than Chinese societies. Expectably, a survey of folk beliefs about disordered eating in Australia

showed that the DSM-III fat phobia criterion for the diagnosis of AN was judged by very few people to be abnormal.[80]

Even though young Chinese women increasingly prefer to *stay* slim,[58] there is less stigmatization of fatness in the Chinese tradition, and slimness does not seem to be as inextricably intertwined with a woman's future as in the West.[81] Partly because of the economic power and robust health that plumpness would symbolize for the family, traditional Chinese notions were that "fat people have more luck" and "gaining weight means good fortune." Chinese gods are nearly always portrayed as being fat and rarely exhibit the ascetic refusal of food.[47] By contrast, thinness was considered a sign of ill health and would pejoratively be associated with active pulmonary tuberculosis, or even heroin addiction. Even today, saying, "You've lost weight" may be less a compliment than an expression of concern about somebody's health.[13]

The globalizing of fat phobia notwithstanding, AN remains a rare condition in nearly all non-Western societies with the exception of Japan.[20, 21, 58] As Yap[82] stated when he discussed the CBS status of *koro*, "the fact that isolated cases may be seen in widely separated cultures does not invalidate the conclusion, since it is still necessary to account for the consistent and relatively frequent occurrence of cases within a particular culture area which allows a model to be distinguished" (p. 48).

Criterion Three: Diagnosis Relies on Culture-Specific Technology as Well as Ideology

Since the diagnosis of fat phobic AN requires "standardized" criteria which were formulated only one to two decades ago, its recognition and diagnosis may be said to rely on culture-specific technology and ideology.[83] This statement receives support from the historical and cross-cultural studies of AN, which have attested to the fact that fat phobia is not the sole rationalization for the afflicted women to refuse eating. These "non–fat-phobic" anorectic subjects, for reasons discussed in details elsewhere,[55, 69] used abdominal bloating, loss of appetite no hunger, distaste for food, and/or simply no appetite to explain the restriction of food intake. Despite an overall resemblance to their fat phobic counterparts and their indisputable place in the cultural history of AN, they failed to be diagnosed as AN according to contemporary Western nosology.[8, 47, 55, 73, 74, 84, 85] Instead, they are pigeonholed into the category of "atypical eating disorders," a rubric which has no real classificatory or explanatory power. More importantly, these patients challenge the claim of the DSM system to have escaped considerations of etiology[39]

In a historical review, Habermas[86] found that 7 out of 12 nineteenth century French publications on AN mentioned a fear of obesity, whereas this was recorded by only one German author and no British or American author in the same period. As the cultural pursuit of slimness might have been more prevalent in France then, he took the view that culturally mediated ideology played a constitutive part in influencing clinicians' observations and construction of medical knowledge, in this case the assignment of self-starvation to fat phobia. In a related article, Habermas[87] suggested that J. M. Charcot, a renowned French physician, was probably the first to discern fat phobia in anorectic patients. Because of Charcot's nationwide influence, he alerted many French doctors to "discover" some of the patients' motivation to avoid fatness. Logically, Habermas surmised that there might have been simultaneous national influences on both medical thinking and on neurotic symptom formation, such as "possibly a national preoccupation with cuisine and food in the case of France" (p. 364), implying that professional and lay epistemologies may lie on the same cultural continuum.

From an interactionist perspective, had the DSM manual been as rhetorically disseminated in the past as it is today, physicians might have made diagnoses of fat phobic AN more liberally. Equally, some anorectic patients may elect to present a medical account which affirms clinicians' academic explanatory models during the process of illness negotiation.[72] The two parties may thereby enter into what Shorter[8] satirically termed an "implicit conspiracy" (p. 192), a situation which could also be fostered by mental health professionals' inadvertent transmission to anorectic patients of double messages regarding medically versus aesthetically desirable body weights.[88] This sharing of explanatory models often means that the patients will be "liked" by their practitioners (p. 614).[72] It is perhaps of interest to recall here a psychiatric case report of a young Ethiopian woman with psychogenic vomiting and weight loss following torture. During hospitalization in a specialist unit in London where she spent "a great deal of time" with anorectic patients and attended their treatment groups, she was noted to have acquired "anorectic attitudes" about becoming fat and the desire to remain inordinately thin. This apparently motivated the authors to make a diagnosis of AN.[89]

The imperceptible and yet powerful impact of biomedical technology on Asian clinicians' diagnostic practice can be located in the literature on AN. In reporting a young anorectic woman in Hong Kong, Chiu[90] remarked that "this case was atypical in that the relentless pursuit of thinness was not present. Instead, her dieting seemed to be merely a way to divert her family members' attention from severe mutual conflicts to her." Despite the absence of fat phobia, a DSM-III diagnosis of AN was tacitly made. In another paper describing seven anorectic patients in Singapore, Ong and Tsoi[19] underscored in the abstract that their clinical features were typical of Western AN, but the case histories clearly indicated that fat phobia was obvious only in three patients. A 17-year-old girl, in fact, "admitted that she was thin" and "there was no desire at any time for a thin body image" (pp. 259–260). These case reports demonstrated that a locally occurring illness reality may be distorted in accordance with a preconceived template during the biomedical process of diagnosing AN. The latter may be more culture-bound than the disease of self-starvation itself.

Criterion Four: Successful Treatment Is Accomplished Only by Participants in That Culture

This is, for biomedical practitioners in particular, a provocative thesis.

While it seems axiomatic that mental illness is optimally treated by members of the sufferer's culture, and anecdotal evidence shows that "indigenous practitioners successfully heal" in significant portions of the world,[91] Ritenbaugh's proposition has not been substantiated with regard to either biological or psychosocial therapy. To the extent that all therapy operates in, and is constrained by, its own context, this may be because the empirical evaluation of the connection between culture and psychotherapy is fraught with both conceptual and methodological difficulties.[92] It is perhaps not surprising that previous reviews of research on Western psychotherapy did not show a strong or even consistent relationship between treatment outcome and therapist/client characteristics such as ethnicity, socioeconomic status, gender, and age.[93]

Nonetheless, Cheng and Lo,[94] two Western-trained Chinese psychiatrists in Canada, contended that a minority therapist/mainstream dyad during intercultural psychotherapy might bring about four areas of distinct advantages, namely, language independence, culture independence, posi-

tive transference, and analogous experiences. They believed that because Western psychiatry and psychotherapy are culture-bound, mainstream therapists may easily be "culturally addicted" (p. 386), as opposed to a minority therapist who can maintain cultural neutrality. They also submitted that biculturism, contrary to expectations, would not only foster the challenging of culturally encapsulated taboos and assumptions, but also promote the acceptance of alternative worldviews and a wider repertoire of coping strategies.

A clearly pertinent issue in the relationship between culture and treatment of AN is that of gender. Some feminist scholars have submitted that women and men are psychologically in "worlds apart," and that each gender's modus operandi for perceiving and communicating reality may represent a distinct culture.[95, 96] In the case of such a gendered disorder as AN, the sufferer's culture is obviously that of female. Eating disorders have, in fact, been seen to represent a crucial topic in the psychology of women, and form part of a complex constellation of female disorders in Western societies.[11, 25, 53, 74, 97]

Thus, to consider the provocative argument of some feminist writers that the treatment by a male therapist for such a predominantly "female malady" as AN is "cross-cultural" and problematic is of heuristic interest.[98] Grounded on case studies, Zunino and coworkers[99] argued that therapist gender, by affecting the quality of transference–countertransference interaction, could have a pronounced impact on the course and content of psychotherapy with eating-disordered women. Wooley[100] also contended that female therapists are in a better position than their male counterparts to treat these patients because the latter are hard-pressed to behave in ways that are not traditionally masculine, and this leads to bans on therapist self-disclosure, touch, and display of strong emotion by either therapist or patient. By contrast, the same demeanor is far less conflictual and more easily integrated into therapy for female therapists (p. 334), who may be perceived by female clients to possess more empathic understanding than male therapists.

However, while gender will undeniably influence the process of psychotherapy, a successful outcome of treatment may depend less on gender similarity than egalitarianism, attitudinal flexibility, competence, and perhaps charisma of the therapist.[93, 95] Gender dissimilarity is not only compatible with a harmonious matching of patient and therapist, but may also lead to an advantageous crisscrossing of gender-specific worldviews and coping strategies. More research is clearly needed.

Ritenbaugh's proposal on the benefit of cultural congruence between healer and patient may also be challenged by the empirical finding that bulimia nervosa, which comprises multiple fat phobic cognitive distortions, can be treated successfully without focusing directly on these culture-specific cognitions. A randomized controlled trial involving 75 DSM-III-R bulimia nervosa patients showed that interpersonal psychotherapy, which enhanced their interpersonal malfunctioning without addressing the disturbed eating attitudes and habits, worked as efficaciously as cognitive behavioral therapy, which specifically modified fat phobic concerns. The authors postulated that interpersonal psychotherapy brought about positive changes in patients' social relationships and ameliorated their eating disorder via certain indirect mechanisms[101]

There is much more to the debate over culture and healing, but even the brief commentary here is to suggest that the mode of interaction between patient culture and healer culture, and their richly embedded therapeutic encounter, are complex.[102] Hsu[103] wrote that a "baffling array of treatments has been advocated for anorexia nervosa in the last 30 years," but a precise therapy is lacking. Somatic treatments ranging from vitamin and

hormone treatments to electroconvulsive therapy were tried in uncontrolled studies but none has been shown to have specific value.[71] Psychotherapy, generally considered the single most important form of treatment for AN, does not rely on any distinctive theoretical approach. The "core psychopathology" of fat phobia[69] in particular is ironically said to be an inconsequential clinical focus that need not be directly challenged.[104] Intended to rectify fat phobia, the so-called body-oriented therapy embraces video confrontation as well as diverse therapeutic elements such as massage, dance, and even wrestling for fun.[105] Clearly, these treatment considerations question Ritenbaugh's thesis.

Unlike some feminist therapists who may incorporate sociopolitical elements into their treatment models,[79] biomedical practitioners are less concerned with these facets of AN. In clinical practice, patients usually receive an eclectic amalgamation of nutritional counselling, psychotherapy, behavioral modification, social interventions such as removing them temporarily from an adverse family situation, and various medications of uncertain efficacy. Despite such multimodal treatment, they frequently resist clinicians' admonition that aspects of their lives are pathological.[106] It has even been suggested that behavioral modification, one of the most commonly used techniques for bringing on weight gain, is experienced by patients as a humiliating form of brutal coercion by which they may be reduced to utter helplessness and suicidality.[107] Perhaps as a form of protest against the power differential between biomedical doctors and themselves in patriarchal hospital settings, patients may relate to nonmedical staff (e.g., student nurses) more willingly than to doctors.[13, 47, 53, 108, 109] Some of them may also recover "spontaneously," that is, without specific biomedical interventions.

Historical records[110] and clinical experience in Hong Kong[13] as well as China[14, 23, 25] indicate that similar treatment strategies, none of which seemed culture-specific, were used. In Beijing where specialist eating disorder units are understandably lacking, Chen[23] reported that seven child AN patients were treated successfully with a combination of behavioral techniques, adjunctive diazepam, nutritional therapy, and, above all, an initial period of removal from perpetuating family environments. This was followed by educating their parents to adopt an "unconcerned" attitude vis-à-vis their eating behavior. One of them also received insulin-induced hypoglycemic therapy to increase hunger and food intake.[111] Regarding short-term outcome, five patients were reported to be recovered and two improved. So too, Song and Fang[14] in Beijing reported significant weight gain in eight out of nine AN patients by the use of nutritional counselling, "dredging" psychotherapy,[112] low-dose tricyclic antidepressant and insulin therapy. An amalgamation of supportive measures, psychotherapy, and moderate doses of antidepressants was also used with varying success in a series of 19 AN patients in Nanjing, China.[25] At an eating disorder unit in the Czech Republic, a similar synergy of approaches was apparently used.[113]

As Swartz[5] suggested, the greatest weakness of Ritenbaugh's definition of CBS may occur in the context of treatment. It is hard to contend, even though comparative treatment studies are wanting, that the successful treatment of AN can only be accomplished by participants in one specific culture. Wohl[102] has even submitted that because no one culture is homogeneous and all psychotherapy is thus cross-cultural, intracultural and intercultural psychotherapy should be seen as lying on a continuum. "Cross-cultural" therapeutic success, so conceived, is little surprise.

More likely is that a variety of problem solvers with very different armamenteria and traditions are able to deal with anorectic patients effectively. Anorexia nervosa may therefore fail to fulfill Ritenbaugh's 4th crite-

rion.[114] This may be because anorectic subjects' personal difficulties are fundamentally similar,[55] and that practitioner–patient transactions in the healing process are inherently complex in all cultures (p. 10).[63] Intended or not, certain "universal" healing factors such as listening, empathy, dispelling of ambiguity, and the boosting of morale,[102] dominate many forms of symbolic healing, be they "Western" psychotherapies, faith healing, poetic incantations, performative magic, *qiu qian* (a popular form of Chinese divination using bamboo sticks), or the magnanimous use of endocrine extracts during the "pituitary era" of AN.[115] Given the extremely nebulous link between clinical phenocopies and pharmacoresponsivity, the CBS concept may also be redundant for psychopharmacologists who find that they successfully treat many different CBSs with the same class of psychotropic drugs.[4, 116]

But there are arguments in defense of Ritenbaugh's criterion. To recognize similarities among different forms of healing, and to acknowledge their therapeutic role in a variety of contexts, should not obscure the fact that we cannot translate one form of therapy to another without the loss of situated meanings. To the extent that notions of the self, the definition of health, the application of theories of disease, the experience of treatment, and the conception of what constitutes "successful treatment" may be culturally constrained,[34, 63] the treatment of AN in a particular social world *is* culture-bound. For example, harmonious familial interdependence, not personal autonomy or the resolution of parental conflicts,[56, 117] may be considered the main goal of healing in a sociocentric Chinese context. A Chinese anorectic subject and her mother, whose main worry is over marriageability and lineage prolongation, may see as a symbol of cure the return of menses (with herbal recipes) rather than individuation (with psychoanalytic psychotherapy), self-actualization (with humanistic psychotherapy), or the cessation of binge-eating (with cognitive-behavioral therapy).[118] In the clinical context, these nonconsensual patient attitudes may be carefully concealed from their healers.

Alternatively, a previously obese Western anorectic patient may view a biomedically suboptimal body weight as aesthetically desirable and, by opposing further weight gain, continue to be amenorrheic. Although menstruation is biomedically required as one of the principal outcome criteria of AN, Bordo[11] noted that the "disgust with menstruation" is typical of anorectic patients (p. 87). In the specific setting of psychoanalytic psychotherapy, this may then be interpreted as evidence of psychological resistance vis-à-vis the resolution of adolescent turmoil.[56] Similarly, the psychodynamic model that AN represents an endeavor to forestall sexual maturity, repress sexual drives, and prevent the development of an appealing female figure may expressly require that the attainment of normal heterosexual relationship should be the main goal of successful treatment.[119] Impaired social relationship, however, is common in follow-up studies of recovered anorectic subjects.[13, 56, 71, 103] Adequate weight gain, one of the cardinal yardsticks of success of behavioral modification, may nonetheless be regarded as a "misleading sign of recovery" from a psychodynamic viewpoint (p. 1422).[107] These meaning-oriented considerations lend credence to Ritenbaugh's notion that, as a corollary of the CBS concept, "treatment judged as successful in one cultural context may not be understood as successful from another perspective."

CULTURE IN PSYCHOPATHOLOGY AND THE PSYCHOPATHOLOGY OF CULTURE

Referring to the need for a "critical sociology of psychiatric knowledge and practice," Good[44] reminded us that psychopathology must be studied as "socially and historically produced" (p. 200). One instance of the reciprocal interaction between culture and psychopathology may be the sociohistorical transformation of the symptomatology of AN.

An increasing number of reviews on the history of AN have concluded that females who exhibited obdurate self-starvation could be traced back to as early as the fifth century. These fasting girls' remarkable quest for spiritual piety made them both a curiosity and medical mystery. The strong attention they drew from the public and physicians then furnished the psychosocial context in which the transformation of self-starvation from a religious to a medical matter occurred.[97]

In an erudite review published in 1958, Nemiah[120] made no allusion whatsoever to fat phobia, but attributed American anorectic patients' psychogenic starvation to "the wish not to eat," "food phobia," "aversion to food," or a "true loss of appetite" (p. 253). It was only after 1930 that the characteristic "fear of fatness"[39, 40] started to emerge as a rationale for food refusal in AN.[8, 110, 121] More specifically, Casper[121] stated that "the drive towards thinness does not emerge as a common and predominant motive until about 1960." She ascribed this to an increasingly weight-conscious society generated by economic prosperity and the surplus of food, which together projected fat phobia into the foreground as an explanation for women's widespread pursuit of slimness.

In discussing the relationship between social change and the mutability of psychopathology, Murphy[122] suggested that changes in symptomatology of a mental disorder could be thought of as "the by-product of social problem solving" (p. 51). From this vantage point, what social problem is solved by the transformation of voluntary self-starvation into its fat phobic rendition.[55]

Lee[123] invoked the concepts of "structure" and "anti-structure," developed by the acclaimed symbolic anthropologist Victor Turner, to explicate the dialectical relationship between CBS and cultural reality. Within this conceptual frame, the normative phenomenon of dieting to pursue thinness represents "structure" (proper behavior or normality), while AN may be treated as "anti-structure" (improper behavior or abnormality). According to the ICD-10,[40] a 1.62 m tall woman is not anorectic if she weighs 46 kg (BMI = 17.5 kg/m²). But she is authentically so if, in the presence of fat phobia and amenorrhea, she weighs 45.5 kg (BMI = 17.3 kg/m²). By throwing the slimness ideal publicly into question and thus evoking negative societal reactions, AN, so precisely and yet arbitrarily defined, should serve both to delegitimate the pursuit of thinness and to endorse "simple" dieting as a normative part of cultural reality. Since Western people now diet to pursue an aesthetically prescribed low body weight which may be at odds with normal biological functioning,[48] the designation of AN as a potentially fatal psychiatric disease can be construed as health professionals' attempt to pathologize the everyday fear of fatness in order to admonish weight-conscious individuals that they should accept a broad range of bodily shapes as healthy. As Karp[31] says, AN may be seen to "emerge out of the lifeworld and reflect back upon it, perhaps even against it" (p. 224).

According to Turner's theory, had AN not been reified as an intrapersonal pathology which can be "grasped and fixed" (p. 59),[53] an even higher prevalence of dieting might have been found in Western society. The anorectic disease thus equilibrates, albeit precariously, the ongoing medical-aesthetic contradiction over the physical body and the metaphorical "body-as-experienced."[11] The existence of this homeostatic role of AN receives empirical support from an Australian community survey, in which the majority of females perceived that their knowledge about eating disorders came predominantly from the mass media and made them more cautious about dieting behavior.[124] But at a cost, for 8 percent of the subjects in this same study believed

that the power of the media was also responsible for the rising incidence of eating disorders. In Barcelona, Spain, a recent study showed that anorectic subjects were more subject to media pressure on slimming than were nonanorectic girls of the same age, and were thus more likely to accept the behavioral patterns dictated by such advertising.[125] These findings recall Swartz,[72] who inferred that "an environment receptive to the understanding of eating disorders may be one in which they will flourish" (p. 617). Inasmuch as fat phobia may *both* cause and follow AN,[126] culture and psychopathology form a dynamically interlocked whole.

That the categorical distinction between AN and innocent dieting is arbitrary may be supported not only by the resonance between the anguish of some AN sufferers and the fat phobic distress of ordinary women, but also by studies that have unambiguously demonstrated a continuum of disordered eating attitudes and behavior in the community. A large-scale survey of American adolescents, for example, showed that as many as 63 percent of high school girls dieted in the last year with an average weight loss of 10–12 pounds, while 6 percent exhibited recurrent binge-eating episodes.[127] In nearly all epidemiological surveys on eating disorders, "partial" AN and bulimia nervosa syndromes, in which varying degrees of emotional distress often eclipse the modest eating problem, are typically more common than the biomedically designated disorders.[58, 128] When empowered by nosologic authorities, small changes in the extant psychiatric diagnostic criteria may therefore create a marked change in the manifest prevalence of eating disorders. The latter can sociologically be conceived as a form of norm violation.[6]

At the same time as AN appears to increase in prevalence in the last few decades,[103, 129] it is perhaps no accident that its diagnostic criteria have been slackened by the psychiatric profession. Thus, the amount of weight loss required for the diagnosis of AN has decreased from 25 percent or more of premorbid weight in Feighner's[130] or the DSM-III criteria[131] to 15 percent of standard body weight in the DSM-III-R[39] and the DSM-IV.[9] In the ICD-10 draft,[132] a BMI of less than 16 kg/m² was essential for diagnosis. In the formally published ICD-10, a more lenient BMI of less than 17.5 kg/m² is required.[40] The latter criterion would, paradoxically, cast some 16 percent of slim but healthy young Chinese women in Hong Kong,[58] as well as 69 percent of the *Playboy* centerfolds and 60 percent of Miss America contestants over a 10-year period (1979–1988), into the anorectic weight domain.[133]

These slackened criteria may have arisen from, and concurrently contributed to, the increased prevalence of mild forms of AN in modern times. As Lucas[129] wrote, regarding this process of pathologization and the "apparent epidemic" of AN, "prior to the 1980s it was likely that a patient was quite symptomatic, undernourished, and significantly ill by the time she was taken to a physician," (p. 746) while "it is my belief that the mild form has increased in frequency as a result of sociocultural pressures, and that it is this form of the illness that has been increasingly recognized and identified" (p. 750). The frequently cited "epidemic" of this socially reconstructed form of AN[11, 51, 55] is therefore contingent on a relaxed definition of AN, which may be seen to be as normalizing as it is pathologizing.[134] Shorter[8] drew attention to the proliferation of eating disorder specialty clinics and the coverage on AN that went with them. He ascribed to the biomedical establishment the notoriety responsible for the escalation of AN, and justifiably regarded this as a form of iatrogenesis (p. 191).

Unlike the sporadic cases of early anorectic patients who were shockingly marasmic,[110, 135] the mild forms of "me-too" AN, which arise *en masse* and display proto-

typical illness narratives and routinized patterns of behavior,[44] may recover spontaneously. Conjuring more fascination than horror, they confute the historical and clinical description of AN as a potentially fatal disorder of self-starvation that resulted from debilitating family and characterological pathology, for which "parentectomy" and intensive psychotherapy were fundamental solutions.[8, 13, 23, 54, 56, 110] In 1958 when people were presumably thinner than nowadays, Nemiah[120] wrote that the mean amount of weight loss of anorectic patients was 45 percent (p. 255), which was considerably higher than the DSM-IV or ICD-10 threshold.[9, 40] Similarly, Bruch in 1974 referred to emaciation as "the most prominent symptom" of AN.[107] Because frightful cachexia, not fat phobia, governed the diagnosis of AN in the past, "mild" AN seemed not to be encountered.[136] By contrast, the contemporary diagnosis of AN chooses to deemphasize emaciation and, at the same time, highlights fat phobia. This position was exemplified by Lacey,[137] who contended that even when the weight loss criterion was not clearly fulfilled, weight phobia[138] would still be "the pathognomonic feature of AN, i.e., the feature which clearly demarcates anorexia from all other psychological and physical conditions." In a case report entitled "anorexia nervosa following torture in a young African woman," similarly, the authors[89] labeled a patient with psychogenic vomiting as AN because of her having acquired a certain fear of becoming fat, even though her amenorrhea was only transient, and her scores on the Eating Attitudes Test[139] were atypically low.

Starting as an interpretive tool[56] but drawing upon powerful cultural symbolism and social momentum because of the apparent success of the thinness-as-beauty hypothesis in explaining the epidemiology of AN, fat phobia is then built into the biomedical diagnostic criteria and preeminent explanatory model for AN.[9, 40] This has encouraged not only what Bruch[138] called a copycat phenomenon of mild AN on the one hand, but also psychiatry's adamantine silencing of core messages pertaining to the sociopolitical, religious, and moral contexts of self-starvation on the other.[47] The hindrance thus caused by the exclusive use of the fat phobia model to comparative studies, where more loosely articulated epistemologies and disease theories are desirable, is ignored.[69]

According to Lee's perspective,[123] the reification of the mild forms of AN will diminish the bases of contrast between structures and antistructures, and therefore curb the intended function of promulgating AN in order to combat community-wide dieting. Far from invoking social censure and serving a premonitory role, fat phobic AN may even be legitimized as a "model of misconduct" for Western females to articulate personal suffering. Indeed, borderline anorectic shapes are often rated as being highly attractive[140, 141] and AN itself, for all its known mortality, has been glamorized in the West.[142] Branch and Eurman,[143] for example, demonstrated that the friends and relatives of anorectic patients often honored their appearance as well as their self-discipline, and might even reinforce their behavior with tangible rewards. Of course, the culturally instilled fear of fatness and the attendant activities by which women discipline their bodies help maintain a large "keep-fit industry" in business, attesting to the connection between medicalization and commercialization in present-day consumer society.

To the extent that culture and psychopathology are interdependent facets of a socially constructed world, psychiatric theory cannot deny its participation in the epistemology and social trajectory of the anorectic discourse, which articulates personal miseries as much as it does public concerns.[144] An immediately relevant task confronting both anthropology and psychiatry is to decipher the cultural forces which so efficiently reconstruct fat phobic AN as a social malaise in an expanding number of societies irrespective of their indigenous cultures, and to devise preventative measures thereof.

NOTES

1. Henry J. *Culture Against Man*, p. 322. Vintage Books, New York, 1963.

2. The overly generalizing terms of "Western" and "non-Western" do not homogenize culture. Throughout this paper, they will be used loosely with the recognition that differences exist among ethnic groups, socioeconomic groups, and other subcultures even within any one (necessarily pluralistic) society.

3. Littlewood R. From categories to contexts: a decade of the 'New Cross-Cultural Psychiatry.' *Br. J. Psychiat.* **156**, 308, 1990.

4. Prince R. The concept of culture-bound syndromes: anorexia nervosa and brain-fag. *Soc. Sci. Med.* **21**, 197, 1985.

5. Swartz L. Anorexia nervosa as a culture-bound syndrome. *Soc. Sci. Med.* **20**, 725, 1985.

6. Bottero A. Anorexia nervosa: a culture-bound syndrome? *Cahiers d'Anthropologie et Biométrie Humane (Paris)* **4**, 61, 1986.

7. Rothblum E. D. Women and weight: fad and fiction. *J. Psychol.* **124**, 5, 1990.

8. Shorter E. Youth and psychosomatic illness. In *From the Mind into the Body: The Cultural Origins of Psychosomatic Symptoms*, chapter 6, pp. 149–255. The Free Press, New York, 1994.

9. American Psychiatric Association. *Diagnostic and Statistical Manual of Mental Disorders*, 4th edn, DSM-IV. APA, Washington, DC, 1994.

10. Pate J. E., Pumariega A. J., Hester C., and Garner D. M. Cross-cultural patterns in eating disorders: a review. *J. Am. Acad. Child Psychiat.* **31**, 802, 1992.

11. Bordo S. Anorexia nervosa: psychopathology as the crystallization of culture. *Philosophical Forum* **17**, 73, 1985–1986.

12. Oyewumi L. K. and Kazarian S. S. Abnormal eating attitudes among a group of Nigerian youths: II anorexic behaviour. *East Afr. Med. J.* **69**, 667, 1992.

13. Lee S. Anorexia nervosa in Hong Kong—a Chinese perspective. *Psychol. Med.* **21**, 703, 1991.

14. Song Y. H. and Fang Y. K. A clinical report of nine cases of anorexia nervosa. *Chin. Ment. Hlth. J.* **4**, 24, 1990.

15. Tseng M. C., Lee M. B., and Lee Y. J. A clinical study of Chinese patients with eating disorders. *Chin. Psychiat.* **3**, 17, 1989.

16. Goh S. E., Ong S. B. Y., and Subramaniam M. Eating disorders in Hong Kong. *Br. J. Psychiat.* **162**, 276, 1993.

17. Chadda R., Malhotra S., Asad A. G., and Bambery P. Socio-cultural factors in anorexia nervosa. *Ind. J. Psychiat.* **29**, 107, 1987.

18. Khandelwal S. K. and Saxena S. Anorexia nervosa in people of Asian extraction. *Br. J. Psychiat.* **157**, 784, 1990.

19. Ong Y. L. and Tsoi W. F. A clinical and psychosocial study of seven cases of anorexia nervosa in Singapore. *Sing. Med. J.* **23**, 255, 1982.

20. Suematsu H., Ishikawa H., Kuboki T., and Ito T. Statistical studies on anorexia nervosa in Japan: detailed clinical data on 1,011 patients. *Psychother. Psychosom.* **43**, 96, 1985.

21. Suzuki K., Higuchi S., Yamada K., Komiya H. and Takagi S. Bulimia nervosa with and without alcoholism: a comparative study in Japan. *Int. J. Eating Disorders* **16**, 137, 1994.

22. Condit V. K. Anorexia nervosa: levels of causation. *Human Nature.* **1**, 395, 1990.

23. Chen J. Behavioural therapy of seven cases of childhood anorexia nervosa. *Chin. Ment. Hlth J.* **4**, 26, 1990.

24. Xu S. H., Gao Z. X., and Xu B. X. The application of the diagnostic criteria of the Chinese Classification of Mental Disorders. *Chin. J. Ment. Dis.* **19**, 59, 1993.

25. Zhu Y. H., Sheng S. N., Li B. L., Fu S. W., and Zhai S. T. A clinical and follow-up study on anorexia nervosa. *J. Clin. Psychol. Med.* **4**, 206, 1994.

26. In an academic meeting held in September 1994, in Shenzhen, China, I was told that up to three AN patients were treated at one and the same time in the psychiatric ward of a hospital in Beijing, China (Xu Y. X., personal communication).

27. Weiss M. Eating disorders and disordered eating in different cultures. *Psychiat. Clin. N. Am.* (in press).

28. Nasser M. Screening for abnormal eating attitudes in a population of Egyptian secondary school girls. *Soc. Psychiat. Psychiat. Epidemiol.* **29**, 25, 1994.

29. Yap P. M. Classification of the culture-bound reactive syndromes. *Aust. N. Z. J. Psychiat.* **1**, 172, 1967. Although Yap regarded culture-bound syndromes as atypical variations of generally distributed psychogenic disorders and, in the tradition of the old cross-cultural psychiatry,[3] placed them into the acultural symptom clusters of Western psychiatric nosology, there is little doubt that his creation of the term was groundbreaking, and has helped raise important questions and research agendas for cultural psychiatry and medical anthropology.[30]

30. Landy D. Medical anthropology: a critical appraisal. In *Advances in Medical Social Science* (Edited by Ruffini J. L.), pp. 185–314. Gordon and Breach Science Publishers, New York, 1983.

31. Karp I. Deconstructing culture-bound syndromes. *Soc. Sci. Med.* **21**, 221, 1985.

32. Kroll J. Cross-cultural psychiatry, culture-bound syndromes and DSM-III. *Curr. Opin. Psychiat.* **1**, 46, 1988.

33. Cassidy C. M. Protein-energy malnutrition as a culture-bound syndrome. *Cult. Med. Psychiat.* **6**, 325, 1982.

34. Littlewood R. and Lipsedge M. The butterfly and the serpent: culture, psychopathology and biomedicine. *Cult. Med. Psychiat.* **11**, 289, 1987.

35. Hahn R. A. Culture-bound syndromes unbound. *Soc. Sci. Med.* **21**, 165, 1985.

36. This tendency, however, may arise more from the researcher's own limitations than the concept itself. Thus, researchers with both biomedical and social science backgrounds may integrate the neurobiological and psychosocial study of culture-bound conditions. Kleinman's study of Chinese neurasthenic patients' response to tricyclic drugs is an example,[37] while the study of autonomic and perceptual vulnerability in subjects prone to *koro* and its treatment with tricyclic antidepressant may be another.[38] Contrary to Hahn,[25] I believe that the CBS concept does not need to be seen to fragment human functioning.

37. Kleinman A. Neurasthenia and depression: a study of somatization and culture in China. *Cult. Med. Psychiat.* **6**, 117, 1982.

38. Turnier L. and Chouinard G. Effet anti-koro d'un antidépresseur tricyclique. *Can. J. Psychiat.* **35**, 331, 1990.

39. American Psychiatric Association. *Diagnostic and Statistical Manual of Mental Disorders*, 3rd edn. revised, DSM-III-R. APA, Washington, DC, 1987.

40. WHO. *The ICD-10 Classification of Mental and Behavioural Disorders—Clinical descriptions and diagnostic guidelines*. World Health Organization, Geneva, 1992.

41. There is a glossary containing the names and brief descriptions of 25 culture-bound syndromes (AN is not included) in the DSM-IV (pp. 844–849),[9] but they are not accepted as axis-I diagnoses.

42. Hughes C. C. Ethnopsychiatry. In *Medical Anthropology: Contemporary Theory and Method* (Edited by Johnson T. M. and Sargent C. F.), p. 141. Praeger, New York, 1990.

43. Helman C. G. Heart disease and the cultural construction of time: the type A behaviour pattern as a Western culture-bound syndrome. *Soc. Sci. Med.* **25**, 969, 1987.

44. Good B. J. Culture and psychopathology: directions for psychiatric anthropology. In *New Directions in Psychological Anthropology* (Edited by Schwartz T., White G. M. and Lutz C. A.), pp. 181–205. Cambridge University Press, Cambridge, 1992.

45. Simons R. C. and Hughes C. C. *The Culture-Bound Syndromes: Folk Illnesses of Psychiatric and Anthropological Interest*. Reidel, Dordrecht, 1985. These authors composed a fairly comprehensive glossary and synonymy of about 200 folk illnesses of psychiatric and anthropological interest. Anorexia nervosa and bulimia nervosa were not included.

46. Prince R. and TCheng-Laroche F. Culture-bound syndromes and international disease classifications. *Cult. Med. Psychiat.* **11**, 3, 1987.

47. Banks C. G. Culture in culture-bound syndromes: the case of anorexia nervosa. *Soc. Sci. Med.* **34**, 867, 1992.

48. Ritenbaugh C. Obesity as a culture-bound syndrome. *Cult. Med. Psychiat.* **6**, 347, 1982.

49. Hill R. F. and Fortenberry J. D. Adolescence as a culture-bound syndrome. *Soc. Sci. Med.* **35**, 73, 1992.

50. My reliance on Chinese data was due both to my familiarity with them as well as their availability in reasonable details. Where possible, data from non-Chinese cultures were also included. I believe that the theoretical aspects of some of my arguments are extendible to other contexts.

51. Prince[4] proposed a more restrictive definition of CBS based on the presence of specific psychosocial features. By intentionally disregarding culture-specific notions of cause, it may be less desirable for making a comparative analysis. Although this paper focused on Ritenbaugh's interpretive model, there are of course other theoretical models for understanding CBS, such as the structural model of Littlewood and Lipsedge, pertaining to sex roles and complementary notions of personal identity and attribution[34]

52. Prince,[4] Swartz,[5] Banks[47] and Gremillion[53] discussed AN from the standpoints of the usefulness of the concept, hermeneutics, religious asceticism, and feminism, respectively. They made little or no reference to data in non-Western societies.

53. Gremillion H. Psychiatry as social ordering: anorexia nervosa, a paradigm. *Soc. Sci. Med.* **35**, 57, 1992.

54. Bruch H. *Eating Disorders: Obesity, Anorexia Nercosa, and the Person Within*. Basic Books, New York, 1973.

55. Lee S., Ho T. P. and Hsu L. K.G. Fat phobic and non-fat phobic anorexia nervosa—a comparative study of 70 Chinese patients in Hong Kong. *Psychol. Med.* **23**, 999, 1993.

56. Crisp A. H. *Anorexia Nervosa: Let Me Be*. Plenum Press, London, 1980.

57. Mennell S. On the civilizing of appetite. *Theory, Cult. Society* 4, 373, 1987.

58. Lee S. How abnormal is the desire for slimness? A survey of eating attitudes and behaviour among Chinese undergraduates in Hong Kong. *Psychol. Med.* **23**, 437, 1993.

59. Mumford D. B., Whitehouse A. M. and Choudry I. Y. Sociocultural correlates of eating disorders among Asian schoolgirls in Bradford. *Br. J. Psychiat.* **158**, 222, 1991.

60. BMI is derived from the formula: body weight in kilograms/(height in meter)^2. It is a much better reflection of overall body shape than absolute body weight, but does not distinguish among boniness, muscularity, and fattiness. It ranges from 20–25 kg/m^2 in non-obese Western adult women, but within this biomedically "normal" range a high proportion of them feel fat and desire to lose weight.

61. Chun Z. F., Mitchell J. E., Li K., Yu W. M., Lan Y. D., Jun Z., Rong Z. Y., Huan Z. Z., Filice G. A., Pomeroy C. and Pyle R. L. The prevalence of

anorexia nervosa and bulimia nervosa among freshman medical college students in China. *Int. J. Eating Disorders* **12**, 209, 1992.

62. Gandhi D. H., Appaya M. P. and Machado T. Anorexia nervosa in Asian children. *Br. J. Psychiat.* **159**, 591, 1991.

63. Kleinman A. Major conceptual and research issues for cultural psychiatry. *Cult. Med. Psychiat.* **4**, 3, 1980.

64. Lee S. Unpublished data from a survey on "folk theories of anorexia nervosa."

65. Ritenbaugh's definition is generous since any one of the four criteria is sufficient for defining a condition as culture-bound. To the extent that these criteria were used primarily for the analysis of social discourse, this breadth of definition is not a matter for concern in this evaluative essay.

66. *The Shorter Oxford English Dictionary on Historical Principles*. Vol. 1, p. 223. Oxford University Press, Oxford, 1973.

67. Rodin J. Cultural and psychosocial determinants of weight concerns. *Ann. Intern. Med.* **119**, 643, 1993. The author discussed the media-promoted myth that willpower should guarantee that anyone can be slim, and hence a willingness for people to try almost any weight-loss strategy, resulting more often than not in frustration, shame, and defeat.

68. Just as the ICD-10[38] stipulates that culture-specific disorders "were first described in, and subsequently closely or exclusively associated with, a particular or cultural area" (p. 176), the DSM-IV[9] similarly defines CBS as a "locality-specific" pattern of aberrant behavior (p. 844). This geographical denotation of culture-specificity excludes AN as a culture-bound disorder nowadays.

69. Lee S. Self-starvation in contexts: towards the culturally sensitive understanding of anorexia nervosa. *Soc. Sci. Med.* **41**, 25, 1995.

70. DiNicola V. F. Anorexia Multiforme: self-starvation in historical and cultural context. Part II: Anorexia nervosa as a culture-reactive syndrome. *Transcult. Psychiat. Res. Rev.* **27**, 245, 1990.

71. Garfinkel P. E. and Garner D. M. *Anorexia Nervosa: A Multidimensional Perspective*. Basic Books, New York, 1982.

72. Swartz L. Illness negotiation: the case of eating disorders. *Soc. Sci. Med.* **24**, 613, 1987.

73. Yager J. and Davis C. Letter to the editor. *Transcult. Psychiat. Res. Rev.* **30**, 295, 1993.

74. Steiger H. Anorexia nervosa: is it the syndrome or the theorist that is culture- and gender-bound? *Transcult. Psychiat. Res. Rev.* **30**, 347, 1993.

75. Schmolling P. Eating attitude test scores in relation to weight, socioeconomic status, and family stability. *Psychol. Rep.* **63**, 295, 1988.

76. Dixon R. A. A note on the analysis of causation in psychological research: the influence theory. *Psychol. Record* **30**, 271, 1980.

77. The Aristotelian tetrad of causality also includes "material" and "formal" causes. These four causes are points of reference used in understanding developmental process and are not, in the modern sense, causes at all. The analysis of causation and the assignment of a cause, Dixon[76] argues, is in itself a highly theory-laden endeavor.

78. This variable relationship between fat phobia and AN may be likened to the increased but not consistent risk caused by cigarette smoking to lung cancer.

79. Seid R. P. Too "Close to the bone": The historical context for women's obsession with slenderness. In *Feminist Perspectives on Eating Disorders* (Edited by Fallon P., Katzman M. A. and Woolley S. C.), pp. 3–16. The Guilford Press, New York, 1994.

80. Huon G. F., Brown L. B. and Morris S. E. Lay beliefs about disordered eating. *Int. J. Eating Disorders* **7**, 239, 1988.

81. Szekely E. A. Women's anxious pursuit of attractive appearance. *Phenomenol. Pedagogy* 5, 108, 1987.

82. Yap P. M. Koro—A culture-bound depersonalization syndrome. *Br. J. Psychiat.* **111**, 43, 1965.

83. Here technology may consist of familiarization with the DSM manual and, where "scientific" research is concerned, official training in the use of structured biomedical interview schedules such as the SCID[84] which generates DSM-III-R diagnoses reliably. Ideology refers to the belief that fat phobia is the predominant rationale for food denial as well as being the cause of AN.

84. Spitzer R. L., Williams J. B. W., Miriam G. and First M. B. *Structured Clinical Interview for DSM-III-R— Patient Edition* (SCID-P, Version 1.0). American Psychiatric Press, Washington, DC, 1990.

85. Parry-Jones W. L. I. and Parry-Jones B. Implications of historical evidence for the classification of eating disorders. A dimension overlooked in DSM-III-R and ICD-10. *Br. J. Psychiat.* **165**, 287, 1994.

86. Habermas T. H. The psychiatric history of anorexia nervosa and bulimia nervosa: weight concerns and bulimic symptoms in early case reports. *Int. J. Eating Disorders* **8**, 259, 1989.

87. Habermas H. The role of psychiatric and medical traditions in the discovery and description of anorexia nervosa in France, Germany, and Italy, 1873–1918. *J. Nerv. Ment. Dis.* **170**, 360, 1991.

88. Szekely E. A. From eating disorders to women's situations: extending the boundaries of psychological inquiry. *Counsel. Psychol. Q.* **2**, 167, 1989.

89. Fahy T. A., Robinson P. H., Russell G. F. and Sheinman B. Anorexia nervosa following torture in a young African woman. *Br. J. Psychiat.* **153**, 385, 1988.

90. Chiu L. P. W. Anorexia nervosa in a young Chinese woman in Hong Kong. *Can. J. Psychiat.* **34**, 162, 1989.

91. Kleinman A. and Sung L. H. Why do indigenous practitioners successfully heal? *Soc. Sci. Med.* **13B**, 7, 1979.

92. Lee S. Applicability of psychotherapy for non-Western people. *Br. J. Psychiat.* **161**, 413, 1992.

93. Beutler L. E., Crago M. and Arizmendi T. G. Therapist variables in psychotherapy process and outcome. In *Handbook of Psychotherapy and Behaviour Change* (Edited by Garfield S. L. and Bergin A. E.), pp. 257–310. John Wiley and Sons, New York, 1986.

94. Cheng L. Y. and Lo H. T. On the advantages of cross-culture psychotherapy: the minority therapist/mainstream patient dyad. *Psychiatry* **54**, 386, 1991.

95. Kaplan A. G. Female or male psychotherapists for women: new formulations. In *Women's Growth in Connection* (Edited by Jordan J., Kaplan A., Miller J. B., Stiver I., and Surrey J.), pp. 268–305. The Guilford Press, New York, 1991.

96. The notion of gender, namely, that there are two natural and opposing categories of normative personhood, accompanied by a variety of identifying symbols, is itself a cultural production. Men may be as feminine as women may be masculine.

97. Brumberg J. J. *Fasting Girls: The Emergence of Anorexia Nervosa as a Modern Disease.* Harvard University Press, Cambridge, MA, 1988.

98. A recent advertisement on "The Renfrew Center" in the *Int. J. Eating Disorders* (December, 1994 issue, last page) stated that because "women are different, their therapy needs are different." At this "Most Insurance Accepted" Center, women can expect to "find inspiration and a new experience of themselves through intensive, therapeutic treatment programs which combine a respect for the unique psychology of women, the strength of a caring community and the active participation of each woman in her own recovery."

99. Zunino N., Agoos E. and Davis W. N. The impact of therapist gender on the treatment of bulimic women. *Int. J. Eating Disorders* **3**, 253, 1991.

100. Wooley S. C. The female therapist as outlaw. In *Feminist Perspectives on Eating Disorders* (Edited by Fallon P., Katzman M. A. and Woolley S. C.), pp. 318–338. The Guilford Press, New York, 1994.

101. Fairburn C. G., Jones J., Peveler R. C., Hope R. A. and O'Connor M. Psychotherapy and bulimia nervosa: longer-term effects of interpersonal psychotherapy, behaviour therapy, and cognitive behaviour therapy. *Arch. Gen. Psychiat.* **50**, 419, 1993.

102. Wohl J. Integration of cultural awareness into psychotherapy. *Am. J. Psychother.* **XLIII/43**, 343, 1989.

103. Hsu L. K. G. *Eating Disorders*, p. 130. The Guilford Press, New York, 1990.

104. Garner D. M. and Garfinkel P. E. Body image in anorexia nervosa: measurement, theory and clinical implications. *Int. J. Psychiat. Med.* **11**, 263, 1981.

105. Vandereycken W. The relevance of body-image disturbances for the treatment of bulimia. In *Bulimia Nervosa: Basic Research, Diagnosis and Therapy* (Edited by Fichter M. M.), p. 326. John Wiley and Sons, Chichester, 1990.

106. Goldberg S. C., Halmi K. A., Eckert E. D., Casper R. C., Davis J. M. and Roper M. Attitudinal dimensions in anorexia nervosa. *J. Psychiat. Res.* **15**, 239, 1980.

107. Bruch H. Perils of behaviour modification in treatment of anorexia nervosa. *JAMA* **230**, 1419, 1974.

108. Anorectic patients commonly complain about being exploited, dominated, coerced, and mistrusted by hospital staff.[106, 107] Psychodynamic theory holds that anorectic patients' battle with practitioners represents their need to strive for autonomy in the therapeutic situation, and results from their interpretation of external therapeutic

efforts as over-controlling. The resolution of their conflicts around self- and social control is seen as a foremost therapeutic goal.[54] By contrast, feminist writers believe that anorectic patients' "uncooperative" attitude during inpatient treatment is due to the intrinsically nonegalitarian relationship between therapist and client in a patriarchal setting. This inequality replicates the pattern of oppression which anorectic patients have experienced outside of the "therapeutic" milieu.[109] Feminist therapy aims to minimize this power differential and demystify the therapy relationship.

109. Sesan R. Feminist inpatient treatment for eating disorders: an oxymoron? In *Feminist Perspectives on Eating Disorders* (Edited by Fallon P., Katzman M.A. and Woolley S. C.), pp. 251–271. The Guilford Press, New York, 1994.

110. Shorter E. The first great increase in anorexia nervosa. *J. Soc. Hist.* **21**, 69, 1987.

111. Insulin therapy is rarely used by Western psychiatrists because anorectic patients are considered to be highly preoccupied with food[56] (p. 3), but deny it merely as a form of defensive self-control. Within this conceptual frame, "anorexia" is a misnomer. Nonetheless, a study in Hong Kong showed that 16 percent of Chinese anorectic patients used primarily "no appetite/hunger," a convenient and irrefutable argument[8] (p. 166), to explain food refusal.[55]

112. Lu L. G. *Dredging Psychotherapy*. Shanghai Science and Technology Press, Shanghai, 1989. Established by a Chinese psychiatrist, Long-guang Lu, this form of psychotherapy is said to combine the philosophy of psychological treatment in traditional Chinese medicine with the principles of Western cognitive-behavioral therapy. It promotes psychological health by cleaning out ("dredging") psychological blocks in oneself (p.25). In Western terms, it is probably "eclectic" in nature.

113. Faltus F. Anorexia nervosa in Czechoslovakia. *Int. J. Eating Disorders* **5**, 581, 1986.

114. From a clinical vantage point, it may be argued that few, if any, psychiatric conditions will fulfill Ritenbaugh's fourth criterion completely. Anthropologists are typically chided by clinicians for overemphasizing the importance of cultural factors in the inherently complex process of healing (see Steiger's commentary on two papers[47,53] which offered an anthropological analysis of AN and its treatment failures[74]). However, Ritenbaugh's crite-

rion undoubtedly has heuristic value in stimulating needed reflections on culture and treatment.

115. Lucas A. Toward the understanding of anorexia nervosa as a disease entity. *Mayo Clin. Proc.* **56**, 254, 1981.

116. For example, although tricyclic drugs are biomedically labelled as antidepressants, they ameliorate not only depression, but also a diversity of disease categories including panic disorder, obsessive compulsive disorder, generalized anxiety disorder, phobia, negative symptoms of schizophrenia, bulimia, *koro*, narcolepsy, sleep apnea, and even somnambulism and nocturnal enuresis in children.

117. Minuchin S., Rosman B. and Baker L. *Psychosomatic Families: Anorexia Nervosa in Context*. Harvard University Press, Cambridge, MA, 1978.

118. My clinical experience in Hong Kong indicated that overeating was frequently tolerated in the Chinese family. Few Chinese parents were aware that it could signify a psychiatric disease.

119. Beoporad J. R., Ratey J. J., O'Driscoll G. and Daehler M. L. Hysteria, anorexia, and the culture of self-denial. *Psychiatry* **51**, 96, 1988.

120. Nemiah J. C. Anorexia nervosa: fact and theory. *Am. J. Digest. Disorders* **3**, 249, 1958.

121. Casper R. C. On the emergence of bulimia nervosa as a syndrome: a historical view. *Int. J. Eating Disorders* **2**, 3, 1983.

122. Murphy H. B. M. History and the evolution of syndromes: The striking case of Latah and Amok. In *Psychopathology—Contributions from the Social, Behavioural and Biological Sciences* (Edited by Hammer M., Salzinger K. and Sutton S.), chap. 2, pp. 33–55. John Wiley and Sons, New York, 1973.

123. Lee R. L. M. Structure and anti-structure in the culture-bound syndromes: The Malay case. *Cult. Med. Psychiat.* **5**, 233, 1981.

124. Murray S., Touyz S. and Beumont P. Knowledge about eating disorders in the community. *Int. J. Eating Disorders* **9**, 87, 1990.

125. Toro J., Salamero M. and Martinez E. Assessment of sociocultural influences on the aesthetic body shape model in anorexia nervosa. *Acta Psychiat. Scand.* **89**, 147, 1994.

126. In the Aristotelian model of causality, a final cause may *follow* its effects.[76]

127. Whitaker A., Davies M., Shaffer D., Johnson J., Abrams S., Walsh B. T., and Kalikow K. The struggle to be thin: a survey of anorectic and

bulimic symptoms in a non-referred adolescent population. *Psychol. Med.* **19**, 143, 1989.

128. King M. B. Eating disorders in a general practice population: prevalence, characteristics and follow-up at 12 to 18 months. *Psychol. Med. Monogr. Suppl.* **14**, 1, 1989.

129. Lucas A. The eating disorder 'epidemic': more apparent than real? *Pediatr. Ann.* **21**, 746, 1992.

130. Feighner J. P., Robbins E. and Guze S. B. Diagnostic criteria for use in psychiatric research. *Arch. Gen. Psychiat.* **26**, 57, 1972.

131. American Psychiatric Association. *Diagnostic and Statistical Manual of Mental Disorders*, 3rd edn, DSM-III. APA, Washington, DC, 1980.

132. W.H.O. *ICD-10: 1986 Draft of Chapter V—Categories F00–F99. Mental, Behavioural and Developmental Disorders.* Division of Mental Health. World Health Organization, Geneva, 1987.

133. Wiseman C. V., Gray J. J., Mosimann J. E. and Ahrens A. H. Cultural expectations of thinness in women: an update. *Int. J. Eating Disorders* **11**, 85, 1992.

134. Business as well as politics have contributed to the scene. A diagnostic criterion based on >25 percent weight loss may mean that some AN subjects in the West will receive delayed treatment because of the lack of insurance coverage, or that some eating disorder clinics will have to close down.

135. Gull W. W. Anorexia nervosa (apepsia hysterica, anorexia hysterica). *Transact. Clin. Soc. (London)* **7**, 22, 1874.

136. Patients with AN in Hong Kong were also associated with marked weight loss of over 33 percent (mean BMI = 13.35 kg/m²). Rarely, if ever, did they know about relatives or friends who suffered from AN, or read about the anorectic literature.[55] The situation in Taiwan appeared similar.[15] The Western reports of anorectic patients recommending books for their doctors to read[53] (p. 59), and feeling unauthentic for not practicing self-induced vomiting,[72] were not encountered.

137. Lacey J. H. Anorexia nervosa and XY gonadal dysgenesis. *Br. J. Psychiat.* **161**, 276, 1992.

138. The term *weight phobia* was coined by Crisp (n. 56, p. 78), in this clinically derived theory of psychobiological regression, to refer to anorectic patients' panicky avoidance of a normal body weight and the adult responsibilities it symbolized. He postulated a subpubertal threshold weight of 38–41 kg. at which patients should exhibit defiance toward further weight gain in order not to reinstate the process of maturation. This phenomenon was not consistently encountered in the author's clinical experience, as patients' resistance could occur at different times during the course of treatment. The allied term of *fat phobia*[58] is more phenomenologically oriented and less interpretive in nature. It describes anorectic patients' immediate experience of feeling fat and refusing food as a result. Unlike weight phobia, it may also refer to the disparagement of specific body parts in subjects with a relatively normal overall body shape.

139. Garner D. M. and Garfinkel P. E. The Eating Attitudes Test: an index of the symptoms of anorexia nervosa. *Psychol. Med.* **9**, 273, 1979.

140. Bruch H. Four decades of eating disorders. In *Handbook of Psychotherapy for Anorexia Nervosa and Bulimia* (Edited by Garner D. M. and Garfinkel P. E.), pp. 7–18. The Guilford Press, New York, 1985.

141. Furnham A. and Alibhai N. Cross-cultural differences in the perception of female body shapes. *Psychol. Med.* **13**, 829, 1983.

142. Hence the joke "how do I catch anorexia nervosa?".

143. Branch C. H. H. and Eurman L. J. Social attitudes towards patients with anorexia nervosa. *Am. J. Psychiat.* **137**, 631, 1980.

144. On 24 November 1994, a 15-year-old Chinese student who weighed 32 kg and presumably suffered from AN collapsed and died while she was walking in a street in Hong Kong. As no person was publicly known to die from AN in the past, this led to unusually extensive media coverage which centered on dieting as the cause of her death, and publicized AN as much as they warned people about its lethality. Two widely read newspapers used "dying to look perfect" and "dieting disorder hits affluent Hong Kong" as their headlines, respectively. Potentially harmful compensatory behaviors such as self-induced vomiting were freely referred to.

THE MISSING VOICE OF THE CRITICALLY ILL: A MEDICAL SOCIOLOGIST'S FIRST-PERSON ACCOUNT

David A. Rier
Bar-Ilan University, Israel

Existing sociological studies of critical illness deal mainly with providers and families, but seldom with patients, themselves. Moreover, most of the literature on the patient's experience involves chronic illness. Based on the author's experience as an intensive care unit (ICU) patient, this paper demonstrates that certain concerns of the post-Parsonian literature, such as full disclosure of information to patients and patients' negotiation and collaboration with physicians, are of minimal relevance for critically ill patients. This paper also discusses the notebook the author used in the ICU to communicate while on a respirator, thus unintentionally leaving a concurrent record of his experience, in a form of "inadvertent ethnography." This allowed him to reconstruct experiences rarely accessible to sociologists. Such notebooks can help us construct accounts of the ICU patient's experience, and move us toward a sociology of the critically ill patient. Potential topics for this new research area are suggested.

INTRODUCTION

In the intensive care unit (ICU), wrote Zussman (referring to depersonalization), "patients vanish" (1992: 43). Medical sociology largely replicates this disappearing act: The voice of the critically ill is virtually absent from the contemporary literature. This paper is grounded in a first-hand account of my own critical illness. Beyond drawing attention to the missing voice of the critically ill, this paper describes how my ICU experience led me, as a medical sociologist, to reassess current thinking on such issues as disclosure of information to patients and patient partic-

ipation in treatment. Its secondary aim is to propose a particular type of data source (notebooks kept by intubated ICU patients) with which to capture the experiences of the critically ill, and to outline how this might move us toward a sociology of critical illness from the *patient's* perspective.

Critical illness is hardly terra incognita to the sociology literature. However, studies typically focus on the perspective of physicians (e.g., Zussman 1992; Harvey 1996) or nurses (e.g., Strauss [1968]1975; Asch et al. 1997), or else emphasize provider–family interaction (e.g., Sosnowitz 1984; Heimer and Staffen 1995). Though some research does tap patients' words, these exceptions are limited. Robillard (1994), a sociologist already unable to speak because of an existing disease, described his months as an ICU patient with

Reprinted from *Sociology of Health & Illness*, vol. 22, no. 1 (2000), pp. 68–93, by permission of Blackwell Publishers Ltd./Editorial Board.

pneumonia. He discussed his relation to the technology on which he depended, and the cultural and communication gaps between him and his nurses. Though on a respirator for at least part of the time, he wrote as if he retained full mental faculties throughout; while in the ICU, he even worked on a book (1994: 385)! This, combined with his existing condition, makes his experience of critical illness a highly atypical one. Moreover, he barely engaged with the medical sociology literature at all; instead, he interpreted his experience via postmodernism. At the opposite end of the spectrum is Richman (1996), a sociologist who spent two months comatose in the ICU. He recalled virtually nothing of the actual ICU experience; instead, his work explored the dreams he had while comatose. Cowie's (1976) study of heart attack patients focused mainly on prehospital help-seeking behavior, and tapped only subjects' retrospective reconstructions. Similarly, Speedling's (1980) retrospective interviews with heart attack patients and their families focused on how they interpreted the ICU experience. However, few patients' voices were presented; and these were usually describing the period before they entered the ICU, or as they were leaving it. Jablonski's (1994) paper, based on retrospective interviews with former intubated ICU patients, is strictly descriptive, and included no sociological analysis.

Even in the literature of sociological illness narratives, with its avowed focus on the patient's experience (Hyden 1997), the voices of the critically ill are scarce, for this literature is dominated by accounts of chronic illness (e.g., Charmaz 1991; Paget 1993; Hyden and Sachs 1998; Zola 1982). There do exist some first-hand sociological narratives involving critical illness. Hart (1977) described her shifts in status and identity from expectant mother to patient, as her childbirth process grew increasingly medicalized, culminating in a misdiagnosed, near-lethal case of puerperal fever. Mapes

(1977) explained how he "worked the system" to secure appropriate care for his pneumothorax. Frank (1991) described his heart attack, including how he and his physician discussed it, and how this illness differed from his subsequent bout with cancer. Timmermans (1994) wrote of how he came to understand that his mother would eventually succumb to the effects of her stroke. However, these pieces scarcely included the perspective of the patient during the weakest, impaired state. Timmermans did not include the patient's perspective at all, and the other works, like most accounts, glossed over the truly critical phase (Hart 1977: 104–105, 108; Mapes 1977: 35; Frank 1991: 9). Instead, these accounts emphasized the prior or subsequent phases, often highlighting patients' bargaining and negotiation with the medical staff. We will return to this literature later. Meanwhile, it is clear that there is a lack of first-hand accounts grounded in concurrent (as opposed to retrospective) recording of the critical stage of illness,[1] including the "altered states" phases in which mental faculties are impaired. Still rarer are reflexive versions of such accounts, in which medical sociologists discuss how being critically ill influenced them as medical sociologists. Such gaps in the literature are important, because the critically ill, too, have their stories to tell.

Early in 1997, I learned this the hard way. Soon after beginning the winter intersession at the Israeli university where I teach medical sociology (and one month after the birth of our fifth child), I was admitted to the ICU of a Jerusalem hospital in acute respiratory and kidney failure, the products of a pneumonia of rare virulence. I was 34 years old and, until then, healthy. Two days after entering the hospital, I was sedated, intubated, and placed on a respirator, where I remained for the next 15 days. During my first two weeks in the ICU, I surprised my physicians by failing to respond to very intensive treatment, and (as I was told later) it was not clear to them that I would live. In any position save that of sitting up, I felt as though I were drowning. Due to my sedation and weakness, I slept often. Even while awake, I was not always fully alert. At one point, the combination of high fever and sedation produced auditory hallucinations. My disorientation would have been greater had my wife not wisely persuaded the staff to let me wear my glasses 24 hours a day (as an added bonus, I soon realized that, should my respirator fail, I could hurl my glasses into the center of the room to attract attention). Eventually, I began slowly to improve, and finally made a full recovery (but for having acquired my first real *chronic* illness, mild asthma, in the wake of the pneumonia). In all, I spent nearly three weeks in the ICU, and another five days on a general medical unit before my discharge. Though it would be over 18 months before I regained all my energy, I was able to return to work after five weeks of home rest.

SETTING

My ICU was dominated by an open area that also contained the nursing station; off this area were six cubicle-like open bays. Each held one bed, assorted equipment, and a chair or two. Curtains could be closed to screen off a cubicle from the main area. My own cubicle lay at the end of the main area, directly opposite the front door to the unit. For my first 10 days on the respirator, I was confined to bed. Since I was tethered to the respirator, my field of vision was restricted. Subsequently, I began to spend increasing periods in a lounge chair near my bed, in an effort to improve lung drainage. Though still attached to the respirator, I could now look out into the main ICU area, including both the nursing station and the entrance to the unit. This gave me a view of both staff and visitors.

And there *were* visitors. In the United States, visits to very sick patients in the ICU are generally limited to immediate family,

and for very short periods at that. In the two American ICUs studied by Zussman, visitors were mostly limited to 10- to 15-minute visits every two hours (1992: 15). Yet in my Israeli ICU, the number, duration, and timing of visits were virtually unlimited. My wife was able to spend much of the day at my bedside. This was possible partly due to the availability of a side room, within the ICU, in which my wife could nurse our newborn daughter. She could then leave her there with a volunteer or with my mother (who had rushed to Jerusalem from the United States after my condition deteriorated). Many others visited as well, ranging from the commander of my army reserve unit to rabbis under whom I studied (one of whom came nearly every night, for an hour).

METHODOLOGY

The primary data source for this paper is the notebook I used to communicate (by writing) while I was on the respirator, when an endotracheal tube made speech impossible. Actually, I began to write even before I was placed on the respirator, as I was already too short of breath to speak easily. According to my wife, a nurse, seeing that I was desperate to communicate, brought me a pad and pen. After I had written about 30 pages in the pad, my wife replaced it with an 8 × 10½ inch spiral notebook, in which I wrote another 110 pages while on the respirator (in this paper, the term *notebook* covers both the pad and the spiral notebook).

This notebook was not a diary. Neither was it intended as a sociologist's record of his experiences in the ICU. While I was in the ICU, the notebook was strictly a means of communicating with others. As such, most of the journal entries are, in and of themselves, quite banal. We will see further however, that these entries were a potent tool in recapturing experiences rarely documented in the sociological literature.

I was not always able to write, nor could I always write coherently or legibly. My spelling in both English and Hebrew deteriorated. Though I seldom dated the pages, one can track the course of my illness by noting the phases in which the lines written in the notebook appear in lazy arcs all over the paper, with words sometimes trailing off in the middle, uncompleted. Sometimes, there are more explicit clues to my mental status: At one point, for instance, I wrote, "I often hear many voices. . . . Am I crazy?" However, at many other points, the writing suggests I was in fairly full command of my faculties. In the preparation of this paper, the notebook was supplemented by copies of faxes exchanged daily between my wife and our respective parents in the United States during my illness, as well as subsequent conversations with the staff, my wife, other family members, and others who visited during my hospitalization. Unless otherwise noted, all descriptions of my hospitalization recorded herein come from my own memories, usually aided by consultation with the notebook.

One advantage I had in interpreting my experience in the ICU was a better than layman's grasp of medical details. Eight years earlier, our premature triplets had spent almost three months in a neonatal ICU. I was thus already familiar with such staples of ICU routine as respirators, blood gases, and monitors. Moreover, I had once volunteered in an emergency room and trained as an emergency medical technician (EMT). Finally, my doctoral training combined public health and medical sociology.

CRITICAL ILLNESS: A PARSONIAN WORLD?

Before proceeding, it is worth noting key aspects of my illness experience that affected my relationship to my wider social surroundings. First, unlike chronic illnesses, which may begin with a twinge not diagnosed or treated for many months (e.g., Davis [1963]1991; Bury 1982), the onset of my own illness was acute, sudden. This telescoped trajectory offered little chance to reflect on or prepare for the experience. By the time I woke up sick the first morning, I was already so weak that I often could not think clearly. I had very high fever, chills, and difficulty breathing. The day I entered the hospital (two days later), I deteriorated rapidly, to the point that the struggle to breathe consumed nearly all my attention. This leads to a second characteristic of my illness, immediacy: the focus on the next breath, or the next painful procedure. This focus on the present was reinforced by my tendency while heavily sedated to forget the events of one day nearly completely by the next. Third, as my horizon of time was compressed, so too was my social horizon, which rapidly narrowed to that of my doctors, nurses, and visitors. Similarly, my authority and responsibilities of home and work quickly and decisively fell away. Curiously, this acute, critical illness seemed to disrupt my life far less than did many of the non–life-threatening chronic illnesses described by Bury (1982) and Charmaz (1991). Because my illness seemed simply to *replace* my earlier life, rather than *compete* with it, I was spared the stress (so prominent in accounts of chronic illness) of trying to manage my normal obligations while ill. However, perhaps the crucial point is that my condition rendered me fully dependent on my doctors and nurses, with little physical or mental strength with which to challenge them.

For a medical sociologist, being ill offers a priceless opportunity to engage, in the most intimate manner possible, with the subject of one's lifework. My own illness constituted a proving ground of the medical sociology theories to which I had subscribed, and which I had been teaching my students. In fact, we will see that my illness transported me across ethnic groups and back two generations, leading me to reevaluate these theories. Indeed, several aspects of my illness provided practical lessons in the interaction between theory and lived experience.

For instance, I've always enjoyed teaching Zborowski's ([1952]1960) classic work on cultural responses to pain. It will be recalled that, whereas the Italian-American patients in his study trusted their doctors and were happy once drugs relieved their pain, the Jewish patients were more suspicious. Continuing to worry that the painkillers merely masked a serious, undetected problem, the Jews were not appeased when their pain abated, and questioned their physicians' competence. Until this bout with pneumonia, by far the most serious malady I've ever experienced, I had fitted Zborowski's typology for my ethnic group (Jewish) perfectly. I'd always been particularly suspicious of painkillers, and extremely concerned with identifying the ultimate cause of the illness. To that end, I often conducted my own searches of the medical literature, sought second opinions, paid close attention to physicians' specific credentials, asked detailed questions, and otherwise adopted an activist patient stance.

Yet I now know that Zborowski's categories are not fixed, that they can vary with the intensity of illness: In the ICU, I exchanged my Jewish patient identity for that of an Italian patient. First, I had complete confidence in my physicians and nurses. Second, I judged my medical progress mainly by the ease with which I could breathe, and the frequency with which the staff had to perform painful procedures on me. In this I was alone: Everyone else defined my medical condition in more empirical terms. I found it disconcerting that every single visitor to my bedside, even before greeting me, would first peer intently at a point 12 inches over my head. I was only marginally aware and minimally interested that they were looking at a wide array of gauges and dials detailing my status. I was at a loss to understand everyone's preoccupation with such trivia. After all, I was able to tell them (by writing in my notebook) how I felt. If I was

breathing comfortably on the respirator, I could not understand the long faces over a discouraging blood oxygen saturation value. If I was feeling poorly that day, I felt left out by the general elation over a robust PO_2 reading.[2] But regardless of how I felt, I was for the first time in my adult life content mainly to leave the details to the medical staff. As I wrote to a visitor at one point, "I'm very low-key—not my curious old self."

This new passivity had corollary implications, which would place the gap between theory and experience into sharp relief. I'd often joked with my medical sociology students that much of the course could be called, "Talcott Parsons and Why He's Wrong." I'd then explain that Parsons (1951: 428–479) defined the patient role as a passive one of simply seeking medical attention and complying with the doctor's orders. Indeed, this theoretical outlook substantially mirrored typical doctor–patient relations in the America of the 1950s. I would continue by explaining that Parsons's work set the agenda for subsequent generations of sociologists. However, I'd demonstrate that Parsons has since been criticized as being paternalistic, as too readily assuming that patients should place their trust in the physician, as paying insufficient attention to the patient's perspective, to the patient's ability to challenge, negotiate, collaborate with, or circumvent the physician (Gerhardt 1989; Gallagher 1979; Levine and Kozloff 1978; Turner 1990). Such critiques have become a "cottage industry in medical sociology" (Frank 1997: 132). By the time I'd started graduate school in the 1980s, class discussions often treated Parsons's approach as obsolete, almost a "1950s model."

As I taught my students, much of this shift is bound up with social changes, particularly concerning the relationship of patients to the medical profession. This relationship has changed greatly since Parsons's day, partly because of the influence of social movements such as feminism (Boston Women's Health

Book Collective 1979) and consumerism (Reeder 1972). Especially for chronic diseases, patients today often prefer an active or at least collaborative role in treatment decisions (Coyle 1999: 115; Degner et al. 1997: 1490). Indeed, what Donovan and Blake wrote regarding medication compliance could be said about many areas: "Today's patients want more information and greater opportunities to be active in their dealings with medical practitioners" (1992: 508). As Crossley observed, many now advocate a "patient empowerment ideology" (1998: 508), and a "popularised discourse of empowerment" is common among consumer and patient groups (1998: 528). Illness narratives frequently reflect such "post-Parsonian" themes. Since the 1970s, narratives have often manifested a critical stance, in which Parsonian trust in the medical establishment has been replaced by fear, anger, or scepticism (Hawkins 1993: 4–9).

Similarly, today's sociological literature describes and frequently endorses patient behavior far different from that portrayed in Parsons's model, and different too from what was common in Parsons's era. This is frequently expressed in terms of full disclosure of information and participation in clinical decision making (e.g., Cooper 1997; Stewart and Sullivan 1987). Medical sociologists often explicitly advocate such patient behavior (e.g., Donovan and Blake 1992: 512; Indyk and Rier 1993). Sociological thinking on disclosure, in particular, has long been critical of physicians' withholding information from patients (Davis 1960; Glaser and Strauss 1965; Millman 1977). Sociologists' first-person illness narratives often portray a quest for self-determination, with patients challenging or negotiating with their physicians to extract maximal information, collecting their own information, exploring alternative medicine, using impression management to manipulate the system to their advantage, and attempting to play as active a role as possible in their treatment (Macintyre and Oldman 1977; Paget 1993;

Butler and Rosenblum 1991; Mapes 1977; Hart 1977; Webb 1977).

Medical sociology's embrace of the empowerment model is not entirely uncritical (Lupton 1997; Coyle 1999; Crossley 1998; Crossley and Crossley 1998). Still, it permeates the literature, and published anthologies, designed for classroom use, help to codify and transmit this post-Parsonian critical, activist tradition (e.g., Conrad and Kern 1990; Wallace 1990). The field of bioethics expresses congruent trends in its contemporary emphases on patient autonomy and self-determination (Smith 1996). This preoccupation is part of a wider "culture of rights" (Zussman 1992: 9–12). Certainly, the "empowered patient" model is the tradition in which I was trained, and which had guided my own writing and teaching.

Apart from the social forces mentioned above, there is another explanation for medical sociology's contemporary thinking on patient–provider relations: an explicit focus on chronic illness. Parsons's sick-role model has often been criticized for over-emphasizing acute illness (Turner 1990: 47; Gallagher 1979). Subsequent researchers have sought to correct this, with a new focus on chronic illness (e.g., Strauss et al. 1982: 978; Stewart and Sullivan 1987: 40–41; Bury 1991: 452). Such work often emphasizes, *contra* Parsons, how active patients can or should be. Thus, (as in many of the accounts cited above) the chronically ill are often described as negotiating with physicians over treatment and the interpretation of symptoms (e.g., Hyden and Sachs 1998; Bury 1991: 460), or as manipulating settings and appearances (e.g., Bury 1991: 462). We are much the richer for research exploring such facets of the patient experience. Yet medical sociologists' enthusiasm to move beyond Parsons seems to have led us also to move beyond (if not abandon) studies of acute illness.[3] It is as if sociologists, having conceded that acute, critical illness is Parsonian territory, deserted the field for the next several decades in pursuit of topics more amenable to non-Parsonian analysis. In so doing, perhaps we have thrown out the baby with the bathwater (as Fahy and Smith 1999: 71 suggest of Parsons's critics in another context), leaving certain kinds of questions unanswered (as will be discussed in the final section). As for myself, in what is the most lasting result of my unaccustomed passivity in the ICU, my illness provoked me to reassess the critique of Parsons I had been teaching only weeks before.

For, despite my deep commitment to disclosure, negotiation, and patient participation, the reactionary truth is that I was too sick to know certain details of my case, too weak to be a partner in decision making. Coyle (1999: 115) has also noted that patients facing critical illness reject full disclosure and avoid assuming responsibility for their care. As Haug and Lavin observed, a patient when *critically* ill may "abandon a consumerist stance and accept the doctor's control in a desperate need to get well" (1981: 223). In this sense, one might say that I had travelled back in time, that I had a "1950s-model" illness—one which turned me into a 1950s-style patient— which is more amenable to interpretation by Parsons's 1950s model than by theories of more recent vintage.

NEGOTIATION AND PARTICIPATION, DISCLOSURE AND TRUST

For example, no informed consent forms were offered to me or my wife during my entire hospitalization, though a range of diagnostic procedures were performed. Nor were my personal preferences or values sought. Generally, decisions were made about my treatment, and I was told something about them later. Most of my physicians were friendly and warm, but little doctor–patient partnership existed.

Of course, my case was straightforward, involving no quality of life or ethical dilemmas. I wanted to live, and had a chance at full recovery. Unlike the pattern common to a chronic illness trajectory, moreover, my status as an acute, critical patient meant that decisions often had to be made quickly. Then, too, my condition presented only a narrow range of clinical options. Given the extent to which my lungs were compromised, and the difficulty I was having breathing, I understood, for example, that I *needed* the respirator. No other delivery device came close to providing as much oxygen, and the struggle to breathe was rapidly exhausting me. Overall, there was not the same potential for negotiation or partnership often present (for most of the trajectory, at least) with a disease such as breast cancer, where various treatment options may exist, and there is often sufficient time to explore them. As Zussman (1992: 36) has observed, truly critically ill patients rarely make effective advocates or partners in treatment.

Interestingly, the true nature of their relationships with the doctors may not always be clear even to alert critically ill patients. For much of my time in the ICU, I *believed* that my doctors and I were engaged in a "mutual participation"–model relationship. In fact, our relationship was much closer to the Parsonian "activity-passivity" model (in which the doctor does something to the passive patient, without the latter's participation), to use Szasz and Hollender's ([1956]1987) formulations.

Consider my intubation. On my second morning in the ICU, my doctors broached the subject of the respirator, explaining why they thought it might be a useful option down the road. They respectfully answered my questions, which focused on the implications of the endotracheal tube it would necessitate. I was especially concerned that the sedation required to tolerate the tube would probably render me unconscious for most of the time I would be on the respirator. Yet since, even with a facemask delivering high-concentration oxygen, I was already too short of breath to speak or eat without great difficulty, I agreed that a respirator might eventually come in handy. I had the definite impression that I was a full partner in this decision. Thus, when my wife arrived shortly thereafter, I wrote to her explaining that "we" had decided that I might eventually need a respirator. I proudly stressed that I had been part of the decision-making process. What neither my wife nor I knew was that, from the moment I was admitted to the ICU, the doctors had considered the respirator inevitable, given the amount of fluid in my lungs. They had merely decided to wait a bit, given my general health and youth, in case I improved.

Yet the staff had given me the impression that the respirator was merely a possible option for the future. I was therefore surprised to see them converge on me that very night, with palpable urgency, saying, "We're putting you on a respirator *now*." Shocked, I protested. I was particularly disturbed about the prospect of being unconscious for an indefinite period at such short notice; I tried to think of last-minute instructions to leave my wife. One nurse immediately engaged in a deft piece of "cooling out the mark."[4] She very calmly observed:

> Look, they may want to intubate you later. It'll help you breathe and make it easier for them to do bronchoscopies if they want. If you're going to get the respirator later, you may as well get it now, when it's not an emergency, right?

I was so impressed by this reasoning that I graciously gave my assent (even as the staff clustered around my bedside quite rapidly preparing to intubate), happily returning to my delusion of partnership in the "elective" decision to use the respirator. Only much later did my wife tell me that she was given a far different picture when the staff subsequently called to tell her of my intubation. When she too protested that this was supposed to have been just a "down-the-road" possibility, she was bluntly told, "We had to intubate him immediately: His blood gases dropped suddenly."

The next day, I later learned, one physician explained to my wife that my intubation had

actually been inevitable. My wife responded that she did not want any further information withheld from her. From then on, this doctor fully honored her request, sparing her little. Though many of the other physicians were reluctant to divulge bad news to her unless pressed, my wife did manage to extract most of the details—and their sobering implications—from the physicians and nurses on the unit. In some ways, in fact, my wife noted much wider availability of patient information and records than is common in an American ICU. Both she and other visitors were able to peruse portions of my chart (including information on medications, lab values, and vital signs) in detail. My colleagues and students who telephoned the ICU were sometimes given detailed updates of my blood gas values, etc. My wife regularly faxed such data to my uncle, former chief of a coronary-care unit in the United States. He was flabbergasted at the amount of information to which she was allowed access.

As for myself, despite surprising the staff by remaining mostly awake and often alert despite heavy sedation, all this time I only *thought* I was being told everything. The doctors did give me status reports and explanations, and both they and the nurses were careful to explain procedures they were about to perform on me. Yet they spared me most of the more distressing details, particularly regarding prognosis. One ICU doctor (my wife later told me) seemed always to give my wife the most grim interpretation possible of my situation, yet even *this* physician radiated optimism in my presence. The selective withholding of information applied not only to mortality risk. Nobody mentioned the long-term risks of using the respirator, which I viewed innocently as simply the machine that was doing all the hard work for me. Nor did I know until after discharge that, had I not begun to improve just when I did, the doctors would have performed a tracheotomy to prevent complications from the endotracheal tube. Hearing the word "tracheotomy" would have scared me more than thoughts of death, because I would have feared it could end my career as a university lecturer.

Like many other patients in my situation (Jablonski 1994), I was spared even nonmedical upsetting news, whether family- or current events–related. I am very grateful for this, because I was then so sick and weak that I simply could not have handled such news. This assessment is based partly on what happened upon my finally hearing one particular piece of bad family news (which my family had been concealing from me) a full 11 days after being taken off the respirator, when I had been out of the ICU for nine days and home from the hospital for four. Even then, this news nearly overwhelmed the limited physical strength I could marshal to absorb it. While true that my reactions when at my sickest were unpredictable, I am convinced that hearing this news while in the ICU could have killed me.

As it was, I was remarkably confident throughout my illness, and felt secure even while on the respirator—a common response (Jones et al. 1979; Bergbom-Engberg and Haljamae 1988). Even in the two days before intubation, I never worried about the fact that I was having such difficulty breathing that, as mentioned above, speaking or eating demanded great effort. I simply assumed that the staff would reverse the situation. After all, I recall thinking, isn't that why one goes to the hospital? Throughout most of my stay in the ICU, I maintained the same happy assumption.

Much of my confidence was generated by the optimistic air projected by the staff. In his ethnography of two ICUs, Zussman (1992), like Strauss ([1968]1975) before him, claimed that, whereas "sentimental work" (cultivating trust, personal relationships, and preserving patients' individual identities despite serious illness) is important to medical treatment, this is not true in the ICU, where the patients are often unable to communicate. In the ICU, argued Zussman, "patients vanish" (1992: 43). Indeed, one doctor in Zussman's work spoke

of ICU patients as being reduced to "a little bit of a science project" (1992: 32); another compared ICU care to "veterinary medicine" (1992: 33). The focus is on the technical; "[p]ersonhood has little to do with the tasks at hand. Doctors and nurses . . . do not imagine it as part of the process of treatment." (1992: 40). My own experience was far different. Not only did the staff engage quite actively in sentimental work, but I consider this to have been critical to my recovery (as discussed below). Of course, for part of my time in the ICU, I was the only patient on the unit awake and able to communicate with the staff. As one nurse told my wife, the staff particularly enjoyed communicating with alert patients. In any event, according to both my own recollections and those of my wife, the staff were consistently patient and kind, as well as cheerful. Both doctors and (especially) nurses took great pains to preserve my "personhood," which task, one nurse later explicitly informed me, they considered part of their job. They protected my dignity insofar as possible, often had the extra minute to come over and kid around with me, and always—always—met my requests with a smile, treating me as a friend or relative. Indeed, one older Russian-immigrant physician treated me as if I were her nephew; she even pinched my cheek whenever she examined me. My relationships with staff were so friendly that I was occasionally nonplussed when, during rounds, the staff approached my bed and did not joke around or chat: I had forgotten that medical work in the ICU does involve more than social calls. During the difficult extubation procedure, when I was briefly unable to breathe, both doctors and nurses literally cheered me on, counting out the seconds. Later, a nurse reporting for her shift entered the unit. Before even taking off her coat, she happened to see me sitting up, detached from the respirator. She ran straight into my room, whooping for joy.

As could be predicted from the nursing literature (Bergbom-Engberg and Haljamae

1988), the staff's cheerfulness, and the personal attention they lavished on me, gave me a strong sense of security. As mentioned earlier, this conviction that everything was under control and would turn out all right remained with me through most of even the most critical phase of my illness. But given my weakness, not even the staff's smiles and attention could have sustained this security had they given me the full, discouraging story they were giving to my wife. Though it might seem that my sense of security was really a function of the sedation, this served mainly as a tranquillizer; it would not necessarily have prevented my growing depressed upon hearing bad news about my prognosis.

These points are crucial, because I am convinced that this cocoon of optimism helped save my life. I remember quite vividly lying in bed one night during the week I was at my sickest, sorting out my situation. I knew that they don't put young men on respirators because they're *too* healthy. I could certainly tell I was getting sicker and weaker, despite the most intensive treatments the ICU could provide. In fact, I could actually feel myself slipping away. I put two and two together, and realized that I was dying (subsequent discussions with the staff, family, and visitors have largely corroborated my assessment). For several minutes I mulled that over, marvelling at what a unique experience death would be: *There's* something I've never done, I told myself. I wondered what it would feel like. Actually, it didn't strike me as being all that difficult: Dying seemed to involve just relaxing and letting go. I understood that I might even die that night. How about that? I asked myself. A bit later, however, I happened to look across the room at the wall, which was covered with drawings and cards from our children. I instantly snapped out of it: "Hey! I've got five kids! I've got a wife! We've got a newborn baby! *I'm* not allowed to die!" I resolved to pull myself together. I told myself that: (1)I was young, and a nonsmoker; (2) people all over

the world were praying for me,[5] as my wife kept reminding me; and (3) the ICU staff had me in good hands: They didn't seem too worried, and were knocking themselves out trying to cure me; so (4) all I had to do was lie there, keep breathing, and rely on them (with G-d's help) to get me out of this. Apart from confirming what other ICU survivors have written about the power of social supports and religious faith (Baier and Schomaker [1986]1995; Simpson 1982: 135), this demonstrates the importance of confidence in the staff, and of their ability to cultivate a sense of security which kept me hopeful enough to resist "letting go" and sinking further.

As stated above, part of this feeling of security also depended on selective disclosure of information. My physicians avoided telling me of my deteriorating prognosis. As we have seen (and will see again below), there were moments when I sensed I was close to death, and I was calm enough in confronting them. But, as I learned, the reactions of patients are most unpredictable. While in the ICU, I had been carefully shielded from the news that another ICU patient had died. However, after I had left the ICU and moved to the general medical floor, I was profoundly disturbed one night when a great wail suddenly rose up from relatives visiting an Arab patient down the hall, signalling that he had just died. I had never laid eyes on this patient, was already well on the road to recovery, and my overall mood by then was buoyant. Yet this incident frightened me more than almost anything that happened to me back in the ICU. Certainly, while still critically ill, I would never have welcomed official confirmation that I was, in fact, dying. In the ICU, part of my equipoise rested on the fact that I was merely flirting with the possibility of death. Receiving an official death sentence (or even hearing the reports the doctors were giving my wife) would have been quite another matter. As one survivor of a critical case of meningitis noted: "believable, *believed* lies can be useful if they prevent despair and the abandonment of effort" (Simpson 1982:108). Speaking of her own case, Simpson observed:

> We who are seriously ill draw on the faith of others . . . the beliefs of others . . . come through as objective reality even if it is not necessarily so. It was a long time before I realised that, for my own protection, the direct information . . . I was getting from these professionals was partial and incomplete. They knew it when I did not (1982: 116).

More generally, in research conducted among Scottish cancer patients in the early 1970s, even among those patients who did try to extract information from the staff about their prognosis, *not one* wanted to know if or when the disease would be expected to claim his or her life:

> They wanted to know the truth about their condition, but only up to a point. . . . they had no wish to be informed that they were definitely done for, that their case was hopeless (McIntosh 1977: 122).

Looking back, then, it seems clear to me that my survival while in the ICU is partly due to the staff's upbeat demeanor *and* to their selective disclosure of information. Selective disclosure has a long tradition in medicine, dating back to Hippocrates (Konner 1993: 5). As Oliver Wendell Holmes (Sr.), MD, long ago advised:

> Your patient has no more right to all the truth you know than he has to all the medicine in your saddlebag. . . . He should get only so much as is good for him. . . . It is a terrible thing to take away hope, even earthly hope, from a fellow-creature ([1871]1962: 181).

However, as one senior physician recently observed, "[t]he prevailing notion today is very different. Paternalism has been rejected in favour of patient autonomy and the view that 'full disclosure' is requisite for good medical practice." (Lowenstein 1997: 76). Indeed, "truth telling has become so routine that it is virtually inescapable, however bad and potentially unsettling the news" (Konnor 1993: 5). In the United States, for example, physicians are now far more likely than in the past to disclose cancer diagnoses to patients (compare Oken 1961 with Novack et al. 1979). The lifesaving potential of selective disclosure is easily neglected in today's climate of consumerism, empowerment, informed consent, and the "right to know."

As a medical sociologist, my original thinking on such issues had been shaped by certain key studies. As early as my undergraduate introduction to medical sociology, I had been impressed by Glaser's work on disclosure of terminal illness, which included an explicit suggestion that doctors disclose the truth more frequently to terminal patients ([1966]1979: 237). In graduate school, I was strongly influenced by Davis's (1960) classic account of how physicians failed to inform parents of polio patients of their child's poor prognosis, even after it was clear to the physicians. Instead, they allowed parents to hope for a recovery long after such hope was actually groundless. According to Davis, the main reason for this failure was that it allowed physicians to avoid the unpleasant, time-consuming chore of managing parents' expected reaction to bad news. Ever since reading that piece, I had been committed to full disclosure. This commitment was only strengthened by my sustained exposure to the contemporary critical bent in the medical sociology literature. One work typifying such an approach (and typical, too, of the kind of material I'd been using in the classroom) is Millman's (1977) ethnography of three American hospitals. Millman portrayed a "collusion" to cultivate trust among surgical patients so as to protect—not the patients' health—but the "comfort, schedule, and convenience of the medical staff" (1977: 19). More generally, "[k]eeping the patient uninformed" is a means to "limit the power and autonomy of patients" (1977: 137). According to Millman, while physicians may rationalize the suppression of upsetting medical details from patients "on the grounds of 'protecting' the patient . . . in fact they are more precisely protecting themselves and their colleagues" (1977: 137).

The evidence adduced by Davis, Millman, and others seems convincing. Such work had surely made me (like many medical sociologists) suspicious of medicine's paternalistic justifications for shielding patients from information about their illnesses. Indeed, society has gained much by moving beyond uncritical trust in medicine.

Yet how much of this is relevant to *critically ill patients*, as opposed both to their families, and to patients with chronic or noncritical illness? The contemporary discourse of disclosure (such as that represented by the works cited earlier) has been shaped by chronic or terminal, but seldom *critical*, illness. The paradigm is fatal cancer, not acute heart attack. Because of this, the debate pays insufficient attention to a key aspect of the critical patient experience: Death may not be immediately inevitable, but *could become so* by full disclosure. As one ICU survivor wisely cautioned in a related context:

> Remember, now: the sick person is a *living* person, not a dead or dying one, right up to that final moment. Do not bid farewell too early; a premature conclusion may be the shove that speeds the parting (Simpson 1982:32).

During my own illness, trust certainly assumed quite a different aspect from that commonly discussed by today's medical sociologists. As a critically ill patient, my trust in the staff, and my confidence that I would recover, were, I am convinced, major factors in my survival (as noted above). This demonstrates a too-readily overlooked flip side of Millman's view of a "conspiracy" against the patient: Patients may well benefit from putting their trust in the staff, and from being spared the full truth.

Of course, even my own experience suggests that the patient's stance on disclosure depends on the phase of illness. After all, I was not a terminal cancer patient. I had an acute, life-threatening, but potentially curable disease. My condition did improve, and I began to pass out of the critical stage. As I was gradually weaned off the respirator, my morphine was reduced. I began to feel the endotracheal tube in my body and suffer from feelings of being gagged and choked. Still, I was recovering, and the restoration of physical strength and mental function steadily returned me to my customary identity as a patient of the post-Parsonian era: I preferred to know all the details of my treatment.

However, not all the staff adjusted instantly to my evolving orientation. My impending removal from the respirator (extubation) was a case in point. I was well aware that extubation symbolized recovery. Yet I feared it, because of something which had happened several days earlier, when the physiotherapist briefly disconnected me from the respirator so that I could stand up and walk on the spot for a few moments. During those moments, I had found breathing normal room air almost impossible, as though it were the atmosphere of a different planet. This naturally raised some important questions. How, I asked the staff, would I manage without the respirator? Were they *sure* I wouldn't suffocate? Could they *promise* me? Perhaps because of this, some of the staff decided that the news that I was soon to be extubated should be broken to me in stages. Thus, one Tuesday morning I heard, from behind the drawn curtain of my cubicle, one of the senior physicians tell my wife (in a voice louder than he realized), "We're planning to extubate him tomorrow, but we don't want him to know it's coming so soon. So, we'll just tell him it may happen by the end of the week." Of course, since some of the staff *had* adjusted to my newly retrieved inquisitiveness, his indiscretion was moot. One of the nurses (ironically, the very one who had sweet-talked me into agreeing to be intubated) had already matter-of-factly told me to expect extubation the next day. In fact, she had fully honored my request that there be "no surprises." Thus, where one physician had earlier spoken vaguely of "some discomfort" to be expected during extubation, this nurse correctly explained that I'd feel as though I were drowning.

My identity as a patient continued evolving (or "reverting") even after leaving the ICU for the general medical floor. I grew stronger, began to ask lots of questions of doctors, and engaged in keen—if friendly—bargaining with them over things like my date of discharge and the best location for insertion of painful arterial lines. I tried hard to extract as much information from my physicians as possible without being labelled a troublemaker, just like patients in most other illness narratives. The fact that, with my improving condition, I did engage in such behavior suggests that my far different behavior while in the ICU was not the result of a natural tendency toward optimism, submissiveness, or of my religious faith, but rather of being critically ill.

Another consequence of my having passed out of danger was that several of my ICU physicians began indirectly telegraphing the information that I had almost died. Upon seeing me, they would stare piercingly into my eyes for several seconds before greeting me. At times, they would shake their heads, as though clearing them of an unpleasant vision, before speaking to me. This was socially inappropriate behavior, and I thought it odd. As I gradually noticed that this was becoming a pattern, I came to understand: They were looking at me as though I should not have been there. This was perhaps my first external confirmation that my own estimate, while on the respirator, had been accurate. Later, many physicians became a shade more direct, allowing that they had been "*very* worried" about me. As they said this, they looked meaningfully at me.

INADVERTENT ETHNOGRAPHY AND THE MISSING VOICE OF THE CRITICALLY ILL

There are real methodological difficulties in portraying the lifeworld of the acutely, critically ill. First, such patients often can neither record their own impressions nor be interviewed about them. It is thus not surprising that many students of critical illness do not make even an attempt to interview ex-ICU patients, presuming them to be unable to remember their experiences (e.g., Harvey 1996: 82). Of course, one Swedish study of 304 ex-ICU respirator patients found that 52 percent could remember their experiences on the respirator, and 90 percent of these were able to describe certain experiences in detail (Bergbom-Engberg et al. 1988). Still, my own experience suggests that, by the time a patient *is* strong enough to be interviewed or to record retrospective impressions, much can be lost without a written record to refer to. Moreover, the extent to which the passage of time reshapes and colors recollections is far greater without a "real-time" (i.e., concurrent) written record from the critical phase to serve as a check. Second, not all such patients return to tell the tale: They may not recover with their full faculties, or they may die. Third, observers can only watch from the sidelines, often only guessing at the thoughts and feelings of the patient. Family members might seem useful surrogates for first-person accounts of the critically ill. However, my own experience taught me that there is much the patient does not convey even to close relatives. Finally, as my wife points out, even in a hospital with a liberal visiting policy, as mine had, the staff often shoo visitors out of the room during key moments, such as performance of difficult procedures, patient examinations, nurses' report or doctors' rounds, as well as when the patient is being bathed or dressed.

Taking all this into account, it is no surprise that most existing depictions of the critical illness experience emphasize the pre- or post-critical phases, glossing over the critical phase, as discussed above. This is another reason why the literature lays so much emphasis on practices such as bargaining to secure information or to negotiate an identity as a "good patient." Yet, during the critical stage of my own illness. I was too sick and weak to worry consciously about such concerns. Therefore, I have come to view the emphasis on bargaining and negotiation in accounts of serious illness as limited. It covers but part of the story, the part in which the patient is both strong and clear-headed enough to engage in them, and better able to remember and record experiences. Describing a serious illness *only* in such terms fails to capture the full range of experience.

Of more direct methodological importance, my notebook indicates that I was beyond the point of thinking sociologically while in the ICU. I am not sure I would even have recognized the names of Anselm Strauss or Eliot Freidson, and I know I could not remember what I'd learned from their work. I do not think that I remembered, during parts of my time in the ICU, that I even *was* a sociologist. In fact, it took a week or two after leaving the hospital until I began to remember fragments of the sociological literature. Despite this, I was often fairly alert to my immediate surroundings in the ICU, and often able to communicate.

Because the tube forced me to communicate mainly via writing. I was unwittingly *inscribing fieldnotes* of my experiences, in a process I have come to call "inadvertent ethnography." As explained earlier, what I wrote in the notebook was written for the purposes of communication alone. I had no thought of (nor energy for) recording impressions of the experience for posterity. Even less had I the intention (or the ability) while in the ICU of recording a sociologist's observations, and my notebook includes none. In fact, the notebook contains just one reference to sociology (made while communicating with a

visitor), and it neatly captures my disengagement: "As a medical sociologist, I'm always so curious about hospitals. Now, I just want get better [*sic*]."

I thus occupied an uncommon methodological position. While in the ICU, I experienced my illness purely as a patient. Yet I left a written, "real-time" record of the experience which was available to me when, a few weeks after discharge, I was prepared to relive my hospitalization by reading the notebook for the first time. This afforded me the retrospective identity of sociological observer.

My experience demonstrates the layers of memory that such a notebook can capture, and those it can't. Since I had the methodological good fortune to be able to analyze my own notebook. I could use it to retrieve vivid memories accessible to no one else, and, possibly, by no other means. Since, while sedated, I forgot many things completely by the next day, the notebook often helped me recall key events which otherwise may have been forgotten forever. Only through my notebook, for example, did I remember the aftermath to the following episode. Once, when the staff suctioned off my accumulated secretions, I had a violent coughing fit, which made it impossible to breathe. I began turning blue, and (as one ICU physician later informed me) my pulse plunged from 124 to 14. In the only time that the ICU staff dropped their masks of calm confidence, they instantly began rapping out orders in loud, agitated voices, and I was stabilized by a more or less "crash" effort. Even before I read the notebook, I had remembered some of this, if only in its bare outlines. However, only when reading the notebook did I remember *at all* something that happened soon after this crisis. I saw that I had written to the nurse asking if I would ever need to be suctioned again (when I wrote this, I had already forgotten that the staff had been suctioning me for the whole four days I'd been on the respirator till then). She replied it would be done regularly, several times each day. I next wrote to her requesting that, just before the next suctioning, she should please get someone to help me say *Viduy*, the Jewish prayer before dying. Reading those few short words instantly triggered a flood of detailed memories that reminded me that, when I wrote them, I did not expect to survive another such procedure. Though it was already over a month after the fact, and I was sitting in the safety of my own living room, I was jolted to read this record of something I had forgotten totally, and which I had never mentioned to anyone else. Moreover, within a second or two of reading these words, I relived the original episode. Sights, sounds, and emotions—of the suctioning, of feeling suffocated, of fear, of the staff's yelling, of being resuscitated—flooded over me, leaving me shaken and drained. There were other remarkably dramatic events that I had forgotten totally until reading my notebook.

However, there are certain other events about which my wife told me, but which appear neither in my notebook nor in my memories at all. One example is having my chest fluids drained by insertion of a long needle. My wife tells me that I was aware it had been done, and had found it most unpleasant. Today, I remember nothing of it at all. I also have only the vaguest memories of having bronchoscopies done and of being taken (respirator, gauges, and all) for a CAT scan. Apparently, I had been too sick to record such events in the notebook. Conversely, there are also memories of certain events that have stayed with me since they occurred, though they appear nowhere in the notebook (and of which I told no one until after leaving the ICU). One example was the episode quoted earlier in which, while contemplating my anticipated demise, I looked over at my children's pictures and experienced myself as "snapping out of it."

Though there exists great controversy over just which methodological stance is appropriate when conducting fieldwork (Van Maanen 1988; Denzin and Lincoln 1994), few would recommend doing it while critically ill, under sedation. Yet this is how I stumbled over the fact that notebooks kept by ICU respirator patients constitute an undiscovered data source[6] with which to tap the experience of the critically ill. In fact, this may be the only way to construct a first-hand patient's account of the critical portion of the illness spectrum.

It is not often that medical sociologists can build our own first-hand accounts of this phase. Yet we can harvest notebooks kept by others while on respirators, and supplement them by interviewing their authors. Ideally, interviews would take place in two stages: while still in the hospital (though not, presumably, while still in the ICU), and after discharge, once both the former patient and the researcher have had time to review the notebooks. For former patients, reading the notebook would serve as a memory aid. Based on my own experience, this would allow them to flesh out the events recorded in only their barest form in the notebook. By looking at even such seemingly trivial, fragmentary inscriptions as, "Why no feel throat?" or "Where old nurse?", the former patient might recall whole worlds of feeling and meaning completely inaccessible to others. Without the notebook, some of these memories would probably remain lost even to the patients, themselves. For the researcher, the patient interviews could help decipher and interpret the contents of the notebooks.

Not every ICU patient is sick enough to need such a notebook, and perhaps most of those sick enough are too weak to use one, or are discouraged by busy nurses from using one (Albarran 1991; Jablonski 1994; Hafsteindottir 1996). Moreover, many illnesses do not call for intubation, so many patients are not forced to use a written record in order to communicate. Still, respirator use is widespread. One large-scale survey of American intensive care units found that "respiratory insufficiency/failure" was the leading admission diagnosis (24 percent of all admissions) in medical ICUs, and that fully 44 percent of all medical ICU patients received respirator treatment (Groeger et al. 1993). Overall, the potential population for writing in notebooks is that portion which is both intubated *and* alert while in the ICU. Among the total of 348 patients in the two ICUs observed by Zussman, while 200 (57 percent) were classified as alert, only 74 (21 percent) were both alert *and* intubated (1992: 33). Thus, there will remain many portions of the illness spectrum among ICU patients that we will not so readily be able to reconstruct. Primo Levi (1989:16–18) wrote that those who left records of Auschwitz were the relatively more "privileged." That is, their experiences were milder than those of the vast majority of inmates, whose stories were lost. A similar problem confronts us as we attempt to use ICU survivors' accounts to build a sociology of critical illness. Nonetheless, those ICU patients who *do* leave such a record afford us a rare glimpse of a world seldom portrayed in the existing literature. Moreover, advances in ICU technology and technique are causing a shift toward ICU patients being less heavily sedated and more alert than they were in the past. As one ICU physician observed:

> In these times of patient-focussed ventilators, minimal sedation and early tracheostomy, many ICU patients who are not therapeutically or pathologically obtunded are able and keen to communicate in written form (Banerjee 1998).

Future studies of the ICU therefore may *not* find, as did Zussman, that patients "vanish" (1992: 43).

CONCLUSION: TOWARD A SOCIOLOGY OF THE CRITICALLY ILL PATIENT

Do medical sociologists know as much as we think we do? On how broad a database do we construct our theory? In fact, methodological obstacles to capturing the world of the critically ill have combined with the effects of a reaction

to Parsonian analysis to produce a dearth of first-person accounts of the acute, critical phase of illness. This lack suggests that part of what we know and think about patients, illness, and providers rests on data more limited than we realize.

Indeed, my own first-hand account demonstrates critical illness in the ICU to be something quite different from the stuff of most current sociological descriptions of the patient's experience. But the implications go beyond simply addressing a gap in the literature. The aftermath of my time in the ICU was an exercise in reflexivity. My experiences led me, as a medical sociologist, to reassess my theoretical orientation, and to recognize that the current discourse on participation, negotiation, and disclosure is not universally relevant.

First, my experience reminds us that, during the critical phase, at least, physicians' concealment of information can be more than just a device for the convenience or protection of the medical staff. By gliding over or ignoring the critical phase, we ignore precisely that phase, that context, in which physicians' traditional paternalism makes the most sense: when patients are at their weakest and least stable, and their lives hang in the balance. In this phase, concealing information from the patient (although not from the family) to cultivate confidence may well find compelling justification on medical *and* moral grounds. This does not require us to deny the analyses of Millman (1976) or Davis (1960), but it does help us to place them in perspective. If confronted with the question, most medical sociologists presumably could see the logic in concealing certain details from, say, an unstable, critically ill cardiac patient. However, because our collective gaze has been directed elsewhere, toward the chronic phase, we seldom confront such issues. Yet these issues are very real ones, which many physicians face daily. For, it must be stressed, the critical phase is a common one. The *accounts* are rare; the phenomenon isn't: Heart attacks and car crashes happen all the time, for example.

Second, negotiation and partnership are concepts bearing only limited relevance to critically ill patients (though this is not necessarily true of their families). Such patients often lack the strength and clarity either to challenge or to collaborate with the physician, and their clinical picture may vastly constrain treatment options. ICU care certainly does raise ethical issues; these are a focus of Zussman's (1992) book. Yet such decisions are often made *about*, not *by* the patient in the critical phase. My experiences in the ICU demonstrate that existing accounts of fully sentient patients plotting strategy, consciously negotiating turf, defining and redefining their roles and statuses (while they may be valid in and of themselves) tell only part of the story. They represent only one portion of the full spectrum of the patient career, one possible type of illness trajectory.

By capturing the voice of the critically ill, we could lay the foundation for a wider sociology of the critically ill patient. The present account is merely a small, exploratory step in this direction. It must be extended, ideally by analyzing the notebooks that other critically ill patients leave. Future studies could thereby investigate to what extent the disparities between my own ICU experience and those described in Zussman's (1992) study, for example, are attributable to cross-cultural differences, or to the fact that many ICU patients are not as young as I was, are not treated by so motivated a staff, have weaker social supports on which to rely, or face a different clinical course and prognosis.

More broadly, sociology's abandonment of a Parsonian focus on acute, critical illness has left much unfinished business. Potential topics for a new research program on critically ill patients include policies of information disclosure, and how patients perceive them; cultivation of the patient's trust in staff, and the maintenance of hope; interactions between patients, staff, and families; the extent to which ICU patients desire, achieve, or merely have the illusion of, participation and collaboration in their care; the frequency with which patients attempt negotiation, and the extent of their success; the intense need of intubated patients to communicate, and their dependence for this on staff with the requisite skill, time, and patience; and differences between medical and surgical ICUs. Ultimately, such research could help improve the care of critically ill patients.

Meanwhile, we still know very little about the patient's experience of critical illness. This author is currently planning a study involving in-depth interviews with ICU survivors, particularly (where possible) those who kept notebooks in the ICU. The primary goal is to discover, via grounded theory analysis (Glaser and Strauss 1967), key areas for empirical and theoretical work on critical illness.

Sociologists need not go out and get critically ill in order to redress existing gaps in the literature. We simply must recognize that what we think we know corresponds all too closely to what we can readily measure. And that this suggests we know less than we think we do.

NOTES

1. Throughout his book, Frank (1991) speaks of cancer as "critical" illness. Frank uses this term to mean "life-threatening." However, this paper applies a narrower definition: the critical *phase* of illness, in which life is immediately hanging in the balance. Chronic or acute diseases may have their critical phase, or they may not. This paper is primarily interested in the critical phase of acute illness, although much of the analysis extends to the truly critical phase of chronic illness as well. In this paper, the term *chronic illness* will often be used to denote the "noncritical phase."

2. PO_2 is an index of how much oxygen is contained in the arterial blood, and is used in assessing the extent of respiratory failure (Pagana and Pagana 1983: 89).

3. Another factor is of course the growing awareness that chronic illness accounts for an increasing share of morbidity and mortality.

4. See Goffman's (1952) famous discussion of devices to help social actors adjust to undesirable situations and statuses.

5. As a believing Jew, I derived real encouragement from knowing I was being prayed for. In addition, a measure of my tranquillity while at my sickest came from my conviction that everything was part of G-d's plan, and was ultimately for the best. Yet this faith has been a constant in my life, and had never prevented me from being an inquisitive, assertive patient. I am therefore led to conclude that my quite different patient identity in the ICU is more readily ascribed to the nature of critical illness, and less to faith.

6. Adamson (1997) kept a diary of his experience with chronic illness. Though his wife had to record his impressions when he was too weak (1997: 155), he does not describe the critical phase.

REFERENCES

ADAMSON, C. (1997) Existential and clinical uncertainty in the medical encounter: an idiographic account of an illness trajectory defined by inflammatory bowel disease and avascular necrosis, *Sociology of Health and Illness*, 19, 133–59.

ALBARRAN, J. W. (1991) A review of communication with intubated patients and those with tracheostomies within an intensive care environment, *Intensive Care Nursing*, 7, 179–86.

ASCH, D. A., SHEA, J. A., JEDRZIEWSKI, M. K. and BOSK, C. L. (1997) The limits of suffering: critical care nurses' views of hospital care at the end of life, *Social Science and Medicine*, 45, 1661–8.

BAIER, S. and SCHOMAKER, M. Z. ([1986]1995) *Bed Number Ten*. New York: CRC.

BANERJEE, A. [ashokeb@ICU.wsahs.nsw.gov.AU] (1998) Re: Writing by intubated ICU patients. Electronic posting to ccm-1 [Critical Care Medicine; ccm-1@list.pitt.edu] Internet discussion list. 19 October.

BERGBOM-ENGBERG, I. and HALJAMAE, H. (1988) A retrospective study of patients' recall of respirator treatment (2): Nursing care factors and feelings of security/insecurity, *Intensive Care Nursing*, 4, 95–101.

BERGBOM-ENGBERG, I., HALLENBERG, B., WICKSTROM, I. and HALJAMAE, H. (1988) A retrospective study of patients' recall of respirator treatment (1): Study design and basic findings, *Intensive Care Nursing*, 4, 56–61.

BOSTON WOMEN'S HEALTH BOOK COLLECTIVE (1979) *Our Bodies, Ourselves* [revised and expanded]. New York: Simon and Schuster.

BURY, M. (1982) Chronic illness as biographical disruption, *Sociology of Health and Illness*, 4, 167–82.

BURY, M. (1991) The sociology of chronic illness: a review of research and prospects, *Sociology of Health and Illness*, 13, 451–68.

BUTLER, S. and ROSENBLUM, B. (1991) *Cancer in Two Voices*. Duluth, MN: Spinsters Ink.

CHARMAZ, K. (1991) *Good Days, Bad Days: the Self in Chronic Illness and Time*. New Brunswick, NJ: Rutgers University Press.

CONRAD, P. and KERN, R. (eds) (1990) *The Sociology of Health and Illness: Critical Perspectives* [3rd Edition]. New York: St. Martin's.

COOPER, L. (1997) Myalgic encephalomyelitis and the medical encounter, *Sociology of Health and Illness*, 19, 186–207.

COWIE, B. (1976) The cardiac patient's perception of his heart attack, *Social Science and Medicine*, 10, 87–96.

COYLE, J. (1999) Exploring the meaning of 'dissatisfaction' with health care: the importance of 'personal identity threat', *Sociology of Health and Illness*, 21, 95–124.

CROSSLEY, M. L. (1998) 'Sick role' or 'empowerment'? the ambiguities of life with an HIV positive diagnosis, *Sociology of Health and Illness*, 20, 507–31.

CROSSLEY, N. and CROSSLEY, M. L. (1998) HIV, empowerment and the sick role: an investigation of a contemporary moral maze, *Health*, 2, 157–74.

DAVIS, F. (1960) Uncertainty in medical prognosis: clinical and functional, *American Journal of Sociology*, 66, 41–7.

DAVIS, F. ([1963]1991) *Passage through Crisis: Polio Victims and their Families*. London: Transaction.

DEGNER, L. F., KRISTJANSON, L. J., BOWMAN, D., SLOAN, J. A., CARRIERE, K. C., O'NEILL, J., BILODEAU, WATSON, P., and MUELLER, B. (1997) Information needs and decisional preferences in women with breast cancer, *Journal of the American Medical Association*, 277, 1485–92.

DENZIN, N. K. and LINCOLN, Y. S. (eds) (1994) *Handbook of Qualitative Research*. London: Sage.

DONOVAN, J. L. and BLAKE, D. R. (1992) Patient non-compliance: deviance or reasoned decision-making? *Social Science and Medicine*, 34, 507–13.

FAHY, K. and SMITH, P. (1999) From the sick role to subject positions: a new approach to the medical encounter, *Health*, 3, 71–93.

FRANK, A. W. (1991) *At the Will of the Body: Reflections on Illness*. Boston: Houghton Mifflin.

FRANK, A. W. (1997) Illness as moral occasion: restoring agency to ill people, *Health*, 1, 131–48.

GALLAGHER, E. B. (1979) Lines of reconstruction and extension in the Parsonian sociology of illness. In Jaco, E. G. (ed) *Patients, Physicians, and Illness* [3rd Edition]. New York: Free Press.

GERHARDT, U. (1989) *Ideas about Illness: an Intellectual and Political History of Medical Sociology*. New York: New York University Press.

GLASER, B. G. ([1966]1979) Disclosure of terminal illness. In Jaco, E. G. (ed) *Patients, Physicians, and Illness* [3rd Edition]. New York: Free Press.

GLASER, B. G. and STRAUSS, A. L. (1965) *Awareness of Dying*. New York: Aldine de Gruyter.

GLASER, B. G. and STRAUSS, A. L. (1967) *The Discovery of Grounded Theory*. New York: Aldine de Gruyter.

GOFFMAN, E. (1952) On cooling the mark out: some aspects of adaptation to failure, *Psychiatry*, 15, 451–63.

GROEGER, J. S., GUNTUPALLI, K. K., STROSSBERG, M., HALPERN, N., RAPHAELY, R. C., CERRA, F. and KAYE, W. (1993) Descriptive analysis of critical care units in the United States: patient characteristics and intensive care unit utilization, *Critical Care Medicine*, 21, 279–91.

HAFSTEINDOTTIR, T. B. (1996) Patient's experiences of communication during the respirator treatment period, *Intensive and Critical Care Nursing*, 12, 261–71.

HART, N. (1977) Parenthood and patienthood: a dialectical autobiography. In Davis, A. and Horobin, G. (eds) *Medical Encounters: the Experience of Illness and Treatment*. New York: St. Martin's.

HARVEY, J. (1996) Achieving the indeterminate: accomplishing degrees of certainty in life and death situations, *Sociological Review*, 44, 78–98.

HAUG, M. R. and LAVIN, B. (1981) Practitioner or patient—who's in charge? *Journal of Health and Social Behavior*, 22, 212–29.

HAWKINS, A. H. (1993) *Reconstructing Illness: Studies in Pathography*. West Lafayette, Indiana: Purdue University Press.

HEIMER, C. A. and STAFFEN, L. R. (1995) Interdependence and reintegrative social control: labelling and reforming 'inappropriate' parents in neo-natal intensive care units, *American Sociological Review*, 60, 635–54.

HOLMES, O. W. ([1871]1962) The young practitioner. In Davenport, W. H. (ed) *The Good Physician*. New York: MacMillan.

HYDEN, L.-C. (1997) Illness and narrative, *Sociology of Health and Illness*, 19, 48–69.

HYDEN, L.-C. and SACHS, L. (1998) Suffering, hope and diagnosis: on the negotiation of chronic fatigue syndrome, *Health*, 2, 175–93.

INDYK, D. and RIER, D. A. (1993) Grassroots AIDS knowledge: implications for the boundaries of science and collective action. *Knowledge: Creation, Diffusion, Utilization*, 15, 3–43.

JABLONSKI, R. S. (1994) The experience of being mechanically ventilated, *Qualitative Health Research*, 4, 186–207.

JONES, J., HOGGART, B., WITHEY, J., DONAGHUE, K. and ELLIS, B. W. (1979) What the patients say: a study of reactions to an intensive care unit. *Intensive Care Medicine*, 5, 89–92.

KONNER, M. (1993) *Medicine at the Crossroads*. New York: Pantheon.

LEVI, P. (1989) *The Drowned and the Saved* (trans. Raymond Rosenthal). New York: Vintage.

LEVINE, S. and KOZLOFF, M. A. (1978) The sick role: assessment and overview, *Annual Review of Sociology*, 4, 317–43.

LOWENSTEIN, J. (1997) *The Midnight Meal and Other Essays About Doctors, Patients, and Medicine*. London: Yale University Press.

LUPTON, D. (1997) Consumerism, reflexivity, and the medical encounter, *Social Science and Medicine*, 45, 373–81.

MACINTYRE, S. and OLDMAN, D. (1977) Coping with migraine. In Davis, A. and Horobin, G. (eds) *Medical Encounters: The Experience of Illness and Treatment*. New York: St. Martin's.

MAPES, R. (1977) Patient manipulation of the system: an ethno-biographic account. In Davis, A. and Horobin, G. (eds) *Medical Encounters: The Experience of Illness and Treatment*. New York: St. Martin's.

MCINTOSH, J. (1977) *Communication and Awareness in a Cancer Ward*. New York: Prodist.

MILLMAN, M. (1977) *The Unkindest Cut: Life in the Backrooms of Medicine*. New York: Morrow Quill.

NOVACK, D. H., PLUMER, R., SMITH, R. L., OCHITILL, H., MORROW, G. R. and BENNETT, J. M. (1979) Changes in physicians' attitudes toward telling the cancer patient, *Journal of the American Medical Association*, 241, 897–900.

OKEN, D. (1961) What to tell cancer patients: a study of medical attitudes, *Journal of the American Medical Association*, 175, 1120–8.

PAGANA, K. D. and PAGANA, T. J. (1983) *Understanding Medical Testing*. New York: New American Library/Mosby.

PAGET, M. A. (1993) *A Complex Sorrow: Reflections on Cancer and an Abbreviated Life*. Philadelphia: Temple University Press.

PARSONS, T. (1951) *The Social System*. New York: Free Press.

REEDER, L. G. (1972) The patient-client as a consumer: some observations on the changing professional-client relationship, *Journal of Health and Social Behavior*, 13, 406–12.

RICHMAN, J. (1996) Coming out of ITU crazy: dreams of affliction. Paper presented at the annual conference of the Medical Sociology section, British Sociological Association. Edinburgh, Scotland, September.

ROBILLARD, A. B. (1994) Communication problems in the intensive care unit, *Qualitative Sociology*, 17, 383–95.

SIMPSON, E. S. (1982) *Notes on an Emergency: a Journal of Recovery*. London: W. W. Norton.

SMITH, D. H. (1996) Ethics in the doctor-patient relationship, *Critical Care Clinics*, 12, 179–97.

SOSNOWITZ, B. G. (1984) Managing parents on neonatal intensive care units, *Social Problems*, 31, 390–402.

SPEEDLING, E. J. (1980) Social structure and social behavior in an intensive care unit: patient-family perspectives, *Social Work in Health Care*, 6, 1–22.

STEWART, D. C. and Sullivan, T. J. (1987) Illness behavior and the sick role in chronic disease: the case of multiple sclerosis. In Schwartz, H. D.

(ed) *Dominant Issues in Medical Sociology* [2nd Edition]. New York: Random House.

STRAUSS. A. ([1968]1975) The intensive care unit: its characteristics and social relationships. In *Professions, Work, and Careers*. New Brunswick, NJ: Transaction.

STRAUSS, A., FAGERHAUGH, S., SUCZEK, B. and WIENER, C. (1982) The work of hospitalized patients, *Social Science and Medicine*, 16, 977–86.

SZASZ, T. S. and HOLLENDER, M. H. ([1956]1987) The basic models of the doctor-patient relationship. In Schwartz, H. D. (ed) *Dominant Issues in Medical Sociology* [2nd Edition]. New York: Random House.

TIMMERMANS, S. (1994) Dying of awareness: the theory of awareness contexts revisited, *Sociology of Health and Illness*, 16, 322–39.

TURNER, B. S. (1990) *Medical Power and Social Knowledge*. London: Sage.

VAN MAANEN, J. (1988) *Tales of the Field: on Writing Ethnography*. London: University of Chicago Press.

WALLACE, S. P. (1990) Institutionalising divergent approaches in the sociology of health and healing: A review of medical sociology readers, *Teaching Sociology*, 18, 377–84.

WEBB, B. (1977) Trauma and tedium: an account of living in on a children's ward. In Davis, A. and Horobin, G. (eds) *Medical Encounters: the Experience of Illness and Treatment*. New York: St. Martin's.

ZBOROWSKI, M. ([1952]1960) Cultural components in responses to pain. In Apple, D. (ed) *Sociological Studies of Health and Sickness*. New York: McGraw-Hill.

ZOLA, I. K. (1982) *Missing Pieces: a Chronicle of Living with a Disability*. Philadelphia: Temple University Press.

ZUSSMAN, R. (1992) *Intensive Care: Medical Ethics and the Medical Profession*. Chicago: University of Chicago Press.

Part VI

HEALING OPTIONS

Have you ever visited or thought about visiting a chiropractor, acupuncturist, naturopath, hypnotherapist, or faith healer for sickness or injury? If you have, you are not alone. Some people periodically seek the assistance of such practitioners. Why you or anyone else would contemplate such an alternative is a topic of interest among medical sociologists.

The activities of chiropractors, spiritualists, and herbalists are healing options. But, you might ask, options for what? In modern societies, any approach that deviates from the dominant Western medical paradigm constitutes a healing option. Yet, in developing nations, potions from a folk healer or acupuncture may be commonly accepted treatment modalities. Under these circumstances, Western medicine may represent the alternative. Thus, social, cultural, and historical factors influence what is and is not defined as a healing option.

Legitimacy is another issue to take into account in any discussion of alternatives. Take, for example, the trend toward a more holistic approach in Western medicine. Over time, certain healing options, such as midwifery, meditation, and acupuncture, have gained in legitimate standing, whereas others continue to be held in low regard (faith healing, folk healing, voodoo). As such, healing options, not uniformly accepted or respected, are variously judged as legitimate by those in power to determine conventional medical practices.

We are now aware that healing options exist, that they are not equally viewed as legitimate, and that many individuals avail themselves of these services. The question remains, Why? Why and under what conditions would you or someone else choose alternative medicine? Data collected by medical sociologists uncover multiple reasons for this behavior. Individuals use healing options because alternative medicine practitioners are friendly, considerate, sensitive, nonthreatening, affordable, and geographically accessible. Additionally, they share similar cultural values and traditions, spend time with their patients or clients, instill optimism and hope, and exercise a more holistic style in treating suspected causes of emotional and physical maladies. Most of all, they are perceived as supportive and helpful whether their remedies succeed or not.

Generally, healing options can and will be employed at any time during the course of an illness. At the first signs or symptoms of an emotional or physical problem, some individuals seek options other than mainstream medicine. In other instances, people use healing options concurrent with or instead of conventional medical care. At still other times, they turn to healing options after scientific medicine has failed to cure mental, chronic, or terminal illnesses. In this sense, alternative medicine constitutes a treatment of last resort.

We have chosen the article "Religion, Health, and Nonphysical Senses of Self" by Ellen L. Idler for this section in order to show the various ways in which religion is used by people to cope with problems of physical health. She notes that past research shows that religious involvement has a protective effect on health as religious people tend to have positive health lifestyles and live longer. She observes that higher religiousness can also be associated with poorer, not better, health, when people turn to religion in times of crisis concerning illness and disability. Her research, however, focuses on a third way of thinking about religion and health. She found that people who are strongly religious may not find their sense of self threatened by physical ailments; rather, they deemphasize their physical abilities and attributes and focus instead on their spiritual, nonphysical being that allows them to obtain satisfaction and meaning in their lives in context in which their physical body does not matter so much.

The second paper is by Mary Abrums and is entitled "Jesus Will Fix It after Awhile: Meanings and Health." This paper focuses on the health of African Americans and provides an account of the responses of a group of working-class women who belonged to a store-front church in Seattle, Washington. This study examines the beliefs of these women about their health and health care providers in the context of their religion. In encounters with white doctors, the women maintained control over the situation because they believed outcomes were determined by God.

RELIGION, HEALTH, AND NONPHYSICAL SENSES OF SELF

Ellen L. Idler
Rutgers University

The relationship between religion and physical health is a complicated one. In the Durkheimian tradition, and in longitudinal epidemiological studies, religious involvement is shown to have a protective effect on health. Cross-sectionally, however, and even in short follow-up periods, we sometimes see higher levels of religiousness associated with poorer, not better, health, as people in the midst of crises often turn to religion for comfort and social support. A third way of thinking about the relationship involves self-ratings of health, which appear to represent broad conceptions of self in which physical health and abilities may be deemphasized and nonphysical characteristics, including religious or spiritual self-identities, may be relied upon. Quantitative and qualitative data from a cross-sectional sample of disabled clients of an urban rehabilitation clinic support both of the latter perspectives.

Social scientists in the past several decades, who have been very much interested in health and social life, have generally shown very little interest in the subject of religion and health. For one thing, data sets in which both these complex phenomena are adequately measured are rare; even rarer are follow-up studies in which causal direction can be accurately assessed. The primary source of funding for health research in the social sciences has been the federal government and, although no explicit restrictions are placed on survey research on religious practices, a de facto restriction has arisen from the principled separation of church and state. The comparative lack of research on religion may also reflect some absence of interest on the part of health researchers. Another reason may be that the relationship between religion and health is so complicated. Alternative causal orders are

equally plausible, and even the sign of the association is uncertain. *The Oxford English Dictionary* says *complicated* means that which has been "folded, wrapped, or twisted together, combined intimately, and mixed up with in an involved way." This describes the relationship of religion and health very well. Moreover, neither religion nor health is itself a single strand. Religious involvement can mean a mix of practices, beliefs, and identities; health is an even more global concept combining mental, physical, and even social well-being. The purpose of this article is not really to untwist the two, since they appear to occur as naturally interwoven, but simply to look at the knot from several vantage points.

VIEW 1: RELIGION'S PROTECTIVE EFFECT ON HEALTH

One way to think about religion and health is the way Durkheim ([1897] 1951; [1915] 1965) did. Religion has a beneficial effect on human social life and individual well-being because it regulates behavior and integrates individuals in caring social circles. It provides stability and support, structure and intimacy. Ritual religious practices especially provide these benefits, and religious faiths with high levels of ritual in their worship and private devotional practices tend to benefit more from lower suicide rates (Durkheim [1897] 1951) and better health among the elderly (Idler & Kasl 1992). Even more directly, religious belief systems may include prohibitions against certain behaviors such as smoking, excessive alcohol use, or sexual experimentation, lowering the incidence among religious group members of diseases for which these behaviors are risk factors (Levin & Schiller 1987). Less directly, religious beliefs may provide an overarching cognitive framework for interpreting events," plausibility structures" that are readily available to individuals to provide coherent meaning for both the small events of the life course and the large events of history (Berger 1967). These mechanisms have sometimes been called the health behavior, social cohesiveness, and sense of coherence hypotheses (Idler 1987; see also Idler 1993a). Because of its multidimensionality, religious involvement could have multiple causal pathways for its effect on physical health.

The causal order in this view is that religious involvement precedes health status; the direction of the association is positive. As in any research on the effect of risk factors on health, the most conclusive research comes from epidemiological studies of large populations with extensive initial health assessments and longitudinal follow-up of subjects, just the kind of data that do not usually include measures of religious involvement, let alone richly multidimensional ones.

VIEW 2: RELIGION IN ILLNESS AND SUFFERING

Paradoxically, the mirror image of the relationship between religion and health also has a compelling logic. People often turn to reli-

gion in times of trouble, including, and especially, during crises of serious illness. Religious groups can offer both spiritual and practical help to the sick: prayers, visitors, and hot meals. Perhaps even more important, they offer to the faithful a comforting belief in divine authority over human affairs (Pollner 1989). As C.S. Lewis (1962) wrote,

> Nor have I anything to offer my readers except my conviction that when pain is to be borne, a little courage helps more than much knowledge, a little human sympathy more than much courage, and the least tincture of the love of God more than all (p. 10).

Here too, religious involvement is multidimensional. In the language of social research, turning to religion is a kind of emotional coping strategy, one that is especially effective at reducing distress and restoring hope (Kaplan, Munroe-Blum, & Blazer 1993) among the elderly (Koenig, George, & Siegler 1988) and those experiencing illness or loss (Mattlin, Wethington, & Kessler 1990). Religion legitimates the marginal human situations of illness and death by giving them a place in a single sacred reality (Berger 1967). Religious faith, exercised as private prayer, is a cognitive and emotional resource immediately accessible to the sick or disabled (Koenig 1993); the "social" support received from divine others (Pollner 1989) is similarly available, whatever the situation of need. Empirically, then, we should see data in which religious involvement is associated with poorer health cross-sectionally, and even over short follow-up periods (for examples, see Idler & Kasl 1992; King, Speck, & Thomas 1994). In this view, the sign of the association is negative, and the causal order is reversed: Health problems precede religious involvement.

In some extreme cases of the religious life, the strength of the negative association can even be intensified. A recent novel, *Mariette in Ecstasy*, is a fictional account of an intensely religious young girl who enters a convent and receives the *stigmata*, the wounds of Christ, in her hands, feet, and sides (Hansen 1991). This is a miraculous occurrence that was first experienced by St. Francis of Assisi, and subsequently by a small number of others whom the Catholic church has recognized and canonized. A negative association between religion and health would result from individuals turning to religion in times of illness, but an even more negative association would be seen when extremely devout individuals actually seek out physical suffering as a means of spiritual purification. Christians believe that not only Christ's death on the cross, but also his suffering there, atoned for their sins. For some, although not many perhaps, physical suffering may take on the religious meaning of identity with Christ; with the mortification of the flesh, the spirit is purified. These are extraordinary individuals, of course, "religious virtuosi," but the issue shows just how complicated things can get.

VIEW 3: RELIGION AND SELF-RATINGS OF HEALTH

A third way of thinking about religion and health hinges on the way health is defined and measured. It involves the self-ratings of health that people give as responses to the survey question, "Would you rate your health as excellent, good, fair, or poor?" Their responses, often considered too subjective to be of use in epidemiological studies, have been shown repeatedly to predict mortality over both short- and long-term periods of follow-up, even after adjusting for the respondent's medical condition (Mossey & Shapiro 1982; Schoenfeld et al. 1994). While the meaning of these self-ratings of health remains uncertain, they apparently reflect a respondent's definition of health that encompasses more than just disease status, at least as it has been measured by surveys, medical records, or standard exams by a physician (Idler 1992). In fact, when asked

about the meanings attached to their ratings ("When you answered the last question about your health, what did you think of?"), people offer answers citing their ability to work, their feelings of distress, their good or bad health habits, their own health in the past, or the health of others, in addition to their pain and present illness or injury (Groves, Fultz, & Martin 1992). Students of the cognitive aspects of survey design have recently become very interested in the multiple meanings respondents assign to their answers to this apparently simple question (Feinberg, Loftus, & Tanur 1985; Schechter 1994).

The breadth of the answers suggests that individuals are evaluating many areas of their life when assessing their health—including the health of others in comparison with their own, their emotional well-being, their social relationships, and their ability to perform valued activities in addition to their physical health. The relative weight placed on each of these areas and their patterns will differ from one individual to another. For example, one respondent in the present study, a 28-year-old Asian male with post-polio syndrome, answered that his health was excellent (in spite of the braces on his legs and the cane he walked with):

> My health is excellent. In general, I'm in that part of my life. I'm 28 years old. A lot of people help me get through my life before I go to surgery. I went through the surgery 14 times. Now I can walk. I can do better than before. I'm satisfied with my life that's for sure. Also my family helps me and my friends help me. You have to have other personalities to help you.

Thus in spite of having a debilitating chronic condition, this man emphasizes the support of his social network, his overall satisfaction with life, and his improvement from an earlier period in his life, and it allows him to evaluate what some might consider poor health as excellent.

One can see these evaluations of health as reflecting underlying concepts of the self; for some individuals, peak physical health may be an important aspect of their identity, for others it may be only incidental. The level of physical health necessary for this latter group to perform their social roles effectively or to gain satisfaction from valued activities may be minimal. Stephen Hawking, the physicist with severe multiple sclerosis, or Chuck Close, the painter who was partially paralyzed in midlife, would be extreme examples of people who have made major intellectual or artistic accomplishments despite severe physical debility.

We might very crudely break these areas of the self into two, and call them physical and nonphysical senses of self. Nonphysical senses of self would include cognitive or intellectual abilities; aesthetic interests in music, literature, or art; being a member of a profession; or having satisfying social relationships. The balance of one's physical and nonphysical senses of self might be stable throughout life, or it may shift as we age or experience illness. Charmaz (1991: 259) writes that ill people who "define essential qualities of self as distinct from their bodies," especially those who are encouraged by others to do so, are more likely to transcend the situation of their illness; they have "defined a valued self beyond a failing body." Development or possession of an intact nonphysical sense of self would then be associated with better global self-ratings of health even in the presence of chronic illness.

A religious or spiritual sense of self, the focus of this article, would certainly be among these aspects of identity. We might specifically predict that people who think of themselves as strongly religious or spiritual people would not find that identity threatened by illness or disability; indeed, the socially supportive attention of the religious group, and comfort received from prayer and ritual activities, could strengthen religious beliefs and reinforce such an identity. The sign of the association and the causal order in this third view are identical to the first: Religious involvement precedes and is associated with better health. What differentiates the two is the meaning and measurement of the concept of health: Self-ratings of health may be relatively positive, even in the presence of serious or chronic illness. There is some evidence for this association: One recent study shows religious practices to be positively related to an index containing two self-ratings of health (Ferraro & Albrecht-Jensen 1991).

Although the three views have been presented as incompatible with each other, their incompatibility is to some extent a heuristic simplification. Ultimately, all causal processes and directions of association could have a place in a complicated picture of processes that occur over time as people age, health events occur, and religious involvement declines or grows.

The hypotheses for this study are derived from the latter two ways of thinking about religion and health. First, with respect to the religious response to illness and suffering, we expect to see that respondents with poorer health or greater disability are more likely to say they have sought help from their religion. Second, with respect to religious and nonphysical senses of self, we expect to see that respondents with stronger religious senses of self-identity and better self-ratings of health will have a stronger nonphysical sense of self.

METHOD

Sample

The participants in this study were randomly selected from clients of an urban rehabilitation clinic. The present study was part of a larger effort to better understand the meaning of self-ratings of health, with the eventual goal of discovering the processes by which these highly predictive self-ratings are generated. The strategy for the study was to focus on clients whose self-ratings were different from what might be expected from their observed physical health.

To identify such individuals, two instruments from the NHANES-I (National Center for Health Statistics 1977) were used to compare data on the same condition from two independent sources: a physician's examination of the client's musculoskeletal system and the patient's own self-report of pain in those same joints. The protocol for the physician's exam was the musculoskeletal exam portion of the first National Health and Nutrition Examination Survey (NHANES-I) (National Center for Health Statistics 1977). The examination requires the physician to manipulate, flex, extend, bend, and rotate the client's joints, noting tenderness, swelling, deformity, limitation of motion, pain, and other symptoms of the knees, hips, back, neck, shoulders, elbows, wrists, ankles, feet, fingers, and toes. The second instrument, measuring the respondent's perceptions, was the *Arthritis Supplement* to the NHANES-I (National Center for Health Statistics 1977), a detailed set of questions about the individual's experience of pain, stiffness, and swelling in the knees, hips, back/neck, and other joints, which corresponds closely to the physician's examination.

Two hundred clients were screened with both instruments, representing a completion rate of 63.3 percent, to locate individuals who were reporting more pain than might be expected on the basis of their physical exam, and also those who reported less. These "pain" and "exam" scores could then be compared to the nationally representative NHANES-I sample from which the measures were taken.

Scores for the physician's evaluation (Exam) and the corresponding client reports of joint pain (Pain) were converted to Z-scores and the difference was taken, so that higher (positive) scores represented relatively greater physician findings, and lower (negative) scores represented greater reported pain. A similar difference variable was calculated for the entire original NHANES-I sample. Respondents in the clinic sample whose scores were one or more standard deviations away from the mean of the same variable for the NHANES-I sample were asked to participate in

the psychosocial interview. Ironically, the screening was mostly unnecessary. In the NHANES-I sample, approximately 15 percent of the sample fell outside the one standard deviation line; in the clinic sample it was 88 percent. In other words, the great majority of the clients screened had pain reports that were different from what would be expected on the basis of their physician's exam. Because the clinic respondents' scores were compared to the NHANES-I distribution, not their own, this finding is *not* an artifact of the distribution of clinic scores. Most important, these scores were about evenly split between overreporters and underreporters.

Of the 176 clients who were screened into the second part of the study, 7 refused to participate further, 3 died or were hospitalized, and 20 could not be recontacted with the information they had given. This yielded 146 psychosocial interviews, or an 83 percent completion rate for the second part of the study.

Measures

Findings from the NHANES-I physician exam were summed for all sites.

For the *Arthritis Supplement*, if clients responded *no* to each of five screening questions, they were considered to have no musculoskeletal pain. As the emphasis in the present study was also on the interpretation of current states, respondents who reported pain of any duration that had not recurred in the last year were also considered to have no pain.

The health assessment instrument also includes the 38-item chronic conditions history of the NHANES-I Medical History Questionnaire (National Center for Health Statistics 1977), a body systems symptom review instrument—from which musculoskeletal symptoms were omitted for the purposes of this study (Cameron, Leventhal, & Leventhal 1993); a 10-item physical abilities battery used in the Rand Health Insurance Experiment (Brook et al. 1979) that asks the respondents about their ability to do simple activities (such as dressing

and walking inside the house) and more difficult tasks (such as housecleaning and participating in sports), sociodemographic variables,
health practices, and the single-item self-rating
of health ("in general, would you say your
health is excellent, very good, good, fair, or
poor?"). This questionnaire was administered
to the clients as soon as possible after the
physician's examination, usually immediately.

The chronic-condition items were developed into two measures, one summarizing
the respondent's chronic disease burden that
puts them at risk for mortality and the other
for chronic diseases that do not have a mortality risk but do cause disability. The measures were based on analyses of 16-year
age-adjusted mortality risks by condition in
data from the 1987 NHANES-I Epidemiologic
Followup Study (NHEFS) (National Center
for Health Statistics 1992).

The psychosocial interview took about one
hour to complete. It combined frequently
used scales and open-ended questions on a
variety of subjects, including religion. Because self-ratings of health appear to reflect
broad areas of emotional and social well-
being and outlook on life (Adelman 1994;
Maddox 1964), topics covered in the interview included social networks and support
(Norbeck, Lindsey, & Carrieri 1981), depression (Radloff 1977), neuroticism (Eysenck
1958), optimism (Scheier & Carver 1985),
body consciousness (Miller, Murphy, & Buss
1981), religious affiliation, activities, beliefs,
and self-rated religiousness (Hoge 1972;
McCready & Greeley 1976), and a set of items
measuring the nonphysical sense of self. The
last scale was developed specifically for this
research, to elicit the importance the respondent placed on various aspects of nonphysical
(social, intellectual, aesthetic, spiritual) identity. Thus, they were asked, on a scale of 0 to
10, "to what extent do you think of yourself as
a *musical* person? (Probe: If 10 is the most
musical you could be, and 0 is not *musical* at
all . . . ?)" The 15-item scale appears in the
appendix to this article.

We used three measures of religious
involvement. The first is a self-assessment of
religiousness, based on the two asterisked
items in the appendix. The second is a
measure of religious activities, including atten-
dance at services and other religious activities,
reading the Bible, knowing other people in
the congregation, and watching religious programs on television. Finally, because of this
article's concern with the issue of seeking help
from religion for health problems, responses
to an open-ended question were coded
dichotomously for whether the respondent
had received help or not. The respondent's
religious affiliation was also recorded.

Analysis

Cronbach's alphas were calculated for the
appropriate scales: self-rated religiousness
alpha = .63, religious activities alpha = .76,
neuroticism alpha = .72, optimism alpha =
.77, social body consciousness alpha = .67,
depression alpha = .91, and nonphysical
sense of self = .77.

Scale analysis, bivariate, logistic regression,
and ordinary least-squares regression analyses
were conducted for the two dependent variables: help from religion and nonphysical
sense of self. Multivariate analyses were given
a hierarchical structure, with the religion variables entering the model first, to distinguish
the dependent variable from other dimensions of religiosity. Sets of variables were then
introduced one at a time; in the second step
the key independent variables for health were
added, and possible confounding demographic variables at the third step. Possible
explanatory factors of health practices were
added at the fourth step, social networks and
support at a fifth step, and psychological
characteristics and distress were added at the
sixth step. Variables were included in the sets
only if they had a significant bivariate association with the dependent variable in initial
analyses; nonsignificant variables ($p < .10$)
were dropped to reduce the number of variables in the model at any one time.

RESULTS

Because this study adopted some of its instruments from those used with a nationally representative sample, the disability clinic sample can be compared with the larger sample (Idler 1993b). Respondents in the clinic sample were about evenly split between males and females, but the clinic respondents were much more likely to be non-white and unmarried, and they were somewhat more educated than the NHANES-I sample. The clinic sample had poorer self-rated health, more mortality-risk and disability-risk chronic conditions, poorer musculoskeletal status by physician's evaluations, and greater reports of pain.

Variables to be included in the analysis are described in Table 1. The two dependent variables, help from religion and nonphysical sense of self, are not at all correlated with each other.

Self-rated religiousness is highly correlated with receiving help from religion, as are race, education, and income. The other measures of religious involvement (activities and beliefs) do not appear because, while they were also highly correlated with receiving help from religion, they were too highly correlated with self-rated religiousness to be included together in a multivariate analysis. Nonphysical sense of self is not highly correlated with anything, although it has small associations with social support and neuroticism.

Table 2 shows the religious heterogeneity of the sample. Protestant respondents were more often non-white and younger than Jewish and other respondents. Roman Catholics were about evenly split between white and non-white and had the least education of the groups. Jewish respondents were more likely to be female, were all white, and had the oldest average age. Those with "other" or no religious affiliation were the most educated. Because of the demographic differences between the groups, and because of the similarities between Jewish and other/none respondents, two dummy variables, for Protestants and Catholics, were coded and included in all analyses. Jewish and other/none respondents were far less likely to report receiving help from religion. Nonphysical senses of self do not differ significantly among the groups.

The multivariate analysis begins in Table 3. The hypothesis whose testing is displayed in this table is that respondents with poorer health will be more likely to have sought help from religion. Variables included in the table are entered in sets from those that were significantly associated with receiving help from religion in Table 1. Tables 3 and 4 show standardized coefficients.

The analysis begins with model 1, considering just the religion variables. Respondents who think of themselves as strongly religious people are much more likely to say they have received help from religion, as are Protestants when compared with the Jewish/other/none respondents.

In model 2 we add the health measures that had a significant association with receiving help in Table 1, functional disability, cognitive status, and chronic disease disability risk. Only the disability measure is associated with receiving help, and this measure is retained throughout. In model 3 are added the sociodemographic factors; non-white respondents were much more likely to say they had received help, and lower levels of income and education were marginally significant, so all three are retained. Note that the significant effect of being Protestant disappears because of the strong effect of race.

In model 4 the health risks of alcohol use and inactivity are added; inactivity has a negative association with receiving help. In model 5 the psychological characteristics of neuroticism, optimism, body consciousness, and depression are added, but there are no significant relationships among them.

Thus, for view 2, the hypothesis is confirmed: The more disabled people are, the more likely they were to say they had sought help from religion. The direction of the asso-

TABLE 1 Descriptive Statistics for Variables Used in Analysis, Disability Clinic Study

Variable	N	Minimum	Maximum	χ	Pearson r Help	Pearson r Nonp.
Help from religion	138	0 = Not mentioned	1 = Mentioned	0.6	1.00	.01
Nonphysical sense of self	143	23 = Low	111 = High	75.8	.01	1.00
Protestant	143	0 = Other	1 = Protestant	0.3	.24	.04
Catholic	143	0 = Other	1 = Catholic	0.3	.09	−.05
Self-rated religiousness	143	0 = Not at all religious	20 = Highly religious	12.1	.51	.17
Self-rated health	145	1 = Poor	5 = Excellent	2.7	−.04	.16
Disability	200	0 = None	20 = Severe	7.1	.19	.01
Chronic disease: Disability risk	200	0	1	0.5	−.18	.07
Cognitive status	200	1 = No impairment	3 = Impaired	1.2	.16	.06
Female	200	1 = Male	2 = Female	1.6	−.14	.05
Age	200	18	92	47.8	−.31	−.01
Race	200	1 = White	2 = Non-white	1.5	.57	.03
Income	188	$7,500	$80,000 $19,700		−.42	.07
Education	199	4 years	26 years	13.1	−.43	.11
Alcohol use	200	0 = Never	365 = Daily	47.4	−.27	.08
Inactivity	200	2 = Much exercise	6 = Little or no exercise	4.5	−.15	−.19
Social support: From respondent	144	9 = Little support	510 = Much support	178.4	.02	.21
Social support: To respondent	144	12 = Little support	487 = Much support	165.1	−.01	.23
Social network size	144	1 person	20 people	7.4	.02	.21
Frequency of social contacts, per year	145	18	4,468	1,166.5	.07	.18
Depression symptoms	145	20 = Rarely	67 = Most of the time	36.5	.13	−.16
Neuroticism	142	0 = Low	6 = High	2.9	.14	−.21
Optimism	142	6 = Low	20 = High	14.7	.23	.19
Social body consciousness	144	0 = Low	12 = High	9.4	.21	.11
Physical body consciousness	144	0 = Low	16 = High	10.2	.16	−.08

*Correlations larger than .17 significant at $p < .05$.

ciation is that poorer health is associated with greater religiousness. This association is net of the respondents' ratings of their own religiousness, race, education, and activity levels.

In Table 4 we see the analysis of nonphysical sense of self. The direction of the hypothe-

sized relationship with self-rated religiousness is the same as it was for help from religion; people with a stronger religious or spiritual sense of self should have a stronger overall nonphysical sense of self. The hypothesized direction for self-rated health, however, is dif-

TABLE 2 Descriptive Statistics for Religious Affiliation Categories

Religious Preference	Percent	Percent Female[a]	Percent White[b]	Mean Age[c]	Mean Educ.[d]	Percent w/Help from Religion[e]	Mean Nonphys. Sense of Self[a]
Protestant	31.5	55.6	20.0	43.2	12.7	31.2	76.9
Catholic	30.8	61.4	47.7	43.4	12.1	31.9	74.5
Jewish	17.5	80.0	100.0	65.1	14.4	16.7	73.6
Other/none	20.3	62.1	51.7	53.0	15.1	20.3	78.1

[a] No significant differences between groups.
[b] $\chi^2 = 41.3$, 3 df, $p < .0001$.
[c] $F = 11.46$, 3 df, $p < .0001$. Bonferroni adjustment shows Jewish respondents older than all others.
[d] $F = 6.68$, 3 df, $p < .0003$. Bonferroni adjustment shows Roman Catholics with less education than all others, Other with more.
[e] $F = 7.3$, 3 df, $p < .0001$. Bonferroni adjustment shows Jewish respondents less likely than all others to receive help from religion.

TABLE 3 Regression of Help from Religion on Religion, Health Status, and Psychological Factors, Disability Clinic study

	Model 1 B	Model 2 B	Model 3 B	Model 4 B	Model 5 B
Protestant	.293*	.287*	.049	.087	.131
Catholic	.233+	.170	−.069	−.060	−.071
Self-rated religiousness	.684***	.688***	.686***	.752***	.747***
Chronic disease		−.169			
Disability risk					
Disability		.263*	.315+	.468*	.498*
Cognitive status		.101			
Female			−.031		
Race (non-white)			.590**	.591**	.669***
Income			−.291+	−.287	−.251
Education			−.355+	−.405+	−.490*
Age			−.146		
Alcohol use				−.194	
Inactivity				−.424*	−.397*
Neuroticism					−.035
Optimism					−.064
Body consciousness:					
Physical					−.272
Social					.021
Depression					.272
−2 Log likelihood χ^2	45.8	53.2	89.0	93.4	93.6
Degrees of freedom	3	6	9	9	13
N	138	138	129	129	128

*$p < .05$ **$p < .01$ ***$p < .001$.

TABLE 4 Regression of Nonphysical Sense of Self on Religion, Health Status, and Psychological Factors, Disability Clinic Study

Variables	Model 1 B	Model 2 B	Model 3 B	Model 4 B	Model 5 B	Model 6 B
Self-rated religiousness	.184*	.203*	.226*	.220*	.225*	.219*
Protestant	−.042	−.111	−.055	−.071	−.086	−.071
Catholic	−.075	−.122	−.053	−.075	−.031	−.041
Self-rated health		.198*	.181*	.149+	.146+	.132
Education			.150+	.143	.173+	.130
Inactivity				−.136		
Social support:						
To respondent					.202	
From respondent					−.067	
Social network size					.009	
Frequency of social contacts					.113	
Neuroticism						−.158
Optimism						.081
Depression						−.003
Adjusted R^2	.01	.04	.05	.06	.07	.06
N	143	142	141	141	140	140

$*p < .05$ $+p < .10$.

ferent from the disability/help from religion association in the same way that view 2 is opposite to view 3: We expect people with a stronger nonphysical sense of self to have better self-rated health.

The analysis follows a similar strategy. In model 1, including just the religion variable self-rated religiousness is associated with nonphysical sense of self, but Protestants and Catholics show no differences from the Jewish/other/none respondents. These associations are not changed when self-rated health is added.

In the next column, the sociodemographic factor of education is added. It is marginally significant and is retained in further steps; as one would expect, higher levels of education correspond with greater nonphysical senses of self. Among the health practices, which originally included smoking, alcohol and illicit drug consumption, and inactivity (lack of exercise), only lack of exercise was associated at the bivariate level with either help from religion or nonphysical sense of self.

Lack of exercise is entered in the fourth column here, and it shows no significant association with nonphysical sense of self.

Several aspects of social networks and support were associated at the bivariate level with nonphysical sense of self, but none of the associations are significant when tested in the multivariate model.

Last, we look at some psychological characteristics, which had significant bivariate associations. None of them, however, is significant in the multivariate analysis.

Thus, the most parsimonious model containing all significant effects is model 3, in which the nonphysical sense of self is associated with higher levels of religiousness, better self-ratings of health, and to some extent, higher levels of education, as was hypothesized.

DISCUSSION

This study has many limitations; at best it can be considered illustrative and preliminary. The sample is small and highly selected for individuals with health problems. Moreover, it is a cross-sectional study in a field in which the causal directions are especially problematic. At most it can suggest directions for future studies of religion and health.

With these limitations in mind, however, the seemingly paradoxical hypotheses for this study were both supported, and they show that religion does have a complicated relationship with health. The first hypothesis was that respondents with greater disability would be more likely to say they had sought help for their health problems from their religion. This yes/no response was coded from what was actually an open-ended question in the interview: "Do your religious beliefs help you at all with your health problems? Can you tell me in what way, or give me any specific examples of help that you received?" There were many interesting answers to this question; 62 percent of the sample gave a positive response. In fact, the respondents' stories illuminate both findings of the study; they especially provide insight into the meaning of identities based on spiritual or religious criteria.

Spiritual Awakenings

First there are accounts from respondents who felt that help from God or their religion changed everything in their lives. Perhaps the most dramatic stories were of religious awakenings that took place directly as a result of a sudden illness or injury.

> I don't know . . . I felt so spiritual, you know [after the stroke]. It was such a—you know—a beautiful experience. I get like that every now and then. . . . I got this relaxed feeling and feel so good. I don't think you could feel that good all the time. We couldn't walk around feeling like that daily. One thing, I stopped worrying as much as I used to, and I been able to let go of certain things that I couldn't let go of before. And, you know, I used to sit and cry because I was so happy. Yeah, it's a great way to feel. . . . I learned to be by myself. I get lonely sometimes . . . but I can deal with it more now. So in a sense I look at my stroke

as a blessing. . . . I think . . . through this stroke I started to feel more spiritual.

These are the words of a 51-year-old black Protestant woman who had been a typist before her stroke. She is still partially paralyzed and speaks elsewhere of looking down at her hands, which she cannot move. Rather than regret, however, at her loss of her skill and ability to earn a living, she thinks of those who have had a stroke and died, and she feels lucky to be alive. More than that even, she feels that her life has been enriched by the experience, so much that she used to "sit and cry because I was so happy" and actually speaks of her stroke as a blessing. There were other such stories. Another was from a 35-year-old black Protestant woman who had also been a secretary and had also had a stroke:

> At the time before my stroke I had no experience with my God. With my stroke I learned from him. It happened with faith. My pastor and my friends talked to me about religion. I was not very serious about religion. I take God seriously, deeply. People in my church pray for me and visit me all the time. They call me and give me support.

Both these women identified their illnesses as real turning points in their religious lives, although they imply that they had had some connection with religion ("my pastor and my friends talked to me") before the event. One man, also a Protestant, 52 years old, white, a fabric designer who was paralyzed after a mugging in which he was stabbed in the back, explained:

> When your life drastically changes I think if you had any religious training or background you tend to resort or turn to it or think of it or find it more enhancing or helpful. Due to my injury I've become more religious.

Whether they are awakenings or reawakenings isn't really important. What is important is that these respondents saw a growth in their spiritual lives that coincided with, and came about as a direct result of, their shrinking physical capacity. A loss in one area of life became a gain in another. It is especially clear when the respondents had some degree of paralysis, an unambiguous loss of physical ability. It is a causal chain these people are telling us about, one in which they consciously make the direct connection between the helping functions of religion and the nonphysical, religious or spiritual sense of self. One more example is from a 25-year-old Protestant Hispanic male who had injuries that resulted in memory loss and speech problems:

> Through my injuries I'm so depressed. When I go to church, I feel so much better. It relieves me. A few times I've been to church, I "caught the Spirit." And after that I felt so much better.

Discovering Purpose in Life

There were some other respondents who spoke about religious awakening in a different way, not as a feeling of spirituality, but as a conviction that God had a purpose for them. A number of these people's illnesses or injuries had brought them close to death, and the very fact of their survival took on a religious meaning, causing them to see their lives in a new way. One man was a 42-year-old Russian immigrant, a bus driver, who had fallen five flights of stairs and injured his pelvis and head and had nerve damage (his religious affiliation was "other," for Russian Orthodox):

> When I had my accident, I had spent time in a coma for three weeks. And finally I survived, and was on my way to recover, and I think that if God saved my life, he had a purpose. So I believe him, and I'm not going marching down.

Another man, a 40-year-old Hispanic, Roman Catholic man whose legs had both been amputated after a train accident said simply,

> I thank God. There is a purpose to why I'm still alive.

Healing, Strength, and Comfort

In many other cases, there was, in addition to gratitude for being alive, also gratitude for the recovery they had experienced, which they often framed in terms of religious healing. Perhaps the single most dramatic example came from a pretty young Protestant Hispanic woman who had suffered severe head injuries in a car accident. She limped slowly into the interview room on crutches and with braces on both legs. She told me she had been in a coma for three months:

> [The doctors] told me I would never walk again. [What helps me is] trusting in God, knowing when it's his time. I ask for his help and he always helps me. He is there caring for me, he's dependable.

The interviewer said, "And you just walked in here." And she beamed. Another woman (Roman Catholic) who asked God directly for healing and felt she received it was 63 years old and had immigrated from the Virgin Islands. She had had a stroke, was using a walker, and still had partial paralysis in one arm:

> When I was in the hospital, when I woke up and I couldn't feel nothing, I figured that I would be an invalid. I would be in a wheelchair, and people would have to do things for me. And then I started praying, asking Jesus to help me, give me strength, that I could do the things, and have nobody wait on me. My prayer was answered. I've come a long way, and I have to give thanks to almighty God. I have to thank my God every day.

Another example is from a young black Protestant woman who fell four stories from her apartment in a fire:

> I think that believing in God . . . a lot of people thought I was going to die. I'm making it. Even the doctor told me that I have nine lives because they almost gave me up. With God's help I'm walking around. I didn't move around for eight months. I was on my back. I couldn't

do anything for myself. Now with the help of God I'm doing all these things.

There were several other respondents who reflected directly on the relationship between the healing that comes from medicine and the healing that comes from faith. For example,

When medicine can't help, God does. He's the doctor of all doctors.

A 45-year-old black auto repairman, a Protestant, who had had a stroke said:

[My religious beliefs] helped 100 percent. When I was going to the church I couldn't walk. I prayed a lot and I noticed I made an improvement. I believe it was partly because of the prayer. Again, it's the Lord who made us. He's the one who knows about us. Doctors are directed by the Lord. The physician's knowledge comes from God. I'm sick with a stroke and the doctor might say I'm not going to walk or I may not be able to live again. They are directed by the Lord. I think all my improvement comes from God.

Respondents conceived of "help" in many different ways. Short of attributing any healing to their faith, many respondents at least felt they gained peace, encouragement, strength, and comfort. Here is a sampling of responses:

I try to think of the hereafter. That gives a little optimism I think. Just the occasional dropping into church gives some encouragement. (69-year-old white Roman Catholic woman, former secretary with back pain)

The doctor said if the car hit me by another inch I would have been crippled. God helped me with that. In my depression I've asked him to give me the strength and to lift my burdens. (43-year-old black Protestant man, computer supervisor)

It's helped me overcome. I didn't take public transportation, but now I take it. God makes me feel brave. I feel more independent. (32-year-old Asian woman, Protestant, data entry worker with post-polio syndrome)

If I'm in pain whether it be physical or mental, I pray for strength and guidance and I feel that I've gotten it. (36-year-old black woman, Protestant, clerical worker with epilepsy)

Yes, it's comforting knowing that God is there to help me deal with pain and everything else in life. (40-year-old black man, Roman Catholic, office associate with vascular problem)

Finding a Meaning in Suffering

There was also a theme of enduring suffering that several respondents developed. Some framed their experiences in terms of being tested by God, and believing that their faith would be rewarded in the future. These were respondents who could point neither to tangible physical healing nor to intangible emotional comfort, but who believed that their present suffering must have some religious meaning. Here are some examples:

I am attending a group that believes in reincarnation. We discuss what the soul is, what a person is. I believe life is a learning experience. I believe the soul goes through many lifetimes. I believe that my disability is something that I have to go through to sort of get back on the right path of evolution. We are all evolving into something perfect. People who choose difficult lives choose them to learn from them. (43-year-old Jewish female, newsstand worker with arthritis of the knee)

Job suffered and endured due to his faith in God. His reward then was twice as much. Endurance is the most important thing and faith that he does exist and that if we do his will the rest comes. (49-year-old Hispanic Protestant woman, salesperson suffering pain and depression)

My friend, when she was sick, she never thought that she was going to die. She thought that maybe God was thinking about her and wanted to see if she really had faith in him. (22-year-old Hispanic woman with lupus. She spoke so often during the interview of "her friend" that one wonders if she wasn't really talking about herself)

Because they say God has no respect for individual persons. Anyone can get sick because tomorrow isn't promised to anyone. Just thank God for one more day. Anything can happen. It's scary, you have people, family, kids. The environment around us, you tend to worry about families. I feel prayer helps. Reading in the Bible that Job had to go through sickness even though he was a perfect and upright man and everything. God blessed him more and gave him a new family. (24-year-old black Protestant woman with multiple sclerosis)

These accounts are among the most thoughtful and subtle that were given. They show a poignant level of reflection, a sense of prayers prayed but not answered, a struggle, a real groping for meaning that does not come easily. Their identification with the biblical figure of Job, especially, shows the unresolved nature of their suffering.

Like Job, some respondents were also angry with God for allowing evil in the world, or cruelty, or neglect. One 76-year-old actress who had no religious affiliation and had suffered a stroke was being interviewed during the Los Angeles riots. She said:

You could make a case for that [that religious beliefs help people with their pain or health problems]. I could make a case. I sometimes read things and I become completely swayed by what I read and then I think, well, I get cynical about it. I can't answer that question. I wish I had that connection, I really do. I've prayed in my life. I prayed a lot when I was little. When something happens like it's happening now in Los Angeles, how can you think that this God in heaven cares about you? It's stupid.

Another woman, a 53-year-old Hispanic Roman Catholic who had had an aneurysm, gave a classic account of the problem of the existence of evil in the world:

I should be more closer to God, you know. I can't believe that I'm like this. God is supposed to be kind, love, you know. People say that, I can't. If

God is supposed to be so kind, so helpful, he would cure me if I was sick. Quote the Bible, blind people, crippled people heal ye . . . from death. How come he wants people to go hungry? To be paralyzed, even kill each other? God cannot be giving me this cause I refuse, coming from the Devil, the Devil is mean. But that's different stuff. Or maybe I wicked in my own self and I don't know it, and I deserve this. We've been punished ever since Adam and Eve. So maybe I would say well then why should I worry about it. They did it and that's how we have to pay for it. Maybe I should take this penalty, but I can't. Because I should not pay for what they did.

Another woman blamed God more indirectly, for the failings of the people around her to help her as she thought they should. This was a 36-year-old Hispanic woman, a Roman Catholic:

God helps me in a lot of ways. But he put people in this world to help and I don't see anyone helping me in the things I really need. I need physical therapy, understanding, and to treat me like a normal person. I'm just like everybody else. I'm not getting the help I need.

The Spiritual, Nonphysical Self

The argument in this article has been that one of the benefits of religious involvement will be in refocusing the respondent on aspects of the self to which a painful, or nonfunctioning, or unattractive physical body is irrelevant. The inner, spiritual self can be beautiful and whole even when the material, physical body is broken or diseased. As these are important teachings of the Christian religion, it is not surprising that the preceding responses come almost exclusively from Protestants and Roman Catholics. But there was another important group of responses from people who were Jewish or identified their religious affiliation as other or none, and who also regarded their spiritual self as very important. One woman, a 37-year-old writer with Guillan-Barré syndrome said,

Yes [her religious beliefs helped her] because of the meditation. You lay down and localize where your pain is. From there you take the pain and you have a spirit at the end of the bed that receives the pain. You watch the pain go off. You go over every step of relaxation until the pain goes away. I've only been going there for two months. . . . there is a Science of Mind Center that I go to on the weekends. They have a healing circle and prosperity groups that focus on living a happy and healthy life-style without medication. There are practitioners there and a reverend. There is a religious aspect to it.

Another woman, a 48-year-old Jewish musician who had Ehlers-Danlos syndrome, a hereditary disease of the connective tissue, said:

My inner values, my nonmaterial world values, are very helpful with my pain. I don't call it religion. I work with my body energy and my emotional energy. I use my visualizing techniques to manipulate my mind. To me they are spiritual exercises, choosing life as opposed to being struck down by my situation.

Finally, here are some passages from the very lengthy response of a 65-year-old European immigrant; she had had breast cancer some years before and was currently seeking treatment for arthritis. She was a professor and identified her religious affiliation as "other":

As I come close to my exit, I come to what Erikson calls "the closing of the circle." I was inspired by Herbert Benson and Norman Cousins. It is the state of being you are in, I am at peace with myself—our bodies can fight cancer themselves. I pat my breast, I say "Tootsie, we have to coexist. If I am cremated you are too." If it is not to be, God whoever you are, okay then please let me stay a little longer, and then go as fast as possible. I don't think suffering is noble. . . . I'm trying to explain what is beyond language. I'm smarter than this, it is liberating, I can go into any of them [churches] and feel at home. I don't live in fear—I am in resolution in my unconscious.

This woman was an intellectual, well-read and thoughtful, a professional who told me with great pride about students she had trained; and she reveals a remarkable separation between her physical self and her "real" nonphysical self in imagining conversations with her own body parts. She also was a lonely person, with no family, and she had recently lost her best friend to a recurrence of breast cancer; her self-rating of health was "fair."

Religion is a complicated thing. People seek help from it when they are in trouble, especially when they have been brought up with a traditional faith, and especially when that religious tradition speaks to their situation. So the data show, quite straightforwardly, that people with greater disability were more likely to say they had sought help from religion. The respondents' own words, which I have used liberally, seem to convey a consistent theme that people turn to religion in need, and that one of the ways religion helps them is by letting them "rise above" their problems, so to speak, by putting them in a context in which the physical body does not matter that much.

Well, I know that some people if they believe in God and if they believe in prayer would pray to be relieved of their pain. But I always could see others that were worse off than me so when I went to pray, I couldn't pray for myself when the guy next door was so much worse so I wound up praying for him and it helps to take my mind off my own problems. (54-year-old Roman Catholic woman who had had a stroke)

In these voices speaking of religion and health there are themes of new insight, of the relevance of religious beliefs to some of the most challenging and threatening of human experiences, and of the growth and development of the self. Above all, they speak of the authenticity of these experiences. Self-ratings of health, another expression of subjective experience, are being taken more and more seriously by researchers because of their apparent ability to communicate vital health information. Their relationship with eventual health outcomes should also underscore for us the validity and importance of the patient/respondent's point of view, a view some have argued is increasingly absent in the historical development of Western medicine (Reiser 1993).

The coherence of these voices belies the contradictions in the relationship between religion and health presented at the beginning of this article. People say they do turn to religion in crises of illness, and religion also seems to be associated with more positive views of health when the spiritual self becomes more prominent. Ultimately, however, longitudinal data are necessary to establish causal order in these processes that appear contradictory at the cross section.

APPENDIX   Sense of Self Scale

Here are some ways in which people think about themselves. For these questions, I would like you to think about your whole life, not just the way you are today.

On a scale of 0 to 10, tell me to what extent you think of yourself as:

1. a musical person?
2. a reader?
3. an artistic person?
4. a social person?
5. an intellectual?
6. a family person?
7. a conversationalist?
8. a writer?
9. a spiritual person?*
10. someone who is good with numbers?
11. someone who is good at solving problems or puzzles?
12. a scientific person?
13. a professional?
14. someone with a sense of humor?
15. a religious person?*

*Treated as a separate scale for the purpose of this study.

REFERENCES

ADELMAN, PAMELA K. 1994. "Multiple Roles and Physical Health among Older Adults." *Research on Aging* 16:142–66.

BERGER, PETER L. 1967. *The Sacred Canopy: Elements of a Sociological Theory of Religion.* Doubleday.

BROOK, ROBERT H., JOHN E. WARE, ALLYSON DAVIES-AVERY, ANITA L. STEWART, CATHY A. DONALD, WILLIAM H. ROGERS, KATHLEEN N. WILLIAMS, and SHAWN A. JOHNSTON. 1979. "Overview of Adult Health Status Measures Fielded in Rand's Health Insurance Study." *Medical Care* 17 (Supplement):1–131.

CAMERON, LINDA, ELAINE LEVENTHAL, and HOWARD LEVENTHAL. 1993. "Symptom Representations and Affect as Determinants of Care-Seeking in a Community-Dwelling, Adult Sample Population." *Health Psychology* 12:171–79.

CHARMAZ, KATHY. 1991. *Good Days, Bad Days: The Self in Chronic Illness and Time.* Rutgers University Press.

DURKHEIM, EMILE. [1897] 1951. *Suicide.* Translated by John A. Spaulding and George Simpson. Free Press.

———. [1915] 1965. *Elementary Forms of the Religious Life.* Translated by Joseph W. Swain. Free Press.

EYSENCK, H.J. 1958. "A Short Questionnaire for the Measurement of Two Dimensions of Personality." *Journal of Applied Psychology* 42:14–17.

FEINBERG, STEPHEN E., ELIZABETH F. LOFTUS, and JUDITH M. TANUR. 1985. "Cognitive Aspects of Health Survey Methodology: An Overview." *Milbank Memorial Fund Quarterly* 63:547–64.

FERRARO, KENNETH F., and CYNTHIA M. ALBRECHT-JENSEN. 1991. "Does Religion Influence Adult Health?" *Journal for the Scientific Study of Religion* 30:193–202.

GROVES, ROBERT M., NANCY H. FULTZ, and ELIZABETH MARTIN. 1992. "Direct Questioning about Comprehension in a Survey Setting." Pp. 49–61 in *Questions about Questions: Inquiries into the Cognitive Bases of Surveys,* edited by Judith M. Tanur. Russell Sage.

HANSEN, RON. 1991. *Mariette in Ecstasy.* Harper Collins.

HOGE, DEAN R. 1972. "A Validated Intrinsic Religious Motivation Scale." *Journal for the Scientific Study of Religion* 11:369–76.

IDLER, ELLEN L. 1987. "Religious Involvement and the Health of the Elderly: Some Hypotheses and an Initial Test." *Social Forces* 66:226–38.

———. 1992. "Self-Assessed Health and Mortality: A Review of Studies." *International Review of Health Psychology* 1:33–54.

———. 1993a. *Cohesiveness and Coherence: Religion and the Health of the Elderly.* Garland.

———. 1993b. "Perceptions of Pain and Perceptions of Health." *Motivation and Emotion* 17:205–24.

IDLER, ELLEN L, and RONALD J. ANGEL. 1990. "Age, Chronic Pain, and Subjective Assessments of Health." *Advances in Medical Sociology* 1:131–52.

IDLER, ELLEN L., and STANISLAV V. KASL. 1991. "Health Perceptions and Survival: Do Global Evaluations of Health Status Really Predict Mortality?" *Journal of Gerontology: Social Sciences* 46:S55–65.

———. 1992. "Religion, Disability, Depression, and the Timing of Death." *American Journal of Sociology* 97:1052–79.

KAPLAN, BERTON H., HEATHER MUNROE-BLUM, and DAN G. BLAZER. 1993. "Religion, Health, and Forgiveness." Pp. 52–77 in *Religion in Aging and Health,* edited by Jeffrey Levin. Sage.

KING, MICHAEL, PETER SPECK, and ANGELA THOMAS. 1994. "Spiritual and Religious Beliefs in Acute Illness—Is This a Feasible Area for Study?" *Social Science and Medicine* 38:631–36.

KOENIG, HAROLD G. 1993. "Religion and Hope for the Disabled Elder." Pp. 18–51 in *Religion in Aging and Health,* edited by Jeffrey Levin. Sage.

KOENIG, HAROLD G., LINDA K. GEORGE, and ILENE C. SIEGLER. 1988. "The Use of Religion and Other Emotion-Regulating Coping Strategies among Older Adults." *The Gerontologist* 28:303–10.

LEVIN, JEFFREY S., and P.L. SCHILLER. 1987. "Is There a Religious Factor in Health?" *Journal of Religion and Health* 26:9–36.

LEWIS, C.S. 1962. *The Problem of Pain.* Macmillan.

MADDOX, GEORGE L. 1964. "Self-Assessment of Health: A Longitudinal Study of Selected Elderly Subjects." *Journal of Chronic Disease* 17:449–60.

MCCREADY, WILLIAM C., and ANDREW GREELEY. 1976. *The Ultimate Values of the American Population.* Sage.

MATTLIN, JAY A., ELAINE WETHINGTON, and RONALD KESSLER. 1990. "Situational Determinants of Coping and Coping Effectiveness." *Journal of Health and Social Behavior* 31:103–22.

MILLER, LYNN C., RICHARD MURPHY, and ARNOLD H. BUSS. 1981. "Consciousness of Body: Private and Public." *Journal of Personality and Social Psychology* 41:397–406.

MOSSEY, JANA, and EVELYN SHAPIRO. 1982. "Self-rated Health: A Predictor of Mortality among the Elderly." *American Journal of Public Health* 72:800–808.

NATIONAL CENTER FOR HEALTH STATISTICS. 1977. *Plan and Operation of the Health and Nutrition Examination Survey, United States, 1971–1973.* (DHHS Publication no. PHS 79–1310). U.S. Public Health Service.

———. 1992. *Plan and Operation of the NHANES-I Epidemiologic Followup Study, 1987.* (DHHS Publication no. PHS 92–1303). U.S. Public Health Service.

NORBECK, JANE S., ADA M. LINDSEY, and VIRGINIA L. CARRIERI. 1981. "The Development of an Instrument to Measure Social Support." *Nursing Research* 30:264–69.

POLLNER, MELVIN. 1989. "Divine Relations, Social Relations, and Well-Being." *Journal of Health and Social Behavior* 30:92–104.

RADLOFF, LENORE S. 1977. "The CES-D Scale: A Self-Report Depression Scale for Research in the General Population." *Applied Psychological Measurement* 1:385–401.

REISER, STANLEY JOEL. 1993. "The Era of the Patient: Using the Experience of Illness in Shaping the Missions of Health Care." *Journal of the American Medical Association* 269:1012–17.

SCHECHTER, SUSAN (ed.). 1994. *Proceedings of the 1993 NCHS Cognitive Aspects of Self-Reported Health Status.* U.S. Department of Health and Human Services, Public Health Service, CDC, National Center for Health Statistics.

SCHEIER, MICHAEL F., and CHARLES S. CARVER. 1985. "Optimism, Coping, and Health: Assessment and Implications of Generalized Outcome Expectancies." *Health Psychology* 4:219–47.

SCHOENFELD, DAVID E., LYNDA C. MALMROSE, DAN G. BLAZER, DEBORAH T. GOLD, and TERESA E. SEEMAN. 1994. "Self-Rated Health and Mortality in the High-Functioning Elderly—A Closer Look at Healthy Individuals: MacArthur Field Study of Successful Aging." *Journal of Gerontology: Medical Sciences* 49:M109–M115.

"JESUS WILL FIX IT AFTER AWHILE": MEANINGS AND HEALTH

Mary Abrums
University of Washington

There are many myths and stereotypes related to the health of people of color in the United States. Many research studies are done and statistics proliferate on the health status of nondominant groups. Few studies attempt to understand the meaning systems of poor and working-class African-American women in relationship to health and health care. This study uses an ethnographic approach including narrative analysis of life history interviews in order to examine how the life experiences and belief systems of a small group of poor and working-class African-American women from a storefront church in Seattle, Washington, inform and influence the women's opinions and inter-actions with the dominant white health care system. This paper will examine specific dimensions of the women's belief systems and discuss how these beliefs are applied as the women interpret, confront, and examine the meaning of health and the meaning of their own experiences in specific health care encounters. The women's belief systems, learned and reinforced within the context of their daily lives, enable the women to offer a unique critique of the health care system, as well as to maintain a powerful subjectivity in the face of an objectifying system, the dominant white Western health care system.

INTRODUCTION

There are many myths and stereotypes that relate to the health of people of color in the United States. Statistics proliferate on the poor health of nondominant races on innumerable parameters. News articles in the popular press are written daily, discussing and speculating on the reasons for the poor health of African Americans, Native Americans, Asian refugee groups, and so forth. Most of these articles cite scientific research as the basis for the discussions. Health professionals are typically trained to utilize research which presents race as an influential factor related to health problems. However, according to Cooper and

Reprinted from *Social Science & Medicine*, vol. 50 (2000), pp. 89–105, by permission of Elsevier Science.

David (1986) "the uncritical use of the traditional biological concept of race" has created multiple problems in the health care arena. The authors state that such use of information "has distorted etiological thinking in public health and has proven an obstacle in the development of effective intervention strategies" (p. 97). The United States Institute of Medicine has recently advised scientists to "abandon traditional racial categories because they are 'of limited utility for the purpose of health research' " (as cited in Schmid 1999: A4). The Institute notes that the "concept of race rests on the unfounded assumption that there are fundamental biological differences among racial groups" (ibid), and suggests that data could be more useful if collected on more specific ethnic or regional groups which would allow researchers to examine such variables as the impact of communities on health.

However, the racial categorization of health problems is deeply entrenched in the social and professional consciousness and in the discourse of health in Western society. Health professionals and researchers are taught by other professionals who utilize this traditional approach to race in statistical information, and then inevitably incorporate this same approach in the education of clinicians. The educators of health professionals simultaneously integrate this information with their own clinical experiences, bringing their own personal histories, fears, and stereotypes into their teaching and caregiving activities and into the clinical judgments that they make about their clients. Some fairly straightforward examples of clinical beliefs about African Americans that have become commonly accepted as true, are that they are at high risk for hypertension, that they have an unusually high infant mortality rate, and that poverty and lifestyle predispose many African Americans to a wide variety of serious health problems. Clinicians typically, having been exposed to this information over and over again, accept these beliefs as innocuous "facts" without critically examining the repercussions of the relationship of the use of race as it corresponds to physiological problems and as the two terms are used as parallel indicators of poor health status.

Schiller (1992) notes that "instead of accepting that the concept of risk group is 'useful,' we must ask 'useful for whom to do what?'" (p. 249). She points out that epidemiology constructs "a sense of citizenship, as those who belong to the strong and healthy general population of the nation are distinguished from the weak and vulnerable subjects of study . . . the 'at risk'" (ibid).

Analysis of the negative ramifications of categorizing groups in the AIDS crisis has been particularly illuminating in understanding the problems inherent in categorizations of certain groups of people (Crawford 1994; Schiller 1992; Singer 1998;

Sobo 1993). Schiller (1992) found in her study of "at risk" groups and AIDS, that the construction of AIDS risk groups as culturally distinct served to compound the AIDS crisis in the following ways: by leading to misunderstandings about who is at risk and who is not; by creating poor targeting of health education attempts; by contributing to the spread of the disease because of confusion about who is "at risk"; by stigmatizing and marginalizing people with AIDS; by concentrating on the disease itself without noting that the disease is proliferating under the conditions "of unemployment and growing structurally caused poverty, the subsequent development of the informal economy of drugs, the lack of primary and preventive health care, the oppression of women and people of color" (p. 246). Schiller stresses that "the concept of risk group . . . has perpetuated these consequences through what it does not allow us to see as much as through the type of thinking it promotes" (ibid). Sobo's (1993) study gives a graphic example of how "risk" categorizations can backfire in the public health arena. In the face of negative labels, HIV/AIDS risk denial has become "part of a self protective strategy adopted in the face of racist finger-pointing and blame-laying" (p. 462). She notes that sexism, racism, and other oppressions create forces on people's beliefs about HIV/AIDS risks and on their perceived power to address risks that, in reality, are enmeshed in social, cultural, and economic problems.

In order to examine more deeply why the statistical use of race as a dimension of health is problematic, we turn to the social sciences for discussions on how race is used in Western society. Rothenberg (1990) points out that "the construction of difference is essential to racism, sexism, and other forms of oppression" (p. 42). She notes that claims about difference "are offered under the guise of value-free descriptions yet smuggle in normative considerations that carry with them the stigma of inferiority" (p. 43). Rothenberg discusses how "difference" in race, as well as in gender, as defined by nature/biology "performs certain critical functions" (p. 45). These are as follows: First, this difference implies a natural hierarchy, that is, it is the natural order of things to have a superior and inferior group; second, since it is the natural order, those in power are absolved from responsibility for the condition of the inferior group and thus the victim is blamed for his/her own victimization; and third, since the difference is seen as "one of kind not degree," relationships are difficult to alter and significant change is unachievable.

According to Harding (1986), racial categorizations and comparison projects demonstrate many of the problems inherent in U.S. society as a whole. She notes that categorizations which divide groups into white and "other" (choose any race or ethnic group) show residues of colonialism, that is, they speak to the development of a "universal other" for purposes of domination and exploitation; they assume that people are without history prior to their relationships with whites; and they assume more commonality among *like* groups and more differences *between* unlike groups than may actually exist.

Crawford's (1984, 1994, 1998) work demonstrates how social beliefs about who becomes ill and who remains healthy compound and intensify the ability of one group (in this research, the middle class) to create "an external other, people and groups that are negatively stereotyped" (Crawford 1994: 1355). In his research, Crawford (1984) found that the language of health is commonly used as a metaphor for "self-control, self-discipline, self-denial and will power . . . concepts that are fundamental to the Western system of values" (p. 77). In Western society, "the healthy body is the property of a deserving owner" (Crawford 1994: 1356). Health has come to be "something that could be achieved . . . a social idea . . . an essential foundation of character . . ."

(ibid, p. 1349). Just as health has come to be seen as a characteristic that is justly deserved by the person who performs all the correct behaviors (as advised by the barrage of health promotion efforts), ill health has come to be seen as being justified as well. Disease is related to a person's "inability to care for himself with 'healthy behaviors' "; and illness appears to be tied to "a fatal flaw of character or a personality defect, in an unconscious predisposition toward illness, or in living 'a high stress' life with poor 'stress management' . . ." (ibid, p. 1356). Crawford (1994) emphasizes that, in this consciousness about health, there is "a social distancing from the 'unhealthy,' a further stereotyping of already stigmatized groups who then, because of their 'irresponsible' habits are confirmed in their Otherness" (p. 1356). Crawford points out that,

> the statistical basis of attributes that connect particular diseases to certain groups and behaviors only gives an appearance that rational influences are at work. The connections, however, often resonate with deeply ingrained, implicit meanings and powerful moral judgments. The sick are made not only responsible for their illness, they are also made different (p. 1356).

He demonstrates how, since the nineteenth century,

> the language of health [has come] to signify those . . . who were responsible from those who were not, those who were respectable from those who were disreputable, those who were safe from those who were dangerous, and ultimately, those who had the right to rule from those who needed supervision, guidance, reform or incarceration (p. 1349).

Crawford (1994) notes that "in a risk conscious era, the 'healthy' self develops an even greater investment in the delineation of boundaries." In short, "self needs other." As social distance between groups widens, "attributions of self-destructive disregard and irresponsibility also increase." These beliefs are often deeply enmeshed in ideas of "victimization from a destructive social and physical environment" and this only serves to magnify judgments, thus "[converging] with other victim blaming ideas about the poor and the marginalized." As such, "high risk" is a label given to individuals "who, unlike the privileged, are 'locked' into 'cycles' of deviance and self destruction . . . The otherness of the sick or the high risk individual . . . is, in short, a boundary maintaining device that serves multiple agendas" (pp. 1357–1359).

There have been profound consequences historically to the classification of people into categories related to race, class, or gender in the health care arena. The Tuskegee Syphilis Study where 399 black men from Macon County, Alabama, were denied treatment for syphilis in order to study the course of the disease, is perhaps the most well known project that treated a group of people as "other." As Gamble (1997) states, this experiment "has come to symbolize racism in medicine, misconduct in human research, the arrogance of physicians, and government abuse of black people" (p. 1773).

Gamble (1997) demonstrates that this situation is not an isolated event, rather it must be placed within its broader social and historical context. She specifies that this experiment reflects a historical pattern of dehumanization of black people by the medical establishment. Black peoples' fears and feelings of mistrust, even today, are based on an extensive history of experimentation, on receiving the worst care from student doctors in the poorest segregated wards, on the stories of black bodies being stolen from graveyards by "night doctors" for study, and on fears of deliberate genocide from exposure to syphilis, to AIDS, and to drugs within black communities. Sobo (1993) found that, "in discussing the origins of AIDS, many black women reported having heard talk of laboratory accidents, contaminated water, or

information that was being withheld . . . men spoke openly of AIDS as a part of a racist plot to eliminate blacks" (p. 466). Sobo (1994) notes that

> the experience of racism and the legacy of the negative encounters that African Americans have had with the public health system, as well as the mistreatment that women and the poor historically received from the biomedical sector fuel the misgivings that many African American women have about health care workers' motives and interests (p. 21).

Gamble (1997) points out that "the powerful legacy of the Tuskegee Syphilis Study endures, in part, because the racism and disrespect for black lives that it entailed, mirrors black peoples' contemporary experiences with the medical profession" (p. 1776).

Young (1982) discusses how "many medical practices develop and persist because they are useful for other people and for reasons unconnected with curing and healing" (p. 271). Taussig (1987) points out that social problems and health care are intimately interrelated. He states that the health sciences can be used for "political goals in a large number of complicated and interacting ways" (p. 19). He discusses how health care often "takes the political edge off some of the outstanding social problems that the system as a whole produces, without necessitating deep changes in the system itself [noting that] medicine is a specifically privileged tool in that its humanitarian image allows for the penetration of forces that might otherwise be unacceptable" (p. 19). It is important to understand how health care research and its subsequent discourse, that is, ways of presenting information, *can both reflect and determine* overall societal attitudes and values toward a group of people, as well as predispose this same group to receiving a particular type of care in the health care system. West (1995) notes that race does matter in the health care discourse, but not necessarily for health reasons. Rather, race matters because categorizations present black people (and other nondominant races) as "problem people." Health care funds are directed at this or that "problem" of poor African Americans without ever questioning "[what] this way of viewing black people reveals about us as a nation" (p. 557) or more specifically, what this view reveals about the U.S. health care system.

In order to adequately address issues of oppression in health care, Baer, Singer, and Johnson (1986) call for "the dialectical examination of contending forces in and out of the health arena that impinge on health and healing" (p. 95). They stress that, in analyzing health and health care, the questions of power must be addressed on several levels— the macrosocial level (health agencies, multinational drug firms, agribusiness), the intermediate level (health administration), the microsocial level (doctor/patient interaction), and the individual level (patient's support, experiential response to illness). Singer and Baer (1995) note that it is essential for critical medical anthropology to "seek to understand the play of power, as exercised both *during* (in the immediate structuring of provider–patient relations) and *through* the interaction (in the reinforcement of existing class, gender, or racial relations)" (p. 73). These authors see that the U.S. medical system is a "reflection of class, racial/ethnic, and gender relations in the larger society . . . [it] constitutes an arena of struggle among these social divisions" (p. 182). They note that "whole worlds come together in the clinical encounter" (p. 73); and that, inevitably, through the doctor–patient "encounter and the expression given thereby to underlying contradictions, medicine is established as both an arena of social conflict and a structure of social control" (p. 34).

Taussig (1980) develops this idea, pointing out that in the Western biomedical model of health care, the clinician–patient relationship has become reified into diagnosis and treatment, and behind this screen lies a social relationship of control that supports the dominant order. There is a false illusion of reciprocity in the clinician–patient relationship and the patient receives the message: "Do not trust your senses, but leave the facts of physical matter to the doctor's control" (p. 9). The patient becomes both subject and object and the term *health care provider* has come to mean "one who provides health," that is, one who has the power to give health. Hidden behind this term and behind the reification of the clinician–patient relationship are issues of control, of helping the patient "to comply for his/her own good." Taussig states, "It is a strange 'alliance' in which one party avails itself of the other's private understandings in order to manipulate them all the more successfully" (p. 12).

Scheper-Hughes and Lock's (1987) work on the "three bodies" provides partial insight into this issue of social/medical/scientific control as an objectifying process in Western medicine. These authors see that there are three bodies: the mindful body, the social body, and the body politic. The medicalization of the body misses the connections between the individual, the phenomenological self, and the social, instead transforming the social into the biological. Scheper-Hughes and Lock find that the body is a symbol, a convenient means of justifying particular social values, and social arrangements such as the "natural" dominance of males over females or perhaps the "natural" predisposition of certain races to have physical problems, such as hypertension.

Under the auspices of the body politic, societies reproduce the "correct" body or individual for the particular time. For example, the "correct" body for a people under threat has historically been a strong, aggressive warlike individual. In today's dominant society the politically correct body is "lean, strong, androgynous and physically fit"

(Scheper-Hughes and Lock 1987: 25). The authors see, like Crawford (1984, 1994), that health has come to be seen as deserved. They state, "Health is viewed as an achieved rather than an ascribed status . . . Ill health is no longer viewed as . . . a mere quirk of nature, but rather is attributed to the individual's failure to live right, to eat well, to exercise . . ." (Scheper-Hughes and Lock, 1987: 25). Proliferation of disease categories and labels contribute to this view by labeling who is "normal," thus creating "a sick and deviant majority" (ibid). Scheper-Hughes and Lock believe that individuals are mostly unaware of these forces that control them. It is only during times of intense emotion, such as in sickness or in moments of deep trance or sexual transport that the "mind and body, self and other become one" (p. 29).

Comaroff (1985) describes how individuals can be both knowing and unknowing about the process of being formed and/or influenced by the political and social forces surrounding them. She discusses how persons who have been decentered by forces beyond their control attempt to "reconstruct themselves and their universe" (p. 3). She sees that resistance to controlling forces is demonstrated through "novel symbolic orders" that come into existence (p. 119).

Taussig, Scheper-Hughes and Lock, and Comaroff all portray the self primarily in its "unknowing" state, created by social forces, with the self enacting its subjectivity through symbolic forms or during times of intense emotion. According to these authors, development and enactment of subjectivity is seen as mainly a *reaction* to the objectification processes.

However, it is important to stress that there are multiple dimensions in any interchange of power and social conflict. Singer and Baer (1995) note that socially constituted categories of meaning and the political-economic system are strong forces that shape the day-to-day realities of individual lives. However, they

state that they do not mean "to imply that individuals are passive" (p. 101). Singer (1998) believes that it is critical to incorporate the macrosocial level in any analysis, but it is also crucial to understand the relationship between "structure and agency" (p. 330).

It must be noted that theories that portray the development of subjectivity as a *response* to a dominant power support the notion that subjectivity develops from an objectification process, rather than as a creative endeavor. The feminists, such as Harding (1986) and Alcoff (1988), question this concept, bringing about a subtle shift in emphasis by seeing that experiences, rather than outside forces, are primary to an embodied self. Subjectivity (and the subsequent development of meaning for an individual) is thus formed by positionality within context. Throughout life an individual finds herself in many positions within many contexts. In short, she has many experiences. Not all are oppositional ones, not all are in response to a dominant order. In addition, these feminist theorists see that there is no subject/object split, and that so-called "objects" are, in reality, active, not passive. Thus, individuals/subjects are constructed and construct themselves and their meaning systems through experience; that is, through active interchange with political, economic, social, cultural, and historical processes with which they come in contact. Although these outside processes do have an influence on the experience of the individual, that experience is an *active interchange*, thus the individuals influence the world around them and they are actively involved in the creation, construction of their own ever-changing subjectivities.

Although science, and particularly biomedicine, has often tried to objectify women of color for its own purposes and for societal purposes, it has not been very successful in its project. Hence the same frustration is often heard or implied from health professionals: "If *they* would only do what we tell them to, [choose one: they, their health, their babies, the society] would get better." This project of objectification has not belonged to women of color. It has been an outside project perpetuated by the dominant order and has failed to grab *their* attention, much less to control the women. Although it is important to acknowledge that the attempt to objectify women of color has been made and that some women do feel alienated from the system at times, they are not alienated from themselves. As the pastor of the church in this study says. "She knows who *she* is."

It is certainly impossible to entirely escape the idea of "outside forces" having an influence on the shaping of an individual and her beliefs; however, individual agency can be seen as at least as important as these forces. If academic theorists can recognize that we have all been formed, in part, by the structures of domination and power in our society, so can others. Within this recognition itself is a knowing subjectivity. As Pratt (1986) says, "Subjective experience is spoken from a middle position already within or down in the middle of things, looking and being looked at, talking and being talked at."

According to Jaggar (as cited in Martin 1987), there may even be a decided advantage to being on the margins when striving to understand systems of power. She states, " . . . many members of the ruling class are likely to be convinced by their own ideology. . . . Oppressed groups, by contrast suffer directly from the system that oppresses them. . . . Their pain provides them with a motivation for finding out what is wrong . . ." (p. 190).

Martin (1987) finds that the black working-class women in her study, women who suffered from the "triple jeopardy of race, class and gender" seemed to come closer to achieving a critical stance about their health care than did women in other groups (p. 193). She states, "those at the bottom of the heap tend to see more deeply and clearly the nature of the oppressions exacted at the top of the heap" (p. 202).

A STUDY OF BLACK CHRISTIAN WOMEN

The relationship between the macrosocial level, the intermediate level, the microsocial level and the individual level (Baer, Singer, and Johnson 1986) in health and healing can only be fully understood by examining social forces, by understanding health care systems, by studying clinical encounters, by examining the day-to-day lived experiences of the people involved and by listening to the views of the people experiencing both oppression and creating agency in their world. This study seeks to understand the views and experiences of a group of poor and working-class black women (the women self-referred, choosing the term *black*) from a small storefront church. The women in this research study had clear views about the health care system which they shared with me during the 18 months of my project. In casual conversations and in interviews, the women made frequent reference to the historical legacy of racism, to the racism they experienced daily in their health care encounters, and to the everyday management of the messages they received. Thus, they readily moved back and forth between the micro- and the macrosocial worlds that affected them every day, and they employed individual agency as a counterforce. As Young (1982) states, "informants' statements seem complex . . . because they often juxtapose different kinds of knowledge. A speaker does not necessarily know all of his facts in the same way, and he often gives different, epistemologically distinctive accounts of his sickness at the same time" (p. 272). As the women voiced their views, it was clear that they both created their own meaning and understood that this creation was influenced by the world around them.

This qualitative ethnographic research project was conducted with a group of black women, their families, and church leaders, who attended the Morning Sun Missionary Baptist Church (pseudonym), located in a residential area of the Central District in Seattle, Washington, U.S. There were 35 members in Morning Sun Church, and since this research was done with a very small church membership, its results cannot be generalized to other groups. Of these 35 church members, five of the women (along with the pastor and his wife) did the majority of the work of the church. Two core intergenerational families, each with four generations in the church, made up the majority of the church membership. In addition, there were a few isolated elderly women whose children were "raised in the church" but who were now grown and gone. The families in the church had all originated in Louisiana or Georgia. Family members had come north during the Great Migration of the 1940s, seeking opportunities, mostly with Boeing aircraft or with the shipyards in the booming World War II industries in the area. The women participating in the interview portion of the study ranged in age from 19 to 82. Their incomes varied—some were on welfare or disability; some were the "working poor" (one had an annual take-home pay of around $9,000 which supported between four and nine family members, the number depending on the situation of grown children and their offspring); some were employed at "good" jobs as bus drivers or as computer operators. One family, with both spouses working (the wife as a bus driver, the husband as a city disposal worker), made a combined income of $50,000. The women varied in their level of education. One elderly woman had finished the fourth grade, others had dropped out of high school. Still others had "some college" and the pastor's wife was one academic term short of attaining her master's degree.

METHODOLOGY

Two research methodologies guided my research approach and process, traditional ethnographic participant-observation method and feminist methodology. This combined approach allowed for a rich generation of data that incorporated the following: my observations and the women's views about day-to-day experiences with race, class, and gender; their views and my observations on clinical encounters and health experiences; the women's *interpretations* of their experiences with power and oppression; their views and mine on how their philosophies related to God and prayer functioned both as creative healing forces and as resistances to dominant ideology.

From the anthropological literature, I drew on concepts related to "thick description," symbolism, and the incorporation of self-reflection throughout every step of the research process (Bowen 1954; Comaroff 1985; Geertz 1973; Hurston 1963[1935]; Martin 1987; Meyerhoff 1978; Rabinow 1977; Pratt 1986; Shostak 1983). From feminist methodology, I utilized principles of feminist participatory research in designing and implementing the project. Moore (1988) states that feminist ethnography is "based on the multiple authorship of anthropological texts [and represents] both the interlocutory process of fieldwork and the collaboration between anthropologist and informant on which the practice of social anthropology rests" (p. 174). Kingman (1997) notes that feminist participatory research includes "a non-hierarchical . . . approach in which the context surrounding phenomena is acknowledged and studied and the impact of the researcher's values and emotions on the research process is acknowledged" (p. 251). According to Thompson (1991), feminist participatory research is committed to a gender focus, is oriented toward the transformation of gender-power relations, and is committed to understanding a diverse range of women's struggles and experiences within context. A model of feminist participatory research "requires that the researcher/s and the participants establish the focus, direction/s, process and product of the research together" (Thompson 1991: 31).

A key issue in feminist participatory research is the establishment of a nonhierarchical relationship between researcher and participants. Although anthropologists have clearly dealt with power differentials in their work, I found that the feminist literature was helpful in clarifying the difficulties I faced in doing research as a white, well-educated middle class woman studying with poor and working-class African-American women. I was realistically concerned that the power differential inherent in our relationship would influence every step of the research process and I wanted to neutralize this as much as was humanly possible throughout the research study.

Like Stack (1974), I believed that the question of "entry" into the research setting was very important. Thus, I chose to do this research about health in a church where the church members "held the cards" rather than in a clinic or a school setting where the power rested in the dominant white values and ideology. I found that it was important to access the church hierarchy correctly. I first met with the church's designated "missionary," a person who works with outsiders and teaches them about the church mission. Missionary Lake advised me to seek permission from the pastor to observe and participate in the church services. Pastor Kent sanctioned my work. However, neither he nor Missionary Lake granted permission to do interviews. Rather, I was told, "We'll see about that." In reality, the members of the church needed to get to know me in order to trust me. It was only after I had participated at the church for 15 months, and only after the women had been strongly encouraged by the pastor's wife, that they agreed to share their life histories in an interview process.

Prior to initiating the interviews. I tried to be true to the principles of feminist participatory research in other ways, some of which were successful, some of which were not. For instance, although I asked two of the women leaders to help me design the research method and questions, they refused to do this, saying "You know what you want to find out, so just ask." However, I found that "just asking" was not that simple and I received minimal responses to my questions for a long time.

Communicating with the women seemed fraught with difficulties and it was only after much trial and error on my part that I learned that some of my most innocuous (to me) questions held undertones of racist assumptions that were offensive. My most basic inaccurate assumption in casual conversations and in interviews was that the women saw themselves as I had been trained to see them, and as they were presented in the popular and academic literature, as an "at risk" vulnerable group. This assumption was, at best, puzzling to them, and at worst, it was insulting and racist. It became clear that my "subjectivity" was influencing the presumed "objectivity" of my research questions. In addition, it was apparent to me on a "feeling level" that there were some issues of power and control at play and that the women were successfully resisting my questions. After an initial unsuccessful and tense "researcher-led" interview with Missionary Lake, I recognized that my questions and the assumptions behind them were a problem, as was the interaction of one person questioning another about her life. Minister (1991) points out that, in the standard oral history frame,

topic selection determined by the interviewer questions, one person talking at a time, the narrator "taking the floor" with referential language that keeps within the bonds of selected topics—

denies women the communication form that supports the topics women value (p. 35).

Minister notes that women value same-sex equality, but this "interviewer-led" style sets up an immediate hierarchy. Thus, it becomes important to equalize power differential through one's approach in the interview. I found that the following were important "equalizers" in the interview process with this particular group of women: (1) the women took greater control of the interviews when we met in their homes versus a neutral setting or my home; (2) I incorporated the idea of "making meeting" (Banks-Wallace and Saran 1992) by always bringing a gift of food (sometimes lunch, but often fruit and cookies for impatient children); (3) I let the women determine how long the interview should take (anywhere from 2–6 h over a 1–2 day period); (4) I discarded all of my questions, seeing that the women's stories could take me places where I wanted to go; (5) I held conversations with the women during the interview, that is, I fostered dialogue by sharing my reactions, my beliefs and values, and my experiences; (6) I protected the women's privacy by encouraging them to turn off the tape recorder at any time, by assuring them of anonymity (the women chose their own pseudonyms—often the name of their mother or an idealized individual such as a gospel singer), and by giving them the opportunity to read and delete any portion of their life history before publication; (7) I followed the advice of Missionary Lake and the pastor's wife that the women would be insulted if I offered to pay them for the interviews. Instead I offered them favors or small gifts in return for their time. (For example, I made a genogram for one large extended family, I helped one family without a car with transportation, I gave Christmas gifts to the children of one family with whom I had a close relationship, etc.)

In order to allow for the most open-ended type of interview possible, I adapted Minister's (1991) feminist approach to interviewing and used an unstructured interview format to prevent myself from controlling topics. Each woman was asked, at the beginning of her interview, to tell the story of her life as if she were writing it. She was told that the story could begin and end at any point. Concepts such as "spirituality," "death," "how you manage," and "feeling good" were written on a single sheet of paper and were used to "trigger" topics that the storyteller might address in the course of the interview (see Fig. 1).

Life history interviews were conducted with nine of the women, seven of whom were from two of the "core" church families. This intergenerational approach enabled me to interview three generations of women in each of

Tell the story as if you were writing the story of your life

History of family	Development as a woman
	Life as a child, young adult, middle adult, older adult
Spirituality	
Birth	Health
	Feeling good
Illness	
Feeling bad/ hard times	Death
Racism/experiences with medical care	Who helps you?
How you manage	Prayer

Basic: age, education, job history, number of siblings, children.

FIGURE 1 Interviewing tool: life story topics. Adapted from Minister, K. (1991) A feminist frame for the oral history interview. In: Gluck S. B. & Patai D. (eds.) *Women's Words: A Feminist Practice of Oral History*, pp. 27–42. Routledge, New York.

the core families, providing fascinating familial, developmental, and historical perspectives to the experiences of large extended families. In addition, two elderly women, widows, living alone whose children were grown and gone were interviewed. All of these interviews were much more than simple narrations of life's events. As the women described their experiences and the context of these experiences, they related their fears and beliefs about motherhood, death, racism, men, health, God, children, the public schools, work, and the dominant white social system that touched nearly every aspect of their lives.

During the 18 months that I studied at the church, in addition to the interviews, I collected traditional ethnographic information from a variety of experiences. I participated in Sunday services, went to social events, attended Bible study groups, and went with church members to "fellowship" with other churches. I also spent time with the women and their families outside of church functions. I went to dinner with them and went shopping for clothes and groceries and Christmas trees. I visited with them in their homes and went with them to doctors' appointments, to visit relatives in the hospital, and to sign their children up for school.

In analyzing the data, I incorporated feminist principles in that I began my analysis with the women's life stories. Thus, I attempted to firmly ground myself in the reality of the women's day-to-day experiences, interpretations, and context. I agreed with Cantarow's (as cited in Scott 1991) notion that "the people who have lived through particular events are the ones best qualified to talk about them" (p. 9). In writing the women's stories I simply organized the stories into readable form, preserving the women's self-interpretations (again, using feminist methodology in recognizing the women's ability to understand

meaning within the context of their every day lives). In other words, narrative interpretation of the women's life stories was done by the women themselves as they told their stories. The women organized the importance of various events, analyzed how particular incidents had changed the courses of their lives, and clearly described the meaning of interactions, both positive and negative, with the dominant white society.

Once I had centered myself in the women's stories, I began to analyze all of the data—including my own reactions to specific events. The incorporation of this self-reflective process was essential for me to understand my subjective influence on the interactions and on the analysis of the content. There were four principles that I held as I did every step of the analysis: (1) the pastor's wife had often pointed out to me that "the simple is the most profound" and I tried to keep my analysis and my writing clear so that anybody who wanted to could read the study (Collins 1990; hooks 1981; Spradley 1980); (2) since I have a tendency to see women, especially black women, as victims, I tried to keep them firmly in mind as agents [as Mohanty (1984) points out, there is no universal oppression, only a universal struggle]; (3) As I did the analysis, I continually asked the question "How" instead of "Why" (Hancock 1989) to prevent myself from making judgments and to stay firmly centered in the women's reality; (4) I acknowledged that whatever I wrote could be used for political purposes to either hurt or to help black women and so I attempted to examine my writing carefully from every angle to see if it would contribute to the liberation or the oppression of black women. (In the end I was not sure I could control how the reader would choose to use the information.)

Only after I had thoroughly grounded myself in the women's voices and in my own subjective biases, did I begin to search for themes throughout the data—consistent patterns in what the women said and did, words repeated over and over in sermons and music, in Sunday school, during social times, throughout the interviews, when we went shopping or for a ride in the car. Research data from these interviews, from casual conversations in the community and at church, as well as more formal material from sermons and songs during church services and Bible study was compiled, coded, and arranged categorically in broad themes, then analyzed for subthemes. (I was confident in my decision to combine church-related data with the "everyday" data and the information from the interviews, because the women's everyday lives were closely enmeshed with their religious beliefs and practices. The women spent anywhere from two to 12 hours in church every week, they described themselves as praying several times a day, and they stated firmly that their beliefs in God and Jesus guided them in all aspects of their lives.)

There were several subthemes that emerged from the health-related data. These themes were as follows: (1) general beliefs or theories that helped the women to cope with life's problems and challenges in general; (2) beliefs about the body and who has power over healing the body; (3) experiences with health and feelings related to personal experiences in the health care system; (4) views about the discourse generated about black women in the health care macrosocial system (specifically discourse related to statistical information); (5) descriptions of how the women responded to and took power in an often discriminatory and judgmental health care system when forced to seek care for themselves or their families. The remainder of this paper will discuss these subthemes related to the women's beliefs and views on health, healing, and the health care system.

THE WOMEN'S THEORIES

This section will begin by exploring some of the women's belief systems that helped the women live their lives and deal with times of trouble, that is, their "theories." The word *theory* is deliberately used and is defined as follows: "an explanation based on thought; explanation based on observation and reasoning, especially one that has been tested and confirmed as a general principle explaining a large number of related facts" (Barnhart and Barnhart 1993). The women's theories were, in fact, "explanations based on observations and reasoning" that had been "tested and confirmed," not just historically, but by the women themselves in their everyday experiences.

One of the most central of the women's theories, addressed over and over again by the church members and church leaders, was that there was a difference between *education* and *intelligence*. The pastor's wife spoke often of the false intellectualism that came with advanced degrees. She stated, "When we get a little academic training, we get 'the big head,' but we ain't nothing without the Lord . . . you never get so academic that you don't need the Lord." She believed that "it is easier for the simple people to accept Jesus. If a mind is analytical, it's a little hard to get through to." She pointed out that the multitude was unwilling to believe in Jesus because he was a carpenter's son and the people were focused on prestige—they were waiting for the son of a king. She stated, "Some people think they know everything. They look down on people who may not be as well-learned, but the depths of things come from the unlearned." It is important to note that these comments were from a woman with an advanced degree who strongly valued education. The pastor's wife always admonished the children to further their education, but added that they must "put God first."

There were many traditional black sayings that addressed this same issue. A visiting preacher said, "Up here will fool you [pointing to his head], in here will school you" [pointing to his heart]. Another preacher quoted Rosetta Carr, "You can go to college, you can go to school. But if you haven't got religion, you an educated fool."

Collins (1990) described a similar concept in her work. She pointed out that life as a black woman required wisdom because it was essential for survival. Thus, black people were quick to ridicule "educated fools" with "book learning" but no "mother wit" (p. 208). Concrete experience was the criterion for credibility: "Personal experience is considered very good evidence. With us, distant statistics are certainly not as important as the actual experience of a sober person" (Nelson as cited in Collins 1990). According to Collins, "ideas cannot be divorced from the individuals who create and share them. . . . Every idea has an owner and that owner's identity matters" (pp. 215, 218).

For the church members of Morning Sun, there was a very important concept which related the meaning of intelligence to the body and to healing. One had to understand that Jesus was in charge of the body. The pastor's wife stated this eloquently, "He's my mind, my feet, my hands. If He doesn't let me do it, I can't do nothing. . . ."

This belief system about the meaning of the body and its relationship to intelligence was explored more deeply in a sermon by the pastor on nature and the body. The pastor often utilized metaphors taken from nature, demonstrating the rural roots of the congregation whose original members had migrated from Southern farms and small towns. The pastor entreated his congregation to look to nature for the answers to their questions. He led them carefully in his sermon, first discussing the phenomena of all of nature, then applying these concepts as he spoke of the wonders of the body. He spoke with amazement of the mother hen who knew how to protect her "ten or twelve or fifteen little chicks" from the hawk. He marveled at the stripes on a watermelon saying, "I want you to take it and count the stripes . . . they say it's even and to me, it looks like they have to be—stripes all around, don't run out . . .Who make it that way? Can't nobody make it like God. . . ." He laughed about the wisdom of the design—that God did not have melons growing in a tree, "it'd be dangerous"; but instead He put the tiny cherries in a tree and the melons on the ground where they could not hurt anybody. The pastor spoke in wonder about the flower that bloomed only at night—one could not see it, but it was the most fragrant flower so its beauty could be known. The pastor discussed how God made the elephant's hind legs and forelegs to bend in the same direction—pointing out that otherwise the elephant could never raise up from the ground.

Only after the pastor had marvelled at the beauty of nature was he ready to talk about the meaning of the human body. He began by emphasizing that man was made in the image of God. He then described the wonders of the body, simply, graphically, and with humor:

It would be terrible if our nose was turned the other way—it would rain in there! Look how God shapes us, how He makes us, looks out for us . . . To make people with ears so they could wear glasses! What if your ears wasn't there? (laughter) Ain't you glad you're you?! Isn't that love? . . . It's a good thing God didn't make our elbows up here [indicating his shoulders]. Without elbows . . . our arms would just bend backwards and go all to pieces. He love us and give us five senses and that's why He say "I would not have you be ignorant! I'm an intelligent God and I want you to be intelligent!" He wants you to be in His likeness . . . Touch all you fingers together. I can see you laugh, but . . . You couldn't write, you couldn't pick up a little pin . . .Can you see? Can you hear? Can you walk? . . . God made you with hands, made you with a brain . . . If you don't use it, you got no business with it! . . .

The "intelligent" person recognized the most essential meaning of the body, that it was a beautiful gift from God, given so that one could know God. The intelligent person also held another truth, that only God had power over the body.

There were other core elements of the meaning system related to health and healing. No matter what happened to one in life, the members of Morning Sun Church encouraged one another to count their blessings. One member quoted her mother saying, "Child, don't worry that you have no shoes because some people have no feet." The pastor always wanted hair like his brother, but finally he realized that "I could have no head!" The pastor urged members who did not always have the right foods to think about people eating out of garbage cans.

The pastor tried to help members cope with illness by ascribing meaning to illness, saying, "Sometimes we bring it on ourselves, sometimes it's hand down . . . be way back there in the family. Mighta been your mother's side . . . Mighta been your father's side . . ." He saw that sickness was sometimes related to sin. He stated, "Sin causes us to be sick a lot of time. We may bring it on ourselves a lot of time."

In addition to seeing that the individual could control aspects of illness related to sin, the pastor encouraged patience and hope when coping with illness or with other problems. He pointed out that "there's waiting times" just as there were for Abraham. He tried to help his church members be philosophical about these times saying, "But when we done worrying, we in the same place." He reminded them of how God told Job, "Look at the stars and the sun . . . if I did all these things, I can take care of your little problems."

One of the most effective methods that the pastor used to inspire hope in his congregation was the repetition of simple but meaningful phrases (often taken from the Bible). The following are examples of these hopeful messages:

- Weeping comes in the night, but joy comes in the morning.
- After a long drive, you can see the lights of the city and know "I'm gonna make it now."
- Trouble don't last always.
- There's a bright day somewhere and I can find it.
- Stand at the door and knock and it'll open.

The pastor believed that the best action anyone could take when ill was to pray. He stressed his point, using a medical metaphor, by saying that "when you got problems . . . what you need to do is 'Operation Pray.'" He noted that often "we'll try *everything* else and then we'll try Jesus last." The members of Morning Sun learned to pray in a particular way. They asked God to grant their request, but added "if it be Your will," or prayed the words, "Fix and change *as You see fit.*" They believed that they did not have the comprehension that God did, and thus could not know all of the circumstances. In their experience they had sometimes received what they had asked for, but the situation had not turned out the way they had hoped. Thus, they had learned to acknowledge their limited power and experience; and in the end, they turned it over to God.

If prayer was seen as a healing force, then, according to the pastor, the purpose of the church was "to be a hospital to all kinda people." The church "should be a place where someone in distress can come," and "it rescues us from the forces that hurt us." The church was a "place people come to be revived . . . when the Spirit comes in sometimes, it speaks to the individual and takes away their problems." As members became more and more "like Him," they left behind physical ailments—at least for a time. One woman said, "If you feeling bad and you in church and you get in the Spirit, at least them couple of hours of church . . . When you walk out the door, that pain might hit you again, but when you sitting there, you feeling good." Often during a particularly moving sermon, one of the women exclaimed aloud, "Medicine! Medicine!" acknowledging the healing power of the Word.

Baer (1981) notes that these views of illness and healing stress the importance of the individual and of certain magical-religious rituals. These aspects of a religious faith offer important coping mechanisms, but simultaneously imply that the blame for the illness lies with the individual, ignoring societal influences. The "medicine" of the church and the Holy Spirit offer a healing therapy which acts as a palliative for the individual and discourages him from seeking social change. These approaches, according to Singer and Baer (1995) "tend to be compensatory and accommodative rather than corrective" (p. 295). However, church members interpret the influence of prayer and the healing power of the Spirit in a different way. They would agree that "the Spirit" heals the individual, but they would *not* deny that societal change is also necessary. However, they see that the most powerful tools for societal change lie in prayer and in the power of the Holy Spirit. Their most well-educated member, the pastor's wife, who was often their spokesperson, reacted indignantly when it was pointed out that some people believed that religion could lull people into an acceptance of the status quo. She stated vehemently that Jesus had changed the world more than any other person and that the church members followed his teachings. The pastor discussed this belief often saying, "Christ is love and love is the answer. It changes things!" The church members and the pastor often repeated, "Prayer changes things!!" Thus, although the members saw prayer as therapy acting at the individual level, they also saw it as an active and powerful force that could create change in the social world.

The women's theories about intelligence, the body, healing, and prayer enabled them to deal with illness, to approach healing, and to cope with the health care system utilizing a particular framework that held meaning for them. These central beliefs that the women held and emphasized over and over in church and in their daily lives were as follows: There was a difference between intelligence and education; having intelligence meant that one recognized that only God had power over the body; it was important to count one's blessings; illness could be caused by sin, but this might have been a sin that occurred in a prior generation and as such would not be under the control of the person experiencing the illness; there were "waiting times" and one needed to learn to be patient and to trust in God's wisdom and power; there was always hope in any situation; and prayer was the most effective way to influence healing and to create social change.

LIVED EXPERIENCES

In addition to understanding the women's belief systems or theories, it is essential to recognize the reality of the women's lives. It must be acknowledged that the women experienced all of the major medical problems that we have come to expect from people who live in poverty and/or who are subjected to continual stress and poor medical care for a variety of reasons. However, the purpose of this section is not to reiterate the women's health problems, nor to discuss actual health encounters, but to give the reader a sense of some of the *feelings* that the women shared about their health care experiences. These feelings relate directly to the development of the women's belief systems about health and health care.

There were two major "feeling-level" concepts that were repeated often as the women talked about their experiences in the health care system: the feelings of fear and distrust.

The pastor's wife was extremely frightened of doctors and hospitals. She described her feelings, "You know, fear of the unknown. I get so scared. Oh, my stomach, my heart. My husband practically has to drag me." She knew it was "silly" but she could not help it. She spoke often about her doctor's nurse who "knew about black people" and soothed her gently with conversation about her garden. When one of the adolescents in the church needed minor surgery, the girl was extremely frightened and could not speak when the doctor asked her questions. The pastor's wife commented about this situation. "You know how black women are—scared of the doctor—she thinks she will die because people go in the hospital and never come out." If the pastor's wife had to go to the hospital, she preferred the Catholic Hospital because the sisters would pray with her and the priest would come. Another church woman protested at this choice of hospitals, however, saying she had heard that they "experiment" on people in this same hospital. This woman was terrified when she had had to spend the night in a hospital and begged to go home the next day. She was afraid of the openness of the hospital, and she felt that anyone could wander in off the street and hurt her. The church members expressed similar fears in other areas. They spoke of deeply held fears in isolated areas of town, or in heavily wooded areas, or they described fear of the dark in unfamiliar parts of town. One woman explained her fear of the woods, saying, "Just the woods, the woods!" Her daughter elaborated, "there's too much woods to disappear into." One man's comment about his fear of the dark was revealing: "I'm not scared of the dark; I'm scared of what's *in* the dark." They acknowledged that their fear of the woods and the dark, like their fear of doctors, might be "silly," but they could not get around it.

hooks' (1992) notion about how "whiteness makes itself felt as a terrorizing imposi-

tion" in black life is applicable to this discussion. People of all races who have been trained by the dominant order have been taught to see whiteness as "synonymous with goodness, with light, with safety" (p. 341). Because white people see whiteness in this way, they assume that black people (and others), conceptualize whiteness in the same way. However, hooks demonstrates that to black people whiteness "makes its presence felt in black life as a terrorizing imposition, a power that wounds, hurts, tortures . . ." (p. 341). Njeri (as cited in hooks 1992) sees that her own terror with white people and white institutions is linked "with the history of the black people in the United States, seeing it [as] an imprint carried from past to present" (p. 342). hooks (1992) notes,

In the absence of the reality of whiteness, I learned as a child that to be "safe," it was important to recognize the power of whiteness, even to fear it, and to avoid encountering it. There was nothing terrifying about the sharing of this knowledge as a survival strategy . . . (p. 344).

To hooks (1992) the terror is confounded by the fact that whiteness is masked as a benign, even benevolent representation which "obscures . . . the sense of threat" (p. 345). She adds,

The eagerness with which contemporary society does away with racism, replacing this recognition with evocations of pluralism and diversity which further mask reality . . . has become a way to perpetuate the terror by providing a cover, a hiding place. Black people still feel the terror, still associate it with whiteness, but are rarely able to articulate the varied ways we are terrorized because it is easy to silence by accusations of reverse racism or by suggesting that black folks are merely evoking victimization to demand special treatment (ibid).

Some might ask: "Isn't this going a bit far—seeing major institutions, systems, and policies as 'terrorizing'?" However, McIntosh

(1995) points out that we are often taught to "recognize racism only in individual acts of meanness by members of [our own] group, never in invisible systems conferring unsought racial dominance on [our] group from birth" (p. 13).

Realistically, the women's fears *were* based on actual experiences with life and death that took place within the context of the dominant white health care system. When Missionary Lake was 10 years old she saw her father die of diabetes after having had both legs amputated. Her maternal aunt suffered the same fate and the family believed that she had become a diabetic when the doctor started giving her insulin shots before she needed them. Both Sister Jackson and Sister Strong had come close to death as children from ruptured appendices. Both were treated in hospitals for months, far from their rural homes, as the doctors fought their infections without antibiotics. Sister Strong's mother died at age 40 from a "real bad heart problem," and Sister Strong herself lost five infants who were "blue babies." The pastor's wife's mother had 21 children but only nine of them lived. She herself was only 16 when her mother died. Sister Smith had come close to death from an IUD infection. Sister Lander, a young church mother, had had one stillborn baby in the hospital and a second baby who died of leukemia at six weeks of age. These traumatic events in the lives of these women, most of which occurred when the women were children or young women, no doubt affected them. Thus, the fear of doctors and hospitals, like hooks' terror of whiteness, came from perhaps unrecognized associations of whiteness and doctors and hospitals and physical pain and mortal sorrow.

"I Don't Trust 'Em"

hooks' idea of whiteness as a terrorizing presence as well as the actual traumatic experiences the women had suffered, seemed to relate to this issue of fear that some of the women described. However, an even more common reaction to health care interactions, was a sense of uneasiness, of mistrust, perhaps of cognitive dissonance, as the women's impressions of the doctor's words or actions did not correspond with the women's belief systems or their definition of self or their understanding about what was going on between clinician and patient.

The women themselves talked openly about this sense of distrust. Sister Lander, a 40-year-old mother of four, told me, "I don't trust 'em" (doctors). When her six-year-old daughter, Shani, was hospitalized for kidney surgery (she had been born with a defective ureter and risked losing a kidney), Sister Lander was clear that she would not leave the child in the hospital without a family member, and she would only leave those family members whom she could trust to speak up assertively. Her distrust was obviously warranted when Shani became more and more ill after surgery, stoically refusing to speak or sleep or move or admit to discomfort. While Sister Lander and Shani's grandmother watched their child uneasily for two days, the doctors tried to discover the source of the problem, finally recognizing that Shani's ureter had not been reconnected to her bladder during surgery. Although the mother had spoken to the experienced faculty surgeon at the children's teaching hospital, and been assured that he would be doing the surgery, one cannot help but wonder if the surgeon would have made such a gross error, or if, in fact, someone else, possibly a student, did the surgery.

Sister Lander told another story about a time when her youngest daughter Bebe had meningitis. The lab results confirming the diagnosis had not yet come back when the clinic sent Bebe home on antibiotics. The mother, without knowing the lab results, was told to bring Bebe back to the clinic the next day, but Bebe was sleeping soundly and Sister

Lander decided to wait. Soon the police came to the door and told her to take Bebe to the hospital. Although the police "were real nice" and Sister Lander "understood," she was surprised at the presence of the police and wondered why the clinic had not tried to call her first.

There were other situations where the women expressed their distrust and uneasiness regarding doctors and control issues. Missionary Lake told me, "You can't contradict no doctors." Sister Lander replied, "It doesn't do much good." Missionary Lake fumed angrily after her meetings with the medical evaluation team on the placement for her disturbed grandson, saying "Who know that child? You do! *You* raised him! . . . I *know* his problem, know how to handle him." She complained bitterly about the "medical terms" doctors used when "you *know* that child!"

Marie Jones, a 50-year-old church member, described a time when she was hospitalized and near death from an IUD infection. She told the nurses that her ex-husband, a physician, would be calling to consult, but the nurses thought she was hallucinating, not believing that Sister Jones, a black woman, could be married to a doctor. Her care changed dramatically when her ex-husband, a physician, advocated for her. Sister Lander told another story about how she had watched the doctors in the labor and delivery room have a race to see who could stitch up a patient the most quickly after the woman had given birth. Sister Newton, a woman who had a child in her thirties, told the doctors she did not want spinal anesthesia during labor and "not to mess with my back," but states that the providers tried to "psychologize" her into having the medication. Although she had requested a tubal ligation after birth, the doctors refused to do the procedure after her baby was born, and, without giving her any explanation, simply said that she would have to return several months later for the proce-

dure. The doctors put her on birth control pills even though she was hypertensive and anemic.

These stories were not dissimilar to the stories of many women of all races and ethnic groups (Singer and Baer 1995; Martin 1987). However, the possibility that the women's treatment was due to racism on the part of the health care providers was an additional factor for them to contend with and try to process during vulnerable times.

Did Taussig's (1980) "reification" or Scheper-Hughes and Lock's (1987) "objectification process" enter into these experiences? Many of the women's experiences suggested that these ideas were applicable. The women's reports supported the idea that a social relationship of control that sustained the dominant order was at play. Although there were some positive comments about the health care providers, more often there were stories of fear, mistrust, and racism. Encounters with health providers were generally, at best, an exercise in frustration fraught with wasted time, and, at worst, occasions for humiliation and a basic sense of dislocation about the validity of one's own impressions. The women's descriptions and experiences held a common thread: that they were being judged. Thus, Sister Lander was potentially neglecting her child's meningitis, Sister Jones was "hallucinating" about her doctor husband, Sister Newton was incapable of knowing what was best for herself. And yet not one of these women refused to go to the doctor, all of them wanted good care and they appreciated it once they had experienced it. They *wanted* to trust in those to whom they had entrusted themselves and their children. There was just little or no evidence that this was a wise thing to do. They were accustomed to their treatment, and stated, "I just go ahead on." But it did not feel good.

But were these women unknowingly objectified? Absolutely not!! They resisted passively when they were in the middle of the encounter (averted gaze, refusal to ask questions, refusal to accept medication, monosyllabic answers), and they resisted actively with loud storytelling and complaining when they were among friends and relatives. The younger adolescent women were sometimes "unknowing" about the control issues involved, but as they grew in experience, this social relationship of control became more and more apparent to them. Whether the women were "knowing" or "unknowing," however, they never gave up their position as subject and they never ceased to influence the interchange.

THE WOMEN'S CRITIQUE: THE GAZE THAT JUDGES AND THE GAZE THAT LOOKS BACK AND SEES

One of the most important ways in which the women demonstrated their understanding (their "knowing subjectivity") of how the health care system objectified them was in their interpretation of the meaning of health care statistics. From a research point of view, the women "fit" the reported statistics for health problems for African-American women. As a researcher, I assumed that the women accepted these statistics, were concerned about them, and might have some insights about why their health was statistically so problematic. However, when the women were asked: "Why do you think the infant mortality rate for African-American babies is so high?" or "What do you think are the causes for the hypertension rates in African-American women?", the women gave some startling answers.

These answers demonstrated that the women understood that there was far more to the statistics about them than "objective facts." Like Brown (as cited in Singer and Baer 1995), they rejected "the widely held belief that epidemiology is a value-free scien-

tific activity" (p. 364). Since the women (as was discussed earlier in the paper) distinguished between "education" and "intelligence," they did not automatically believe that statistics were true, simply because educated people had generated them. From the women's perspective, experience, not education, was the criterion for intelligence. Hence, distant statistics were not necessarily to be believed, unless they fit with one's lived experience or with the experience of a trusted friend or relative. Although the women knew that they had health problems, their comments demonstrated that they understood that the purposes of health care statistics were often not to their benefit. In fact, they saw clearly that the health care discourse about them judged them, researched them, presented them to the public, and ultimately hurt, rather than helped, them. This extremely profound and revealing aspect of the women's critique can be seen as "the gaze that judges and the gaze that looks back and sees" (Abrums 1995).

A specific example will help to clarify the women's viewpoint. When asked about infant morbidity and mortality rates, the women said that they did not know of babies who had died or who had been ill. At times they gave this response even when there were family members with children who were developmentally disabled or when infants in the family or church had died. But when confronted with this discrepancy, the women said they did not see these babies as part of the statistics. They stated that those statistics applied only to girls who were "too young, girls on drugs, girls drinking." In other words, the women felt that the statistics did not apply *because of the way they were framed*—the women knew that they had taken good care of themselves during their pregnancies and that they took good care of their babies, therefore they were not part of the statistics. The women pointed out that, because of how the statistics were presented, they were no longer objective statements of fact, but in reality they served a very different *function*—that of perpetuating myths and stereotypes about African-American women. These statistics, like Taussig's (1980) health care relationships, had been reified into what they were not. Statistics, ostensibly to improve health, provided a screen, hiding a social relationship of control and judgment. Because of the way the statistics were framed and presented, they were utilized to make a group of people, a race, look bad, weak, diseased, uneducated, and unable to care for themselves and their children. The women saw that health research had rarely been to their benefit—rather that others benefited economically while they remained the "guinea pigs" and looked worse and worse on paper.

The women noted that the research system, like other institutions, perpetuated itself by pumping out more data, and that studies were developed so somebody else (never them) could make money. Thus, any health statistics were highly suspect because they were heavily influenced by both "the almighty green dollar" and by racism. The statistics were also suspect because they belied the women's experience of having taken good care of themselves and their children. Embroiled in this whole issue of women of color, subjectivity, and medicine, and at the heart of the women's critique, is the issue of public policy. Health professionals commonly believe that public health policy is based on scientific, biomedical research. However, the women's critique demonstrates that one of the unrecognized dimensions of social and scientific systems such as health care systems is that myths and stereotypes are often disguised within scientific as well as within historical research. This idea does not assume *intent*, that is, that racism is purposefully perpetuated by the way statistics are presented, rather it demonstrates *function*, how the statistics function in

the society. The manner in which statistics have characteristically been translated into supposedly benevolent public policy supports the same function. Thus, the statistics function, not just to make a group look bad, but also to provide support for continuation of projects that perpetuate the dominant order—the continuation and growth of the health care and research industries.

There are several ways in which statistics, purposefully or inadvertently (it really does not matter), serve these functions. hooks' (1992) idea of the concept of "white" as good and "black" as bad comes into play here, as does Harding's (1986) notion about the damaging aspects of projects which compare one group to another, thus creating a "universal other" without power of history, an "other" that is more dissimilar than similar. As Cooper and David (1986) point out:

> . . . races do exist. They are a powerful force in determining health, not for biological but for social reasons. Black people in our society are imprisoned by institutional racism: This is the attribute of blackness which at bottom determines their health status (p. 114).

The stereotypes which underlie the presentation of health statistics regarding people of color function as political myths which justify racist policy and approaches. While perhaps not as seemingly deadly as Stannard's (1989a,b) analysis of the function of political myths in the colonization of the Hawaiian natives or Taussig's (1987) description of the use of these myths in exterminating and controlling the natives of the Puntamayo, these stereotypes are just as damaging in their own way. There is really not much difference between the colonizer's myth of the "precontact" Hawaiian people as diseased, weakened barbarians committing infanticide and today's statistics which represent African Americans as having more physical problems than other races, or statistics which imply that black infant mortality rates are related to prenatal neglect. As hooks (1992) states:

> Stereotypes, however inaccurate, are one form of representation. Like fictions, they are created as substitutions, standing in for what is real. They are not to tell it like it is but to invite and encourage pretense. They are a fantasy, a projection onto the Other that makes them less threatening. Stereotypes abound when there is distance. They are an invention, a pretense that one knows when the steps that would make real knowing possible cannot be taken—are not allowed (p. 343).

The most important issue to be raised by the church women's critique, is not that the statistics have been and are often racist (although this too is very important), but rather that statistics presented in a racist framework prevent policymakers and caregivers from questioning *the true causes* for the poor health of some African Americans and of other groups in poverty or on the margins. Thus, the manner in which the statistics are framed provides a screen, a distracter, from what is really going on. Statistics that blame the victim obscure the fact that it is *the essential racism* of our society that maintains situations of poverty, stress, poor nutrition, and polluted environments. It is this racism, not the statistics themselves, that creates and perpetuates the conditions that lead to poor health. However, it is the statistics that support the myths that sustain the conditions.

MEANING AND SUBJECTIVITY: "YOU DON'T KNOW BECAUSE I'M NOT YOURS"

The women of Morning Sun might not have had control over all of the effects of poverty, racism, and sexism in their lives, but they could and did refuse some of the information from the dominant ideology that attempted to objectify, control, and judge them. They could and did "remain subject" in the face of the objectifying data and the control of the health care system because of a core meaning system that sustained and supported them. Using their intelligence, the women had developed a healthy skepticism about their encounters with the health care system and the information generated by the system about them. They had created a meaning system that enabled them to understand their experiences and to take control of their own healing. The anchor for this meaning system that overshadowed all other influences was the belief that the body was a gift from God and that only God had the ultimate say over what would happen to the body. An "intelligent" person recognized and believed this. This belief did not emerge solely as a reaction to oppressive forces, rather it grew primarily from a creative center within the women. This belief, along with the ability to critique the health care system from the margins (which was facilitated by their knowledge that education did not always beget intelligent information), enabled the women to cope when they encountered the health care system.

A final story will best illustrate how the women enacted their subjectivity. A visiting preacher, Sister Light, told of a time when she was in a coma with a body temperature of 60 degrees when the doctors said, "No way!" and gave her 12 hours to live. She said adamantly:

> I admire doctors but they don't know it all. Doctors don't accept nothing they don't understand!! Doctor said he was ready to sign my death certificate, but I said "Doctor, you don't know, because I'm not yours!!"

When the women told this and other stories about God's power over the doctor (told over and over again), their beliefs about God's power were solidified and the frailty of the human doctor was reinforced. When the women told stories such as this one, they were strong and justified, happy and powerful. They held a truth that few people knew.

The women of Morning Sun remained in control in their encounters with health care because of their belief system. They knew and chose Who was really in control. They chose their own Master, their own Healer and they knew Him well. To paraphrase this thinking, "If Jesus is in charge of the doctor, as He is in charge of us all, and Jesus is my Friend, then I may have to give up control, but I know Who I am giving it up to and it is the Right Person. I am in Good Hands."

In this way the women of Morning Sun Church, in a sense, co-opted the power of the doctor (wouldn't the doctor be surprised?). The women "reified," so to speak, the health care encounter into their belief system of power. In this system the Power was on their side. This Power used the doctor as an instrument, a tool to carry out His will, His intention for the women. Thus, there was no objectification process for them. If anyone became an object, it was the doctor as Jesus used his hands, brain, and heart for healing the sick. This belief system was not simply a reaction to the power and control of the dominant society. Rather, it was centered in the knowledge that the body, like the perfectly symmetrical stripes on the watermelon, was a beautiful gift from God. The power to "change and rearrange" and heal the body remained firmly in the hands of God. Thus, the women remained subject by choosing their own Healer.

REFERENCES

ABRUMS, M. E., 1995. Jesus Will Fix It After Awhile: A Study of Black Christian Women and Their Church. Unpublished doctoral dissertation, University of Washington, Seattle.

ALCOFF, L., 1988. Cultural feminism versus post-structuralism: the identity crisis in feminist theory. *Signs* 13(3), 405–436.

BAER, H., 1981. Prophets and advisors in black spiritual churches: therapy, palliative, or opiate? *Culture, Medicine and Psychiatry* 5, 145–170.

BAER, H. A., SINGER, M., JOHNSEN, J. H., 1986. Introduction: toward a critical medical anthropology. *Social Science and Medicine* 23 (2), 95–98.

BANKS-WALLACE, J., SARAN, A., 1992. Sisters in Session. Paper presented at the Women's Health Research Group, University of Washington, Seattle.

BARNHART, C. L., BARNHART, R. K., 1993. *The World Book Dictionary*, World Book Inc, Chicago.

BOWEN, E., 1954. *Return to Laughter*. Harper and Row, New York.

COLLINS, P. H., 1990. *Black Feminist Thought: Knowledge, Consciousness and the Politics of Empowerment*. Routledge, New York.

COMAROFF, J., 1985. *Body of Power, Spirit of Resistance*. University of Chicago Press, Chicago.

COOPER, R., David, R., 1986. The biological concept of race and its application to public health and epidemiology. *Journal of Health Politics, Policy and Law* II (1), 97–116.

CRAWFORD, R., 1984. A cultural account of 'health': control, release and the social body. In: McKinlay, J. (Ed.), *Issues of the Political Economy of Health Care*. Tavistock, London, pp. 60–103.

CRAWFORD, R., 1994. The boundaries of the self and the unhealthy other: reflections on health, culture and AIDS. *Social Science and Medicine* 38 (10), 1347–1365.

CRAWFORD, R., 1998. The ritual of health promotion. In: Williams, S. J., Gabe, J., Calnan, M. (Eds.), *Theorizing Health, Medicine and Society*. Sage, London, pp. 1–27.

GAMBLE, V. N., 1997. Under the shadow of Tuskegee: African Americans and health care. *American Journal of Public Health* 87 (11), 1773–1777.

GEERTZ, C., 1973. Thick description: toward an interpretive theory of culture. In: Geertz, C. (Ed.), *The Interpretation of Culture: Selected Essays*, Basic Books, New York, pp. 3–30.

HANCOCK, E., 1989. *The Girl Within*. Fawcett Columbine, New York.

HARDING. S., 1986. *The Science Question in Feminism*. Cornell University Press, Ithaca.

HOOKS, b. 1981. *Ain't I a Woman: Black Women and Feminism*. South End Press, Boston.

HOOKS, b. 1992. Representing whiteness in the black imagination. In: Grossberg, L., Nelson, C., Treichler, P. (Eds.), *Cultural Studies*. Routledge, New York, pp. 338–346.

HURSTON, Z. N., 1963. *Mules and Men.* Indiana University Press, Bloomington [1935].

KINGMAN, L. A., 1997. European American and African American men and women's valuations of feminist and natural science research methods in psychology. In: Vaz. K. M. (Ed.), *Oral Narrative Research with Black Women.* Sage, Thousand Oaks, pp. 250–259.

MARTIN, E., 1987. *The Woman in the Body.* Beacon Press, Boston.

MCINTOSH, P., 1995. White privilege and male privilege. In: Anderson, M. L., Collins, P. H. (Eds.), *Race, Class & Gender: An Anthology.* Wadsworth Publishing Co, California. pp. 76–87.

MEYERHOFF, B., 1978. *Number Our Days.* Simon and Schuster Inc, NY.

MINISTER, K., 1991. A feminist frame for the oral history interview. In: Gluck, S. B., Patai, D. (Eds.), *Women's Words: A Feminist Practice of Oral History.* Routledge, New York, pp. 27–41.

MOHANTY, C. T., 1984. Under Western eyes: feminist scholarship and colonial discourses. *Boundary* 2 XII (3/XIIII), 333–358.

MOORE, H. L., 1988. *Feminism and Anthropology.* University of Minnesota Press, Minneapolis.

PRATT, M., 1986. Field work in common places. In: Clifford, J., Marcus, G. (Eds.), *Writing Culture: The Poetics and Politics of Ethnography.* University of California Press, Berkeley.

RABINOW, P., 1977. *Reflections on Fieldwork in Morocco.* University of California Press, Berkeley.

ROTHENBERG, P., 1990. The construction, deconstruction, and reconstruction of difference. *Hypatia* 5 (1), 42–57.

SCHEPER-HUGHES, N., LOCK, M. M., 1987. The mindful body: a prolegomenon to future work in medical anthropology. *Medical Anthropology Quarterly.* New Series 11, 6–41.

SCHILLER, N. G., 1992. What's wrong with this picture? The hegemonic construction of AIDS research in the United States. *Medical Anthropology Quarterly* 6 (3), 237–254.

SCHMID, R. E., 1999. Report: don't use race labels in study of cancer in minorities. *The Seattle Times,* p. A4.

SCOTT, K. Y., 1991. *The Habit of Surviving.* Ballantine Books, New York.

SHOSTAK, M., 1983. *Nisa: The Life and Words of a Kung Woman.* Vintage Books, New York.

SINGER, M., 1998. Forging a political economy of AIDS. In: Singer, E. (Ed.), *The Political Economy of AIDS.* Baywood Publishing Co, New York, pp. 3–31.

SINGER, M., BAER, H., 1995. *Critical Medical Anthropology.* Baywood Publishing Co Inc, New York.

SOBO, E. J., 1993. Inner-city women and AIDS: the psycho-social benefits of unsafe sex. *Culture, Medicine and Psychiatry* 17 (4), 455–485.

SOBO, E. J., 1994. Attitudes toward HIV testing among impoverished inner-city African American women. *Medical Anthropology* 16 (1), 17–38.

SPRADLEY, J. P., 1980. *Participant Observation.* Holt, Rinehart, and Winston Inc, New York.

STACK, C. B., 1974. *All Our Kin.* Harper and Row, New York.

STANNARD, D., 1989a. Recounting the Fables of Savagery: Infanticide in Ancient Hawaii and the Functions of Political Myth. Paper. University of Hawaii, Honolulu.

STANNARD, D., 1989b. *Before the Horror: The Population of Hawaii on the Eve of Western Contact.* Social Science Research Institute, Hawaii.

TAUSSIG, M. T., 1980. Reification and the consciousness of the patient. *Social Science and Medicine* 1 (B), 3–13.

TAUSSIG, M. T., 1987. *Shamanism, Colonialism and the Wild Man: A Study in Terror and Healing.* University of Chicago Press, Chicago.

THOMPSON, J. L., 1991. Exploring gender and culture with Khmer refugee women: reflections on participatory feminist research. *Advances in Nursing Sciences* 13 (3), 30–48.

WEST, C., 1995. Race matters. In: Andersen, M. L., Collins, P. H. (Eds.), *Race, Class, and Gender: An Anthology,* 2nd ed. Wadsworth Publishing Co, Belmont, California, pp. 550–560.

YOUNG, A., 1982. The anthropologies of illness and sickness. *Annual Review Anthropology* 11, 257–285.

Part VII
DOCTOR–PATIENT INTERACTION

As William Cockerham (2001) points out, doctor–patient interaction constitutes a structured relationship and mode of discourse that is inherently social. Talcott Parsons's seminal concept of the sick role (1951) is most notable in this regard, pointing to the respective obligations of patients and physicians toward each other. These obligations clearly take the doctor–patient interaction out of a medical and disease-specific arena, to encompass a medical-sociological framework that includes such concepts as norms, expectations, meanings, negotiation, compliance, and power. Parsons's original formulation has generated numerous theoretical discussions and empirical studies on the sick role (see Glasser 1991) as well as alternative conceptualizations of the interaction between doctor and patient. This part presents two papers that illustrate modern forms of physician–patient interaction as well as a third article on the rising prominence of the use of the Internet as a source for health information.

The first article in this section is by Rose Weitz, who studied family interaction with the intensive care unit (ICU) doctors treating her badly burned brother-in-law. Entitled "Watching Brian Die: The Rhetoric and Reality of Informed Consent," this paper provides an extreme case of physician–patient interaction in which doctors regarded communication with the family as a burden and provided little information. They took a one-word response from the barely conscious patient as an assent to proceed with aggressive treatment in an apparently hopeless case and to keep family members from exercising any decision-making authority. Although the general model of doctor–patient interaction today is mutual participation, this study illustrates the effects on a family when doctors take total control.

The second paper, by Mary Warren, Rose Weitz, and Stephen Kulis, acknowledges the fact that the context of medical practice has changed dramatically in the past 20 years. Based on a study in Arizona, Warren and her colleagues found that most physicians accept a more collaborative relationship with their patients, recognize the desire of their patients to participate in medical decisions about their own health, and do not find knowledgeable patients to be a source of dissatisfaction. Rather, dissatisfactions by doctors about their work stemmed largely from the constraints of managed care systems that they were more or less required to accept if they practiced medicine where most patients belonged to such systems.

The third paper, "Doctor in the House: The Internet as a Source of Lay Health Knowledge and the Challenge of Expertise" by Michael Hardey, investigates the use of the Internet as a source of health information. This development has profound implications for changing the physician–patient relationship, as users of the Internet, not doctors, decide what health information is accessed and how it is to be used. What this situation implies for the debate over the deprofessionalization of physicians and doctor–patient interaction is discussed.

REFERENCES

COCKERHAM, WILLIAM C. 2001. *Medical Sociology*, 8th ed. Upper Saddle River, NJ: Prentice Hall.

GLASSER, MICHAEL L. 1991. *Physician-Patient Relationships: An Annotated Bibliography*. New York: Garland.

PARSONS, TALCOTT. 1951. *The Social System*. Glencoe, IL: The Free Press.

WATCHING BRIAN DIE: THE RHETORIC AND REALITY OF INFORMED CONSENT

Rose Weitz
Arizona State University

Two years ago, my brother-in-law was injured in a catastrophic industrial accident, which left him with second- and third-degree burns over 95 percent of his body. Writing both as a family member and as a sociologist, I analyze how his doctors increased their decision-making authority at the expense of informed consent, explore why they did so, and discuss the consequences for families when informed consent is not obtained. I also discuss the difficulties of achieving informed consent when family members have conflicting views on treatment. The conclusions use this story to reflect on the problems of implementing informed consent in clinical practice and on what these problems tell us about U.S. doctors' continuing power and clinical autonomy.

Two years ago, my brother-in-law, Brian,[1] was injured in a catastrophic industrial accident, which left him with second- and third-degree burns over 95 percent of his body and with strong indications that he had suffered a severe inhalation injury.

Brian's accident occurred literally in sight of a major hospital with a regional burns unit, and he was brought to the hospital within minutes. Following the accident, Brian remained in a strange limbo between life and death—unconscious although not comatose, and kept alive by aggressive medical treatment and an ever-increasing assortment of drugs and machines. Burned everywhere except his genitals and the soles of his feet, bandaged from head to toe with only his face showing, and swollen grotesquely, Brian's appearance was literally nightmarish; no one

who saw him slept well afterward. Each day brought minor crises, and each week brought a major crisis that made death seem imminent—as indeed it was, for Brian died three and a half weeks after the accident.

During the days following the accident, various members of my family increasingly began to wonder whether the doctors were making treatment decisions that should have belonged to Brian's wife, Lisa; withholding information she needed to make treatment decisions; or taking actions that could result only in a certain death or an unbearable life. Probably no one could fully avoid this last thought, given the sight we saw each day as we entered the burns unit: a woman, burned six months earlier and far less severely than Brian, staring at a television on the ceiling while wrapped in bandages from head to toe, with her arms and legs splinted, immobilized, and stretched out as if she were crucified on her bed. This was the fate awaiting Brian should he survive.

Reprinted by permission of Sage Publications Ltd from *Health*, vol. 3, no. 2, pp. 209–27. Copyright © 1999, by Sage Ltd.

These issues weighed heavily on my mind. My husband and I had first received word of Brian's injuries by telephone soon after the accident, and had flown a thousand miles to join the family later that night. As a medical sociologist, I knew something of the devastation wrought by severe burns and thus had assumed both that Brian would die and that death would be a mercy (see Kliever 1989). I also, however, knew that medical culture trains doctors to value technological interventions and to view death as failure (Katz 1984; Guillemin and Holmstrum 1986; Klass 1987; Weir 1989), and as a result feared that Brian's doctors might adopt a recklessly aggressive course of treatment.

On the other hand, I also knew that, before beginning treatment, doctors must obtain informed consent from the patient or, if the patient is not competent, from the patient's closest relative (in this case, Lisa). Yet I knew that doctors typically believe that they alone should make clinical decisions, and that they therefore establish typically hierarchical rather than egalitarian relationships with patients and their families (e.g., Mishler 1981; Guillemin and Holmstrum 1986; Anspach 1993). This ideology is so firmly held that the rise of living wills, hospital bioethics review committees, and professional ethics committees designed to change it appears to have had little impact on medical decision making (Guillemin and Holmstrum 1986; Annas 1991; Anspach 1993; SUPPORT Principal Investigators 1995; Bosk and Frader 1998).

Previous studies have documented several ways doctors, whether intentionally or not, can increase their decision-making authority and reduce that of patients and families (Katz 1984; West 1984; Mannon 1985; Fisher 1986; Guillemin and Holmstrum 1986; Waitzkin 1991; Zussman 1992; Anspach 1993). First, doctors may make decisions without asking the patient's or family's opinion, on the assumption that they would agree with the doctors. Second, doctors can respect a patient's or family's wishes, but only after first shaping those wishes through selectively providing information about the situation. In addition, doctors can cut off discussions and questions that they consider irrelevant or uncomfortable, give general rather than specific answers to questions, give information only when directly asked, or use euphemisms that confuse lay persons. Finally, in the rare cases in which patients or families actively challenge medical decisions, doctors can ignore them, arguing that lay persons who disagree with doctors must be too psychologically disturbed to decide rationally, that lay persons are unqualified to make what the doctors view as essentially technical decisions, or that families that take responsibility for life and death decisions experience additional guilt and grief in the long run. As a result, only the most determined, assertive, and resourceful lay persons can challenge doctors' decisions successfully (Zussman 1992). This knowledge led me to fear from the start that the doctors would not give Lisa the information and authority that she needed to act as Brian's surrogate decision maker—a fear that would soon prove warranted.

Since Brian's death, I have had the chance to reflect more on our experiences, and have come to see them as an example both of the difficulties of implementing informed consent in the complex, murky terrain of clinical practice and of the consequences for families when informed consent is not obtained. This article is my attempt to make something useful from this tragedy. Writing, then, both as a family member and as a sociologist, I first describe how the doctors, whether intentionally or not, arrogated decision-making authority, and compare the actions of Brian's doctors to those observed in other studies of intensive care units. I then describe the impact of this on the family, explore why the doctors arrogated decision making, and discuss what this suggests about the continuing power and clinical autonomy of U.S. doctors.

As a case study, some of the limitations of this article are obvious. In addition, although I spoke extensively about these issues at the time and afterward with Lisa and her family, I spoke only minimally with Brian's brother and parents. Similarly, all adult members of Lisa's immediate family read and commented on this article in draft, but none of Brian's relatives did so. As I will describe, tensions developed between the two families during the days following the accident, and I feared that talking with Brian's family about the issues might worsen these already strained relationships. I did, though, speak briefly with Brian's brother. An evangelical Christian who, like us, lived in another state, he had spent most of the first week after the accident at the hospital in prayer, and had then returned home. He claimed that he had not discussed Brian's treatment with either his parents or the doctors.[2]

I had hoped to interview the doctors, but did not want to do so until after I received a copy of Brian's medical records, for fear that an interview might either irritate the doctors or raise fears of a lawsuit, and that subsequently they might make it difficult for us to get the records. Unfortunately, although not surprisingly, Lisa (the only person who legally could request the records) could not bear to go to the hospital for some months after the accident. By the time I received the records, enough time had elapsed that I concluded that contacting the doctors would not be useful, especially since I would have had to do so by telephone. Thus, I can only tell this story from my perspective and, to a lesser extent, that of Lisa and her family.

ARROGATING DECISION-MAKING AUTHORITY

Throughout his hospital stay, decisions about Brian's care were complicated by two facts: that he never regained consciousness after leaving the emergency room and that Brian's father, Jack, and his wife, Lisa, held somewhat different views regarding treatment and decision making. These facts would make it harder for the burns unit doctors to involve the family in decision making and easier for the doctors, whether intentionally or not, to arrogate decision-making authority for themselves.

Because Brian remained unconscious, no one could truly know what he would have wanted for himself. He left neither a living will nor a medical power of attorney. He had, however, told Lisa previously that he would not want to live if his quality of life was ever compromised substantially. This seemed a likely outcome of his injuries, especially since he worked with his hands as a skilled technician and found many of his greatest pleasures in physical activities.

When first brought to the emergency room, Brian was briefly conscious. At that point, the attending doctor from the burns unit, Dr. Thompson, told him that he was severely burned, that his chances of survival were very small, and that any treatment would be "long, arduous, and painful." Dr. Thompson then asked Brian if he wanted to live, and Brian replied affirmatively (although it seems highly unlikely that Brian—in shock, in pain, and with little understanding of his situation—had either the information or the capacity to make an informed decision at this point).

In an emergency of this sort, of course, any additional time spent trying to inform Brian would have reduced his chances of survival. In these circumstances, legal precedent, medical protocols, and insurance regulations authorize doctors to begin treatment if they consider it warranted, postponing any decisions about the appropriateness of continuing treatment until either the patient's prospects become clearer, the patient regains decision-making capacity, or a spouse or other legally accepted surrogate decision-maker arrives on the scene. According to Robert F. Weir, recent legal cases suggest an emerging consensus that

> [such a] surrogate has the legal authority to refuse all forms of life-sustaining treatment on the behalf of the patient . . . as long as the surrogate's decision reflects the patient's own views on life-sustaining treatment or is based on a determination of the patient's best interests (1989: 147).

The right to refuse treatment is legally clearest in cases like Brian's, in which treatment is highly invasive and prognosis is poor (Weir 1989: 150).

Lisa reached the hospital not long after the accident. The doctors briefly informed her of the situation, but did not indicate that she needed to make any decisions about Brian's treatment. At this point, then, the doctors apparently assumed that Lisa would agree with their decisions (see Mannon 1985; Guillemin and Holmstrum 1986; Zussman 1992; Anspach 1993).

My husband and I arrived at the hospital early the next morning, where the other relatives already had gathered. I was startled to find Brian still alive—I had not thought such injuries were survivable—and worried that the doctors might have embarked on a course of futile and perhaps even cruel treatment. Both Brian's relatives and mine—all of whom were closer to Brian than I because they lived much nearer to him—seemed stunned and traumatized, neither supporting nor questioning the doctors' actions. This led me to wonder from the start what I could or should say to them, especially to Lisa.

In the meantime, I dealt with my fears primarily intellectually rather than emotionally by focusing on obtaining information. I began by speaking privately that first day with the senior resident. Choosing my words carefully, so as not to become labeled a troublemaker, I asked who held legal decision-making authority. He answered that Lisa held sole authority as long

as Brian remained unconscious, and mentioned that she might consider issuing a "do not resuscitate" (DNR) order. He explained, however, that doing so was of little importance, because something else almost certainly would kill Brian before cardiac failure and because resuscitation almost certainly would not succeed. That same day he privately told Lisa that she had legal decision-making authority and that she could issue a DNR order, although he did not offer any details.

I then asked the doctor if there were *any* circumstances in which they would ask Lisa's permission before beginning various treatments—mentioning as examples the decision to use kidney dialysis, to give antibiotics, or to use a ventilator. His answer was that there were none. He mentioned without explanation that in some parts of the country, doctors routinely offer only palliative care to any patient who suffers more than a 70 percent burn—much smaller than Brian's injuries—but stated that he regarded withholding any treatment as unethical, for "we have no right to play God."

Like the argument that medical intervention is purely a technical matter, the argument that intervention is a straightforward moral imperative makes it impossible for lay persons to challenge doctors' treatment decisions. This argument serves doctors well only if they favor continuing aggressive treatment while families favor discontinuing it. In most cases, however, both doctors and families favor aggressive treatment. Moreover, when disagreements arise, most often it is doctors who favor discontinuing and families who favor continuing treatment (Mannon 1985; Guillemin and Holmstrum 1986; Zussman 1992; Anspach 1993). This may explain why previous studies of ICUs have not observed doctors making this argument.

My conversation with the senior resident reinforced my fears regarding both the doctors' commitment to aggressive treatment and their unwillingness to involve Lisa in decision making. Subsequent discussions similarly indicated that the doctors regarded Brian's one-word assent to treatment—given when he was less than fully informed and had substantially diminished decision-making capacity—as sufficient authorization not only to begin but also to continue aggressive treatment. For example, a week after the accident, Dr. Thompson met with the family following rounds to discuss the case. (We had returned home the day before, after concluding that we could not predict when the doctors would meet with us or when the situation might change.) This meeting marked the first time that family members publicly—if tentatively—questioned what survival might mean for Brian. In response to their questions, Dr. Thompson stated that he "was not ready to discuss these issues now," and that, based on his interchange with Brian, he would proceed with aggressive treatment unless Brian woke up and instructed him otherwise. When Lisa mentioned her previous conversation with Brian regarding whether he would want to survive if severely disabled, Dr. Thompson told the family—in a manner that both Lisa and her parents described as dismissive—that he routinely ignored "kitchen table discussions" patients might have had while still healthy about withholding life supports. It seems, then, that although the doctors formally recognized both Brian's and Lisa's legal rights to informed consent, they defined those rights very narrowly, providing themselves with an additional means (not previously noted by scholarly observers) for maintaining decision-making authority.

Lisa herself would soon come to the same conclusion. When I tape-recorded her recollections six months after the accident, and asked what she thought the doctors defined as her role in decision making, she replied:

> To say "okay" to whatever they wanted. I think the only reason they ever asked me for consent was because they were required to in certain situations. In the beginning I'm sure they defined my role as "stand back and let us do our job." There was no consultation at all with me for the first 24 hours or so after the accident. And then later when I would try to get more info, their reactions ranged from "this does not compute"—as if they had never heard questions like these before—to almost animosity.

The difficulties Lisa faced in getting information about Brian's prospects left her highly ambivalent about the care he was receiving. She never concluded that it would be best if Brian died or if treatment were halted. Yet questions about Brian's quality of life should he survive continued to haunt her. As she put it: "The one thing I stressed from the beginning to Thompson is 'I don't want [Brian] to survive as just a technological miracle. I'm really clear about that.'" As the days passed, however, first Brian's lungs, then his stomach, and then his kidneys failed, while pneumonia and, increasingly, other bacterial, viral, and fungal infections assaulted his body. Each of these events led Lisa to raise at least tentative questions with the doctors about whether Brian's continued survival was in his best interests and whether certain treatments, especially kidney dialysis, made sense. The responses she received, however, like those given to the families observed in other ICUs by Guillemin and Holmstrum (1986), Zussman (1992), and Anspach (1993), were both too vague and too narrow to answer her questions. As she explained:

> What was frustrating for me was . . . grappling with the issue of whether we are just prolonging his pain or are we really treating him toward recovery? In asking some of the things that I needed to know to understand about the future, that's where it got really frustrating. I kept getting the response "well, he'll keep his hands and his feet," and had trouble getting them to move beyond that. Or they would say "we can arrange for you to talk to Ray" [a survivor of a severe burn who now worked for the hospital], who was a success story. But nobody

wanted to point to the room next door to Bob, where that woman had been lying for six months. . . . There was this black hole whenever you wanted to know "well, what if it isn't a success story?"

In the first few days after the accident, Lisa also raised similar questions with me, giving me the chance to share with her some of the information I had been gathering. In addition to talking with the senior resident, I also had talked on one occasion to Brian's nurse, had several long telephone conversations with friends who were doctors, and had gone to the hospital library and later to a local medical school library to read about severe burns. The pictures I saw and descriptions I read in this library research left me, for the first time since the accident, sobbing near-hysterically, and more horrified than before at Brian's treatment, which increasingly seemed like mere experimentation.

When I told Lisa of my research, and asked her whether she wanted to know what I had learned, she unequivocally said yes. I then told her that burns of this sort would likely lead to lifelong pain and risk of death from infection. I also told her that, according to Brian's nurse, the pain would impair Brian's ability to concentrate to such an extent that he would be unable to read or attend college (a prospect that had offered the one potentially positive outcome of the accident) for some time. I did not explicitly state my views on Brian's treatment, both because I lacked the courage and because I wanted Lisa to form her own opinion, but I am sure that something of my own views came through.

I was not the only family member who questioned whether aggressive treatment made sense. Those of us who did so, however, discussed our views only guardedly and only with those we suspected would agree. Similarly, those who favored aggressive treatment tended to keep their views to themselves. The one exception was Brian's father, Jack, who quickly emerged as a vocal supporter of aggressive treatment, stating that he wanted everything possible done to keep Brian alive, regardless of Brian's eventual quality of life. Indeed, Jack's commitment to aggressive treatment extended to possibilities that the doctors had ruled out explicitly, such as a lung transplant. That philosophy also led Jack to tell Lisa that he would have trouble forgiving her should she withhold any treatments and to tell her father that withholding treatment would be the same as killing Brian. Brian's mother, on the other hand, never discussed her views with any member of Lisa's family. Her silence "spoke" eloquently about the difficulties we were all facing in trying to sort out and communicate our views.

In an ideal scenario, either the doctors or other members of the "care team"—nurses, pastoral counselors, social workers, psychologists—would have facilitated discussion of the issues, helping individuals to explore their feelings and options, seek needed information, and reach consensus or at least tolerance for divergent viewpoints. This was never attempted, despite Lisa's request for such a discussion.

Instead, the doctors seemed to avoid these issues while the social workers, psychologists, and pastoral counselors seemed to view their job as "cooling out" the family. For example, when Lisa's mother and father (a minister who had served for five years on a hospital medical ethics committee) asked one of the pastoral counselors to facilitate a family discussion about possibly terminating care, the counselor dismissed the request with the statement that: "Well, I'd trust any family member of mine to Dr. Thompson." A similar meeting with a social worker also yielded no results. Even worse, both the pastoral counselor and one of the social workers implied in conversations with Lisa that she was only questioning the doctors' decisions because she did not want to be burdened with a sick husband. (Similarly, Stinson and Stinson 1979; Guillemin and Holmstrum 1986; Anspach 1993;

found that parents who opposed aggressive treatment for premature infants were labeled by staff as either psychologically disturbed or as not really wanting a baby.)

These responses particularly infuriated Lisa's father. His concerns led him to request information about the hospital's ethics committee. The glossy brochure he received from one of the chaplains mentioned that the committee had established ethical guidelines for medical care. Despite two attempts by Lisa's father and one by her brother (a local lawyer), neither was able to obtain the guidelines. After returning home, I tried to obtain more information about how ethics committees work, and whether the ethics committee at this hospital could or should play a role. My conversations with a friend who works in health law and a bioethicist familiar with this particular hospital led me to conclude that ethics committees typically are structured to assist doctors in dealing with patients and their families rather than to help patients and families. (See for similar conclusions Paris et al. 1993; Bosk and Frader 1998.) I debated calling the ethics committee myself, but concluded that it would be unlikely to make much of a difference and that it was improper for me to do so without Lisa's permission—which I was loath to seek for fear I would seem to be pushing my views on her. With much trepidation, I did ask the bioethicist with whom I had talked earlier to look into the situation, but did not speak with her subsequently. As far as I know, the committee played no role in Brian's case; none was noted in his medical records.

Similarly, no one from the hospital helped the family to accept Lisa's decision-making authority. I do not know if the doctors ever told Brian's parents that Lisa had sole decision-making authority, but I do know they did not tell any member of Lisa's family other than me. Nor, according to Brian's brother, did they tell him. Moreover, they continued to involve Jack in all discussions about Brian's

treatment, making it difficult for Lisa to raise her concerns privately with the doctors despite her request that they set aside time to speak with her alone:

> And then I had to constantly battle the burn unit staff—especially the doctors—because they wanted everything to be a family thing. I talked to the social worker, chaplain, doctors, and tried to get someone to hear that I understand it is best if there is family participation, but what we have here is a conflict between my views and Brian's parents' views, and I need some help. Because in this situation it's not necessarily beneficial to have these joint conferences with the whole family. And I couldn't get them to listen.

In addition, Dr. Thompson often talked to Jack early in the morning before Lisa arrived at the hospital, relying on Jack to relay information to Lisa. In one instance Dr. Thompson decided to hold the weekly family meeting earlier than had been agreed on and before Lisa had arrived, on the grounds that he could always "fill her in" later (although he did not in fact do so). Finally, according to Lisa and her parents, when meeting with the family, he and the other doctors often seemed both verbally and nonverbally to address their comments to Jack rather than to Lisa. These actions led Lisa to believe that Dr. Thompson and the other doctors were avoiding her and instead communicating to the family through Jack. Since Jack had no legal decision-making authority, undercutting Lisa's authority reinforced the doctors'.

Other factors also reinforced the doctors' authority at the expense of Lisa's. Most critically, and as researchers have documented in other ICUs (Mannon 1985; Guillemin and Holmstrum 1986; Zussman 1992; Anspach 1993), the doctors never gave the family enough information to develop an informed understanding of Brian's prospects or to reach an informed decision about his treatment. After the first day, when we were told that he had only a 1 percent chance of surviving, the doctors offered almost no information about Brian's long-term prospects. They did not change this 1 percent estimate until Brian's final hours, and never gave us any meaningful information about what his life would be like if he did survive. We were told, for example, that Brian was not currently in any pain, but never told that individuals who survive severe burns always experience significant disability and long-term, debilitating pain, making suicide all too common. Similarly, when asked what Brian's life would be like in the long run, the doctors either gave vague answers ("he won't have fine motor skills in his hands") or explicitly told us not to worry about these issues until we knew whether he would survive that long. The latter answer, of course, begged the question as to how we could know if it was worth helping Brian to survive without knowing what his life would be like if he did. For this reason, I encouraged Lisa to develop a specific list of questions for the doctors that could not be dismissed with vague answers, such as how long it would be before Brian could hold and read a book, type at a keyboard, or pick up his two young daughters. Lisa did not act on this suggestion because of her increasing sense that, with each question she asked, the doctors became more dismissive and, occasionally, hostile, and that she was therefore helpless to affect Brian's care. Moreover, the apparent differences between her perception of the situation and the doctors' perception, and her increasing marginalization in Brian's care, led her to wonder whether she was losing her ability to judge the situation rationally.

The doctors' withholding and selective offering of information seemed to reflect a desire to convince the family to accept their decision to treat aggressively. Thus, when Brian's mother asked in a family conference if Brian would retain his ears, the doctor replied that it would not matter, given recent advances in plastic surgery. Similarly, according to several family members, Dr. Thompson told them that "so long as Brian's lungs begin working, we can fix everything else"—a statement that was patently untrue, as the greatest danger to burn patients comes from infections. When Brian, who had been hooked to a ventilator from the start, began taking an occasional breath, the doctors claimed that he was now "breathing on his own." When asked, however, the nurses (who always proved far more forthcoming than the doctors and were much more helpful to Lisa than any other hospital staff) showed us on the monitor how his breaths were both too shallow and too infrequent to sustain life. By the same token, with each physical crisis that Brian survived, thanks to the doctors' intensive interventions, the doctors emphasized how he was a strong man with a "strong will to live." One could have argued with equal logic that Brian was fighting to die, but the doctors would not let him do so.

In the end, Brian's condition began deteriorating so rapidly and completely that the doctors had no further treatments to try. A few days earlier, a new resident had joined the staff. Alone among his colleagues, this doctor seemed to take Lisa's concerns seriously. A long conversation with him during Brian's final days greatly helped Lisa, both by allowing her to express her feelings and by giving her a much greater understanding of how the doctors made their decisions about treatment. When this resident recommended that Lisa give permission to withdraw the drug that kept Brian's heart beating, Lisa accepted his recommendation, and Brian died that night.

THE IMPACT OF ARROGATING DECISION-MAKING AUTHORITY

The doctors' inability or unwillingness to share decision-making authority with the family had both positive and negative effects.

On the positive side, by removing decision-making from the family, the doctors left Jack with the belief that he had done everything in his power to fight for his son's life, and enabled Lisa to avoid responsibility for making some heart-wrenching decisions. As she later observed:

> I can see positive consequences in the way it ended. . . . The positive about all this was that after the fact for whatever reason I'm glad that every possible avenue was tried. Because there's enough questions you ask yourself and enough guilt you lay on yourself that for me I think it's good to know that every possible thing was done. So I don't have the guilt of maybe I terminated things too early.

The doctors' actions also allowed Lisa to avoid confronting Jack directly and risking permanent damage to their relationship. This was especially important to Lisa, as she recognized from the start that her girls might lose their father and would need a relationship with their grandfather. It is also possible (although unverifiable) that keeping Brian alive for so long benefited the family by giving some individuals time to come to terms with his eventual death.

On the other hand, the doctors' lack of commitment to shared decision making had several harmful effects. The doctors' consistently optimistic interpretation of Brian's condition and unwillingness to answer hard questions about his prognosis left some family members woefully unprepared for his eventual decline and death. Conversely, those family members who believed Brian had virtually no chance to survive, and dreaded even more what his life might be like if he did, experienced three and a half weeks of anguish, during which they could only regard Brian's treatment as a medical experiment rather than meaningful clinical care. In addition, the doctors' actions added to Lisa's trauma, by leading her to question her sanity and judgment.

Not surprisingly, this experience left some family members cynical about and even fearful of medical care, by suggesting that doctors might be more interested in their own careers or egos than in their patients' welfare. Fortunately, several of us had turned to friends who were doctors for advice during this experience. Almost unanimously, these friends were appalled by the situation, which helped us to avoid generalizing from Brian's doctors to all doctors. Nevertheless, some family members (including my husband) subsequently wrote living wills to protect themselves from overly authoritarian doctors. (I had had a living will for some time.) Others have not done so in part because they no longer believe such documents offer much protection. As Lisa said to me six months after Brian's death:

> I remember when [your husband] sent his living will to Mom and Dad and I read it and I applied Brian's experience to that. I realized that that piece of paper isn't worth hardly anything. If a doctor thinks it doesn't apply to your situation or defines some of the key terms in ways differently from you, you're powerless to do anything about it.

To the extent that the doctors' unwillingness to share decision-making authority prolonged aggressive treatment, that refusal also had the effect of threatening the family's financial resources, and thereby adding to the emotional stress of the situation. Fortunately, Brian's medical bills were covered by workers' compensation, but each additional day away from work put Lisa's job further in jeopardy. Lisa was fortunate that she was paid; others might not have been. In addition, Brian only had accidental death insurance, rather than regular life insurance, to protect his wife and their daughters should anything happen to him. That policy only paid if he died within 30 days after an accident. If extraordinary medical measures had continued to keep Brian hanging on to life for even a few days longer, the policy would have been worthless. No one, of course, would have regretted the loss of the insurance money if Brian had a reasonable chance of surviving. If, however, he had no real chance of doing so, then the loss of insurance money would have been a cruel additional blow.

Equally important, each day in limbo further strained the family's emotional resources. During the three and a half weeks in intensive care, Brian's two young daughters lost not only all meaningful contact with their father, but also much of their usual contact with their mother, who spent many hours at the hospital. Normal daily routines, too, fell by the wayside. Thus, the time in intensive care added a month of chaos, especially for the girls, to what would have been a devastating loss in any circumstances. In addition, that month of chaos was punctuated by medical crises that sapped the family's emotional resources by forcing us repeatedly to confront Brian's imminent death.

Finally, a palpable division developed between some members of Brian's and Lisa's families. Given the different philosophies and subject positions that these individuals had brought to the situation, this division may have been inevitable. Nevertheless, it is possible that had the hospital staff encouraged and mediated open discussions among family members, some middle ground might have been found, and individuals might have been able to express their views in ways that did not threaten their relationships with each other.

DISCUSSION

The central question that emerges from this story is why were Brian's doctors so unwilling to share decision-making authority? The simplest answer is *because they were ICU doctors*. Previous studies consistently have found that ICU doctors define informed consent in ways that give them tremendous leeway to assert their own decisions (Man-

non 1985; Guillemin and Holmstrum 1986; Zussman 1992; Anspach 1993). Those studies find that except in the most hopeless of cases, ICU doctors almost invariably begin aggressive treatment without consulting the patient or the family. As the clinical situation becomes clearer, doctors either define the situation in ways that secure the family's support for their decisions or find grounds for ignoring the family's decisions. Brian's story adds to our knowledge of how ICU doctors arrogate decision-making authority, while confirming what others have observed about medical decision making.

In Brian's case, the doctors' unwillingness to share decision-making authority also may have reflected their commitment to aggressive treatment and consequent concern that Lisa might press to limit treatment. For this reason, we need to look further into the philosophical, legal, professional, and psychological reasons why these doctors appeared to support aggressive treatment.

A basic premise of medical culture is that aggressive, invasive treatment is more valued than other treatments (Katz 1984; Guillemin and Holmstrum 1986; Klass 1987; Weir 1989). This is especially true among surgeons. It is thus not surprising that Brian's doctors—who, unlike the ICU doctors studied by other sociologists, were all surgeons—seemed philosophically committed to aggressive treatment, even in a case that seemed almost certainly hopeless.

Legal factors also may have encouraged Brian's doctors to favor aggressive treatment, and thus to resist involving in decision making anyone who might want to limit treatment. Recent court decisions unanimously suggest that doctors who withhold or withdraw treatment will not be found legally liable when patients die, so long as those deaths are caused by an underlying medical condition and the doctors believe they are acting in the patient's best interests (Weir 1989: 152). However, the high malpractice premiums that U.S. doctors pay yearly, combined with recurrent stories about doctors who have been sued, have created an atmosphere in which doctors' fear of lawsuits sometimes may affect their clinical decisions. Such fears naturally would have been amplified for Brian's doctors by Jack's stated opposition to limiting treatment and by Lisa's ambivalence about doing so.

In addition, professional factors—specifically, the research mandate of regional burns units—may have encouraged Brian's doctors to support aggressive treatment and therefore to resist sharing decision making. Sociologists have concluded that the unusual commitment of doctors on neonatal ICUs to aggressive care reflects the strong research mandate of these units, which emphasizes studying how to keep alive ever-younger babies (Guillemin and Holmstrum 1986; Anspach 1993). I would hypothesize that the main mandate of burns unit doctors is to learn how to keep alive those with ever-more-extensive burns, in the hopes that such knowledge will help other patients in future. By this measure, keeping Brian alive for three and a half weeks was a success—even though he died. Research interest in Brian's case would have been further heightened by the highly unusual source of his burns—no similar burns cases appear in the medical literature except for one very famous case in which all victims died immediately—as scholars have observed often that medical culture teaches doctors to place the most value on treating and researching rare illnesses and conditions (e.g., Ludmerer 1985; Mizrahi 1986; Klass 1987; Scully 1994).

Finally, it is possible that the doctors' commitment to aggressive treatment and apparent unwillingness to share decision making reflected their unusually high sense of identification with Brian. As mentioned earlier, most burns patients are working or lower class. Although neither Brian nor Lisa

had finished college, the other members of the family—all of whom were at the hospital within hours of the accident—had. Since Brian was unconscious and Lisa less outspoken than other family members, the impression the doctors were left with may have been that of a family much more like their own than was typical. In addition, the majority of burns in adults are obviously caused by the burned individual, and linked to smoking, alcohol or drug use, or psychiatric disturbances (including suicide attempts) (MacArthur and Moore 1975; Brodzka et al. 1985; Mannon 1985). Studies repeatedly have found that doctors have limited sympathy for patients of this sort (e.g., Klein et al. 1982; Mizrahi 1986; Smith and Zimmy 1988). In contrast, Brian's injuries resulted from a "normal accident" (Perrow, 1984), caused more by a complex technological system than by any single individual's actions. These factors, coupled with the fact that Brian was a big, healthy man with young children, may have increased the doctors' commitment to doing everything they could to improve his chance of surviving.

The second major question to emerge from this story is why, given the doctors' apparent unwillingness to involve Lisa in clinical decision making, they seemed more willing to involve Jack? Again, part of the answer to this latter question can be found in previous studies. Other scholars have found that doctors are most likely to involve patients and families in decision making when those individuals are college-educated professionals (Mannon 1985; Street 1991; Zussman 1992; Anspach 1993). Although Lisa is intelligent and well read, she had not graduated college and did not hold a fully professional position. In contrast, Jack is a confident and wealthy businessman. In addition, previous research suggests that male doctors feel most comfortable speaking with male patients and relatives (West 1984; Fisher 1986; Waitzkin 1991). This would also partially explain the different reactions to Jack and to Lisa, as all Brian's doctors were male.

Similarly, previous studies suggest that doctors are most likely to share decision-making authority with patients and families who aggressively seek information and involvement (Mannon 1985; Street 1991; Zussman 1992; Anspach 1993). Whereas Jack is comfortable stating his position assertively and aggressively seeking his goals, Lisa tends to make statements and decisions deliberately and quietly. It is possible that, if Lisa had more forcefully asserted her wishes about Brian's treatment or about her role in that treatment, the doctors would have involved Lisa further in decision making—but it is equally possible that they would simply have become more hostile.

The differences between the doctors' communications with Jack and Lisa also may have reflected their stated commitment to a "family model of care." Ironically, rather than helping the family, this model gave the doctors an ideological justification for treating family members as interchangeable units, creating problems for Lisa not discussed in previous studies. Thus, if they told Jack something, they appeared to feel no obligation to inform Lisa, despite their stated belief that she held sole decision-making authority. This occurred more and more often over time, for, as Lisa's differences with Jack grew, she began coming to the hospital only at night to avoid him. As a result, the doctors were far more likely to encounter Jack than Lisa.

Finally, I would argue that although the doctors spent more time talking with Jack, they in fact did *not* offer him any greater involvement in decision making: Jack received no more information than Lisa, and no additional opportunities to challenge the doctors' decisions. Overheard conversations between Jack and the doctors consisted mostly of vague statements from the doctors about Brian's condition and "will to live" and laudatory comments from Jack about the terrific job the doctors were doing. The doctors had no reason to avoid such conversations, which bolstered their authority and sense of moral goodness while in no way challenging their authority. Indeed, Mannon (1985) notes that doctors define showing gratitude as an essential part of family members' role on a burns unit. In contrast, although Lisa never openly challenged the doctors, neither did she show gratitude to them. Thus, speaking with Lisa was never a fully comfortable experience for the doctors.

CONCLUSIONS

Previous studies have documented the different ways doctors, whether intentionally or not, can increase their decision-making authority (Katz 1984; West 1984; Mannon 1985; Fisher 1986; Guillemin and Holmstrum 1986; Waitzkin 1991; Zussman 1992; Anspach 1993). As was true in those studies, Brian's doctors made decisions without asking Lisa's opinion, ignored her wishes when they disagreed with her opinions, or respected her wishes only after first shaping them through selectively providing information. They limited the information available to her by cutting off discussions and questions which they considered irrelevant or uncomfortable, giving general rather than specific answers to questions, giving information only when directly asked (if then), or using euphemisms (such as "breathing on his own") that made it difficult for Lisa to understand Brian's situation. At the same time, and also as documented in other studies, doctors defused challenges by defining their actions as purely technical matters that lay persons could not comprehend, while hospital staff defused challenges to doctors' authority by implying that lay persons who disagreed with doctors must be psychologically disturbed.

Brian's doctors also increased their decision-making authority in ways not observed in previous studies of ICUs. First, by defining Brian's one-word assent to treatment in the emergency room as "informed consent," and by defining prior "kitchen table discussions" as irrelevant to understanding Brian's wishes, they could define themselves as the persons best able to speak for Brian's wishes. Second, by defining medical intervention as a moral imperative, they could define any discussions about withholding or withdrawing care as immoral. Third, by declaring themselves the only arbiters of what constituted an appropriate question, they could avoid questions that might have led to challenges to their decisions. It seems, then, that although the doctors formally recognized both Brian's and Lisa's legal rights to informed consent, they defined those rights very narrowly.

In addition to expanding our understanding of how, whether intentionally or unintentionally, doctors can subvert informed consent, Brian's story also suggests that, even if doctors value informed consent, achieving it will be difficult when family members have conflicting views. It is possible that with sufficient commitment and resources, hospital staff could have resolved the differences within the family, but it is equally likely that those differences were irreconcilable and the problems inevitable. The sources and consequences of such differences and the best ways for dealing with them remain as issues requiring further study.

At a broader level, this story demonstrates the continuing power and clinical autonomy of doctors in the United States. For more than a decade, sociologists have argued that bureaucratic, legal, and financial changes in U.S. health care are threatening doctors' professional dominance and clinical autonomy (McKinlay and Arches 1985; McKinlay 1988; Stoeckle 1988; McKinlay and Stoeckle 1989; Hafferty and McKinlay 1993; Light 1993). Yet none of these changes seems to have affected Brian's care. The development of a bureaucracy specifically to monitor bioethics—the

hospital ethics committee—had no impact on his medical care, probably because it was structured to respond to doctors' needs, rather than those of patients or families. In addition, ethics committees are primarily staffed by doctors, while most other members are hospital employees. Professional loyalties, as well as the need to maintain good relations with colleagues, make it unrealistic to expect these individuals to view doctors' actions critically (Bosk and Frader 1988). Moreover, doing so might place their employer at legal risk, by providing grounds for a lawsuit by patient or family. Thus, only the most foolish or selfless of individuals would do so. For the same reasons, the increased use of pastoral counselors and social workers to meet families' psychosocial needs had no impact on Brian's care. These individuals advocated for family members when they needed help with insurance forms and temporary housing, but advocated for the doctors when doctors and family came in conflict. Legal changes, too, which theoretically have given patients and families greater rights (Annas 1989), had relatively little impact in Brian's case; like most legal changes, changes in the area of "patients' rights" only have empowered unusually determined individuals with unusually good access to resources (Zussman 1992). Finally, the financial constraints (such as "diagnostic-related groups") that public and private insurers have imposed in recent years on U.S. doctors (Dolenc and Dougherty 1985; Dunn et al. 1988) have many loopholes. In Brian's case, the most important loophole is that these financial constraints rarely apply in emergency situations (unless individuals reach the lifetime maximum that some insurers set for total covered medical costs); all Brian's treatment—which totaled about $300,000—was covered by worker's compensation, the state-run program that pays for treatment for occupational illnesses and disabilities. For all these reasons, then, we should expect to continue hearing stories like this one in future.

NOTES

1. All names in this article have been changed. None of the persons discussed in this article share my last name.

2. In any story like this one, it is difficult to balance ethical obligations to one's profession against those to one's family. I decided to write this article despite these difficulties both because I needed to do so, and because Lisa and her family wanted me to, as a way of giving some meaning to this tragedy through helping others understand the problems with informed consent in intensive care. I have left out some minor details of family dynamics that might hurt either individuals or relationships between individuals, but nothing that would substantially change the story.

REFERENCES

ANNAS, G. J. (1989). *The rights of patients: the basic ACLU guide to patient rights.* Illinois, IL: Southern Illinois University Press.

ANNAS, G. J. (1991). Ethics committees: from ethical comfort to ethical cover. *Hastings Center Report, 21* (May–June), 18–21.

ANSPACH, R. R. (1993). *Deciding who lives: fateful choices in the intensive-care nursery.* Berkeley, CA: University of California Press.

BOSK, C. L. and FRADER, J. (1998). Institutional ethics committees: sociological oxymoron, empirical black box. In R. DeVries and J. Subedi (Eds.), *Bioethics and society: constructing the ethical enterprise,* pp. 94–116. Upper Saddle River, NJ: Prentice Hall.

BRODZKA, W., THORNHILL, H. L. and HOWARD, S. (1985). Burns: causes and risk factors. *Archives of Physical Medicine and Rehabilitation, 66,* 746–52.

DOLENC, D. A. and DOUGHERTY, C. M. (1985). DRGs: the counterrevolution in financing health care. *Hastings Center Report, 15(3),* 19–29.

DUNN, D., HSIAO, W. C., KETCHAM, T. R. and BRAUN, P. (1988). A method for estimating the preservice and postservice work of physicians' services. *Journal of the American Medical Association, 260,* 2371–8.

FISHER, S. (1986). *In the patient's best interest: women and the politics of medical decisions.* New Brunswick, NJ: Rutgers University Press.

GUILLEMIN, J. and HOLMSTRUM, L. L. (1986). *Mixed blessings: intensive care for newborns.* New York: Oxford University Press.

HAFFERTY, F. W. and MCKINLAY, J. (1993). Conclusion: cross-cultural perspectives on the dynamics of medicine as a profession, in F. W. Hafferty and J. B. McKinlay (Eds.), *The changing medical profession: an international perspective,* pp. 210–26. New York: Oxford University Press.

KATZ, J. (1984). *The silent world of doctor and patient.* New York: Free Press.

KLASS, P. (1987). *A not entirely benign procedure: four years as a medical student.* New York: G.P. Putnam's.

KLEIN, D., NAJMAN, J., KOHRMAN, A. and MUNRO, C. (1982). Patient characteristics that elicit negative responses from family physicians. *Journal of Family Practice, 14,* 881–8.

KLIEVER, L. D. (1989). *Dax's case: essays in medical ethics and human meaning.* Dallas, TX: Southern Methodist University Press.

LIGHT, DONALD W. (1993). Countervailing power: the changing character of the medical profession in the United States. In F. W. Hafferty and J. B. McKinlay (Eds.), *The changing medical profession: an international perspective,* pp. 69–79. New York: Oxford University Press.

LUDMERER, K. M. (1985). *Learning to heal: the development of American medical education.* New York: Basic Books.

MACARTHUR, J. D. and MOORE, F. D. (1975). Epidemiology of burns: the burn-prone patient. *Journal of the American Medical Association, 231,* 259–63.

MCKINLAY, J. B. (1988). Introduction. *The Milbank Quarterly, 66,* 1–9.

MCKINLAY, J. B. and ARCHES, J. (1985). Towards the proletarianization of physicians. *International Journal of Health Services, 15,* 161–95.

MCKINLAY, J. B. and STOECKLE, J. D. (1989). Corporatization and the social transformation of doctoring. *International Journal of Health Services, 18,* 191–205.

MANNON, J. M. (1985). *Caring for the burned: life and death in a hospital burn center.* Springfield, IL: Charles C. Thomas.

MISHLER, E. G. (1981). Viewpoint: critical perspectives on the biomedical model. In E. G. Mishler (Ed.), *Social contexts of health, illness, and patient care.* Cambridge: Cambridge University Press.

MIZRAHI, T. (1986). *Getting rid of patients: contradictions in the socialization of physicians.* New Brunswick, NJ: Rutgers University Press.

PARIS, J. J., SCHREIBER, M. D., STATTER, M., ARENSMAN, R. and SIEGLER, M. (1993). Beyond autonomy: physicians' refusal to use life-prolonging extracorporeal membrane oxygenation. *New England Journal of Medicine, 329,* 354–7.

PERROW, C. (1984). *Normal accidents: living with high-risk technologies.* New York: Basic Books.

SCULLY, D. (1994). *Men who control women's health: the miseducation of obstetrician-gynecologists.* New York: Teachers College Press.

SMITH, R. C. and ZIMMY, G. (1988). Physicians' emotional reactions to patients. *Psychosomatics, 29,* 392–7.

STINSON, R. and STINSON, P. (1979). On the death of a baby. *Atlantic Monthly, 244(1),* 64–72.

STOECKLE, J. (1988). Reflections on modern doctoring. *The Milbank Quarterly, 66,* 76–91.

STREET, R. (1991). Information-giving in medical consultations: the influence of patients' communicative styles and personal characteristics. *Social Science and Medicine, 32,* 541–8.

SUPPORT PRINCIPAL INVESTIGATORS (1995). A controlled trial to improve care for seriously ill hospitalized patients. *Journal of the American Medical Association, 274,* 1591–8.

WAITZKIN, H. (1991). *The politics of medical encounters.* New Haven: Yale University Press.

WEIR, R. F. (1989). *Abating treatment with critically ill patients: ethical and legal limits to the medical prolongation of life.* New York: Oxford University Press.

WEST, C. (1984). *Routine complications: troubles with talk between doctors and patients.* Bloomington, IN: Indiana University Press.

ZUSSMAN, R. (1992). *Intensive care: medical ethics and the medical profession.* Chicago, IL: University of Chicago Press.

PHYSICIAN SATISFACTION IN A CHANGING HEALTH CARE ENVIRONMENT: THE IMPACT OF CHALLENGES TO PROFESSIONAL AUTONOMY, AUTHORITY, AND DOMINANCE

Mary Guptill Warren
Rose Weitz
Stephen Kulis
Arizona State University

For some time, sociologists have debated whether physicians still retain dominance in the health care world, public faith in their moral and scientific authority, and the autonomy to set work conditions and make clinical decisions. Using ideas derived from this debate, we analyze the impact of changes in the health care environment on physician satisfaction. Our data come from a mailed survey of 510 Arizona physicians. Our results show that background physician attributes did not predict satisfaction, nor did most organizational attributes. However, participation in IPAs (Individual Practice Associations) predicted higher satisfaction, while payment according to a third-party payer's fee-for-service schedule predicted lower satisfaction. In addition, physicians were more likely to be satisfied if they wrote the orders that nonphysicians had to follow, were paid what they wanted, did not need to subordinate their clinical judgment to that of nonphysicians, and believed that their patients had confidence in physicians. Our conclusions discuss both theoretical and policy implications of our findings.

From at least the turn of the century until the mid-1970s, medicine seemed the consummate example of a profession—an occupational group characterized by specialized technical knowledge, public faith in its moral and scientific authority, the autonomy to make decisions and regulate its work condi-

tions and members, and dominance over other occupations in its work sphere (Freidson 1970, 1994; Parsons 1951; Starr 1982). However, changes during the last 20 years—especially the rise of patients' rights and managed care plans (in which medical treatment is closely supervised to control costs)—have led some sociologists to argue that medicine has lost much of its status as a profession (e.g., Haug 1977; Haug and Lavin 1981; McKinlay 1988; McKinlay and Arches

Reprinted from the *Journal of Health and Social Behavior,* vol. 39 (1998), pp. 356–67, by permission of the American Sociological Association.

1985; McKinlay and Stoeckle 1989). Others, on the other hand (e.g., Freidson, 1986, 1994; Hafferty and Light 1995), have argued that medicine's professional status remains largely intact and that medicine remains the dominant profession in the health care field. (For an excellent summary of this debate, see Light and Levine 1988.)

Curiously, these debates about the professional status of physicians have rarely been grounded in data on physicians' assessments of their situation. Of course, these theories were developed to explain the status of medicine as a profession, not the situations of individual physicians. Nevertheless, each of these theories provides us with valuable concepts for understanding the situation of contemporary physicians. In this paper, we use concepts taken from these theories to identify factors that may increase or decrease physician satisfaction in this rapidly changing health care environment. Using these theories in this way seems particularly appropriate as their proponents sometimes have linked changes in the professional status of medicine to physician satisfaction (e.g., Haug 1988; McKinlay 1988; Stoeckle 1988).

Physician satisfaction is a critical topic not only for physicians but also for patients and health care administrators. When physicians are satisfied, they are significantly more likely to stay in a given practice (Lichtenstein 1984; Mick et al. 1983). As a result, plan administrators are saved the financial costs associated with high turnover, as well as the decline in patient satisfaction that often accompanies high turnover. Patients, meanwhile, may receive not only greater continuity of care but also a higher quality of care (Skolnik, Smith, and Diamond 1993). This may explain why physician satisfaction and patient satisfaction are strongly correlated (Linn et al. 1985). Finally, when patients are satisfied, they are less likely to leave a plan, which is obviously a benefit for any health care administrator.

In this study, we look specifically at the impact on physician satisfaction of changes in patient–physician relationships and of changes associated with the rise of managed care. Managed care was developed as a way to contain costs without sacrificing quality of care in the absence of a national health care system. Given the large and growing role played by managed care in the United States, it is critical that we learn how managed care affects physician satisfaction and what factors can ameliorate any negative effects of managed care.

As others have noted (Lammers 1992; Linn et al. 1985; Schulz, Girard, and Scheckler 1992), surprisingly few recent studies have looked at physician satisfaction. Moreover, none have looked at the impact of changing patient–physician relationships, and almost none have looked at the impact of managed care (Hadley and Mitchell 1997). Studies conducted in the last two decades, during which managed care has flourished, suggest that satisfaction may be correlated with self-employment (Baker and Cantor 1993); perceived intellectual rewards (Chuck et al. 1993); working in group rather than solo practice (Skolnik et al. 1993); control over the work environment and lack of bureaucratic regulations (Chuck et al. 1993; Lammers 1992); and, for those working in staff model HMOs, participation in organizational decisions on such issues as hiring, adopting new services, or resolving patient grievances (Barr and Steinberg 1983). Age and sex have not been found correlated with satisfaction.

These results must be considered very tentative, however, given the small number of studies on these issues and the limitations of those studies. Two of these studies (Baker and Cantor 1993; Chuck et al. 1993) present only bivariate relationships and use no control variables. A third compares doctors in markets with high versus low managed care penetration rather than comparing doctors with high versus low proportions of patients from managed care (Hadley and Mitchell 1997). As a result, this last study is more useful for understanding the market than for understanding the situation of physicians.

The best data on how managed care affects physician satisfaction comes from two cross-sectional studies of physicians in the Madison, Wisconsin, metropolitan area conducted in 1986 and 1993 (Schulz et al. 1992, 1997). About 85 percent of patients in that area belong to managed care plans, so physicians essentially cannot avoid participating in managed care. Both studies found that satisfaction with HMO work was higher among primary care physicians, those in group practice, and those who obtained more than 25 percent of their patients from HMOs (probably because those with lower percentages faced severe economic difficulties). In addition, satisfaction with HMO work was highest among those who believed they had substantial clinical autonomy and who were satisfied with their income. Neither age nor sex was correlated with satisfaction in these studies.

THEORETICAL OVERVIEW

According to John McKinlay and his colleagues John Stoeckle and Joan Arches (McKinlay 1988; McKinlay and Arches 1985; McKinlay and Stoeckle 1989; Stoeckle 1988), contemporary physicians have far less autonomy than physicians in past decades. From their perspective, physicians have lost control over who become their patients, the terms and content of their work, the equipment and facilities needed for their work, and the amount and rate of remuneration for their labor. These changes stem primarily from two sources: (1) the increasing attempts by the federal government to control health care costs, such as through the Diagnosis Related Groups system and the Resource-Based Relative Value Scale, and (2) the rise in managed care plans, which enrolled 6 million

Americans in 1976 but 51 million in 1995 (Group Health Association of America 1995). Under managed care, physicians' clinical autonomy may be compromised, as they often must obtain approval before beginning care, prescribe only authorized drugs, or follow specified treatment plans for given ailments (Hafferty and McKinlay 1993; Light 1993; Schneller, Hughes, and Hood-Szivek 1994). In addition, managed care has threatened physicians' autonomy to make everyday decisions about work conditions; it has pressed them to abandon entrepreneurial solo practices and their own fee-for-service schedules and to accept working in ever-larger group practices and receiving payment via capitation, salary, or third parties' fee schedules. Finally, under managed care, physicians have considerably less control over their patient pool, as patients enter and leave their practices based on the contracts with managed care firms that physicians and employers sign. For all these reasons, then, McKinlay and his colleagues argue that physicians have lost professional autonomy.

Marie Haug and Bebe Lavin (Haug 1977, 1988; Haug and Lavin 1981) also believe that physicians' status as professionals is threatened, but emphasize the role played by challenges to professional authority. They define authority as "the *right* to influence and direct behavior, such right having been accepted as valid and legitimate by others in the relationship" [emphasis in original] (Haug and Lavin 1981: 212). They argue that in past decades, the public assumed physicians had a wealth of knowledge far beyond that available to consumers and trusted physicians to use that knowledge for the public's good. With the rise of the patient rights and medical self-care movements, however, public knowledge of and involvement in medical matters has increased while public trust in physicians has decreased. As a result of these challenges to professional authority, physicians are becoming only expert consultants whose advice may be taken or left, rather than members of a profession, as earlier sociologists (e.g., Freidson 1970) had defined that term.

Eliot Freidson (1994), on the other hand, argues that despite any changes in physicians' work environment or relationships with patients, they retain their dominance in the health care world. This position is also supported by various other observers, such as Frederic Hafferty and Donald Light (1995). According to Freidson, "the [medical] profession is accepted as the authoritative spokesman on affairs related to its body of knowledge and skill, and so its representatives serve as expert guides for legislation and administrative rules bearing on its work. Furthermore, the profession has an administrative or supervisoral monopoly over the practical affairs connected with its work; its members fill the organizational ranks that are concerned with establishing work standards, directing and evaluating work. 'Peer review' rather than hierarchical directive is the norm"—even if that peer review is based partly on data from modern information systems established and administered by non-physicians (Freidson 1994: 163–164). Thus, although the position of individual physicians may have changed, and their autonomy and authority may be threatened, the dominance of the profession remains intact.

METHODS

Study Site

Data for this study come from a mailed survey conducted by the authors in Maricopa County, Arizona. Maricopa County is home to the city of Phoenix and to 59 percent of Arizona's physicians. This area was chosen as research site both for logistical reasons and because the impact of managed care has been particularly acute here. Eighty-six percent of physicians in Arizona have at least one contract with a managed care plan (Group Health Association of America 1995). All Arizonans who belong to AHCCCS (the state's substitute for Medicaid) are enrolled in managed care plans. So are 72 percent of commercially insured persons residing in the Phoenix metropolitan area (Edlin 1994), as compared to 52.6 percent of Americans nationally (Edlin 1994). Finally, Arizona is tied with California for having the highest proportion of Medicare recipients enrolled in managed care programs: 37 percent, compared with 13 percent nationally (Health Care Financing Administration 1997).

Sample

The survey was mailed in 1995 to a random sample of 1,070 licensed medical doctors in active, federal or nonfederal, clinical practice in Maricopa County, stratified by primary versus specialty care. Seventy-nine individuals were later removed from the sample because they had retired, died, or moved. Final response rate was 51.5 percent ($n = 510$) of the 991 potential respondents. There were no significant differences in gender, age, group size, or participation in various types of managed care plans between our respondents and Maricopa County respondents to the 1994 Arizona Board of Medical Examiners (BOMEX) survey; that survey is required for licensure and was answered by more than 95 percent of Arizona physicians.

Eighty-two percent of survey respondents were male, compared to 79.2 percent of physicians nationally (Randolph et al. 1997). Respondents ranged in age from 28 to 78 with a mean of 46. Arizona physicians were somewhat younger than physicians nationwide; 81 percent were under age 55, compared to 70 percent nationally (Randolph et al. 1997). Twenty-four percent of respondents practiced as solo practitioners, compared to 29 percent nationally (Kletke, Emmons, and Gillis 1996). Thirty-seven percent practiced in groups of three or more compared to 33 percent of nonfederal physicians nationally. An average of 11 physicians practiced per group, as was the case nationally (Kletke et al. 1996). Almost all respondents to our survey (97%) indicated that they participated in at least one type of managed care plan, and many reported participating in more than one type.

Measures

Table 1 shows all variables used in this study. Items were recoded if necessary so that higher scores would reflect greater perceived challenges to professional autonomy, authority, or dominance. The dependent variable, satisfaction, was measured using responses (on a Likert scale from 1 = strongly disagree to 5 = strongly agree) to this item: "I am satisfied with being a physician today." In this paper, those who disagreed or strongly disagreed are referred to as the percentage dissatisfied.

Data Analysis

Because this research is based on a cross-sectional survey, we cannot directly investigate how changes over time in the practice of medicine have affected physician satisfaction. Instead, the data analysis is designed to compare levels of satisfaction between physicians whose working conditions are more like those prevailing in the past (e.g., solo practice, low percentage of patients from managed care) to those whose working conditions are more like those expected in the future (e.g., group practice, high percentage of patients from managed care).

We first present bivariate correlations with satisfaction for all physician and organizational attributes and for all variables measuring perceived challenges to professional autonomy, authority, or dominance. We then present five multiple regression models. The first model looks at the impact on satisfaction of the physician and organizational attributes. Each of the next three models adds to this the

TABLE 1   Survey Questions Used for Variables

Physician attributes
1. In what year were you born?
2. In what year did you begin practice?
3. Are you male or female? (coded female = 1, male = 0)
4. Are you a primary care physician? (coded yes = 1, no = 0)

Organizational attributes
5. In addition to you, how many physicians work in your practice?
6. About what percentage of your patients are from managed care plans?

In which types of managed care plans do you participate?
7. PPOs? (coded yes = 1, no = 0)
8. IPA HMOs? (coded yes = 1, no = 0)
9. Group/Staff HMOs? (coded yes = 1, no = 0)

I am paid by:
10. the fee-for-service schedule I set. (coded yes = 1, no = 0)
11. the fee schedule set by third parties. (coded yes = 1, no = 0)
12. capitation. (coded yes = 1, no = 0)
13. salary. (coded yes = 1, no = 0)

Attitudinal Measures[a]
  Challenges to professional autonomy
14. I own or rent my office.*
15. I own most of the diagnostic technology (from low to high tech) I use in daily practice.*
16. By and large, I am paid what I want to be paid for my services.*
17. Sometimes I must ignore my own clinical judgment and follow the directives of nonphysicians regarding patient care.
18. I do not determine my work schedule.
19. In order to get new patients, I generally must sign managed care contracts.
20. Third-party payers have considerable effect on how I treat my patients.

  Challenges to professional authority
21. In general, my patients have a great deal of medical knowledge.
22. Most of my patients do not want to participate in their treatment decisions.*
23. My patients have little confidence in physicians.

  Challenges to professional dominance
24. I write the orders that nonphysician health care workers must follow when treating my patients.*

  Satisfaction
25. I am satisfied with being a physician today.

[a]Responses to attitudinal questions ranged from 1 = strongly disagree to 5 = strongly agree. Items marked with an asterisk (*) were reverse coded.

Note: IPA = individual practice association. PPO = preferred provider organization.

variables derived from one of the three sets of challenges to physicians' professional status. The final model includes all physician and organizational attributes plus all variables measuring challenges to physicians' professional status.

Due to problems with multicollinearity, we use only age and not first year in practice in the multiple regressions. No other variables presented problems with multicollinearity.

RESULTS

Satisfaction

Just over half of our respondents (56.5%) describe themselves as satisfied or very satisfied with being a physician today. Mean satisfaction was 3.457 with a standard deviation of 1.178. In contrast, other surveys have found higher levels of satisfaction with between 65 percent and 87 percent considering themselves satisfied or very satisfied. These studies all used Likert-type scales, but each used a different measure of satisfaction. As a result, it is very difficult to compare these findings and to try to understand why—or if—our respondents were more dissatisfied than those answering other surveys.

Bivariate Analysis

Physician and Organizational Attributes. Before looking at the theoretical models, we first looked at the impact of physician and organizational attributes on physician satisfaction. To do this, we used t-tests for differences between means for dichotomous variables and Pearson correlations for continuous variables (Table 2).

Neither age, first year in practice, nor gender are significantly related to satisfaction, nor are primary care physicians more satisfied than specialists.

Organizational attributes proved better predictors of satisfaction than physician attributes. Satisfaction is positively correlated

with size of practice. The percentage dissatisfied drops from 33 percent among solo practitioners, to 29 percent among those in groups of two to four. It drops further to 14 percent among those in groups of 5 to 10. However, dissatisfaction rises somewhat (to 24%) among those in groups of more than 10.

Satisfaction is inversely correlated with percentage of patients from managed care. Seventeen percent of those with less than one-quarter of patients from managed care and 18 percent of those with 25–49 percent of patients from managed care are dissatisfied. In contrast, 29 percent of those with 50–74 percent of patients from managed care and 31 percent of those with three-quarters or more of patients from managed care are dissatisfied.

Satisfaction is less likely if one is paid by a third party's fee schedule. Twenty-eight percent of those paid by a third party's fee schedule are dissatisfied compared to 21 percent of those who are not. Conversely, satisfaction is more likely if one is paid by salary: Twenty-three percent of those paid by salary are dissatisfied compared to 27 percent of those who are not.

Challenges to Professional Autonomy, Authority, and Dominance. Table 2 also shows bivariate relationships between satisfaction and challenges to professional autonomy, authority, and dominance. Seven items on the survey measure challenges to professional autonomy. Two of these looked at the entrepreneurial aspects of medical practice: owning or renting one's office or owning most of one's diagnostic equipment. Neither item was significantly correlated with physician satisfaction. However, the remaining items, which measured physicians' perceptions of loss of control over work conditions and clinical autonomy, were all significantly and negatively correlated with physician satisfaction. The strongest challenges to satisfaction come from not being paid what one wanted for one's services and having to

TABLE 2 Descriptive Statistics and Bivariate Relationships with Physician Satisfaction (Using Pearson Correlations for Continuous Variables and Mean Difference T-Tests for Dichotomous Variables)

	All variables			Continuous variables	Dichotomous variables		
Independent variables	N	Mean	Standard deviation	Pearson correlation with satisfaction	Mean satisfaction among those answering "yes" (N)	Mean satisfaction among those answering "no" (N)	Mean difference t-value
Physician attributes							
Age	504	46.545	9.956	-.082	—	—	—
First Year in Practice	505	80.229	9.662	.064	—	—	-.105
Female	507	.183	.387	—	3.444(90)	3.459(414)	-.105
Primary Care Physician	505	.546	.498	—	3.504(274)	3.395(228)	1.031
Organizational attributes							
Size of Practice	506	10.598	28.352	.101*	—	—	-.439
Percentage Patients from Managed Care	491	53.947	28.819	-.098*	—	—	
Participate in PPOs	507	.791	.407	—	3.445(398)	3.500(106)	-.439
Participate in IPAs	507	.723	.447	—	3.473(364)	3.414(140)	.498
Participate in HMOs	507	.437	.496	—	3.473(222)	3.443(282)	.282
Paid by Own Fee Schedule	507	.447	.497	—	3.529(225)	3.398(279)	1.249
Paid by Third-Party Fee Schedule	507	.696	.460	—	3.360(350)	3.675(154)	-2.777***
Paid by Capitation	507	.351	.477	—	3.528(176)	3.418(328)	1.045
Paid by Salary	507	.398	.490	—	3.617(201)	3.350(303)	2.488*
Challenges to professional autonomy							
Don't Own or Rent Office	490	2.557	1.796	.029	—	—	—
Don't Own Diagnostic Equipment	496	3.526	1.645	.040	—	—	—
Not Paid What I Want	503	3.725	1.220	-.319***	—	—	—
Must Ignore Clinical Judgment	503	2.501	1.279	-.295***	—	—	—
Don't Set Work Schedule	505	2.439	1.327	-.166**	—	—	—
Must Sign Contracts to Get Patients	497	3.621	1.380	-.148***	—	—	—
Third Parties Affect Treatment	501	3.351	1.385	-.188***	—	—	—
Challenges to professional authority							
Patients Have Medical Knowledge	503	2.636	.951	.119**	—	—	—
Patients Want to Participate	503	3.681	.928	.036	—	—	—
Patients Lack Confidence in Physicians	503	2.685	.886	-.302***	—	—	—
Challenges to professional dominance							
Don't Write Orders for Nonphysicians	491	2.145	1.097	-.130**	—	—	—

*p < .05; **p < .01; ***p < .001.

yield one's clinical judgment to nonphysicians. One-third (33%) of those who are not paid what they want are dissatisfied, compared to only 10 percent of those who are paid what they want. Similarly, 44 percent of those who sometimes must yield their clinical judgment to nonphysicians are dissatisfied, compared to only 18 percent of those who need not do so.

In addition, the percentage dissatisfied was higher among those who do not set their own work schedule, must sign managed care contracts to get patients, and believe that third-party payers affect their treatment of patients. One-third (32%) of those who do not set their work schedules are dissatisfied compared to 20 percent of those who do. Similarly, 29 percent of those who must sign managed care contracts to get patients are dissatisfied compared to 19 percent of those who do not need to do so, while 31 percent of those who agree that third-party payers have considerable effect on how they treat their patients are dissatisfied compared to 19 percent of those who disagree.

Three items measured challenges to professional authority. Surprisingly, those who agree that their patients have a great deal of medical knowledge are *less* likely to be dissatisfied than those who disagree (18% versus 32%). Whether one's patients want to participate in treatment decisions had no impact on physician satisfaction. However, those who agree that patients lack confidence in physicians are considerably more likely to be dissatisfied than those who disagree (47% versus 18%).

Only one item in this study measures challenges to professional dominance. One-third (34%) of those who do not write the orders for nonphysicians to follow are dissatisfied compared to less than one-quarter (23%) of those who do write such orders.

Regression Analysis

To further explore the sources of physician satisfaction, we used multiple regression (Table 3). The relative stability of the regres-

sion coefficients across the table indicates few problems with interactions in the data.

Model 1 tests only for the impact of physician and organizational attributes. In this model, size of practice, participation in IPAs, and payment by one's own fee-for-service schedule are predictors of higher satisfaction ($p < .05$) while percentage of patients from managed care contracts and payment by third-party payers' fee schedules are predictors of lower satisfaction ($p < .05$ and $p < .01$, respectively). The effect of the last variable is particularly strong. The explanatory power of the equation ($R^2 = .05$) is low but significant ($p < .01$).

Model 2 includes the items measuring challenges to professional autonomy and the items on physician and organizational attributes. In this model, neither size of practice, percentage of patients from managed care contracts, or payment by own fee schedule have a significant effect. However, participation in IPAs remains a predictor of higher satisfaction ($p < .05$), and payment according to a third-party payer's fee-for-service schedule remains a predictor of lower satisfaction ($p < .01$). In addition, those who do not set their own work schedule are significantly less likely to be satisfied ($p < .05$) as are those who are not paid what they want to be paid and those who believe they must ignore their clinical judgment ($p < .001$). The percentage of explained variance is higher ($R^2 = .166$) than in model 1 and remains significant at $p < .01$.

Model 3 includes the items measuring challenges to professional authority and the items on physician and organizational attributes. As in model 1, physicians in larger practices report higher satisfaction while satisfaction is lower for those with higher percentages of patients from managed care ($p < .05$). As in models 1 and 2, satisfaction is lower for those who are paid according to a third-party payer's fee-for-service schedule ($p < .05$ and $p < .001$, respectively). However,

TABLE 3 Multiple Regression of Physician Satisfaction ($N = 440$)[a]

Independent variables	Model 1	Model 2	Model 3	Model 4	Model 5
Physician attributes					
Age	−.007	−.008	−.008	−.007	−.007
	(.006)	(.006)	(.006)	(.006)	(.005)
Female	.022	−.029	.121	.080	.086
	(.151)	(.145)	(.148)	(.150)	(.144)
Primary Care Physician	.018	.032	−.003	.023	.016
	(.121)	(.115)	(.117)	(.120)	(.111)
Organizational attributes					
Size of Practice	.004*	.003	.005*	.004*	.003
	(.002)	(.002)	(.002)	(.002)	(.002)
Percentage Patients from Managed Care	−.005*	−.002	−.004*	−.005*	−.001
	(.002)	(.002)	(.002)	(.002)	(.002)
Participate in PPOs	.064	.088	.146	.111	.191
	(.185)	(.175)	(.178)	(.183)	(.171)
Participate in IPAs	.347*	.390*	.265	.365*	.351*
	(.161)	(.154)	(.155)	(.159)	(.150)
Participate in HMOs	−.085	−.053	−.046	−.080	−.033
	(.118)	(.113)	(.114)	(.117)	(.110)
Paid by Own Fee Schedule	.263*	.098	.187	.290*	.083
	(.127)	(.123)	(.122)	(.126)	(.120)
Paid by Third-Party Fee Schedule	−.687***	−.568**	−.710***	−.711***	−.590**
	(.201)	(.203)	(.194)	(.199)	(.197)
Paid by Capitation	.219	.167	.254	.205	.194
	(.141)	(.132)	(.135)	(.139)	(.129)
Paid by Salary	−.013	−.059	−.039	.005	−.060
	(.161)	(.157)	(.154)	(.159)	(.153)
Proletarianization model					
Don't Own or Rent Office	—	−.004	—	—	−.001
	—	(.049)	—	—	(.048)
Don't Own Diagnostic Equipment	—	−.015	—	—	−.013
	—	(.041)	—	—	(.040)
Not Paid What I Want	—	−.176***	—	—	−.164***
	—	(.046)	—	—	(.045)
Must Ignore Clinical Judgment	—	−.196***	—	—	−.148***
	—	(.042)	—	—	(.041)
Don't Set Work Schedule	—	−.096*	—	—	−.061
	—	(.042)	—	—	(.041)
Must Sign Contracts to Get Patients	—	−.034	—	—	−.051
	—	(.045)	—	—	(.044)
Third Parties Affect Treatment	—	−.041	—	—	−.049
	—	(.039)	—	—	(.038)
Patient empowerment model					
Patients Have Medical Knowledge	—	—	.050	—	.026
	—	—	(.057)	—	(.054)
Patients Want to Participate	—	—	−.039	—	−.030
	—	—	(.061)	—	(.059)
Patients Lack Confidence in Physicians	—	—	−.381***	—	−.288***
	—	—	(.062)	—	(.061)
Dominance model					
Don't Write Orders for Nonphysicians	—	—	—	−.172***	−.126**
	—	—	—	(.050)	(.047)
Intercept	4.071***	5.574***	5.081***	3.280***	5.594***
Adjusted R^2	.050	.166	.130	.074	.221

[a]Unstandardized regression coefficients are reported. Standard errors are in parentheses.

*$p < .05$; ** $p < .01$; *** $p < .001$.

participation in IPAs is not related to satisfaction. In addition, believing that patients lack confidence in physicians is a significant predictor of lower satisfaction ($p < .001$). On the other hand, whether respondents believe that their patients have much medical knowledge or want to participate in their own care has no effect on satisfaction. The percentage of explained variance ($R^2 = .13$) is lower than in model 2, but higher than in model 1, and remains significant at $p < .01$.

Model 4 includes both the item measuring challenges to professional dominance and the items on physician and organizational attributes. In this model, as in model 1, size of practice, participation in IPAs, and payment by one's own fee-for-service schedule are significant predictors of higher satisfaction ($p < .05$), while percentage of patients from managed care contracts and payment by third-party payers' fee schedules predict lower satisfaction ($p < .05$ and $p < .001$, respectively). In addition, those who believe they do not write the orders for nonphysicians to follow are less satisfied than those who do ($p < .001$). The percentage of explained variance is higher than in model 1 ($R^2 = .074$) and is significant ($p < .01$). However, it is lower than in models 2 and 3, perhaps because this model has fewer variables than the other theoretical models.

The final model, model 5, includes all the variables and has the greatest predictive value ($R^2 = .221$, $p < .001$). In this model, size of practice, payment by own fee schedule, and percent of patients from managed care are no longer significant predictors of satisfaction. However, participation in IPAs once again predicts higher satisfaction ($p < .05$), while payment according to a third-party payer's fee-for-service schedule predicts lower satisfaction ($p < .001$). In addition, each of the theoretical items that had proven statistically significant in the previous models remains significant in this model except whether one sets one's own work schedule. As

in the other models, physicians are more satisfied if they believe they write the orders that nonphysicians must follow ($p < .01$), are paid what they want for their services ($p < .001$), do not need to ignore their clinical judgment and follow the advice of nonphysicians ($p < .001$), and believe that their patients have confidence in physicians ($p < .001$).

CONCLUSIONS

Theoretical Implications

We began this project by looking at the theories of Eliot Freidson, John McKinlay, Marie Haug, and their colleagues. Each of these theories pointed to specific changes in the health care environment that may have affected the status of medicine as a profession. In this paper, we tested whether these same changes may play a role in enhancing or reducing satisfaction for individual physicians. The results suggest that some but not all of these changes do have clear and measurable consequences for physicians.

To Eliot Freidson, professional dominance is the critical factor in physicians' professional status. In a recent work (1994), Freidson has argued that so long as physicians as a group remain dominant in the division of labor in health care, they will retain their status as professionals even if individual physicians lose some of their clinical autonomy. Our research suggests as well that retaining dominance is critical to physician satisfaction.

Whereas Freidson deemphasizes individual clinical autonomy, McKinlay and his colleagues consider it a central aspect of physicians' professional status. And, indeed, our research suggests that clinical autonomy plays an important role in physician satisfaction. In addition, John McKinlay and his colleagues also have argued that medicine's status as a profession has declined due to physicians' loss of autonomy in setting work conditions. Our research suggests that only some of these changes affect physician satisfaction: So long as physicians retain control over their work schedule and are paid what they want to be paid, they do not care whether they must sign managed care contracts to get patients or whether they own or rent their own offices or equipment.

Finally, Marie Haug and Bebe Lavin argue that physicians' professional status has declined because patients now have more medical knowledge, want to participate in treatment decisions, and lack confidence in physicians. Our research suggests that only the last of these three variables affects physician satisfaction.

The context in which physicians practice has changed dramatically in the last 20 years. Our data suggest that this context has changed to such an extent that regardless of age or years in practice, many physicians accept a somewhat more collaborative relationship with patients as the norm rather than invidiously comparing their positions to those of physicians in some ideal past. Similarly, whereas physicians 20 years ago may have been horrified at the prospect of managed care, physicians now accept it as the rules of the game—at least in areas in which high percentages of patients belong to such plans—and recognize that the price of refusing to play by those rules is bankruptcy. As a side effect, physicians may now view the entrepreneurial aspects of medical practice—owning or renting one's office or equipment—as an unnecessary nuisance rather than as a professional prerogative. Similarly, physicians now accept that patients will seek medical knowledge and desire to participate in medical decisions and thus do not find such patients an impediment to work satisfaction. We cannot say from our data, however, whether changes in patient–physician relationships have had little effect on physician satisfaction because physicians have learned to manage such patients without spending much time or giving up clinical autonomy or because physicians

have concluded that educated patients are easier to work with and have better outcomes.

Practical Implications

From a practical perspective, probably the most useful conclusion to be drawn from this study is that participation in managed care does not have to lead to physician dissatisfaction (cf. Schulz et al. 1997). Percentage of patients in managed care plans appears not to affect satisfaction so long as doctors retain clinical autonomy and control over their work schedule and are paid what they want to be paid for their services. Interestingly, even if physicians ultimately are paid what they want, they find it particularly unsatisfying (or perhaps just aggravating) to be paid according to a third party's fee schedule. Conversely, they find it particularly satisfying to work in IPAs, which offer more clinical autonomy, entrepreneurial autonomy, and control over work conditions than any other options available under managed care. Finally, the beliefs that patients lack confidence in physicians and that physicians do not write orders for nonphysicians both reduce satisfaction, independently of the effect of percentage of patients from managed care.

Managed care plans cannot afford to ignore physician satisfaction as it affects both quality of care and patient satisfaction. Our results suggest several steps that managed care programs can take to protect physician satisfaction. First, managed care administrators can review the limits they place on clinical autonomy—such as requiring physicians to obtain prior authorization before offering or recommending certain treatments—and can explore whether plans can offer physicians greater latitude without sacrificing financial or health care goals. Second, managed care administrators can strive to increase patient confidence in physicians while increasing physicians' belief that their patients have confidence in them. Plans can take such steps as informing patients of the strategies they use to select high-quality physicians and to ensure that their physicians offer high-quality care and then informing physicians of these actions. Third, managed care administrators can involve physicians in the processes of setting reimbursement and work schedules. Finally, given that managed care plans will have to continue to limit clinical autonomy and control work conditions, physician satisfaction may be increased if (1) physicians play a larger role in setting those limits (including establishing parameters for data collection and analysis) and (2) plans better educate physicians regarding how patients and physicians benefit from those limits. It is particularly crucial that for-profit managed care plans do so as physicians might otherwise reasonably conclude that the sole purpose of these limits is to benefit stockholders.

In an ideal managed care scenario, contracts between managed care plans and physicians would link physician pay to patient outcomes. Those outcomes would include both medical indicators (such as number of hospital admissions) and patient-satisfaction indicators (such as survey responses and number of patient-initiated malpractice complaints or suits). These contracts would give both the most clinical autonomy and the most reimbursement to physicians with the best outcomes—satisfied, healthy patients. Thus, physicians who use referrals, diagnostic tests, and medical interventions wisely—offering patients neither too much nor too little care—and those who have a good bedside manner that engenders patient confidence will receive both the most income and the most autonomy from managed care plans. In such a scenario, physicians, patients, and managed care plans will all benefit.

REFERENCES

BAKER, LAURENCE C. and JOEL C. CANTOR. 1993. "Physician Satisfaction Under Managed Care." *Health Affairs* 12:258–70.

BARR, JUDITH K. and MARCIA K. STEINBERG. 1983. "Participation in Organization Decision Making: Physicians in HMOs." *Journal of Community Health* 8:160–73.

CHUCK, JOHN, THOMAS NESBITT. JULIE KWAN, and SHERILYNN KAM. 1993. "Is Being a Doctor Still Fun?" *Western Journal of Medicine* 159:665–69.

EDLIN, M. 1994. "HMOs Cry 'Eureka!'" *Managed Healthcare* October: 40.

FREIDSON, ELIOT. 1970. *Professional Dominance: The Social Structure of Medical Care*. New York: Atherton Press.

———. 1986. *Medical Work in America: Essays on Health Care*. New Haven: Yale University Press.

———. 1994. *Professionalism Reborn: Theory, Prophecy and Policy*. Chicago: The University of Chicago Press.

GROUP HEALTH ASSOCIATION OF AMERICA. 1995. *National Directory of HMOs*. Washington, DC: Group Health Association of America.

HADLEY, JACK and JEAN M. MITCHELL. 1997. "Effects of HMO Market Penetration on Physicians' Work Effort and Satisfaction." *Health Affairs* 16:99–111.

HAFFERTY, FREDERIC W. and DONALD LIGHT. 1995. "Professional Dynamics and the Changing Nature of Medical Work." *Journal of Health and Social Behavior* 1995: 132–53.

HAFFERTY, FREDERIC W. and JOHN B. MCKINLAY. 1993. "Conclusion: Cross-Cultural Perspectives on the Dynamics of Medicine as a Profession." Pp. 210–26 in *The Changing Medical Profession: An International Perspective*, edited by F. W. Hafferty and J. B. McKinlay. New York: Oxford University Press.

HAUG, MARIE. 1977. "Computer Technology and the Obsolescence of the Concept of Profession." In *Work and Technology*, edited by M. Haug and J. Dofny. Beverly Hills, CA: Sage.

———. 1988. "A Re-examination of the Hypothesis of Physician Deprofessionalization." *The Milbank Quarterly* 66:48–56.

HAUG, MARIE and BEBE LAVIN. 1981. "Practitioner or Patient—Who's in Charge?" *Journal of Health and Social Behavior* 22:212–29.

HEALTH CARE FINANCING ADMINISTRATION. 1997. *Medicare Managed Care Contract Report*. Retrieved January 1998 (http://www.hcfa.gov/stats/mmcc. htm).

KLETKE, PHILLIP E., DAVID W. EMMONS, and KURT D. GILLIS. 1996. "Current Trends in Physicians'

Practice Arrangements: From Owners to Employees." *Journal of the American Medical Association* 276:555–60.

LAMMERS, JOHN C. 1992. "Work Autonomy, Organizational Autonomy, and Physicians' Job Satisfaction." *Current Research on Occupations and Professions* 7:157–75.

LICHTENSTEIN, ROBERT. 1984. "The Job Satisfaction and Retention of Physicians in Organized Settings: a Literature Review." *Medical Care Review* 41:139–79.

LIGHT, DONALD W. 1993. "Countervailing Power: the Changing Character of the Medical Profession in the United States." Pp. 69–79 in *The Changing Medical Profession: An International Perspective*, edited by F. W. Hafferty and J. B. McKinlay. New York: Oxford University Press.

LIGHT, DONALD W. and SOL LEVINE. 1988. "The Changing Character of the Medical Profession: A Theoretical Overview." *The Milbank Quarterly* 66 [supplement 2]: 10–32.

LINN, LAWRENCE S., ROBERT H. BROOK, VIRGINIA A. CLARK, ALLYSON R. DAVIES, ARLENE FINK, and JACQUELINE KOSECOFF. 1985. "Physician and Patient Satisfaction as Factors Related to the Organization of Internal Medicine Group Practices." *Medical Care* 23:1171–79.

MCKINLAY, JOHN. 1988. "Introduction." *The Milbank Quarterly* 66:1–9.

MCKINLAY, JOHN and JOAN ARCHES. 1985. "Towards the Proletarianization of Physicians." *International Journal of Health Services* 15:161–95.

MCKINLAY, JOHN and JOHN D. STOECKLE. 1989. "Corporatization and the Social Transformation of Doctoring." *International Journal of Health Services* 18:191–205.

MICK, STEPHEN S., SHELDON SUSSMAN, LYDIA ANDERSON-SELLING, CARLOS DELNERO, ROBERT GLAZER, ELIZABETH HIRSCH, and DANIEL S. ROWE. 1983. "Physician Turnover in Eight New England Prepaid Group Practices: An Analysis." *Medical Care* 21:323–37.

PARSONS, TALCOTT. 1951. *The Social System*. New York: Free Press.

RANDOLPH, LILLIAN, BRADLEY SEIDMAN, and THOMAS PASKO. 1997. *Physician Characteristics and Distribution in the U.S.* Chicago: American Medical Association.

SCHNELLER, EUGENE, ROBERT HUGHES, and PAMELA HOOD-SZIVEK. 1994. "The Future of Medicine." Pp. 13–37 in *New Leadership in Health Care Management: The Physician Executive*, 2d ed. edited by W. Curry. Tampa, Florida: The American College of Physician Executives.

SCHULZ, ROCKWELL, CHRIS GIRARD, and WILLIAM SCHECKLER. 1992. "Physician Satisfaction in Managed Care Environments." *The Journal of Family Practice* 34:298–304.

SCHULZ, ROCKWELL, WILLIAM E. SCHECKLER, D. PAUL MOBERG, and PAULEY R. JOHNSON. 1997. "Changing Nature of Physician Satisfaction with Health Maintenance Organization and Fee-for-service Practices." *The Journal of Family Practice* 45: 321–30.

SKOLNIK, NEIL, DAVE R. SMITH, and JAMES DIAMOND. 1993. "Professional Satisfaction and Dissatisfaction of Family Physicians." *The Journal of Family Practice* 37:257–63.

STARR, PAUL. 1982. *The Social Transformation of American Medicine: The Rise of a Sovereign Profession and the Making of a Vast Industry*. New York: Basic Books.

STOECKLE, JOHN. 1988. "Reflections on Modern Doctoring." *The Milbank Quarterly* 66:76–91.

DOCTOR IN THE HOUSE: THE INTERNET AS A SOURCE OF LAY HEALTH KNOWLEDGE AND THE CHALLENGE TO EXPERTISE

Michael Hardey
School of Nursing, University of Southampton

This paper investigates the new and unique medium of the Internet as a source of information about health. The Internet is an inherently interactive environment that transcends established national boundaries, regulations, and distinctions between professions and expertise. The paper reports findings from a qualitative study of households who routinely used the Internet to access health information and examines how it affected their health beliefs and behaviors. The public use of previously obscure and inaccessible medical information is placed in the context of the debate about deprofessionalization. It is shown that it is the users *of Internet information rather than authors or professional experts who decided what and how material is accessed and used. It is concluded that the Internet forms the site of a new struggle over expertise in health that will transform the relationship between the health professions and their clients.*

INTRODUCTION

One of the central areas of debate in medical sociology concerns the nature of the relationship between those with medical expertise and their patients or clients. Since Parsons's (1951) account of the "sick role" the general picture that arises out of accumulated research findings is one of patients more or less (depending on such variables as social class, race, and gender) being transformed into disembodied cases depicted in a medicalized discourse. The literature has provided various accounts of the way medical professionals use their "social monopoly of expertise and knowledge" (Turner 1995: 47) to

manage encounters and perpetuate their position of power. Nevertheless, the processes of proletarianization and deprofessionalization have been identified as a threat to the dominant position of medicine (Elston 1991). Proletarianization represents the process whereby organizational and managerial changes divest professions of the control they have enjoyed over their work. This is reflected in claims by some advocates of "cybermedicine" that new technology is being used by administrators to restrict doctors' autonomy (Slack 1997). At a more general level deprofessionalization is associated with a demystification of medical expertise and increasing lay skepticism about the health professionals (Haug 1973; Beck 1994). In Britain these changes have been reinforced by the redefinition of patients as "consumers" that began in the 1970s and became a central

Reprinted from *Sociology of Health & Illness*, vol. 21, no. 6 (1999), pp. 820–35, by permission of Blackwell Publishers Ltd/Editorial Board.

plank of state policy in the 1980s, with a series of interventions into the health services signalled by the White Papers *Working for Patients* (DOH 1989) and *The Patient's Charter* (DOH 1991) that offered to "empower" the users of health and social services. The realignment of public services around market mechanisms was essentially driven by the informed decisions of the consumers of health care (Shackley and Ryan 1994). As part of a vision of a networked society the Green Paper *Our Healthier Nation* (DOH 1998) anticipates a government Internet resource, "Wired for Health" as a source of health information for schools and colleges as well as the public. The focus on the provision of information is also reflected in the *Patient Partnership Strategy* (NHS Executive 1996) and *The New NHS* (NHS Executive 1997) which place an emphasis on patients' active involvement in discussions about their health. This inclusive approach is also evident in the patient-centered models of care used in general practice (Laine and Davidoff 1996).

A central theme in the move toward consumerism is the need to provide clients with information; a theme prominent in Giddens's (1991) account of life in our "late modern" society. Giddens suggests we live in an information-rich society in which life plans and strategies have to be negotiated via a potentially confusing mass of competing and sometimes contradictory sources of information. As he makes clear, this applies just as much to those who are ill as it does to those who are healthy. In a fictional account of a woman's search for information about her back pain, for example, he describes how she finds information from various sources that provide a diversity of material from which she can make "a reasonably informed choice" (1991: 141). What is of most interest in his account for the purposes of this paper is that one important source of information was the Internet. Like the participants in the study reported in this paper, Giddens's subject was engaged in those core activities of the reflexive consumer of evaluating and at times challenging expert knowledge (Lupton 1997).

The Internet is a relatively new, unique, and extremely rich source of information that is available to anyone with access to a computer that is linked to a network. It has a short history that began in 1969 when four computers in the United States were linked together so that military information could pass between them (Hobbs 1994). Until the end of the 1980s communication between computers was largely confined to text-based email. At the European Nuclear Research Centre (CERN) the need for a simple computer-based tool to support the coordination of research projects led to the development of what was called a *browser*. In a break with past approaches to computer communication, the browser was designed on the assumption that users should be allowed to search for information rather than be reliant on authors deliberately distributing it to them (King et al. 1997). The concept was christened the World Wide Web (WWW) at CERN in 1990. In 1993 a browser application called Mosaic that provided a graphical user interface and the seamless integration of text and graphics caught the attention of the popular press. Two years later, the WWW was a core topic at the G7 meeting of the world economic powers. Today almost the entire globe has access to the Internet and many businesses and households are linked directly to it (Holderness 1998). The Web browser is now familiar to anyone who has used the Internet and often provides the model for the interface to library catalog systems and electronic learning material. It enables users to access both the WWW and use other resources such as email and newsgroups that constitute part of the broader Internet.

The rapid expansion of the Internet has been fueled by fierce competition within the computer industry that continues to drive down the price of high-performance computers and telecommunications equipment. In Britain the introduction of a competitive telecommunications market has seen the expansion of cable and satellite communications systems. This provided the basis for the delivery of digital consumer technology and opened up new markets for Internet Service Providers (ISPs) that connect homes and organizations to the Internet. At present, the ownership of home computers and use of the Internet at home reflects the social class hierarchy. The General Household Survey recently reported that 64 percent of households in social class one and 48 percent of households in social class two owned a home computer in 1996. Although there is a higher rate of domestic computer ownership in the United States, a similar pattern is evident, with lower-income households being less likely to own a computer (Bikson and Panis 1997). However, in both cases there is a rapidly increasing rate of computer ownership and domestic use of ISPs. Furthermore, the convergence of digitally based consumer services provides the means to incorporate access to the Internet within familiar broadcast media. There is also evidence that falling costs and increased ease of use have undermined educational and gender barriers in the adoption of home computers which are being perceived as another "technology appliance" (Lin 1998). It should also be remembered that many people have access to the Internet at work or through the increasing number of cybercafes and computers in public libraries and schools.

This paper argues that the Internet constitutes a new and unique medium in which expert knowledge is accessible to anyone with a computer linked to a network or modem. Medical dominance is challenged not only by exposing exotic medical knowledge to the public gaze (Good 1994) but also by the presence of a wide range of information about and approaches to health. At the heart of

medical autonomy is exclusive access to "expert knowledge" (Giddens 1991) and the ability to define areas of expertise and practice. The Internet provides a possible threat to this situation. Anyone with a few technical skills and access to a suitable computer can add to the mass of health information on the Internet (McKenzie 1997). Users need only know of a convenient starting point that is likely to have a link to the desired resource or use any one of a number of search engines such as Yahoo! and Lycos as well as various specialist health resources (e.g., Medical Matrix, CliniWeb, OMNI) that provide annotated hierarchical links. Pallen, writing in the *British Medical Journal*, describes a search for the unusual condition of Recklinghausen's neurofibromatosis which

> . . . was completed in two minutes and provided links to seven web pages at four sites. One particularly informative site at the Massachusetts General Hospital provided a description of the condition, complete with magnetic resonance scans, information about clinical services, research, conferences, and self-help groups (1995: 1552).

The challenge presented by self-help groups to medical dominance can be traced back to the late 1960s. Since then they have grown to such an extent that few chronic illnesses are not represented by a national if not international group. A search for information about cancer, for example, will provide links to sites that range from centers of clinical excellence to individuals advocating unconventional approaches to treatment. Commonly used search engines do not discriminate between material provided by those with clinical expertise and those, for instance, advocating astral healing. A search conducted for information about cancer may take users to a site that provides evidence about cures based on "dissonant energy waves."[1] This site advocates the approach of a biologist who believed that energy waves could destroy cancers and that his work was suppressed by "medical interests." Herbal remedies are advocated as a cure on another site, while users are encouraged to purchase a book of potential cures elsewhere on the Internet.[2,3] The search may also find OncoLink[4] which provides up-to-date clinical trial and treatment information, as well as acting as an educational resource for cancer patients and their families (Buhle et al. 1994). This has hyperlinks to the British-based Cancer Web which provides a range of material for patients and practitioners as well as links to support groups.[5] Pressure groups of all kinds have quickly colonized the Internet and warn users of threats that range from global ecological dangers to the consumption of genetically modified food.

This paper, therefore, examines the Internet as a source of knowledge about health in relation to the broader sociological debates about deprofessionalization and consumerism. The paper draws on a qualitative case study of people who use the Internet as a source of knowledge about health. Although of limited scope, it is probably the first attempt to examine in depth how people with no persistent chronic illness use the Internet as a source of information about health.

THE STUDY

There are few empirical studies of Internet users, and methodologies for studying information and communications technologies are diverse and range from email surveys to ethnomethodological approaches (December 1996; Slack 1998). The research that forms the basis for this article follows a case-study approach which is particularly useful when examining new phenomena (Yin 1994). An invitation to take part in the study was sent to subscribers of three different email lists that contained members largely confined to the South of Britain. The invitation was also sent to subscribers of a locally based ISP. This invi-

tation contained information about the study and appeared in users' email utility as a "health on the Net study." Users who responded to this initial request were sent a letter outlining the project and a short questionnaire so that they could be screened for inclusion in the research. Questions about household composition, locality, employment, and health were asked. This exercise produced a group of 28 potential participants who were from Kent to Cornwall. Nine households, who were willing to participate in at least two interviews over a year and lived within reasonable travelling distance, constituted an initial sample. Contact was made by telephone to confirm participation in the study and to arrange interview dates. To take advantage of a snowball approach, at the end of each initial interview participants were asked if they could suggest another household that could be approached to take part in the study. This strategy was used to include households not reached by the initial request for participation. Three households were subsequently sent the screening questionnaire and one household was recruited to the research. Households that fulfilled the characteristics for inclusion in the study but were not interviewed have taken part in an email-based survey. Two pilot interviews were undertaken for both phases of the research. As they were not substantially different from the other interviews, they were included in the general sample.

Two interviews in participants' homes were undertaken with each household over a year with both parents present where there were children. The interviews covered a range of issues related to health and the Internet. The majority of interviews lasted between one and two hours. Research notes were also kept as respondents were asked to demonstrate the use of their computers and some of the resources that they had discovered. The interviews were transcribed, and recurring themes and issues were identified in the resulting data following a grounded theory approach. This technique is based on the generation of analytically based categories through the "constant comparative method" that validates the categories against the data they are grounded in (Strauss and Corbin 1990). Research data remain confidential and the names used to report findings in this paper have been changed. While it is not possible to generalize from such a small-scale study, the experiences and concerns reported here may not be untypical of Internet users.

The final case study consisted of 10 households in the South of Britain. The main income earners were aged between 28 and 52, worked full time in managerial and other jobs that are classified as social class one and two. This reflects the current relationship between social class and the ownership of home computers. Five women worked full time, only one of whom worked at home. None of the households contained a family member with a chronic condition except asthma and eczema which were present in four instances. All the families regarded themselves as "healthy" apart from the "usual" childhood complaints. None of the participants regarded themselves as "experts" in relation to computers and no household had owned a home computer with a modem link for more than 16 months.

READING THE INTERNET

Using the Internet is an inherently interactive process that involves users in a continual process of decision making. The WWW is underwritten by hypermedia protocols that, through a browser, enable users to point and click their way across the Internet. Users are actively involved in the construction of a narrative which they read as they search through the Internet for information. By *read* I mean to include text and other forms of information that users may identify on the Internet. The reader in a hypermedia environment

uses search strategies and hyperlinks to trace paths through a virtual space of endless possibilities. Participants in the case study were familiar with the use of Web browsers and routinely used search engines to identify information. The process of finding information is anchored in experiences of print media:

> Even the kids know how to search for stuff they're interested in. The only frustration is the time it takes sometimes. Though if you think about how long and difficult it can be to find something in a book or a library the Internet is far more efficient. Of course you also know that whatever it is you are looking for it is bound to be there somewhere.

This perception of the inclusiveness of information on the Internet means that unfruitful or overlong searches for information are regarded as due to the users' failure to define appropriate key words or use search-relevant resources. A little ingenuity may be required:

> It can take a bit of lateral thinking to come up with the right terminology. It is also important to use the right search engine. I've found the Home Doctor page really simple and helpful.

The Home Doctor Web site allows users to enter or browse through symptoms that are linked to products available from pharmacists in Britain.[6] A research project in the United States designed a Web site that provided information on the recognition and treatment of cardiac arrhythmias (Widman and Tong 1997). The site included an interactive demonstration and explanation of complex cardiac rhythms and allowed users to send questions to the site's authors. Over a month in 1995 the site received 10,732 visits for information from some 50 countries. The authors also received and responded to enquiries from users that were almost always appropriate to the clinical nature of the site. This demonstrates that users can not only identify material relevant to them but also use it as a resource to make further appropriate enquiries. The researchers also note that they usually responded to such enquiries within 24 hours which points to a further advantage of Internet-based consultation for users.

When useful material has been identified, it often contains hyperlinks within the text and/or highlighted links to other sites that may be of interest to users. A simple mouse click on a hyperlink takes users from one Web site to another. This produces what can be regarded as a "narrative" that consists of the material that may be read on the computer screen, stored on the computer, and/or printed to resemble a conventional text. This narrative is assembled by the users so that openings, middles, and ends are what he or she desires (Joyce 1994). In a sense, there is no "ending" in hypertext because the reader can link to another text before reaching the end of the original text. The recent introduction of frames that break up the screen allow users to hyperlink to other Web resources without leaving the original site. The distinction between what is "inside" one site and "outside" it therefore becomes unclear. To the user, material that is accessed through hyperlinks may appear to come from the site that presents the frame. Users may move between Web sites that originate in different countries and continents without realizing that they have left the site they first accessed. The undertow of commercialism can be detected in the use of frames as they enable the originally accessed site to retain a degree of control over the user (for example, advertisements can be presented to users). Hypertext therefore releases material from the context in which it was written and presented as well as from the control of authors, publishers, national and professional regulations and constraints.

As texts pass seamlessly across different readership groups they are subject to different interpretive strategies. For example, a research scientist may write a paper for a medical audience that is published in the electronic version of a medical journal and is available to anyone with access to the Internet. Furthermore, users may arrive at the paper from a hyperlink within a different source and depart from it in a similar manner. The process of constructing a narrative is comparable with accounts of reflexivity that emphasize continual monitoring, criticism, and assessment of knowledge (Beck et al. 1994). A participant explained the process:

> It's not like reading a magazine. You can slip into a skimming mentality which is what the kids tend to do. . . . Unlike a book, you choose what you see and put things together as you go along. One quickly learns to reject the rubbish as you go along. When I'm looking for something specific I usually feel fairly confident when I have got what I wanted.

THE STRUGGLE OVER EXPERTISE

The equity of presentation offered by the Internet dissolves the boundaries around areas of expertise upon which the professions derived much of their power. Furthermore, the illusion of authority given to computer-mediated material may benefit nonorthodox medicine which lacks the symbols of power and authority routinely available to orthodox medicine (Saks 1992). This diversity and the resulting uncertain nature of Internet health information has provided grounds for dismissing the Internet as a "serious tool" for professionals (Information Market Observatory 1995), and for others to represent it as dangerously confusing to clients. At the heart of the debate about the unity and impact of the Internet lies the question of the quality of the material that is available on it. The issue of quality can be used to illustrate how lay users define and cope with the problem and the way it is used by the medical profession to attempt to retain and redefine boundaries around medical expertise.

There are two main dimensions to this problem of quality. The first relates to Web material that is authored by health professionals, and the second concerns the boundary between medical and other approaches to health. A recent study of Internet advice for the home care of feverish children made a comparison between medical guidelines and the Internet advice (Impicciatore et al. 1997). It was found that only four out of 41 sites studied matched medical guidelines in the management of childhood fever. However, as the researchers note, "fever in children is rarely harmful, and treatment may not always be necessary." Part of the problem here is the global nature of the Internet that is highly subversive of national boundaries and guidelines to clinical treatment. It should be remembered that users from countries other than the originating site may experience problems related to the different labels used for proprietary drugs as well as national differences in the recognition of treatments. This raises the question of how and whether lay users are able to manage contradictory or misleading information. Differences with the narratives constructed by users were viewed as problems that were a "natural" characteristic of the Internet:

> I think there is room for people to be misled. Some of the things you find simply contradict each other. Actually it only needs a little common-sense to make your mind up about what is useful. . . . At the end of the day you have to rely on your own judgement.

Another respondent was similarly confident in her ability to discern reliable material but had adopted a reflexive approach:

> If you are a bit doubtful about something it is a simple matter to ask a slightly different question to get more information. I mean, one thing about the Net is that you only have to think about what you are looking for . . . so one piece of information makes you think a little differently so you get a different slant on what

you want. . . . I would say that it (contradictory or misleading information) was not a problem any more than it is on TV or a magazine.

These quotations suggest that users were aware of the quality problem and that they felt they could assess narratives that enabled them to resolve the difficulty. As a participant suggested previously, the clinical quality of health-related CD-ROMs, advice in popular magazines, or "family doctor" books may be no more reliable than much of the information available on the Internet. Furthermore, direct comparison can be made with the medical consultation:

> My GP is very busy and does not have time to answer questions fully. Actually it is much easier to think about what you want to ask when you look things up on the Net. I don't get that nagging feeling that I'm needlessly taking up his time.

The unregulated electronic space of the Internet echoes the diversity of the market for health that existed before medicine secured its professional status (Stacey 1988). Once established the profession invested much time and energy in reinforcing and expanding the boundaries of its practice within the paradigm of natural science. Analysis of case-study material suggests that participants had an inclusive view of health information which is anchored in the diversity of the consumer market:

> I'd heard about osteopathy but I hadn't realised that it would be any use for my back ache. I like to know what I might be letting myself into . . . so it was useful to get the background information, so I felt I could make a sensible choice. . . . The osteopath was clearly right for me . . . and I would recommend it to anyone now.

Several participants mentioned how beginning a search to look for information about prescription drugs or symptoms had led them to information about nonorthodox approaches to health:

> I was given these anti-biotics but they gave me thrush and I couldn't sleep. My GP wasn't terribly helpful but when we looked up antibiotics we found a lot about what they could do to you . . . you know, side effects that they don't bother explaining to you. Anyway we also found a lot about natural treatments that did not involve drugs as such. . . . Allergies are probably a lot to do with my problem so I'm trying this diet we found out about and I'm seeing a homeopath.

As the preceding quotation suggests, the Internet may act as a conduit to nonorthodox therapy. It can also be instrumental in challenging a course of treatment:

> I was diagnosed as having high blood pressure and they gave me these pills. OK I was told I might get some side effects but I felt pretty bad sometimes after taking them. Anyway I found this place in the States [USA] that had a whole lot of information about this drug. Turns out that my symptoms happen to some people and there was this other pill that works better. . . . When I got to see my GP she was surprised about what I knew about the prescription and put me on this other drug which works fine. I actually showed her some print outs from the Web that clearly show these tests that had been run on the drug and the symptoms that people in my circumstances had as a result. She was a bit taken aback but took me seriously and spent longer than I have ever had going through the details with me.

A number of participants reported that they had renegotiated treatment for themselves or their children with their GP on the basis of information they had found on the Internet.

Participants in the study accessed the Internet in the familiar space of the home with only self-imposed limits on time. This is a very different venue from the consulting room with its trappings that reinforce medical dominance (Heath 1984). Embarrassing or difficult questions can be asked and answers may only be shared with the computer. Furthermore, physical location is largely irrelevant to users of the Internet. This provides scope for minority communities to seek information about Ayurvedic, Unani, and other approaches to health which may not be easily available where they are resident or not be encouraged by GPs. Those who live in rural areas or in parts of the globe with less developed services for particular conditions can participate in support groups and read information about their health problem. The breakdown of the local/global distinction has also been seen as one of the benefits of telemedicine. However, such narrowband communication is limited compared to the Internet that offers integrated digital media (McGee and Tangalos 1994).

The medical profession anchors the problem of quality within a natural science model that is reinforced by the concept of evidence-based practice and the traditional role of the professions as a protector of the public interest (Saks 1992). A particularly apt example of this is provided by the Quackwatch site.[7] Constructed by a retired psychiatrist and sympathetic doctors in the United States, the mission of Quackwatch is to warn users about what is regarded as unscientific or inappropriate health information. The site rejects all but "proven" medical material following a review by clinicians, and includes examples of unsound health material. In doing this the site appears to follow a strict evidence-based hierarchy that gives priority to material based on randomized controlled trials. Over a hundred dubious practices are listed and include acupuncture and traditional Chinese medicine. In a good example of boundary keeping, the site also offers selective and sometimes vitriolic comments together with a commentary emailed to it by users advocating alternative approaches to treatment. There is little evidence for "new modesty" (Beck 1994) about medical expertise in the Quackwatch site that discredits all but narrowly defined health knowledge.

Perhaps more representative of the response from the medical profession are the calls for the creation of an international standard for Internet health material. The provision of a "gold standard" or "kitemark" for health-related Web sites would allow the medical profession to establish boundaries around the medical expertise that is represented on the Internet. Institutes like Mitretek (1998) have developed criteria for assessing the quality of health information that include clear statements about sites' objectives, intended audience, and accuracy of content. However, organizations that provide a rating system may not make the criteria on which reviews are based explicit. A survey of 47 instruments used to indicate quality revealed that only 14 made the criteria used explicit (Jadad and Gagliardi 1998).

DISCUSSION AND CONCLUSION

The potential of the Internet as a source of health information has yet to be widely recognized. A recent review of evidence-based information for clients concluded that it was "too early to know whether it will be a widely used source by patients for health information" (Hope 1996: 20). Theoretical and popular analyses of information technology, however, have focused on its ability to change economic and social relationships in an egalitarian direction (e.g., Bell 1974; Toffler 1980; Castells 1996). At a microlevel, it has been argued that "by the mid-1990s, people can be expected to view personal computers as knowledge sources rather than as knowledge processors . . . gateways to vast amounts of knowledge and information" (Tennant and Heilmeier 1991: 123). The participants in this study took advantage of their computers to find health material in this ever-expanding body of knowledge. They did this in the familiar space of the home, largely with only self-imposed limits on time. This is a very different venue from the consulting room. Embarrassing or difficult questions they wanted to ask were shared only with the computer or anonymous others.

The Internet as a global market that offers new opportunities for consumerism continues to attract much media attention and considerable investment in electronic commerce. Access to the global health market enables users to undergo, for example, cosmetic surgery in Eastern Europe or visit India for hip replacement operations. This suggests that the "local" medical encounter and medical expertise should be seen in the "global" context. It is therefore possible for individuals from different traditions to access "local" expertise about, for example, Ayurvedic or Unani approaches to healing from practitioners situated in communities where these are the predominate models of healing. This multiplicity of therapeutic regimes, self-improvement guides, and self-help groups provides resources for users to construct and reconstruct narratives to maintain or alter their sense of self-identity in a manner which goes way beyond that implied by Parsons's sick role (Giddens 1991, cf. Parsons 1951). Advice and advertising about diets, exercise plans, muscle-building drugs, and so forth continue to proliferate on the Internet. The capacity of the Internet to reassure people anxious about the "external" and "internal" health of their bodies is central to this process, and the Internet provides a unique resource for users to cultivate their bodies within a discourse on "lifestyle" (Shilling 1993). Such tendencies challenge the efforts of national governments' attempts to erect barriers to the importation of drugs that are not licensed locally or, as in the recent case of Viagra, have an uncertain status in local health care systems.

It would be wrong to prioritize a model of modernistic health consumerism mediated by the Internet whereby users become detached from the emotional and caring dimensions of health in the face of a sea of information. Rather, the resources available on the Internet encourage pluralist approaches to health. At one level, the information available transcends established scientific, political, and professional boundaries, and at another, interactive resources create the space for the construction of new narratives about health and lifestyle. Within newsgroups, chat rooms, and other interactive resources, people "open up" to others in an environment where anonymity promotes trust in strangers. Such electronic communities offer new opportunities for people with chronic or debilitating conditions to participate on an equal basis in community life. Global self-help groups provide a space for strangers who are bound within an environment that minimizes the "gamble" (Giddens 1991) involved in sharing intimate feelings. The anonymity of such places provides fertile ground for giving meaning to life crises or what Giddens refers to as "fateful moments." This reflects the roots of electronic health information which can be traced back to the email-based online support groups that emerged in the 1980s and were often originated by people with HIV/AIDS. Such resources have developed into sophisticated collaborations between health professionals and user groups like the European-based SEAHORSE project, which provides information and support in relation to HIV/AIDS and acts as an interactive conduit for the sharing of expertise. *Expertise* here is defined holistically to include lay knowledge whether from patients, carers, or family members.

The research noted in this paper supports Gidden's contention that "provided that the resources of time and other requisites are available, the individual has the possibility of a partial or more full-blown reskilling in respect of specific decisions or contemplated courses of action" (1991: 139). This exposure of the health profession's knowledge base to the public gaze represents the challenge to medical expertise envisaged by Haug's (1973) notion of deprofessionalization. Moreover, from within the medical paradigm, the provision of detailed information about treatment has been shown to be welcomed by patients and to be associated with measurable improvements in health (Weinman 1990). In a recent review of the research literature, Coulter (1997) concluded that there was a demand from patients for more information and involvement in their treatment. In the process of "reading" described here, users dynamically assess the usefulness and quality of the information they collect. This protects them from information overload because they actively decide when they have read enough material for their needs. In line with the original idea behind the design of the browser, it is *the users* of information rather than authors or professional experts who decide what is delivered to them. This represents a break with the print-based tradition of health information that is devised by health professionals and often distributed by them so that they control the content and flow of information (Buckland and Gann 1997). The basic design of the Internet therefore represents a challenge to previously hierarchical models of information giving. This shift in control is central to the deprofessionalization thesis and may be seen as contributing to the decline in awe and trust in doctors. The internally referential and provisional nature of medical knowledge and the division between experts is evident in the debate about the quality of Internet health information. Lay challenges to medical expertise noted in this paper produced a re-negation of treatment and in some instances the use of non-orthodox therapies. The blurring of boundaries between orthodox and nonorthodox beliefs encourages a definition of health that embraces spiritual and emotional dimensions often marginal in conventional medicine. However, it would be wrong to conclude that Western medicine becomes simply one option which consumers can choose to include in the construction of meaning about health, and to incorporate in self-care strategies. The dominant discourse about health and healing on the Internet is Western, and, as has been shown here, there are ranges of activities under the umbrella of "quality" that are being used to limit the space or credibility given to non-Western medical knowledge. Further research is needed to understand how and whether doctors view patients' use of the Internet as a threat to their clinical autonomy or as a resource to promote a partnership in care.

REFERENCES TO INTERNET SITES

1. <www.kalamark.com/essiac/sunrest/html>
2. <www.healthfree.com/schulze>
3. <www.ismall.com/zheng/prorder.html>
4. <www.oncolink/upenn/edu>
5. <www.graylab.ac.uk/cancerweb.html>
6. <www.medetail.co.uk/home-doc>
7. <www.quackwatch.com/index.html>

REFERENCES

BECK, U. (1994) The reinvention of politics: towards a theory of reflexive modernization. In Beck, U., Giddens, A. and Lash, S. (eds) *A Reflexive Modernization: Politics, Tradition and Aesthetics in Modern Social Order*. Cambridge: Polity Press.

BECK, U., GIDDENS, A., and LASH, S. (eds) (1994) *A Reflexive Modernization: Politics, Tradition and Aesthetics in Modern Social Order*. Cambridge: Polity Press.

BELL, D. (1974) *The Coming of Postindustrial Society: A Venture in Social Forecasting*. Harmondsworth: Penguin.

BIKSON, T. K. and PANIS, C.W.A. (1997) Computers and connectivity: current trends. In Kiesler, S.

(ed) *Culture of the Internet*. New Jersey: Lawrence Erlbaum Associates.

BUCKLAND, S. and GANN, B. (1997) *Disseminating Treatment Outcomes Information to Consumers: Evaluation of Five Pilot Projects*. London: King's Fund Publishing.

BUHLE, E. L., GOLDWEIN, J. W., and BENJAMIN, I. (1994) OncoLink: a multimedia oncology information resource on the Internet, proceedings of the symposium on computer applications in medicine, *Journal of the American Medical Informatics Association, Symposium Supplement*, 1994, 103–7.

CASTELLS, M. (1996) *The Rise of Network Society Vol. I*. Oxford: Blackwells.

COULTER, A. (1997) Partnership with patients: the pros and cons of shared clinical decision-making, *Journal of Health Services Research Policy*, 2, 2, 112–20.

DECEMBER, J. (1996) Units of analysis for Internet communication, *Journal of Communication*, 4, 324–45.

DEPARTMENT OF HEALTH (1989) *Working for Patients*. London: HMSO.

DEPARTMENT OF HEALTH (1991) *The Patient's Charter*. London: HMSO.

DEPARTMENT OF HEALTH (1998) *Our Healthier Nation*. London: HMSO.

ELSTON, M. A. (1991) The politics of professional power: medicine in a changing health service. In Gabe, J., Calnan, M. and Bury, M. (eds) *The Sociology of the Health Service*. London: Routledge.

GIDDENS, A. (1991) *Modernity and Self-Identity*. Cambridge: Polity Press.

GOOD, B. J. (1994) *Medicine, Rationality and Experience: an Anthropological Prospective*. Cambridge: Cambridge University Press.

HAUG, M. (1973) Deprofessionalization: an alternative hypothesis for the future. In Halmos, P. (ed) *Professionalisation and Social Change*. Keele: University of Keele.

HEATH, C. (1984) Participation in the medical consultation: the co-ordination of verbal and nonverbal behaviour between the doctor and the patient, *Sociology of Health and Illness*, 2, 3, 311–38.

HOBBS, Z. R. (1994) *Hobbes' Internet Timeline*. http://www.amdahl.com/internet/events/timeline.html.

HOLDERNESS, M. (1998) Who are the world's information-poor? In Loader, B.D. (ed) *The Governance of Cyberspace*. London: Routledge.

HOPE, T. (1996) *Evidence-based Patient Choice*. London: King's Fund Publishing.

IMPICCIATORE, P., PANDOLFINI, C., CASELLA, N. and BONATI, M. (1997) Reliability of health information for the public on the world wide web: systematic survey of advice on managing fever in children at home, *British Medical Journal*, 314, 1875–9.

INFORMATION MARKET OBSERVATORY (IMO) (1995) The quality of information products and services. Luxembourg, September, *IMO Working Paper* 95/4. <http://www2.echo.lu/impact/imo/9504.html>.

JADAD, A.R. and GAGLIARDI, A. (1998) Rating health information on the Internet: navigating to knowledge or to Babel? *Journal of American Medical Association*, 279, 8, 611–14.

JOYCE, M. (1994) *Of Two Minds: Hypertext Pedagogy and Poetics*. University of Ann Arbor: Michigan Press.

KING, J. L., GINTER, R. E., and PICKERING, J. M. (1997) The rise and fall of netville: the saga of a cyberspace construction boomtown in the Great Divide. In Kiesler, S. (ed) *Culture of the Internet*. New Jersey: Lawrence Erlbaum Associated.

LAINE, C. and DAVIDOFF, F. (1996) Patient centred medicine; a professional evolution, *Journal of American Medical Association*, 275, 152–6.

LIN, C. A. (1998) Exploring personal computer adoption dynamics, *Journal of Broadcasting and Electronic Media*, 42, 95–112.

LUPTON, D. (1997) Consumerism, reflexivity and medicine, *Social Science and Medicine*, 43, 3, 373–81.

MCGEE, R. and TANGALOS, E.E. (1994) Delivery of health care to the underserved: potential contributions of telecommunications technology, *Mayo Clinical Procedure*, 69, 1131–6.

MCKENZIE, B. C. (1997) Quality standards for health information on the Internet, *Society for the Internet in Medicine*: Quarterly, Issue 3.

MITRETEK (Health Information Technology Institute) (1998) *Criteria for Assessing the Quality of Health Information on the Internet*. <http://www. mitretek.org/hiti/showcase/>.

NHS EXECUTIVE (1996) *Patient Partnership: Building a Collaborative Strategy*. London: HMSO.

NHS EXECUTIVE (1997) *The New NHS. Modern, Dependable*. London: HMSO.

PALLEN, M. (1995) The world wide web, *British Medical Journal*, 311, 1552–6.

PARSONS, T. (1951) *The Social System*. Glencoe: Free Press.

SAKS, M. (1992), *Professions and the Public Interest*. London: Routledge.

SHACKLEY, P. and RYAN, M. (1994) What is the role of the consumer in health care, *Journal of Social Policy*, 23, 4, 517–41.

SHILLING, C. (1993) *The Body in Social Theory*. London: Sage.

SLACK, R. S. (1998) On the potentialities and problems of a WWW based naturalistic sociology, *Sociological Research Online*, vol. 3, no. 2. <http://www.scoresonline.org.uk/scoresonline/3/2/3.html >.

SLACK, W. (1997) *Cybermedicine*. New York: Jossey-Bass.

STACEY, M. (1988) *The Sociology of Health and Healing*. London: Unwin Hyman.

STRAUSS, A. and CORBIN, J. (1990) *Basics of Qualitative Research: Grounded Theory Procedures and Techniques*. London: Sage.

TENNANT, H. and HEILMEIER, G.H. (1991) Knowledge and equality: harnessing the tides of information abundance. In Leebaert, D. (ed) *Technology 2001: the Future of Computing and Communications*. Cambridge, MA: MIT Press.

TOFFLER, N. (1980) *The Third Way*. London: Pan.

TURNER, S. S. (1995) *Medical Power and Social Knowledge*. London: Sage.

WEINMAN, J. (1990) Providing written information for patients: psychological consequences, *Journal of the Royal Medical Society*, 83, 303–5.

WIDMAN, L. E. and TONG, D. A. (1997) Requests for medical advice from patients and families to health care providers who publish on the World Wide Web, *Archives of Internal Medicine*, 157, 209–12.

YIN, R. K. (1994) *Case Study Research: Design and Methods*. Thousand Oaks: Sage.

Part VIII

PHYSICIANS
IN A CHANGING SOCIETY

Professional autonomy and social control of medical practice are hallmarks of the medical profession. No other profession has been granted equivalent powers of self-regulation and self-direction. As William Cockerham (2001) points out, organized medicine has continued to pursue a pattern of professional behavior based on the image of medical practice at the turn of the century, when the physician worked on a solo basis as an independent, fee-for-service, private practitioner. However, at present, challenges to the autonomy of the medical profession come mainly from three sources: government regulation; changes in the patient–physician relationship associated with consumerism; and corporations in the business of health care in the coming era of managed care. Physicians remain powerful in health matters but not to the same extent as earlier in the twentieth century. In this part, two papers address the professional status of physicians and the changing nature of their work.

In the first paper, "Professional Dynamics and the Changing Nature of Medical Work," Frederic Hafferty and Donald Light review major sociological writings to examine the status and professional dynamics of medicine in a changing environment. The authors summarize the historical context of medicine's power and prestige, and discuss both the internal and the external forces that are shaping medicine and the nature of medical work. Hafferty and Light state that they are deliberately provocative in organizing their arguments, drawing conclusions, and offering recommendations—an approach that proves effective in challenging the reader to rethink the current and future status of the medical profession.

The authors point to five groups that challenge medicine's boundaries: government, at all levels; corporate purchasers of health care for their employees; corporate sellers, such as providers of services and manufacturers of medical products, including pharmaceuticals; consumers; and other health care providers. In relation to changing dynamics, Hafferty and Light observe that, although no one suggests that organized medicine has become an insignificant player in health care issues and reform, its ability to exert influence in an increasingly crowded policy environment appears "greatly diminished." Further, the authors, following through on their promise on provocation, state that the basic overall thrust of professionalism is toward a loss and not a continuation or strengthening of medicine's control over its work. The time has come to begin structuring health policy that emphasizes the presence of a partnership between rank-and-file physicians and the public at large.

Particularly important is Hafferty and Light's conceptual and research agenda for medical sociology. They state that sociologists need to reevaluate the concept of profession in general, including the dynamics of professionalism and the nature of professional work. Related to this is reconsideration of the concepts of autonomy and uncertainty as these relate to the medical profession. The sociological research agenda should include studies on the new "knowledge elite" emerging within the ranks of medicine, better understanding the regulatory environment in which medicine operates, the changing nature of medical work not only within medicine but across the various health professions, and cross-cultural comparisons between professional dynamics in the United States and other countries.

The second paper, by Susan Hinze, is entitled "Gender and the Body of Medicine or at Least Some Body Parts: (Re)Constructing the Prestige Hierarchy of Medical Specialties." Hinze interviewed male and female physicians in a resident-training program about their choice of specialty, seeking to determine whether men opted for higher-prestige specialties such as surgery, surgical subspecialties, anesthesiology, and radiology and women chose lower-status specialties such as family practice, pediatrics, obstetrics and gynecology, dermatology, and psychiatry. She was particularly interested in the physicians' perceptions of the hierarchy and their criteria for the top specialties. Regardless of the gender of the physician respondents, the highest-prestige specialties are characterized as "macho, action-oriented, physical, and technically sophisticated," whereas the less-prestige specialties are described as more "passive, emotional, and soft." Hinze found that women are not prevented from participating in high-prestige specialties by male "gatekeepers," but there was a more subtle structural barrier of masculine images associated with the higher-status specializations that applied to women in those jobs as well. Some female physicians, however, reject the male-oriented prestige system and place greater value on specialties ranked lower by men.

PROFESSIONAL DYNAMICS AND THE CHANGING NATURE OF MEDICAL WORK

Frederic W. Hafferty
University of Minnesota, Duluth
Donald W. Light
University of Pennsylvania

The organization and delivery of health care in the United States is undergoing significant social, organizational, economic, political, and cultural changes with important implications for the future of medicine as a profession. This essay will draw upon some of these changes and briefly review major sociological writings on the nature of medicine's professional status to examine the nature of professional dynamics in a changing environment. To this end, we focus on the nature of medical work and how this work impacts on and is impacted by medicine's own internal differentiation and the presence of contested domains at medicine's periphery. We trace this dynamic through a number of issues including the multidimensional nature of medical work, the role of elites in that work, and how changes in the terms and conditions of work can exert changes at medicine's technical core. We close with some thoughts on the relationship of public policy to medicine's professional status, the role health policy might take in shaping a new professional status, the role health policy might take in shaping a new professional ethic for medicine, and the role sociologists might play in this process.

The rise of medicine to the status of a dominant profession in the United States has been fostered by two compatriot trends. One was the emergence of a more autonomous state, ushered in by the rise of populism in the 1890s, the peaking of laissez-faire capitalism, and the ascendancy of the notion that government had a proactive role to play in advancing the general welfare and health of the populace. The second trend was the continued evolution of a capitalistically based, corporate-industrial presence, fueled by industrial expansion and a continuing indus-

trial revolution, and holding important implications for the rationalization and reorganization of work (Zhou 1993). As unskilled workers turned to unions to protect their interests, more elite occupational groups turned to state legislatures to establish their interests through practice laws and licensure provisions (Zhou 1993).

Medicine was uniquely positioned to take advantage of these trends. Having formed its national association in 1847, nearly a half century earlier, the decision to evolve as a professional entity rather than a trade union placed it in a regulatory environment that favored professional rather than business interests. Although it would be incorrect to frame the state as nothing more than a leg-

Reprinted from the *Journal of Health and Social Behavior*, extra issue (1995), pp. 132–53, by permission of the American Sociological Association.

islative handmaiden to medicine's monopolistic interests, the historical record makes clear that during the first half of the twentieth century medicine did acquire an extraordinary degree of cultural legitimacy along with extensive legal protections and legislatively based entitlements (Brown 1979; Champion 1984; Starr 1982; Stevens 1971). In turn, medicine was able to resist corporate efforts to employ physicians directly (as "company doctors") or to organize them into prepaid group practices that would provide services under contract to corporations and large business enterprises (Light 1991).

Medicine's powers and prestige reached their zenith in the 1950s and 1960s, a period widely characterized as the "Golden Age of Medicine." The watershed would come in 1965 with the passage of Medicare and Medicaid legislation. Evidence of medicine's continued influence could be found with the inclusion of Section 1801 of the Medicare Act. This section specified that the federal government would not exercise "supervision or control over the manner in which medical care services were provided . . . or over the administration or operation of any . . . institution, agency, or person providing health services" (Thompson 1981). On the other hand, by mandating (via economic incentives) the delivery of medical services to two previously disenfranchised groups (the elderly and the poor), the state clearly announced that it considered itself a legitimate source of social welfare legislation in the arena of health care. Over the next two decades, the rise in expenditures remained unchecked by various remedial strategies such as certificates of need and peer review organizations, government, and private payers. This lead to a "buyers revolt" (Light 1988), accompanied by renewed efforts to control the terms, conditions, and the content of medical work.

As the state struggled to devise effective mechanisms for controlling health care costs, a long-dormant corporate presence began to exert its own presence—and interests (Relman 1980, 1987, 1991; Starr 1982). Traditional distinctions between payers and providers (e.g., insurance companies versus hospitals and clinics) became blurred as both sides moved to horizontally expand by purchasing businesses in the other's domain. The political defeat of the Clinton Administration's health reform bill in 1994 served only to highlight how much of the reorganization of health care was taking place within the private as opposed to the public sector.

The changes being wrought within this fluid environment of shifting alliances and organizational arrangements are staggering. In less than a generation of providers, the solo practitioner has given way to the group practice, which itself has become buried under a mosaic of practice networks, institutional arrangements, and organizational schemes (e.g., health maintenance organizations [HMOs], independent practice arrangements [IPAs], preferred provider organizations [PPOs], third-party administrators [TPAs], and integrated service networks [ISNs]). Managed care arrangements and practice networks are being supplemented by practice protocols, treatment guidelines, and a litany of requirements for prior authorization (Kelly and Toepp 1994). Patterns of practice, once arranged informally around loose networks of individual providers, are becoming more routinized (Luce, Bindman, and Lee 1994). Assessments of quality, once privately conducted almost exclusively by peers and in a ritualistic and cordial fashion (Bosk 1980; Freidson 1975; Millman 1977), have been replaced by, among other things, physician "report cards" and related assessment tools developed and deployed by employers and payers to measure—and control—provider behavior (Brouillette 1991; Winslow 1994). Billing and claims records, long the chief primer of medicine's revenue pump, are being turned against medicine by government and corporate payers in efforts to limit and manage the practices and practice patterns of physicians (Luce et al. 1994). In turn, national organizations collect and disseminate information on hospital mortality and morbidity rates, physician performance indicators, and even patients who have filed malpractice claims (Irving 1993; Maier 1994; Millenson 1993).

In the following pages, we first present an overview of sociological thinking on the nature of professions and professional dynamics. We then briefly outline some of the major forces that are shaping medicine currently both from within and at medicine's periphery. In both instances, our focus is on how these dynamics influence the content and control of medical work. We follow this with a more detailed examination of two phenomena that reflect the intersection and interaction of external and internal forces: (1) the rise of administrative and technical elites within medicine (as an example of a source of internal tension); and (2) the emergence of medical effectiveness research and practice protocols (as an example of externally based forces). Once again, we focus on examining these trends in terms of their impact on the core of medicine's professional identity . . . its control over the content of its work. Given our emphasis on the interdependent nature of state-professional-corporate relations, including the fact that the state has emerged as a major sponsor of effectiveness research and as a producer of practice guidelines, we turn to some observations on the role played by health policy in the process of professionalism and make some suggestions for how policymakers might be informed by a sociology-of-professions perspective. We close with some recommendations for medical sociology itself, including conceptual issues that need to be explored

and research that needs to be undertaken, all with the hope of improving our understanding of professional work and the role that work plays in addressing public health problems.

Across all of these issues, we seek to maintain an analytic framework that locates the evolving nature of medical work within the symbiotic relationship that exists between medicine's own internal dynamics and the shifting tensions among countervailing interests marshaled at the boundaries of medicine's professional domain. The explicit recognition that medicine's trajectory of professionalism is shaped interdependently by dynamics both internal to the profession itself as well as external (e.g., such as major institutions and sectors of society including the state, the public, related occupational groups, and corporate interests) serves as the cornerstone of this essay.

Although it has become increasingly clear that data from cross-national studies are critical to any concerted understanding of professionalism (Hafferty and McKinlay 1993; Hafferty 1995), we confine our focus in this essay primarily to the case of the United States. Finally, we have sought deliberately to be provocative in organizing our arguments, drawing our conclusions, and advancing our recommendations. We prefer forceful counterarguments to quiet acceptance.

SOCIOLOGICAL OBSERVATIONS ON THE NATURE OF PROFESSIONS

Sociological writings on professions have tended to parallel the evolving relationship between state, professional, and corporate interests. Weber's concern that the rise of capitalism, along with the forces of rationalism and bureaucratization, would result in an iron cage of servitude (Weber 1952, 1968) was paralleled by Durkheim's hope that professions would function to organize scientific and expert knowledge into associations of colleagues, forming a "moral authority" that would serve as a buffer between the public and the onslaught of industrialization (Durkheim 1933: 26).

This notion of professions as experts in the service of public interests became part of the Progressive Movement, the ideas of which were reflected in E. A. Ross's *Social Control: A Survey of the Foundations of Order* (1901). Physicians were perceived as an important occupational class who sought to advance public welfare by strengthening licensing laws, by opposing commercialism in medicine, by driving out proprietary medical schools, and by attacking the hucksterism of the nostrum industry (Light 1989). Early sociological writing on the professions (e.g., Carr-Saunders by himself [1928] and with Wilson [1933]) chronicled the emergence of a middle-class fashion and zeal for professional work. As was true for Durkheim and many other distinguished sociologists of the time, Carr-Saunders regarded the rise of professions as an important source of standards, service, and moral authority in the modern world of corporations and markets (Bledstein 1976). Less well-appreciated is the degree to which this drive also constituted a more silent war against emergent forms of corporately organized and competitively structured health care (Light 1989).

This idea of professional life as the embodiment of service reached its most formal apogee when Parsons (1939) characterized professional work as universalistic yet functionally specific, rational, and altruistic. Reflecting the tenor of the postwar period, Parsons (1951, 1954) formalized the earlier writings on the nature of professional work into his typology of pattern variables and into a normative view of doctoring that presented the profession's image of ideal practice as sociological reality. Parsons seemed relatively innocent of the idea that the restraint of self-interest in a professional guild is the key to its economic, cultural, and institutional

power and therefore best serves the collective interests of its members. No attention was given to the ways in which the enlightened paternalism of doctoring, which Parsons extolled, resulted in part from cultivating ignorance, helplessness, and a sense of incompetence in patients as techniques of social control (Waitzkin and Waterman 1974; Light 1979).

The economic, cultural, and institutional power of medicine grew apace during the 1950s and 1960s. By the late 1960s, accusations of greed, hubris, fragmentation, and insensitivity to patients had proliferated and led to seminal works by Freidson on professional dominance (1968, 1970a, 1970b). A key element in Freidson's early writings was his recognition that the interpersonal basis of professional authority is weak and unstable. Parsons may have emphasized that authority emanates from technical knowledge, but that locus alone leaves professionals with little more than their powers of persuasion. To solve this problem, professions seek to institutionalize their authority. They use licensure and public identity to attract clients suffering from a persistent problem. They gain control over valued services and facilities, like prescription drugs and hospitals and medical excuses from work. Related observations on the efforts of professional groups to establish a market shelter and to gain status, privilege, and legal protections at the cost of a service orientation came with the writings of Johnson (1972) and Larson (1977).

The print was hardly dry on Freidson's conclusions about medicine's status as a dominant profession, balanced as they were by his critiques of medicine's loss of a service ethic, when other sociologists' pronouncements of medicine's fall from professional grace began to surface. Principal among these critiques were Haug's thesis of "deprofessionalization," (1973, 1975, 1988; see also Haug and Lavin 1978) and a related but theoretically distinct concept of "proletarianization" advanced by

McKinlay (1973, 1977, 1988; see also McKinlay and Arches 1985; McKinlay and Stoeckle 1988). Freidson responded throughout the 1980s with a series of rebuttals (see Freidson 1983, 1984, 1985, 1986a, 1986b, 1987, 1989), in which he dismissed evidence of the profession's weakening grip and affirmed the continued dominance of the profession in clinical affairs. Although proponents of all three of these perspectives have retreated somewhat from their earlier arguments (Hafferty and McKinlay 1993), and while the accelerating rise of a corporate presence in medicine and the computer-facilitated monitoring of physician work appear to bolster the arguments of McKinlay and Haug respectively, most observers continue to conclude that medicine is retaining its professional dominance both in this country and abroad (Hafferty 1988, 1995; Hafferty and McKinlay 1993; Hafferty and Salloway 1993; Mechanic 1991).

Most recently, two interrelated trends have contributed appreciably to our understanding of professional dynamics. The first, more empirical in nature, is the growth in the number of cross-national examinations of professional dynamics.[1] The second, more theoretically oriented, is the evolution of a theory of countervailing powers formed by the work of Abbott (1988), Halpern (1988, 1992), Light (1993, 1995), and others. The emergence of recent cross-national studies, with their focus on state, professional, and corporate forces in countries other than the United States and Great Britain, have made it amply clear that in each country medicine takes on a different professional character as it is shaped by the particular configuration of countervailing institutional powers, and all within a framework of professional dynamics that includes professional ascension as well as professional maintenance and professional decline (Hafferty 1995).

Building upon these observations, the notion of countervailing powers locates professions within a field of institutional and cultural forces and parties in which one party may gain dominance (e.g., the state in the former Soviet Union and the medical profession in the United States) by subordinating the needs of significant other parties who, in time, mobilize to counter this dominance.[2] In a situation in which a currently dominant group (e.g., the medical profession in the 1960s) seeks to maintain its privileges and power, change takes place over decades, partly from the excesses and neglects of dominance and partly from the mobilization of other parties. Extrinsic forces, such as technological advances, significant changes in resources or economics, demographic changes, and societal changes outside the field of forces also influence the balance of power and make countervailing powers more than a zero-sum game.

FERMENT AT THE CORE AND TENSIONS AT THE PERIPHERY

Structurally, organized medicine never did fit Goode's (1957) idyllic characterization of the profession as a "community of equals." Claims heralding the death of the generalist began to surface as early as the turn of the century (Shryock 1967; Konold 1962), with trends supporting a specialty-oriented and procedurally based medicine continuing well into the 1990s. Despite a policy emphasis on primary care in the 1970s and again in the 1990s, this trend toward specialization and thus toward internal differentiation has accelerated in recent years.[3]

Faced with tightening revenue streams, individual specialties have taken up arms to control particular diagnostic or therapeutic modalities. In the summer of 1993, for example, the American Society for Gastrointestinal Endoscopy and the American College of Gastroenterology hired a major Washington, D.C., law firm and undertook a national campaign to convince hospitals that allowing family practitioners to perform endoscopies would be tantamount to condoning malpractice (Castro 1994). Their efforts were reasonably successful even though this call to limit the availability of endoscopies made it more difficult for patients to receive this service. Similar struggles have arisen over who is qualified to do flexible sigmoidoscopies, first pitting gastroenterologists and internists against family practitioners and more recently pitting physicians in general against nurse practitioners (Maule 1993). Other clashes have evolved between gynecologists and family practitioners over colposcopy and within hospital systems about general (Can chiropractors receive privileges?) or specific (Who is qualified to deliver babies, do laparoscopic surgery, or work with patients in intensive care units?) staff privileges (Chene 1986; Dent 1991). Even the entitlements that have traditionally accompanied specialty certification (e.g., the "exclusive right" to perform certain procedures) are coming under fire as provider organizations such as hospitals and HMOs begin to employ their own competency-based assessments to establish who is eligible to perform particular clinical activities (Pelberg 1989). A related conflict has been drawn between generalists and specialists over who should function as a legitimate source of primary care services (Barondess 1993; Rivo, Jackson, and Clare 1993; Schwartz, Ginsburg, and LeRoy 1993). With the growing presence of capitation contracts, the stakes have become enormous. As managed care and related "gatekeeper" systems stress a stepwise delivery model that restricts "front door" access to subspecialists, providers such as rheumatologists, oncologists, and cardiologists are attempting to reposition themselves as primary providers for their chronically ill patients, and thus to tap into the primary care as well as the subspecialty revenue streams. Even more threatening,

the very presence of capitation reduces the overall need for subspecialists in managed care systems, thus producing an oversupply of these provider types (Weiner 1994).

In recent years, one of the more bitter conflicts among specialties has been around the introduction of resource-based relative value scales (RBRVS), a payment scheme based on cost (as opposed to charges) for reimbursing physician services under Medicare. RBRVS was designed (at least initially) to redress the traditional imbalance in reimbursement patterns that have favored technical and procedurally based medical work (and thus subspecialty-oriented activities of listening, questioning, and explaining) (Hsiao et al. 1988, 1992). As the federal government, in its role as buyer seeking fair prices based on cost, moved to implement RBRVS, lines of allegiance were quickly and predictably drawn. RBRVS was praised by primary care specialty groups and vilified by subspecialty—particularly surgical—interests (Werner 1992; Gott 1993). Opposing camps wasted little time in attacking each other as well. "Master organizations" such as the American Medical Association (AMA) and the American College of Physicians found themselves betwixt and between as they scrambled to answer to multiple constituencies.

But RBRVS did more than exacerbate the frictions that lurked beneath the surface of medicine's public facade of internal equanimity. The development of RBRVS also reflected the resolve and power of Medicare and Congress to ascertain the cost and value of different medical and surgical procedures. Using practice-based data, RBRVS sought to measure (1) the time, skill, and intensity of each procedure; (2) all direct and indirect costs of practice; and even (3) a return on the income forgone when physicians pursue additional years of specialty training rather than enter practice. Work itself was quantified along four major dimensions: (1) time;

(2) mental effort and judgment (including knowledge and diagnostic acumen); (3) technical skill and physical effort; and (4) psychological stress. These formulas were intended not merely to reflect the relative value of physician work but ultimately to alter the way physicians delivered services. Perhaps most importantly, the RBRVS methodology legitimated the idea of measuring something (medical work) that had for so long been considered enigmatic and idiosyncratic—and therefore unqualifiable. In many respects, the arrival of RBRVS has helped to set the stage for subsequent efforts to measure quality of care and to assess medical outcomes. RBRVS also represented a loss of control for medicine over the setting of reimbursement rates, something long dominated by physicians.

Important rifts within medicine have appeared along a number of other "fault" lines as well. Over the past several years, the AMA and the American College of Surgeons have been split bitterly over a number of issues including the issue of work-hour limits for residents (Deaconson et al. 1988; Van 1989; Kelly et al. 1991). Health reform and proposals for fee caps and for a single payer plan placed the AMA (con) and the American College of Medicine (pro) on opposite sides of the table (Neus 1992). Internally, the AMA has been deeply divided over the issue of whether physician ownership of laboratories or other diagnostic facilities represents a conflict of interests and thus unethical behavior on the part of providers so situated (Priest 1992).[4] As the media began to report examples of referral abuses and as studies tied physician ownership to higher referral patterns (Mitchell and Scott 1992; Scott and Mitchell 1994), the already fragile trust between medicine and the public became further strained (Hafferty 1991). Correspondingly, the perceived failure of medicine to satisfactorily police itself has led to a variety of legislative actions (and thus externally

derived controls) such as those spearheaded by California Representative Pete Stark to cover physicians' facility ownership and referral practices.[5]

Matters of physician supply, including the system-straining effect of physician oversupply, constitute another dimension of medicine's internal dynamics. Although not yet a visible issue in the United States, physician unemployment has been reported in other countries, and linkages between oversupply and the forces of proletarianization have long been a part of the sociological literature on issues of medicine's professional dominance (Hafferty and Wolinsky 1991; Hafferty and McKinlay 1993). In the United States, recent projections based on HMO staffing patterns make it clear that medicine continues to produce too many physicians, particularly subspecialists (Weiner 1994). Evidence of oversupply—or at least fear of a shrinking marketplace—is reflected in the above-referenced turf battles among various physician groups.

The presence of these turf battles, along with the emergence of the state as an arbiter of medicine's internal conflicts, stands as a witness to medicine's inability or unwillingness to satisfactorily control its own affairs, to the growing role of the state in exerting its regulatory presence, and to the inability of medicine to resist such incursions. These turf battles also bring us to the second of our territories, the topic of boundary maintenance and matters of external relations.

Tensions at the Periphery

Five broad groups make up the external locus of countervailing pressures that exist along medicine's boundaries: (1) *government*, including local, state, and federal; (2) *corporate purchasers* of health care for their employees (e.g., GE, IBM) and their agents, such as insurance and managed care companies; (3) *corporate sellers*, such as providers of services (e.g., Humana) and manufacturers of medical products, equipment, and pharmaceuticals (e.g., Merck, Kodak); (4) *consumers*, as represented by government and consumer groups (e.g., AARP, Citizen Action, and various disability advocacy groups), but also reflected by activities such as consumer spending and the changing tides of cultural legitimacy; and (5) *other providers*, such as nurses, physical therapists, and alternative providers such as chiropractors and herbalists.

Here too, the overall pattern has been one of increasing differentiation and greater complexity. Government action on issues of health care financing and organization unfolds at federal, state, and even local levels, sometimes in a complementary and sometimes in a conflicting fashion. Corporations routinely compete—and seek to acquire a dominant position (and thus a minimization of competition) in the medical marketplace. Turning to other providers, we find the evolution of a highly complex web of occupational groups, each seeking to establish a distinctive sphere of work (and thus influence) along with a concurrent desire to bask in the sun of professional prerogatives. Turf wars exist not only between medicine and other provider groups such as nursing, chiropractic, and pharmacy, but among and within these groups as well.[6] Other examples of external tensions highlight the interrelatedness of some of these domains. The rise in the number of alternative practitioners ("other providers") has been accompanied by a startingly broad acceptance by the public ("cultural legitimacy") of alternative therapies and "unconventional medicine" (Eisenberg et al. 1993; also, see Letters to the Editor [1993] for responses to the Eisenberg et al. article). HMOs, particularly those employing providers directly ("corporate sellers"), have moved aggressively to transfer clinical services down the traditional medical hierarchy ("other providers"). Today, the majority of babies delivered within the Kaiser system are delivered by midwives. Taken as a whole, these patterns indicate a diminished presence and role for physicians in the actual delivery of services and lessening influence over the degree to which other groups participate in delivering those services.

The dynamics surrounding the Clinton Administration's health reform efforts, including the formation of Hillary Rodham Clinton's health care task force, illustrate this complexity as well as medicine's overall marginalization. Long accustomed to a privileged seat at the policy table, the AMA and other major physician organizations found themselves unexpectedly, purposefully, and pointedly excluded from direct task force participation (McCombs 1993; Pear 1993; Priest 1993). Vice President Gore warned the AMA that it would no longer dominate health reform (SoRelle 1993), while President Clinton labeled the AMA just another "special interest group" (Hall 1993). As the national debate swirled on, registered lobbying groups with an interest in health reform, now numbering over 1,500, circled Washington intent on restructuring the traditional roster of key players (Feder 1993). Physicians, once disdainful of practice arrangements such as HMOs and IPAs, are now fighting a series of legal battles to *require* these organizations or networks to hire them under "any willing provider" provisions (that is, if a provider is willing to abide by the rules of the network or organization, then that provider must be hired or included in that plan).[7] Meanwhile, medicine's legislative presence appears less decisive and less well-orchestrated. Between 1989 and 1992, for example, the AMA contributed significantly more to House members who wound up *opposing* AMA positions on three key health issues (including the "gag rule" on abortion counseling) than to those who supported AMA interests (Sharfstein and Sharfstein 1994).

While no one is suggesting that organized medicine has become an insignificant player, its ability to exert its influence in an increasingly crowded policy environment appears greatly diminished. Only an influential few (e.g., see Mechanic 1991; Freidson 1994) still insist that physicians, as medicine's traditionally high-priced free agents, continue to dominate the playing field. As medicine continues to experience internal tensions, and particularly as these differentiations are reflected in strains between a governing elite and a clinically based rank-and-file, we anticipate that the basic overall thrust of professionalism is toward a loss and not a continuation or strengthening of medicine's control over its own work. It is becoming increasingly clear that the ranks of medicine will be populated with both winners and losers, something that does not bode well for medicine's internal solidarity, its ability to effectively secure its boundaries, and thus its ability to maintain control over the content of its work.

THE RISE OF THE NEW ELITES

Organized medicine has not been untouched by the swirl of activity along its boundaries. One important effect of the buyers revolt has been the rise of two groups within the ranks of medicine: a knowledge elite exerting technical and cognitive power, and a more recent administrative elite wielding economic and organizational power (Freidson 1984, 1987). Although a knowledge elite has been present within the ranks of medicine since at least the time of the Flexner Report and the related development and evolution of the academic medical center, it is only in the past decade that attention has been focused not so much on developing individual diagnostic and treatment procedures as on establishing their efficacy based on outcomes, on the utilization of clinical trials, and on assessing entire systems of care including their financing and organization. The presence of physician administra-

tors, while also long-standing, has shifted from the traditional informality of rotating chair or clinical chief positions to a trend for clinicians to establish themselves more permanently within the boardroom or executive suite.

Two different scenarios have surfaced in writings on these elites. On the one hand, there is concern that the presence of these two elites signals a growing rift between them and the rank-and-file physicians and thus a growing tension between the knowledge generators and the knowledge consumers, the rule setters and rule followers, the managers and those being managed, and those who function as owners versus those who perform as employees. In short, it has been anticipated that the rise of these elites, particularly an administrative elite, would constitute a "critical change" in the organization of medicine and one that might hold "dire consequences" for medicine's status as a profession (Freidson 1987). "When you have one elite setting the standards and another elite directing and controlling and other professions doing the work, you have altered the organization of the body and relations between its members which may have serious implications for its corporate character" (Freidson 1984: 14).

The possibility that these elites might function as a source of structural instability and thus undermine medicine's professional status brings us to a counterscenario. Medicine's powers and prerogatives are being maintained because physicians—not laypersons—are serving in critical decision-making positions and thus securing medicine's control over the technical core of its work and the organizations in which it is clinically applied. It is physicians, the argument runs, who are creating the databases, writing the guidelines and protocols, conducting the relevant research on matters critical to the nature of medical work, organizing and distributing the resources so that these tasks can be done, and serving as ministers without portfolios (Freidson 1987). In short, it appears that these new elites have been cast as both *necessary* to medicine's maintenance of its professional status and as *potentially destructive* to that status. How are we to think sociologically about these possibilities?

This issue may be viewed from several vantage points. First, it is important to recognize that although the rise of the academic medical center and the large-scale federal funding of biomedical research within such centers during the 1970s and 1980s facilitated the growth of new career paths for physicians in research and administration, the declaration that medicine continues to exert definitive control over its work by virtue of the fact that MDs are functioning in these roles, remains just that—an assertion. Although the ranks of physician-researchers and physician-administrators have grown, so too have the number of non-MD researchers and administrators, bringing with them alternative disciplinary backgrounds, differing paradigms, and contrasting cultures and orientations toward work. To the best of our knowledge, there has been little effort to examine the proportion, respective roles, and the influence of physicians versus nonphysicians in either the production of new medical knowledge or the administration of medical resources. Thus, there has been little empirical information about the relative influence of a physician versus a nonphysician elite at the core of medical work.

More central than issues of composition or even ascribed influence are those of hierarchy, power, and role. The notion that the attainment of an MD degree (or lack thereof) is the critical factor around which the control of medical work revolves is tenuous at best. There are two grounds on which to question such assumptions about professional fidelity. The first is empirical and asks whether physicians who enter the administrative ranks con-

tinue to identify with their earlier allegiances as clinicians or whether they adopt more of a managerial orientation. The second, more conceptual, concerns the relative influence of prior socialization versus current work setting on professional behavior.

Data on the first question are linked to work done by Montgomery (1990, 1992). She found that, even at the earliest stages in the development of physician executives as an occupational type (during the mid- to late 1980s), those moving from clinical into management ranks engaged in a process of "individual reprofessionalization" as they began to shift their identity and commitments from the medical profession to the organization for which they worked. Moreover, it appeared that management identity intensified as time and involvement in administrative duties increased.

Turning to our second point, Freidson is quite clear in both *Profession of Medicine* (1970a) and *Professional Dominance* (1970b) that he views current work environment as being more influential than education and prior socialization both in determining and explaining "professional performance." But if this indeed is the case, then should we not expect physician-administrators or managers, as individuals who spend the bulk of their working day administering resources, conducting basic science or clinical-outcomes research, organizing conferences or establishing national research priorities, to identify more with the problems and exigencies "at the top" than with the day-to-day contingencies and murkiness of life in the clinical trenches? Montgomery suggests that this is exactly what is happening, and Freidson provides, in part, the interpretive framework for why this might be so. To date, only Wolinsky (1988: 43) has suggested a criterion for "physician membership," which although stringent (requiring that a loss of one's physician identity would occur only when physicians had "fully and permanently divested themselves of actual medical practice") does emphasize the influence of work setting over that of medical training or the attainment of a particular degree.

In sum, although the whole issue of physician control over the content of his or her work needs substantial empirical examination, the evidence gathered to date about the case of physician-administrators suggests that this elite does not represent the points of view of the rank-and-file. Furthermore, it appears that the critical issue is not one of degree attainment (MD or otherwise) but rather the notion of orientation toward work, toward organization and power, and toward those who pay one's salary.

An alternative approach to the depiction of these two elites as necessary but potentially destructive is to frame their appearance in a more dynamic fashion. Thus, while their *arrival* may initially have provided organized medicine with at least the appearance of an "in-house" resource base along with a locus of functional control, any *subsequent movement* toward an elite status may render the profession increasingly vulnerable to outside control. That control tightens particularly as the profession becomes more internally differentiated and as outside forces, such as corporate interests, attempt to coopt the expertise of these elites as a part of more general efforts to restrict the clinical discretion traditionally exercised by rank-and-file clinicians. In other words, steps taken by organized medicine to populate the ranks of the knowledge and administrative elite with physician "insiders," and thus to maximize its control over the process of rationalization and the technical core of medical work, also set in motion forces that might undermine that very control.

As we have noted earlier, there are few reasons to believe that these elites will represent the interests of organized medicine—if this has ever been the case. Clearly it is in the interests of capital and the state to persuade these elites to adopt points of view other than those that resonate within hospital corridors and clinic hallways. Furthermore, it is more than reasonable to expect that as these elites establish their positions of power and influence, they will become estranged from those they were intended to save . . . in this case the rank-and-file clinician. Similar to Freidson's observations on the self-corrupting nature of autonomy (Freidson 1970a: 368–82, 1970b: 42; Hafferty 1988),[8] we can imagine that these groups might become as estranged from the rank-and-file as medicine has become from the general public. This possibility is exacerbated because, unlike the more general relationship between medicine and society, there is no implied social contract between these elites and the rank-and-file. There is no promise that they will hold themselves accountable for acting in the best interest of their "members." Furthermore, at least in the case of the knowledge elite, there are no mechanisms for "external" review or a mandated process of accountability—at least with respect to issues of fidelity and service orientation. In short, there is no guarantee that these elite groups will align themselves with the interest of medicine as opposed to non-MD health researchers (in the case of the knowledge elite) or corporate interests (in the case of both the knowledge and the administrative elite).

A related issue is whether these two groups themselves might come to represent antagonistic as opposed to complementary interests. We do not attempt to answer this question here, but note that it is an extremely complicated issue and one linked to a number of related factors including respective work settings (the knowledge elite being more likely to function in academic settings; the administrative elite in a corporate environment), the extent to which each is able to organize itself as a special interest group (the administrative elite appearing much further along in this regard than the knowledge elite),[9] their relative status within the culture of medicine as well as the broader societal culture (it is unclear at this time which group is accorded greater legitimacy either within medicine or within society at large), and the degree to which the work of each might come to be considered "problematic" or "tainted" by those in power (e.g., if medical technology becomes cast in too negative a light, then the administrative elite may be accorded greater license to rein in these advances).

In summary, we view the rise of these elites within medicine's own ranks as one part of a more general process of rationalization that has accompanied medicine's rise to professional status. At the present time we see few reasons to believe that these new elites will "identify with the ideals of their profession and concern themselves with sustaining the integrity of the work for which they have taken responsibility" (Freidson 1987: 144). Rather, these new elites will not only fail to identify with the rank-and-file or with broader professional values but they themselves will evolve in disparate directions, with the administrative elite becoming the more dominant of the two as it develops closer working and ideological ties with corporate interests and bureaucratic structures.

INCURSIONS INTO MEDICINE'S TECHNICAL CORE

The impact of the knowledge and administrative elites on medical work brings us back to the nature of that work and some observations on factors that are influencing change in the content of medical work. Change in the content of work can occur in two fundamental ways. First, changes in dimensions other than content of work (e.g., technical core), such as in the terms of work (e.g., pay, hours) and the conditions of work (e.g., organizational structure, employment status), may exert a determining influence on that very core. Thus, while it remains important to differentiate between terms, conditions, and content for analytical reasons (see Freidson 1970a), this importance should not blind us to exploring how change in one realm might influence change in the others. The second route for change involves efforts to alter the content of work more directly, such as recent efforts to develop practice protocols and to conduct research on medical effectiveness. Here, the specific intent is to limit what some view as an excessive level of clinical discretion held by practicing physicians.

In the first instance, greater attention needs to be given to examining how changes in the terms or the conditions of work may play an instrumental role in altering the content of that work. Studies of medicine in the former Czechoslovakia (Heitlinger 1991, 1993), China (Henderson 1993), and the former Soviet Union (Field 1988, 1993) suggest that while state control over critical resources does not unduly impact on the decision-making control exercised by physicians *relative to that exercised by other health care workers*, shifts in resource availability may affect the decision-making process itself, including the clinical outcomes of those decisions.

There appears to be a somewhat analogous situation emerging in this country as third-party payers, corporate purchasers of health care, and the state itself become more aggressive in attempting to influence resource availability and conditions under which clinical services are delivered. Examples include the use of formularies that dictate a specific and limited number of medicines available for prescribing, tighter scheduling of patient visits, in-home referral requirements, requirements for prior authorizations, and the hotly debated linkage of physician reimbursement to lower resource utilization by patients. Thus, while it would remain at least true literally that physicians retain the legal right to order any test they might deem appropriate or to treat the patient in the manner they deem "best," it is also true that the threat of review along with the intimidation fostered by the threat of nonreimbursement, effectively limits the number of clinical practice options. In these ways, HMOs, managed care plans, and related practice arrangements leave the physician in charge of clinical decision making, but do so within a range of incentives (positive and negative) that are intended to alter at least the terms and conditions under which medicine is practiced.

In short, administrators may never set foot in the examining room, politicians may assume office without clinical training, and insurance agents may never add the laying on of hands to their complement of business practices; but the availability of clinical resources, including the establishment of a prevailing organizational (work) culture (e.g., how many patients are to be seen per hour, how much revenue needs to be generated, and the redefining of patients as customers, in short, the "nature" of clinical work, including norms governing that work) places managers, payers, and purchasers near the heart of the clinical encounter. Over time, choices based on technical-scientific considerations or on professionally controlled norms may be replaced by institutional mandates concerning cost containment or efficiency, by political considerations, or by an organizational hierarchy based on rules and a uniform work product. As the decision-making process expands to represent interests other than technical/medical, those clinical activities not supported or "sanctioned" by critical resources may recede into an unused and distant netherland, eventually slipping out of one's differential diagnosis or clinical armament altogether. Restrictions on certain types of services that at one time may have elicited energetic challenges from clinicians may become the norm as physicians find themselves less

inclined to rock the organizational boat and thus advocate on behalf of their patients. Ethical principles, such as the AMA's call for physicians to seek changes in laws that are contrary to the best interests of the patient (Clause 3 in the AMA's Principles of Medical Ethics [American Medical Association 1994]) slip into an even greater obscurity. As the nature of clinical work is transformed, a new clinical culture is created.

The second and more direct avenue for change includes more direct attempts by payers and the government to alter the content of work without necessarily involving the terms or the conditions of that work. An example of this type of intervention can be seen in the recent surge of interest in medical effectiveness research (MER) along with the proliferation of practice protocols and clinical guidelines. The growing importance—and influence—of research on quality of care and health outcomes is reflected in the passage of P.L. 101–239 in which Congress replaced the National Center for Health Services Research and Technology Assessment with a new agency level office, the Agency for Health Care Policy and Research (AHCPR). AHCPR was charged with improving the effectiveness and efficiency of the health care system by undertaking projects that would differentiate between effective, equivocal, and ineffective clinical interventions (Raskin and Maklan 1991). The goal was to reduce the amount of "unnecessary" variability and uncertainty in clinical practice. Related goals included bringing empiricism to the clinical decision-making process and the conjoint empowerment of both providers and patients through increased knowledge.

The new law and subsequent AHCPR activities place the state and matters of effectiveness research at the hub of health care reform with a significant—and growing—health policy presence. In addition to supporting research, AHCPR was charged with developing and disseminating practice guidelines based on its own work along with that of the multiagency federal MEDTEP (Medical Treatment Effectiveness Program). These guidelines will be used to provide health care organizations and clinicians with a scientific rather than a tradition-laden basis for guiding treatment and diagnostic decisions.

But protocols backed by the collection of primary data and the causally oriented methodology of clinical trials represent only a few of the guidelines that currently are circulating within the medical marketplace. A larger presence is occupied by panels or groups of individuals who have come together to establish some form of practice norms. These "expert panels" include federally funded undertakings involving international authorities, exhaustive literature reviews, and the employment of meta-analysis; more nationally based efforts underwritten by third-party payers, corporate purchasers, or corporate providers of medical care; regionally configured efforts by state medical societies, payers, or deliverers; as well as efforts by physicians at individual clinics who wish to establish some agreed-upon approach for handling common clinical problems within their own practices. In most of these instances, the emphasis is not so much on collecting new data as it is on compiling and assessing state-of-the-art knowledge or on agreed-upon methods of approaching particular clinical problems (Brook and Lohr 1985).

Without taking sides as to the relative validity of these two approaches, the expert panel, although more efficient, gives greater weight to tradition, convention, and custom than does the more primary data-driven effectiveness research model. The expert panel thus offers organized medicine a greater opportunity to exert its traditional powers and influence. In sum, protocols based on expert panels are more likely to maintain medicine's traditional professional

prerogatives than protocols generated by primary research.

At first glance, it appears obvious that the advent of medical effectiveness research represents a serious challenge to medicine's professional status. The intent of AHCPR (and P.L. 101–239) to limit clinical discretion almost mandates such a conclusion. Such a threat appears all the more serious if the establishment of effectiveness research-based protocols are controlled by nonmedical interests—regardless of whether the research work itself is carried out by MDs. In these ways, protocols generated by effectiveness research, grounded as they are in the paradigm of science, represent a serious "external" threat to medicine's traditional practice of legitimating its work based on the notions of "usual and customary." Although the boundary between science and "nonscience" is itself ideologically based (Gieryn 1983), the arrival of medical effectiveness research raises the very real possibility that medicine's long-standing claim to a professional status based on its scientific expertise is about to be hoisted with its own petard.

On the other hand, advocates of effectiveness research argue that their mission is a scientifically neutral one and that the issue is not one of limiting physician discretion per se, but rather of removing ineffective and even dangerous options from the examining room (Raskin and Maklan 1991). Such protests aside, it appears clear that the payer-driven movement to assess effectiveness clearly threatens the autonomy of individual physicians. At the same time—and to the extent that effectiveness research involves the elimination of questionable and unscientific clinical practices—this overall trend may strengthen medicine's overall professional status by placing professional work on a more scientific footing. Thus, we are left with a paradox: the presence of less autonomy at the individual practitioner level along with a possibly stronger profession at the corporate

level—with the major impetus provided, ironically, by outside payers who unintentionally
have begun to rescue medicine from the
inner-directed and self-deceiving nature that
accompanies the attainment of autonomy.
Such speculation aside, it will be important to
keep a watchful eye on corporate initiatives to
place cost considerations at the core of their
efforts to evaluate health care practices
including outcomes. To the widely noted
fears that decisions about the content of
medical work may come to be dictated more
by matters of cost than by considerations of
technical appropriateness and quality (Relman 1987), we point out that establishing
indicators of cost-appropriateness is an
undertaking that does *not* reside within the
boundaries of medicine's technical expertise
and therefore is one that must remain vulnerable to the legitimate participation of
interests other than medical-professional.

PROFESSIONALISM
AND HEALTH POLICY

Matters of health policy and medicine's professional status must straddle two conflicting
views of professions: (1) professions as a type
of occupation whose activities reflect those of
a simple monopoly and whose main goal (as
revealed in social action rather than in
rhetoric) is to leverage their privileged status
for their own gain—and thus an occupational
group whose predilections require the need
for external control; or (2) professions as
institutions which function in the public
interest and for that reason should be preserved (Dingwall 1983). Twenty-five years ago
the prevailing observation was that medicine's successful quest for autonomy had rendered it incapable of regulating its work in
the public's interest as well as undertaking
any substantive remedial measures on its own
(Freidson 1970a, 1970b). More recently, this
conclusion has been supplanted by calls to
seat the professional model (stressing flexi-

bility and discretionary judgment) rather
than the bureaucratic model (stressing stan-
dardization and reliability) at the heart of
health care policy (Freidson 1994).

Calls to place professionalism rather than
bureaucracy at the core of health policy are
not new, but they do invite us to return to
several issues previously covered in this paper,
including the corrupting nature of discretionary work (e.g., autonomy's "critical
flaw"), medicine's historical inability to exercise control over its members, the need for
external reins to be placed over medicine's
autonomy, and the increasing differentiation
and stratification within the ranks of
medicine. While the ultimate goal of both
public policy and medical practice is to serve
that elusive "public good," the pursuit of that
goal appears increasingly to place medicine
and policy in antagonistic roles, particularly
around issues of clinical discretion.

Calls for policies that will nourish professionalism and strengthen the profession's collective commitment by encouraging things
such as peer review and the exercise of
internal controls (Freidson 1994) are steps in
the right direction, but one needs to
remember that peer review is something generated and supported within a system characterized by collegial-peer relationships. It is
not supported by a system composed of technical and administrative elites who function
to define and control the clinical work
carried out by the rank-and-file. As argued
earlier, there is no evidence to date suggesting that these new elites will share either
a core set of values in common with the rank-
and-file or values reflecting a fiduciary or
service orientation. At the same time, the
absence of administrative and knowledge
elites within the profession renders medicine
vulnerable to the incursions of "outside"
experts, individuals whose agendas may be
not only antagonistic to medicine but anti-
thetical to the necessary presence of discretion in medical work.

This paradox asks us to frame issues of health policy in a more inclusive fashion, particularly how policy can strengthen medicine's legitimate control over its technical core and strengthen its service orientation without encouraging the structural divisiveness that often accompanies the presence of a knowledge and/or administrative elite. The goal here is to resist pressures to distance the technical core of medical work from those asked to act on its behalf—the rank-and-file clinicians. As a related issue, health policy needs to keep a wary eye on the tendency of elites to extend medicine's dominance into realms of knowledge application rather than the more delimited domain of knowledge determination.

The connection between a service orientation and discretion over clinical activities is subtle but real. A service orientation defined by the presence of a uniform product translates the notion of service from something that entails responsiveness and flexibility into something that is more of a technical commodity. *As a first task then, policy experts must wrestle with the question of whether they consider discretion to reside at the core of medical work.* In part, this asks policymakers to reflect on the nature of medical work and on the role that uncertainty plays in that work. The goal may be to reduce uncertainty—as it is with medical effectiveness research (Raskin and Maklan 1991, forthcoming)— but the line between uncertainty and discretion is a fine one. Many of the protocols circulating today represent consensus, not science, and while consensus may provide us with uniformity, it also may hinder our ability to respond effectively to that which resides at either end of medicine's grand bell-shaped curve (Mechanic 1994).

But perhaps the maintenance of clinical discretion should not be defined as a key goal of policy? Perhaps decision making should rest more with the goals of uniformity, a hierarchy of rules, and with issues of cost. If so,

then we must begin to think of medicine not so much as a profession but as a technical undertaking. The gain will be uniformity, but at the cost of autonomy. In this respect, we must resign ourselves to being served by clinicians who are linked more by broadly established and technically oriented norms of practice (e.g., protocols) than by some more amorphous (and difficult to maintain) commitment to service and to addressing clinical problems at the individual patient level. Here we do not wish to lament some romanticized version of a "paradise lost" but rather to frame the question of how the nature of medical work is being altered fundamentally as issues of clinical discretion and autonomy become ideologically relegated to an increasingly small corner of the health care picture.

Whether current health policy will engender positive or negative consequences in these regards has yet to be seen or even reasonably predicted. One possibility is a health care system in which most of the problems of most of the people are handled routinely and expeditiously (whether the outcome be cure, alleviation, palliative maintenance, or death) but where unusual and/or nonroutine matters are handled in a less satisfactory manner. The issue is not so much one of disease complexity, limits to coverage, or restrictions governing treatment availability, but rather one of how strategies that limit clinical discretion (such as practice protocols or requirements for prior authorization) will alter the way physicians process clinical data, think about matters of health and disease, and act on the basis of that knowledge.

Health policy must become more anticipatory on a range of fronts and must keep an eye toward muting the inevitable presence of such unanticipated consequences. We suggest two principal "screens." The first screen would subject all health policy initiatives to the question of how that policy might have an impact on medicine's sense of community, of a distinctive mission, and on a sense of shared values. This first screen does not seek to promote medicine's hegemony so much as it does the reemergence of a service ethic and orientation within the medical ranks. Policies that fuel the divisive cracks of elitism within medicine and/or call for physicians to be "managed" run the risk of creating a hostile environment for the delivery of clinical services. The second screen asks how a particular policy might affect the discretion exercised by rank-and-file clinicians in the organization and delivery of their services. An example relating both screens is the degree to which rank-and-file clinicians are thought to play a central role in conducting effectiveness research and in the development of practice protocols. These are the individuals best able to assess the level and type of clinical uncertainty at the practice level. These also are the troops within which any esprit de corps must reside.

A related health policy trend that might benefit from the application of both screens is the effort to link malpractice immunity to the use of practice protocols. To date, such initiatives have appeared in several states including Maine, Minnesota, Oregon, New York, and Florida, with Maine's *Medical Liability Demonstration Project* being the most fully developed (Atchinson 1994; AHCPR 1994). While particulars vary by state, one underlying theme is the willingness of organized medicine to trade some aspect of its traditionally coveted autonomy for malpractice protection. A second feature of these initiatives is the general absence of direct references to an ethic of service and altruism. The overall topic of malpractice reform is a complicated one, touching upon territory claimed by two professions (law and medicine) and including issues of money and ego. Nonetheless, medicine's apparent eagerness to keep a critical distance from what it views as the onerous and stifling threat of external review, particularly as it involves

decision making by the public (the jury system along with the "court" of public opinion) provides us with some indication of the diminished sacredness of autonomy relative to the threat of malpractice in today's practice environment.

None of this is to suggest that health policy should hesitate to undertake initiatives to restructure inequities or imbalances in the organization and delivery of health services, including issues of geographic and specialty maldistribution. If too many specialists are skewing the delivery picture, then steps should be taken to rectify the situation. Similarly, none of this should be interpreted as a suggestion that health policy must undertake specific efforts to ensure medicine's hegemony over other health occupations or domains that do not fall within the narrow limits of medicine's technical expertise. As we have already suggested, conflict at the "outposts" may prove to be more facilitative than disabling in developing core knowledge about matters of health and disease as well as in implementing that knowledge. Nonetheless, neither the public nor medicine itself is well served by health policies that move to expand medicine's control over matters—particularly matters of knowledge application—rightly retained by the public. In this respect, health policy needs to evaluate its own tendency to blithely accept medicine's claims of expertise as well as its own proactive tendency to contribute to the general medicalization of society (Conrad 1992).

The pendulum of medicine's status as a profession may have swung more to the side of avarice than altruism, but medicine can never return to its promise of placing the public's interests ahead of its own so long as policymakers create an incentive structure that treats—and thus defines—professionals as economically motivated entities. This is not to argue that economic incentives are not an effective or rational vehicle for change. But, policy that treats physician behavior as economically determined will play a role in creating such a beast.

The alternative is to create policy that maximizes a profession's leanings toward the values of service and altruism. Pollyannish sentiments aside, we can begin by structuring health policy, particularly policy dealing with matters of quality, to emphasize the presence of a necessary partnership between rank-and-file physicians (as opposed to administrative and technical elites) and the public at large. This is not a new suggestion, but it is one that needs constant repetition and reinforcement.

Relatedly, if an emphasis on accountability can be raised as a counterbalance to that of autonomy, if clinical practice can be placed within the larger context of prevention, early intervention, self-management, and interprofessional programs for managing chronic problems, perhaps medicine and society will be the better for it. But the policy question is, whose ends will this serve? At the moment, the balance among countervailing powers is shifting rapidly toward insurers and managed care corporations. They are supposed to be the agents of payers/buyers, but they seem most bent on establishing market share and on maximizing profits. Furthermore, competitive markets mean that cost-shifting and favorable selection are the easiest ways to make money and win contracts. One needs long-term subscriber contracts for managed competition and for the medical profession to be harnessed to the interests of patients. The policy danger is that the medical profession will go from being the seduced handmaiden of corporate purveyors of medical technologies and pharmacologies as elaborate clinical interventions, to being the kidnapped handmaiden of corporations making money by *limiting* clinical interventions. The object of policy efforts is to establish incentives and constraints that balance the countervailing powers in health care so that they serve to benefit society and its members.

CONCLUSIONS: A CONCEPTUAL AND RESEARCH AGENDA FOR MEDICAL SOCIOLOGY

From the very outset, a sociological fascination with professions was grounded in the anticipation that this organizational type would function (hopefully) to buffer the public from the abuses of state powers and the unrelenting march of bureaucratic rationalism. These early hopes faded as it became obvious that the attainment of professional status was accompanied by monopolistic tendencies, organizational insularity, and a loss of service orientation.

In the twenty-first century, sociologists need to reevaluate the concept of profession, including the dynamics of professionalism and the nature of professional work. Over the past century, the notions that professions embodied a core of technical expertise and represented a service orientation have stood at the center of sociological discussions about these matters. Over the past 25 years it has become increasingly obvious that medicine's claims in both of these regards have contained as much rhetoric as fact. So, where do we go from here?

We need to rethink whether autonomy should remain the pivotal issue in understanding professional dynamics. Driven by medicine's abuse of its prerogatives, its failure to control its own work, and by the revolt of the buyers, we now find the notion of accountability appearing forcefully alongside the more traditional view that esoteric knowledge and technical expertise legitimate exemption from outside review. The emergence of a movement to better establish effectiveness and quality in clinical services offers medicine the hope that its work can be placed more squarely on the altar of scientific rationality, but at the risk of incursions by outside experts into its domain. In addition, the arrival of practice guidelines and protocols may well facilitate medicine's loss of control over clinical activities to other kinds of providers. As sociologists, we need to explore aggressively how the concepts of clinical discretion and autonomy can coexist with that of accountability, as well as how undesirable and unanticipated consequences may come to dominate the quest for greater rationality in health care services.

A related issue involves the concept of medical uncertainty and the presence of ambiguity in medical work. Both themes have a long tradition within medical sociological circles. The former is linked closely to the work of Renee Fox (1980) and the latter with the writings of Robert Merton and Elinor Barber (1976). Sociologists need to examine how the notions of science and uncertainty are being created by, as well as driving, effectiveness research and how these assumptions are related to issues of health, disease, and medical work. While the goal of effectiveness research is to make medicine less governed by custom and tradition, it is also true that the growth of this discipline, along with the deployment of clinical guidelines, will develop its own normative structure accompanied by its own taken-for-granted assumptions about the nature of things. While individual assessments may sparkle with data that are reliable and valid, the overall process is not immune to developing its own myths about its objectivity and the superior nature of its approach to overcoming the ambiguities embedded in clinical decision making. Sociologists can monitor this process. At the very least, sociologists can point out that the goal of reducing the amount of "unnecessary" variability in clinical practice need not lead to the reduction of uncertainty in medical work. There is also the issue of whether the elimination of uncertainty is an attainable or appropriate vision for guiding research on health care and disease. Sociologists are aptly positioned to question whether advances in scientific knowledge will reduce

the amount of uncertainty present in a system or whether such advances will create a new arena of uncertainty. The challenge for both sociologists and policymakers is not to make medicine more scientific—that will happen, for better *and* for worse—but to understand whether this latest push to rationalize medicine will cause us to expect too much from effectiveness research and at the same time cause us to neglect a more fundamental challenge in health care: how the restoration of an ethic of service and altruism can accompany medicine's reenergized scientific engine. The real danger will be in equating a "greatly improved product" (clinical services) with the existence of a service orientation as if the presence of the former establishes or guarantees the latter. The development of knowledge and the application of that knowledge are two different things. The former is a technical matter that belongs within the domain of science and medicine. The latter resides in a more social domain and should be controlled by the public.

A sociological research agenda on the dynamics of professionalism and the changing nature of medical work should reflect and inform the above issues. Work by Montgomery (1990, 1992) on physician executives and their orientations toward work should be replicated and extended. The number of physician executives has grown dramatically since Montgomery conducted her research a decade ago. But our understanding about who becomes a physician executive, following what career paths, with what role expectations and strains, and with what implications for the structuring and control of medical work has not kept pace. Perhaps the resocialization Montgomery found was more the product of a nascent occupational group than of a fundamental transformation in the value climate of physicians-turned-administrators? Currently, we lack the data to address these issues. Similar questions need to be asked about the careers and work of the new knowledge elite emerging from within the ranks of medicine, particularly those who study clinical effectiveness and quality and, thus, those who set the standards that will govern the way medicine is practiced in the future. The values that guide their work are not clear, and ascertaining whether these elite labor to enhance a corporate rather than a professional service orientation would be an important dimension of any inquiry.

Moving our focus from matters of internal dynamics to medicine's periphery, sociologists need to develop a clearer understanding of the regulatory environment in which medicine operates, both from the bottom up and from the top down. Beginning on the shop floor, we need to look more closely at how the various rules and regulations that emanate from government and corporate purchasers actually impact on the delivery of clinical services in the examining room and at the bedside. Exactly what is changing in the way services are being delivered at the provider-patient level? Similarly, we need to examine what countervailing steps are being taken by practitioners to dampen, modify, or otherwise shape the impact of these regulations. We need a framework for understanding which influences are being formed as "beneficial" versus "detrimental," by whom, and to what ends. We also need a better understanding of how rules governing medical work, including protocols and guidelines, reach the physician and, for example, whether attaching reimbursement to their use plays a role in how physicians respond to them. In addressing all of these issues, a commitment to conducting fieldwork in clinical settings will play a critical role. Moving to a macrolevel, we need a better assessment of the overall regulatory environment that surrounds medicine. Following the lead of Friedman (1965), we need

to establish the degree of licensing legislation that is favorable to medicine as a profession (e.g., "friendly") versus legislation that seeks to regulate the behaviors of both the profession as a corporate entity and as individual practitioners (e.g., "hostile"). We also need to be sensitive to major shifts in that balance in order to ascertain the direction of change, if any.

Relatedly, we need to examine the changing nature of medical work as it is reconfigured across the various health occupations. The rise of the clinical nurse specialist and the expanding of clinical responsibilities for nurse practitioners and physician assistants have implications for the professional status of medicine. Like medicine, other health occupations are becoming highly stratified. The ability of other providers to establish a common value system and sense of community has implications for their ability to mount an effective challenge to medicine's hegemony. We need to examine their own internal dynamics as well as how these occupational groups are positioning themselves relative to other players in the health care sector.

Finally, although this paper has focused on the medical profession in the United States, a better understanding of professionalism, the interplay of state, professional, and corporate interests, and the broader dynamics of countervailing powers can only occur in the presence of an appreciable and sustained cross-national focus. Work done to date represents an important beginning, but one that has been more focused on industrialized countries and major world powers. Less well understood, and in many cases completely unexamined, is the organization of medical work and the dynamics of professionalism in Third World and developing countries in Africa, Central and South America, Asia, and the Pacific Rim. What is the nature of state, professional, and corporate relations in these countries? More importantly, how do notions of expertise and altruism intersect in different political, social, and economic environments?

Within this litany of conceptual issues and research agendas, the key challenge is how to organize expert knowledge in the service of public problems, and how the dynamics of professionalism and the changing content of medical work can best be directed to this end.

NOTES

1. Notable examples include Abbott (1988), Heidenheimer (1989), Wilsford (1991), and edited volumes by Jones (1991), Hafferty and McKinlay (1993), and Johnson, Larkin, and Saks (1995). Works in progress include Krause's (1995) study of professions in five countries and Freidson's (1995) forthcoming look at five professions across five countries.

2. As an imperfect analogy, one might imagine a tetrahedron (or larger polyhedron) with cables stretching from each corner to a central ring. Each cable is attached to a winch at the corner, and the parties or institutions so situated work with more or less energy to crank the ring toward them. Any given location of the ring defines the current relations among the countervailing powers but the ring remains in tension, even at dead center. The closer the ring is to one corner or another, the more difficult it becomes for individual parties to pull the ring back—but also the more likely it is that their combined efforts, however individually motivated, will have a systemwide effect of moving the ring away from the currently dominant position.

3. Between 1916 and 1971 medicine expanded from a single specialty (ophthalmology) to a body composed of the interests of 22 specialty organizations. Over the next 20 years, however, this number would more than triple. By 1992, the Accreditation Council for Graduate Medical Education (ACGME), one of the two major accrediting bodies, had recognized a total of 25 specialties and 56 subspecialties with the majority of these subspecialties (35/36) receiving their accreditation since 1987. Similarly, the American Board of Medical Specialties (ABMS) now recognizes 70 subspecialty

areas with 40 of these being approved since 1980, and 13 of them since 1990. In addition, both organizations have an ongoing log of pending applications (Martini 1992). So great was this proliferation that, in 1992, the ACGME established a one-year moratorium on new specialties and subspecialties. Although subspecialty incomes are beginning to weaken (Mitka 1994; Page 1994) and while medical school graduates are beginning to show increased interest in generalist residency programs (Kassebaum and Szenas 1994), subspecialty medicine remains well entrenched within organized medicine.

4. For example, in June of 1992, the AMA House of Delegates voted to ignore the recommendations of the AMA's Board of Trustees and the AMA's Council on Ethical and Judicial Affairs and reverse its own six-month ban on physicians referring patients to facilities in which they have a financial interest. Instead, the House of Delegates voted 216 to 210 to recommend (but not require) that physicians inform patients of ownership interests and post their fees (Burton 1992; Pearson et al. 1992).

5. These pieces of legislation are widely known as Stark I and Stark II. There is also a proposed Stark III bill currently that would extend earlier and more limited self-referral provisions to all payers and all services (see Johnson 1994).

6. Examples of between-group struggles include physical therapy and chiropractic over who can undertake "rehabilitation" and who can do "manipulation" (physical therapy claiming the former and chiropractic the latter but each eyeing the other's turf); struggles between nursing and pharmacy over the right to prescribe medicine and make diagnostic determinations; and similar turf wars between optometrists and ophthalmologists, psychiatrists and clinical psychologists, and podiatrists and orthopedists, among others.

7. Plan and network managers contend that such a provision would severely restrict their right to hire only the best (e.g., cost-effective) providers, thus limiting their ability to compete effectively in the health care marketplace.

8. Freidson posited that the mandate or right to be the exclusive judge of one's own work leads over time to a dysfunctional and corrupting isolation in which the group in question "inevitably"

develops "a distorted view of itself, its knowledge, and its mission" (1970b). This insulation from external review leads to (1) the construction of "sanctimonious myths" about its superior qualities; (2) a self-deceiving view of the objectivity and reliability of its knowledge base. What ensues is a "self-deceiving" callousness and insincerity in which attitudes toward clientele become "at best patronizing and at worst contemptuous" (Freidson 1970a: 370); and (3) an increasing inability and unwillingness on the part of the professional group to regulate itself in the public interest, including the incapability of the group to undertake any substantive remedial measures on its own. All of this led Freidson to conclude that necessary controls must come from outside the profession—a step that would include restricting the dominant profession's control over areas "for which its competence does not equip it, *areas including the regulation of the profession itself*" (Freidson 1970a: 372, emphasis ours).

9. Physician executives are organized under the banner of the American College of Physician Executives. No comparable organization exists for physician researchers, who are organized more by substantive area rather than type of work.

REFERENCES

ABBOTT, ANDREW. 1988. *The System of Professions: An Essay on the Division of Expert Labor.* Chicago, IL: University of Chicago Press.

AGENCY FOR HEALTH CARE POLICY AND RESEARCH. 1994. *Medical Effectiveness Research, Clinical Practice Guidelines, and Practice Pattern Profiling: Implications for State Government: A Workshop for Senior State Officials.* U.S. Public Health Service, Agency for Health Care Policy and Research, Center for Research Dissemination and Liaison, User Liaison Program.

AMERICAN MEDICAL ASSOCIATION. 1994. *Code of Medical Ethics: Current Opinions with Annotations.* Chicago, IL: American Medical Association.

ATCHINSON, BRIAN K. 1994. "Maine Medical Liability Demonstration Project." *Medical Effectiveness Research, Clinical Practice Guidelines, and Practice Pattern Profiling: Implications for State Government: A Workshop for Senior State Officials in Washington, D.C.*, U.S. Public Health Service, Agency for Health Care Policy and Research.

BARONDESS, JEREMIAH A. 1993. "The Future of Generalism." *Annals of Internal Medicine* 119: 153–60.

BLEDSTEIN, BURTON. 1976. *The Culture of Professionalism.* New York: W.W. Norton.

BOSK, CHARLES L. 1980. "Occupational Rituals in Patient Management." *New England Journal of Medicine* 303:71–76.

BROOK, ROBERT H. and KATHLEEN N. LOHR. 1985. "Efficiency, Effectiveness, Variations, and Quality: Boundary Crossing Research." *Medical Care* 23(5):710–22.

BROUILLETTE, J. N. 1991. "Grading is Degrading: Doctors' Report Card." *Journal of the Florida Medical Association* 78(1):37–38.

BROWN, E. RICHARD. 1979. *Rockefeller Medicine Men: Medicine and Capitalism in America.* Berkeley, CA: University of California Press.

BURTON, THOMAS M. 1992. "Physicians Who Own Labs May Refer Patients to Them for Tests AMA Says." *Wall Street Journal,* June 24, p. B6.

CARR-SAUNDERS, ALEXANDER M. 1928. *Professions: Their Organization and Place in Society.* Oxford, England: The Clarendon Press.

CARR-SAUNDERS, ALEXANDER M. and PAUL A. WILSON. 1933. *The Professions.* Oxford, England: The Clarendon Press.

CASTRO, JANICE. 1994. *The American Way of Health.* Boston, MA: Little, Brown, and Company.

CHAMPION, FRANK D. 1984. *The AMA and U.S. Health Policy.* Chicago, IL: Chicago Review Press.

CHENE, ARTHUR R. 1986. "Hospital Privileges: Speak Softly, But Carry a Big Lawyer." *Connecticut Medicine* 50(8):541–43.

CONRAD, PETER. 1992. "Medicalization and Social Control." *Annual Review of Sociology* 18:209–32.

DEACONSON, TIMOTHY F., DANIEL P. O'HAIR, MARLON F. LEVY, MARTHA B. LEE, ARTHUR L. SCHUENEMAN, and ROBERT E. CONDON. 1988. "Sleep Deprivation and Resident Performance." *JAMA* 260(12):1721–27.

DENT, THOMAS L. 1991. "Training, Credentialing, and Granting of Clinical Privileges for Laparoscopic General Surgery." *American Journal of Surgery* 161(3):399–403.

DINGWALL, ROBERT. 1983. *The Sociology of the Professions.* New York: St. Martin's.

DURKHEIM, EMILE. [1902] 1933. *The Division of Labor in Society.* New York: Macmillan.

EISENBERG, DAVID M., RONALD C. KESSLER, CINDY FOSTER, FRANCES E. NORLOCK, DAVID R. CALKINS, and THOMAS L. DELBANCO. 1993. "Unconventional Medicine in the United States: Prevalence, Costs, and Patterns of Use." *The New England Journal of Medicine* 328(4):246–52.

FEDER, BARNABY, J. 1993. "Medical Groups Battle to be Heard Over Others on Health-Care Changes." *New York Times,* June 11, p. A22.

FIELD, MARK G. 1988. "The Position of the Soviet Physician: The Bureaucratic Professional." *Milbank Quarterly* 66 (Suppl. 2): 182–201.

———. 1993. "The Physician in the Commonwealth of Independent States: The Difficult Passage from Bureaucrat to Professional." Pp. 162–171 in *The Changing Medical Profession: An International Perspective,* edited by F. W. Hafferty and J. B. McKinlay. New York: Oxford University Press.

FOX, RENEE C. 1980. "The Evolution of Medical Uncertainty." *Milbank Memorial Fund Quarterly* 58(1):1–49.

FREIDSON, ELIOT. 1968. "The Impurity of Professional Authority." Pp. 25–34 in *Institutions and the Person,* edited by H. S. Becker, B. Geer, D. S. Riesman, and R. S. Weiss. Chicago, IL: Aldine de Gruyter.

———. 1970a. *Profession of Medicine: A Study of the Sociology of Applied Knowledge.* New York: Harper & Row.

———. 1970b. *Professional Dominance: The Social Structure of Medical Care.* New York: Atherton Press.

———. 1975. *Doctoring Together.* New York: Elsevier.

———. 1983. "The Theory of Professions: State of the Art." Pp. 19–37 in *The Sociology of Professions, Lawyers, Doctors, and Others,* edited by R. Dingwall and P. Lewis. London, England: Macmillan.

———. 1984. "The Changing Nature of Professional Control." *Annual Review of Sociology* 10:1–20.

———. 1985. "The Reorganization of the Medical Profession." *Medical Care Review* 42:11–35.

———. 1986a. "The Medical Profession in Transition." Pp. 63–79 in *Applications of Social Science to Clinical Medicine and Health Policy,* edited by L. Aiken and D. Mechanic. New Brunswick, NJ: Rutgers University Press.

———. 1986b. *Professional Powers: A Study of the Institutionalization of Formal Knowledge.* Chicago, IL: University of Chicago Press.

———. 1987. "The Future of the Professions." *Journal of Dental Education* 53:140–44.

———. 1989. *Medical Work in America: Essays on Health Care.* New Haven, CT: Yale University Press.

———. 1994. *Professionalism Reborn: Theory, Prophecy, and Policy.* Chicago, IL: University of Chicago Press.

———. 1995. *The Fate of Knowledge.* Cambridge, England: Polity Press.

FRIEDMAN, LAWRENCE M. 1965. Freedom of Contract and Occupational Licensing, 1890–1910: A Legal and Social Study. *California Law Review* 53:487–534.

GIERYN, THOMAS F. 1983. "Boundary-Work and the Demarcation of Science from Non-Science: Strains and Interests in Professional Ideologies of Scientists." *American Sociological Review* 48:781–94.

GOODE, WILLIAM J. 1957. "Community Within a Community: The Professions—Psychology, Sociology, and Medicine." *American Sociological Review* 25:902–14.

GOTT, VINCENT L. 1993. "RBRVS and Cardiothoracic Surgery." *Annals of Thoracic Surgery* 55(1):5.

HAFFERTY, FREDERIC W. 1988. "Theories at the Crossroads: A Discussion of Evolving Views on Medicine as a Profession." *Milbank Quarterly* 66 (Suppl. 2):202–25.

———. 1991. "Trust Ideology and Professional Power." Paper presented at the 86th Annual Meeting of the American Sociological Association, August 23–27, Cincinnati, OH.

———. 1995. "Global Perspectives on Health Care." Pp. 231–43 in *Lessons from Some Cross-National Case Studies,* edited by E. B. Gallagher and J. Subedi. Englewood Cliffs, NJ: Prentice Hall.

HAFFERTY, FREDERIC W. and JOHN B. MCKINLAY. 1993. *The Changing Medical Profession: An Inter-*

national Perspective. New York: Oxford University Press.

HAFFERTY, FREDERIC W. and JEFFREY C. SALLOWAY. 1993. "The Evolution of Medicine as a Profession: A Seventy-Five Year Perspective." *Minnesota Medicine* 76(1):26–35.

HAFFERTY, FREDERIC W. and FREDRIC D. WOLINSKY. 1991. "Conflicting Characterizations of Professional Dominance." Pp. 225–49 in *Current Research on Occupations and Professions*, edited by J. Levy. Greenwich, CT: JAI Press.

HALL, MIMI. 1993. "Clinton Tells AMA Task Force is no Place for Special Interests." *USA Today*, March 5, p. A6.

HALPERN, SYDNEY. 1988. *American Pediatrics: The Social Dynamics of Professionalism, 1880–1980.* Berkeley, CA: University of California Press.

———. 1992. "Dynamics of Professional Control: Internal Coalitions and Cross-professional Boundaries." *American Journal of Sociology* 97(4):994–1021.

HAUG, MARIE R. 1973. "Deprofessionalization: An Alternative Hypothesis for the Future." *Sociological Review Monographs* 20:195–211.

———. 1975. "The Deprofessionalization of Everyone?" *Sociological Focus* 8:197–213.

———. 1988. "A Reexamination of the Hypothesis of Physician Deprofessionalization." *Milbank Quarterly* 66 (Suppl. 2):28–56.

HAUG, MARIE R. and BEBE LAVIN. 1978. "Methods of Payment for Medical Care and Public Attitudes Toward Physician Authority." *Journal of Health and Social Behavior* 19:279–91.

HEIDENHEIMER, ARNOLD J. 1989. "Professional Knowledge and State Policy in Comparative Historical Perspective: Law and Medicine in Britain, Germany, and the United States." *International Social Science Journal* 41:529–53.

HEITLINGER, ALENA. 1991. "Hierarchy of Status and Prestige within the Medical Profession." Pp. 207–32 in *Professions and the State: Expertise and Autonomy in the Soviet Union and Eastern Europe,* edited by A. T. Jones. Philadelphia, PA: Temple University Press.

———. 1993. "The Medical Profession in Czechoslovakia: Legacies of State Socialism, Prospects for the Capitalist Future." Pp. 172–83 in *The Changing Medical Profession: An Internal Perspective,* edited by F. W. Hafferty

and J. B. McKinlay. New York: Oxford University Press.

HENDERSON, GAIL. 1993. "Physicians in China: Assessing the Impact of Ideology and Organization." Pp. 184–94 in *The Changing Medical Profession: An International Perspective,* edited by F. W. Hafferty and J. B. McKinlay. New York: Oxford University Press.

HSIAO, WILLIAM C., PETER BRAUN, DANIEL L. DUNN, and EDMUND R. BECKER. 1988. "Resource-Based Relative Values: An Overview." *JAMA* 260:2347–53.

———. 1992. "Resource-Based Relative Value Scale: An Overview." *JAMA* 260:2347–353.

IRVING, CARL. 1993. "National HMO Report Card in Works." *San Francisco Chronicle,* June 13, p. A6.

JOHNSON, JULIE. 1994. "First Federal Salvo Against Doctor Incomes." *American Medical News,* October 3, Pp. 3, 32.

JOHNSON, TERRANCE J. 1972. *Professions and Power.* London, England: Macmillan.

JOHNSON, TERRY, GERRY LARKIN, and MIKE SAKS. 1995. *Health Professions and the State in Europe.* London, England: Routledge.

JONES, ANTHONY. 1991. *Professions and the State: Expertise and Autonomy in the Soviet Union and Eastern Europe.* Philadelphia, PA: Temple University Press.

KASSEBAUM, DONALD G. and PHILIP L. SZENAS. 1994. "Graduates Interest in Generalist Specialties Rises For a Second Year." *Academic Physician and Scientist* (November):2–3.

KELLY, AMALIA, FRANCES MARKS, CAROLYN WESTHOFF, and MORTIMER ROSEN. 1991. "The Effect of the New York State Restrictions on Resident Work Hours." *Obstetrics and Gynecology* 78(3 Pt. 1): 468–73.

KELLY, JOHN T. and MARGARET C. TOEPP. 1994. "Practice Parameters: More than 1,500 Have Been Developed Since 1989 and More Are in the Works." *Michigan Medicine* 93(3):36–40.

KONOLD, DONALD E. 1962. *A History of American Medical Ethics 1847–1912.* Madison, WI: The State Historical Society of Wisconsin.

KRAUSE, ELIOT. 1995. Death of the Guilds: Professions, States, and the Advance of Capitalism—1930 to the Present. New Haven, CT: Yale University Press.

LARSON, MAGDALI S. 1977. *The Rise of Professionalism: A Sociological Analysis.* Berkeley, CA: University of California Press.

LETTERS TO THE EDITOR. 1993. *New England Journal of Medicine* 329(16):1200–204.

LIGHT, DONALD W. 1979. "Uncertainty and Control in Professional Training." *Journal of Health and Social Behavior* 20:310–22.

———. 1988. "Towards a New Sociology of Medical Education." *Journal of Health and Social Behavior* 29:307–22.

———. 1989. "Social Control and the American Health Care System." Pp. 456–74 in *Handbook of Medical Sociology*, 4th ed., edited by H. E. Freeman and S. Levine. Englewood Cliffs, NJ: Prentice Hall.

———. 1991. "The Restructuring of American Health Care." Pp. 53–65 in *Health Politics and Policy*, 2d ed., edited by T. Litman and L. Robins. New York: Wiley.

———. 1993. "Countervailing Power: The Changing Character of the Medical Profession in the United States." Pp. 69–79 in *The Changing Medical Profession: An International Perspective*, edited by F. W. Hafferty and J. B. McKinlay. New York: Oxford University Press.

———. 1995. "Countervailing Powers: A Framework for Professions in Transition." Pp. 25–41 in *Health Professions and the State in Europe*, edited by T. Johnson, G. Larkin, and M. Saks. New York: Routledge.

LUCE, JOHN M., ANDREW B. BINDMAN, and PHILIP R. LEE. 1994. "A Brief History of Health Care Quality Assessment and Improvement in the United States." *Western Journal of Medicine* 160(3):263–68.

MAIER, THOMAS. 1994. "Hospital 'Report Cards' to be Made Public for First Time." *Los Angeles Times*, October 25, p. D2.

MARTINI, CARLOS J. M. 1992. "Graduate Medical Education in the Changing Environment of Medicine." *JAMA* 268(9):1097–105.

MAULE, WILLIAM FOREST. 1993. "Screening for Colorectal Cancer by Nurse Endoscopists." *New England Journal of Medicine* 330(3):183–87.

McCOMBS, PHIL. 1993. "A Delicate Operation: The AMA's James Todd Steps Up to the Table in the Health Care Debate." *Washington Post*, February 4, p. C1.

McKINLAY, JOHN B. 1973. "On the Professional Regulation of Change." *Sociological Review Monographs* 20:61–84.

———. 1977. "The Business of Good Doctoring or Doctoring as Good Business: Reflections on Freidson's View of the Medical Game." *International Journal of Health Services* 7(30):459–87.

———. 1988. "The Changing Character of the Medical Profession: Introduction." *Milbank Quarterly* 66 (Suppl. 2):1–19.

McKINLAY, JOHN B. and JOAN ARCHES. 1985. "Towards the Proletarianization of Physicians." *International Journal of Health Services* 15:161–95.

McKINLAY, JOHN B. and JOHN D. STOECKLE. 1988. "Corporatization and the Social Transformation of Doctoring." *International Journal of Health Services* 18(2):191–205.

MECHANIC, DAVID. 1991. "Sources of Countervailing Power in Medicine." *Journal of Health Politics, Policy, and Law* 16:485–98.

———. 1994. "Managed Care: Rhetoric and Realities." *Inquiry* 31:124–28.

MERTON, ROBERT K. and ELINOR BARBER. 1976. "Sociological Ambivalence." Pp. 3–31 in *Social Ambivalence and Other Essays*, edited by R. K. Merton. New York: Free Press.

MILLENSON, MICHAEL L. 1993. "Report Cards on Health Care." *Chicago Tribune*, December 31, p. 1.

MILLMAN, MARCIA. 1977. *The Unkindest Cut: Life in the Backrooms of Medicine.* New York: William-Morrow.

MITCHELL, JEAN M. and ELTON SCOTT. 1992. "Physician Ownership of Physical Therapy Services: Effects on Charges, Utilization, Profits, and Service Characteristics." *JAMA* 268(15):2055–59.

MITKA, MIKE. 1994. "Higher Pay for Primary Care: Group Practice Salary Survey Shows Declines, Smaller Raises for Specialties." *American Medical News*, October 3, Pp. 3, 6–7.

MONTGOMERY, KATHLEEN. 1990. "A Prospective Look at the Specialty of Medical Management." *Work and Occupations* 17(2):178–98.

———. 1992. "Professional Dominance and the Threat of Corporatization." Pp. 221–40 in *Current Research on Occupations and Professions*, vol. 7, edited by J. Levy. Greenwich, CT: JAI Press.

NEUS, ELIZABETH. 1992. "Doctors' Health Plan Includes Caps on Fees." *USA Today,* September 15, p. A1.

PAGE, LEIGH. 1994. "Early Signs of a Shakeout: Specialists Face the Future." *American Medical News* 37(37):1, 7–8.

PARSONS, TALCOTT. 1939. "The Professions and Social Structure." *Social Forces* 17:457–67.

———. 1951. "Social Structure and Dynamic Process: The Case of Modern Medical Practice." Pp. 428–79 in *The Social Structure,* edited by T. Parsons. Glencoe, IL: Free Press.

———. 1954. *Essays in Sociological Theory.* New York: Free Press.

PEAR, ROBERT. 1993. "White House Shuns Bigger AMA Voice in Health Changes." *New York Times,* March 5, p. A1.

PEARSON, RICK, MIKE CAMPBELL, MICHAEL L. MILLENSON, and ALEXEI MARRIONUEVO. 1992. "AMA Softens 'Self-Referral' Stance." *Chicago Tribune,* June 21, Sec 3, p. 1.

PELBERG, ARTHUR L. 1989. "Credentialing: A Current Perspective and Legal Background." *Quality Assurance and Utilization Review* 4(1):8–13.

PRIEST, DANA. 1992. "AMA Delegates Spar Over Self-Referral." *Washington Post.* December 7, p. A11.

———. 1993. "AMA Seeks Voice on Health Care Task Force." *Washington Post,* March 4, p. A8.

RASKIN, IRA E. and CLAIRE W. MAKLAN. 1991. "Medical Treatment Effectiveness Research: A View From Inside the Agency for Health Care Policy and Research." *Evaluation and the Health Professions* (June): 161–86.

———. Forthcoming. "Outcomes Research: Early Findings and Lessons of Experience." *Annual Public Health Review.*

RELMAN, ARNOLD. 1980. "The New Medical-Industrial Complex." *New England Journal of Medicine* 303:963–70.

———. 1987. "Practicing Medicine in the New Business Climate." *New England Journal of Medicine* 316:1150–51.

———. 1991. "Shattuck Lecture—The Health Care Industry: Where is it Taking Us?" *New England Journal of Medicine* 325(12):854–59.

RIVO, MARC L., DEBBIE M. JACKSON, and LAWRENCE CLARE. 1993. "Comparing Physician Work Force Recommendations." *JAMA* 270(9):1083–84.

ROSS, EDWARD A. [1901] 1969. *Social Control: A Survey of the Foundations of Order.* Cleveland, OH: The Press of Case Western Reserve University.

SCHWARTZ, ANNE, PAUL B. GINSBURG, and LAUREN B. LEROY. 1993. "Reforming Graduate Medical Education: Summary Report of the Physician Payment Review Commission." *JAMA* 270(9): 1079–82.

SCOTT, ELTON and JEAN M. MITCHELL. 1994. "Ownership of Clinical Laboratories by Referring Physicians: Effects on Utilization, Charges, and Profitability." *Medical Care* 32(2):164–74.

SHARFSTEIN, JOSHUA M. and STEVEY S. SHARFSTEIN. 1994. "Campaign Contributions from the American Medical Political Action Committee to Members of Congress. For or Against the Public Health." *New England Journal of Medicine* 330(1):32–37.

SHRYOCK, RICHARD HARRISON. 1967. *Medical Licensing in America, 1650–1965.* Baltimore, MD: Johns Hopkins University Press.

SORELLE, RUTH. 1993. "Gore Warns AMA that Doctors Won't Dominate Health Reforms." *Houston Chronicle,* March 25, p. A5.

STARR, PAUL E. 1982. *The Social Transformation of American Medicine: The Rise of a Sovereign Profession and the Making of a Vast Industry.* New York: Basic Books.

STEVENS, ROSEMARY. 1971. *American Medicine and the Public Interest.* New Haven, CT: Yale University Press.

THOMPSON, FRANK. 1981. *Health Policy and the Bureaucracy: Policies and Implementation.* Boston, MA: MIT Press.

VAN, JON. 1989. "Study of Doctor Training Says Long Hours Must End." *Chicago Tribune,* February 10, p. 1:13.

WAITZKIN, HOWARD D. and BARBARA WATERMAN. 1974. *The Exploitation of Illness in a Capitalist Society.* Indianapolis, IN: Bobbs-Merrill.

WEBER, MAX. 1952. *The Protestant Ethic and Spirit of Capitalism.* New York: Scribner.

———. 1968. *Economy and Society: An Outline of Interpretive Sociology,* vols. 1–3. New York: Bedminster.

WEINER, JONATHAN P. 1994. "Forecasting the Effects of Health Reform on U.S. Work Force Require-

ments: Evidence from HMO Staffing Patterns."
JAMA 272(3):222–30.

WERNER, ELLIOT B. 1992. "Ophthalmologists Lose Big Under RBRVS." *Archives of Ophthalmology* 110(9):1200.

WILSFORD, DAVID. 1991. *Doctors and the State: The Politics of Health Care in France and the United States.* Durham, NC: Duke University Press.

WINSLOW, RON. 1994. "Health: Health-Care Report Cards are Getting Low Grades From Some Focus Groups." *Wall Street Journal,* May 19, p. B1.

WOLINSKY, FREDRIC D. 1988. "The Professional Dominance Perspective, Revisited." *Milbank Quarterly* 66 (Suppl. 2):33–47.

ZHOU, XUEGUANG. 1993. "Occupational Power, State Capacities, and the Diffusion of Licensing in the American States: 1890–1950." *American Sociological Review* 58:536–52.

GENDER AND THE BODY OF MEDICINE OR AT LEAST SOME BODY PARTS: (RE)CONSTRUCTING THE PRESTIGE HIERARCHY OF MEDICAL SPECIALTIES

Susan W. Hinze
Case Western Reserve University

Understanding the disproportionate location of women physicians in lower-status medical specialties necessitates knowing how women and men view the prestige hierarchy of specialties. Previous research on status ranking has been largely quantitative and based upon male respondents. Using narratives from face-to-face interviews with male and female resident physicians, this study finds that, although residents are fairly consistent in their rankings, women were more likely to resist the concept of a prestige hierarchy. In addition to explicit dimensions conferring prestige are implicit justifications grounded in the physician's body. Specifically, high prestige is associated with active interventionist hands and "balls," body parts that I argue are not gender neutral. The findings shift the focus from individual-level gender differences toward a gendered examination of the medical specialty hierarchy. The physicians interviewed here give voice to the silent, symbolic, embodied work of gender that shapes the structure of medical specialties into a ladder with a masculine top and a feminine bottom, regardless of whether male or female bodies occupy the rungs.

The concept of a prestige hierarchy of occupations is generally well documented (Blau and Duncan 1967). Most members of society agree that certain occupations deserve higher status and compensation because of their greater value to society, longer training periods, and difficult or complex skills (Davis and Moore 1945). Intraoccupational hierarchies exist as well. For example, in academia, physicists are generally accorded more respect, status, and compensation than, say, sociologists. Corporate lawyers are more esteemed than public defenders. And surgeons are "kings" in medicine, while pediatricians and psychiatrists vie for the bottom rungs of the ladder.

Feminist scholars, among others, have examined why women more often than men find themselves on the lowest rungs of occupational hierarchies. Research on general occupational sex segregation is voluminous (e.g., Bielby and Baron 1986; Jacobs 1989), and recently much attention has been paid to hierarchical or vertical segregation within occupations and occupational categories (Pavalko 1988; Reskin and Roos 1990; Williams 1989). The concentration of women in less-rewarded subspecialties within specific occupations is termed occupational resegregation (England and McCreary 1987) or female ghettoization (Miller-Loessi 1992).

Are females "ghettoized" in the medical profession? In "A Welcome to a Crowded Field: Where Will the New Female Physicians Fit In?" Judith Lorber (1987) argues that women will be tracked into lower-status, lower-prestige specialties and men will retain dominance in the occupational hierarchy. Currently, women physicians are underrepresented in surgery, the surgical subspecialties, anesthesiology, and radiology and overrepresented in pediatrics, obstetrics and gynecology, dermatology, psychiatry, and family practice (AMA 1994). But is their location due, as Lorber suggests, to tracking, discrimination, and constraint? In other words, are women grabbing the lowest rungs of the intraoccupational ladder because that is all that is available to them?

This article focuses on resident physicians' perceptions of the specialty hierarchy in medicine. Testing hypotheses about gatekeeping and constraints that keep women out of the "top" specialties necessitates knowing how residents perceive the prestige hierarchy. Do they perceive a "top" and "bottom" and, if so, do they agree with the prestige differential? Why do some specialties deserve more status and income? What are the criteria for being on top? This article is based on face-to-face interviews with male and female resident physicians from a major research university. The residents were asked to describe the hierarchy and give reasons for their rankings.

What emerges from the narrative suggests a more complicated view of hierarchy than current formulations allow. Although residents' descriptions of the hierarchy are fairly uniform, women in particular resist the idea of and justifications for a hierarchy based upon prestige. Furthermore, the narrative exposes a definite organization of medical specialties "along the lines of gender" (Acker 1992). The language reveals that medicine, independent of sex or gender as an individual category, is an institution demarcated by symbolic bodies, both masculine and feminine. The bodies, whether female or male, that occupy the highest prestige specialty are described as macho, action-oriented, physical, and technologically sophisticated. The bodies, whether male or female, that occupy the lower prestige specialties are described as passive, less physical, and affective. This article focuses primarily on the body of the physician; however, equally relevant is how the body of the patient factors into perceptions of the specialty hierarchy (Hinze 1997).

LITERATURE REVIEW

Early studies on specialty choice and status rankings were primarily conducted with male medical students, residents, or physicians. Howard Becker, Blanche Geer, Everett Hughes, and Anselm Strauss's classic *Boys in White: Student Culture in Medical School* (1961) focused solely on the socialization of male medical students. Using qualitative methods, they used 140 criteria to assess specialties (from field notes) and 1502 separate comments (from interviews). From this information, they developed 12 general categories of specialty choice criteria. Surprisingly, although the researchers had assumed that length of residency, money, and prestige would be key factors in considering specialties, the medical students studied were more interested (in descending order) in intellectual breadth, responsibility, special personal traits, manageability, comfortable patient relationship, and hours worked. Notably, only 2 percent of the fieldwork comments and 3 percent of the interview comments had to do with prestige of the specialty. Becker and his colleagues concluded that professional colleagues use a different set of criteria than do laypersons, a notion supported by Andrew Abbot (1981) in his discussion of intraprofessional status.

Since Becker's study, the medical profession has changed dramatically. Most significant is the explosion of specialization. In 1875, the International Medical Congress listed eight medical sections. Currently, there are 23 American boards that certify in 33 general areas and 50 subspecialty areas (*ABMS* 1990). Accordingly, the number of doctors who specialize has risen dramatically, spawning recent concerns about a paucity of primary care physicians. For example, one study documents a rise in the percentage of senior medical students interested in specialization from 64 percent to 85 percent between 1982 and 1992 (Xu, Rattner, Veloski, Hojat, Fields, and Barzansky 1995).[1] Along with the increase in specialization came a dramatic influx of female medical students. In 1960, approximately 5 percent of medical students were female (Martin, Arnold, and Parker 1988); by 1993, almost 42 percent were female (Xu et al. 1995). A final change accompanying the increase in specialization and the influx of women is a widened gap in earnings between those at the top of the specialty prestige hierarchy and those at the bottom. The income gap differential between specialists and primary care physicians is due largely to the government's Medicare fee schedule, which reimburses excessively for procedures (Starr 1981). Thus surgeons averaged $255,200 per year in 1994 compared to $126,200 per year for pediatricians (AMA 1995–1996).

In the past three decades research on specialty choice has also changed dramatically. The grounded theory approach employed by Becker and his colleagues has given way to more quantitative studies that tend to rely on a methodological paradigm (i.e., highly structured quantitative analyses of survey data utilizing closed-ended questions with forced

choice items) that precludes the individual's own perceptions of specialty prestige (Anderson 1975; Lieu, Schroeder, and Altman 1989; Matteson and Smith 1977; McGrath and Zimet 1977a; 1977b; Zimet and Held 1975). Studies of medical students' specialty rankings (Bruhn and Parsons 1964; Matteson and Smith 1977; Kritzer and Zimet 1967; Zimet and Held 1975) and the public's specialty rankings (Rosoff and Leone 1989; 1991) rarely explore reasons for the rankings, and none rely upon open-ended explanations. Generally, surgery and internal medicine are ascribed the highest status while pediatrics, psychiatry, and family medicine hover near the bottom. Historically, few studies of specialty status examine gender differences largely because so few women were available for comparison.

Recently, much attention has focused on women's greater interest in primary care specialties (Burkett and Gelula 1982; Bland, Meurer, and Maldonado 1995; Lieu et al. 1989; Xu et al. 1995), but explanations for gender differences in specialty choice vary. I will highlight three types of explanations here. One strand in the specialty choice literature, which I term the "social roles perspective," suggests that women choose specialties that are less time-consuming and demanding (but also less rewarded) because of family responsibilities (Marder, Kletke, Silberger, and Wilke 1988; Martin et al. 1988). In this vein, women's choices are seen as personal choices contingent on familial responsibilities.[2] Another body of evidence supports the notion that specialty choices of women physicians are contingent on the desire for more active patient-participants and for less invasive, less technological, and more holistic approaches to medicine and patients (Hinze 1995).[3] Studies in this vein, which I term the "cultural feminist perspective," emphasize the possibility of women's distinct values as determinants of choice (Davidson 1979; Kutner and Brogin 1990; Leserman 1981; Schobot,

Cayley, and Eliason 1996). Finally, a more critical structural perspective, termed the "liberal feminist perspective," holds that women have experienced tracking, discrimination, and constraints (Lorber 1984; Quadagno 1976). Women's "personal" choices are viewed as situated within a larger structural context where men subtly discourage or even actively prevent (through the system of informal sponsorship or sexist treatment and/or sexual harassment) women from pursuing the most coveted, highest prestige niches in the occupational hierarchy. Implicit in the liberal feminist perspective is the assumption that, all things being equal, women would want access to these specialties and that women view the hierarchy in terms similar to men's perspective. The purpose here is not so much to test these explanations against each other; that has been done elsewhere (Hinze 1995). Rather, I wish to explore how the hierarchy is perceived and to test the assumption that women and men physicians perceive the hierarchy in similar fashion.

Following Myra Marx Ferree (1985), I argue that scholars tend to think about the professions in ways that derive from men's experiences. Ferree notes that much of our research on professional work focuses on how individuals are motivated to acquire professional training and what structural impediments exist to professional credentialing for women and minorities. However, our understanding of professional work is not drawn from women's experiences or voices. Similarly, too often in the medical specialty choice literature, the assumption is that all residents, both male and female, internalize a prestige hierarchy and that all residents desire to be as high on this hierarchy as possible. In order to test such assumptions, it is important to have physician voices, both female and male, at the center. How they think about the specialty hierarchy may differ markedly from the perceptions of academic researchers, a point supported in Becker's work on medical stu-

dents and Abbott's work on professionals. Furthermore, with the increased number of women in the medical profession, a qualitative assessment of the hierarchy and why it exists is timely.

DATA AND METHODS

Data are drawn from open-ended, face-to-face interviews conducted with a subsample of female and male resident physicians ($N< = 18$) who were interviewed as part of a larger study ($N< = 405$; 84 percent response rate) of physicians' specialty choices (Hinze 1995). The 405 respondents who participated in the larger study were asked about their willingness to be recontacted for follow-up interviews; 76 percent of respondents in the telephone interview ($N< = 308$) said they would participate. Three criteria guided my selection of 20 respondents for the follow-up: gender, specialty, and degree to which the respondent engaged in the interview process. Prior to conducting the telephone survey with the full sample, interviewers were asked to evaluate the quality of each interview conducted. Respondents received a score from 0 to 4 depending upon how interested, enthusiastic, or thoughtful the respondent was about the issues explored. In selecting the subsample, the primary investigator (myself) set up three tiers of high-scoring respondents representative by sex and specialty. If someone from position five in tier one (e.g., a male pediatrician) was unavailable or unwilling to be interviewed, then I would substitute someone from position five, tier two and so on. It is noteworthy that all of the respondents selected in tier one agreed to the lengthy face-to-face interviews. Eighteen interviews were successfully conducted; two fell victim to scheduling problems. Ten women (three surgeons, two obstetrician-gynecologists, and one each from psychiatry, pediatrics, dermatology, internal medicine, and anesthesiology) and eight men (two surgeons, two internal medicine physicians, and one each from obstetrics and gynecology, radiology, pathology, and psychiatry) were interviewed.

The resident physicians are located at "Southern" University, a major research institution. The residency program is designed to encourage academic research; a majority of residents perform what is known as a research rotation. In addition, Southern is skewed toward training residents in specialties other than primary care specialties. Compared with programs nationwide, Southern has more surgeons and anesthesiologists, fewer internal medicine physicians, and no family practice program (see Hinze 1995). It is important to note that the emphasis on surgery and surgical subspecialties may skew the determinants of specialty prestige compared with residents nationwide.

The semistructured face-to-face interviews lasted from one to three hours; the average interview length was approximately one hour and 30 minutes. Interviews were conducted at the time and location of the respondent's choice. Eleven interviews were conducted in a private office secured in a local hospital (convenient to the residents), and four were conducted in semiprivate settings in other hospitals. One interview was conducted in a respondent's home, another in a local pub, and a third in a call room. All interviews were taped and notes were taken during the interviews. Twelve of the interviews were subsequently transcribed; due to technical difficulties, six were untranscribable. Hence, although all 18 interviews form the basis for this article, the actual quotes are drawn from the 12 transcribed interviews. The interviews generally focused on the resident's own specialty choice decision and his or her perceptions of what mattered for the choices of his or her peers. During the course of the interview, the resident physicians were asked to describe the prestige hierarchy of medical specialties and then to discuss why they thought it existed.

The methodology used is best described as, following Clifford Geertz (1973), an interpretive approach in which the corporeal metaphors that emerge from the narrative are analyzed to reveal respondents' understandings of the embodied organization of medicine. Central to the interpretations is the question of how the gendered metaphors figure in respondents' medical specialty choices. This article aims for, in Geertz's words, "thick description" that allows us to draw large conclusions from small but very densely textured facts.

FINDINGS

Hierarchy Description

Consensus. There are four notable findings with regard to the specialty rankings. First, residents were fairly consistent in their descriptions of the prestige hierarchy of medical specialties. The hierarchy or "ladder" they described consisted of anywhere between 4 and 10 levels or rungs with an average of about 6. Most resident physicians ranked surgeons as the most prestigious (level or rung 6), followed by internal medicine physicians (level 5), a "lump" that included anesthesiologists, radiologists, pathologists, and others (level 4), followed by obstetrician-gynecologists (level 3), then pediatricians (level 2), and finally psychiatrists at the bottom as the least prestigious (level 1). Residents were quicker to describe a top and bottom and tended to lump together specialties in the middle levels (especially level 4). Similar prestige rankings have been reported over time and across sites (Cassell 1998; Kutner and Brogin 1990; Matteson and Smith 1977; Merton, Bloom, and Rogoff 1956; Zimet and Held 1975), indicating that the hierarchy described by Southern residents is fairly standard. Interestingly, there is not a perfect correspondence between income and prestige. Average incomes in 1994 were highest for (in descending order) surgery, radiology, anesthesiology, obstetrics-gynecology, pathology, internal medicine, psychiatry, pediatrics, and finally, family practice (AMA 1996).

Second, although residents were fairly consistent, there was some jockeying for position between surgeons and internists. Sixteen of the 18 residents placed surgery at the top, two ranked internal medicine as highest or equal to surgery, and several commented on the rivalry between surgery and internal medicine for the top ranking. One female psychiatrist viewed internal medicine and surgery as vying for top dollar. As the following quote illustrates, whereas surgeons make more money and work harder, internal medicine physicians are considered more cerebral:

> There's a big kind of a thing between medicine and surgery, you know? Like, the [internal] medicine people think that they're the cerebral people, and they think about things and they're the real doctors, and they're what the "M" in M.D. stands for. And the surgeons, they think that, "Well, we're the real bright people, and we have to work really hard, and we make more money." And each of those thinks that they're the top specialty.

One female internist remarked that surgeons

> obviously see themselves at the top of the pile and I think what they don't realize is that a lot of medical people just laugh at them and shake their heads. And they let them continue to think they're at the top of the pile because they scream and yell and make a lot of noise and tell everyone how important they are, and no one wants to fight with them.

Indeed, the strength of surgery at Southern University may eclipse other departments. One female obstetrics and gynecology physician suggested that surgery is a "hugely strong department and it's very nationally recognized. That's why anesthesia's not very strong here, because they have to compete with surgery. So here, surgeons are kings. They're the real men." She suggested that in other programs with weaker surgery departments (relative to other surgery departments), anesthesiology may fare better in terms of prestige, perhaps a notch or two higher than other nonsurgical specialties.

Third, residents had a slight tendency to rank their own specialty higher than others ranked it. Although most residents placed radiology in the great "middle morass" (in the words of one resident, referring to what I've termed level 4 and including pathology and anesthesiology) of specialties, one male radiologist put his specialty on a par with surgical subspecialties. In addition, most physicians placed dermatologists in the internal medicine category since they do a year of internal medicine and really "subspecialize." But some placed dermatologists below that great "middle morass," perhaps only a step above psychiatrists or pediatricians. However, one female dermatology resident placed cardiothoracic surgery and neurosurgery at the top of the hierarchy and then said: "I'd personally perceive dermatology probably next [to] or even above the other subsurgical subspecialties." She continued with internal medicine physicians, followed by radiology, obstetrics and gynecology, pediatrics, and finally, psychiatry.

Fourth, residents often gave more detail to an intraspecialty hierarchy. For residents whose specialties contained several subspecialties, "ranking" subspecialties becomes the focus because the internal hierarchy was more familiar than a comparison of one's own specialty to more distant specialties. Consider the words of a surgeon:

> I'd say surgical subspecialties are at the top like cardiac surgeons, neurosurgeons, then vascular surgeons maybe. Then I'd say the other, general surgeons are probably just a tier below that, you could put transplant surgeons, otolaryngologists, other subspecialties. Then down

from there I'd say invasive subspecialties in medicine like cardiology, GI [gastrointestinal], pulmonary. And then you get down to the, you know, run of the mill internists, et cetera. I would say ob/gyn would probably be above internists, probably, then I'd say, hovering down at the bottom, unfortunately, pediatricians, psychiatrists, and stuff like that.

Notice his reference to 7 categories of surgeons and 4 categories of internal medicine physicians, but the further he gets away from his own specialty, the less detail he gives. In fact, he neglected to mention pathology, radiology, and dermatology. When prompted, he located them, but he seemed less sure the further "away" specialties were on the prestige scale. The finding that residents make finer distinctions in specialties or subspecialties nearest them is consistent with the literature on social class distinctions.

Resistance.   Four of the 10 women and one of the eight men interviewed made comments revealing their resistance to the concept of a prestige hierarchy. For example, one female obstetrician-gynecologist asked, "Who defines prestigious?" She prefaced her comments on the hierarchy by arguing that medical students pick up on the prestige hierarchy very early, so clearly one exists, but "that doesn't make it right. I mean, that's a hierarchy based on the majority's opinion or the most outspoken people's opinion, from the people who set the standards, the people in power." She struggles with the hierarchy and possible hypotheses or explanations for women's place in it, arguing that men set up this "hierarchy" and "women are going into fields because they choose to, and tough shit, and we just don't happen to care that we're not high on *their* hierarchy" (emphasis added).

One female psychiatrist acknowledged that "psychiatry is totally at the bottom. People consider psychiatrists as, like, not really docs." However, she argued that the value system is male and "women in medicine

tend not to buy into that as much." She said men are concerned about "how much money you make, and what kind of car you drive, and what kinds of women will sleep with you" whereas "women tend to think about things differently" and value, as she does, "time for myself and to feel like my work itself is rewarding." She asserted that just because women are different "doesn't necessarily mean we're inferior." The only man critical of the prestige hierarchy was an obstetrician-gynecologist who, while ranking psychiatrists at the bottom of the hierarchy, remarked: "I think society probably should value psychiatrists the most, because much of what is wrong with us is psychological." Another female obstetrician claimed:

> Psychiatry . . . always ends up being ranked down lower because it's not a classic medicine that you're taught. . . . I think they should not be at the bottom. . . . I've seen just too many unusual cases here at Southern that psychiatrists made the biggest difference—postpartum depression, trauma after pregnancy loss—where everything I could do, nothing could accomplish what a psychiatrist could accomplish.

Although resistant voices are few, their emergence is surprising. I did not expect respondents to challenge the hierarchy I so matter-of-factly asked them to describe. However, finding a *gender difference* among the resistors is not altogether surprising. The 405 residents who participated in the larger study were asked how important prestige of a specialty was to their choice; 58 percent of the women reported it was not at all important compared to 40 percent of the men ($p \leq .01$). The gender difference in the quantitative study parallels the narrative comments because women are less likely to see prestige as important for their choice of a specialty and are less likely to validate the concept of a prestige hierarchy.

The resistors bring up two important questions. First, are women more likely to resist because they see the hierarchy as male-defined or because they tend to be lowest in the hierarchy? In the interviews conducted here, women toward the middle or top of the hierarchy (i.e., the three surgeons, one anesthesiologist, and one internist) did not resist. Rather, like the men at the top, they went to great lengths to describe why they were more "valuable" and deserved higher status. This suggests that status defines resistance more than gender. Only one man in the "lower-status" specialties resisted the hierarchy and prestige differentials. If status defines resistance, then lower-status men should resist, too. This is not a quantitative study and the resistant voices are few, but it seems plausible that, independent of gender, status predicts resistance, and independent of status, gender predicts resistance. But these variables are not independent. Since women tend to be located in lower-status specialties, they are doubly marginalized and most resistant—along gender *and* status lines. Status tempers resistance for higher-status women (women are more likely to resist a male-defined hierarchy but their position in the hierarchy keeps them from it), and gender tempers resistance for lower-status men (lower-status residents are more likely to resist but maleness causes them to buy into it). Interestingly, the only man who resisted the hierarchy is an obstetrician and one who, in his own words, "likes working with women" and throughout his life "always had better friends that were women than [were] men."

The second important question is: What is the resistance based upon? The comments explored here reveal resistance to the concept of a prestige hierarchy and the lower status of certain specialties within it. The narrative explored in the next two sections suggests that the resistance is based largely upon resistance to the high value attached to interventionist specialties. However, respondents also resist the value placed upon the "macho" nature of higher-level specialties and the consequent pressure for those women choosing high-status specialties to adopt male personae (while at the same time preserving outward femininity).[5]

In summary, residents were fairly consistent in their rankings, although there was a slight tendency to overrank one's own specialty and to be more familiar with intraspecialty rankings than interspecialty rankings. Finally, the women interviewees were more likely to challenge the concept of a prestige hierarchy, and their resistance may be interpreted variously through a gender lens (resisting a male-defined hierarchy) and a status lens (resisting their subordination on the prestige hierarchy). The following section examines the types of explanations given for the prestige hierarchy as defined above.

Explanations

Some residents initially claimed that certain specialties were more prestigious because practitioners in those specialties earned more money, an observation that begs the question. Hence, respondents who gave "money" as an explanation were prompted to reflect upon why they thought certain specialties earned more. A couple of residents resisted explanations. For example, when asked why some specialists earned more than others, one woman psychiatrist replied: "I'm a really bad person to ask 'cause I don't really care about those things. I mean, it's just not part of my value system." However, most residents argued that specialty prestige is not only about earnings; indeed, many high-earning specialties (e.g., radiology) are lower in prestige than specialties where incomes are often less (e.g., internal medicine).

What defines specialty prestige? In general, the explanations focused on the extent to which the *training* is rigorous and tough (longer hours and more years) and the extent to which residents learned concrete, measurable *skills*, especially those that resulted in heroic measures. Thus, the dimensions conferring prestige are time, effort, and skills.

According to one resident, surgery is highest on the prestige hierarchy because: "You put so many hours, so many years into it, so there's a big time commitment. Delaying gratification . . . gosh, it took them that long to learn [those skills], they must be smart!" Later, she claimed that the "end result, what people see," is important to surgery's prestige. "It's like, 'Ah, you saved our little girl with that heart.'"[6]

Implicit in much of the narrative is a subtext that provides a richly detailed, in-depth view of how specialty prestige is organized in the minds of the residents. Specifically, what is striking is the extent to which prestige is not easily categorized by money, lifestyle, or skill level. In fact, only a few of the residents gave such standard responses, and even then they elaborated upon other, less easily categorizable reasons for prestige. Clearly, there was something more important to their sense of why some specialties were "worth more" than others. The residents often talked at length about the body of the physician, or parts of the physician's body, and how that body was engaged with the patient's body. What emerges is the body as an organizing framework for explanations about the prestige hierarchy. Furthermore, the body is not gender neutral. After detailing how the body of the physician matters for specialty prestige, I will address how gender figures into this conceptual framework.

Body Part I: The Hands. Several residents placed surgery and the surgical subspecialties at the top of the hierarchy because the surgeon's hands touch, enter, or probe the human body. The hands are not just any hands, they are active hands. The more somatic intervention, the more prestigious the specialty. This finding is consistent with Stephen M. Shortell's (1974) study in which

physicians, medical students, and patients accorded higher status to physicians who fell into Szaz Hollender's activity-passivity model, where patients are essentially passive and physicians have control over patient outcomes. Consider the following:

> I'm not here to sit on the sidelines. I don't know what God wants me to do, but I'm here to do something, not to stand still. It is to move, it is to be active, it is to do something, to participate . . . and medicine is to save someone's life, relieve the pain, somehow change the course of that human's life and hopefully to make it better. And with that comes responsibility. . . . Surgery demands an action, demands a simulation of information, demands a translation into manual, usually manual, physical actions, which I like. I like using my hands, I like touching things, I like doing things, and you translate taking information and coming to a conclusion and then performing the act and watching, participating in the recovery of a patient. . . . That's what I like about surgery, it is an active subspecialty of medicine whereas a lot of others are passive.

A female surgeon, when asked why she chose surgery, said, "I like working with my hands." She also emphasized the extent to which the specialty is action-oriented, dynamic, and challenging both "medically and technically." For her, the prestige of the specialty is linked to the manual skills of the specialty as well as to the extent to which surgeons "outwork" other specialists and "sacrifice" more. The anthropologist Joan Cassell (1998) argues that some specialties are more embodied than others and that having "good hands" is seen as fundamental to being a surgeon. Furthermore, she suggests: "The extent of embodiment seems roughly parallel to the prestige system among doctors: psychiatrists are on the lowest rung, while at the other end surgeons loftily disdain the less embodied specialties" (p. 33).

Nonsurgeons also ranked surgery as the most prestigious because of their ability to "know" what is going on inside the body and to "fix" it with their hands. An internal medicine resident acknowledged that those in his specialty are less experienced than surgeons with the body. He added, "We feel a belly, you know, and there's something going on there. We don't really know what it is. We don't know how to operate on people so we don't know." The implication is that the deeper one enters the body, the more one *knows* about the patient's condition. Because of the surgeon's hands-on, interventionist experience with the body, internists must often rely on their judgment. The same physician said, "We call them [the surgeons] and they feel: 'Oh, it's nothing, why did you call me?' Just 'cause they've felt a lot more [of] what we call acute abdomens, they know when somebody needs to be opened up and looked at."

One pathologist placed surgeons above internal medicine physicians because surgeons "are in a position to physically save lives, and they're sort of frequently in that position. . . . Medicine people kinda hem and haw around. They think about it, they deliberate about it, they mess around with it, then they call the surgeon and the surgeon fixes it, you know?"

An obstetrician-gynecology resident argued that surgery is more valued

> because surgeons *take a life right into their own hands*. Medicine people, god knows, the way they change their medicines around. Scares me to death. But it's not perceived as much as taking someone's life into their hands because they're never cut open, you know. I mean, all you're doing is changing medicine. That's not a big deal. (emphasis added)

Again, the hands figure prominently. Surgeons hold life in their hands and the actual movements of their hands can dramatically alter someone's life. Also, as one resident suggested, the harder certain body parts are to get at, the more prestigious the specialty or subspecialty. In the following quote, a female obstetrician-gynecologist recognizes that working on basic organs that most of us never get to see raises the prestige of some specialties and subspecialties: "Oh, neurosurgery! Works on a brain. I mean, that's even more mysterious. Not only do you never see the surgeon, you don't even see the brain. I mean, it's such a fantastical thing." Clearly, physicians who touch or feel our most hidden, distant organs (namely, the heart and brain) have status in the eyes of other physicians and the public. Also, notice the comment "never see the surgeon." She argued that surgeons are distant and, hence, godlike to the patients. It is difficult to get an appointment with the surgeon; even when a patient does, the surgeon rarely talks at length, and the major work with the patient is done while patient is sleeping. According to this resident, such distance makes them "unseen magical workers" with enormous power.

According to another obstetrician-gynecologist, psychiatry is at the bottom of the prestige hierarchy because "it's sitting down, talking. . . . Psychiatrists just sit there and they take your money and you lie there and talk, and that's what most people's perceptions are," whereas surgeons save lives and bring about dramatic outcomes and are perceived as "fixing things." She said, it is "very sad" because "reimbursement is set up for taking care of it, fixing it, that sort of thing, but not for preventing it. And so then we have the lower class and the upper class doctor. . . . It's not fair." She gave the example of surgeons amputating a leg when more aggressive preventive medicine might have arrested the vascular disease from going as far as it did in the first place. "If that [smoking] had been changed umpteen years ago, then you wouldn't be the surgeon taking the gangrenous leg off."[8]

Using one's hands to bring about dramatic outcomes is financially rewarded. Active physician bodies are more valued than bodies that are considered passive or inactive, such as psychiatrists (who just sit down and talk) and pediatricians. One male surgeon claimed:

> Pediatricians, they are morons. I'll say that right now into the tape. I know pediatricians. They are morons, they are worse than internists. They are the prime example of *inactivity* in medicine. I mean, they sit around all day with their little teddy bears and stuff like this on their stethoscopes. . . . And basically, I mean, you've probably heard that pediatricians are the children of medicine. I mean, if you think like a child, act like a child, behave like a child, you go into pediatrics because you feel comfortable with children. If you are an active, assertive, hands-on type of individual, that usually goes into surgery, you feel very uncomfortable around children because children are, the entropy is maximum and the surgeon hates entropy. The surgeon likes order and children are disordered. Surgeons are the big boys on the block, the parents who spank the children. (emphasis added)

A great deal is revealed in this quote, but note especially the surgeon's emphasis on inactivity and the association of inactivity with low status to the point of being childlike (and deserving of a spanking given, of course, by an active surgeon). Internists (residents in internal medicine) are also perceived as inactive by this surgeon, consistent with the notion of "hemming and hawing around" offered by the pathologist (quoted earlier) to account for the lower prestige of internal medicine physicians relative to surgeons.

In summary, surgery is perceived by surgeons and nonsurgeons alike as a hands-on, active subspecialty where the goal is to "fix" a broken body. Surgeons hold life in their hands and use their hands to save lives. Since results are less dramatic or heroic, physicians who practice preventive medicine, engage a person in talk therapy, or are "inactive," such as pediatricians and internists, are viewed as less prestigious.

In addition to the emphasis on hands-on, somatic intervention, the resident physicians studied here repeatedly evoked the image of "balls" as important for specialty prestige. As the next section reveals, in addition to having aggressive, highly skilled hands, the highest prestige specialists, whether male or female, have enlarged "balls."

Body Part II: The "Balls." Many residents, whether male or female, recognize and clearly state the importance of the toughness factor, sometimes referred to as the presence and size of one's testes. When asked why the prestige hierarchy exists as it does, one female anesthesiology resident argued:

> Some of it has to do with how hard you slave. The reason, I think, that psych residents are looked down upon is because, whether or not this is true, people perceive them as rolling in at nine o'clock and rolling out at five and, you know, taking calls. My friend who is a psych resident at UCLA took [a] call once every ten nights. And so, it's, you know, "You don't work as hard as I do; therefore, you are not worth as much." I think that comes in. Same with radiologists. . . . They don't put in the hours that other trainees do. Puts them lower down.

In contrast, according to this resident, surgeons are

> just brutalized. There's just no way around it. They're brutalized for four years. And without being genderish about it. I think it's just—you know, it's like, "*My balls are bigger than yours because I'm here every night of the week*," that kind of deal. (emphasis added)

One female obstetrician-gynecologist claimed: "Surgeons are kings. They're the real men. They have the biggest testicles." When pushed as to what she meant by having "the biggest testicles," she elaborated on the concept of toughness, seeing it as connected to "people who work harder":

> When I come off a service where I've been workin' really hard, I feel like the toughest person. I am so tough; I am so superior to you because I work longer hours than you; I have

stayed awake more days in a row than you will ever stay awake, you know; I am so cool . . . that's exactly what it is. So I think it's—god, that's such a good question. I think it's imposed on us by the people in this field. I don't think it's as important to pediatricians to be big macho people.

The same resident also identified an intraspecialty hierarchy along the lines of balls or toughness within obstetrics and gynecology. She asked if I knew any "gyn-onc docs" (gynecological oncologists) and then stated:

These guys are so macho. Dr. X, do you know her? . . . I always talk about how her testicles are bigger than anybody else's in the department. I mean, she is so macho. This woman is so tough. And she walks; she's tough; and she sits like this, you know. She's tough. And she went through six million years of training in one of the hardest training programs in the country, no doubt. She is an incredible surgeon and she's incredibly intelligent. And why is she so damn macho? Because she worked so hard for so long; because she doesn't actually save lives. She just prolongs them for a little while. That's what oncology surgeons do. But she does big, huge, major surgeries that I would never dare to touch. Well, that makes her much more macho than I am because she's not scared of anything, you know?

One dermatologist said, "In my eyes, I've got a lot of respect for them [surgeons]. . . less 'cause of how much they get paid, but because of how much work they put into it. And they've been through a lot. I mean. The guys get *harassed emotionally* in the surgical profession" (emphasis added). For this resident and several others, it was not just the long hours but the extent of the harassment during medical training. One female psychiatrist viewed the more macho specialties as those that not only worked the most hours, but also "suffered." When asked why some specialties are seen as more prestigious than others, she responded, "I think it's the macho

thing. I mean, people perceive that surgeons and otolaryngologists and—people like that—must be suffering a lot and so, you know, what they achieve must be good."

She continued:

It isn't just working hard—surgeons work an eighty-hour week and people are abusing them all the time and they can't complain or even talk about how hard it is because then someone thinks they are weak or have a bad attitude. Whereas peds, *you can work the same number of hours* but you're playing with kids, you're having the fun, your coworkers are commiserating with you over the hours: "Oh, you're post-call. You must be tired. "You know? Whereas in surgery. "Oh, you're post-call. Well, you know, that's just part of the life, you know? Stop whining." (emphasis added)

One female pediatrician elaborated: "Talk about delayed gratification, you know. They go through more years than just about anybody. It's very grueling. It is grueling. It is really grueling."

A male surgeon, reflecting on why so few women are in the highest prestige specialty, argued:

Surgery is . . . compared to the military. And, a lot of women don't feel comfortable in the military. And if you don't feel comfortable in the military, you are not going to feel comfortable in a surgical . . . and again, this, you are going to say this is chauvinistic . . . but . . . there is something . . . I think it is socialization, that it is alright for males to, like the kids in the playground, you know, the kids fight, the boys are able to fight and you know, scruff 'em up and throw mud at each other and they are best buddies afterwards. Well, girls can't do that. . . . It's not as acceptable for women to spar, but for men it is.

Militaristic images were evoked repeatedly in descriptions of surgery. This resident's comments are revealing in light of Judy Wajcam's (1991: 3) observation: "The cultural stereotype of science as inextricably linked with masculinity is also crucial in explaining the small number of women in science. If science is seen as an activity appropriate for men, then it is hardly surprising that girls usually do not want to develop the skills and behaviors considered necessary for success." Whether the surgeon's words reveal a deeply entrenched stereotype ("women don't feel comfortable in the military") or not, the reality is that he perceives the discipline as inappropriate for women.

According to one female resident, "this is still a male-oriented profession. And I know that my testosterone level has gone up remarkably—really! Not my actual blood test, my psychological testosterone level is elevated—from the day I hit medical school until now, nine years later. So, I mean, there's a certain amount of macho."

A woman can symbolically grow balls and her "psychological" testosterone level rises during the harsh medical training. Hence, women can compete with men as long as they are perceived as macho and tough. However, as the words of one female surgeon reveal, the costs can be high. She explained: "I think I've changed probably for the worst these last twelve months because you work so hard and you get the shit beat out of you on a daily basis and they want you to be a man and act like a man and then when you do, it's like you have some big personality disorder . . . you are not feminine anymore." The resident began to cry but continued:

> The goal was never to be perceived as a bitch or something, uh, or to beat up on men and to be some big, I didn't want to be a man, I didn't want to be like real tough and have to chew people out and play hardball with them, that wasn't the goal. . . . [crying harder now]. You know, if this is what, you know, if everyone hates working with me then it wasn't worth it at all.

Toughness, being macho, having balls, suffering—together these contribute to the prestige of surgical specialties. Women can be perceived as macho as men but, as the above resident indicated, there are consequences. Furthermore, as the following quotes reveal, women who choose tough specialties play the macho role but must also emphasize their femininity, at least in physical appearance.

One male surgeon described the female "chairman" [*sic*] of a surgery program as "a competent surgeon, an impressive woman." He continued, "She started off as, yeah, everyone called her a bitch, she's a bitch, *but attractive, dresses well*, professional, is competent, and her surgical skills were good, above average I think, at least average or maybe a little better than average" (emphasis added). He insisted, "If you are a female in a profession, *you maintain your femininity* but you assert yourself as a professional. . . . You will be respected and you will advance yourself" (emphasis added). One female surgeon claimed that the only women she knew in surgery were "not very warm and were not feminine." She added:

> And I think I have maintained my femininity over the seven years, really, pretty well. Post-call or like when I'm extremely tired then, like now, what the hell . . . I didn't put eye shadow on this morning because I knew it would be a long hard day and I'm not going home until tomorrow night, but if I'm, like, going home in the evening, if I'm getting up and going home, then I like to wear nice things. I wore scrubs in today because I figure, like, why bother. But I have my skirt that I wore up there like yesterday, actually, two days ago. . . . I wore my skirt and my hose and these are my . . . I mean, like, I wear girl shoes, I mean, a lot of these women in surgery are pretty unfeminine, the great majority of them are not very feminine. If I've been any kind of role model, sometimes I think it would be to be more of a feminine role model, a feminine surgeon role model, but then like I say, the thing that worries me is maybe I'm this hard-ass that everyone hates working with.

In her study of women physicians, Cassell (1998) finds that women surgeons are an oxymoron for many in the medical profession. According to one woman surgeon, male surgeons viewed female surgeons as "not women" (i.e., they were lesbians or dogs) or as not surgeons (i.e., they were incompetent). Male mentors in two different cases advised women surgeons to wear lipstick, which Cassell interprets as "embodied refutation of *not-woman* status" (p. 42). The men and women quoted above focus on the importance of women maintaining feminine bodies and suggest that women actively shape their bodies (by dressing well, wearing eyeshadow and "girl" shoes) to fit the embodied expectations. This is not unlike the observation that women athletes in masculinized sports must emphasize their femininity (e.g., runner Florence Griffith Joyner) and men athletes in feminized sports must emphasize their masculinity (e.g., figure skater Elvis Stojko). But for women physicians in masculine specialties, the pressure to "be tough" while looking feminine is contradictory and can be a difficult balancing act, one that men are not expected to perform.

In summary, the highest-prestige specialties are perceived as filled by those who have slaved and suffered and consequently have the largest balls. That is, one's balls grow larger through training. Women as well as men can have balls, but the costs of acquiring them are high; women may be perceived as too tough and must work extra hard to preserve their feminine gender identity or, to echo the surgeon quoted above, they will not be accepted.

Residents' beliefs about the existence of and explanation for a prestige hierarchy are complex. In general, most carry a similar mental map of the hierarchy, although lower-status women are most likely to resist it. Moreover, for most residents, certain specialties (e.g., surgery) deserve higher status but the explanations residents gave for deserving

that status are not as clearly organized around standard sociological concepts of prestige as we might expect. In addition to time, effort, and skills, residents invoked the concept of activity, especially as related to the physician's hands and the concept of balls, which symbolize toughness and the ability to survive grueling schedules. In the next section, I explore the relationship between gender and residents' perceptions of what makes a specialty prestigious.

DISCUSSION

Past research on occupational sex segregation in medicine has focused almost exclusively on where individual men and women are located in prestige hierarchies and neglected the extent to which the hierarchies themselves are socially and culturally constructed in gendered ways. It is not enough to ask how women are kept out or, in the words of Karen Miller-Loessi (1992), ghettoized; rather, we must examine the cultural meanings embedded within the existing structure or hierarchy of specialties. The narratives presented here reveal that residents' perceptions of a prestige hierarchy in medicine, of why some specialties are "worth more," are grounded in symbolic body parts that are gender linked. After reviewing how gender figures into the "body of medicine" as described by residents, I conclude by arguing that the images of specialties are not gender neutral and discuss how they may influence women's location in the specialty hierarchy.

Hands

Women as healers have been central across time and place, within families, and at various institutional levels (Perrone, Stockel, and Krueger 1989). Throughout history, women have "laid hands" upon the laboring, sick, and dying or dead. Only as medicine professionalized did this role fall to men, or more accurately, to male physicians (Ehrenreich and English 1973; Morantz-Sanchez 1985; Starr 1983). However, as women have entered medicine in increasing numbers, they have continued to locate in specialties that are least likely to be associated with the kinds of invasive, hands-on activity that is, according to the residents, what confers prestige. For example, women are overrepresented in psychiatry and pediatrics, which residents perceive as "inactive" specialties where nothing is "fixed," and they are underrepresented in the most "active" (and prestigious) specialties such as surgery, the surgical subspecialties, and invasive internal medicine specialties. Certainly, pediatricians and psychiatrists use their hands, but using hands merely to diagnose or soothe the body or catch a baby is not considered high status.[9] The hands must intervene, they must probe, manipulate or cut the body open, often assisted by sophisticated technologies. Implicit in much of the narrative is that the more technology, especially technology that intervenes, the more prestigious the specialty.

The "active hands" invoked by resident physicians are not gender neutral. The classical Western dualism of male activity and female passivity pervades the social world (Hochschild 1983). While much work deconstructs such hierarchical oppositions (Collins 1990), others' work (Bordo 1993) recognizes that those dualisms are embedded in this culture and shape the way we think, in this case, about the prestige of specialties and why some physicians are worth more than others. The historian Christopher Lawrence examines how corporeal images of physicians were employed to enhance the prestige of physicians, especially those engaged in active, interventionist, hands-on medicine that was seen as "inappropriate" for women. Lawrence (1998: 194) quotes an anonymous author from 1845 who wrote, "No man can know much of Anatomy, who is too finical or too lady-like to soil his delicate fingers."

Feminist critiques of the scientific revolution of the sixteenth and seventeenth centuries highlight how science emerged based on masculine projects of reason and objectivity (Wajcam 1991). Wajcam (1991: 5) writes that the critiques "characterized the conceptual dichotomizing central to scientific thought and to Western philosophy in general as distinctly masculine. Culture vs. nature, mind vs. body, reason vs. emotion, objectivity vs. subjectivity, public vs. private." In each dichotomy, the former dominates the latter, and the latter is systematically associated with the feminine.[10] In a similar vein, practitioners of Western biomedicine invoke dualistic metaphors that reveal underlying social meanings: activity versus passivity, fixing versus maintaining, hands-on versus hands-off, invasive versus noninvasive, technological versus personal care—and in each, the former dominates the latter, and the latter is associated with the feminine. The dualism inherent in the residents' narratives is important if we accept, as Evelyn F. Keller (1992) argues, the power of language and the extent to which language, in which beliefs are encoded, has the force to shape what men and women think, believe, and do. Furthermore, the narratives reveal the power that body images have for conveying status and prestige and the extent to which women and men attempt to conform to the appropriate embodied images, a process that may be below the level of language. Our knowledge of what it means to be a man or woman in a particular social setting is embodied, wordless, and transmitted, according to the philosopher Moira Gatens (1996), from the images, symbols, and beliefs encoded in both tangible and imaginary bodies.

"Balls"

While the relationship between the hands/activity terminology and gender may be somewhat subtle, the relationship between balls or testes and gender is anything but subtle. Perceptions of toughness and masculinity pervade resident explanations for the prestige hierarchy. As noted by the residents, women can be tough and have balls, but requiring that women "grow them" to compete in the top specialties is problematic for three reasons. First, as Sandra Harding (1986) and others have argued, conceptually, the problem becomes women (their socialization, aspirations, and values), and the larger question, of how medicine as an institution could be reshaped to accommodate women, is ignored. In other words, if women are confined to lower prestige, less tough specialties, it is their fault for lacking testicles. If only they had more balls or were less passive, then they, too, could be surgeons. As Gatens (1996: 71) notes, "It is beside the point to 'grant' equal access to women and others excluded from the traditional body politic, since this amounts to 'granting' access to the body politic and the public sphere in terms of an individual's ability to emulate those powers and capacities that have, in a context of male/masculine privilege, been deemed valuable by that sphere." Moreover, the presence of women with masculine hands and balls does not change the value system, which is still male defined. Women can successfully adapt but by doing so they become symbolic men and leave the larger structure intact.

A second problem with requiring women to grow balls and devalue noninterventionist medicine is that for women to survive in the highest-prestige specialty and subspecialties asks them to "exchange major aspects of their gender identity for a masculine version without prescribing a similar 'degendering' process for men" (Wajcam 1991: 2). As earlier quotes reveal, the "degendering" can be painful. Women must act like men to survive, but then they fear, as the woman surgeon confided, that everyone hates them for it.

The third and final problem with requiring a certain level of toughness and macho in order to compete in surgery is that, as Wajcam (1991) notes in her work on technology, institutional structures are founded upon the division of labor in larger society in which men are expected to work hard in the public sphere and women are still expected, whether employed or not, to carry the lion's share of the private sphere. Being "tough" because one has endured a long residency with an intense call schedule is more easily attained by those—men—who have less responsibility for the home.

In summary, the bodies, whether female or male, that occupy the top of the hierarchy are hands-on, active, and tough. The bodies, whether male or female, that occupy the lower rungs of the ladder, are perceived as passive, emotional, and soft. The prestige hierarchy is not a gender-neutral concept; as resident perceptions reveal, it is infused with gender. Although there may be a conflation (in the minds of both the public and physicians) of these symbolic, gendered body parts with physiologically based attributes, the narrative makes clear that biological women can make it to the top despite the unsuitability of their bodies; presumably, biological men can and do adapt to the femininity associated with the bottom of the hierarchy.

CONCLUSION

Research on women's location or underrepresentation in scientific and technological fields has recently undergone a massive shift, from studies focused on sexual difference (or, as some scholars have insisted, the lack thereof) to how masculine and feminine meanings are constructed (Keller 1992; Wajcam 1991). Initial research on women's occupational choices utilized gender as an explanatory variable, an individual-level characteristic that reflects the psychosocial development of individual men and women. The focus in such research might have been on the values or social roles of women that eliminated them from the competitive world of surgery and the surgical subspecialties and, increasingly, more technologically sophisticated (and highly remunerated) specialties like radiology and anesthesiology. Alternatively, more explicitly feminist analyses, particularly from a liberal feminist perspective, have analyzed how women's choices were constrained by men in positions of power or by stereotypes about women that caused them to be tracked into lower-level specialties presumed to be more compatible.

More recently, as Keller's (1992: 16) work on women and science reveals, gender has come to be seen as a "cultural structure organizing social (and sexual) relations between men and women." The final step in this progression away from individuals as gendered is to view gender as "the basis of a sexual division of cognitive and emotional labor that brackets women, their work, and the values associated with that work from culturally normative delineations of categories intended as 'human': objectivity, morality, citizenship, power, often even, 'human nature' itself" (Keller 1992: 17). Keller views gender and gender norms as "silent organizers of the mental and discursive maps of the social and natural worlds we simultaneously inhabit and construct—even of those worlds that women never enter." She calls this "the symbolic work of gender" and argues that "it remains silent precisely to the extent that norms associated with masculine culture are taken as universal" (p. 17).

The narratives presented here shift our focus from the tastes, similarities, and differences of individuals, from passive women and mean men, toward the structure of the gendered prestige hierarchy itself with a cultural top characterized by masculine images and symbols. My findings are consistent with Joan Acker's (1990) work on gendered organizations, revealing that organizational structures are not gender neutral. Rather, images of men's bodies and masculinity pervade organizational processes and hierarchies; such images, according to Acker, marginalize women and contribute to gender segregation. Acker argues that women's bodies cannot be adapted to hegemonic masculinity: to function at the top of male hierarchies requires that women render irrelevant everything that makes them women. My findings suggest that women's bodies can adapt but not without significant work and costs.

If, in residents' minds, activity (cutting, fixing, probing, doing) is juxtaposed to passivity (listening, talking, waiting, emotion work), and toughness, as symbolized by having balls and denoted by surviving grueling schedules, is juxtaposed to softness, and if the former in each case is more esteemed and associated with masculinity, then we see a sexual division of labor where bodies at the bottom of the prestige hierarchy, whether male or female, are devalued by association with feminized work. Along similar lines, Rosabeth Moss Kanter's (1977) classic work on men and women in the corporation reveals a masculine ethic of rationality and reason identified in image of managers. The traits assumed to belong to men are elevated: being tough; setting aside personal, emotional considerations; and exhibiting cognitive superiority. According to Kanter (1977: 46), "While organizations were being defined as sex-neutral machines, masculine principles were dominating their authority structures."

Attempts to understand women's disproportionate location on the bottom rungs of the occupational prestige ladder have been largely quantitative, expert defined, and male defined. While the earliest sociological studies on specialty choice used a grounded theory approach, more recent studies have been quantitative and more often from a medical perspective. The few studies by sociologists, particularly liberal feminists, have brought us closer to understanding the persistence of sex segregation among physicians but have at their core male-centered assumptions, namely, that women see the prestige hierarchy in ways similar to men. The voices heard here, while admittedly few and from a training program that may not be particularly representative of national medical education programs, expose the silent, symbolic work of gender and suggest resistance. Does the resistance lend support to the cultural feminist perspective that women's values differ from men's? Perhaps, but the cultural feminist perspective does not allow for variation (only some women resisted) and ignores the extent to which differences might be a reaction to perceived structural barriers.

Do masculine images of activity and toughness that pervade descriptions of higher-status specialties contribute to women's ghettoization in the medical specialty hierarchy? Such a conclusion is problematic if we take seriously women's own words, such as those of the obstetrician-gynecologist: "Women are going into fields because they choose to, and tough shit, and we just don't happen to care that we're not high on *their* hierarchy" (emphasis added). This individual clearly resists what ghettoization implies: that structural forces (and individuals in higher-level positions) conspire to keep some individuals (i.e., women) out of higher-status worlds. However, the same person evoked gendered images ("her testicles are bigger than anybody else's . . . she is so macho") that may function as symbolic barriers. Furthermore, it is possible that some women actively construct symbolic barriers as a guard against entry into marginalized specialties that are rife with pitfalls to avoid, such as grueling, militaristic training schedules.

The structural-agency divide is deep and dates back to Karl Marx's (1852) classic observation that men make their own history but not under circumstances of their own choosing. Structuralist theories, such as those posited by liberal feminists who argue that the informal system of sponsorship and sexist treatment effectively keep women out of more prestigious specialties, tend to minimize the role of human agency. As H. Giroux (1983: 108) notes. "Too often they ignore the complex ways in which people mediate and respond to the interface between their own lived experiences and structures of domination and constraint." However, cultural theories, such as the feminist theory that posits that women hold different values, are flawed as well. Jay MacLeod (1995: 148) asserts, "Culturalist theories . . . too often fail to contextualize attitudes and behavior as responses to objective structures." The present narratives offer a way over the structure-agency divide, at least for the issue of gender and specialty choice.

Based on the respondents' voices, I propose an alternative liberal feminist perspective that allows for more agency. Whereas the traditional liberal feminist perspective emphasizes a male-dominated structure that, either indirectly through an informal system of sponsorship or more directly through sexist treatment, effectively keeps females out of the more prestigious medical specialties, my research suggests two "twists." First, the voices recorded here did not support the notion that male gatekeepers prevent women's entrance into desirable, high-status specialties; rather, the narrative indicates a range of embodied masculine images and symbols embedded in those specialties—a much subtler structural barrier. Furthermore, while women emphasized that they did what they wanted and no one "kept them" from anything, their own words suggest that the images encoded in the highest-status specialties might be inconsistent with their own sense of self and body. Future studies might benefit from tending closely to perceptions of the embodied hierarchy and how women and men view their place within it.

The second twist to the liberal feminist perspective lies in the active resistance of hierarchical interpretations of medical specialties. Recall the argument by one resident that the value system is male and that women "tend not to buy into that as much." This suggests not only a recognition of the maleness of the system but also an active rejection of it, rather than a passive acquiescence to a male-dominated structure. Utilizing a small sample from an admittedly atypical training institution does not justify sweeping generalizations. (And keep in mind that only four of the 10 women interviewed resisted the concept of a prestige hierarchy.) However, it is possible that resistant attitudes reveal oppositional behavior in the specialty choices of women, behavior rooted in a critique of the gendered ideology undergirding the medical specialty hierarchy. Rather than submitting to a dominant gender ideology by being forced into more feminine specialties, women struggled against the gendered structure of medical specialties but chose feminine specialties anyway as an "in your face" move. (One resident that I interviewed informally before beginning my research described how horrified her peers were when she turned down an extremely high-status specialty—neurosurgery—for the lower-status specialty of obstetrics-gynecology because, to paraphrase, she loved the daily miracle of birth. In fact, she admitted that she had trouble accepting her own choice of a "girl" specialty because, as one of the best and brightest, she could have done anything she wanted.)

I would argue, following MacLeod (1995: 21–22), that studies *focused* on resistance (which was not the intent of this study) are key to understanding "the ongoing, active experiences of individuals while simultaneously perceiving in oppositional attitudes and practices a response to structures of constraint and domination." Women's location in lower-status specialties may not be simply a result of the power of the gendered images encoded in the hierarchy that weigh on the choices of women. Rather, women may valorize or rescue what has been devalued as an act of resistance. Future research on specialty choice would do well to focus on the use of embodied metaphors and the presence of resistance in its varied forms. While these narratives capture resistance, it emerged during the data analysis and did not allow me to address openly the range of oppositional attitudes and practices.

In conclusion, these findings shift the focus from individual-level gender differences toward a gendered examination of the medical specialty hierarchy. Through their words, these women and men give voice to the silent, symbolic, embodied work of gender that shapes the structure of the medical specialties into a ladder with a masculine top and feminine bottom, regardless of whether female or male bodies occupy the rungs.

NOTES

1. Some recent evidence suggests that the trend toward specialization is tapering off as more physicians are encouraged to become primary care doctors. Specifically, Xu and colleagues (1995) report an increase in the percentage of medical students interested in primary care careers, from 14.6 percent in 1992 to 22.8 percent in 1994. However, they note that interest in primary care falls well short of the stated goal of the Association of American Medical Colleges that half of all graduates should choose generalist careers.

2. Articles written by medical professionals and published in medical journals tend to invoke (their research did not always support) the social roles perspective. In fact, two of the specialties with the most controllable lifestyles are radiology and anesthesiology; women are underrepresented in both (AMA 1994).

3. As far as I know, my study is the only one designed to test empirically the cultural feminist perspective against the liberal feminist and social roles perspectives. The hypotheses were developed by drawing some of the "classic" (albeit nonmedical) cultural feminist works, such as Gilligan's *In a Different Voice* (1982), Belenky, Clinchy, Goldberger, and Tavule's *Women's Ways of Knowing* (1986), and Ruddick's *Maternal Thinking* (1989).

4. According to scholars of Western biomedicine, the current trend in psychiatry toward biochemical approaches has been prompted, in part, by the higher prestige attached to bodily manipulation than to psychoanalysis (Gaines 1992).

5. I am indebted to a *TSQ* reviewer for pushing me to think about the variety of forms inherent in resistance.

6. The residents' words suggest that patient perceptions of what doctors do is important to how doctors think about what they do. A few studies reveal that lay perceptions differ from professional perceptions (Matteson and Smith 1977; Rosoff and Leone 1991); I'm not aware of any studies that examine the influence of lay perceptions on professional perceptions.

7. It is interesting that the brain generates prestige only if a surgeon invades it. Manipulating brain processes through drugs (as a psychiatrist might) does not boost the prestige ranking of that specialty.

8. Moving farther back in the causal chain, the sociologist or public health worker might point out that if income inequalities were minimized, or tobacco companies reigned in, we would see less smoking to begin with.

9. The status of obstetrician-gynecologists is often contested because they are viewed as passive baby catchers by some (namely, surgeons), although they do perform surgeries. Cassell (1998) uncovers this tension in her work as well. Although the American College of Surgeons and the Association of Women Surgeons include obstetrician-gynecologists, she opted to exclude them from her study of women surgeons because their training is different and because most surgeons view them as "different."

10. Because the body was associated with the feminine as medicine evolved and as surgical skills and knowledge grew in the nineteenth century, the profession worked to cultivate its masculine image by emphasizing its active, hands-on heroic work of fixing the body (Lawrence 1998).

REFERENCES

AMERICAN BOARD OF MEDICAL SPECIALTIES (ABMS). 1990. Evanston, IL.

ABBOTT, ANDREW. 1981. "Status and Status Strain in the Professions." *American Journal of Sociology* 86:819–835.

ACKER, JOAN. 1990. "Hierarchies, Jobs, Bodies: A Theory of Gendered Organizations." *Gender and Society* 4:139–158.

———. 1992. "Gendered Institutions." *Contemporary Sociology* 21:565–568.

AMERICAN MEDICAL ASSOCIATION. 1994. "Graduate Medical Education (AMA), Appendix II." *Journal of the American Medical Association* 272:725–733.

———. 1995–1996. *Physician Characteristics and Distribution in the U.S.* Chicago: American Medical Association.

ANDERSON, BRUCE. 1975. "Choosing a Medical Specialty: A Critique of Literature in the Light of 'Curious Findings.'" *Journal of Health and Social Behavior* 16:152–162.

BECKER, HOWARD, BLANCHE GEER, EVERETT HUGHES, and ANSLEM STRAUSS. 1961. *Boys in White: Student Culture in Medical School.* Chicago: University of Chicago Press.

BELENKY, MARY F., BLYTHE M. CLINCHY, NANCY R. GOLDBERGER, and JILL M. TARULE. 1986. *Women's Ways of Knowing: The Development of Self, Voice, and Mind.* New York: Basic Books.

BIELBY, WILLIAM and JAMES BARON. 1986. "Men and Women at Work: Sex Segregation and Statistical Discrimination." *American Journal of Sociology* 91:759–799.

BLAND, CAROLE J., LINDA N. MEURER, and GEORGE MALDONADO. 1995. "Determinants of Primary Care Specialty Choice: A Non-Statistical Meta-Analysis of the Literature." *Academic Medicine* 70:620–641.

BLAU, PETER and OTIS DUNCAN. 1967. *The American Occupational Structure.* New York: John Wiley and Sons.

BORDO, SUSAN. 1993. *Unbearable Weight: Feminism, Western Culture, and the Body.* Berkeley: University of California Press.

BRUHN, JOHN G. and OSCAR A. PARSONS. 1964. "Medical Student Attitudes Toward Four Medical Specialties." *Journal of Medical Education* 39:40–49.

BURKETT, G. and M. H. GELULA. 1982. "Characteristics of Students Preferring Family Practice Primary Care Careers." *Journal of Family Practice* 15:505–512.

CASSELL, JOAN. 1998. *The Woman in the Surgeon's Body.* Cambridge, MA: Harvard University Press.

COLLINS, PATRICIA H. 1990. *Black Feminist Thought: Knowledge, Consciousness and the Politics of Empowerment.* Boston: Unwin Hyman.

DAVIDSON, LYNNE R. 1979. "Choice by Constraint." *Journal of Health, Politics, Policy, and Law* 4:200–220.

DAVIS, KINGSLEY and WILBERT E. MOORE. 1945. "Some Principles of Stratification." *American Sociological Review* 10:242–249.

EHRENREICH, BARBARA and DEIDRE ENGLISH. 1973. *Witches, Midwives, and Nurses: A History of Women Healers.* New York: Feminist Press.

ENGLAND, PAULA and LORI MCCREARY. 1987. "Gender Inequality in Paid Employment." Pp. 286–320 in *Analyzing Gender: A Handbook of Social Science Research,* edited by Beth Hess and Myra Marx Ferree. Thousand Oaks, CA: Sage.

FERREE, MYRA MARX 1985. "Between Two Worlds: German Feminist Approaches to Working-Class Women and Work." *Signs: Journal of Women in Culture and Society* 10:517–536.

GAINES, ATWOOD. 1992. "From DSM to III-R: Voices of Self, Mastery and the Other: A Cultural Constructivist Reading of U.S. Psychiatric Classification." *Social Science and Medicine* 35:3–24.

GATENS, MOIRA. 1996. *Imaginary Bodies: Ethics, Power and Corporeality.* New York: Routledge.

GEERTZ, CLIFFORD. 1973. *The Interpretation of Culture.* New York: Basic Books.

GILLIGAN, CAROL. 1982. *In Different Voice: Psychological Theory and Women's Development.* Cambridge, MA: Harvard University Press.

Giroux, Henry. 1983. *Theory and Resistance in Education.* London: Heinemann Educational Books.

GLASER, BARNEY G. and ANSLEM STRAUSS. 1967. *The Discovery of Grounded Theory: Strategies for Qualitative Research.* New York: Aldine de Gruyter.

HARDING, SANDRA. 1986. *The Science Question in Feminism.* Ithaca, NY: Cornell University Press.

HINZE, SUSAN W. 1995. "The Intra-Occupational Sex Segregation of Physicians: Why Gender Matters." Unpublished Doctoral Dissertation. Vanderbilt University.

HINZE, SUSAN W. 1997. "I Think It's the Macho Thing: Resident Perceptions of the Prestige of Medical Specialties." Presented at Southern Sociological Society Conference, April 3–6. Atlanta, GA.

HOCHSCHILD, ARLIE. 1983. *The Managed Heart: The Commercialization of Human Feeling.* Berkeley: University of California Press.

JACOBS, JERRY A. 1989. "Long-Term Trends in Occupational Segregation by Sex." *American Journal of Sociology* 95:160–173.

KANTER, ROSABETH M. 1977. *Men and Women of the Corporation.* New York: Basic Books.

KELLER, EVELYN F. 1992. *Secrets of Life, Secrets of Death: Essays on Language, Gender and Science.* New York: Routledge.

KRITZER, H. and C. N. ZIMET. 1967. "A Retrospective View of Medical Specialty Choice." *Journal of Medical Education* 42:47–53.

KUTNER, NANCY K. and DONNA P. BROGIN. 1990. "Gender Roles, Medical Practice Roles, and Ob-Gyn Career Choice: A Longitudinal Study." *Women and Health* 16(3-4):99–117.

LAWRENCE, CHRISTOPHER. 1998. "Medical Minds, Surgical Bodies: Corporeality and the Doctors." Pp. 156–201 in *Science Incarnate: Historical Embodiments of Natural Knowledge,* edited by Christoper Lawrence and Steven Shapin. Chicago: University of Chicago Press.

LESERMAN, JANE. 1981. *Men and Women in Medical School: How They Change and How They Compare.* New York: Praeger.

LIEU, T., S. SCHROEDER and D. ALTMAN. 1989. "Specialty Choices at One Medical School: Recent Trends and Analyses of Predictive Factors." *Academic Medicine* 64:622–629.

LORBER, JUDITH. 1984. *Women Physicians: Career, Status and Power.* New York: Tavistock Publications.

———. 1987. "A Welcome to a Crowded Field: Where Will the New Women Physicians Fit in?" *Journal of American Medical Women's Association* 42:149–152.

MACLEOD, JAY. 1995. *Ain't No Makin' It: Leveled Aspirations in a Low-Income Neighborhood.* Boulder, CO: Westview Press.

MARDER, WILLIAM, PHILLIP KLETKE, ANNE SILBERGER, and R. WILKE. 1988. *Physician Supply and Utilization by Specialty: Trends and Projections.* Chicago: American Medical Association.

MARTIN STEVEN C., ROBERT M. ARNOLD, and RUTH M. PARKER.1988. "Gender and Medical Socialization." *Journal of Health and Social Behavior* 29:333–343.

MARX, KARL. 1852. *The Eighteenth Brumaire of Louis Bonaparte.* New York: International Publishers.

MATTESON, M. and S. SMITH. 1977. "Medical Specialty Choice: A Note on Status Rankings." *Social Science and Medicine* 11:421–423.

MCGRATH, ELLEN and CARL N. ZIMET. 1977a. "Female and Male Medical Students: Differences in Specialty Choice Selection and Personality." *Journal of Medical Education* 52:293–300.

———. 1977b. "Similarities and Predictors of Specialty Interest among Female Medical Students." *Journal of the American Medical Women's Association* 32:361–373.

MERTON, R. K., S. BLOOM, and N. ROGOFF. 1956. "Studies in the Sociology of Medical Education." *Journal of Medical Education* 31:552–565.

MILLER-LOESSI, KAREN. 1992. "Toward Gender Integration in the Workplace: Issues at Multiple Levels." *Sociological Perspectives* 35(1):1–15.

MORANTZ-SANCHEZ, REGINA M. 1985. *Sympathy and Science: Women Physicians in American Medicine.* New York: Oxford University Press.

PAVALKO, RONALD. 1988. *Sociology of Occupations and Professions.* Itasca, IL: Peacock.

PERRONE, BOBETTE, H. H. STOCKEL, and VICTORIA KRUEGER. 1989. *Medicine Women, Curanderas, and Women Doctors.* Norman: University of Oklahoma Press.

QUADAGNO, JILL. 1976. "Occupational Sex-Typing and Internal Labor Market Distributions." *Social Problems* 23:442–453.

RESKIN, BARBARA F. and PATRICIA A. ROOS. 1990. *Job Queues, Gender Queues: Explaining Women's Inroads into Male Occupations.* Philadelphia, PA: Temple University Press.

ROSOFF, STEPHEN M. and MATTHEW C. LEONE. 1989. "The Prestige of Dermatologists." *International Journal of Dermatology* 28(6):377–380.

———. 1991. "The Public Prestige of Medical Specialties: Overviews and Undercurrents." *Social Science and Medicine* 32(3):321–326.

RUDDICK, SARA. 1989. *Maternal Thinking: Toward a Politics of Peace.* Boston, MA: Beacon Press.

SCHOBOT, DAVID B., WILLIAM CAYLEY, JR., and B. C. ELIASON. 1996. "Personal Values Related to Primary Care Specialty Aspirations." *Educational Research and Methods* 28(10):726–731.

SHORTELL, STEPHEN M. 1974. "Occupational Prestige Differences within the Medical and Allied Health Professions." *Social Science and Medicine* 8:1–9.

STARR, PAUL. 1982. *The Social Transformation of American Medicine.* New York: Basic Books.

WAJCAM, JUDY. 1991. *Feminism Confronts Technology.* University Park: Pennsylvania State University Press.

WILLIAMS, CHRISTINE L. 1989. *Gender Differences at Work: Women and Men in Nontraditional Occupations.* Berkeley: University of California Press.

XU, GANG, SUSAN L. RATTNER, J. J. VELOSKI, MOHAMMADREZA HOJAT, SYLVIA K. FIELDS, and BARBARA BARZANSKY. 1995. "A National Study of the Factors Influencing Men and Women Physicians' Choices of Primary Care Specialties." *Academic Medicine* 70:398–404.

ZIMET, CARL and MARK L. HELD. 1975. "The Development of Views of Specialties During Four Years of Medical School." *Journal of Medical Education* 50:157–166.

Part IX
NURSES

Have you ever watched "ER," "Chicago Hope," or "General Hospital"? Have you read articles or books situated in a medical setting? Have you been to a clinic, hospital, or nursing home? Based on these experiences, what are your images of nurses? What are their responsibilities and duties? Why are they so important to you when you are sick or ill?

Historically, nineteenth-century nursing, particularly in the United States, attracted women who sometimes received specialized training and who frequently served as subordinate handmaidens of the more powerful physicians. Valued for her stereotypically feminine qualities, the female nurse to a large extent provided nurturing care to alleviate physical and emotional pain and suffering. Over time, however, nursing and the traditional nurse–physician relationship has changed. Government policies, organizational priorities, and provider behavior were involved in these transformations, but so, too, were expanding educational opportunities, the reemergence of the women's liberation movement, employment shortages, and the entry of men into nursing. As a result, nursing has evolved and continues to evolve in response to the surrounding social environment.

Compared to the past, nurses today perform a wide range of tasks within a diverse health care arena. They may minister to a patient's physical and emotional needs, monitor life-saving equipment, apprise physicians of a patient's medical status, and carry out various administrative and supervisory functions. Additionally, they may conduct physical examinations or deliver babies as nurse practitioners or midwives and teach nursing students at community colleges or four-year institutions of higher learning. In the future, nurses may replace physicians in the provision of primary care, assume greater administrative responsibilities, and serve as vital policy analysts. All in all, nurses are on track to enhance their occupational standing as respected members of the health care community.

In the article "Women in a Women's Job: The Gendered Experience of Nurses," Sam Porter examines the contemporary situation of nurses in a metropolitan hospital in the north of Ireland. He wanted to determine how the social structure of gender influences the working lives of nurses. Through participant observation and informal conversation, he discovered that a nurse's gender does not impact interactions with physicians, as female and male nurses tend to be treated similarly. In contrast, physicians' gender matters, as female doctors are more egalitarian than male colleagues in their dealings with nurses and patients. Gender also plays a role in female nurses' interpretation of their occupational status—especially when they observe more career opportunities and social mobility for their male counterparts. Becoming increasingly assertive, nurses desire more directness and openness in their association with physicians. Contrary to popular mythology, nurses are not sexually permissive, promiscuous playthings. Ironically, gender inequality appears to have lessened among nurses and physicians while increasing in the male nurse manager and female nurse relationship. Hence, gender remains a salient factor overshadowing nurses' working lives.

Do Sam Porter's research results coincide with your images of nursing? What are the similarities? What are the differences? Whatever the images, we have learned that gender equality still eludes female nurses. However, unwilling to passively accept their position, female nurses are becoming more actively involved in challenging the gender barriers that obstruct their professional advancement.

WOMEN IN A WOMEN'S JOB: THE GENDERED EXPERIENCE OF NURSES

Sam Porter
The Queen's University of Belfast

The aim of this paper is to examine how the structural influence of gender affects nurses in their working lives. Gender segregation exists both within and between the occupations of medicine and nursing. It is largely founded on the social construction of a skills/caring dichotomy. An analysis of how the gender of nurses and doctors affects their interactions with coworkers reveals that the increasing proportion of female doctors has attenuated power differences between the two occupations. Examination of nurses' attitudes to gender demonstrates that they are very aware of the problem, despite a tendency to accept credentialist justifications of inequality. As a result of this they are becoming more assertive. The issue of sexual stereotyping is addressed and it is noted that popular mythology about sexual relations between doctors and nurses is highly misleading. Privatized aspirations are having a decreasing influence over nurses' working lives. In conclusion, while gender inequality is losing some of its power in nurse–doctor relationships, it is becoming an increasingly significant factor in the relationship between male nurse managers and female workers.

INTRODUCTION

Issues of gender have been identified as being of considerable importance in explaining the position of nurses (for example, Mackay 1990). Gender affects nursing in three interconnected ways. First, because nursing is popularly seen as mundane "women's work," it is devalued (Abbott and Wallace 1990). Second, because nursing is situated within a stark sexual division of labor alongside the predominantly male occupation of medicine, gender over-determines interoccupational inequalities (Gamarnikow 1978). Third, with the development of a predominantly male managerial elite, gender inequalities are increasingly becoming an issue within nursing (Hearn 1982; Carpenter 1977, 1978).

The purpose of this paper is to illuminate, largely through qualitative analysis, how the social structure of gender affects actors within specific social situations, namely two units in a general hospital. Four major substantive areas are addressed: first, how gender affects power relations between doctors and nurses; second, how gender affects power relations between male and female nurses; third, how nurses interpret issues of gender, and finally, how sexual stereotyping affects relations between doctors and nurses.

Reprinted from *Sociology of Health & Illness*, vol. 14, no. 4 (1992), pp. 510–27, by permission of Blackwell Publishers Ltd/Editorial Board.

THE SEXUAL DIVISION OF LABOR

The most striking difference in the composition of medicine and nursing is gender. Since its rise as an organized profession, medicine has been a predominantly male occupation while nursing has long been regarded as one of the archetypal female occupations. Gamarnikow (1978) has argued that Victorian doctor-nurse-patient relationships could be equated with husband-wife-child relationships. Through their monopoly over diagnosis and prescription, doctors decided who should be a patient and what should be done to them. Nurses were limited, according to Florence Nightingale's precepts, to assisting their medical superiors and to maintaining a hygenic and comfortable environment for their charges who in turn had little knowledge of or authority over what was happening to them. The shadow of these formative role relations remains (Dingwall and McIntosh 1978).

Female disadvantage is not limited to differences between these occupations, it is equally notable within them. Despite recent increases in the number of women entering medical schools, the profession remains firmly in the hands of men (Elston 1977). This is evidenced by vertical segregation within the occupation which means that women occupy proportionately far fewer senior posts than their male counterparts, and also by horizontal segregation. In general surgery, for example, less than 1 percent of consultants are female. Women tend to be concentrated in specialities such as child and adolescent psychiatry (Oliver and Walford 1991).

Numerically, male entry into nursing has been considerably less significant than female entry into medicine. In 1987, fewer than 10 percent of nurses in Britain were men (Gaze 1987). The fate of this small male minority has, however, been considerably more auspicious than that of its female counterpart in medicine. Since the introduction of an industrially modelled line management system following the Salmon Report (1966), men have come to dominate the management of both nursing practice and education, to the point where by 1987 they held over 50 percent of chief nurse and director of nurse education posts in Britain (Gaze 1987). There was an implicit sexism in the Salmon Report; it regarded the "feminine qualities" of nurses as appropriate to bedside care but as a profound hindrance to efficient administration, in that they encouraged concentration on minutiae at the expense of decisiveness. Salmon saw the direction forward as the promotion of a "rational," "masculine" style of management (Carpenter 1978).

It can be seen that gender segregation correlates strongly with both inter- and intra-occupational differentials. The gender inequalities occurring in these two areas can be mutually reinforcing. The successful entry of a male minority into nursing, rather then diluting gender as a major defining factor in occupational differentiation, has exacerbated it by adding male managers to the nurse's burden of male doctors. Conversely, there is some evidence that the increasing entrance of women into medicine is leading to a degree of democratization in the nurse–doctor relationship (Webster 1985).

CURING VERSUS CARING, SKILL VERSUS SYMPATHY

One of the main themes emerging from the above discussion is that women's second-class status both within and between the occupations of nursing and medicine is in part the result of assumptions founded upon a reductionist sociobiological model of gender role differentiation. According to such a model, women, as an extension of their maternal functions, possess expressive, emotional, and caring qualities, while men are naturally more instrumental, rational, scientific, and decisive. This social construction of the female role has been described by Hearn (1982) as the "patriarchal feminine"; feminine because it accords to the feminine, "caring" stereotype; patriarchal because in doing so it reinforces female subordination.

The patriarchal feminine is not simply a descriptive exercise, but involves judgment about the value of various human activities. Those activities which are categorized as being in the male domain are valued more highly than those adjudged appropriate for women (Sayers 1982).

The patriarchal feminine is not, however, the only interpretation open to those who accept "given" gender differences. An alternative position attaches positive rather than negative evaluations to what are seen as immutable womanly traits. A number of radical feminists (for example, de Beauvoir 1983; Firestone 1979) posit biologistic explanations for the sexual division of labor, treating it as a natural, rather than socially generated division (Gamarnikow 1978).

In consonance with such a position, many nursing theorists accept the existence of a skills/caring, male/female dichotomy. This is hardly surprising, given that caring is seen as a core, and indeed unique, attribute of nursing. Defense of the importance of emotional labor is therefore central to the affirmation of nursing's worth (Robinson 1991).[1] The battleground therefore becomes how the various attributes of nursing and medicine are to be evaluated:

> As long as fields that are stereotypically male, highly technological and illness orientated are held in higher esteem than those that have been stereotypically female, focusing on long-term care, quality of life and health maintenance, there is little reason to foresee major changes in interprofessional relationships. . . . (Webster 1985: 317).

Claims for occupational equality are based on the assertion that natural female attributes are at least equal to male characteristics and that the "feminine" tasks performed by nurses are of equal worth to the "masculine" work of doctors (Gordon 1991). As Salvage puts it, "Nurses/women should realise that doctors/men have much to learn from them" (1985: 171).

AIMS AND METHOD

Thus far I have examined how gender inequalities influence the structure of medicine and nursing. However, this does not illustrate how these inequalities affect action, nor indeed, how action maintains or transforms structural inequalities. My empirical enquiries were directed to the question of how the social structure of gender inequality influences social action and vice versa.

The empirical material for this paper was gathered over a three-month period in 1989, during which I was employed as a staff nurse in a large metropolitan hospital in the north of Ireland. It was hoped that the size and urban location of the hospital would mean that local idiosyncracies would be minimized, thus enhancing the external validity of the research. Being within the British jurisdictional zone, public health provision in this part of Ireland is subsumed within the British National Health Service. Health service structures are similar, though not identical, to those in Britain. For example, implementation of the Griffiths management system has been considerably more tardy here than in the rest of the NHS. When this research was undertaken, the Salmon system of management was extant in the hospital observed.

Most of the information came from the intensive care unit in which I was temporarily employed as a staff nurse. The number of subjects observed, disaggregated for occupation, sex, and position were:

	Female	Male
Nurses		
Sister/Charge Nurse	4	0
Staff Nurse	22	3
Nursing Auxiliary	4	0
Total	30	3

	Female	Male
Doctors		
Consultant	0	10
Registrar	1	2
Senior House Officer	5	3
Total	6	15

Data were obtained both by participant observation and by informal discussions between myself and the actors involved. The research might be described as quasi-covert in that while I informed my subjects that I was carrying out a project to examine how nurses communicated with other health care occupations, I did not emphasize my interest in the sensitive issues of power and gender.

Initiating talk about gender issues was easy. One factor that helped was my own sex. The fact that I am male had the ironic and useful effect of encouraging female nurses to be extremely frank about their views. Given the latent resentment harbored by many female nurses about what they perceive as the unfair occupational advantages of their male colleagues, the opportunity provided by a male nurse asking them to tell him what they really thought about men in health care was too good to miss.

Working in an intensive care unit facilitated observation. First, six out of the eight beds in the unit were situated in one room. As a consequence, a large proportion of staff activity was easily observable. Second, the nature of intensive care nursing, with its high nurse–patient ratio, meant that I had time to observe and record interactions. Nevertheless, pressure of work meant that there were

occasions when a considerable period of time elapsed between observation of data and their recording.

Additional data were obtained by a colleague from a general medical ward.[2] The empirical work conducted in this area was guided by the tentative conclusions that emerged from my own data collection, in an attempt to support or falsify them. This was especially important in instances where the numbers involved in the intensive care unit were small. For example, a further five male nurses were observed on the ward. The method of data collection here was solely that of participant observation.

The final source of information for this paper is the most difficult to quantify, but I suspect it was of considerable importance, especially in determination of the direction that the formal research took. This was my seven and a half years of participation in the subject milieu as a clinical nurse.

My method of analysis was based on analytic induction. Questions concerning gender and nursing had emerged from my previous experience as a clinical nurse and from reviewing the literature. These initial questions were:

1. What form did interaction between doctors and nurses take in decision-making sequences?[3]
2. Did gender permutations influence the nature of inter- or intraoccupational interaction?
3. Did female nurses utilize the concept of gender in their understanding of their occupational position?
4. How assertive were female nurses with their male coworkers?
5. Was there any basis for the popular stereotyping of nurses' sexual habits?
6. What did nurses think about their stereotype?

Observation of interactions with these questions in mind led to the formulation of tentative answers. These were then tested to ascertain if they could explain the most common forms of interaction. "Deviant" cases were examined to see if they could be the basis of alternative explanations.

The next step was to test whether my explanations could adequately explain social action occurring in another arena, a general medical ward. Given the variation of divisions of labor between different units, even within a single hospital (Strauss et al. 1985), I felt it was important to test the generalizability of my conclusions. Because intensive care is in many ways unique as a therapeutic regimen, considerable caution needs to be exercised in the extrapolation of results obtained from an ICU[4] to more general claims about the nature of nurse–doctor interactions. Three pertinent specificities of this social situation should be noted. First, the high level of medical intervention that intensive care entails means that there is far more interaction between nurses and doctors in an ICU than in most other units, where a large proportion of care tends to be performed by nurses on their own. Second, emphasis on technology reinforces instrumental aspects of care, a factor that might be seen as strengthening medical superordination. Finally, the unit studied was fairly small, which meant that the number of personnel observed was rather low.

The final stage of analysis was an ex post facto formal quantification of some of the data. The purpose of this exercise was not to offer strong proofs for my claims. Rather, simple counting techniques were used to strengthen the evidence gained from other methods; to render explicit quantification; and to give a general impression of the data, thus contextualizing the extracts of interaction included in the paper (Silverman 1985).

GENDER PERMUTATIONS AND POWER

The effects of gender upon nurse–doctor interactions were measured by observing the interactions of four different combinations:

male doctors and nurses, female doctors and nurses, female nurses and doctors, male nurses and doctors; and by studying the attitudes of female nurses to their gender roles. The first thing I noted was that the gender of a nurse appeared to have little effect on their interaction with doctors. The male nurses studied were not observed to have any marked increase in authority in relation to doctors as compared to their female counterparts. Indeed the quality of interaction between male nurses and doctors and female nurses and doctors seemed to be identical.

Support for this contention came from counting the number of times male and female nurses were observed to make evaluative comments to doctors in reply to medical requests (see Table 1). While lack of comment by nurses does not necessarily reflect subservience in that silence can mean considered consent, the act of comment is indicative of assertiveness in that it entails an assumption by the nurse that her/his opinion is important.

In contrast, the interactions of female doctors with nurses were markedly different from some of their male colleagues. Two instances which occurred on the same day illustrate this point. The first involved a male senior house officer who was preparing to

TABLE 1 Occurrences of Evaluative Verbal Responses by Staff Nurses in Reply to Doctors' Clinical Requests by Sex of Nurse

	Female %	Male %
Commented to doctor about request	28	22
Complied without comment	72	78
Base	53	36

($\chi^2 = 0.15$; 1 d.f.; $p < 0.05$).

The association between gender and likelihood of talking back to doctors was not statistically significant.

perform an aseptic procedure, and who was being assisted by a nurse. His sole verbal communication with the nurse during the entire episode consisted of the demand "Gloves!" At the end of the procedure he left the bedside without a word, leaving the nurse to clear up his debris.

The second involved a female SHO who was also performing an aseptic technique. As well as talking to the patient, the doctor also greeted the nurse, engaging in small talk with both nurse and patient throughout the procedure. Her requests were also expressed in a far more polite manner:

> Sorry, would you mind opening these gloves for me . . . thanks.

On completing the procedure, she tidied away all her waste rather than leaving the nurse to do it.

This is not to say that all male doctors were as pompous as the one noted above. Indeed, there was considerable variation in the behavior of male doctors toward nurses. Nor was it the case that there were no exceptions to the rule of sisterly love, as the following interaction between a staff nurse on the medical ward and a newly arrived doctor demonstrates:

> SN(F): Hello, I'm Forename, I staff here. You must be the new JHO.
> SHO(F): Actually, Staff Nurse, I am Doctor Surname and I happen to be a senior house officer.

Nevertheless, it was generally true that most female doctors were considerably more egalitarian than most of their male counterparts.

A quantitative indication of this came from counting the number of times doctors were prepared to tidy up after themselves, rather than leaving debris for nurses to dispose of. While 65 percent of female doctors observed cleaned up their clinical waste after procedures, the figure was only 36 percent for male doctors. Even when (male) consultants, who

were notably cavalier in their attitude toward procedures, were excluded from the question, the difference remained statistically significant.

The individual variations in behavior noted are a reminder that while gender may be an important factor in interoccupational interaction, it is not the only one. Other aspects of status difference have considerable influence. These may be formal prescriptions about occupational roles (Johnson 1972) or reflections of the immediate situational context within which interactions take place (Hughes 1988). These factors can either reinforce or countervail against the influence of gender.

The fact that nurses' gender had far less impact on the quality of interoccupational interaction than that of doctors probably indicates the power differential that exists between the two groups overall. Being in a weaker occupation means that nurses have less opportunity to engineer the quality of relationships. The inability of male nurses to utilize the advantages of their gender is the result of the ascription to nursing of a position of female subordination. The very factors that afford male nurses intraoccupational advantage work against them in interoccupational power relations. Conversely, because of their position of authority, doctors have considerable latitude in deciding how they are going to interact with members of other occupations. They have the opportunity to avail themselves of the power that they implicitly possess if they wish to, or to act in a more egalitarian fashion if they do not.

NURSES' ATTITUDES TO GENDER ISSUES

There was a militancy apparent in many nurses concerning doctors' assumptions about their inferior gender and occupational roles. Even when they acceded to performing "handmaiden" activities, they often did so with bad grace, as the following incident demonstrates:

The phone in the doctors' room rang. As all the doctors and nurses on duty were busy with other tasks and unavailable to answer it, a female staff nurse left her tea break to take the call. It was a message for a consultant who was on another phone at the time. The nurse spent several minutes standing in silence beside the consultant until he had finished his call and then informed him of the content of the other. She then returned to her tea and exclaimed to the other nurses on their break:

> SN(F): Nurse, cleaner, secretary, receptionist, that's all they think we are. The old sod didn't even say thank you!

Female nurses were conscious that their gender was a significant factor affecting the status of their occupation, though the value judgments that they attached to this fact differed considerably. A minority (four out of the 19 nurses specifically asked) expressed the view that occupational gender differences were to be explained by men having careers while women simply had jobs until they started a family. These differences in work experiences were seen as reflecting natural differences in the roles of the sexes. These nurses tended to accept their lot with equanimity. Others were considerably more assertive in their attitudes, as the following comment of a ward nurse immediately after an altercation with a junior house officer demonstrates:

> SN(F): If that boy thinks we're little women here at his beck and call, he's going to have to learn the hard way. He's nothing but a wee male chauvinist pig!

Criticism like this was reserved for those male doctors who were openly bombastic or sexist. While nurses were often prepared to explain the position of their own occupation in terms of gender, they rarely applied the same critique to doctors. Sexism was seen as an individual phenomenon of specific doctors rather than an institutional ethos. However, the individualist explanations found in this study may not be entirely representative of nurses' attitudes, as the published opinion of one student nurse demonstrates:

> So why do we nurses find ourselves in this [subservient] situation? Nursing is, and always has been, "women's work" and medicine a man's world (Jones 1987:59).

Female nurses in this study were far more willing to ascribe general categorizations to male nurses. The success of senior male nurses was often put down to their sex. Male nurses in the clinical area, and therefore relatively junior in the nursing hierarchy, were invariably regarded as being on their way to higher things, once again because of their sex. My position as a former clinical nurse now studying at a university meant that I did not escape the brunt of this perception.

While their gender opened up greater career opportunities for male nurses, this did not mean that it gave clinical male nurses any advantage over their female counterparts in the immediate situation that they worked in. Barring an underlying resentment of female nurses about the unfairness of promotional opportunities for men, I found no difference in the attitudes and behaviour of other nurses toward male and female ward nurses of the same grade.

Within the clinical focus of this study, the mechanisms by which men were able to advance themselves within nursing administration were not observed. This is significant, because it means that the generation of male hegemony within nursing management lies outside the doing of nursing. Examination of what these mechanisms are would be a fruitful point of departure for further research.

THE PERSUASIVENESS OF CREDENTIALISM

It may seem strange that while nurses viewed the position of their own job in terms of gender, they did not extend this outlook to their analysis of the position of medicine. After all, the positions of the two occupations are inextricably linked, and the brute fact of gender segregation appears to be obvious. However, the difference in attitude of female nurses to male nurses and to male doctors may be due to a difference in familiarity that they have about the processes of occupational advancement.

Because of a high degree of occupational segregation, nurses do not have a great deal of knowledge about how occupational advancement operates for doctors. They are confronted by doctors as people already possessing enabling qualifications and legal licence. These entitlements to occupational superiority are portrayed as being the unproblematic and exclusive result of a meritocratic process. It is hardly surprising, therefore, that nurses find it difficult to form a generalized gendered critique of the position of their medical counterparts.[5] This is testament to the justificatory power of credentialism in the maintenance of occupational closure (Berlant 1975).

Because nurses have had direct experience of the conditions pertaining in the processes of occupational advancement within their own occupation, they take a more cynical attitude toward them. Often either they, or someone they know, has been passed over in favor of a male colleague. This familiarity means that gender bias can less easily be hidden by the guise of functionalist justifications such as educational or experiential differentials.

INCREASING ASSERTIVENESS

While most nurses accepted that the position of doctors was largely due to their accrued credentials, this did not mean that they necessarily saw doctoring as a more important facet of health care than the activities that nurses were involved in. A number of nurses expressed their belief in the importance of nursing care in the promotion of health. The debate about the relative merits of techno-logical intervention and human kindness was illustrated by a brief altercation between a junior doctor and a senior staff nurse:

> JHO(M): Anyone can do a nurse's job, but there's not many people that can do what I can do.
> SN(F): Oh yea? You wouldn't know how to care for your own granny if you had to. There's more to helping people than sticking needles in them, you know.

This interaction is interesting both because it indicates the positive evaluation many nurses put upon the caring role of nursing and as an example of the degree of assertiveness of nurses in their relationships with medical colleagues. The emphasis that nursing theorists such as Salvage (1985) place upon the autonomy and importance of nursing actions has gained acceptance by at least a segment of clinical nurses.

This assertiveness was also displayed in more formal interactions with doctors. I noted many instances where nurses were prepared to challenge medical orders, and indeed, their challenges were often successful, as this instance of a junior house officer requesting a female staff nurse to alter the feeding regimen of a patient demonstrates:

> JHO(M): Mrs. Surname should be eating by now. Can you start her on a soft diet?
> SN(F): Well, she's still very nauseated. I think she could stay on fluids for a while longer.
> JHO(M): That's fine, we'll leave her until tomorrow and see if she's up to it then.

It can be seen that nurses do not act in an unreflexively subordinate way toward their medical colleagues (Porter 1991). While nursing input into decision making in instances like the above does not enjoy official sanction, in that the doctor still has the legally grounded option to ignore the nurse's input, the fact that it occurs, and occurs frequently, may indicate a changing relationship between these occupations.

In the 1960s, Stein (1967) developed the idea of the "doctor–nurse game" to characterize the nature of interoccupational interaction. Stein argued that while nurses were ostensibly deferent to doctors, their deference masked a considerable input into health care decision making. The doctor–nurse game involved nurses making implicit recommendations through the use of statements about the condition of a patient. This masquerade enabled doctors to utilize nurses' knowledge while maintaining the pretense of their own omniscience.

In a study of interaction in a casualty department in 1980, Hughes (1988) noted that while the doctor–nurse game was still played, in certain circumstances nurses were quite prepared to be openly assertive with their medical colleagues.

In the present study, nurses' open assertiveness, rather than being dependent upon specific enabling situational circumstances, appears to have become a more generalized phenomenon.

The impression that there has been an alteration in the relationship between doctors and nurses since the 1960s is reinforced by Stein in his recent reassessment of the doctor–nurse game:

> The 1967 game was an intricate interaction carefully developed over time in which both players were willing participants. What is happening now is that one of the players (the nurse) has unilaterally decided to stop playing the game and instead is consciously and actively attempting to change . . . how nurses relate to other health professionals (Stein et al. 1990: 547).

However, the extent of nursing's autonomy should not be exaggerated. Davies (1977) has argued that the occupational strategies that informed nursing during the Nightingale era, which included deference to doctors, remain influential. In addition, not all efforts to increase the independence of nursing have been entirely successful. Despite the introduction of a formalized procedure of diag-

nosis, prescription, and evaluation known as the nursing process, nursing has not, as yet, successfully attained effective diagnostic autonomy (Porter 1991).[6] This is of significance if one accepts Johnson's (1972) contention that control over diagnosis is the key to interoccupational authority.

SEXUAL STEREOTYPING

The final aspect I wish to deal with is that of sexual stereotyping. This entails the image of nurses as being sexually permissive, most notably with young male doctors. These stereotypes are important because, if they bear any relation to real life, it is obvious that gender inequalities will be considerably overdetermined by sexual attitudes.

Muff (1982) has argued that the sexual stereotyping that nurses are subjected to is the result of myths generated by a male fear of the feminine other. However, while Muff's psychoanalytic approach demonstrates the depth of these attitudes, it tends toward an ahistorical and immutable conception of mythical stereotypes. Kalisch and Kalisch (1982a,b,c) have argued that this particular portrayal of nurses is an historically recent phenomenon. Up until the 1960s, media portrayal of nurses was largely that of chaste young women. During the era of sexual "liberation" this altered radically, with nurses being increasingly portrayed as promiscuous playthings of their medical colleagues.

Kalisch and Kalisch do not speculate as to why this may be so. However, if it is accepted that the images of nurses reflect the images of women in general, a pattern can be identified. Sexual liberalization was a double-edged sword. While it allowed for greater personal freedom, it also brought into starker relief the subordination of women through their sexual roles. If male power and supremacy is expressed through sexuality (Millett 1971), then openness about sex will exacerbate its significance for male domination. In eras when sex is repressed, the domestic, caring roles of women are more prominent aspects of justificatory ideologies for their oppression. Thus, the image of nurses prior to the 1960s was often one of altruistic angels.

Because of the nature of their work, which involves intimate contact with bodies, and indeed with unpleasant bodily functions and dysfunctions, nurses seem to be singled out more than most female occupational groups as the butt of sexual stereotyping. The fear of the other is exacerbated by the other's intrusion into physical aspects of life which are normally closely guarded secrets. Consequently, the mythical stereotypes employed are all the more grotesque. Nurses' intrusions into the bodies of others are countered by the demeaning of nurses' own bodies.

Despite the ubiquity of images in popular culture which portray nurses as the sexual chattels of their medical colleagues, I found no empirical evidence to suggest that the hospital units studied were simmering fleshpots whose primary purpose was to facilitate the libidinous proclivities of young doctors. While occasional instances of sexual innuendo and mild flirtation were noted, these were of a fairly innocuous nature. No evidence of intimate relationships between doctors and nurses was discovered, although it has to be admitted that by their very nature such interactions would tend to be discreetly handled by those involved. Analysis of the company nurses reported keeping on evenings out showed that the people they socialized with were rarely medical personnel. Indeed, only twice did nurses inform me that they had been in the company of doctors, and even then it had been in the context of group outings. While it would be overstating the case to say that intimate contacts between male doctors and female nurses never occur, it does seem that the myths about nurses' sexual behavior are exactly that—myths.

It is hardly surprising that nurses find this state of affairs particularly galling. The level of their resentment was displayed in a discussion about a grossly sexist portrayal of nurses in a daily newspaper. The conversation was concluded with the following comment on the writer of the piece by a young staff nurse:

> *SN(F)*: I just wish that one day that bastard becomes sick and I get to nurse him. I tell you, he'll never have another sexual thought in his life by the time I've finished with him.

THE INFLUENCE OF LATERAL "FEMALE" ROLES

Paradoxically, given that the fixation with the sexuality of nurses appears to be a relatively recent phenomenon, it appears that the dearth of romantic involvement between doctors and nurses that now pertains was not always the case. A significant proportion of senior doctors were married to nurses or former nurses. The lack of interest shown by younger doctors in their nursing colleagues seems to be partially the result of the large influx of women into medicine. With the progressive equalizing of the gender ratio, male doctors have an increasing opportunity to develop personal relationships with their peers. A number of doctor–doctor personal relationships were noted in the study.

There may also be a change in the way nurses view the prospect of doctors as future partners. Earlier studies of nursing almost universally identified an ambivalence on the part of nurses toward their occupation (Davis and Oleson 1963; Dingwall 1977; Simpson 1979; Weitzman 1982). These writers, whose ideological bent ranges from interactionism and phenomenology, to functionalism and feminism, all seem to agree that occupational commitment was compromised by lateral female roles and the prospect of family life and motherhood. If nurses gave their private ambitions precedence over their career aspirations, then seeking a high-status partner from the medical profession would seem a feasible tactic.

Contrary to the conclusions of previous studies, which posited that, because of their gender, nurses rarely regarded their employment as a career, I would argue that for many nurses this is no longer the case. While I have already noted that a minority of nurses in my study continued to regard their work as an interval before the adoption of the domestic role, most were quite definite that they were in the occupation for reasons to do with the occupation itself, whether this was simply to earn a wage, or because of the satisfaction that being in a "caring profession" brings. Moreover, a number of nurses (nine out of the 19 with whom it was discussed) explicitly stated that, notwithstanding their desire to marry, they saw their job as a career which they expected to follow throughout their working lives.

Male doctors' attentions toward female doctors rather than nurses caused amusement rather than resentment in the female nurses observed. This was evidenced by nurses' reactions to several emotional imbroglios between female and male doctors which occurred on the medical ward where more junior medical personnel worked. Their attitude was summed up by one rather cynical staff nurse:

SN(F): It's great fun watching them break each other's hearts!

With the increasing perception of nursing as a career in itself, the instrumental motivation of using it to find a marriage partner has become, if not completely defunct, at least increasingly anachronistic.

CONCLUSION: ONE STEP FORWARD AND ONE STEP BACK

In conclusion, it can be seen that gender remains one of the most important factors in nurses' experience. Its effect, however, may be changing over time. I would contend that these changes reflect general trends in the position of women in our society. If the subordination of nurses in the Nightingale era was an extension of the overtly oppressed situation that women found themselves in at that time, the rather more convoluted and mutable nature of nurses' relations with doctors that pertain today reflect the gradual alteration of the position of women as a whole. We should be cautious, however, about seeing this process as a uniform, if exceedingly gradual, march toward gender equality.

Certainly, there were a number of aspects identified in this study that indicated that change was taking place in this direction. Most notable of these was the refusal of many nurses to acquiesce without objection to the subordinate position that some doctors expected them to take. These actions were predicated upon an increasingly positive self-evaluation of nurses about their role as female workers. The fact that the ideology of feminism is alive and well on hospital wards can only augur well for future developments in the position of nurses. In addition, the increasing proportion of female doctors seems to be leading to an attenuation of gender as a factor in nurse–doctor power relations.

On the other hand, the increase in male authority within nursing over the last quarter of a century must be taken into account. While female nurses are certainly aware of this process, to date little has been done to tackle it. Indeed, the indications are that nursing will increasingly become an occupation divided between male managers and female ward workers. Following the Griffiths report (1983) into NHS management, the Salmon system has been abandoned, with lines of authority exclusive to nurses being replaced by a flexible, generic system of management. While I am unaware of any quantitative measurements of the effects of Griffiths on the gender ratio, there is good reason to suppose that, if anything, gender imbalance will be exacerbated because nurse managers will now have to compete for their positions with managers from predominantly male occupations such as medicine and private business.

There is bitter irony in the fact that at a time when the problems of gender in relation to doctors are being at least partially resolved, the issue has reappeared with just as much vigor in a different locus. Because of its increasing salience, the problem of male domination within nursing indicates a need for further analysis.[7]

NOTES

1. While nursing theorists tend to concentrate on the expressive, "feminine" aptitudes of nurses, this identification is by no means unproblematic in that it does not take into account the manual nature of the job (Symonds 1991).

2. Observation of interactions on the general medical ward were carried out by Sandra Ryan. I would like to record my appreciation for her significant contribution to this paper.

3. I have discussed this question in a previous paper (Porter 1991).

4. The abbreviations used in this paper denote the following:

ICU:	Intensive Care Unit
SN:	Staff nurse
JHO:	Junior house officer
SHO:	Senior house officer
(F):	Female
(M):	Male

5. This facet of social interaction has been noted by Bhaskar, who observes that while society is a skilled accomplishment of active agents, "the social world may be opaque to the social agents upon whose activity it depends . . ." (1989: 4). One of the aspects of this opacity is the existence of what he calls "unacknowledged conditions." It would seem that the role gender plays in the occupational advancement of medicine is at least partially unacknowledged by nurses.

6. It is possible to frame this problem in terms of structuration theory. Giddens (1976) argues that the processes of structuration involve an interplay of meanings, norms, and power. It might be observed that while the meanings and norms involved in interoccupational relations between nursing and

medicine have significantly altered, format power has not because it is embedded in the relatively immutable structure of state-sanctioned legality.

7. This article is based on a paper given to the 1991 annual conference of the Sociological Association of Ireland, 19–21 April, Termonfeckin, Co. Louth.

REFERENCES

ABBOTT, P. and WALLACE, C. (1990) The sociology of the caring professions: an introduction. In Abbott, P. and Wallace, C. (eds.) *The Sociology of the Caring Professions.* London: Falmer.

BERLANT, J. L. (1975) *Profession and Monopoly.* Berkeley, Cal.: University of California Press.

CARPENTER, M. (1977) The new managerialism and professionalism in nursing. In Stacey, M. et al. (eds.) *Health and the Division of Labour.* London: Croom Helm.

CARPENTER, M. (1978) Managerialism and the division of labour in nursing. In Dingwall, R. and McIntosh, J. (eds.) *Readings in the Sociology of Nursing.* Edinburgh: Churchill Livingstone.

DAVIES, C. (1977) Continuities in the development of hospital nursing in Britain, *Journal of Advanced Nursing*, 2, 479–93.

DAVIS, F. and OLSEN, V. L. (1963) Initiation into a woman's profession: identity problems in the status transition of coed to student nurse, *Sociometry*, 26, 89–101.

DE BEAUVOIR, S. (1983) *The Second Sex.* Harmondsworth: Penguin.

DINGWALL, R. (1977) *The Second Organization of Health Visitor Training.* London: Croom Helm.

DINGWALL, R. and McINTOSH, J. (eds.) (1978) *Readings in the Sociology of Nursing.* Edinburgh: Churchill Livingstone.

ELSTON, A. M. (1977) Women in the medical profession: whose problem? In Stacey, M. et al. (eds.) *Health and the Division of Labour.* London: Croom Helm.

FIRESTONE, S. (1979) *The Dialectic of Sex: The Case for Feminist Revolution.* London: The Women's Press.

GAMARNIKOW, E. (1978) Sexual division of labour: the case of nursing. In Kuhn, A. and Wolpe, A. (eds.) *Feminism and Materialism.* London: Routledge and Kegan Paul.

GAZE, H. (1987) Men in nursing, *Nursing Times*, 83, 25–7.

GIDDENS, A. (1976) *New Rules of Sociological Method.* London: Hutchinson.

GORDON, S. (1991) Fear of caring: the feminist paradox, *American Journal of Nursing.* February, 44–8.

GRIFFITHS, R. (1983) *Enquiry into NHS Management.* London: Department of Health and Social Services.

HEARN, J. (1982) Notes on patriarchy, professionalization and the semi-professions, *Sociology*, 16, 184–202.

HUGHES, D. (1988) When nurse knows best: some aspects of nurse/doctor interaction in a casualty department, *Sociology of Health and Illness*, 10, 1–22.

JOHNSON, T. J. (1972) *Professions and Power.* London: Macmillan.

JONES, C. (1987) Handmaiden mentality, *Nursing Times*, 83, 59.

KALISCH, P. A. and KALISCH, B. J. (1982a) Nurses on prime-time television, *American Journal of Nursing.* February, 265–70.

KALISCH, P. A. and KALISCH, B. J. (1982b) The image of the nurse in motion pictures, *American Journal of Nursing.* April, 605–11.

KALISCH, P. A. and KALISCH, B. J. (1982c) The image of nurses in novels, *American Journal of Nursing.* August, 1220–4.

MACKAY, L. (1990) Nursing: just another job? In Abbott, P. and Wallace, C. (eds.) *The Sociology of the Caring Professions.* London: Falmer.

MILLETT, K. (1971) *Sexual Politics.* London: Sphere.

MUFF, J. (1982) Handmaiden, battle-ax, whore: an exploration into the fantasies, myths, and stereotypes about nurses. In Muff, J. (ed.) *Socialization, Sexism and Stereotyping: Women's Issues in Nursing.* Prospect Heights, Ill.: Waveland.

OLIVER, D. and WALFORD, D. (1991) Chairpersons of the Working Party on Women Doctors and their Careers, *Women Doctors and their Careers.* London: Department of Health.

PORTER, S. (1991) A participant observation study of power relations between nurses and doctors in a general hospital, *Journal of Advanced Nursing*, 16, 728–35.

ROBINSON, J. (1991) Working with doctors: educational conditioning, *Nursing Times*, 87, 28–31.

SALMON, B. (1966) *Report of the Committee on Senior Nursing Staff Structure.* London: HMSO.

SALVAGE, J. (1985) *The Politics of Nursing.* London: Heinemann.

SAYERS, J. (1982) *Biological Politics: Feminist and Anti-Feminist Perspectives.* London: Tavistock.

SILVERMAN, D. (1985) *Qualitative Methodology and Sociology.* Aldershot: Gower.

SIMPSON, I. H. (1979) *From Student to Nurse: A Longitudinal Study of Socialization.* Cambridge: Cambridge University Press.

STEIN, L. (1967) The doctor-nurse game, *Archives of General Psychiatry*, 16, 699–703.

STEIN, L., WATTS, D. T., HOWELL, T. (1990) The doctor-nurse game revisited, *New England Journal of Medicine.* 322, 546–9.

STRAUSS, A., FAGERHAUGH, S., SUCZEC, B. and WEINER, C. (1985) *The Social Organization of Medical Work.* Chicago, University of Chicago Press.

SYMONDS, A. (1991) Angels and interfering busybodies: the social construction of two occupations, *Sociology of Health and Illness*, 13, 247–64.

WEBSTER, D. (1985) Medical students' views of the role of the nurse, *Nursing Research*, 34, 313–17.

WEITZMAN, L. J. (1982) Sex-role socialization, in Muff, J. (ed.) *Socialization, Sexism and Stereotyping: Women's Issues in Nursing.* Prospect Heights, Ill.: Waveland.

Part X

HEALTH CARE DELIVERY IN THE UNITED STATES

The provision of health care to the general population has been a major source of debate in the United States during the late twentieth and early twenty-first centuries. Rising costs, equity in the provision of services, and the unequal distribution of health care providers and facilities are the primary issues. The principal issue is cost containment, given the increasingly higher expenses paid for health care, which have caused patients, the business community, and state and federal governments to demand cost controls. Additionally, some 16.3 percent of the American population was without any type of health insurance in 1998—a national disgrace for an affluent nation. All other advanced societies have national health insurance programs providing general coverage for their citizens. The United States has public health insurance providing coverage to only two groups: Medicare for the elderly and Medicaid for the poor. The third issue—that of the maldistribution of providers and facilities—results from the concentration of health care in urban and more-affluent areas, leaving rural and inner-city ghettos with relatively few health care sites.

High costs and the lack of equity in health insurance have made health care reform a major political issue. In 1994, the Clinton administration presented Congress with a historic health reform bill, which would have provided health insurance to all Americans, but the bill failed to gain the necessary support. Intense lobbying by various interest groups, especially small businesses, which would have had to provide health insurance to their employees and absorb most of the costs; physicians; insurance companies; pharmaceutical companies; and others opposed the plan. The issues and their solutions were complex, and delays in bringing the health reform bill forward through various congressional committees gave vested interests time to mobilize opposition.

The articles in this part provide insight into the health care reform debate in the United States. The first paper, "Playing by the Rules and Losing: Health Insurance and the Working Poor," by Karen Seccombe and Cheryl Amey, addresses the problem of the working or near-poor—people who have jobs but do not make enough money to pay for health insurance. The authors find that, although they are playing by the rules (working and being economically productive), over half of the working poor are uninsured.

The concluding paper in this part is by Karen Donelan and her colleagues, entitled "Whatever Happened to the Health Insurance Crisis in the United States? Voices from a National Survey," presents findings from a national survey examining the experience of people with health insurance. Among those with insurance, many still have problems paying their medical bills because of out-of-pocket costs. Among the uninsured, about half say they are still able to get medical care, yet the authors note that all persons without health insurance face a disproportionate burden in obtaining medical care. They conclude that the health insurance crisis persists.

PLAYING BY THE RULES AND LOSING: HEALTH INSURANCE AND THE WORKING POOR

Karen Seccombe
Portland State University
Cheryl Amey
University of Florida

Using a sample of 7,734 employed adults from the National Medical Expenditure Survey, this research compares the sources of health insurance coverage and the antecedents of employer-sponsored insurance among the working poor to those at higher income thresholds. Concern with the working poor is warranted because they constitute the majority of the uninsured, they do not qualify for public health programs, and their health insurance benefits have eroded substantially. The data reveal that (1) the working poor are only one-third as likely to receive insurance from their employer as are the non-poor, and are over five times as likely to be without insurance from any source; (2) employment characteristics are critical antecedents of employer-sponsored insurance and, as a set, explain variation in coverage beyond that provided by human capital/socioeconomic factors; and (3) most employment characteristics have a similar effect on the odds of coverage across income categories, except for unionization and minimum wages. Implications for health care reform are addressed.

INTRODUCTION

The United States has experienced a substantial increase in the inequality of the economic structure, with household income becoming more concentrated among persons with the greatest wealth (U.S. Bureau of the Census 1993). Social stratification is usually operationalized in terms of occupational earnings, prestige, or total accumulated wealth. A cogent argument can be made that, in the United States at least, *health insurance* constitutes another resource that is unequally distributed. Data from the Current Population Survey indicate that over 38 million persons

Reprinted from the *Journal of Health and Social Behavior*, vol. 36 (June 1995), pp. 168–181, by permission of the American Sociological Association.

had no health insurance from any source at any time during 1992 (Employee Benefit Research Institute 1994). These individuals are likely to postpone or forgo visits to health care practitioners for all but the most urgent conditions, and are consequently disadvantaged with respect to health (St. Peter, Newacheck, and Halfon 1992; U.S. Congress, Office of Technology Assessment 1992).

The high number of persons without health insurance, the escalating number of persons with inadequate insurance, and the increasing costs of health care (over $473 billion in 1991) (Levit et al. 1993) contribute to the dissatisfaction felt toward the U.S. health system. In a survey of residents in 10 countries regarding the adequacy of their health care system, the U.S. system had the fewest advocates—only 10 percent of Americans expressed that their health care system "works pretty well and only minor changes are needed" (Blendon et al. 1990). In response to such concerns, health care reform has become a national priority (Clinton 1992; Clinton 1994) and is the subject of congressional debate. The reforms proposed vary considerably, and include discussions of managed competition (Staines 1993), health insurance purchasing cooperatives (Kronick 1993), and pay or play schemes (Holahan and Zedlewski 1992). The common thread of these proposals is their continued reliance upon *employers* to finance the health insurance of their workers (Field and Shapiro 1993; Zelman 1994), unlike in other industrial countries where health care benefits are provided by right of citizenship and are financed by progressive taxes (Starfield 1991). Most proposals do, however, provide exclusions for factors that would prove detrimental to business (e.g., excluding small businesses or part-time workers). We anticipate that these types of exclusions will affect subgroups of workers differently. As a consequence, it is critical that we understand the factors that account for differences in the receipt of insurance among underrepresented groups in the population.

The purpose of this research is to examine the health insurance patterns of the *working poor* (defined here as workers with household incomes below the poverty line), and to compare the antecedents of employer-sponsored coverage of this group to those of higher incomes.[1] The problems faced by the working poor are of particular interest for several reasons. First, despite popular folklore that contends that a job is a ticket to a "better" life, this is not always the case, at least with respect to insurance coverage. National data reveal that 84 percent of the uninsured are either employed or are dependents of employed persons (House Energy and Commerce Subcommittee on Health and Environment 1993). Data from the 1977 National Medical Expenditure Survey (NMES) indicate that the working

poor were two times *more likely to be uninsured* than were poor persons without jobs (Berk and Wilensky 1987). Berk and Wilensky (1987) justifiably conclude that being employed may in fact serve to *restrict* access to medical care for the poor rather than enhance it.

Second, most of the working poor do not qualify for public health insurance programs even when their employers fail to insure them. Medicaid was created to fill in the gaps in coverage among the poor who were without insurance, but stringent eligibility requirements prevent most poor persons from accessing this program. Only 46 percent of the poor and 10 percent of persons with incomes between the poverty level and 200 percent of poverty level have Medicaid coverage (House Energy and Commerce Subcommittee on Health and Environment 1993). The employed are overrepresented among those poor deemed ineligible for Medicaid.

Finally, health insurance benefits have eroded during the past decade, with the erosion occurring more heavily among working poor and low-income individuals. Seccombe (forthcoming) reports that the percentage of persons without insurance increased by 52 percent between 1977 and 1987 among the working poor, whereas it decreased by 10 percent among those with household incomes over 200 percent of poverty level. Moreover, other data indicate a trend toward part-time, part-year, and temporary work (Pfeffer and Baron 1988); a growth in the number of small firms (U.S. Department of Labor 1993); a decline in union membership (Goldfield 1987); and an increase in service sector jobs (Colatosti 1992), factors experienced disproportionately by poor and low-income workers.

Hypotheses

Despite the plethora of data indicating a positive relationship between income and the odds of receiving employer-sponsored coverage, we have a poor understanding of the antecedents of coverage within a multivariate context, and how these antecedents may vary across income categories. Specifically, why do poor workers have such low rates of coverage as compared to other workers? Many of the sociodemographic characteristics and employment contexts which are associated with the receipt of employer-sponsored coverage vary by income, such as race and ethnic background, education level, gender, age, marital status, residential location, number of hours employed, type of industry, workforce size, and union membership (Chollet 1994; Cooper and Johnson 1993; Levil, Olin, and Letsch 1992; Seccombe 1993; Seccombe, Clarke, and Coward 1994; U.S. General Accounting Office 1992). It is not known whether these correlates of employer-sponsored insurance coverage operate in a similar fashion across income categories, particularly in a multivariate context.

A number of scenarios could account for the differences in insurance coverage across income categories that have been observed. It could be that the same relationships are operative in all settings but are present to varying degrees among income groups. For example, working in a large firm may increase the odds of having employer-sponsored insurance in all income groups; however, poor workers may simply be underrepresented in large firms compared to higher-income workers. Or, it could be that variables influence coverage differently across income groups, resulting in the discrepancies in rates that have been observed. For example, union membership may increase the odds of receiving employer-sponsored insurance for those in only one income category, and have no effect on others.

Toward the goal of illuminating the plight of the working poor with respect to employer-sponsored coverage, several hypotheses are tested. Using a sample of employed adults, we anticipate the following relationships.

(HI)   The working poor are less likely to receive employer-sponsored health insurance,

and they are more likely to remain completely uninsured, as compared to higher-income workers.

We do not expect government programs to compensate for lower-than-expected rates of employer-sponsored coverage because poor workers generally do not meet eligibility requirements. Moreover, we do not expect the working poor to purchase private coverage, in large numbers, because of cost. Consequently we anticipate that the working poor comprise a disproportionate number of the uninsured.

(H2)   The employment context includes critical antecedents of employer-sponsored coverage which, as a set, explain variation in employer-sponsored coverage beyond that which is explained by sociodemographic or human capital factors.

Human capital theory articulates that variations in compensation (e.g., pay, job benefits) reflect differences in the investment in personal skills, such as educational level (Becker 1975, 1981). Yet research spanning over a decade calls into question human capital theory. We anticipate here, instead, that occupational characteristics are the most critical antecedents of employer-sponsored coverage. Labor market theories have been employed successfully to explain variations in pay (Bibb and Form 1977), bargaining (Sakamoto and Chen 1991), pensions (Quadagno 1988), other working conditions (Glass 1990), and, recently, health insurance and other medical benefits (O'Rand 1986; Seccombe 1993). Both O'Rand (1986) and Seccombe (1993) suggest that occupational conditions are more critical in determining insurance status than are human capital or sociodemographic factors. We want to extend their research by (1) examining both the independent effects of occupational characteristics using a more recent national sample, and by (2) examining whether employment conditions as a *set* explain a significant portion of the variation in employer-sponsored coverage beyond that which is explained by human capital and sociodemographic factors.

(H3) Employment context is more likely to influence the probability of employer-sponsored coverage among the working poor than among the non-poor.

There is a relatively large pool of lower-skilled workers, and consequently employers are able to secure workers without offering fringe benefits such as health insurance. These employers do not find it necessary to offer benefits as a method to compete for a labor force, and persons filling these jobs are generally powerless to demand them. Thus, the decision of whether to offer health insurance is based on other criteria, such as other features of the occupation. For example, we anticipate that the odds of a janitor receiving insurance will increase if he or she works at a job that is unionized, or works in a large firm, or is employed with a multiple-site employer. That is, we anticipate variation in coverage based upon the occupational characteristics of low-income workers.

In contrast, in order to compete for a relatively smaller pool of highly skilled workers, employers must offer a better and more comprehensive benefits package. Because most employers offer health insurance to their higher-skilled workers (i.e., there is less variation), the employment context is a less critical antecedent of coverage. Thus, for example, we anticipate that the insurance status of the higher-paid computer programmer is less dependent on other features of his or her occupational context.

METHODS

Data and Sample

The data used in this research are from the 1987 NMES, which provides detailed national estimates of health insurance coverage in the United States. Four rounds of interviews were conducted during calendar year 1987, representing the civilian, noninstitutionalized population living in approximately 15,000 households and noninstitutional group quarters during the calendar year 1987. Complete information was obtained from 80 percent of the households selected. Because of the continuing policy interests in vulnerable groups, low-income persons (among others) were oversampled, relative to their proportion in the general population (for additional sampling information, see Edwards and Berlin 1989).

The subsample used in this research is from Round Four (i.e., the last wave of data collection), in order to enable us to ascertain the income of the respondent during the entire calendar year. The subsample consists of one employed adult—aged 18 through 64—from each "insurable unit." Insurable units were constructed within households and families to include individuals who had access to insurance coverage through another family member by virtue of their status as a spouse or dependent. However, two unrelated adults living in the same household, and adult children not attending school, were considered separate insurable units. Due to the dependence of the insurance status of individuals within the same insurable unit, only one individual from each unit was selected for inclusion in the analyses. Our preference was to include full-time workers when available. If only one adult in the insurable unit was employed full-time, he or she was selected for inclusion in the sample. If an insurable unit contained more than one full-time employee, one was randomly selected for inclusion. If it contained no full-time workers, then one part-time worker was selected. Thus, this sample represents those individuals who are most likely to receive insurance from their employer when offered, and therefore should provide conservative estimates of coverage.

The sample was restricted to adults under age 65 because the elderly qualify for health benefits under the Medicare program. It consists of 7,734 adults aged 18 through 64 who were employed at the time of the interview (but not self-employed), with complete data on their poverty status.[2] The data released for public use are weighted to account for the design effects of the sampling strategy employed by the NMES.[3] Missing data are deleted in multivariate analyses.[4]

Nearly 8 percent (7.7%) of the subsample (N = 595) is classified as poor.[5] These employed individuals have household incomes below the poverty line, which in 1987, the year of data collection, was $11,519 for a family of four with two children. Another 15.2 percent of respondents (N = 1,172) had household incomes between the poverty level and 200 percent of the poverty level, or between $11,520 and $23,040 for a family of four in 1987. These individuals are labeled here as "economically vulnerable," because even a modest financial setback (e.g., illness, temporary unemployment) could quickly pull them into poverty. Finally, 77.1 percent of the subsample (N = 5,967) have incomes over 200 percent of the poverty line, or a household income of over $23,040 for a family of four during calendar year 1987 (U.S. Bureau of the Census 1989). These persons are labeled here "non-poor." (See Table 1.)

Variables

The primary variables of interest in this research are the presence and source of *health insurance coverage*. Respondents were initially coded as having health insurance (0) and having no health insurance of any type (1). Those who do have insurance were further categorized by the type of insurance they have: (1) employer-sponsored insurance in the individual's own name through an employer or union; (2) employer-sponsored insurance, but in another person's name

rather than in the name of the individual; (3) public insurance (e.g., Medicaid or similar state-run program); (4) privately purchased insurance; and (5) Civilian Health and Medical Program of the Uniformed Services (CHAMPUS) (for those persons associated with the military). Approximately 5 percent of the sample (N = 405) had two or more types of health insurance coverage, and these are included in all the appropriate insurance categories in Table 2. Of particular interest in the multivariate analyses is whether persons receive *employer-sponsored health insurance in their own name*.[6]

Seven variables were used to describe the occupational characteristics and employment context of the employee. *Number of hours employed* is coded as (1) fewer than 20 hours per week; (2) 20 to 35 hours per week; and (3) more than 35 hours per week. *Union membership* is ascertained (yes or no). Respondents were asked whether they worked for a *multisite* establishment (yes or no). *Workforce size* is measured with a series of dummy variables: (1) fewer than 10 employees; (2) 10 to 25; (3) 26 to 100; and (4) more than 100 employees. A series of six dummy variables represents the *industry* in which respondents work. The categories are collapsed from the U.S. Census Bureau to include (1) construction/repair; (2) agriculture/forestry/fishing/manufacturing; (3) transportation/communications/utilities; (4) sales; (5) finance/insurance/professional/public administration; and (6) personal service/entertainment/recreation. The *respondent's wages* are coded as (1) less than $3.50 per hour; (2) $3.50 to $4.99; (3) $5.00 to $7.49; (4) $7.50 to $9.99; and (5) $10 and over. Finally, *tenure on the job for less than one year* is included (yes or no).

Eight human capital/sociodemographic variables are included since they covary with levels of employee compensation. Previous research has documented that women, younger persons, those who are unmarried,

TABLE 1 Characteristics of Employed Adults (Aged 18–64) by Poverty Status, 1987 (N = 7,734)

Human capital/sociodemographic characteristics:	Poor (N = 595)	Economically vulnerable (N = 1,172)	Non-poor (N = 5,967)	Chi-square
Sex				57.06*
Male	45.0%	53.8%	59.1%	
Female	55.0	46.2	40.9	
Age				138.93*
Under 35	65.1%	61.1%	47.6%	
35 and Over	34.9	38.9	52.4	
Marital Status				79.61*
Married	39.9%	50.4%	56.7%	
Unmarried	60.1	49.6	43.3	
Race/Ethnicity				348.80*
White	56.7%	66.2%	81.9%	
Black	23.1	16.3	9.2	
Other	20.2	17.5	8.9	
Residence				83.71*
Metropolitan	68.8%	70.9%	79.8%	
Nonmetropolitan	31.2	29.1	20.2	
Another Family Member Has Employer-Sponsored Insurance in Own Name				420.42*
Yes	5.9%	12.2%	31.3%	
No	94.1	87.8	68.7	
Child under 18 in Household				154.94*
Yes	46.6%	51.8%	35.0%	
No	53.4	48.2	65.0	
Education				640.09*
Less than High School	43.8%	29.4%	13.2%	
High School Graduate	36.3	42.0	38.1	
More than High School	19.9	28.7	48.7	

Employment context:

Number of Hours Employed				
Fewer Than 20	18.4%	11.3%	5.1%	383.36*
20–35	20.0	12.8	7.5	
More Than 35	61.6	75.9	87.4	
Union Membership				
Yes	8.8%	10.5%	19.6%	99.01*
No	91.2	89.4	80.4	
Multisite Employer				
Yes	49.3%	58.1%	67.3%	115.97*
No	50.7	41.9	32.9	
Workforce Size				
Fewer than 10	30.9%	27.4%	17.1%	249.67*
10–25	22.3	20.6	16.2	
26–100	26.3	24.6	24.8	
More Than 100	20.5	27.4	41.9	
Industrial Code				
Construction/Repair	21.3%	22.0%	24.9%	257.68*
Agricultural/Forestry/Fishing/Manufacturing	12.0	12.5	10.6	
Transportation/Communications/Utilities	5.2	5.5	9.2	
Sales	28.8	26.4	16.6	
Finance/Insurance/Professional/ Public Administration	23.4	26.4	35.5	
Personal Service/Entertainment/Recreation	9.3	7.1	3.1	
Hourly Wage Earned				
Less than $3.50/hour	24.6%	13.6%	5.4%	1308.39*
$3.50–$4.99/hour	37.6	30.5	12.3	
$5.00–$7.49/hour	22.7	30.6	21.3	
$7.50–$9.99/hour	8.3	14.7	20.2	
$10 or more/hour	6.8	10.6	40.9	
Tenure on Job < 1 Year				
Yes	42.7%	31.4%	16.8%	351.88*
No	57.3	68.6	83.2	

*$p \leq .01$.

329

ethnic minorities, and those who live in rural areas are less likely to be insured through an employer than are their counterparts (Coward, Clarke, and Seccombe 1993; Kronick 1991; Levit et al. 1992; O'Rand 1986; Seccombe 1993; U.S. General Accounting Office 1992). Furthermore, persons with these characteristics are also more likely to be poor (U.S. Bureau of the Census 1993). Thus, the effects of these variables are controlled in multivariate analyses using dummy variables. Respondents' *sex* is included. *Age* is coded as (1) less than age 35; or (2) aged 35 and over, in order to distinguish young wage earners from those who have more experience in the labor force. *Marital status* is coded as (1) currently married; or (2) unmarried (including divorced, widowed, or never-married). *Race* and *ethnicity* are coded as (1) White; (2) Black; or (3) other.[7] *Residence* is dichotomized as (1) living in a metropolitan area; or (2) living in a nonmetropolitan area. We include whether the respondent has *any other family member who had employer-sponsored health insurance in their own name* (yes or no). The *presence of one or more children under age 18* in the home is ascertained (yes or no). Finally, respondents' *education* is coded as (1) less than high school; (2) high school graduate; and (3) more than high school.

Table 1 compares the sociodemographic/ human capital and occupational characteristics of the sample, across income categories. The working poor are disproportionately female, young, unmarried, members of racial or ethnic minority groups, and living in nonmetropolitan areas. They are less likely to have other family members who have employer-sponsored health insurance coverage in their own names. They are more likely than the non-poor (although less likely than the economically vulnerable) to have at least one child under age 18 in the home. They also have the lowest mean number of years of education as compared with the other groups. The data also reveal that the working poor are less likely to work

full-time than are either the economically vulnerable or the non-poor; they are less likely to be members of unions, to work for a multisite employer, and to work in large firms. Moreover, the working poor are employed in substantially different industries than are the non-poor, and earn significantly less per hour. Finally, they are also more likely to have been on the job for less than one year.

Analysis

We first analyzed the data to examine differences in the presence and type of health insurance across income categories. Second, using logistic regression models, we examined (1) the extent to which human capital, sociodemographic, and occupational characteristics (both individually and as a set) are associated with the receipt of employer-sponsored health insurance; and (2) whether occupational characteristics influence the odds of being uninsured the same way, across income thresholds. Because the data were weighted to account for the design effects of the sampling strategy, the weights were normed to be equal to our final sample size (Clogg and Eliason 1987).

RESULTS

Table 2 reveals the distribution of health insurance coverage among working poor, economically vulnerable, and non-poor individuals. Our first hypothesis is supported; nearly one-half (48.4%) of the working poor have no health insurance from any source whatsoever, compared to only 9.1 percent of persons with incomes above 200 percent of poverty level.

Among those individuals who do have insurance, differences emerge across income categories in the sources of coverage. For example, only 28.2 percent of the working poor have employer-sponsored coverage in the respon-

TABLE 2 Distribution of Health Insurance Coverage by Poverty Status, 1987 (*N* = 7,734)[1]

	Poor (N = 595)	Economically vulnerable (N = 1,172)	Non-poor (N = 5,967)	Chi-square
No insurance:	48.4%	32.8%	9.1%	1093.30*
Insured:	51.6	67.2	90.9	
Type of Insurance:				
Employer-Sponsored in Own Name[2]	28.2%[3]	49.8%	75.4%	866.91*
Employer-Sponsored but in Another Person's Name	6.7	4.7	9.6	37.06*
Public Insurance	10.2	5.0	.6	375.23*
Private Insurance	6.2	8.4	6.5	7.14
CHAMPUS	3.5	3.2	4.3	3.98

*$p \leq 01$.

Notes:

[1]Data are from Round Four, National Medical Expenditure Survey (NMES), 1987. Percentages are weighted to represent the distribution in the population.

[2]*Persons with employer-sponsored health insurance* includes those who receive coverage through union membership or directly through an employer.

[3]Totals from specific insurance categories do not equal the percentage reporting to be insured because 405 individuals have more than one type of insurance (Poor = 22 or 3.74%; Economically Vulnerable = 49, or 4.2%; and the Non-poor = 334, or 5.6%; Chi-square = 8.12; $p > .01$).

dent's own name, compared to 49.8 percent of the economically vulnerable, and 75.4 percent of the non-poor. Furthermore, the working poor respondents are also less likely than the non-poor to have employer-sponsored insurance in another's name, usually a spouse (6.7% and 9.6%, respectively).

The data reveal that the working poor are more likely to receive public insurance (e.g., Medicaid) than are persons in other income groups. A critical finding remains obvious, however: Very few of the working poor receive public insurance, despite their need. Only 10.2 percent of the working poor receive public insurance while, instead, nearly half remain completely uninsured.

No differences were noted in the percentage of adults who have purchased insurance or CHAMPUS privately. However, it should be emphasized that privately purchased insurance represents a significantly

larger bite out of the budgets of poor and economically vulnerable persons than they do for the non-poor.

Next, we estimate the extent to which human capital/sociodemographic characteristics and employment context are associated with the receipt of employer-sponsored health insurance. Table 3 reports the odds ratios obtained from hierarchical logistic regression models. We want to discern how (1) *each* independent variable, and (2) *sets* of variables, influence the probability of *lacking employer-sponsored* insurance in one's own name (versus receiving employer-sponsored insurance in one's own name).

Model 1 includes the odds ratios for the set of human capital/sociodemographic factors. Females (Odds = 1.72), persons under age 35 (Odds = 2.01), those who are unmarried (Odds = 1.31), racial and ethnic minorities (Odds = 1.48 and 1.49 for Blacks

TABLE 3 Logistic Regression Models Predicting the Lack of Employer-Sponsored Health Insurance in Own Name among Employed Adults (Aged 18–64), 1987

	Model 1: odds ratio	Model 2: odds ratio
Human capital/sociodemographic characteristics:[1]		
Sex		
Female	1.72*	1.21
Age		
Under 35	2.01*	1.35*
Marital Status		
Unmarried	1.31*	1.01
Race/Ethnicity		
Black	1.48*	1.75*
Other	1.49*	1.57*
Residence		
Nonmetropolitan	1.42*	1.22
Other Family Member Has Employer-Sponsored Insurance		
Yes	1.70*	2.77*
Child Under 18 in Household	.97	1.09
Education		
Less than High School	3.42*	2.14*
High School Degree	1.65*	1.35*
Employment context:		
Number of Hours Employed		
Fewer than 20	—	7.17*
20–35	—	3.00*
Union Membership		
No	—	2.82*
Multisite Employer		
No	—	1.84*
Workforce Size		
Fewer than 10	—	3.50*
10–25	—	1.88*
26–100	—	1.48*
Industrial Code		
Construction/Repair	—	.50*
Agricultural/Forestry/Fishing/Manufacturing	—	1.31
Transportation/Communications/Utilities	—	.63
Sales	—	1.18
Finance/Insurance/Professional/Public Administration	—	.63*
Hourly Wage Earned		
Less than $3.50/hour	—	5.00*
$3.50–$4.99/hour	—	3.22*
$5.00–$7.49/hour	—	1.86*
$7.50–$9.99/hour	—	1.21
Tenure on Job < 1 Year		
Yes	—	3.46*
Intercept	−2.17	−4.10
N	7,719	7,103
R^2	.10	.39
−Log Likelihood	4,472.99	3,106.66

*$p \leq .01$.

[1]Reference Categories include Male; Age 35 and Over; Married; White; Metropolitan Residence; No Other Family Member Has Insurance; More than High School Education; Did Not Change Jobs over Past Year; Employed More than 35 Hours; Union Membership; Multisite Employer; Workforce Size over 100; Personal Services/Entertainment/Recreation Industry; Hourly Wage of $10.00 or More.

TABLE 4 Logistic Regression Predicting the Lack of Employer-Sponsored Health Insurance in Own Name by Poverty Status among Employed Adults (Aged 18–64), 1987 (N = 7,403)

	Model 1: odds ratio poor	Model 2: odds ratio economically vulnerable	Model 3: odds ratio non-poor	Odds ratio 1:3
Human capital/sociodemographic characteristics:[1]				
Sex				
Female	1.28	.81	1.27*	n.s.
Age				
Under 35	1.49	1.35	1.30*	n.s.
Marital Status				
Unmarried	1.07	1.06	.95	n.s.
Race/Ethnicity				
Black	1.43	1.55	1.46*	n.s.
Other	1.25	1.40	1.53*	n.s.
Residence				
Nonmetropolitan	1.06	1.40	1.22	n.s.
Another Family Member has Employer-Sponsored Insurance in Own Name				
Yes	.50	1.97	3.30*	$p \le .01$
Child Under 18 in Household				
Yes	.70	.72	1.04	n.s.
Education				
Less Than High School	4.13*	1.82*	1.78*	$p \le .01$
High School Degree	1.82	1.35	1.28*	$p \le .01$
Employment context:				
Number of Hours Employed				
Fewer Than 20 Hours	6.17*	4.44*	8.00*	n.s.
20–35 Hours	2.91*	2.08*	3.19*	n.s.
Union Membership				
No	6.36*	2.44*	2.63*	$p \le .01$
Multisite Employer				
No	2.12*	1.60*	1.82*	n.s.
Workforce Size				
Fewer than 10	2.56*	3.71*	3.49*	n.s.
10–25	1.79	1.77*	1.87*	n.s.
26–100	2.11	1.54	1.37*	n.s.
Industrial Code				
Construction/Repair	1.02	.22*	.64*	n.s.
Agricultural/Forestry/Fishing/Manufacturing	2.16	.66	1.63	n.s.
Transportation/Communications/Utilities	.72	.37*	.82	n.s.
Sales	2.36	.53	1.40	n.s.
Finance/Insurance/Professional/ Public Administration	1.04	.37*	.76	n.s.
Hourly Wage Earned				
Less than $3.50/hour	21.12*	2.10*	4.06*	$p \le .01$
$3.50–$4.99/hour	7.46*	1.32	3.06*	n.s.
$5.00–$7.49/hour	4.35*	.87	1.88*	n.s.
$7.50–$9.99/hour	3.71	.59	1.22	n.s.
Tenure on Job < 1 Year				
Yes	3.46*	2.36*	3.45*	n.s.
Intercept	−5.74	−1.78	−4.34	
N	571	1,110	5,722	
R^2	.43	.31	.33	
−Log Likelihood	211.70	578.82	2,247.44	

*$p \le .01$.

[1]Reference Categories include Male; Aged 35 and Over; Married; White; Metropolitan Residence; No Other Family Member Has Insurance; More than High School Education; Did Not Change Jobs over Past Year; Employed More than 35 Hours; Union Membership; Multisite Employer; Workforce Size over 100; Personal Services/Entertainment/Recreation Industry; Hourly Wage of $10.00 or More.

and others, respectively), nonmetropolitan residents (Odds = 1.42), those who have family members with employer-sponsored insurance in their own name (Odds = 1.70), and persons with relatively lower levels of education (Odds = 3.42 and 1.65 for less than high school and high school degree, respectively) are more likely to lack insurance from an employer. All of these characteristics are more closely associated with the working poor, with the exception that it is higher income groups that are more likely to have other family members with insurance in their own name, as noted previously in Table 1. The only variable here which was not associated with employer-sponsored insurance was having a child under age 18 (Odds = 97).

In Model 2, the respondent's employment characteristics are added. Persons who are employed less than full-time (Odds = 7.17 and 3.00 for less than 20 hours and 20–35 hours, respectively), who are not members of a union (Odds = 2.82), who do not work for multiple-site employers (Odds = 1.84), who work in firms with fewer than 100 employees (Odds = 3.50, 1.88, and 1.48 for under 10, 10–25, and 26–100 employees, respectively), who earn less than $7.50 per hour (Odds = 5.00, 3.22, 1.86, for less than $3.50, $3.50–$4.99, and $5.00–$7.49 per hour, respectively), and who have less than one year tenure on the job (Odds = 3.46) are also more likely to lack employer-sponsored insurance in their own name. Again, these characteristics were found to be associated with the working poor, as previously shown in Table 1. In contrast, those who work in construction/repair, or the finance, insurance, professional, or public administration industries are more likely (than individuals in personal service, entertainment, and recreation) to have insurance through their employer. We also find that the addition of the *set* of employment characteristics to the model reduces the previously significant effects of being female, unmarried, and living in a nonmetropolitan area. Finally, as hypothesized, the inclusion of the employ-

ment context as a set of variables explains the variation in the lack of employer-sponsored health insurance in one's own name beyond the human capital/sociodemographic characteristics by themselves ($p < .001$).

Our next set of analyses was designed to address whether the employment context influences the odds of lacking health insurance from one's employer in the same way across levels of income. In order to determine the appropriate analytical strategy for this question, we conducted a likelihood ratio test for homogeneity of structure. We compared the −2 log likelihood estimate from the model without poverty status minus the sum of the −2 log likelihood estimates from the poverty-specific models. The results of this test provided evidence that the null hypothesis of no difference in the structural relationships across poverty status should be rejected ($p < .05$). Therefore, models were estimated separately for the (1) working poor; (2) economically vulnerable; and (3) non-poor. The odds ratios of the working poor and non-poor (1:3) were then compared across models to ascertain whether differences exist across models— for example, do the predictor variables influence the probability of lacking employer-sponsored insurance for the working poor and non-poor in the same way? A *Z-test* was performed to ascertain whether the odds ratios are significantly different from one another.

The data reveal only modest support for the third hypothesis. Most employment characteristics (and human capital/sociodemographic factors) have similar effects across income categories. The number of hours worked per week, whether one works at a single- or multiple-site employer, the workforce size, the type of industry, wage level, and length of tenure on the job influence the likelihood of a worker having employer-sponsored health insurance in a similar manner regardless of income or poverty status. Of these factors, it appears that the *number of hours employed, wage, workforce size,* and *length of tenure on the job* have a particularly strong impact on the odds of coverage, regardless of income. People who work part-time, have lower wages, who work in small firms, and who have been on the job for less than one year are especially vulnerable to being without employer-sponsored coverage. These data lend support to Colatosti's (1992) contention that workers are increasingly exploited by tenure requirements before they are eligible to receive health insurance.

Two employment characteristics have differential impacts across income groups. First, being in a *union* increases the odds of having insurance more for the poor than for the non-poor (Odds = 6.36 and 2.63 for poor and non-poor, respectively). These data suggest that unions play a critical role in securing benefits for the working poor. Second, the data suggest that a *minimum wage* also has different effects on the odds of being insured by an employer; minimum wage earners in poor households are over 5 times as likely to lack employer-sponsored insurance than minimum wage earners in non-poor households (Odds = 21.12 and 4.06 for poor and non-poor, respectively). In other words, it appears that even minimum wage earners in non-poor households have "better" jobs than workers in poor households, at least with respect to the receipt of health insurance.

Like employment characteristics, most human capital/sociodemographic factors affect the odds of coverage in a similar fashion across income. Sex, age, marital status, race/ethnicity, residential location, and a child under 18 years old in the home all have effects upon the likelihood of receiving employer-sponsored coverage that are similar for the poor and for the non-poor.

However, two human capital/sociodemographic variables have different effects upon the odds of lacking employer-sponsored insurance. First, having *another family member with insurance* in his or her own name increases the odds that the non-poor will lack their own employer-sponsored insurance, with little effect for the working poor (Odds

= 3.30 and .50 for the non-poor and poor, respectively). We speculate that members of non-poor households have choices unavailable to the poor. They may choose to forgo their own employer-sponsored insurance because other members of their insurable unit (i.e., a spouse) have better policies under which they could choose to be included. The data also suggest that low levels of *education* have different effects across income categories, with lower levels of education being an even greater detriment to the working poor than to the non-poor (Odds = 4.13 and 1.78 for poor and non-poor with less than a high school degree, respectively).

DISCUSSION

From a nationally representative sample of U.S. adult workers from the 1987 National Medical Expenditure Survey, this research compared the sources of health insurance coverage, and the antecedents of employer-sponsored insurance of the working poor, to persons with higher incomes. Our findings provide additional evidence that the health insurance system in the United States, as currently configured, is neither inclusive nor equitable.

Several conclusions can be gleaned from these analyses which are relevant to discussions of health care reform. First, only one out of four working poor persons received insurance from their employer, compared to more than two out of three non-poor workers. Government programs, as currently configured, do little to reduce this inequity. One reform strategy that has been suggested is simply to expand Medicaid to uninsured persons. If such a policy is to be effective in reducing the number of uninsured individuals, it must extend coverage to *all* uninsured low-income and poor persons, including those who are employed. This approach would, of course, expand the Medicaid program substantially. However, because Medicaid is viewed by many as "welfare," it is seen in a rather negative light. Consequently, any plans to increase the program's scope considerably will likely be met with considerable public scrutiny and be the subject of widespread criticism.

Second, these data suggest that employment contexts are critical factors in discerning current patterns of employer-sponsored health insurance. Future health care reforms should not be predicated upon individualistic, human capital explanations for differences in coverage. Instead, the lack of health insurance is a byproduct of unequal economic structures—the uninsured are not an idiosyncratic group replete with personal failure. This factor is critical to reform measures because it illustrates that a continued reliance upon employer "good-will" without requiring employers to provide insurance will systematically leave segments of our working population uninsured. If we intend to continue ahead with our previous policy of linking employers and insurance, we must guarantee that certain vulnerable groups (i.e., part-time workers, those in small firms, those who earn low wages) will be included in coverage schemes either by employer mandates or by government intervention.

Third, most of the variables examined here influenced coverage in a similar fashion across income thresholds. This suggests that legislative reforms that address these particular correlates have the potential to have a correspondingly positive effect for workers regardless of household income. For example, because workers at small firms are disadvantaged regardless of income category, policies that create incentives for small employers to purchase insurance for their employees, or mandate all employers to provide health insurance, or policies that create "risk pools" that lessen the costs of insurance for small employers, have the potential to increase the odds of coverage among workers in all income categories. This does not mean, however, that such policies would have the same *magnitude* of effect for

all groups. The working poor are overrepresented in small firms, for example. Therefore, a policy that increased coverage in small businesses would affect a greater proportion of the poor workforce, because nearly one in three working poor is employed in a small business, compared to less than one in five non-poor workers.

Finally, there are several variables that exerted different effects on the odds of coverage across income categories: unionization, minimum wage, level of education, and whether another family member had insurance in his or her name. The differences in employment contexts are of particular interest here, given the very large discrepancy in their effects and the fact that these can be ameliorated more easily by social policy. It appears that poor workers cannot depend upon employers to "look out for them"; instead, they benefit more from the protective structure of a union. These findings are consistent with other research which suggests that unions are critical for securing benefits for disadvantaged groups including ethnic minorities and women (Goldfield 1987; Krecker and O'Rand 1991; Seccombe 1993; Seccombe et al. 1994). We also see, interestingly, that while all minimum wage earners are disadvantaged they are not *equally* disadvantaged. Minimum wage earners who have household incomes above the poverty line are considerably better off with respect to having employer-sponsored health insurance than their counterparts who live in households below the poverty line. Why this is the case is not well understood. Perhaps these two groups are working in different types of jobs—differences that are not measured in these analyses. We anticipate that workers from poor households have fewer choices available to them. They need money now, and do not have the luxury of "shopping around" for the best job (i.e., the one with the most fringe benefits attached). Furthermore, they may have additional structural impediments (i.e., limited English skills, transportation barriers, and so on) which further narrow the opportunities available to them.

One limitation of this research that should be noted is that the NMES public-use tape used in these analyses provides information with respect to the *receipt* of health insurance, not whether it is *offered* by an employer. Given our choice of sample, we have selected respondents who are most likely to accept insurance if it is offered (i.e., full-time workers). However, it is likely that some unknown portion of the employed full-time population deliberately declined coverage, and therefore are coded as not receiving coverage even though it was actually offered by an employer. We have attempted to minimize this error by controlling for selection effects such as having another family member with employer-sponsored insurance in their own name. However, since we did not control for all possible selection effects (e.g., cost of premium), it is likely that some degree of error persists, and therefore the results should be interpreted with this in mind.

In conclusion, it is ironic that nearly half of the working poor are uninsured: They are playing by the "rules" of the health insurance coverage scheme in this country by possessing employment, and they are productive members of our economic system, yet they are without coverage for themselves and for their families. Further discussions of health care reform must recognize the importance of either mandating employers to provide benefits to workers, as is the case in Hawaii, or doing away with the employer-financing mechanism altogether, as is the case in nearly every industrialized (and many nonindustrialized) countries throughout the world. A health care financing system such as is currently found in the United States—one that continues to rely on employer "good will"—further exaggerates the polarization between the "haves" and the "have-nots."

NOTES

1. The term *working poor* is used literally here. It refers to employed persons with household incomes below the federal poverty line, adjusted for year and family size. We use the term *economically vulnerable* to refer to workers with household incomes between the poverty line and 200 percent of poverty. These persons are sometimes referred to as *working poor*, although that term does not correctly describe them. We believe that *economically vulnerable* is a more accurate, and therefore a more appropriate, description. *Non-poor* refers to workers with household incomes above 200 percent of poverty.

2. Individuals who were self-employed ($N = 1,637$) were deleted because the survey did not collect information on certain workplace characteristics that were critical to our analyses. Persons reporting negative income ($N = 27$) were also deleted. Finally, persons assigned a zero weight, indicating that they did not participate in Round Four of data collection, were deleted because their relative poverty status could not be determined ($N = 705$).

3. Individual weights were derived from weights developed at the dwelling-unit level. Dwelling units were first weighted to account for nonresponse, and then poststratified to better reflect the 1987 Current Population Survey (CPS) estimates. The poststratification procedure took into consideration (1) the race/ethnicity of the reference person; (2) the age of the reference person; (3) the number of individuals in the dwelling unit; (4) the census region; and (5) the sex and marital status of the respondent. The weights were then normed to be equal to the final sample size (Clogg and Eliason 1987). The survey data analysis package known as SUDAAN was utilized to account for the effects of the complex sample design (Sha et al. 1991).

4. There are a number of different methods for managing missing cases in the social sciences (Little and Rubin 1990). In these analyses we concluded that there was not a firm basis on which to impute missing values, either from a direct analysis of the incomplete data by the method of maximum likelihood or a multiple imputation method based on explicit and implicit models. Given that the number of respondents eliminated due to missing values ($N = 331$) constituted a rel-

atively small portion of the sample (4.3%), we concluded that no undue bias was being introduced.

5. The poverty variable was constructed by The Agency for Health Care Policy and Research (AHCPR) from income data collected on 26 separate types of income in Supplement Four to the Round Four interview. Data were imputed by AHCPR, if possible, when unavailable. NMES income totals, and means and percentages of the population reporting income by source, were roughly equivalent to the 1988 Marsh Supplement to the CPS for calendar year 1987 for both the total population 15 years of age and older, and the population disaggregated by race/ethnicity and gender of the individual. For further information or procedural details, see AHCPR (1991).

6. The NMES public-use tape employed in this analysis provides information on who is *receiving* coverage through their employer, not on who is *offered* coverage. We recognize that the inability to identify those persons in this data source that were offered coverage by their employer but declined to accept it diminishes our understanding of the precise relationship between the characteristics of a worker and their job that are associated with coverage. However, given our choice of sample (i.e., the fact that we used only full-time workers if available in the household), we have included individuals who are most likely to accept coverage, thereby minimizing this bias.

7. Further race or ethnic breakdowns were not possible, as the small number of Mexican, Puerto Rican, Cuban, Asian, Native American, and other minority groups would have produced unstable estimates.

REFERENCES

AGENCY FOR HEALTH CARE POLICY AND RESEARCH. 1991. *1987 National Medical Expenditure Survey. Public-Use Tape 13 Household Survey. Population Characteristics and Utilization Data for 1987.* File Documentation, August.

BECKER, GARY. 1975. *Human Capital.* New York: Columbia University Press.

———. 1981. *A Treatise on the Family.* Cambridge, MA: Harvard University Press.

BERK, MARC L. and GAIL R. WILENSKY. 1987. "Health Insurance Coverage of the Working Poor" *Social Science and Medicine* 25:1183–87.

BIBB, ROBERT and WILLIAM F. FORM. 1977. "The Effects of Industrial, Occupational, and Sex Stratification on Wages in Blue-collar Markets." *Social Forces* 55:974–96.

BLENDON, ROBERT J., ROBERT LEITMAN, IAN MORRISON, and KAREN DONELAN. 1990. "Satisfaction with Health Systems in Ten Nations." *Health Affairs* 9:185–92.

CHOLLET, DEBORAH. 1994. "Employer-based Health Insurance in a Changing Work Force." *Health Affairs* 1:315–26.

CLINTON, BILL. 1992. "Putting People First: Health Care Our Families Can Afford." *Journal of American Health Policy* 2:17–23.

CLINTON, HILLARY RODHAM. 1994. "Meaningful Health Reform: The Time is Now." *Health Affairs* 1:6–8.

CLOGG, CLIFFORD C. and SCOTT R. ELIASON. 1987. "Some Common Problems in Log-linear Analysis." *Sociological Methods and Research* 16:8–44.

COLATOSTI, CAMILLE. 1992. "A Job without a Future." *Dollars and Sense* no. 176.

COOPER, P. and A. JOHNSON. 1993. "Employment-related Health Insurance in 1987." *Medical Expenditure Survey Research Findings 17.* Rockville, MD: Agency for Health Care Policy and Research (Publication No. 93-0044).

COWARD, RAYMOND T., LESLIE L. CLARKE, and KAREN SECCOMBE. 1993. "Predicting the Receipt of Employer-sponsored Health Insurance: The Role of Residence and Other Personal and Work-place Characteristics." *Journal of Rural Health* 9:28–92.

EDWARDS, W. SHERMAN and MARTHA BERLIN. 1989. "Questionnaire and Data Collection Methods for Household Survey and the Survey of the American Indians and Alaska Natives." *DHS Publication No. PHS 89-3540. National Medical Expenditure Survey Methods 2, National Center for Health Services Research and Health Care Technology Assessment.* Rockville, MD: U.S. Public Health Service.

EMPLOYEE BENEFIT RESEARCH INSTITUTE. 1994. "Sources of Health Insurance and Characteristics of the Uninsured, Analysis of the March 1993 Current Population Survey." *Issue Brief 145.* Washington, DC: EBRI.

FIELD, MARILYN J. and HAROLD T. SHAPIRO, eds. 1993. *Employment and Health Benefits: A Connection at Risk.* Washington, DC: National Academy Press.

GLASS, JENNIFER. 1990. "The Impact of Occupational Segregation on Working Conditions." *Social Forces* 68:779–96.

GOLDFIELD, MICHAEL. 1987. *The Decline of Organized Labor in the United States.* Chicago, IL: University of Chicago Press.

HOLAHAN, JOHN, and SHEILA ZEDLEWSKI. 1992. "Who Pays for Health Care in the United States? Implications for Health System Reform." *Inquiry* 29:231–48.

HOUSE ENERGY AND COMMERCE SUBCOMMITTEE ON HEALTH AND ENVIRONMENT. 1993. *Medicaid Sourcebook: Background Data and Analysis.* Washington, DC: U.S. Government Printing Office.

KRECKER, MARGARET L. and ANGELA M. O'RAND. 1991. "Contested Milieux: Small Firms, Unionization, and the Provision of Protective Structures." *Sociological Forum* 6:93–117.

KRONICK, RICHARD. 1991. "Health Insurance 1979–1989: The Frayed Connection Between Employment and Insurance." *Inquiry* 28:318–32.

———. 1993. "Where Should the Buck Stop: Federal and State Responsibilities in Health Care Financing Reform." *Health Affairs* (Suppl.):87–98.

LEVIT, KATHARINE R., GARY L. OLIN, and SUZANNE W. LETSCH. 1992. "Americans' Health Insurance Coverage, 1980–1991." *Health Care Financing Review* 14:31–57.

LEVIT, KATHARINE R., HELEN C. LAZENBY, CATHY A. COWAN, and SUZANNE W. LETSCH. 1993. "Health Spending by State: New Estimates for Policy Making." *Health Affairs* 3:7–26.

LITTLE, RODERICK and DONALD B. RUBIN. 1990. "The Analysis of Social Science Data with Missing Values." Pp. 374–409 in *Modern Methods of Data Analysis,* edited by J. Fox and J. S. Long. Newbury Park, CA: Sage.

O'RAND, ANGELA M. 1986. "The Hidden Payroll: Employee Benefits and the Structure of Workplace Inequality." *Sociological Forum* 1:657–83.

PFEFFER, JEFFREY and JAMES N. BARON. 1988. "Taking the Workers Back Out: Recent Trends in the Structuring of Employment." Pp. 257–303 in *Research in Organizational Behavior,* vol. 10, edited by B. M. Staw and L. L. Cummings. Greenwich, CT: JAI Press.

QUADAGNO, JILL. 1988. "Women's Access to Pensions and the Structure of Eligibility Rules: Systems of Production and Reproduction." *The Sociological Quarterly* 29:541–58.

SAKAMOTO, ARTHUR and MEICHU D. CHEN. 1991. "Inequality and Attainment in a Dual Labor Market." *American Sociological Review* 56:295–308.

SECCOMBE, KAREN. 1993. "Employer-sponsored Medical Benefits: The Influence of Occupational Characteristics and Gender." *The Sociological Quarterly* 34:557–80.

———. In Press. "Health Insurance Coverage Among the Working Poor: Changes from 1977 to 1987." In *Research in the Sociology of Health Care,* vol. 13, edited by J. J. Kronenfeld. Greenwich, CT: JAI Press.

SECCOMBE, KAREN, LESLIE L. CLARKE, and RAYMOND T. COWARD. 1994. "Discrepancies in Employer-sponsored Health Insurance Coverage Among Hispanics, Blacks, and Whites. The Effects of Sociodemographic and Employment Factors." *Inquiry* 31:221–29.

SHA, B., G. BARNWELL, P. NILEEN, and L. M. LAVANGE. 1991. *SUDAAN Users Manual.* Release 5.50. Research Triangle Park, NC: Research Triangle Institute.

ST. PETER, ROBERT, PAUL W. NEWACHECK, and NEAL HALFON. 1992. "Access to Care for Poor Children: Separate and Unequal?" *Journal of the American Medical Association* 267:2760–64.

STAINES, VERDON S. 1993. "Potential Impact of Managed Care on National Health Spending." *Health Affairs* (Suppl.):248–57.

STARFIELD, BARBARA. 1991. "Primary Care and Health: A Cross-national Comparison." *Journal of the American Medical Association* 266:2268–71.

UNITED STATES BUREAU OF THE CENSUS. 1993. "Poverty in the United States, 1992." *Current Population Report Series P-60,* no. 185. Washington, DC: U.S. Government Printing Office.

———. 1989. "Poverty in the United States, 1987." *Current Population Report Series P-60,* no. 163. Washington, DC: U.S. Government Printing Office.

UNITED STATES CONGRESS, OFFICE OF TECHNOLOGY ASSESSMENT. 1992. *Does Health Insurance Make a Difference—Background Paper.* OTA-BP-H-99. Washington, DC: U.S. Government Printing Office.

UNITED STATES GENERAL ACCOUNTING OFFICE. 1992. *Employer-Based Health Insurance.* GAO-HRD-92-125. Washington, DC: GAO.

ZELMAN, WALTER A. 1994. "The Rationale Behind the Clinton Health Care Reform Plan." *Health Affairs* 1:9–29.

WHATEVER HAPPENED TO THE HEALTH INSURANCE CRISIS IN THE UNITED STATES? VOICES FROM A NATIONAL SURVEY

Karen Donelan
Robert J. Blendon
Harvard University
Craig A. Hill
University of Chicago
Martin Frankel
City University of New York

Catherine Hoffman
Diane Rowland
Drew Altman
Kaiser Family Foundation

In 1992, in the presidential campaign, in major medical journals and medical associations, in the media, and in civic groups, our nation was engaged in a great debate about the best way to provide health insurance coverage to all Americans. By contrast, these debates were conspicuous by their absence in 1996.

The health system reform debate was marked by some controversy about whether there was a health insurance crisis at all.[1] On one side were those who said that most of the uninsured could get care when they needed it, a view that was expressed in a commentary in the *Wall Street Journal* in 1994 that noted that "these [uninsured] citizens are not denied health care" and only 1 in 5 uninsured (about 3% of the population) cannot obtain affordable insurance.[2] On the other side were those who claimed that many of the uninsured faced major barriers to needed health care services and experienced health and economic consequences because of these barriers.

While the political urgency of these concerns has subsided, we know that gaps in

Reprinted from *JAMA*, vol. 276, no. 16 (October 23/30, 1996), pp. 1346–1350, by permission of the American Medical Association.

insurance coverage remain for a sizable number of Americans—recent estimates indicate that approximately 40 million people in the United States were uninsured in 1994 (oral comminication, B. Katherine Swartz, PhD, April 23, 1996, regarding unpublished data from analyses of March 1995 *Current Population Survey*); another 29 million are underinsured.[3] Reports of public opinion surveys have noted that support for reform was driven in large part by anxieties about access to and cost of medical care among both insured and uninsured persons.[4-6]

Prior research has documented decreased access to health care services, and increased burdens of economic hardship, ill health, and mortality that the uninsured and underinsured experience.[7-8] In the midst of the health system reform debate, media reports about this research were frequently augmented with vignettes illustrating the consequences of access and financial problems for individuals and families. While vignettes can add a valuable qualitative dimension to quantitative estimates of problems, they are not randomly selected and may illustrate extreme, rather than average, consequences. Verbatim responses are common in the development of sample surveys, but in larger-scale surveys, structured and coded responses are preferred to minimize cost and increase analytic power.

Now that the politically charged health system reform debate has subsided, we return to the basic questions that marked that discussion. What problems do uninsured people have in getting and paying for medical care in today's changing health care system? How many Americans are affected? How severe are their problems and their consequences? We sought to answer these questions by using a combination of quantitative measures of access to health care and personal qualitative accounts in a recent survey of Americans to determine who has experienced problems getting medical care and paying for it.

DATA AND METHODS

The survey design and instrument were developed by research staff of the Harvard School of Public Health, the Henry J. Kaiser Family Foundation, and the National Opinion Research Center (NORC) at the University of Chicago. NORC conducted the survey by telephone from February 22 to April 27, 1995. A random adult respondent (aged 18 years or older) was selected in each household, with no substitution if that person refused or could not be contacted. At least 16 attempts were made both to select the random adult in each household and to interview the person selected.

In all, 3,993 interviews were conducted. All respondents were asked to respond to a common battery of health status, health services utilization, and demographic questions. Interviewers used computer-assisted software that prompted the survey questions, which were read to the respondents; responses were then typed into the computer. Among all respondents, a subgroup of 1,234 (31%) reported experiencing at least one of three core problems in the past year: an episode of being uninsured (unweighted $n = 596$), a time when they did not get medical care that

they thought they needed (unweighted $n = 636$), or a problem in paying medical bills (unweighted $n = 606$). Respondents with the three core problems of interest were interviewed at greater length in topic-specific modules to explore the nature and consequences of their experiences. Among respondents reporting one of the three core problems, interviews averaged 19 minutes; other interviews averaged 4 minutes.

At the close of the interview, respondents were asked to describe the consequences of their experiences using an open-ended item: "I would like you to tell me in your own words what happened to you as a result of the problems you have experienced. We are especially interested in the consequences of your [insert: not getting medical care that you thought you needed/time without insurance/problems in paying medical bills] on, for example, your physical or mental health, your family relationships, your employment or your household finances." The responses were coded for content in areas of health, employment, family, and financial consequences. Coded and illustrative verbatim responses are reported here. Edits to the verbatim responses are indicated in brackets and were used only to protect respondent identity or correct typographical errors. Where they appear, verbatim responses were selected at random with substitution for cases where responses were unintelligible or missing.

To ensure conformity with known distributions in the national population, the data are weighted to adjust for age, race, sex, religion, education, and marital status, as well as for household size.

The response rate, calculated as complete interviews at all telephone numbers known to be households and not known to be businesses, was 52 percent. In NORC's experience in recent years, this rate is about average for random-digit-dial telephone surveys with random respondent selection. The margin of sampling error for a sample of 3,993 people is approximately ± 1 percent, and increases for smaller subgroups of the sample (e.g., a maximum of ± 3% for 1,234 people, ± 4% for 600 people, and ± 10% for 100 people).

RESULTS

Among all 3,993 respondents surveyed, 18 percent of adults said that there was a time in the past year when they did not get medical care that they thought they needed, and 16 percent said they had a problem in the past year in paying medical bills. Nineteen percent indicated that they were without health insurance either at the time of the survey (12%) or at some point in the year prior (7%). Throughout this article, people who were uninsured at the time of the survey are combined with people who were uninsured for some part of the year prior to the survey; this group is referred to as the "uninsured."

Uninsured and insured respondents reported significantly different experiences (Table 1). The uninsured were four times more likely than the insured to report an episode of needing and not getting medical care and three times more likely to report a problem in paying for medical bills. Differences between the uninsured and the insured are also observed in key health and demographic measures.

Because of these differences, we present study findings for the uninsured and insured separately. Figures 1 and 2 show the distribution of the three core problems (insurance, inability to get care, paying medical bills) encountered by the uninsured and insured as well as the respondents' ratings of the severity of those consequences.

The Uninsured

Who Are the Uninsured and Why Don't They Have Insurance? The findings of this survey confirm many things we know about the uninsured from prior research. The general demographic profile is similar, with about 70 percent of the uninsured saying that they were employed during at least part of the time they were without coverage. Of these, approximately 40 percent worked for employers who provided coverage to at least some employees.

Table 2 shows the reasons for not having insurance coverage as reported by the uninsured. *Cost and the lack of employer-provided coverage are the principal reasons for being uninsured.* Political rhetoric to the contrary, very few Americans are uninsured by choice. Fewer than one in 10 of the uninsured said that they did not want or need health insurance coverage or just did not think about getting it.

TABLE 1 The Different Characteristics and Experiences of the Uninsured and Insured in the United States

	Uninsured (%)	Insured (%)	All respondents (%)
Key study variables:			
Problems getting needed medical care in past year	45*	11	18
Problems paying medical bills in past year	36	12	16
Problems getting needed care and paying medical bills	28	4	5
Health status and demographic variables			
Fair or poor health	21	18	18
Disability or chronic illness limiting daily activities	19*	13	14
Household income ≤$15,000	20*	9	11
Less than high school education	24*	17	18

*$p < .05$.

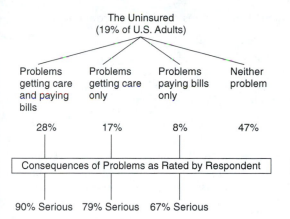

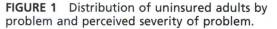

FIGURE 1   Distribution of uninsured adults by problem and perceived severity of problem.

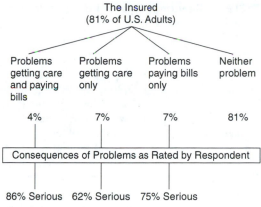

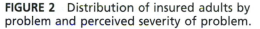

FIGURE 2   Distribution of insured adults by problem and perceived severity of problem.

More than half (59%) of the uninsured said that this was the first time in the past five years that they had been without insurance coverage; 40 percent reported other periods of being without insurance.

Difficulties in Getting Needed Care.   Forty-five percent of the uninsured and 11 percent of the insured report a time in the year prior to the survey when they needed care and could not get it. Among all survey respondents, episodes of not getting needed care were reported by about 25 percent to 35 percent of people with a higher burden of illness (defined as self-reported fair or poor health or disability). Barriers to care are amplified among the uninsured—75 percent of those in poor health and 54 percent of those in fair health said that there was a time in the past year when they experienced this problem.

How often does getting needed care present an obstacle for the uninsured and for

TABLE 2   Reasons for Being Uninsured

Reason cited as "main reason you are/were without insurance"	% Uninsured at time of survey who report this reason	% Insured at time of survey and uninsured during previous year who report this reason
Coverage too expensive	64	41
Change in employment status	7	14
Employer doesn't offer insurance	2	2
Not eligible for employer-provided coverage	6	13
Unemployed	1	2
Change in family/marital status	1	1
Not eligible for public assistance	2	2
Preexisting medical condition and cannot obtain coverage	1	1
Don't want or need insurance	3	6
Reason related to spouse's employment	1	8
Other reason	7	15

TABLE 3 Randomly Selected Uninsured Respondent Descriptions of Medical Problems for Which Care Was Not Received

Sex	Age (y)	Problem
Male	35	Rapid heart rate after walking with friends way too fast.
Female	44	A long-term thing, hypertension.
Male	29	Coughing, tight breathing.
Male	63	I was having angina.
Female	21	Female problems.
Female	33	When I go to bed at night my foot and my toes started swelling every day till they hurt so bad I had to move my big to[e] just to get a cramp out; It hurts.
Male	36	I have heart trouble and I can't stand myself sometimes. I need eye surgery right now. I need another cornea transplant.
Male	36	Imagined it was a pulled tendon or torn.
Male	40	Intermittent pain. We were never quite sure what it was. Would like to have looked into it further, but because of our insurance we were limited.

what symptoms are they delaying care? About half of the uninsured (49%) reported one episode; the remainder indicated that there were multiple occasions. Of those who did not get needed care, 60 percent said that it was for a "specific medical problem" (actual text of question); 17 percent needed preventive care (defined as "checkups, immunizations, cancer screening"); the remainder said that both types of care were needed.

We asked respondents to describe the medical symptoms they had at the time they needed and did not get medical care. Table 3 shows several randomly selected unedited responses for uninsured respondents. Seventy percent of the uninsured said that their symptoms were either "very serious" or "somewhat serious" at the time they could not get care.

For the overwhelming majority of the uninsured, cost and insurance reasons are the predominant reasons for not getting needed medical care. Fifty-one percent said that they could not afford to pay, 25 percent said that they had no insurance at the time, and the remainder indicated other reasons. Only 2 percent said that they didn't think that their symptoms were serious enough to warrant getting care.

Approximately half (52%) of uninsured people who said that there was a time when

they needed care and did not get it tried to get help from a medical professional for the problem they described to us; 75 percent were successful. At the time of the survey, 50 percent of uninsured respondents who said that there was a time when they did not get needed care in the past year (representing about 1 in 4 of uninsured adults surveyed) said that they still had either "pain or disability" as a result of the medical problem or problems they reported.

Problems in Paying Medical Bills. Lack of health insurance coverage may be associated with lower utilization of health services, but it sometimes leaves uninsured people who do need and use medical care with subtantial out-of-pocket medical costs. While 12 percent of people with health insurance coverage had a problem in paying medical bills in the year prior to the survey, more than one-third (36%) of people without health insurance reported this experience (Figure 1). Just as uninsured persons in fair or poor health are more likely than the insured to have difficulty in obtaining care, 48 percent of those in fair health and 67 percent in poor health told us that they had problems in paying medical bills in the year prior to the survey.

Because it is difficult to obtain such information from respondents with unaided recall, out-of-pocket medical expenditures were broadly measured (>$1,000, >$5,000). Among the uninsured who reported problems in paying bills, 49 percent said they paid more than $1,000 out of pocket for medical bills in the year prior to the survey; 8 percent paid more than $5,000. Among all adults surveyed, 34 percent paid more than $1,000 out of pocket; 4 percent paid more than $5,000.

At the time of the survey, two-thirds (67%) of the uninsured who had problems in paying medical bills still owed money for those bills; 70 percent owed less than $1,000, 22 percent owed $1,001 to $5,000, 5 percent owed $5,001 to $20,000, and 2 percent owed in excess of $20,000. Forty-four percent of the uninsured with problems in paying bills have been contacted in the past year by a collection agency.

It is a commonly held assumption that the uninsured can get free or charity care if they need it. Only 37 percent of the uninsured who reported problems in paying medical bills said that they had received medical care "for free or for a reduced charge" in the previous year.

Consequences of Core Problems for the Uninsured. Figure 1 shows that among the uninsured with problems in paying medical bills (but not in getting care) 67 percent say the consequences were "very serious" or "somewhat serious"; a significantly higher proportion (79%) of those with difficulty in getting needed care point to serious consequences. People who are uninsured and report both problems (about 5% of all adults surveyed and 28% of the uninsured) are distinguished from the general adult population in several ways as shown in Figure 3—they are more likely to rate the consequences of their experiences as serious, they are sicker, they are more likely to be female and to have higher out-of-pocket expenses for health care.

In Table 4 we present selected illustrative verbatim accounts for the uninsured who reported somewhat serious or very serious consequences of the three core problems studied (insurance, getting care, and paying

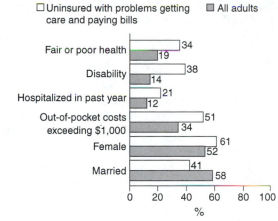

FIGURE 3 Characteristics of uninsured adults who report problems in getting medical care and in paying for it compared with U.S. adult population.

bills). Coding of all the verbatim responses demonstrated that while 37 percent of the uninsured report virtually no consequences of their problems, others mention problems ranging from major health conditions such as heart disease, cancer, and diabetes (16%); problems in paying for food or shelther (6%); employment difficulties (10%); or stress, worry, or fear (22%). Nearly half (42%) of those uninsured who also had difficulty in getting care or in paying medical bills reported a major health condition.

The Insured

We have seen that a number of the health and health care problems studied here disproportionately affect uninsured people (Table 1). However, the sheer magnitude of people in the United States who have health insurance means that even if a small proportion of the population experiences difficulty, millions of people are affected.

Difficulties in Getting Needed Medical Care. As shown in Figure 2, 11 percent of insured adults in the United States reported a time in the year prior to the survey when they could not get medical care that they thought they

TABLE 4 Randomly Selected Verbatim Accounts about the Consequences of Insurance and Medical Care Problems from People Who Rate the Consequences "Very Serious" or "Somewhat Serious"

The uninsured

Problems getting care:
   "Related to the MS (multiple sclerosis) that I have. I need a specific medicine that lessens the exacerbations of the disease and I can't afford to get it. It's very frustrating and makes me angry because I'm progressing in my disease without the medicine that could possibly slow it up."

Problems paying medical bills:
   "My 2 daughters have a problem with eyesight and I don't have the money to go to the eye doctor, and my children have a toothache and I don't have the money to take them to the dentist. If I pay the doctor, I don't have the money to pay the rent and I won't have a roof and it's important to get food."

Both problems:
   "I needed surgery for cataracts but my doctor couldn't do the surgery because I didn't have insurance. The doctor said I had cancer . . . they gave me a hysterectomy because I had cancer. [Program name] paid almost all of the bill and I paid off the rest in payments. I was unemployed for 6 months. It was hard to meet all the payments of the other bills."

The insured

Problems getting care:
   "Family history of colon cancer, was advised to get a screening every 2 years. It affects my finances because we have not met the deductible. We have a $2,500 deductible. I guess that the only gripe I have is that I pay too much for insurance and they're raising it again by $100 a month."

Problems paying medical bills:
   "I have to pay out of a Social Security check of $362 a month for [insurance company name]. They want $500 per month. Something wrong. Medicare doesn't pay full cost of hospital or medicine. I don't take prescriptions then—it costs $100. Other people get food stamps, whatever they want. I was born here, worked here, get nothing."

Both problems:
   "One medical problem I do have is depression. [I'm supposed to go to] the doctor every 3 months. Can't afford it. You get very stressful, it makes the problem worse and you just don't go. . . . It would be nice to go to the doctor to get antibiotics and not have to worry about bills."

---

needed. As in the uninsured population, problems in getting needed care are disproportionately high among insured people in fair or poor health.

When asked to rate the severity of that medical problem as they perceived it at the time, 60 percent (compared with 70% of the uninsured) said that they thought their problem was either very or somewhat serious when they could not get care.

Among the uninsured, cost and lack of insurance coverage predominated among reported reasons for not getting needed medical care. One in four (25%) insured respondents also said that they could not afford to pay for care; one in 10 (11%) said that their problem was not serious enough to warrant care. An additional 20 percent of insured respondents report a variety of problems with insurance coverage, including denial of insurance claims, perceptions of respondents and their physicians that certain services would not be covered, and services used that were not covered by insurance.

Approximately 10 percent reported structural barriers to care such as transportation problems, difficulty in getting time off from work, and problems in getting appointments.

Problems in Paying Medical Bills A previous study conducted in 1992[7] found that 19 percent of Americans reported problems in paying medical bills and 75 percent of those had insurance. In this study we found that 58 percent of people with problems in paying medical bills were insured for the whole year prior to the survey, while another 14 percent who were insured at the time of the survey had had no insurance for some part of the previous year. Twenty-eight percent were uninsured at the time of the survey. These findings underscore the value of considering the dynamics of health insurance coverage over time and of not relying solely on point-in-time measures of coverage in analyses.

We asked insured respondents who had problems with medical bills why their health insurance did not cover the cost of their care. Among more than a third of respondents (38%), costs were part of copayments, deductibles, or coinsurance. Other reasons included services costing more than insurance covered (21%), services not covered by insurance (16%), and care from a provider outside the plan (5%). Only 1 percent reported exclusion because of a preexisting condition, an unmet waiting period for coverage, or failure to get proper approvals from insurance.

Consequences of Core Problems for the Insured As already noted, the proportions of insured people who report difficulty in getting needed medical care and/or in paying medical bills are significantly lower than in the uninsured population (Table 1). However, if we translate these proportions into approximate numbers of adults in the United States, about 28 million had insurance that was inadequate to guarantee freedom from access and cost burdens. This is approximately the same number as the estimated number of the underinsured

reported in 1995.[9] Respondent ratings of the severity of the consequences of their financial and medical care difficulties demonstrate that, as in the uninsured population, the majority of insured people who report these problems see them as severe: 75 perent said the consequences of problems paying bills were serious, and 62 percent of those with problems getting care noted serious consequences. Among the insured who have both problems, 86 percent said there were serious consequences—a proportion that does not differ significantly from the uninsured. In Table 4, we present illustrative verbatim responses about consequences from insured people who reported serious consequences of the core problems studied.

COMMENT

This survey's findings bring us back to central questions raised during the failed health system reform effort. Do we have a crisis in the U.S. health insurance system? How big is the problem? How many people are affected? How serious are the consequences?

As described at the outset of this article, in one view, virtually all the uninsured in America can get all the health care services they need. In another view, virtually all without coverage are at risk for tragedy. This study's findings challenge both extreme views. On one hand, the notions that only 3 percent of the uninsured do not have access to affordable insurance coverage and most do not have problems getting care when they need it[2] are pure speculation; the majority of the uninsured cite cost as the principal reason they do not have insurance coverage and approximately half of the uninsured reported difficulty in getting needed care and/or in paying for medical bills in the course of a year. The overwhelming majority of this group rate the consequences of their problems as serious.

On the other hand, the uninsured are a minority of Americans, and about half of them reported that they did not experience problems in getting or in paying for medical care in the year prior to the survey. Results shown here point to the fact that while many people in this group worry about the future, and we may speculate about their plight in the event of a major accident or illness, about half of the uninsured in America are not experiencing difficulties in obtaining medical care.

Among the insured, approximately one in six people (some 28 million adults) have insurance policies that do not protect them from problems in getting needed medical care or in paying medical bills. The cost-sharing requirements of health plans generate out-of-pocket expenditures that are unaffordable for some Americans.

From these findings, some might legitimately conclude that, even adding the experiences of the uninsured and insured, difficulties with access to needed medical care and the affordability of medical bills affect a minority of the U.S. population and need not be of broader societal concern. Others might conclude that even though these problems affect a minority of Americans, it is a minority of millions of people; one in four insured or uninsured adults surveyed means that approximately 50 million adults are affected. The 70 percent who say that their problems are serious translates into about 34 million people. Problems in getting needed medical care affect about 17 million uninsured adults and 17 million insured adults in America, and problems in paying medical bills are reported by 13 million uninsured and 17 million insured Americans.

Other dimensions of the findings reported here could also be troubling. First, although similar numbers of insured and uninsured people report difficulty in obtaining medical care and paying for it, those without health insurance face disproportionate burdens. Second, aspects of our health care system are especially challenging to negotiate for uninsured and insured people who are sick. People in fair or poor health, people with major chronic illnesses, and people with disabilities

are disproportionately represented in every problem area studied—health insurance, getting needed care, and paying medical bills. One in six of the uninsured noted in verbatim responses about consequences of these problems that they had a concurrent major illness.

Is there a crisis in our health care system? The voices of the people that we surveyed give life to the statistics and tell us a story of millions of individual crises in getting and in paying for health care each year. Are the crises of this minority a crisis for our society? That is a question this study will not resolve.

REFERENCES

1. SWARTZ, K. Dynamics of people without health insurance: don't let the numbers fool you. *JAMA*. 1992;271:64–66.
2. STELZER, I. M. There is no health care crisis, *Wall Street Journal*, January 25, 1994; section A:12.
3. SHORT, P. F., BANTHIN, J. S. New estimates of the underinsured younger than 65 years. *JAMA*. 1995;274:1302–1306.
4. HENRY J. KAISER FAMILY FOUNDATION/COMMONWEALTH FUND/HARRIS POLL. Storrs, Conn: Roper Center for Public Opinion Research; January 31, 1992.
5. HENRY J. KAISER FAMILY FOUNDATION/COMMONWEALTH FUND/HARRIS POLL. Storrs, Conn: Roper Center for Public Opinion Research; August 6, 1993.
6. BLENDON, R. J., DONELAN, K. Public opinion and efforts to reform the U.S. health care system: confronting issues of cost-containment and access to care. *Stanford Law Policy Rev.* Fall 1991;3:146–154.
7. BLENDON, R. J., DONELAN, K., HILL, C. A., CARTER, W., BEATRICE, D., ALTMAN, D. Paying medical bills in the United States: why health insurance isn't enough. *JAMA*. 1994;271:949–951.
8. WEISSMAN, J. S., EPSTEIN, A. M. *Falling Through the Safety Net: Insurance Status and Access to Health Care*. Baltimore, Md: Johns Hopkins University Press, 1994.
9. HENRY J. KAISER FAMILY FOUNDATION. *Uninsured in America: Straight Facts on Health Reform*. Menlo Park, Calif: Kaiser Family Foundation; April 1994. Report 1004.

Part XI

HEALTH CARE
IN SELECTED COUNTRIES

Three papers are included in this final section on health care in selected countries. The first paper, by Martha Livingston, "Update on Health Care in Canada: What's Right, What's Wrong, What's Left," examines Canadian health policy. Although much is right about the system, namely quality care without financial barriers, there are also problems, such as increasing costs. Livingston's article reviews the Canadian debate on health reform.

David Mechanic is author of the second paper, entitled "The Americanization of the British National Health Service." This paper reviews changes in the British system of socialized medicine intended to create an internal market generating competition and more cost-effective care. These measures include allowing hospitals to become self-governing trusts and permitting general practitioners to act as fund holders for their patients. The overall effect is movement in the direction of managed care, which originated in the United States.

The final paper is by William Cockerham on "The Social Determinants of the Decline in Life Expectancy in Russia and Eastern Europe." The author finds that the population group most affected by premature deaths was middle-age, working-class males. The principal cause of increased mortality was not communicable diseases, environmental pollution, genetics, and poor quality health care, but heart disease brought on by unhealthy lifestyles featuring heavy drinking and smoking, high-fat diets, and little or no exercise. Stress and a health policy that failed to contain rising morality from heart disease were contributing factors as well. But the social practices of a particular segment of society in the former socialist states of Europe were the ultimate determinant of the downturn in longevity.

UPDATE ON HEALTH CARE IN CANADA: WHAT'S RIGHT, WHAT'S WRONG, WHAT'S LEFT

Martha Livingston
State University of New York at Old Westbury

Any discussion of health care and health care "reform" in Canada needs three parts: a discussion, first, of what's right with Canada's health care system (medicare), and isn't wrong—that is, the myths about Canadian health care that have been routinely perpetrated in the United States; second, what has always been wrong with a fee-for-service, private-practice-based medical sickness-care system; and, third, the real news: threats to the system, beginning in the 1980s under the Conservative government of Brian Mulroney and deepening ever more dramatically since. Lest the article's title be misinterpreted, what's left of the health care system is substantial; what's also left is the analysis, by progressive Canadians, of budget-cutters' attempts to dismantle the system. This article will examine how, in the current political climate, progressive public health discourse can be and has been hijacked, deformed, and misused by would-be budget-slashers. A further note: The article is based largely on interviews with health care providers, health officials, and progressive researchers and activists, conducted by the researcher in Ontario, Quebec, Saskatchewan, and British Columbia on several visits in recent years.

I: WHAT'S RIGHT, DESPITE WHAT WE HEAR HERE, WITH HEALTH CARE IN CANADA

The Canadian system, flawed and threatened though it is, is nonetheless an enormous achievement, and light-years ahead of the U.S.'s wildly expensive, out-of-control, profit-laden nonsystem. Because many Americans cannot imagine health care as a right, they interpret problems in other nations' health care systems as evidence that a rational national health program cannot work. Nothing could be further from the truth; as

Victoria, B.C., family practitioner Rodney Drabkin[1] put it, "Tell your American physicians that if they came to Canada to practice medicine, they would think they had died and gone to heaven." The statement holds for users as well as providers.

Briefly, because this task has been undertaken elsewhere,[2-5] what's right with Canada's health care system is that it has provided and continues to provide world-class care to all in what remains essentially a one-tiered system. Benefits have never been completely comprehensive as regards prescription, dental, eyeglass, nonphysician, and alternative coverage. The indisputable fact that all Canadians are entitled to medical care without financial barriers has made the system Canada's most popular social program and

Reprinted from the *Journal of Public Health Policy,* vol. 19, no. 3 (Autumn, 1998), pp. 267–88, by permission.

one of the world's most popular health care systems.[6]

What *isn't* wrong in Canada's health care system is the Big Lie that Americans have heard in the mainstream press for years, about long waiting lines for scarce high-tech care, and Canadians pouring south to buy that care in the United States.[2, 7-10] From time to time, in one province or another, a particular service may develop a backlog, usually remedied by the province as soon as the bottleneck is recognized. One reason for some waits is patients' preference for a particular provider; this "problem" can be found in any system in which patients have unlimited choice of provider. Another source of these horror stories is the allegations made by the various parties during yearly fee-setting negotiations between provincial medical associations and health departments. For years, U.S. advocates of a Canadian-style single-payer system have tracked these "horror" stories when they were reported in the U.S. press, invariably finding that the stories had been thoroughly misrepresented. For example, Dr. Charles J. Wright, an orthopedic surgeon and vice president (Medical) of Vancouver General Hospital, the second-largest hospital in Canada, was quoted completely out of context in a *Reader's Digest* article[11] implying that hip replacements in Canada were scarce and determined on economic, not medical, grounds. Dr. Wright[12] was incensed at the misuse of his words, and described a much different scenario to this researcher. British Columbia's Ministry of Health and Ministry Responsible for Seniors tracks waiting times for many types of surgery and produces a "Waiting List Report"[13] several times a year; the report for mid-1997 showed an increase in numbers of surgeries performed, and a decrease in many waiting times. Similarly, Naylor[14] describes the intelligent use of queues for coronary care in Ontario.

In fact, many U.S. residents have flocked north for care.[15, 16] These big lies were designed to scare Americans away from further investigating a possible Canadian-style single-payer

solution to our own, real health care horror story, and do not stand up to closer scrutiny.

II. WHAT'S WRONG: ONGOING PUBLIC HEALTH DEBATES AND THEIR MISUSE BY BUDGET-CUTTERS

Ever since medicare was created, there has been much discussion, especially in progressive public health circles, of "what's wrong with Canada's health care system, and how to fix it."[17-20] This discussion has followed a pattern common in the evolution of national health care systems.[21, 22] Typically, countries first establish a funding mechanism for health care expenses (Canada's beginning with hospital coverage in Saskatchewan in 1947 and comprehensive health care in that province in 1962, and evolving into the current national program in 1971), called a national health insurance system. After a number of years, after the first glow of success, the country begins a process of reexamination, to decide whether the system could be better organized and more value obtained for the money. A typical second step in the evolution of health care systems might then occur, to a national health service (NHS) model, the United Kingdom's being the prototype. There are no laws about this progression, but a number of countries seem to follow this pattern, described by Roemer[21] as the "continuum of government intervention" in the health care market (p. 96). What is new in Canada is the recent use by would-be budget-cutters of many arguments previously thought to be the sole intellectual property of progressive health policy analysts and activists.

1. Community Health Clinics, Fee-for-Service Medicine, and the Evolution of Canadian Health Care

In Canada, even as the community health clinic system was initiated in Saskatchewan in 1962, many argued for a comprehensive, government-run or government-controlled system like the British NHS, with doctors on salary in comprehensive, community-based health centers.[18, 19] The community health clinic movement in Saskatchewan was an effort to put this vision into practice. Community-based health activists established a provincewide clinic network to be run jointly by professionals and community, serving a broad range of health and social needs in addition to the curative care provided by staff doctors. Some feel that settling the 1962 Saskatchewan doctors' strike by establishing a fee-for-service payment method for doctors was a major setback to efforts to establish a more rational NHS-style system of health care at the outset. Although there are community health clinics throughout Canada, with an especially vigorous network of 160 CLSCs in Quebec,[23] private practice, fee-for-service medicine remains the dominant mode of payment for physician services, with over 90 percent of Canada's physicians remunerated this way.[17,24]

Critics of the present system such as Sallie Mahood, M.D., family practice doctor and member of the Family Practice Faculty at the University of Saskatchewan,[25, 26] argue that the FFS model of care has deformed the system both in type and quality of care by paying doctors more to do tests and procedures than careful, lengthier office visits and physical examinations, and encouraging the speedy movement of patients through the office. It creates incentives to overtreat by financially rewarding doctors for follow-up office visits when telephone follow-up would suffice, and perversely provides no incentive for preventive care and health education, particularly when these services are provided by nonphysicians and are therefore not directly reimbursable in a private practice setting. It also contributes to fragmentation and duplication of services. Interestingly, in all the recent health care reform discussion and activity, there has been little discussion by federal or provincial governments of altering the FFS mode of physician reimbursement, without which it is hard to imagine real change in the organization of health care delivery. Physicians account

directly for 15–16 percent of health expenditures, but control 80 percent of expenditures, defining what is and isn't health care.[27] And although many physicians would balk at a switch to salary or capitation, some would welcome it, seeing FFS as a stumbling block to providing the kind of care they would prefer to provide. Some, said Cheryl Anderson, M.D., a public health officer in Vancouver, B.C.,[28] even feel that their incomes would increase were they to work on salary. Others simply do not want financial considerations to impinge on their ability to treat patients as they see fit.

2. Deinstitutionalization and Local Control

Provinces have responded to the continuing funding shrinkage in a number of ways. In both Saskatchewan and British Columbia, for example, the provinces have devolved much power onto a network of newly established local or district health boards charged with administering health care in their areas, and in Quebec decentralization to 17 regions was undertaken in 1992.[29] While in general, local control is a fine principle, current plans are seen by some as a cover for cutbacks, putting local boards in the position of presiding over shrinking funds and allowing provincial and federal governments to avoid taking direct responsibility for service cuts.[30]

In several provinces, including British Columbia, Saskatchewan, and Ontario, deinstitutionalization, especially of many long-term-care patients, seems a reasonable way to trim budgets. Although many see such plans as more humane in keeping all but the sickest in the community, others are critical, noting the pitfalls that accompany deinstitutionalization without a corresponding increase in funding for community-based care. Many still remember mental health deinstitutionalization programs of the 1960s in both the United States and Canada through which hospitals and wards were shut and mentally ill persons brought back into communities ill equipped to care for them without the corresponding provision of community-based care. The result, in the United States at least, was a burgeoning population of untreated, often homeless mentally ill persons in most major cities. Canadians critical of the current trend toward community-based care note that unless sufficient funding is provided, the result will often be that women now paid to provide patient care as health care workers in institutions will be downsized and transformed into unemployed, unpaid family caregivers in communities.[30] And early discharge, resulting in patients' being released from hospital "quicker and sicker," is also seen as a form of privatization, since home care and private nursing care are not usually included in the public system.[31]

3. Social Determinants of Health

Much of the recent discourse on directions for health care reform has taken the form known in public health circles as the "social determinants of health" argument, suggesting that a more effective health system would address contributors to health status such as the environment, workplace, social class, racism, sexism, and poverty as well as primary and preventive care, rather than focusing most of the resources on treatment of disease.[20,24,32] In particular, Rachlis and Kushner's 1989 version of this argument[17] had a national impact.

A number of different versions of the "social determinants" argument have emerged, each proposing its own solutions. One formulation minimizes the "social" in the social determinants and focuses primarily on individual behavior and "lifestyle," resulting in governments investing in health promotion campaigns relating primarily to smoking cessation, substance use, diet and exercise, and the like, as in the Saskatchewan "wellness" program.[33] This formulation of "determinants of health" is also seen in Statistics Canada's National Population Health Survey Overview, which measured "many lifestyle factors considered to be determinants of health, including smoking, alcohol consumption, weight, and physical activity."[34]

In other formulations, the social aspects of social determinants are more fully emphasized, with a corresponding government programmatic focus on shifting funds away from sickness care to social programs such as housing and employment, the better to deploy societal resources to prevent illness. This approach was espoused at least for a time by the British Columbia Ministry of Health and Ministry Responsible for Seniors.[35] Some members of the Ministry[36] enthusiastically described programs they were in the process of initiating in 1995 with this in mind. The National Forum on Health, established by the federal government in 1994 to help formulate policy on health care reform-related issues, focused much attention on the social determinants of health,[37] concluding, in their final report (p. 24)[38] that "there is more to health than health care," and recommending specific action on child and family health, community action, the establishment of an Aboriginal Health Institute, and "explicit acknowledgement of the health and social impacts of economic policies, and action to help individuals who are trying to enter the workforce." The Canadian Public Health Association, not surprisingly, also espouses a social determinants perspective.[39]

At first blush, progressive public health advocates must find it hard to imagine anything wrong with a national discussion of the social determinants of health and a switch away from spending health care dollars on sickness care to spending for preventive care. On closer inspection, however, two major problems emerge. The first is why the social determinants argument is being put forward by government at this time. Can it simply be that after 25 years, government officials have come to recognize that the current system is not the most efficient way to organize health care? Many suspect rather that the social determinants argument is being used as a cover for the recent massive cutbacks in Canada's health care system. After all, if the money isn't really providing health care, it could be better spent elsewhere.

In an interview,[40] Frank Fedyk and Jake Vellinga of Health Canada's Health Policy Division described to this researcher efforts in some provinces to "take a health determinants approach." While in principle the argument makes sense, progressive public health advocates are galled to see money slashed simultaneously from health care and other social programs as well. The resulting drop in income level, increased unemployment, and less funding to education and housing, make it harder for Canadians to stay or become healthy,[32] and reveal the real explanation for the current popularity of the social determinants argument in many official circles. In a 1996 address to a meeting of the American group, Physicians for a National Health Program,[41] Michael Rachlis bluntly summed it up: Government talk of putting more money into the social determinants of health was "just rhetoric."

The other major problem is the potential for victim blaming, focusing on individual behavior such as smoking and minimizing truly social determinants such as workplace hazards. Saskatchewan's formulation of the determinants of health as a "wellness" model, focusing primarily on lifestyle issues, is an example. As Dr. Sallie Mahood pointed out,[25] not every illness is preventable—especially under the present social system.

4. Evidence-Based Medicine

A related argument also current in mainstream circles suggests that much of the Canadian health care dollar is spent on ineffective and downright harmful treatments. Evidence-based medicine, or evidence-based decision making, examines current clinical practice to assess which procedures are demonstrably effective, which possibly ineffective, and which actively harmful. This sort of assessment can be useful in identifying dollars wasted on unproven or actively harmful procedures; according to Rachlis and Kushner,[17] more than 80 percent of clinical medicine is based on no scientific studies at all, and many studies that are done are of poor quality. A new journal inaugurated in 1995 by the American College of Physicians, *Evidence-Based Medicine*, is co-edited by a McMaster faculty member, and also has a number of associate editors from McMaster. But the leap from research to changing clinical practice is often difficult to accomplish.

Saskatchewan's Health Services and Utilization Research Commission (HSURC), funded by but independent of the Saskatchewan Ministry of Health, is also engaged in this research. HSURC was established in 1992 "to promote the wellness of the people of Saskatchewan by fostering the efficient and effective utilization of health services and by stimulating, funding, and promoting research in the healing arts and health sciences" (title page).[42] The organization researches and produces technical reports and clinical practice guidelines on medical procedures to promote evidence-based clinical medical practice, conducting both original studies and meta-analyses of existing studies. Given the respect it is accorded among health care providers throughout the province as well as by the provincial health ministry, HSURC may actually be able to have an impact on clinical practice in the province. This ability is enhanced also by HSURC's method of discussing with providers and communities which issues they see as most urgently needing investigation.

The National Forum on Health included evidence-based decision making as one of its four working groups;[37,38] it examined issues not only of what constitutes evidence and how evidence is or is not acted upon, but also discussed including "non-traditional" evidence and "evidence from other cultures." Once again, while no one can argue with the usefulness of basing health care spending decisions in part on reliable studies of treatment efficacy, some worry that evidence-based decision making can also be used as an excuse for health care cutbacks: If the stuff doesn't work, why waste public money on it? Others are critical of the types of outcomes being measured and the kinds of data being used, worrying that some treatments important to patients' quality of life may not be appropriately researched or considered outcomes.

5. Use of Nonphysician Providers; Alternative and Complementary Medicine

Advocates for the inclusion of nonphysician providers and alternative medical treatments in the system suggest that a fee-for-service, private-practice-based system has been unable to take sufficient advantage of nonphysician providers such as midwives and advanced-practice nurses whose services are well received and can cost the system less than those of medical doctors. Federal health officials Frank Fedyk and Jake Vellinga[40] described the possible use of nurse-practitioners as "a new point of entry into the system."

Many Canadians also feel that a truly comprehensive health care system should include the right to choose nonstandard treatments as well as nonphysician providers. There is much evidence for the efficacy of many nonstandard treatments, as well as evidence that it can often, though not always, provide lower-cost treatment producing positive outcomes with fewer unwanted side effects.[43] Many of these treatments are well accepted and widely used by Canadians. Statistics Canada (pp. 15–16) reported that "in 1994, 15% of adults—3.3 million people—reported using some form of alternative medicine in the past year."[34] The majority of them—12 percent—also consulted a regular physician in that period. (By contrast, a U.S. study,[43] examining all forms of alternative treatment, showed that about one-third of Americans use various forms of alternative medicine.) The most popular form of alternative care in Canada in 1994 was chiropractic care; homeopathy and massage therapy were also mentioned. The survey also found that Canadians with chronic conditions, including back problems, food allergies, ulcers, and urinary incontinence, used more alternative care than those with no chronic

conditions. The survey found (p. 16) that rates of use of chiropractic care were higher in those provinces with some chiropractic coverage: Alberta, British Columbia, Manitoba, Saskatchewan, and Ontario.[34] There was also an increase in use (from 11 to 18%) from the lowest- to the highest-income households, reflecting the fact that provinces typically have treatment limits and payment caps for such care. Another survey[45] found that 20 percent of Canadians had used some form of complementary medicine in 1990.

Health care policymakers sometimes believe that including more kinds of practitioners in a system must inevitably make the system more expensive, since it adds options and providers, and medical doctors are often loath to share the reimbursement pie. Increasing access to often more-innocuous and less-expensive alternative treatments, however, can have the potential to reduce the total amount of money spent on health care.

As with all aspects of health care, policies regarding coverage for nonphysician providers vary by province, based primarily on each province's history of use of such services before medicare's inception nationwide in 1971. An inquiry of all provincial health programs conducted by the author reveals that for the most part, nonphysician provider services to outpatients are not directly reimbursed. Many provinces cover in-hospital services by such allied health professionals as physical, occupational, and speech therapists, and many cover physical therapy services out-of-hospital as well. Some dental, podiatric, and optometric services are also covered by many provinces. Some provinces cover psychological services; psychologists are employed on salary by hospitals or community-based facilities.

Chiropractors and osteopaths are covered in several provinces, and massage therapists are covered in Ontario and B.C. But these services, unlike physician services, often have limits and co-payments. In 1992, chiropractors in Saskatchewan, who had previously functioned wholly within the system, opted for a new arrangement in which user fees were implemented. Since provincial reimbursement had been, in their view, too low, the new arrangement allowed chiropractors to see fewer patients yet maintain their income levels, despite the inevitable loss of those patients unable to pay privately for their services. According to the executive director of the Saskatchewan Chiropractic Association,[46] most patients in this category can access care through workers' compensation or means-tested programs providing care to low-income residents. A similar scenario has occurred in British Columbia, where chiropractors are still included in the system, but where, according to chiropractor Randy Zindler,[47] about 40 percent have opted out because of dissatisfaction with reimbursement rates. Patients of opted-out B.C. chiropractors can file claim forms and receive reimbursement at the provincial rate, but most pay the extra-billed amount out of pocket.

Midwifery is an interesting case in point of the inclusion of nonphysician providers. Much evidence exists[48–50] that midwifery is the preferred method of childbirth management for all but the most high-risk labors, and that where it is legal and accessible, women strongly prefer this care to standard medical management. It is also less costly, because midwife-attended births involve less use of technology and fewer high-tech interventions, resulting in fewer expensive surgical deliveries. Only in Ontario has midwifery been fully included thus far; this popular and well-received development[51] occurred on 31 December 1993.[52] In Quebec, physician opposition to the inclusion of midwives has been fierce, but seven out-of-hospital, midwife-run birthing centers have been established throughout the province as a demonstration project, functioning within rigorous protocols, and will be evaluated within the next few years, according to Josée Briggs, midwife and director of one of the centers, La Maison de Naissance de l'Outouais.[53] The future of midwifery in the province, however, remains

unclear. In British Columbia, midwives working toward inclusion in the system were heartened, in May 1993, when the then-B.C. Minister of Health Elizabeth Cull, announced, at the International Confederation of Midwives' Congress in Vancouver, the legalization of midwifery and establishment of a Midwives' College for British Columbia.[54] The process of implementing midwifery in the province is now underway. In Saskatchewan, midwifery has been viewed as a potential component of the Wellness Program, and the Ministry of Health in 1995 established an advisory committee to investigate its inclusion, according to Regina midwifery advocate Kathy Ellis, a member of the advisory board.[55, 56]

III. HEALTH CARE "REFORM": REAL THREATS TO THE SYSTEM: THE POLITICAL-ECONOMIC CONTEXT

1. "The Deficit Made Me Do It!"

For the last several years, discussion of the fate of all of Canada's social programs, including health care, has been conducted within the framework of a national deficit debate. Since health care is so popular that no politician dares attack it outright, the discourse is generally framed as "everybody loves medicare; unfortunately, given the deficit, we simply can't afford it anymore."

The "strategic deficit" argument as put forward by political conservatives suggests an inevitable, urgent need to cut social spending in order to reduce or eliminate the deficit. Framed in this way, the argument first entered the international geopolitical arena in the early 1980s via President Ronald Reagan's budget director, David Stockman. Stockman's explicit position was that the strategic deficit argument made possible the cutting of otherwise-popular social programs. Coupled with tax cuts to the wealthy, the result, in the United States, has been a dramatic rise in income inequality between the richest few percent and the rest of the American people.

The argument was adopted by Conservative Prime Minister Brian Mulroney in the early 1980s, and has since been used to justify substantial cutbacks in social spending in Canada. Opposition to this view has been widespread.[57,58] Unfortunately for the health of medicare and other social programs, many Canadians accepted the seeming logic of the argument: We're in debt; we have to cut back our spending. When the Liberals came to national power in 1993, they soon reversed their campaign promise to defend social programs, and their positions on these issues started to look more and more like those of the Conservatives they had succeeded. Indeed, Conservative former Prime Minister Brian Mulroney observed[59]:

> They've endorsed our agenda pretty well, and I'm very pleased with that. The free-trade agreement with the United States, the North American free-trade agreement, the GST [a highly unpopular value-added tax], privatizations and our low-inflation policy. . . . and they're taking them a little further (p. 91).

Liberal Prime Minister Jean Chrétien had declared, during the 1993 election campaign, that "I don't want a medical system in Canada where there will be a system for the rich and a system for the poor. . . . We will keep it as it is, and nobody will touch it as long as the Liberal Party is there" (p. 191).[59] Health care advocates breathed a sigh of relief, and Canadians went to the polls to ensure Liberal protection of medicare. But when the Liberals released their first budget, with both changes in the federal health care funding formula and large funding cuts, Chrétien responded to the hue and cry by suggesting that medicare had originally been intended to provide only catastrophic care, and that the original federal funding for the program had been meant only as a temporary measure to "kick-start" the system (p. 192).[59] The deficit argument is usually coupled with another argument not based in fact, that health care spending is out of control. Actually, public spending on health

care has *declined* since the 1970s, from about 76 percent of total health care expenditures to about 72 percent in 1994 (p. 8)[60] and most recently to 70 percent,[31] with the private sector growing correspondingly, a phenomenon known as "passive privatization." (The largest category of private health care expenditure, and one of the fastest-growing, is for pharmaceuticals.) The argument that spending is out of control is seemingly bolstered by the increase in health expenditures' percentage of GDP from 7.1 percent in 1975 to 10.1 percent in 1993, making it the "second most expensive health care system in the world," as Frank Fedyk of Health Canada's Health Policy Division said.[40] In fact, this phenomenon is explained by the "denominator effect." Several recessions during the 1980s resulted in a decline in GDP growth—the denominator—but health care spending did not decline by as much as GDP did. This created the appearance of an increase in health care and other social program spending (pp. 6–7).[60] Recent cuts in health care spending have resulted in a drop from 10.1 percent of GDP in 1993 to 9.8 percent in 1994, 9.5 percent in 1995, and 9.1 percent in 1996.[61]

Another, related myth is that health and other social expenditures are the major reasons for the fiscal crisis in which Canada finds itself. However, critics of this view[57, 62–65] respond that this spending is responsible for only 6 percent of the national debt, whereas tax breaks to corporations and the wealthiest Canadians are responsible for 50 percent, and high-interest-rate policies for 44 percent, of the national debt.

2. Challenges to the Canada Health Act

Although the current system of medicare came into being nationwide in 1971, the Canada Health Act of 1984 consolidated the program and closed loopholes, outlawing balance- or extra-billing by physicians and user fees by facilities, guaranteeing a truly one-tier system nationwide.[66] The Act achieved these goals by requiring the provincial plans to meet five criteria: universality, comprehensive coverage for all medically necessary care (as defined by the provinces; it has for the most part never included universal dental care, eyeglasses, out-of-hospital prescription drugs, or nonphysician or alternative care), accessibility, portability (across Canada and even, to some extent, outside of Canada), and public administration.[4] Provinces which failed to meet these criteria would lose a portion of the federal money transferred to the provinces for medicare. But the 50-50 cash payment by the federal government to the provinces for health care ceased in 1977, when a formula was introduced by which the provinces got some cash and some "tax points," that is, tax relief on the federal level to allow the provinces to raise their own taxes to pay for medicare. This program, called Established Programs Financing (EPF), consisted of one payment to cover the federal portion of both health care (two-thirds) and postsecondary education financing (one-third).[3] Originally, the formula contained built-in increases based on both population and economic growth; but starting in the late 1980s, the federal government reduced the amount paid on the basis of economic growth,[67] accelerating this reduction so that for 1995–1996, the rate was GNP growth *minus* 3 percent, and the per capita figure, at $523, has stayed constant since 1990. Since the EPF's inception in 1977, the cash portion of the federal transfer money has been reduced annually, with a projected decrease to a zero cash transfer to the provinces over the next 10 or 15 years.

The problem with decreasing the cash transfer is that the threat of withheld cash has been the federal government's chief weapon for enforcing the provisions of the Canada Health Act. In the last few years, there have been several provincial challenges to the Canada Health Act, most notably though not exclusively in Alberta, where some facilities started to charge a "facility fee" in addition to what is paid by the province for the service. This form of extra-billing poses a real threat to a one-tier health care system by allowing those with the ability to pay to get services not available to, or faster than, those without. At a less-than-completely cordial meeting of federal and provincial health ministers in September 1995, federal Health Minister Diane Marleau set a deadline of 15 October 1995 for imposing sanctions on provinces (specifically, Alberta) not complying with the Canada Health Act,[68] and the province subsequently retreated.

With the passage of Liberal Bill C76 on 1 April 1996, the funds-transfer mechanism has been dramatically altered so that starting in 1997, health care funds have been block-granted in one Canada Health and Social Transfer (CHST) payment. Whereas health and postsecondary education funds had previously been protected by being transferred separately from other social program monies, now provinces get one payment for all and are allowed to determine how best to spend these monies. Coupled with this change in financing was a decrease in funding of $2.5 billion in the first year (a 3 percent reduction, according to the federal government), and $4.5 billion in the second year. This policy change presented the unappetizing possibility of health and social advocacy groups fighting over their respective slices of a shrinking pie. As Frank Fedyk and Jake Vellinga of Health Canada put it,[40] this decrease "poses major challenges for the provinces," which demanded to know what level of funding they could expect in future years, so that they could start to make long-range plans. They also described nationwide discussion of the minimum dollar amount necessary to ensure the federal government's continued ability to enforce the Canada Health Act and felt that the issue would be successfully resolved. Monique Bégin, former Minister of Health, reported[61] that she "personally believe[s]" that the $12.5 billion the federal government gives the provinces is "still important enough to give the federal minister the clout to enforce the Act."

3. Other Threats: "Death by a Thousand Cuts"

Bégin, who as Liberal Minister of Health crafted the Canada Health Act in 1983,[66] warned, during Free Trade Agreement talks in 1988, that medicare was a fragile system vulnerable to "death by a thousand cuts."[59] Bill Tholl, then-Director of Health Policy and Economics of the Canadian Medical Association, echoed these sentiments[69] in describing recent unremitting assaults on medicare. Even before Bill C76 instituted block-granting, provinces have responded to ongoing medicare budget cuts since the recessions of the early 1980s by de-listing services, closing facilities, and cutting back health care staff. In response, health care advocates, professionals, workers, and recipients have been waging ongoing struggles both to maintain services and to restore funding to programs threatened by cutbacks. Not all of them take on the deficit argument explicitly, but they contend that de-listing or cutting back services has both human and economic consequences. For example, the Province of Saskatchewan's prescription drug program used to provide pharmaceuticals to all people in the province with a $3.50 co-payment. In the early 1990s, in a cutback, residents of the province were made responsible for the first $200 per month of their drug bills, with only people in poverty and "high-end users," the chronically ill, exempted from this deductible. One result, described by Sallie Mahood, M.D.,[25] was an increase in teen pregnancy and demand for abortions by women who could no longer afford birth control pills. Other cutbacks described by Patricia Gallagher, Executive Director of Operations for the Saskatchewan Government Employees' Union,[70] and Larry LeMoal, of the Saskatchewan Union of Nurses,[71] include closed hospitals and beds; de-listing and de-insuring of services and drugs; laying off of workers; and contracting out of management, laboratory, and nursing services. Gallagher described the process by which private corporations insinuate themselves into the system by submitting lowball bids for specific (e.g., laboratory) services. "Once they're in," she said, "they're the only game in town, and can charge whatever they please."

4. Privatization and the NAFTA Threat

A mantra frequently heard south of the border and now sometimes echoed north of the border is that the private sector—in health care and everywhere else—is more efficient. In health care, nothing could be more wrong. Study after study has demonstrated that Canada spends about one-third less on its public system than the United States spends on a health care system which does not guarantee health care to all chiefly because of the private sector's enormous administrative costs, waste, and profiteering.[2,60,72] In fact, expenditures in the private sector in Canada are growing far faster than public expenditures; for example, drug expenditures increased from about 8 percent of total health expenditures in 1977 to about 15 percent in 1993 (p. 5).[60]

Nevertheless, as services get de-listed, more and more costs are shifted to the private sector, threatening to transform a one-tier, universal program into a two-tier, means-tested program in which the poor will receive mediocre public services while the middle class, with private supplemental health policies provided either through the workplace or out of pocket, buy their way out. The American for-profit health care insurance business, ever on the alert for more customers, eagerly seizes every opportunity to make inroads into Canada's potentially lucrative health care market. In 1995, for example, Ontario Blue Cross/Blue Shield, the nonprofit company providing supplemental health insurance to government workers and others, was bought by the for-profit corporation Liberty International.[40] In May 1996, there was an attempt by the Ontario government to hire a notorious American firm, National Medical Care, to provide dialysis care for the province; health care advocates' vigilance resulted in temporary defeat for this privatization attempt,[73,74] but the Ottawa doctor involved in that effort is now suing.[75]

Another threat to the system is seen in the Canada–U.S. Free Trade Agreement (FTA), the North American Free Trade Agreement (NAFTA), and the Multilateral Agreement on Investments (MAI, often referred to as "NAFTA on steroids") now being negotiated. The countries party to these agreements are not allowed to put into place programs which result in one country's having an unfair trade advantage over the others. The result, therefore, is to drive social benefits down to the lowest common denominator—and Canada's health care system would have far to fall. Social programs currently in place are exempted from this "unfair trade advantage" provision under NAFTA's Clause 2C9, which assures governments "the right to perpetuate the kind of social system that they want."[40] But once services are de-listed, U.S. health care corporations, poised at the border, will leap eagerly into the newly privatized health care market. And once a service has been taken over by the private sector, it would become an unfair trade advantage, under NAFTA, to republicize it. So services off-loaded to the private sector will be gone from the public domain forever, or at least until the demise of NAFTA. Conversations in 1995 with Canadian health officials and policy analysts revealed a vast difference in perception of this potential threat to health care. Those within the government with whom I spoke were without exception unconcerned about NAFTA's implications for medicare, firmly believing that Clause 2C9 would protect it. Those outside the government, by contrast, saw a profound threat to the system in the combination of service cutbacks and NAFTA, feeling that the many cuts now being made in the system represent programs that cannot, under NAFTA, be restored.

IV. CONCLUSION

Make no mistake about it; the Canadian health care system as we in the United States have come to know and admire it is in grave danger. Despite the federal government's positive spin—that they are "renewing," rather than reforming the system[40]—Canadians outside government say that they are "in for the fight of our lives."[76] This article has attempted to separate the strands of the debate and to demonstrate how in the current political climate, progressive public health discourse can be and has been hijacked, deformed, and misused by budget-slashers. It is the profound wish of this observer that the Canadian people will find a way to stand on guard for their excellent, if flawed, health care system, and that it will remain for years to come a beacon of hope for those of us still struggling for a just health care system.

REFERENCES

1. INTERVIEW, RODNEY DRABKIN, family practice physician, Victoria, B.C., 19 July 1993.
2. EDITORS OF CONSUMER REPORTS. *How to Resolve the Health Care Crisis: Affordable Health Care for All Americans.* Yonkers, New York: Consumer Reports Books, 1992.
3. TAYLOR, M. G. *Insuring National Health Care: The Canadian Experience.* Chapel Hill: The University of North Carolina Press, 1990.
4. CANADIAN EMBASSY. *Health Care in Canada.* Washington, D.C., 1997.
5. ARMSTRONG, P., ARMSTRONG, H., and FEGAN, C. *Universal Health Care: What the United States Can Learn from the Canadian Experience.* New York: The New Press, 1998.
6. BLENDON, R. J., LEITMAN, R., MORRISON, I., & DONELAN, K. "Satisfaction with Health Systems in Ten Nations," *Health Affairs* 9 (1990): 185–92.
7. BURNEY, D. H. "Letter to the Editor," the *New York Times* (21 November 1991): A26.
8. BURNEY, D. H. "Letter to the Editor," the *New York Times* (11 June 1992): A22.
9. COHEN, T. "Busting the Myths about Canada's Health Care," the *Wall Street Journal* (6 February 1992): A15.
10. MARMOR, T. R., & GODFREY, J. "Canada's Medical System is a Model. That's a Fact," the *New York Times* (23 July 1992): A23.
11. MUNRO, I. R. "How Not to Improve Health Care," *Reader's Digest* (September 1992): 49–53.
12. INTERVIEW, CHARLES J. WRIGHT, Vice President (Medical), Vancouver General Hospital, 14 July 1993.

13. British Columbia Ministry of Health and Ministry Responsible for Seniors. *Waiting List Report.* Fall, 1997.

14. Naylor, C. D. "A Different View of Queues in Ontario," *Health Affairs* 10 (1991): 110–28.

15. Farnsworth, C. "Americans Filching Free Health Care in Canada," the *New York Times* (20 December 1993): A1, A8.

16. Thorne, S. "Health-care Refugee," the *Ottawa Citizen* (27 January 1992).

17. Rachlis, M., and Kushner, C. *Second Opinion: What's Wrong with Canada's Health Care System and How to Fix It.* Toronto: Collins, 1989.

18. Badgley, R. F., and Wolfe, S. *Doctors' Strike.* Toronto: Macmillan of Canada, 1971.

19. Rands, S. *Privilege and Policy: A History of Community Clinics in Saskatchewan.* Saskatoon, Sask.: Community Health Cooperative Federation, 1994.

20. Terris, M. "Lessons from Canada's Health Program," *Technology Review.* February–March 1990: 27–33.

21. Roemer, M. I. *National Health Systems of the World,* Vol. I. New York/Oxford: Oxford University Press, 1991.

22. Roemer, M. I. *National Health Systems of the World,* Vol. II. New York/Oxford: Oxford University Press, 1993.

23. Interview, Pierre Ippersiel, Directeur, CLSC de Hull, 26 September 1995.

24. Mhatre, S. L., and Deber, R. B. "From Equal Access to Health Care to Equitable Access to Health: A Review of Canadian Provincial Health Commissions and Reports," *International Journal of Health Services* 22 (1992): 645–68.

25. Interview, Sallie Mahood, Family Practice Faculty, University of Saskatchewan, 21 July 1993.

26. Interview, Sallie Mahood, Family Practice Faculty, University of Saskatchewan, 21 July 1995.

27. Rachlis, M., and Kushner, C. *Strong Medicine: How to Save Canada's Health Care System.* Toronto: HarperCollins, 1994.

28. Interview, Cheryl Anderson, Medical Health Officer, Vancouver Health Board, 22 July 1995.

29. Pineault, R., Lamarche, P. A., Champagne, F., Contandriopoulos, A.-P., and Denis J.-L. "The Reform of the Quebec Health Care System: Potential for Innovation?", *Journal of Public Health Policy* 14 (1993): 198–219.

30. Armstrong, P., Armstrong, H., Choiniere, J., Feldberg, G., and White, J. *Take Care: Warning Signals for Canada's Health System.* Toronto: Garamond Press, 1994.

31. Fuller, C. "Canada's Health Care Crisis: More and More Health Care Services Being Privatized," *Medical Reform* 17 (1998): 9–11.

32. Wolfe, S., and Badgley, R. F. "Universal Access in Canada: Questions of Equity Remain," *Health/PAC Bulletin* 22 (1992): 29–35.

33. Simard, L. *A Saskatchewan Vision for Health. A Framework for Change.* Saskatchewan Health, 1992.

34. Statistics Canada. *National Population Health Survey Overview* 1994–95. Ottawa: Statistics Canada Health Statistics Division, Pub. #82–567, 1995.

35. B. C. Ministry of Health and Ministry Responsible for Seniors, Office of Health Promotion. *Our New Understanding of Health,* 1993.

36. Interview, John Greschner, Assistant Deputy Minister; Sue Rothwell, Executive Director, New Directions Development Division; Mike Corbeil, Executive Director, Pharmacare; Rick Hudson, Medical Consultant, Strategic Programs, B.C. Ministry of Health and Ministry Responsible for Seniors, 19 July 1995.

37. National Forum on Health. "Seeking Solutions . . .," *InfoForum No. 5* (July 1996).

38. National Forum on Health. *Canada Health Action: Building on the Legacy.* 2 vols. Ottawa, 1997.

39. Interview, Robert Burr, Director of Public Affairs, and Ron deBurger, Director, AIDS Program, Canadian Public Health Association, Ottawa, 25 September 1995.

40. Interview, Frank Fedyk, Assistant Director, and Jake Vellinga, Senior Policy Analyst, Health Policy Division, Policy and Consultation Branch, Health Canada, 25 September 1995.

41. Rachlis, M., keynote address, Physicians for a National Health Program Annual Meeting, Windsor, Ontario, 18 May 1996.

42. Health Services Utilization and Research Commission. *Annual Report* 1993–94, 1994.

43. Fugh-Berman, A. *Alternative Medicine: What Works.* Tucson, Arizona: Odonian Press, 1996.

44. EISENBERG, D. M., et al. "Unconventional Medicine in the United States: Prevalence, Costs, and Patterns of Use," *The New England Journal of Medicine* 328 (1993): 246–52.

45. LaVALLEY, J. W., and VERHOEF, M. J. "Integrating Complementary Medicine and Health Care Services into Practice," *Canadian Medical Association Journal* 153 (1995): 45–49.

46. INTERVIEW, C. JAMES STEWART, Executive Director, Saskatchewan Chiropractic Association, 23 July 1993.

47. INTERVIEW, RANDY ZINDLER, chiropractor, Vancouver, B.C., 20 July 1995.

48. BURTCH, B. *Trials of Labour: The Re-emergence of Midwifery*. Montreal/Kingston: McGill-Queen's University Press, 1994.

49. LIVINGSTON, M. "Choice in Childbirth: Power and the Impact of the Modern Childbirth Reform Movement," *Women and Therapy* 6 (1987): 239–61.

50. MITFORD, J. *The American Way of Birth*. New York: Dutton, 1992.

51. SARICK, L. "Childbirth's Ancient Art Reborn as a Profession," *The Globe and Mail* (14 May 1994): A1, A6.

52. HESS, H. "Midwives Get New Hospital Role," *The Globe and Mail* (20 January 1994): A1.

53. INTERVIEW, JOSÉE BRIGGS, Directeur, La Maison de Naissance de l'Outouais, 22 September 1995.

54. *Newsletter, International Confederation of Midwives*. "Midwives: Hear the Heartbeat of the Future," International Confederation of Midwives Conference (1993):3.

55. INTERVIEW, KATHY ELLIS, midwifery advocate, Regina, Saskatchewan, 27 July 1995.

56. REGINA COMMUNITY CLINIC. *Midwifery Brief, Prepared for the Midwifery Advisory Committee*. 31 January 1995.

57. CHORNEY, H., HOTSON, J., and SECCARECCIA, M. *The Deficit Made Me Do It!* Ottawa: Canadian Centre for Policy Alternatives, 1992.

58. RALPH, D., RÉGIMBALD, A., and ST-AMAND, N. *Open for Business, Closed to People: Mike Harris's Ontario*. Halifax, N.S.: Fernwood Publishing, 1997.

59. BARLOW, M., and CAMPBELL, B. *Straight Through the Heart*. Toronto: HarperCollins, 1995.

60. HEALTH CANADA. *National Health Expenditures in Canada 1975–1993*. Policy and Consultation Branch, Health Policy Division, 1995.

61. BÉGIN, M. Talk on Canadian Health Care, New School for Social Research, New York, 10 February 1998.

62. MIMOTO, H., and CROSS, P. "The Growth of the Federal Debt," *Canadian Economic Observer*, June 1991: 3.1–3.17.

63. McQUAIG, L. *The Wealthy Banker's Wife*. Toronto: Penguin, 1993.

64. McQUAIG, L. *Shooting the Hippo: Death by Deficit and Other Canadian Myths*. Toronto: Viking/ Penguin, 1995.

65. ARMSTRONG, P., and ARMSTRONG, H. *Wasting Away: The Undermining of Canadian Health Care*. Toronto/New York/Oxford: Oxford University Press, 1996.

66. RICHARDSON, B. "Monique Bégin: Ready to Do Battle Again," *Canadian Forum*, October 1996: 14–18.

67. ANGUS, D.E., AUER, L., CLOUTIER, J.E., & ALBERT, T. *Sustainable Health Care for Canada*. Ottawa: Queen's–University of Ottawa Economic Projects, 1995.

68. HEALTH CANADA. News Release 1995-63: *Federal Health Minister Determined to Preserve and Protect Medicare*. Ottawa, 1995.

69. INTERVIEW, BILL THOLL, Director of Health Policy and Economics, Canadian Medical Association, Ottawa, 25 September 1995.

70. INTERVIEW, PATRICIA GALLAGHER, Executive Director of Operations, Saskatchewan Government Employees Association, Regina, 27 July 1995.

71. INTERVIEW, LARRY LeMOAL, Saskatchewan Union of Nurses, Regina, 25 July 1995.

72. HIMMELSTEIN, D. U., LEWONTIN, J.P., and WOOLHANDLER, S. "Who Administers? Who Cares? Medical Administrative and Clinical Employment in the United States and Canada," *American Journal of Public Health* 86 (1996): 172–78.

73. IBBITSON, J. "Ontario Reviews Dialysis-unit Deal with U.S. Firm," *Ottawa Citizen*, 1 May 1996: A1.

74. MEDLINE, E. "Dialysis Firm Faces Three Major Investigations in U.S.," *Ottawa Citizen*, 2 May 1996: A1.

75. INTERVIEW, HUGH ARMSTRONG, Carleton University School of Social Work, Ottawa, 18 November 1996.

76. INTERVIEW, HUGH ARMSTRONG, Carleton University School of Social Work, Ottawa, 22 September 1995.

THE AMERICANIZATION OF THE BRITISH NATIONAL HEALTH SERVICE

David Mechanic
Rutgers University

The core reform of the British National Health Service (NHS) was the establishment of a quasi market with a split between purchasers and providers. Health authorities and general practitioner (GP) fundholders were to be discriminating purchasers seeking more efficient and responsive services. This market orientation was embedded in a larger context of managerial, allocational, public health, and primary care changes. This paper reviews the background and dynamics of these modifications and offers an early assessment. There is evidence that the reforms have unleashed much energy, activity, and thoughtfulness about future health care, but it remains unclear whether the gains justify the increased administrative and other transaction costs and potential threats to equal access.

Both the United States and the United Kingdom have gone through protracted debates on reform of their health care systems in the past several years. In each instance, the debate focused on basic questions of how medical care should be organized to limit costs while maintaining quality and on the responsibilities of government, the private sector, and purchasers, providers, and patients. Although the United Kingdom set out on a new course and the debate in the United States stalemated, both systems of care continue to evolve in response to new challenges in science and technology, the aging of the national populations, increasing public expectations, and the demands of national and local politics.

There is much that differs greatly in the two countries, ranging from their systems of government and policy-making processes to the magnitude of their investments in health care services. The British National Health Service (NHS) is a system under the tight supervision of central government with predominantly a single source of revenue from national taxation. Medical care is universally available, and most care is free at the point of service. The general practitioner (GP) and health center, as the point of first contact, constitute a strong primary care system in which basic health services are readily accessible, but GP gatekeepers are the route to more expensive services such as specialty and hospital referral. Waiting lists are the central mechanism to fit services to demand, and waiting is most common for discretionary surgery.[1] Although recent surveys show considerable public disquiet with developments in the NHS, particularly with perceived underfunding and conditions in hospital outpatient departments, the NHS commands great loyalty among the population.

Reprinted from *Health Affairs* (Summer 1995), pp. 51–67, by permission of the publisher. Copyright © 1995 The People-to-People Health Foundation, Inc., All Rights Reserved.

It may seem curious to expect to learn from contrasts between systems as different as those of the United States and the United Kingdom. Yet, despite these differences, both countries emphasize the role of market forces and competition in seeking new arrangements that are better suited to address the growing tensions between population demands and needs and the capacity of public budgets to meet them. Although not a central participant in either country, Alain Enthoven set the background for framing many of the issues in both nations with his concept of managed competition. His advocacy for an internal market in the NHS was widely discussed in health policy circles and is acknowledged by former Prime Minister Margaret Thatcher to have been the background for the government's reform considerations.[2] Despite their very different starting points, the United States and the United Kingdom have been considering initiatives that could result in greater similarities than have ever been evident in the countries' contrasting approaches to organizing health care services.

BACKGROUND OF THE BRITISH REFORMS

Since its inception the NHS has undergone periodic reorganizations, but not in ways that greatly altered either medical dominance or the expectations of patients using the service.[3] In the early 1980s considerable emphasis was put on improved management, and there was growing awareness that the needs-based formula for allocating funding to regions and districts and compensating areas for utilization across boundaries (the Resource Allocating Working Party formula, referred to as RAWP) was flawed.[4] The allocation formula was modified to better take account of need as measured by mortality differences, age structure, and socioeconomic indicators; this process is continuing. In the

1980s a number of managerial initiatives were introduced in the hospital and community sectors, followed by efforts to monitor primary care more closely and to give greater emphasis to disease prevention and health promotion.[5] Many of these ideas were implemented through a new contract for GPs introduced in April 1990. Thus, the later British reforms were embedded within processes of continuing operational changes affecting resource allocation, the organization of the Department of Health, institutional accountability, and GP contract provisions.

References to the British reforms usually relate to three changes that had greater ideological implications than the iterative modifications in operations and management had. First, these changes sought to separate the financing and purchasing of care from its provision, creating an internal market. Second, hospitals and other health care organizations publicly administered by the local health authority were allowed to become self-governing trusts, having more autonomy for their budgets and self-management and the authority to sell services to any health authority, other hospitals, or the private sector. Third, GPs with larger numbers of patients were allowed to take charge of part of the budget for their patients (approximately 25 percent) and to purchase services on their behalf from any provider.

Despite their unfamiliar descriptions, these reforms involve concepts that are familiar and taken for granted in the American context. The internal market, for example, is similar to public contracting for medical and social services as carried out by many state and local governments in the United States. The British "trusts," although they have less autonomy, resemble nonprofit provider organizations common in the United States. GP fundholding is basically a restricted or mini health maintenance organization (HMO) in which providers are contractually responsible for purchasing necessary services for their enrollees. The details may vary a good bit, but it is not too far-fetched to suggest that the Thatcher reforms were to some degree an Americanization of the NHS.

Uncovering the forces and specific events leading to these changes is the historian's task, but the general picture seems reasonably clear. In the 1970s and 1980s advancing technologies, an aging population, and increased patient expectations focused attention on resource shortages. Tensions were exacerbated by conflicts between the government and the medical profession and increased media attention to shortages, waiting lists, and other incidents that implied failure in maintaining NHS standards. The Labor Party made the NHS and evidence of resource shortages issues in the 1987 election, thereafter putting the Thatcher government on the defensive.[6] No reasonable increment of increased funding by itself was likely to eliminate the rationing tensions. Chancellor of England Nigel Lawson, as chief financial officer of the country, was unwilling to yield to the irresistible pressures to increase NHS expenditures without a review of the inefficiencies and flaws in the NHS.[7]

In January 1988, Prime Minister Thatcher set up a ministerial group, which she chaired. This small group of five members met frequently over most of the year; their efforts culminated in publication of the White Paper, *Working for Patients*.[8] The proposed reforms were strongly opposed by Labor and much of the medical profession, which alleged that the NHS was being privatized and commercialized. Commanding a majority in Parliament and in control of her party, the prime minister was able to legislate her program substantially intact. As the Labor Party prepared for its victorious 1997 election, it stated its opposition to many of these reforms, especially GP fundholding. These measures, however, remained in place in 2000.

Americans familiar with state competitive contracting will appreciate how much the so-called internal market in the United Kingdom deviates from a truly competitive situation, especially considering that the constraints in the British context are greater than in most of our states. Julian Le Grand and his colleagues have described the British "internal market" as a "quasi market," which departs from conventional markets in terms of both supply and demand. In quasi markets, organizations need not be private or seek profits. Nor is purchasing necessarily expressed in money terms.[9] Although privatization was given consideration in early discussions of reform within the Thatcher government, the eventual goal was more modest: making cost more salient for health professionals and patients.[10]

NATIONAL HEALTH SERVICE: REFORMS AND RELATED CHANGES

As noted previously, the key feature of the British reforms was an effort to create a quasi market within the NHS with a separation between the purchasing of services and their provision. The District Health Authorities (DHAs), each encompassing about half a million people, receive an allocation from the central government. Although prior to the reforms the health districts were purchasers and providers of services, they now also are responsible for assessing need and purchasing services from hundreds of provider organizations that have become trusts and are independent of the health authorities. They also are permitted to purchase services from the private sector, although private purchasing is now very limited. Purchasing is allowed anywhere in the country as a means to encourage trusts to be more responsive providers and health districts to be more prudent buyers. The theory is, of course, that the competitiveness of the quasi market will result in improvements in efficiency and quality, or as the British put it, will provide more value for money.

Fundholding

GPs with larger practices are now allowed to apply to become fundholders, for which they receive an allocation for purchasing a defined set of elective, nonemergency services for their patients. Nonfundholders must refer patients to hospitals and specialists who have contracts with the local health authority.[11] While nonfundholders are gatekeepers, they do not work within a budget. Fundholding services may be purchased from wherever the GP decides and from either public or private sources. Savings achieved may be reinvested in the practice or in new services, but not directly in GPs' personal incomes. Some GPs resent the introduction of money into their relationships with patients, and some critics worry about the possibility that fundholders' investments in their own practices can be turned into profit when they retire and transfer their practices. But, by any American standard, the profit incentives for fundholders are extraordinarily weak. Initially, the scheme was to apply to practices of 11,000 patients or more, but it was subsequently reduced to 9,000 patients, then 7,000, and more recently to 5,000.[12] Fundholding now covers about half of the population, although such coverage varies greatly among geographical areas. The range of purchasing also has been extended, and experiments are now in place to examine a much broader capitation covering the entire spectrum of care.[13] Fundholders are not at personal financial risk and are protected against excessive financial risk to their practices by a stop-loss for each patient, with additional costs incurred by the DHA.

Fundholding, initially seen as a small aspect of the quasi market, has gained considerable prominence in the United Kingdom, and the government has been extending the scheme.[14] Fundholding greatly increases the bargaining power of GPs, who can take their contracts elsewhere should hospitals, medical consultants, or other agencies show a lack of responsiveness. Nonfundholders are largely restricted to those providers chosen by the local health authority. Fundholding also allows GPs to purchase a different mix of services. Although GP contracts are a small part of the income of any of the trusts, at the margins the income they provide can potentially affect the economic health or even the survival of these institutions.[15]

Fundholding requires GP practices to engage in considerable contracting activities for which higher levels of practice management and informational capacity are required. The Department of Health has invested considerable funding in introducing managers into practices and upgrading computer systems. While some claim that the Department of Health gives preferential treatment to fundholders, others view the improvements in management and information systems as a prerequisite for high-quality primary care. Current data do not allow an accurate assessment of the extent to which early fundholders received preferential treatment or whether perceived improvements justify the added practice costs.

Community Care

The three basic 1991 reforms were followed by a further initiative in community care that might be seen as an extension of the reforms.[16] The 1991 community care initiative and later clarifications affecting the frail elderly, the mentally ill, and other persons with disabilities clearly distinguished between the responsibilities of the NHS in providing free health care to all and social care, which was to be provided on the basis of a means test. All responsibility for long-term care was given to local government, reducing some of the earlier flexibility in the NHS that allowed the transfer of patients from the health to the social security budget. The open-ended social security system and opportunities to cost-shift relieved pressures on both health and social services, but long-term care social security funding is now capped, with these monies transferred to local governments to distribute on a needs basis. Local authorities were instructed to reduce direct provision and purchase social services largely from the private sector. The reduction in funding flexibility and the budget cap led to charges that long-term care needs were being neglected. Studies by the Department of Health indicate serious continuing difficulties.[17]

The community care initiative is a complex revision of services in which local government, in cooperation with the DHAs, develops and commissions services as a way of reducing fragmentation between these two sectors. Local government case managers are given new authority to assess need and to make disbursements for residential and home care on that basis. A major policy motive was to reduce growing social security entitlements for residential care, shifting the emphasis to less expensive home care and making grants discretionary relative to assessed need. Community care is generally difficult, requiring cooperation from different sectors such as housing, social services, and medical care.[18] Workers from each sector have their own culture and bureaucratic needs, and all function in a context of constrained resources. Also, it is not clear that case managers from local government have the capacity to integrate needed services. Everyone concedes that community care is problematic. The value of the reforms in this sector remains uncertain, and erosion of long-term care is of major concern to the affected groups.

Health Promotion/Disease Prevention

Finally, as in the United States, efforts are being made to promote health through improved lifestyles and public education and practice. Focusing on behavioral change and environmental improvement, the government has set various objectives and priorities such as reducing smoking and lung cancer deaths and suicide in its publication, *The Health of the Nation*.[19] The establishment of objectives is similar to the "year 2000 objectives" in the United States, although less elaborately developed. Both efforts share the same difficulty of developing a clear strategy for implementation. While over the longer run the British effort offers important potential, the challenge remains of translating rhetoric into viable programs that can realistically attain the goals envisioned.

COMPARATIVE CONSIDERATIONS

From the American side, there is much in the United Kingdom to emulate, particularly universal coverage, easily accessible and increasingly well developed primary care services, an impressive capacity to maintain a balance among various levels of care, and control of health care expenditures. But the NHS had become rather set in its ways, somewhat inefficient and unresponsive, and not particularly receptive to innovation or to patient preferences. Although it seemed to muddle through from year to year, periodically modifying its organizational and managerial structures, it has been a service very much dominated by the preferences and practice proclivities of the consultant specialists who controlled their turfs with an iron grip and were not particularly responsive to opportunities to carefully inspect the value of their practice choices. Most are hardworking and conscientious but largely oblivious to issues of efficiency and the need to manage resources well. Global budgets impose financial constraints, but a need remains to allocate fairly within these limits. Innovations in the United States, such as outpatient and day surgery, professional peer review, health services evaluation, and practice guidelines, are slow to develop in a system that goes along with the presumption that the consultant always knows best. Although the British government was ready to intrude when budgetary issues were at stake, it gave doctors a degree of freedom that U.S. physicians can regard with envy.

Rationing and Queues

It should be no surprise that a service that invests so few of its national resources in health care, compared with the United States, would have fewer amenities and longer queues. Certainly the NHS rations the availability of technology—chronic renal dialysis being perhaps the best known and most highly publicized example—although the extent of rationing in this area has been greatly reduced in recent years.[20] Here the result of rationing is clearly death; thus, this example served those who enjoy bashing the NHS. But, for the most part, the constraints on life-extending technology seem to be applied more to interventions such as coronary artery bypass surgery and uncertain cancer treatments for which there is at least an arguable case about the appropriate aggressiveness of intervention. Perhaps more serious are the extended waiting lists for discretionary services such as cataract, knee, and varicose vein surgery and hip replacements.[21] Although people do not die from delays in receiving these treatments, their comfort and level of functioning may be severely limited. The Patients' Charter, part of a national effort to improve the provision of public service, establishes maximum waiting times for various procedures. Despite some improvement, even these targets seem shockingly long to Americans. The quality of health systems must be judged by their capacity to promote health, reduce disability, and enhance quality of life and not solely by their ability to provide life-extending treatments.[22] Indicators of improved functioning are likely to convey a great deal more about the quality of medical care than are mortality outcomes, which are largely a product of broader social and environmental factors.

Competition and Decentralization

The direction of reform is never inevitable and depends much on culture, prior institutional and professional arrangements, dominant ideologies, and politics. During the 1980s both the United Kingdom and the United States followed a common ideology that extolled the virtues of competition in the marketplace and the efficiencies of privatization. In both countries, government, while advocating greater competition and decentralization of decision making, strengthened central control over financial arrangements and, in the United Kingdom, managerial control as well. Central government was prepared to leave micromanagement to the regions and local districts, but not without considerable advice and guidelines from the center. This allows the central government to have a hand in what goes on but also insulates it to some extent from embarrassment stemming from rationing problems or service failures.

The NHS remains largely intact, in the sense that it continues as a tax-funded, universal system, free to all at the point of service. Outside of major revolutions, health care systems evolve from what went before. Within these limits, it is fair to say that Prime Minister Thatcher put her distinctive stamp on Britain's health care services, substantially shaking up the cozy understandings and power relationships that prevailed. At the very least, the reforms have forced all of the major participants to think more carefully about their roles and responsibilities and their connections with other parts of the health and social services systems. From a more optimistic standpoint, the separation of the roles of purchasers and providers of service offers the potential to introduce greater efficiencies and responsiveness to client populations. It will be uncertain for some time whether the large transaction costs of creating a quasi market are justified by the results. Health districts and GP fundholders are now establishing service contracts with hospitals and other community caregivers to meet the needs of their patients. There is a great deal of learning required on the part of all parties as they modify their roles, and it will be some time before the outcomes sort out.[23]

From Theory to Action: Internal Markets

The opportunity for the leadership of the political party in power to make policy in the British context allowed Prime Minister Thatcher to move forward aggressively despite broad opposition and fierce resistance from the medical profession. As the Thatcher government looked around for possible models, it seized on the idea of developing an internal market, but instead of testing the concept in demonstration projects as Enthoven had suggested, it imposed the idea on the entire country by fiat.[24] Enthoven, focusing on efficiency, had argued for developing purchasing at the district level, but the government took a two-prong approach, giving purchasing authority to both the DHAs and the GP fundholders.[25] Initial fundholders were given budgets based on their historical costs for purchasing a defined set of services and were held harmless for expenditures in any year exceeding £5,000 (approximately $8,000) per client. Theory would suggest difficulties with such small purchasing entities and an inclination toward risk selection, as some American commentators warned.[26] Thus far, however, fundholding apparently has been one of the more successful of the new initiatives—energizing many GPs and encouraging provider responsiveness—although it is still early in the game.

There are good reasons why some of the perverse outcomes reasonably to be expected in the United States with such a scheme have not materialized in the British context. The first cohorts of GP fundholders were enthusiastic participants, largely motivated to improve care for their patients.[27] Although savings could be invested in enhanced services in the practice, they could not directly be used to increase GP remuneration. Moreover, with the funds based on historical costs, and with relatively stable practice populations, GPs were unlikely to experience any radical change in case-mix, and emergency services remained the responsibility of the DHAs. If case-mix was altered for unanticipated reasons, being held harmless for extra-large expenditures (a form of reinsurance) protected GPs from large losses. Historical costs vary quite a bit across GP practices for no apparent reason, and the obvious next step is to develop a risk-adjusted capitation formula that will allocate resources in a more equitable way.[28] As more GPs enter fundholding status and as capitation schemes are introduced, it will be important to assess how the capacity of GPs to be independent purchasers develops and how national health objectives are sustained with the decentralization of purchasing responsibility.

While GP fundholding appears to have achieved some success, expanding the scope of fundholding to cover a wider array of health services might prove dangerous. There are indications that many GPs know too little about the potentialities of new specialized services to purchase them appropriately. Moreover, in some specialized areas, such as care for the severely mentally ill, appropriate services are not available in many localities and need to be developed on a geographic basis.[29] Even if GPs are appropriately aware, the fragmentation of purchasing among many purchasers makes it less likely that the necessary service systems will be developed. There also is concern that GPs will divert resources intended for the severely mentally ill to patients who are less sick. Similar considerations apply to other highly specialized medical services.

While district purchasing has been very conservative, largely contracting with historical providers using block contracts, fundholding GPs have been more aggressive and innovative. GPs, who no longer fit the characterization put forth by Lord Moran (an eminent medical educator and Winston Churchill's personal physician) as those who have fallen off the mobility ladder, nevertheless are treated by consultant physicians with less than full equality. Fundholding has given GPs more leverage in dealing with consultants and outpatient departments. They now have the wherewithal to take their business elsewhere should hospitals treat them and their patients discourteously or fail to provide a reasonable service. Studies of early fundholders show that they have had some success at reducing patient waiting times, getting consultants to see patients at GP premises, and generally improving the system's responsiveness to patients.[30] The assumption that the constrained available services provide a zero-sum situation in which improvements are bought only at the expense of nonfundholders has led to concerns about possible inequities resulting from fundholding schemes. As more GPs become fundholders, the risk of differential treatment may abate somewhat, although monitoring of the situation would be prudent. Careful efforts to monitor the scheme thus far have not substantiated the fears and allegations, although the perception of growing inequalities persists.

Having studied general practice in the United Kingdom some 30 years ago, and having expressed skepticism of its capacity to keep pace with medical advances, I am impressed by how well the country seems to have fared since changes in remuneration and other conditions of service were introduced in 1966.[31] One of the real strengths of the NHS is its primary care system, which provides easy access but controls admission to more expensive components of medical care. Single-handed practice has shrunk, and GPs increasingly work in small groups in collaboration with nurses, social workers, and other health personnel. Patient lists are substantially reduced from what they were 30 years ago, and GPs are given incentives to provide preventive care and to respond to other national priorities. GP remuneration has much improved relative to that of specialists, and GPs no longer express the sense of relative deprivation that so poisoned the practice atmosphere of the early 1960s. General practice is now successfully entrenched in the medical schools, and the Royal College of General Practice, which was just a fledgling organization 30 years ago, now plays a major role in encouraging a high standard of practice and in giving GPs a greater sense of esteem. The 1990 legislation that made it easier for patients to change GPs and that increased the capitation component of GP remuneration to 60 percent (to encourage competition for patients) represents another small facet of attempting to build a quasi marketplace that energizes provider responsiveness.

GP Reactions

Many GPs, however, remain angry about their 1990 contract, which set increased expectations and required more practice monitoring and information.[32] Some aspects of the contract provide additional fees for specific services and have not been controversial. But other requirements, such as annual checkups for patients over age 75 and having to provide more information to patients on the services they provide, are seen by some GPs as a waste of their time and practice resources. Also highly controversial are target payments for achieving particular levels of Pap smears and immunizations and health promotion "banding arrangements" in which remuneration is scaled to the proportion of one's patients who are assessed for various health risks. Although the ideas underlying these incentives are apparent, they put new burdens on

practitioners who already perceive themselves
as overextended.

Large disparities in general practice costs
still exist across geographical areas, comparable to the large utilization and cost variations found in the United States. These
reflect differences in GPs' attitudes, referral
opportunities, and other factors that are not
yet fully understood. The expansion of fundholding makes salient the issue of adjusted
capitation, although this remains an area that
the British government will approach especially carefully, given the irritations already
common among GPs.[33]

Resource Distribution

In recent years the national government has
made efforts to achieve greater equity among
regions and districts in hospital services;
resources have been withdrawn from inner
London, an international center for medical
education and research. The new purchasing
arrangements have resulted in fewer referrals
from outside London, leading to an inquiry
into the future of health services in London.
The resulting "Tomlinson Report" recommended closing or merging some of the most
distinguished British hospitals, and this process
is continuing despite years of controversy and
rancor.[34] London was greatly overbedded, but
in the past few years there has been a large
reduction of acute care beds.[35] Strong differences of opinion persist on whether these
reductions exceed reasonable levels, and the
media almost daily feature stories about the difficulties in locating appropriate beds for emergency hospitalization of mentally ill patients,
persons needing intensive care, and other
groups. A 1992 King's Fund report supported
the conclusions of the Tomlinson inquiry, but
more recently concern has been expressed
about the pace of change.[36] This later critique
emphasizes the need for having new services in
place before old ones are abolished, always
having the capacity to deal with emergencies
and crises, and achieving greater consensus

and understanding as the changes proceed.[37]
There is little question that the shrinkage of
resources has cast a pall over London
medicine. Not surprisingly, most London
physicians express hostility not only to the government but also to the reforms.

It is an open question as to whether the
shrinkage of the London medical infrastruc-
ture has been too fast and too deep and
whether the allocation formula on which this
reduction is based is appropriately sensitive
to the special circumstances of London. The
extent to which the problem of acute bed
availability reflects resource shortages or bad
management remains controversial and unresolved. Whatever the merits of opposing
views, the picture of the overall NHS reforms
is soured by the developments that affect
London and some other large cities. Yet these
are the physicians whose voices are best
known in the international community and
who may substantially color how the British
reforms are perceived from the outside.

Practice Variations and Quality Control

Serious problems remain with the implementation of reforms, and dangers lie ahead. No
reform can compensate for an underfi-
nanced health service, and the NHS is greatly
underfunded by the standards of most developed Western nations. Most of these nations
are richer than the United Kingdom, but
rising expectations for access to new technologies have no obvious link to gross
domestic product (GDP). For example, in
the early 1990s rates of coronary artery bypass
graft surgery and coronary angioplasty in the
United Kingdom lagged behind those in
most industrial countries. Rates per million
population for these procedures have been
approximately one-sixth of those in the
United States.[38] U.S. physicians may be doing
far too many such procedures, although
recent studies of appropriateness indicate
that this excess may be exaggerated.[39] Rates in
the United Kingdom, however, are very low.

Variations in the use of such procedures among health districts in the United Kingdom are very large; clearly, too few are being done in many areas of the country.[40] With purchasing fragmented among districts and GP fundholders, who can exercise great discretion, monitoring future performance will be difficult. This may be still a larger problem with less prestigious services, such as for the mentally ill or the disabled, whose needs may be even more poorly understood and neglected at the local level than they were before. With decentralization of purchasing, practice variations and differences in quality of service may become larger. As the reforms proceed, it will be essential to distinguish rhetoric from results. The declaration of goals and aims may be quite different from the allocation of resources. In an interesting study of 100 commissioning authority plans for 1993–1994, Sharon Redmayne, Rudolf Klein, and Patricia Day found relatively stable purchasing patterns despite many new aspirational priorities.[41] In tracing the subsequent allocation of new developmental funding, they found that 58 percent of the total went to acute care relative to acute care's 51 percent proportion of the NHS budget. Mental health, the most commonly endorsed aspirational priority, received only 8 percent of priority expenditures, which is only two-thirds of its share of the overall NHS budget.

However one may regard the direction of NHS reforms and the particular initiatives, the energy in new directions is incontestable. The NHS may not feel a great deal different for the typical patient, but the reforms have initiated a process of examination and local involvement that has brought new enthusiasm to many participants. Thus far, health districts, encouraged by the Department of Health to move slowly, have been extremely conservative, only modifying preexisting service arrangements at the margins, but the potential for more radical shifts as they gain confidence and expertise is evident.[42] Whether the

efforts and new administrative expenses are justified by the results remains to be seen. In the short run, however, the new potential has shaken many entrenched routines.

LESSONS FROM ABROAD?

One might chalk up the varying success of the Thatcher and Clinton governments in reforming health care to differences in determination, political skill, or, more likely, the very different governmental structures in the United Kingdom and the United States. The founding fathers of the United States did not establish a framework that makes it easy to concentrate power or to achieve major shifts in carrying out government's business. Nevertheless, the different outcomes in the two countries are instructive and offer some insights about the increasing difficulties of formulating coherent public policies.

The Thatcher reforms were certainly no more popular than the Clinton proposals were. They were vigorously opposed by the medical profession, opposition parties, and much of the media.[43] Thatcher was not deterred, however, and persisted with her agenda on the basis of ideology, with little evidence that the quasi market could really work. Skeptics might argue that her goal was to divert attention and responsibility from the failure to adequately finance the NHS by decentralizing many decisions to disperse responsibility and to make it difficult to monitor events. Interestingly enough, even left-wing British health care experts now view the reforms as having positive potential.[44]

In accepting many aspects of Enthoven's conception of an internal market, the British government disregarded his reasonable advice to test the theory in selected regions and to work out administrative details. Instead, the reforms were put in place nationally with only the vaguest concept of how they were to be implemented or of the actual costs involved in the elaborate contracting that would become commonplace. Goals and implementation plans were repeatedly modified, and the government directed purchasers to move slowly in modifying preexisting relationships. In a sense, after a major ideological victory, the choice was made to implement social policy by muddling through, amending the process in response to both experience and politics. This process continues now, and implementation of the reforms is still evolving.[45] It is assisted by the flexible legislative framework of the NHS that allows much modification without detailed legislation.

U.S. economists and health services researchers who follow British events were not shy in warning the British about all the ways in which the reforms would not work. The researchers were quick to observe that practices of 11,000 patients were far too small to become purchasers or to assume the risks of possible patient selection. Ironically, there has been no evidence that this constitutes a major problem in the United Kingdom, and the size criterion for a fundholding practice decreased to 7,000 patients and is now 5,000 patients. Indeed, the idea of fundholding itself, which was seen as too inconsequential and inefficient to be pursued, has turned out to be one of the more interesting innovations that has invigorated many GPs and has begun to change the insensitivity of some consultants.

It is naïve to anticipate that approaches to reform or their substance are transferable from one culture and political context to another. Countries certainly get ideas from one another and insights as to what works in varying contexts and why. A recent review of reform in 17 countries in the Organization for Economic Cooperation and Development (OECD) concluded that there was considerable convergence among these countries in reform initiatives, although these ideas were modified to fit local conditions.[46] One lesson, perhaps, from the recent experience of the NHS is that governments not only need a vision, but also a pragmatic willingness to muddle through a bit, to allow reforms to evolve in iterations that build on experience. Although the Thatcher government knew what it wanted to achieve, unlike the Clinton administration, it left most of the details to be worked out over time. Health care reform, whether British or American, can be solved only in stages. As Rudolf Klein, one of the most astute observers of the British scene, recently noted:[47]

There may be much to be learnt from the experience of different countries about the balance of advantages and disadvantages of trying to introduce carefully crafted new models, with every detail worked out, as against designing framework institutions which evolve over time. A comparison of the experiences of the United States and the United Kingdom might suggest that the advantage lies on the side of designing flexible framework institutions. Or it might simply demonstrate that different models of change are contingent on the political institutions in which the health care systems are embedded.

NOTES

1. S. Frankel and R. West, *Rationing and Rationality in the National Health Service: The Persistence of Waiting Lists* (Houndsville: Macmillan, 1993).

2. A. C. Enthoven, *Reflections on the Management of the National Health Service* (London: Nuffield Provincial Hospital Trust, 1985); and M. Thatcher, *The Downing Street Years* (London: HarperCollins, 1993), 607. Although it is clear that Enthoven's analysis was background to reform considerations, these reforms, particularly the internal market, were part of a broader trend to reduce the role of government and increase competition and responsiveness in education, social services, and housing as well as in health care. Thus, the reforms in their more general sense constituted part of a coherent and pragmatic ideology.

3. R. Klein, *The Politics of the NHS*, 2d ed. (London: Longman, 1989).

4. Department of Health and Social Security, *Inquiry into NHS Management* (the Griffiths Report)

(London: Her Majesty's Stationery Office, 1983); and W. Ranade, *A Future for the NHS? Health Care in the 1990s* (New York: Longman, 1994), 56.

5. Department of Health and Social Security, *Promoting Better Health* (London: HMSO, 1987), Cmnd. 249.

6. N. Lawson, *The View from No. 11: Memoirs of a Tory Radical* (London: Corgi Books, 1992), 612.

7. Ibid., 612–619. While Margaret Thatcher confirms Nigel Lawson's resistance to increasing NHS expenditures, she gives his role less importance in initiating the review and developing the reforms. See Thatcher, *The Downing Street Years*, 607–617.

8. Secretaries of State for Health, *Working for Patients* (London: HMSO, 1989), Cmnd. 555.

9. J. Le Grand and W. Bartlett, eds., *Quasi-Markets and Social Policy* (Houndsville: Macmillan, 1993), 10.

10. Thatcher, *The Downing Street Years*, 607–617.

11. Prior to the reforms, GPs could refer patients to any NHS facility, although most referrals were to hospitals and other services within the district. Nonfundholders now have fewer choices for referral than they had before the reforms.

12. NHS Executive, *Developing NHS Purchasing and GP Fundholding* (Quarry House, Leeds: Department of Health, 20 October 1994), EL (94)79.

13. A. Harrison, ed., *Health Care UK, 1993/94: An Annual Review of Health Care Policy* (London: King's Fund Institute, 1994).

14. NHS Executive, *Developing NHS Purchasing and GP Fundholding.*

15. B. Kirkup and L. J. Donaldson, "Is Health Care a Commodity: How Will Purchasing Improve the National Health Service?" *Journal of Public Health Medicine* 16 (1994): 256–262.

16. Secretaries of State for Health, *Caring for People: Community Care in the Next Decade and Beyond* (London: HMSO, 1989), Cmnd. 849.

17. Department of Health, *Implementing Caring for People: Community Care Packages for Older People* (Lancashire: Health Publications Unit, 1994).

18. D. Mechanic, "Challenges in the Provision of Mental Health Services: Some Cautionary Lessons from U.S. Experience," *Journal of Public Health Medicine* (June 1995).

19. Secretaries of State for Health, *The Health of the Nation: A Strategy for Health for England* (London: HMSO, 1992), Cmnd. 1986.

20. H. J. Aaron and W. B. Schwartz, *The Painful Prescription: Rationing Hospital Care* (Washington: The Brookings Institution, 1984); and T. Halper, *The Misfortunes of Others: End-Stage Renal Disease in the United Kingdom* (Cambridge: Cambridge University Press, 1989).

21. Frankel and West, *Rationing and Rationality in the National Health Service.*

22. D. Mechanic, *Inescapable Decisions: The Imperatives of Health Reform* (New Brunswick, N.J.: Transaction Publishers, 1994).

23. R. Robinson and J. Le Grand, eds., *Evaluating the NHS Reforms* (London: King's Fund Institute, 1994).

24. Lawson, in *The View from No. 11*, offers an alternative view: "There was much criticism when the White Paper was published that the Government was being characteristically doctrinaire and arrogant in imposing its reforms without even having a series of pilot projects first. I found this very puzzling. No hospital was obliged to become an NHS Trust Hospital: those that did, volunteered to do so. Similarly, no doctors were obliged to become fundholders: those that did, volunteered to do so. This seemed to me to be the best possible form of pilot project, with the guinea pigs volunteering for their role rather than having it unwillingly thrust upon them" (618).

25. Ibid. Lawson notes: "My own idea had been that the review should be confined entirely to the hospital service. . . . I felt it would be politically prudent to leave the reform of general practice until later, after the reform of the hospital service had been completed. Margaret, however, having initially been too nervous to do anything at all, once she accepted the idea, characteristically decided to go the whole hog, and reform everything at once" (615).

26. R. Scheffler, "Adverse Selection: The Achilles Heel of the NHS," *The Lancet* I (1989): 950–952; and J. P. Weiner and D. M. Fermiss, *GP Budget Holding in the UK: Lessons from America*, Research Report no. 7 (London: King's Fund Institute, 1990).

27. H. Glennester et al., *Implementing GP Fundholding: Wild Card or Winning Hand?* (Philadelphia: Open University Press, 1994).

28. Ibid.

29. Mechanic, "Challenges in the Provision of Mental Health Services."

30. H. Glennester, M. Matsaganis, and P. Owens, *A Foothold for Fundholding* (London: King's Fund Institute, 1992); Harrison, *Health Care UK, 1993/94*; and Glennester et al., *Implementing GP Fundholding.*

31. D. Mechanic, "General Practice in England and Wales: Its Organization and Future," *The New England Journal of Medicine* 279 (1969): 680–689.

32. Ranade, *A Future for the NHS?* 58–59.

33. Here again, Lawson's *View from No. 11* is revealing. He notes that "the general practitioner came face to face with the public all the time, and the political cost of alienating them could be very high" (615).

34. Department of Health, *Report of the Inquiry into London's Health Service, Medical Education, and Research* (the Tomlinson Report) (London: Department of Health, 1992); and S. Boyle, ed., *London Monitor,* no. 2 (London: King's Fund Institute, 1995), 16–20.

35. B. Jarman, "Is London Over-Bedded?" *British Medical Journal* 306 (1993): 979–982.

36. King's Fund Commission, *London Health Care, 2010: Changing the Future of Services in the Capital* (London: King's Fund, 1992).

37. R. Maxwell, "Foreword," in *London Monitor,* no. 2 (London: King's Fund Institute, 1995), 3.

38. Clinical Standards Advisory Group, *Access to and Availability of Specialist Services* (London: HMSO, 1993).

39. See, for example, E. A. McGlynn, "Comparison of the Appropriateness of Coronary Angioplasty and Coronary Artery Bypass Graft Surgery between Canada and New York State," *Journal of the American Medical Association* 272 (1994): 934–940.

40. Clinical Standards Advisory Group, *Access to and Availability of Coronary Artery Bypass Grafting and Coronary Angioplasty* (London: HMSO, 1993). The data reported in this study are from 1991–1992. The authors have indicated that more recent data from 1993–1994 show comparable patterns.

41. S. Redmayne, R. Klein, and P. Day, *Sharing Our Resources: Purchasing and Priority Setting in the NHS,* no. 11 (London: National Association of Health Authorities and Trusts, 1993).

42. R. Klein and S. Redmayne, *Patterns of Priorities: A Study of the Purchasing and Rationing Policies of Health Authorities,* no. 7 (London: National Association of Health Authorities and Trusts, 1992).

43. J. R. Butler, *Patients, Policies, and Politics: Before and After "Working for Patients"* (Philadelphia: Open University Press, 1992).

44. J. Le Grand, "For Better or Worse?" *New Statesman and Society* (19 November 1993): 22–23.

45. R. Klein, *The New Politics of the NHS* (London: Longman, 1995).

46. Organization for Economic Cooperation and Development, *The Reform of Health Care Systems: A Review of Seventeen OECD Countries* (Paris: OECD, 1994).

47. R. Klein, "Learning from Others: Shall the Last Be the First" (Paper presented at the Four-Country Conference on Health Care Policies and Health Care Reform, Amsterdam, February 1995).

THE SOCIAL DETERMINANTS OF THE DECLINE OF LIFE EXPECTANCY IN RUSSIA AND EASTERN EUROPE: A LIFESTYLE EXPLANATION

William C. Cockerham
University of Alabama at Birmingham

This paper examines the social origins of the rise in adult mortality in Russia and selected Eastern European countries. Three explanations for this trend are considered: (1) Soviet health policy, (2) social stress, and (3) health lifestyles. The socialist states were generally characterized by a persistently poor mortality performance as part of a long-term process of deterioration, with particularly negative outcomes for the life expectancy of middle-aged, male manual workers. Soviet-style health policy was ineffective in dealing with the crisis, and stress per se does not seem to be the primary cause of the rise in mortality. Although more research is needed, the suggestion is made that poor health lifestyles—reflected especially in heavy alcohol consumption, and also in smoking, lack of exercise, and high-fat diets—are the major social determinant of the upturn in deaths.

One of the most striking developments in world health is the decline of life expectancy in Russia and Eastern Europe. This situation is without precedent in modern history. Nowhere else has health generally worsened—instead of improved—among industrialized nations. To date, however, it is not fully understood why such a pattern emerged in this region in the late twentieth century, nor has an extensive literature developed about this phenomenon in Western medical sociology. This circumstance is not only a health disaster for the societies and individuals involved, but it is also sociologically provocative because these nations officially espoused a socialist ideology which, theoretically,

should have promoted health for all. Yet the reverse happened and adult mortality significantly increased.

This paper investigates current patterns in longevity in Russia and selected Eastern European countries. The purpose is to identify the major social determinant of the downturn in life expectancy in a global region once claiming to be superpower and officially oriented toward achieving an egalitarian classless society. The focus will be on the persistent poor mortality performance between the mid-1960s and 1980s and its acceleration in the 1990s as a long-term process of deterioration. The evidence for a social basis for the rise in mortality will first be reviewed and three potential explanations will be explored: (1) Societ health policy, (2) social stress, and (3) health lifestyles.

Reprinted from the *Journal of Health and Social Behavior,* vol. 38 (June 1997), pp. 117–30.

It should be noted that the rise in adult mortality in Russia and Eastern Europe is real and not a statistical artifact as the result of improvements in vital registration systems (Eberstadt 1994; Field 1994). Whereas infant mortality rates may be untrustworthy because of incomplete reporting (Anderson and Silver 1990; Keep 1995), infants are not the cohort whose death rates are reported as increasing. Rather, Eberstadt (1994) finds adult mortality rates in the region to be generally reliable and characterized by nearly universal coverage since at least the mid-1960s. Field (1994) questions Russian morbidity statistics, but likewise suggests that the mortality data are generally accurate and straightforward.

SOCIAL CAUSES OF THE RISE IN ADULT MORTALITY

The first question that must be answered is whether or not a social basis exists for the drop in life expectancy. Second, if there is a social basis, what is it? Several factors support the thesis that the downturn primarily resulted from social rather than biomedical causes. First, the rise in mortality was not universal; rather, there were distinct differences in gender, age, urban-rural locale, education, and region. The people most affected in the former Soviet Union were middle-aged males in manual occupations (Godek 1995; Haub 1994; Knaus 1981; Mezentseva and Rimachevskaya 1992; Shkolnikov 1995; Tulchinsky and Varavikova 1996). Other data show a similar pattern in Bulgaria (Carlson and Tsvetarsky 1992), the Czech Republic (Carlson and Rychaříková 1996; Rychtaříková 1996), Hungary (Carlson 1989; Hungarian Central Statistical Office 1996; Józan 1989, 1996), Poland (National Centre for Health System Management 1996; Okólski 1993; Wnuk-Lipinski 1990), and the Soviet Bloc generally, with the exception of East Germany (Bojan, Hajdu, and Belicza 1993; Eberstadt 1994; Okólski 1993).

The mortality situation is depicted in Table 1 for the former Soviet Union and Russia for selected years between 1960 and 1994. Table 1 shows that male life expectancy in the former Soviet Union stood at a high of 65.3 years in 1960, declined to 61.9 by 1980, but improved to 65.1 in 1987. As will be discussed, Russian demographers credit this brief rise in male longevity to Gorbachev's anti-alcohol campaign in the mid-1980s (Andreev 1990; Ponarin 1996; Shkolnikov and Nemtsov 1994). But the campaign was discontinued in late 1987 and by 1989 average life expectancy for Soviet men had declined to 64.2 years.

Following the collapse of the former Soviet Union in 1991, Table 1 shows that life expectancy for Russian males accelerated downward from 63.5 years to a low of 57.5 in 1994. For females, Table 1 shows a slow but consistent upward trend between 1960 and 1987 in life expectancy from 72.7 years to 73.9 years; by 1989, however, life expectancy for Soviet women had stabilized at 73.9 years. In 1991, in the new Russian Federation, females lived 74.3 years on average, but by 1994 life

TABLE 1 Life Expectancy at Birth in the Former Soviet Union and Russian Federation, Selected Years, 1960–1994

Year	Male	Female
Soviet Union:		
1960	65.3	72.7
1980	61.9	73.5
1987	65.1	73.9
1989	64.2	73.9
Russia:		
1991	63.5	74.3
1992	62.0	73.8
1993	59.0	72.0
1994	57.5	71.1

Source: *Population of the USSR* 1962; U.S. National Center for Health Statistics 1991, 1994; Shkolnikov 1995.

expectancy for women had fallen to 71.1 years. Consequently, both Russian men and women had a lower life expectancy in 1994 than their Soviet counterparts in 1960, and since the breakup of the former Soviet Union, mortality for both sexes has increased.

Age-specific contributions to the downturn in life expectancy have been concentrated in middle-aged males throughout the period of decline (Field 1995; Knaus 1981; Mezentseva and Rimachevskaya 1992; Shkolnikov 1995). For example, the greatest increase in death rates for Russian men between 1975 and 1993 is found in the 15–64-year-old age group, with the most pronounced rise occurring at ages 30–34 (Shkolnikov and Nemtsov 1994). By 1991–1992, 54 percent of all age-specific mortality increases for males were associated with 15–44-year-olds and 40 percent with 45–64-years-olds. However, for 1993–1994, the most recent years data are available, 53 percent of the increase in death rates for Russian men was due to excess mortality among 45–64-years-olds, 34 percent to that among 15–44-year-olds, and only 13 percent to that among males age 65 and over. Excess mortality in adult males may be shifting to late middle age, but continues to be a middle-age phenomenon nevertheless (Shkolnikov 1995).

Not only can a social causation argument be supported by the fact that the downturn has been generally caused by early deaths among middle-aged males, but the accelerated decline in life expectancy for both Russian women and men in the 1990s can be linked to a definitive social event: the demise of the Soviet Union. That is, already poor health conditions worsened with the collapse of the Soviet state. And like their male counterparts, it is late middle-aged (45–64 years) Russian women who have contributed the most to the rise in female mortality since 1992 (Shkolnikov 1995).

Life expectancy has also declined for both urban and rural Russian males, but urban males show the greatest decrease. In 1979,

urban males had outlived rural males 3.0 years on average (62.3 years versus 59.3 years) but, by 1994, urban males showed an advantage of only .8 years (57.7 years versus 56.9 years) over rural males (Shkolnikov 1995). Between 1979 and 1994, life expectancy for urban males declined 4.6 years compared to 2.4 years for rural males, which is shrinking the urban-rural difference. Data are lacking on social class differences in mortality, but death rates by level of education in Russia between 1975 and 1994 for males show increases for all educational groups—with the steepest rise among those with the lowest education (Shkolnikov, Ademets, and Deev 1996).

The rise in adult mortality in the former Soviet Union is also related to region. Table 2 compares life expectancy at birth in the former Soviet republics between 1979 and 1980 and either 1991, 1992, or 1993, depending on the availability of data. Surprisingly, Table 2 shows that the most developed republics in the former Soviet Union's European areas showed the greatest declines in life expectancy, while those in the Caucasus and Central Asia generally experienced increases in longevity. The exceptions were Armenia in the Caucasus where life expectancy fell during this period for both males and females, and Uzbekistan in Central Asia where a steep decline occurred for females. As shown in Table 2, the greatest decrease in life expectancy for males was in Russia (2.5 years), followed by Belarus (2.1), Latvia (2.0), Estonia (1.8), Armenia (1.6), and the Ukraine (.6). For females, the decline was greatest in Uzbekistan (3.6 years), with Armenia (1.3), Belarus (1.2), Russia (1.0), Estonia (.4), and Latvia (.1) also showing declines.

The general pattern of the rise in mortality from its inception is therefore centered on middle-aged, urban males in manual occupations in the most developed republics of the former Soviet Union. Exclusively biomedical causes of morbidity would not likely be con-

TABLE 2   Life Expectancy at Birth in the Former Soviet Republics, 1979–1980 and 1991/92/93

	Male			Female		
Country	1979–80	1991/92/93[a]	Change	1979–80	1991/92/93[a]	Change
Slavic and Moldova:						
Belarus	65.9	63.8	−2.1	75.6	74.4	−1.2
Moldova	62.4	63.9	1.5	68.8	71.9	3.1
Russia	61.5	59.0	−2.5	73.0	72.0	−1.0
Ukraine	64.6	64.0	−0.6	74.0	74.0	0.0
Baltic States:						
Estonia	64.2	62.4	−1.8	74.2	73.8	−0.4
Latvia	63.6	61.6	−2.0	73.9	73.8	−0.1
Lithuania	65.5	64.9	−0.6	75.4	76.0	0.6
Caucasus:						
Armenia	69.5	67.9	−1.6	75.7	74.4	−1.3
Azerbaijan	64.2	66.3	2.1	71.8	74.5	2.4
Georgia	67.1	68.7	1.6	74.8	76.1	1.3
Central Asia:						
Kazakhstan	61.6	63.8	2.2	71.9	73.1	1.2
Kyrgyzstan	61.1	64.2	3.1	70.1	72.2	2.1
Tajikistan	63.7	67.6	3.9	68.6	71.9	3.3
Turkmenistan	61.1	62.9	1.8	67.8	69.7	1.9
Uzbekistan	65.9	66.1	0.2	75.6	72.4	−3.2

[a]Refers to 1991, 1992, *or* 1993.

Source: Haub 1994; Kaasik, Hörte, and Andersson 1996; Shkolnikov 1995.

strained by these social parameters, thereby suggesting that the determinants of the downturn in life expectancy are primarily social.

Second, the increased mortality was not caused by a rise in infectious diseases, but primarily resulted from an increase in chronic illnesses having significant ties to specific forms of social behavior—especially heart disease and its connection to unhealthy lifestyles, stress, smoking, and alcohol abuse, along with accidents. Third, a genetic explanation does not seem to apply because the limited time period involved in not enough for large-scale genetic change to have occurred (Adler et al. 1994), nor is there evidence of genetic change.

Fourth, inferior medical care does not appear to be the cause since there is no evidence that the health care system, either by design or inadvertently, promoted early deaths—especially from heart disease among large numbers of middle-aged males. Even though Soviet medicine did not have an overall reputation for high quality, it nevertheless provided a basic, no-frills service to the general population (Cassileth, Vlassov, and Chapman 1995; Davis 1989; Knaus 1981). Furthermore, Soviet medicine claimed to have played an important role in reducing rates of infectious diseases and infant mortality which had also risen in the late 1960s and the 1970s.

And fifth, while extensive environmental pollution has been documented in heavily industrialized areas in Russia and Eastern Europe and there is evidence of an increase in respiratory diseases, hepatitis, lead contamination, and low birth weights in these particular regions (Hertzman 1995; Keep 1995; Potrykowska 1995), the effects of this pollution to date do not seem to be of such a magnitude as to have caused the massive, nationwide decreases in adult male life expectancy (Kulin and Skakkeback 1995; Watson 1995).

For example, in Russia, pollution-related illnesses like cancer and respiratory diseases were responsible for less than 12 percent of the increase in deaths in 1992–1993 (Haub 1994). Cancer deaths caused only 1.7 percent of the increased mortality and respiratory diseases caused an additional 8.9 percent. The leading cause of death was circulatory diseases (48.3%), followed by accidents (13.5%), murder/suicide (7.5%), alcohol (6.1%), and digestive/infectious diseases (4.6%). Other diseases caused the remaining 9.9 percent of the increased mortality. Another problem with the environmental explanation is that the regions that suffered from particularly high levels of pollution did not necessarily have the highest mortality rates (Watson 1995). East Bohemia in the Czech Republic, for instance, has relatively high life expectancy despite poor air quality, while parts of Slovakia with clean air have low life expectancy (Hertzman 1995). Results such as these suggest that environmental pollution, while important, is not the principal cause of the downturn in life expectancy (Kulin and Skakkeback 1995).

It therefore appears that the major causes of rising mortality are largely social in origin, which suggests that Soviet health policy, societal stress, or health lifestyle is the major culprit. Although it can be argued that each explanation represents an important causal factor, the next section will consider each possibility individually in order to locate the likely primary social determinant.

SOVIET HEALTH POLICY

Health care delivery systems and policies are acts of political philosophy; consequently, social and political values influence the choices made, institutions formed, and levels of funding provided for health (Light 1986).

Prior to the collapse of communism in the former Soviet Union and Eastern Europe in 1989–1991, the health care delivery systems in the region were philosophically guided by Marxist-Leninist programs for reshaping capitalism into socialism. The ultimate goal of Marxism-Leninism was the establishment of a classless society, featuring an end to class oppression, private property, worker alienation, and economic scarcity (Bell 1991; Zotov 1985). However, Marxist-Leninist ideology pertaining to health was never developed in depth (Deacon 1984; Marx and Engels 1973; Waitzkin 1983, 1989).

The new Soviet state established in the aftermath of the 1917 Revolution nevertheless faced serious health problems, including large-scale epidemics and famine. More out of practical than theoretical necessity, the Fifth All-Russian Congress of Soviets outlined some fundamental principles of Marxist-Leninist health policy in 1918. The Congress mandated that health care would be (1) the responsibility of the state, (2) provided without direct cost to the user, and (3) controlled by a central authority. Moreover, providing health care for workers, with an emphasis on preventive care, was a top priority (Cassileth et al. 1995; Light 1986). Because of the critical need for doctors and a shortage of manpower due to industrial and military demands, large numbers of women, especially nurses with a proletariat background, were ordered into medical schools where they were given cram courses and certified as physicians (Knaus 1981). Today, Russia has more doctors per capita than any major nation (about one physician for every 259 people) and some 76 percent are women (Cassileth et al. 1995). However, medical professionalism was not rewarded, nor encouraged. The Soviet government provided low wages (about $24 a month, less than what a bus driver would make) and status (the equivalent of a high school teacher) for the great majority of its medical practitioners (Cassileth et al. 1995; Field 1991, 1993, 1994;

Knaus 1981). In 1987, the average salary for health care providers was 71 percent of the national average (Mezentseva and Rimachevskaya 1992).

A hierarchical system of health care delivery facilities provided services, with local polyclinics being the initial point of entry for primary care and the source of referrals to higher-level services. The general public did not have a choice of physicians, but were assigned to a medical practitioner on the basis of residence. Treatment for infectious diseases, immunizations, maternal and child care, and other primary services were widely available (Knaus 1981; Rowland and Telyukov 1991; Tulchinsky and Varavikova 1996). Although quality was uneven and services in some rural areas were provided by physician assistants (feldshers) instead of doctors, the Soviets nonetheless established a nationwide health care delivery system providing free treatment. The initial results were impressive. Between 1928 and 1941, an enormous expansion in numbers of physicians and health facilities took place (Field 1967; Sidel and Sidel 1983). Western medical observers like Sigerist (1947: 32) found the early development of the Soviet health care delivery system to be "stupendous." "The chief impression of the visitor in 1938," states Sigerist (1947: 32), "was that not only was there more of everything but that everything there had been greatly improved." Medical measures, along with some improvement in living standards, were credited with substantially reducing infant mortality and the incidence of many communicable diseases like typhus, cholera, and syphilis (Knaus 1981).

From the end of World War II until the mid-1960s, health progress in the Soviet Union was rapid, steady, and general (Eberstadt 1994; Mezentseva and Rimachevskaya 1990). For example, in the Russian Soviet Federated Socialist Republic, life expectancy for males was 40.4 years in 1938 but reached 64.0 in 1965; for females, life expectancy increased from 46.7 years to 72.1 during the same period (Shkolnikov 1995). A similar situation occurred in Eastern Europe where Soviet-style health care delivery systems had been installed after 1945 (Eberstadt 1994; Okólski 1993). In Hungary, for instance, male life expectancy rose from 54.9 years in 1941 to 67.5 in 1966—the highest ever recorded (Hungarian Central Statistical Office 1996). Life expectancy for Hungarian females increased from 58.2 years to 72.2 during the same time.

However, in the mid-1960s, life expectancy for males began a downward trend throughout the Soviet Bloc and a review of the literature suggests four major shortcomings in the Soviet health care system: funding, quality, access, and strategy. First, health care was not a national priority and was therefore seriously underfunded. In 1989, two years before the Soviet Union collapsed, only 3.4 percent of the GDP—a percentage lower than in any other major industrialized nation—was spent on health care. Turkey (3.9%) and Greece (5.1%) spent larger proportions of their GDP on health that year than the Soviet Union. According to Mezentseva and Rimachevskaya (1992), health care in the Soviet Union was typically financed on the basis of the "residue principle," that is, from funds left over after providing for the needs of the sectors of the economy given a higher priority: defense, heavy industry, and agriculture.

Second, Soviet health care was not generally of a high quality in comparison to the West. Although modern facilities and well-trained physicians existed, the great majority of doctors lacked the training of Western physicians and most hospitals were poorly equipped and had inadequate supplies (Cassileth et al. 1995; Curtis, Petukhova, and Taket 1995; Davis 1989; Keep 1995; Knaus 1981; Light 1992). Rural areas, as noted, were often serviced by physician assistants in relatively primitive health stations. Soviet medical technology reportedly lagged behind that of the West by several years (Makara 1994). Therefore, as Light (1992) points out, the widespread availability of competent physicians with the medical supplies needed for their work has been a fundamental problem.

Third, despite socialist ideology, access to quality health care was inherently unequal in the Soviet system. According to Mezentseva and Rimachevskaya (1992), the existence of social inequality in health was never described by the government as a problem that needed solving, nor widely recognized as a problem by a general public until only late in the final years of the Soviet regime. What Soviet health policy provided was a universal and equal right to health protection, not an end to socially determined differences in health or in the quality of medical care provided (Mezentseva and Rimachevskaya 1990, 1992). There was, for example, a complex, stratified arrangement of clinics and hospitals, with separate closed systems for elite groups, such as top government officials, miners, and other industrial workers, and open systems for residents of Moscow, provincial cities, and rural areas (Davis 1989). In order to receive personal attention and access to better care, patients typically provided gifts or bribes to health care personnel which evolved into a second economy within the overall health care system (Cassileth et al. 1995; Davis 1989; Knaus 1981). Field (1993: 167) referred to the bribery system as the "commercialization of Soviet medicine" and noted that it was paradoxical that payments by patients were reintroduced in a system designed to remove financial incentives from the patient–physician relationship.

Fourth, the strategy emphasizing prevention was not a complete success. Until the 1990s, it was generally effective in controlling the major infectious diseases (Tulchinsky and Varavikova 1996). There was also some improvement in infant mortality as previously noted, and in deaths from cancer and respiratory diseases between 1970 and 1986 (Mezentseva and Rimachevskaya 1990, 1992). However, mortality from heart disease rose significantly, with age-standardized death rates from circulatory diseases increasing in Russia from 814.3 per 100,000 in 1970 to 1,089.3 in 1993 (Shkolnikov and Nemtsov 1994).

Of course, cause-of-death data, especially international comparisons, need to be interpreted with care because of the unavoidable subjectivity in diagnosis and coding for death certificates (Ruzicka and Lopez 1990). While the formerly communist countries of Europe may not have had a higher standard than the West in this regard, Eberstadt (1994) nevertheless observes that these data offer a view of the proximate causes of the region's health problems. Virtually all sources maintain that circulatory diseases (ischemic heart disease, stroke, and hypertension) and trauma (accidents, homicide, suicide, and poisonings) dominate the region's mortality patterns (cf. Eberstadt 1994; Haub 1994; Kaasik, Hörte, and Andersson 1996; Shkolnikov 1995; Shkolnikov and Nemtsov 1994; Tulchinsky and Varavikova 1996).

Whereas Soviet health policy was oriented toward the prevention of infectious diseases, it was ineffective in adjusting to the increased prevalence of heart disease and trauma as chronic, noncommunicable causes of death in the former Soviet Union and elsewhere in countries like the former Czechoslovakia and Hungary (Bojan, Hajdu, and Belicza 1991; Makara 1994). This leads to the paradoxical conclusion that the centralized egalitarianism that succeeded in addressing epidemics and contagious diseases in the early period of Soviet health care delivery functioned poorly when confronted with chronic illnesses and their causes in the late twentieth century. Thus, the Soviet-style health policy did not cause the increase in mortality in the region but rather was unable to address the surge in circulatory problems and traumatic episodes.

The social stress and health lifestyle explanations seem to be more promising lines of inquiry in the search for the major cause of increased mortality.

SOCIAL STRESS

A social explanation maintains that differences in health and life expectancy are based on the different capabilities of the various social classes in buffering the effects of stress. Socioeconomic distinctions in mortality and morbidity are found for practically all diseases and occur at every level of a social hierarchy, not just between the upper and lower class (Adler et al. 1994; Illsley and Baker 1991). Therefore, something more than poverty is operative in determining health differences between social classes, since the upper class lives longer than the upper middle class even though both classes are affluent. Thus, the critical factor in health, according to a social stress explanation, is a person's location in a social hierarchy, with higher socioeconomic status (SES) providing less exposure to negative events and more social and psychological resources in coping with such events when they occur (Adler et al. 1994).

Building on previous research, Evans, Barer, and Marmor (1994) identify stress as the single most important variable in the health of large populations. The basis for this conclusion is largely derived from Marmot's (Marmot et al. 1991; Marmot, Shipley, and Rose 1984) influential Whitehall studies which document a clear social gradient in life expectancy across occupational ranks of British male civil servants. Evans (1994) suggests that the social gradient in life expectancy from high to low is generally caused by differing "microenvironments" (defined as relations at home or work) that facilitate the transfer of strain from stressful life events. The lower one is on the social ladder, the less able one is to transfer stress, and the greater the harm to the individual's

health. Evans claims that it is this ability to transfer or buffer the effects of stress, rather than some mechanical connection to wealth, that ultimately determines the effects of stress on the body. Increasing prosperity and success are also cited by Evans and colleagues as a major source of self-esteem and empowerment which reflects positively on an individual's physical and mental health.

Applying this perspective to macrolevel processes, Evans and colleagues (Hertzman, Frank, and Evans 1994) note that as Japan moved into the upper hierarchy of nations, Japanese life expectancy became the highest in the world. Russia and Eastern Europe, in contrast, moved downward in the world's hierarchy and life expectancy decreased as well, thereby suggesting that changes in status can be translated into changes in mortality as societal stress is either reduced or increased.

However, while this conclusion has a certain logical appeal, it is not at all clear how the relationship between stress and macrolevel social change enhances or lessens the life expectancy of large populations, or particular individuals within those populations. Specific stressors and specific disease outcomes as a result of these stressors have not been identified, which makes it difficult to prove a precise cause and effect. Furthermore, among the Japanese, Okinawans have the highest longevity, but have historically been accorded lower social status by Japanese in the home islands (Lebra 1980). While it might be argued that Okinawan longevity in relation to status is atypical, the fact remains that they are a major exception to any hierarchical theory of human life expectancy.

Is is apparent that Russia and Eastern Europe comprise societies experiencing considerable stress as a result of fundamental economic, political, and social changes in the wake of communism's downfall (Keep 1995; Stokes 1993). Yet is is not evident that this macrolevel stress is the primary cause of increased mortality. Consider for example, the Czech Republic, which, like the other former communist nations, experienced an increase in male mortality beginning in the mid-1960s. But unlike the others, this trend was reversed in the mid-1980s—prior to the end of Soviet domination and the difficulties associated with the transition out of communism—and continues today after a one-year interruption in 1990. Between 1989 and 1994, life expectancy in the Czech Republic increased 1.4 years for males and 1.1 years for females, thereby demonstrating that the Czechs are escaping the general Eastern European trend in mortality (Rychtaříková 1996).

Thus, it can be argued that the Czech Republic has experienced stressful events like its neighbors, but has seen male mortality generally fall instead of rise in the last decade. Declines in deaths from heart disease, stroke, and cirrhosis of the liver for 25- to 44-year-old males and in heart and respiratory diseases for 45- to 59-year-old males are the principal causes of the Czech downturn in mortality. Consequently, Carlson and Rychtaříková (1996: 9) reject a stress hypothesis for the Czech Republic by pointing out that "rapid declines in nearly all causes of death for all age groups after 1990 has coincided with rapid social transformation, economic insecurity, stress, unemployment, new freedom in the marketplace to buy and sell an unprecedented variety of foodstuffs, and in general, an acceleration of the sort of 'westernization' that was supposed to be producing rising death rates."

Thus, the question remains unanswered: Were significant numbers of people in the former Soviet Union and Eastern Europe, primarily middle-aged men, so stressed by their social and psychological circumstances that increasingly higher proportions of them succumbed to heart attacks over a period of 20 years? The stress explanation of increased mortality needs stronger evidence to support its role as the primary social determinant. It may be that stress has a more indirect effect and influences life expectancy by promoting unhealthy lifestyles.

HEALTH LIFESTYLES

The health lifestyles explanation lays the blame for poor health upon unhealthy practices and social conditions. Health lifestyles are collective patterns of health-related behavior based on choices from options available to people according to their life chances (Cockerham, Rütten, and Abel 1997). These life chances include the effects of age, gender, race/ethnicity, and other variables that affect lifestyle choices. The behaviors that are generated from these choices can have either positive or negative consequences on body and mind, but nonetheless form an overall pattern of health practices that constitute a lifestyle.

Sociological thinking on lifestyles generally remains guided by the insight of Max Weber (1978). Weber's work suggests that lifestyles have two major components: (1) life choices (self-direction) and (2) life chances (the structural probabilities of finding satisfaction). Weber's most important contribution to conceptualizing lifestyles is identification of the dialectical interplay between choice and chance in lifestyle determination (Cockerham, Abel, and Lüschen 1993). People therefore have a range of freedom, but not complete freedom, in choosing a lifestyle; that is, they have the freedom to choose within the social constraints that apply to their situation in life.

While this perspective suggests that participation in a healthy lifestyle—which typically involves decisions about food, exercise, coping with stress, smoking, alcohol and drug use, risk of infection and accidents, and physical appearance—is largely up to the individual, Cockerham et al. (1997) indicate this may not necessarily be the case. Structural constraints embedded in life chances may be the dominant factor in the operationalization of health lifestyles. Bourdieu (1984), for example, notes that categories of perception—the basis of self-direction—are largely determined by socialization, experience, and the reality of class circumstances. The habitus which guides social action is limited by its perceptual boundaries. The dispositions produced are typically compatible with the constraints imposed by the larger social order and set the individual on a stable and consistent course of action. These constraints may, in fact, leave people with little or no choice in exposing themselves to unhealthy conditions and practices.

In societies, like those in Eastern Europe, where people lacked information about health and had little or no control over their diet, ecological pollution, or a social environment where smoking and heavy drinking was normative, poor health lifestyles were likely. Nagorski (1993) reports that Eastern Europeans are among the world's heaviest drinkers and smokers, and their diet is loaded with fat. Vodka and cigarettes were cheap and easily available in large quantities to workers, and the average citizen had little choice about which foods to purchase and consume. Nagorski (1993: 189) states: "If Eastern Europeans seemed less concerned about maintaining healthy habits, if they shrugged off warnings about the dangers of drinking, smoking, and lack of exercise more easily than their Western counterparts, if they seemed to take ecological devastation more fatalistically, this was a natural result of the sense of powerlessness the communist system encouraged at every turn."

The major argument against the lifestyle explanation is that it places responsibility for health directly on the individual and his or her lifestyle choices. When people develop poor health or die prematurely, it is their fault because of these choices. This allows the capitalist system and its health care sector to escape blame for unhealthy social conditions or medical mistakes (Navarro 1986; Waitzkin

1983). Consequently, the lifestyle explanation is depicted as a form of "blaming the victim," which permits the state and powerful groups to evade responsibility. There is some justification for this view if lifestyles are considered to be more or less exclusively based on individual choice; however, there is little empirical evidence that lifestyles are merely a deliberate product of independent individuals. As Bourdieu (Bourdieu and Wacquant 1992: 183) explains: "Autonomy does not come without the social conditions of autonomy and these conditions cannot be obtained on an individual basis." Therefore, as noted, life chances and the parameters they set for choice selection play an especially powerful role in determining lifestyles (Cockerham et al. 1997).

If life chances constrain life choices in the more consumption-oriented and individualistic West, they are likely to impose even greater limits on lifestyle choices in the East. During the Soviet era, for example, high-quality foodstuffs were not widely available in Russia (Chamberlain 1982). The food consumed was determined more by what was available than by personal choice over a range of options. Although the diet was nutritionally adequate, it was unbalanced by an excess of carbohydrates and fatty meats, shortages in fresh fruits and vegetables in winter months, and a lack of variety (Keep 1995; Knaus 1981; Tulchinsky and Varavikova 1996). We would argue that such external constraints (life chances) dominate choices and result in relatively unhealthy lifestyle patterns and rising mortality.

Evidence supporting a lifestyle explanation for the rise in mortality comes from at least four sources: (1) prior research, (2) the types of diseases most responsible for the increase, (3) Russia's anti-alcohol campaign, and (4) a recent Hungarian survey of health behavior. First, several studies and research reports suggest that unhealthy lifestyles may be the major cause of the rise in mortality in the former Soviet Union and Eastern Europe in general (Eberstadt 1990; Feachem 1994; Kulin and Skakkeback 1995) and in the former Czechoslovakia (Janecková and Hnilicová 1992) and Poland (World Bank 1992) in particular. Second, a particularly strong association exists between cardiovascular diseases and health lifestyle practices involving diet, exercise, smoking, and heavy drinking (Cockerham 1995), and, as previously discussed, the leading overall cause of the mortality increase in Russia and Eastern Europe is disease of the circulatory system. The increase in heart disease would suggest an increase in risk behavior; and this appears to be the case based on data showing a dramatic rise in the per capita consumption of cigarettes and hard liquor in Eastern Europe between the mid-1960s and 1980s (Eberstadt 1990), increasingly higher levels of alcohol consumption in Russia between 1971–1984 and 1987–1993 (Shkolnikov and Nemtsov 1994), and a rise in the percentage of regular smokers in Hungary between 1984 and 1994 (Antal 1994; Hungarian Central Statistical Office 1996). Moreover, in Hungary, deaths from cirrhosis of the liver and the estimated number of alcoholics doubled between 1987 and 1993 (Hungarian Ministry of Welfare 1995).

Third, while not conclusive, the relationship between a lifestyle involving heavy alcohol use and the rise in male mortality nevertheless appears especially important. As Okólski (1993: 177) puts it: "It seems that of all plausible determinants of adult male mortality increase in Eastern Europe, the most widely accepted underlying factor is growing alcohol consumption." A strong relationship between alcohol consumption and decreased male life expectancy has been found in both Eastern Europe (Okólski 1993) and Russia (Anderson and Silver 1990; Meslé and Shkolnikov 1995; Meslé, Shkolnikov, and Vallin 1992; Ponarin 1996; Shkolnikov and Nemtsov 1994).

The magnitude of alcohol use in the former Soviet Union is illustrated by the fact that tax revenues from sales of vodka accounted for 35 percent of the Soviet budget in 1988. By 1995, vodka generated less than 5 percent of revenues, not because of decreased consumption, but because of the government's loss of the state monopoly on production and sales and inability to control the black market. In 1995, Russians consumed 4.1 gallons of hard liquor per capita—the highest in the world. In an extensive study of the alcohol-mortality relationship in Russia, Shkolnikov and Nemtsov (1994) investigated alcohol sales and consumption between 1971 and 1993. Their focus was on Gorbachev's 1984–1987 anti-alcohol campaign and they determined that both reported and real alcohol consumption declined during this period. Calculating the difference between observed and expected deaths by sex and age, Shkolnikov and Nemtsov found that longevity increased 3.2 years for males and 1.3 years for females during the campaign's duration, with the greatest advances occurring in 1986. Shkolnikov and Nemtsov (1994: 1) concluded that "the rapid mortality decrease in the years 1984 to 1987 can be assumed to reflect a pure effect of reduced alcohol abuse on mortality, because there were no other significant changes in conditions of the public health in that short period." The fact that alcohol abuse was very much a regional (or ethnic) problem (Keep 1995: 269) may help explain why the rise in adult male mortality has been greater in Russia and the Baltic states (where consumption was highest) than in Central Asia.

According to Shkolnikov and Nemstov (1994), the mode of drinking common to middle-aged Slavic males is part of a Northern European lifestyle involving rapid group consumption of large doses of vodka with a light snack; the participant is expected to continue to drink with his fellows even when he feels he has had enough. Apparently little or no social stigma is associated with drunkenness. Earlier in the twentieth century Russian workers typically drank large amounts of alcohol only on their days off (Sundays and Russian Orthodox Church holidays). However, during the Soviet period, heavy alcohol consumption became common throughout the year, which most likely fostered a lifestyle characterized by consistent binge drinking. This situation suggests that it is the normative demands of a particular lifestyle, rather than health policy or stress, that is primarily responsible for the pattern of male drinking in Russia.

Other evidence supporting a lifestyle explanation for rising mortality is found in Hungary's 1994 Health Behavior Survey (Hungarian Central Statistical Office 1995). This nationwide survey of 5,476 households (an 85% response rate) found that the percentage of smokers had increased to 35.0 percent from 31.9 percent in 1986. Some 72 percent of the sample drank alcohol regularly, with 11.6 percent characterized as "excessive drinkers." Only 21.4 percent of the men and 13.5 percent of the women reported regular physical exercise, while less than 10 percent of the men and 12.5 percent of the women ate vegetables almost every day in the winter. Furthermore, over half of all visits to physicians were made by just 10 percent of the respondents. Hungary's health profile is among the worst in Eastern Europe and these data help us to understand why. For example, Hungary's mortality rate rose from 10.2 deaths per 1,000 persons in 1960 to 14.3 in 1994 with the rise in heart disease among middle-aged men serving as the principal cause (Carlson 1989; Hungarian Central Statistical Office 1996; Józan 1989, 1996; Nagorski 1993).

Although Soviet-style health policy and social stress have likely contributed to the downturn in life expectancy in Russia and Eastern Europe, this review of the evidence suggests that unhealthy lifestyle is the primary social determinant of the higher death rates and currently offers the most promising line of inquiry for future research.

EAST GERMANY: AN EXCEPTION?

Of all the Soviet Bloc countries, only East Germany avoided the downturn in male life expectancy. However, reliable statistics show that the East German state did not entirely escape regional trends, and increases in longevity were significantly slowing over time (Jahrbuch der Bundesrepublik Deutschland 1996; Statistisches Bundesamt 1995). Between 1970 and 1991, for example, male life expectancy increased only 1.1 years for East Germans compared to 5.2 years for West Germans. As seen in Figure 1, both East German men and women outlived their Western counterparts until the 1970s when the West Germans moved ahead. By unification in 1991, West German men lived 2.4 years more on average than East German males (72.4 years versus 70.0 years) and West German women had 2.7 years greater longevity than women in East Germany (78.9 years compared to 76.2 years).

Had the health and life expectancy of East Germans been better than that of West Germans, the superiority of Soviet-style health care delivery could have been demonstrated. The division of Germany into distinct capitalist and communist states offered the opportunity to evaluate "a natural experiment in history" (Light and Schuller 1986; Volpp 1991). However, by unification, East Germany's health care system was judged a major failure and none of its features were retained (Apelt 1991; Knox 1993; Niehoff, Schneider, and Wetzstein 1992; Volpp 1991). Like Soviet-style health systems elsewhere in Eastern Europe, the East German approach was becoming

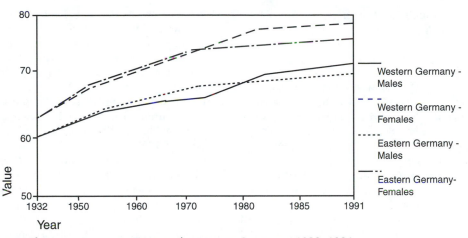

FIGURE 1 Life expectancy, Eastern and Western Germany, 1932–1991.

Source: United Nations *Demographic Yearbook* 1955, 1961, 1966, 1974, 1975; World Health Organization *World Health Statistics Annual* 1986, 1993; *Jahrbuch der Bundesrepublik Deutschland* 1996.

increasingly ineffective in coping with heart disease (Knox 1993).

The role of stress in retarding life expectancy in East Germany is not known because of a lack of data. But there is limited support for a health lifestyles argument in the few existing comparative studies. There are data, for example, that show that the incidence of cardiovascular disease was greater in East Germany than in West Germany, with East German males showing higher levels of cigarette smoking, hypertension, cholesterol, and obesity (Helmert, Mielck, and Classen 1992). East German females showed a similar pattern except for smoking. One result was an age-adjusted mortality rate from heart disease in 1988 that was 40 percent higher for males and 60 percent higher for females in East Germany as compared to West Germany (Knox 1993). Other research suggests that East Germans were less likely to exercise and more likely to consume hard liquor than West Germans (Lüschen, Apelt, and Kunz 1993). Consequently, a health lifestyles approach offers a basis for future comparisons of East and West Germany. While East Germany was

an exception to the general Eastern European mortality pattern, its position was eroding by the time of unification.

CONCLUSION

This paper has examined the rise of adult mortality in Russia and selected Eastern European countries during the late twentieth century. A review of relevant data shows that the socialist states were generally characterized by a persistently poor mortality performance as part of a long-term process of deterioration. Soviet-style health policy was ineffective in dealing with the situation; thus, the centralized system that succeeded in addressing contagious diseases in the early Soviet period functioned poorly in coping with heart disease and trauma in the late twentieth century. While social stress may also be an important factor in the rise in mortality, evidence is lacking that stress per se can account for the sharp rise in male deaths throughout the region. Although more research is needed, the strongest evidence to date suggests that unhealthy lifestyles are the principal social determinant of increased mortality in the region.

REFERENCES

ADLER, NANCY E., THOMAS BOYCE, MARGARET A. CHESNEY, SHELDON COHEN, SUSAN FOLKMAN, ROBERT L. KAHN, and S. LEONARD SYME. 1994. "Socioeconomic Status and Health: The Challenge of the Gradient." *American Psychologist* 49:15–24.

ANDERSON, BARBARA A. and BRIAN D. SILVER. 1990. "Trends in Mortality of the Soviet Population." *Soviet Economy* 3:191–251.

ANDREEV, YE. M. 1990. "Prodolzhiitelnost zhizni I prichini smerti v SSSR [Life Expectancy and Causes of Death in the U.S.S.R.]." Pp. 90–116 in *Demograficheskiye processi v SSSR*. Moscow, Russia: Nauka.

ANTAL, LÁSZLÓ Z. 1994, "Causes of High Mortality Rate in the Former Socialist Countries." Budapest, Hungary: Hungarian Academy of Sciences.

APELT, PETER. 1991. "Gleichheit und Ungleichheit im Gesundheitswesen der DDR [Equality and Inequality in Health Systems in the German Democratic Republic]." *Mensch Medizin Gesellschaft* 16:27–33.

BELL, DANIEL. 1991. "Values and the Future in Marx and Marxism." *Futures* (March): 146–62.

BOJAN, FERENC, PIROSKA HAJDU, and EVA BELICZA. 1991. "Avoidable Mortality. Is It an Indicator of Quality of Medical Care in Eastern European Countries?" *Quality Assurance in Health Care* 3:191–203.

———.1993. "Regional Differences in Avoidable Mortality in Europe." Pp. 125–39 in *Europe Without Frontiers: The Implications for Health* edited by C. Normand and P. Vaughan. Chichester, England: Wiley.

BOURDIEU, PIERRE. 1984. *Distinction*. Translated by R. Nice. Cambridge, MA: Harvard University Press.

BOURDIEU, PIERRE and LOÏC J.D. WACQUANT. 1992. *An Invitation to Reflexive Sociology*. Chicago, IL: University of Chicago Press.

CARLSON, ELWOOD. 1989. "Concentration of Rising Hungarian Mortality Among Manual Workers." *Sociology and Social Research* 73:119–27.

CARLSON, ELWOOD and JITKA RYCHTAŘÍKOVÁ. 1996. "Renewed Mortality Decline in the Czech Republic." Paper presented to the Sawyer-Mellon Conference on Increasing Adult Mortality in Eastern Europe, March, University of Michigan, Ann Arbor, MI.

CARLSON, ELWOOD and SERGEY TSVETARSKY. 1992. "Concentration of Rising Bulgarian Mortality Among Manual Workers." *Sociology and Social Research* 76:81–84.

CASSILETH, BARRIE R., VASILY V. VLASSOV, and CHRISTOPHER C. CHAPMAN. 1995. "Health Care, Medical Practice, and Medical Ethics in Russia Today." *Journal of the American Medical Association* 273:1569–622.

CHAMBERLAIN, LESLEY. 1982. *The Food and Cooking of Russia*. London: Penguin.

COCKERHAM, WILLIAM C. 1995. *Medical Sociology*. 6th ed. Englewood Cliffs, NJ: Prentice Hall.

COCKERHAM, WILLIAM C., THOMAS ABEL, and GÜNTHER LÜSCHEN, 1993. "Max Weber, Formal Rationality, and Health Lifestyles." *Sociological Quarterly* 34:413–25.

COCKERHAM, WILLIAM C., ALFRED RÜTTEN, and THOMAS ABEL, 1997. "Conceptualizing Contemporary Health Lifestyles: Moving Beyond Weber." *Sociological Quarterly* 38:601–22.

CURTIS, SARAH, NATASHA PETUKHOVA, and ANN TAKET. 1995. "Health Care Reforms in Russia: The Example of St. Petersburg." *Social Science and Medicine* 40:755–65.

DAVIS, CHRISTOPHER M. 1989. "The Soviet Health System: A National Health Service in a Socialist Society." Pp.233–62 in *Success and Crisis in National Health Systems*, edited by M. Field. London: Routledge.

DEACON, BOB. 1984. "Medical Care and Health Under State Socialism." *International Journal of Health Services* 14:453–82.

EBERSTADT, NICHOLAS.1990. "Health and Mortality in Eastern Europe, 1965–1985." *Communist Economies* 2:349–65.

———. 1994. "Health and Mortality in Central and Eastern Europe: Retrospect and Prospect." Pp. 198–225 in *The Social Legacy of Communism*, edited by J. Millar and S. Wolchik. Cambridge, England: Cambridge University Press.

EVANS, ROBERT G. 1994. "Introduction." Pp. 3–26 in *Why Are Some People Healthy and Others Not? The*

Determinants of Health of Populations, edited by R. Evans, M. Barer, and T. Marmor. New York: Aldine de Gruyter.

EVANS, ROBERT G., MORRIS L. BARER, and THEODORE R. MARMOR (eds.). 1994. *Why Are Some People Healthy and Others Not? The Determinants of Health of Populations.* New York: Aldine de Gruyter.

FEACHEM, R. 1994. "Health Decline in Eastern Europe." *Nature* 367:313–14.

FIELD, MARK G. 1967. *Soviet Socialized Medicine: An Introduction* New York: Free Press.

———. 1991. "The Hybrid Profession: Soviet Medicine." Pp. 43–62 in *Professions and the State,* edited by A. Jones. Philadelphia., PA: Temple University Press.

———. 1993. "The Physician in the Commonwealth of Independent States: The Difficult Passage from Bureaucrat to Professional." Pp.162–83 in *The Changing Medical Profession ,* edited by F. Hafferty and J. McKinlay, New York: Oxford University Press.

———. 1994. "Postcommunist Medicine: Morbidity, Mortality, and the Deteriorating Health Situation." Pp. 178–95 in *The Social Legacy of Communism,* edited by J. Millar and S. Wolchik. New York and Cambridge, England: Woodrow Wilson Center Press and Cambridge University Press.

———. 1995. "The Health Crisis in the Former Soviet Union: A Report from the 'Post-War' Zone." *Social Science and Medicine* 41:1469–78.

GODEK, LISA. 1995. "The Gender Gap in Ukrainian Mortality." Paper presented to the Sawyer-Mellon Conference on Increasing Adult Mortality in Eastern Europe, December, University of Michigan, Ann Arbor, MI.

HAUB, CARL. 1994. "Population Change in the Former Soviet Republics." *Population Bulletin,* vol. 49. Washington, DC: Population Reference Bureau.

HELMERT, UWE, ANDREAS MIELCK, and ELVIRA CLASSEN, 1992. "Social Inequities in Cardiovascular Disease Risk Factors in East and West Germany." *Social Science and Medicine* 35:1283–92.

HERTZMAN, CLYDE. 1995. *Environment and Health in Central and Eastern Europe.* Washington, DC: World Bank.

HERTZMAN, CLYDE, J. FRANK, and ROBERT G. EVANS. 1994. "Heterogeneities in Health Status and the Determinants of Population Health." Pp. 67–92 in *Why Are Some People Healthy and Others Not?" The Determinats of Health and Populations,* edited by R. Evans, M. Barer, and T. Marmor. New York: Aldine de Gruyter.

HUNGARIAN CENTRAL STATISTICAL OFFICE. 1995. "Preliminary Report on the Health Behavior Survey 94." Budapest, Hungary.

———. 1996. "Main Features of the Hungarian Demographic Situation in the Early Nineties." Budapest, Hungary.

HUNGARIAN MINISTRY OF WELFARE. 1995. "Program of Health Services Modernization: Supplements." Budapest, Hungary.

ILLSLEY, R. and D. BAKER. 1991. "Contextual Variations in the Meaning of Health Inequality." *Social Science and Medicine* 32:359–65.

JAHRBUCH DER BUNDESREPUBLIK [Yearbook of the Federal Republic of Germany]. 1996. Munich, Germany: Beck.

JANECKOVÁ, HANA and HELENA HNILICOVÁ. 1992. "The Health Status of the Czechoslovak Population. Its Social and Ecological Determinants." *International Journal of Health Sciences* 3:143–56.

JÓZAN, PETER. 1989. "Some Features of Mortality in Postwar Hungary: The Third Epidemiological Transition." *Cahiers de Sociologie Démographie Médicales* 29:21–42.

———. 1996. "Health Crisis East of the Elbe: A Consequence of Death-Ended Modernization." Paper presented to the Sawyer-Mellon Conference on Increasing Adult Mortality in Eastern Europe, March, University of Michigan, Ann Arbor, MI.

KAASIK, TAIE, LARS-GUNNAR HÓRTE, and RAGNAR ANDERSSON. 1996. *Injury in Estonia: An Estonian Swedish Comparative Study.* Sundbyberg, Sweden: Karolinska Institute.

KEEP, JOHN. 1995. *Last of the Empires: A History of the Soviet Union 1945–1991.* Oxford, England: Oxford University Press.

KNAUS, WILLIAM A. 1981. *Inside Russian Medicine.* Boston: Beacon Press.

KNOX, RICHARD. 1993. *Germany's Health System.* Washington, DC: Faulkner & Gray.

KULIN, HOWARD E. and NIELS E. SKAKKEBACK. 1995. "Environmental Effects on Human Reproduction: The Basis for New Efforts in Eastern Europe." *Social Science and Medicine* 41: 1479–86.

LEBRA, WILLIAM F. 1980. "The Okinawans." Pp. 111–34 in *People and Cultures of Hawaii: A Psychocultural Profile,* edited by J. McDermott, Jr., W. Tseng, and T. Maretzki. Honolulu, HI: University of Hawaii Press.

LIGHT, DONALD W. 1986. "Introduction: State, Profession, and Political Values." Pp. 1–23 in *Political Values and Health Care: The German Experience,* edited by D. Light and A. Schuller. Cambridge, MA: MIT Press.

———. 1992. "Russia: Perestroika for Health Care?" *Lancet* 339:326.

LIGHT, DONALD W. and ALEXANDER SCHULLER, eds. 1986. *Political Values and Health Care: The German Experience.* Cambridge, MA: MIT Press.

LÜSCHEN, GÜNTHER, PETER APELT, and GERHARD KUNZ. 1993. "Systems in Transition: Health Conduct, Health Care, and Social Stratification in East and West Germany." Paper presented to the Midwest Sociological Society Meetings, April, Chicago, IL.

MAKARA, PETER. 1994. "Policy Implications of Differential Health Status in East and West Europe: The Case of Hungary." *Social Science and Medicine* 39:1295–302.

MARMOT, M.G., J. SHIPLEY, and GEOFFREY ROSE. 1984. "Inequalities in Death—Specific Explanations of a General Pattern." *Lancet* 83:1003–6.

MARMOT, M.G., G.D. SMITH, S. STANSFELD, C. PATEL, F. NORTH, J. HEAD, I. WHITE, E. BRUNNER, and A. FEENEY. 1991. "Health Inequalities Among British Civil Servants: The Whitehall II Study." *Lancet* 337:1387–93.

MARX, KARL and FRIEDRICH ENGELS. [1846] 1973. *The German Ideology.* Moscow, Russia: Progress Publishers.

MESLÉ, FRANCE and VLADIMIR M. SHKOLNIKOV. 1995. "La mortalité en Russie: une crise sanitaire en deux temps." [Mortality in Russia: A Health Crisis in Two Periods]. *Revue d'études comparatives Est-Ouest* 4:9–24.

MESLÉ, FRANCE VLADIMIR SHKOLNIKOV, and JACQUES VALLIN. 1992. "Mortality by Cause in the U.S.S.R. in 1970–1987: The Reconstruction of Time Series." *European Journal of Population* 8:281–308.

MEZENTSEVA, ELENA and NATALIA RIMACHEVSKAYA. 1990. "The Soviet Country Profile: Health of the U.S.S.R. Population in the '70s and '80s—An Approach to a Comprehensive Analysis." *Social Science and Medicine* 31:867–77.

———1992. "The Health of the Populations in the Republics of the Former Soviet Union: An Analysis of the Situation in the 1970s and 1980s." *International Journal of the Health Sciences* 3:127–42.

NAGORSKI, ANDREW. 1993. *The Birth of Freedom: Shaping Lives and Societies in the New Eastern Europe.* New York: Simon and Schuster.

NASELENIYE SSR [*Population of the USSR*]. 1962. Moscow, Russia: Finnasy i Statistika Publishers.

NATIONAL CENTRE FOR HEALTH SYSTEM MANAGEMENT. 1996. "Health Care System in Transition (HiT) Profile Poland." Warsaw, Poland: Ministry of Health and Social Welfare.

NAVARRO, VICENTE. 1986. *Crisis, Health, and Medicine: A Social Critique.* New York: Tavistock.

NIEHOFF, J.U., F. SCHNEIDER, and E. WETZSTEIN, 1992. "Reflections on the Health Policy of the Former German Democratic Republic." *International Journal of Health Services* 3:205–13.

OKÓLSKI, MAREK. 1993. "East-West Mortality Differentials." *European Population,* vol.2, edited by A. Blum and J. Rallu. London, England: John Libbey.

PONARIN, ED. 1996. "Adult Mortality and Alcohol Consumption in Russia." Paper presented to the Sawyer-Mellon Conference on Increasing Adult Mortality in Eastern Europe, March, University of Michigan, Ann Arbor, MI.

POTRYKOWSKA, ALINA. 1995. "The Effects of Environmental Pollution for Population in Poland." Pp. 307–24 in *Population-Environment-Development Interactions,* edited by J. Clarke and L. Tabah. Paris, France: CICRED.

ROWLAND, DIANE and ALEXANDRE V. TELYUKOV. 1991. "Soviet Health Care from Two Perspectives." *Health Affairs* 10:71–86.

RUZICKA, LADO T. and ALAN D. LOPEZ. 1990. "The Use of Cause-of-Death Statistics for Health Situation Assessment: National and International Experiences." *World Health Statistics Quarterly* 43:249–58.

RYCHTÁŘÍKOVÁ, JITKA. 1996. "Will the Czech Republic Escape the Eastern European Crisis?" Paper presented to the Sawyer-Mellon Conference on Increasing Adult Mortality in Eastern Europe, March, University of Michigan, Ann Arbor, MI.

SHKOLNIKOV, VLADMIR. 1995. "Recent Trends in Russian Mortality: 1993–1994." Paper presented at the USAID Conference, October, Moscow, Russia.

SHKOLNIKOV, VLADIMIR AND ALEXANDER NEMTSOV. 1994. "The Anti-Alcohol Campaign and Variations in Russian Mortality." Paper presented to the Workshop on Mortality and Adult Health Priorities in the New Independent States, November, Washington, DC.

SHKOLNIKOV, VLADIMIR M., SERGEY ADAMETS, and ALEXANDER DEEV. 1996. "Mortality Differentials in the Context of General Mortality Reversal in Russia: The Educational Status." Paper presented to the Sawyer-Mellon Conference on Increasing Adult Mortality in Eastern Europe. March, University of Michigan, Ann Arbor, MI.

SIDEL, VICTOR W. and RUTH SIDEL. 1983. A Healthy State: An International Perspective on the Crisis in United States Medical Care, rev. ed. New York: Pantheon.

SIGERIST, HENRY E. 1947. Medicine and Health in the Soviet Union. New York: Citadel Press.

STATISTICHES BUNDESAMT [Statistical Office of the German Government]. 1995. Statistisches Jahrbuch [Statistical Yearbook]. Stuttgart, Germany: Metzler and Pöschel.

STOKES. GALE. 1993. The Walls Came Tumbling Down: The Collapse of Communism in Eastern Europe. New York: Oxford University Press.

TULCHINSKY, THEODORE H. and ELENA A. VARAVIKOVA. 1996. "Addressing the Epidemiologic Transition in the Former Soviet Union: Strate-gies for Health System and Public Health Reform in Russia." American Journal of Public Health 86:313–20.

U.S. NATIONAL CENTER FOR HEALTH STATISTICS. 1991. Health United States 1991. Washington, DC: U.S. Government Printing Office.

———. 1994. Health United States 1993. Washington, DC: U.S. Government Printing Office.

VOLPP, KEVIN. 1991. "The Structure of Health Care Delivery in Communist East Germany." Mensch Medizin Gesellschaft 16:3–13.

WAITZKIN, HOWARD. 1983. The Second Sickness: Contradictions of Capitalist Health Care. New York: Free Press.

———.1989. "A Critical Theory of Medical Discourse: Ideology, Social Control, and the Processing of Social Context in Medical Encounters." Journal of Health and Social Behavior 30:220–39.

WATSON, PEGGY. 1995. "Explaining Rising Mortality Among Men in Eastern Europe." Social Science and Medicine 41:923–34.

WEBER, MAX. 1978. Economy and Society. 2 Vols., edited by G. Roth and C. Wittich. Berkeley, CA: University of California Press.

WNUK-LIPINSKI, EDMUND. 1990. "The Polish Country Profile: Economic Crisis and Inequalities in Health." Social Science and Medicine 31:859–66.

WORLD BANK. 1992. Poland: Health System Reform. Washington, DC: World Bank.

ZOTOV, V.D. 1985. The Marxist-Leninist Theory of Society. Moscow, Russia: Progress Publishers.